Fibre Channel Arbitrated Loop

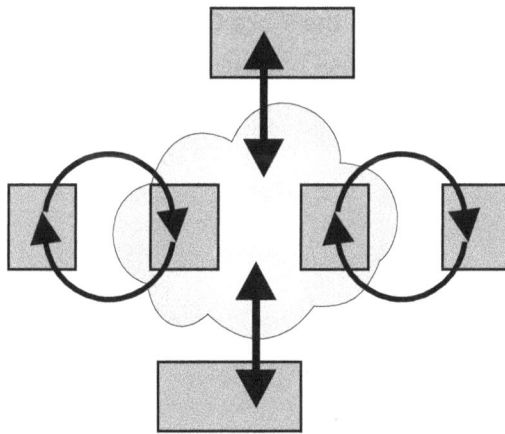

Robert W. Kembel
Horst L. Truestedt

NIA

Cover design by David Fischer, Fischer Graphic Services.

Be sure to check out the other books in the Fibre Channel Consultant series:

Fibre Channel A Comprehensive Introduction   ISBN 978-0-931836-10-7
Fibre Channel Switched Fabric   ISBN 978-0-931836-11-4
Fibre Channel over Ethernet (FCoE)   ISBN 978-0-931836-12-1
Fibre Channel Arbitrated Loop   ISBN 978-0-931836-13-8

ISBN 978-0-931836-13-8

Published by:

Northwest Learning Associates, Inc.
12 Water Street
Hingham, MA 02043
781-626-4746, Fax: 781-626-4751
email: info@nlabooks.com
Visit our web site at www.NLAbooks.com

Printed in the United States of America

20 19 18 17 16 15 14 13

Contents

List of Figures

List of Tables

Foreword

At the opening of this century Fibre Channel and Fibre Channel Arbitrated Loop are not just architectural visions with good potential. They are central players in the high performance systems and products of an immense data storage and retrieval industry. Their conceptually simple architecture has been refined and expanded into a multi-faceted design that enables data to be acquired, stored, shared, and retrieved across multiple sites, with multiple users, at speeds and distances previously unattainable. The unique capability and versatility of Fibre Channel Arbitrated Loop (FC-AL) to connect storage devices and subsystems simultaneously make this technology a natural foundation for the implementation of Storage Area Networks (SANs). With the use of FC-AL and the more recent FC-AL-2 as a cornerstone for SAN implementations, a strong understanding of Fibre Channel and Fibre Channel Arbitrated Loop is essential in the development, deployment, and support of SAN technology.

Even simple designs have complexities that challenge experienced designers, implementers, and technical support teams. This is certainly true for FC-AL and FC-AL-2. The sheer size and intricacies of the standards documentation suggest the value of a companion guide, a basic manual that gives the facts, straightforward explanations, and well-presented tables and figures to complement the wealth of information.

This is such a guide. This book takes you through the basics of Fibre Channel Arbitrated Loop design and function, and also serves as a cross-reference to the standards documents.

The authors of this book are uniquely well positioned to address the topics of Fibre Channel and Fibre Channel Arbitrated Loop. Both have been involved in development and definition of the ANSI standards for Fibre Channel and Fibre Channel Arbitrated Loop for many years. Robert Kembel, author of Fibre Channel: A Comprehensive Introduction and the first edition of this book, was editor of the "Public Loop Direct Attach Profile Technical Report" for Fibre Channel. Horst Truestedt, often regarded by colleagues as the "Father of the Arbitrated Loop" was editor of both the "Fibre Channel Arbitrated Loop" and "Fibre Channel Arbitrated Loop-2" standards. Both men have been teaching these topics to engineers, managers, marketers, and support teams all over the world. Their collective wisdom, experience, and perspective on this topic will be of tremendous benefit to the reader, regardless of the reader's prior knowledge, experience, or application.

Skip Jones

Director of Planning and Technology, QLogic Corporation
President of the Fibre Channel Industry Association
Vice President of the SCSI Trade Association.

Skip is an active campaigner in both speech and print about storage and network technology trends, the role of SCSI, Fibre Channel and other SAN technologies, as well as industry associations and initiatives that accelerate market development of pertinent technologies.

Acknowledgments

When the first edition of this book was written there was one author: Robert W. Kembel. During the life of that edition Fibre Channel Arbitrated Loop technology progressed substantially in capability and refinement. This revised edition of the original book is based on the shared expertise of the original author and Horst L. Truestedt who is the technical editor of the ANSI standards for both "Fibre Channel Arbitrated Loop" and "Fibre Channel Arbitrated Loop-2." Each author recognizes and appreciates the patience and diligence of the other in bringing this book to what the reader has here: a completely updated edition that reflects the second generation of Fibre Channel Arbitrated Loop (FC-AL-2).

Both authors realize that a project of this magnitude doesn't happen without the encouragement, support, and help of many people who work behind the scenes, contributing their time, ideas, and expertise to the final product. This page is dedicated to them.

First and foremost, the authors thank Gary Stephens, founder of FSI Consulting, and David Deming, founder of Solution Technology, who provided the vision and the opportunities that led to the original creation of this book and ultimately, to its revision. Both men have been strong advocates of written materials that accurately reflect the standards upon which FC-AL and FC-AL-2 are based, and of a clear, readable, easy-to-use format for presentation of the information. Gary has been a fellow teacher and mentor in the writing of this book; Dave has opened the doors to a teaching career for both authors that continually challenges them to refine and develop the standards information for their students.

The authors also thank the many colleagues in the ANSI standards community who have contributed immensely to each man's knowledge and skill. In particular, Dave Baldwin, Paul Boulay, Roger Cummings, Jan Dedek, Mike Fitzpatrick, Skip Jones, and Gary Warden have provided something special in support of the authors and this book.

No book is complete without the guidance and contributions of editors, artists, and a team of production staff who turn the authors' words into a finished book. Bonnie Marson and Jim McVeigh took on the monumental task of proofreading a very difficult technical work. Their keen observations and attention to detail have contributed immensely to ensuring that every sentence has at least one noun, one verb, and makes grammatical sense. David Fischer provided an outstanding cover design. Jean Schroeder managed the on-site production staff at Sheridan Books and handled the multitude of details needed to print and deliver this book. To each one of these people, a heartfelt *thank you* for their dedication and good humor.

Most especially, the authors thank their wives, Julie Kembel and Jeanne Truestedt, who shared in this venture in so many ways. Both women are business partners and colleagues. Each is an author and publisher; each manages the day-to-day tasks of running our respective businesses. Each has shared our vision for this project and supported us wholeheartedly throughout the writing of this book.

Finally, a special *thanks* goes to the many students who have helped shape the direction of this book through their generous feedback and comments.

Preface

During the past five years, we have conducted numerous Fibre Channel seminars for a diverse group of engineers, programmers, managers, and other product developers. One thing that has been consistently apparent is the need for more explanatory information about this exciting new technology. Those who read the standards find that while they present a very precise set of rules regarding the behavior and requirements, they do not explain why those behaviors exist, how they came to be, or the implications associated with the available options.

We can't tell you how many times someone has come up to us after a seminar and said, "I've read the standard, and know what it says but I don't understand the reasons behind what it says." In response, we have to tell them that the intent of standards is not to explain why certain requirements exist or how to implement those requirements. Standards define externally observable behavior and do not describe how a design accomplishes that behavior.

In writing this book, we have taken the information provided by the ANSI Fibre Channel Arbitrated Loop standard and expanded it to explain the reasons behind required behaviors. We have provided information that addresses the how, what, and why behind the standards.

This book assumes the reader has a basic understanding of the structure and operation of Fibre Channel and the Small Computer System Interface (SCSI). The focus in this book is principally on the Arbitrated Loop topology—primarily as it applies to SCSI-3 Fibre Channel Protocol (FCP) operations. We have maintained this focus to be consistent with the major direction of current activities and Fibre Channel Arbitrated Loop applications. This activity is mainly directed to current storage systems and subsystems. If you are new to Fibre Channel, we encourage you to read the companion book in this series *"Fibre Channel: A Comprehensive Introduction"* which is available from the same publisher.

We have organized this book in a logical progression, which follows the same format as is used in the professional training seminars. As a result, the book opens with a general introduction that helps illustrate the role the Arbitrated Loop topology plays in the larger Fibre Channel picture as well as the use of Arbitrated Loop as an alternative to other interface options.

After the Arbitrated Loop has been positioned relative to the other Fibre Channel topologies and some potential applications have been explored, the focus shifts to the actual operation of the loop as defined by the ANSI standard. This provides the reader with a comprehensive understanding of the behavior of the Arbitrated Loop. Unlike the Arbitrated Loop standard, however, this description includes discussions of how the loop protocols operate and the implications of different modes of operation. To assist the reader with understanding loop behavior state tables are included in the appendix titled *"LPSM State Tables"* on page 321 precisely defining actions required by the Arbitrated Loop standard.

The last part of the book moves beyond the Arbitrated Loop standard and provides in-depth examinations of practical considerations associated with using the Arbitrated Loop. The operation of the SCSI Fibre Channel Protocol is described with numerous examples of how SCSI commands may use the loop. The chapter on understanding loop performance provides an introduction to techniques that can be used to estimate loop performance and compare different configurations or modes of operation. High-availability applications bring their own set of requirements to the loop environment and these considerations are covered in their own chapter.

With the increasing focus on Storage Area Networks (SANs), it certainly appears there is a bright future for the Fibre Channel Arbitrated Loop. Even though this topology provides an ideal solution for many applications, it should not be viewed as a panacea for all interface situations. Some applications represent a natural fit for the particular attributes provided by the Arbitrated Loop. Other applications may be better served by a Fibre Channel switched fabric environment, or even a different interface altogether. One of the unique strengths of an Arbitrated Loop design is that is can grow with the needs of the application and incorporate the high-aggregate bandwidth capabilities of the switched fabric when required. For the near term, the characteristics of the Arbitrated Loop make it a logical evolutionary path from the parallel SCSI interfaces of today.

Robert W. Kembel
Horst L. Truestedt

1. Introduction

The Fibre Channel Arbitrated Loop is the third addition of the Fibre Channel family of intercon-nection topologies. It is ideal for many small to mid-sized configurations where the cost of a separate fabric switch would be prohibitive. Arbitrated Loop applications include storage sub-systems, processor clustering, work group networking, and many other environments requir-ing modest connectivity combined with high transmission speeds.

Arbitrated Loop was originally conceived to fill the gap between the somewhat limited capabili-ties of the point-to-point Fibre Channel configuration and the relatively expensive switched fab-ric. By simplifying the switching mechanism and distributing the function to each port, Arbitrated Loop strikes a balance of connectivity, cost, and performance that makes it unique. Arbitrated Loops may be attached to a switched fabric to create a larger configuration. This may make a switched fabric more affordable by amortizing the cost of the switched fabric across multiple Arbitrated Loop ports (i.e., the cost of one switch port is spread across multiple Arbitrated Loop ports).

The principal Arbitrated Loop objectives are to:

• provide simple, low-cost connectivity without requiring a separate fabric switch;

• provide performance and connectivity 5x-10x the capabilities of fast-wide SCSI at compara-ble system level costs;

• maintain backward compatibility with the point-to-point and switched fabric topologies; and,

• provide a growth path by attaching one or more loops to a Fibre Channel fabric.

Loop-capable ports (called L_Ports) incorporate additional functionality and loop-specific pro-tocols, self-discover their environment, and automatically adopt the appropriate loop or non-loop behavior.

1.1 Fibre Channel Topologies

The original Fibre Channel standard fully defined the point-to-point topology and introduced the concepts associated with a switched fabric topology. While these two topologies were ap-propriate for many applications, it was apparent that point-to-point was too limited in the num-ber of ports that could be supported while switched fabric was too costly for many uses. A third topology called Buffer Insertion Loop had been discarded because the high-speed buffers were deemed too expensive for a low-cost topology. However, a third topology was needed to fill the gap between the two existing topologies that would provide a moderate amount of con-nectivity without the cost associated with the switched fabric. This topology then became known is Arbitrated Loop where arbitration is used (similar to the SCSI bus) to acquire access to the loop.

1.2 What Is Arbitrated Loop?

Arbitrated Loop is a loop interconnection topology that allows up to 126 participating node ports to communicate with one another without the need for a separate switched fabric. Unlike the switched fabric topology with its centralized approach to routing, Arbitrated Loop distributes the routing function to each L_Port. This reduces the cost of achieving the interconnection because the loop functionality represents a relatively small addition to the normal port functionality.

Arbitrated Loop differs from switched fabric topologies in the number of concurrent connections that are possible. Typical switched fabric environments support multiple concurrent connections by using a non-blocking switch architecture. The term non-blocking indicates that one switch connection between one pair of ports does not block the ability to make another switch connection between a different pair of ports. As a result, the fabric provides a total bandwidth that may be many times the bandwidth of an individual port.

Arbitrated Loop is a fully blocking connection topology that allows a single connection between one pair of L_Ports at any point in time. Connections between other L_Ports are blocked until the first connection ends. As a result, the total bandwidth available in an Arbitrated Loop is limited to the bandwidth of the loop itself (i.e., the bandwidth is shared among all the L_Ports on the loop.

Figure 1 illustrates the three topologies supported by Fibre Channel.

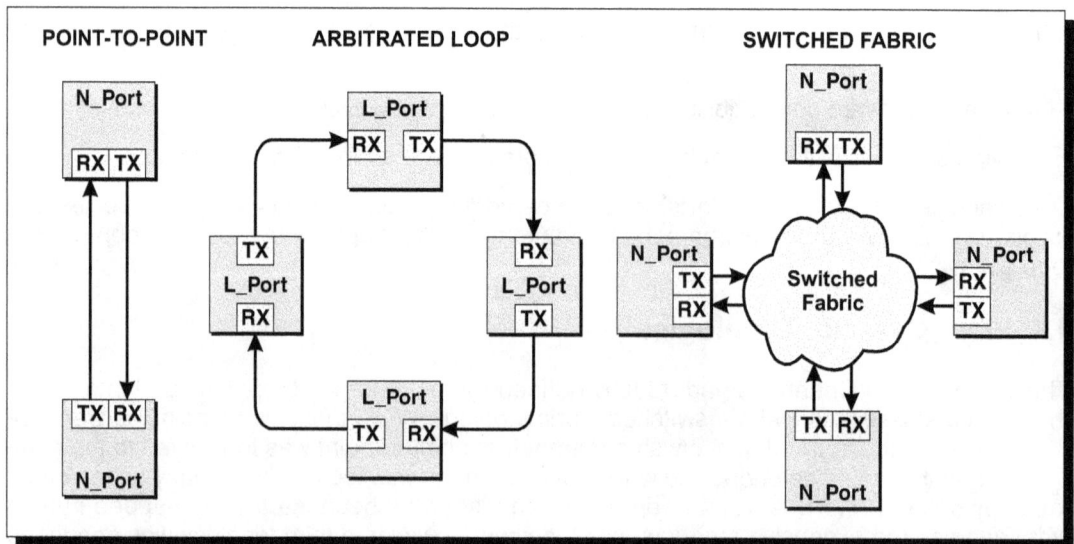

Figure 1. Fibre Channel Topologies

Each topology provides specific characteristics making it more applicable to certain environments than others. A summary of these characteristics is presented in Table 1 on page 3.

Attribute	Point-to-Point	Arbitrated Loop	Switched Fabric
Number of ports	2	2-127	Up to 2^{24}
Maximum bandwidth	Link rate * 2	Link rate * 2	Link rate * num. of ports
Bandwidth allocation	Dedicated	Shared by all L_Ports	Managed by fabric
Address assigned by	N_Port	Loop initialization and Fabric Login	Fabric login
Number of concurrent circuits	1	1	Number of ports/2
Effect of port failure	Link fails	Loop fails (port bypass circuit may be required)	Link fails
Concurrent maintenance	Link is down	May be disruptive	Link is down
Expansion	Add additional N_Ports	Attach to fabric	Expand fabric
Redundancy	Add redundant port	Use dual loops	Use redundant switches
Links rates	All	All	All
Media types	All	All	All
Classes of service	All	All	All
Access to interconnect	Dedicated	Arbitration	Dedicated to switch, managed by switch
Cost per port	Port cost	L_Port cost	Port cost + fabric port

Table 1. Fibre Channel Topology Comparison

- Point-to-point is the basic topology described by the Fibre Channel standard. It allows two N_Ports to be connected via a single link. Larger configurations can be created by providing multiple N_Ports on each node. Each point-to-point circuit provides the full bandwidth supported by the N_Ports.

- Arbitrated Loop allows configurations containing up to 126 participating node ports and one participating fabric port to communicate. More ports than this can be connected to an Arbitrated Loop, however, the additional ports are not able to acquire an address or participate in loop operations.

- The switched fabric topology can theoretically support configurations with over 15 million ports. Because multiple concurrent connections can exist between different pairs of ports, aggregate bandwidths of hundreds or thousands of gigabytes per second are possible.

Because the loop's bandwidth is shared by all participating ports on the loop, an individual L_Port may only be able to realize a small portion of the rated bandwidth. Larger configurations can be created by attaching one or more Arbitrated Loops to a switched fabric. An example of this type of configuration is shown in Figure 2 on page 4 which has two separate Arbitrated Loops attached to a single switched fabric.

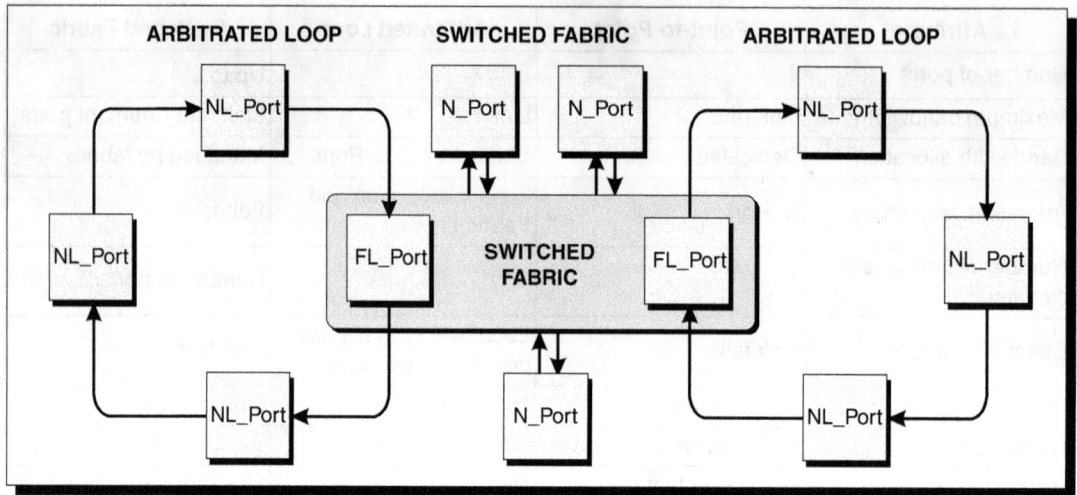

ARBITRATED LOOP   **SWITCHED FABRIC**   **ARBITRATED LOOP**

Figure 2. Hybrid Fabric Attached Loop Topology

The Arbitrated Loop configuration is created by separating the transmit and receive fibres associated with each L_Port and connecting the transmit output of one L_Port to the receive input of the next L_Port. An example of this is shown in Figure 3 on page 5 where the transmit output of Port_1 is connected to the receive input of Port_2, the transmit output of Port_2 is connected to the receive input of Port_3, and so on until the transmit output of the last port is connected to the receive input of the first port.

The Arbitrated Loop architecture allows up to 127 L_Ports to participate in loop operations. More L_Ports may physically be connected to the loop, but due to addressing considerations associated with the loop protocols, the additional ports are not able to participate in loop operations. Of the 127 L_Ports, one can be a fabric L_Port which provides attachment to a switched fabric while the other 126 L_Ports are associated with nodes.

Information from one L_Port flows around the loop from transmitter to receiver through the intermediate L_Ports until it reaches its final destination. Each L_Port contains a repeater function which allows frames and ordered sets to pass through the L_Port. This L_Port interconnection is shown in Figure 3.

To keep the loop hardware simple and cost effective, the repeater function does not buffer frames and contains only a small six-word speed-matching buffer to compensate for clock tolerances. The lack of frame buffers requires that all L_Ports on the loop must operate at the same link speed (i.e., all L_Ports must operate at 1,062.5 megabaud or 2125 megabaud). Because the repeater function operates at the transmission word level and does not buffer frames, L_Ports can retransmit frames larger than they themselves are able to receive in their internal receive buffers. This ability allows low-cost devices with limited receive buffering capabilities to share the same loop with higher-performance devices utilizing larger frame sizes.

The loop is a common resource shared by all L_Ports. To ensure that information from one L_Port does not interfere with information from another, each L_Port must arbitrate for access

Chapter 1. Introduction

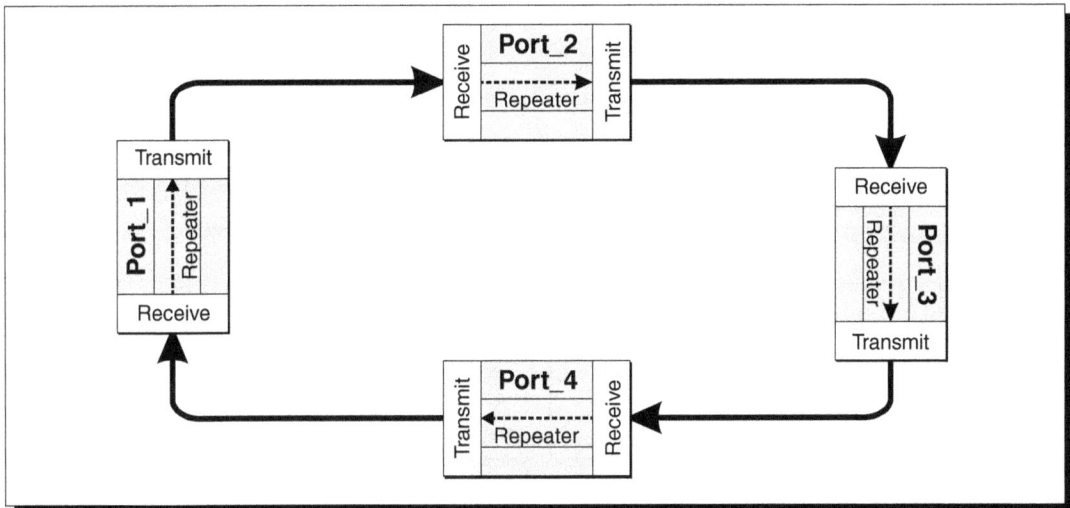

Figure 3. L_Port Interconnection

to the loop before originating information. When the L_Port wins arbitration, it open a destination L_Port to create a circuit between the two L_Ports. Once a loop circuit is established, the two L_Ports can begin frame transmission and reception with each other. As long as the loop circuit is active, the other L_Ports act as repeaters, creating what could be considered a dynamic *point-to-point like* connection as shown in Figure 4.

In the example on the left, Port_1 and Port_3 have established a loop circuit while Port_2 and Port_4 are repeating received transmission words. In the example on the right, Port_2 and Port_4 have established a loop circuit while Port_1 and Port_3 are repeating received transmission words. Any L_Port is capable of establishing a circuit with any other L_Port while all of the remaining L_Ports function as repeaters.

As long as the loop circuit is active, the two L_Ports have full use of the loop's bandwidth, including the ability to operate in full-duplex mode. Each L_Port may simultaneously transmit and receive data at the full link rate (typically 100 megabytes per second in each direction for a total of 200 megabytes per second). When the two L_Ports have completed communication with each other, the circuit is closed and the loop is made available for use by other L_Ports.

Loop-specific protocols are defined to control loop initialization, arbitration, and the opening and closing of loop circuits. These protocols use primitive signals and primitive sequences consisting of loop-specific ordered sets. Each loop-capable port contains a Loop Port State Machine (LPSM) responsible for performing the loop protocols. The LPSM receives controlling inputs from the L_Port's hardware and firmware as well as the ordered sets received from the loop interface. These inputs cause the LPSM to progress through the appropriate states as the loop protocols are performed.

Arbitrated Loop is one of the family of Fibre Channel topologies, not a new architecture. While the actual definition occurred after the initial Fibre Channel standard was developed, several of

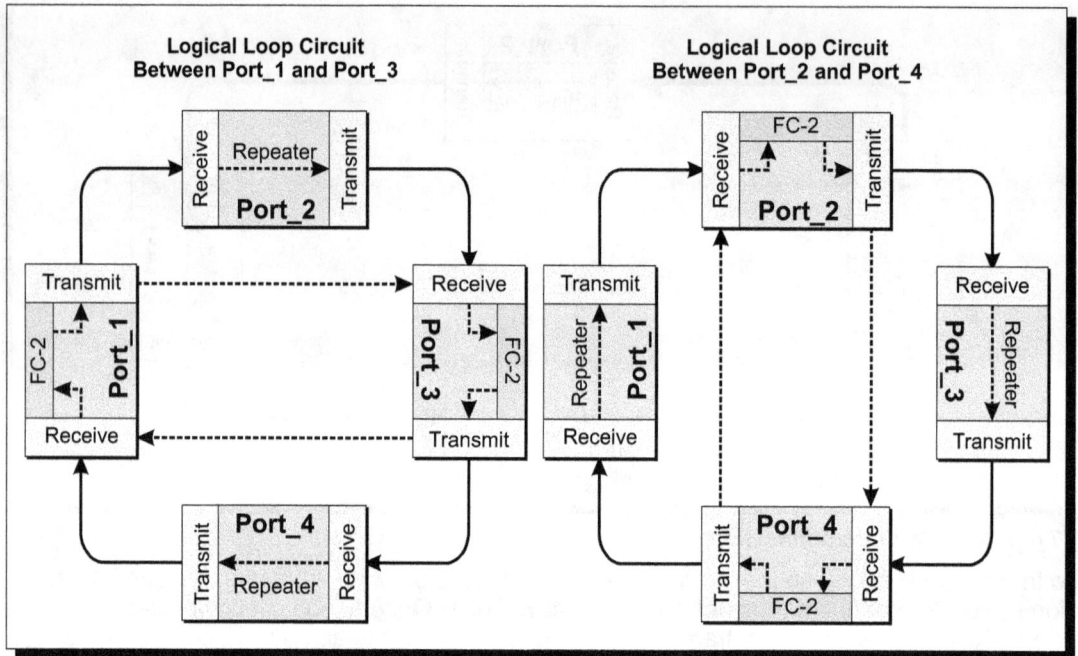

Figure 4. Dynamic Loop Circuits

the architects envisioned the need for additional topologies, such as Arbitrated Loop. As a result, the majority of the existing Fibre Channel architecture applies equally to the loop.

An Arbitrated Loop is capable of supporting all of the protocols currently mapped to Fibre Channel. This includes SCSI-3 (the Small Computer System Interface), TCP/IP (Transmission Control Protocol/Internet Protocol), SBCON (Single Byte CONnectivity protocol, the ANSI standard version of IBM's Enterprise Systems CONnectivity), and several others.

The loop can operate with any of the media types and link rates defined by the Fibre Channel standard. While link rates can't be mixed on a single loop, media types can. This enables an application to use copper media for some portions of the loop to save cost, while using optical media in other portions to gain distance and noise immunity.

The Arbitrated Loop supports the use of any of the existing classes of service defined by the Fibre Channel standard. Class-1/6 service can be used to provide a dedicated connection for one or more sequences with confirmation of delivery. Class-2 and Class-3 provide a frame multiplexed transmission capability allowing sequences to be transmitted over one or more loop circuits. Class-2 provides confirmation of frame delivery, while Class-3 does not. Class-4 service can be used to provide fractional bandwidth connections with confirmation of delivery.

1.3 Port Types

Ports capable of operating in an Arbitrated Loop environment have certain functions not present in non loop-capable ports. These ports are called L_Ports (or loop ports) to indicate that the necessary loop functionality is present. Each L_Port incorporates an LPSM to perform the loop-specific protocols and a repeater function to allow information to pass through the port and around the loop until it reaches its ultimate destination. L_Ports can be associated with either a node or a fabric. If the L_Port is part of a node, it is called an NL_Port (short for Node L_Port). If the loop port is part of a fabric, it is called an FL_Port (Fabric L_Port).

When an L_Port wishes to communicate with an NL_Port on the same loop, it establishes a loop circuit with that NL_Port. When an NL_Port wishes to communicate with a port external to the loop (i.e., attached to a fabric connected to the loop), it establishes a loop circuit with the FL_Port and then sends the frames to the switched fabric via the FL_Port. The switched fabric routes the information to the destination port which may be an N_Port attached directly to the fabric, or an NL_Port on a different loop attached to the fabric by another FL_Port.

Fibre Channel defines a number of architected services that are located at "well known" addresses defined by the various standards. Some of these services are required in a fabric environment, while others are optional. In a fabric environment, when a port wishes to access one of these services, it sends its request to the "well known" address assigned to that service and the fabric delivers the request to the appropriate destination. When the port is on a loop with a fabric attached, it establishes a loop circuit with the FL_Port, and sends its request via the FL_Port to the final destination. See Figure 2 on page 4 for an example of an Arbitrated Loop attached to a fabric.

If the Arbitrated Loop is not attached to a fabric, one NL_Port on the loop may optionally provide one or more of the defined Fibre Channel services (e.g., Name Server, Time Server, Security Server, etc.). An NL_Port that provides this optional functionality is called an F/NL_Port (short for Fabric/Node L_Port). The F/NL_Port mimics the behavior of an FL_Port by responding as the FL_Port would, if it were present. After a loop circuit is established, the F/NL_Port responds to the "well known" addresses associated with the Fibre Channel service or services supported. Whether the service is provide within the fabric or by an F/NL_Port, is completely transparent to the NL_Port requesting the Fibre Channel services.

1.4 Loop Applications

Arbitrated Loop has a number of characteristics that make it attractive in various applications. Among potential applications are storage subsystems, file servers, workgroup or departmental clustering, processor clustering, high-performance networking, high-performance network backbone, and as a high-performance device interface. The following sections provide examples illustrating the use of Arbitrated Loop in each application. The examples use 100 megabytes per second which is the dominant link speed at this moment. However, 200 megabyte ports are already available and higher link speeds have also been defined for Fibre Channel.

1.4.1 Storage Subsystem

The needs of storage subsystems have been a driving factor in the development of Arbitrated Loop. Both RAID (Redundant Arrays of Independent Disks) and JBOD (Just a Bunch of Disks) applications take advantage of Arbitrated Loop's connectivity and high-performance potential. Arbitrated Loop's ability to attach up to 125 disk drives to a single initiator and support full duplex transfers at 100 megabytes per second makes large capacity subsystems practical.

A single Fast/Wide SCSI initiator can attach a maximum of 15 devices and provides an instantaneous bandwidth of 20 megabytes per second (Ultra-SCSI raises the data phase transfer rate to 40 megabytes per second and Ultra-2 to 80 megabytes per second, but the command overheads remain the same). The upper portion of Figure 5 on page 8 illustrates a typical multiple-target SCSI parallel bus configuration with a file server and one or more external enclosures housing up to eight disk drives per enclosure. Due to the addressing limitations of the SCSI wide parallel bus, a maximum of 15 drives can be attached to one initiator.

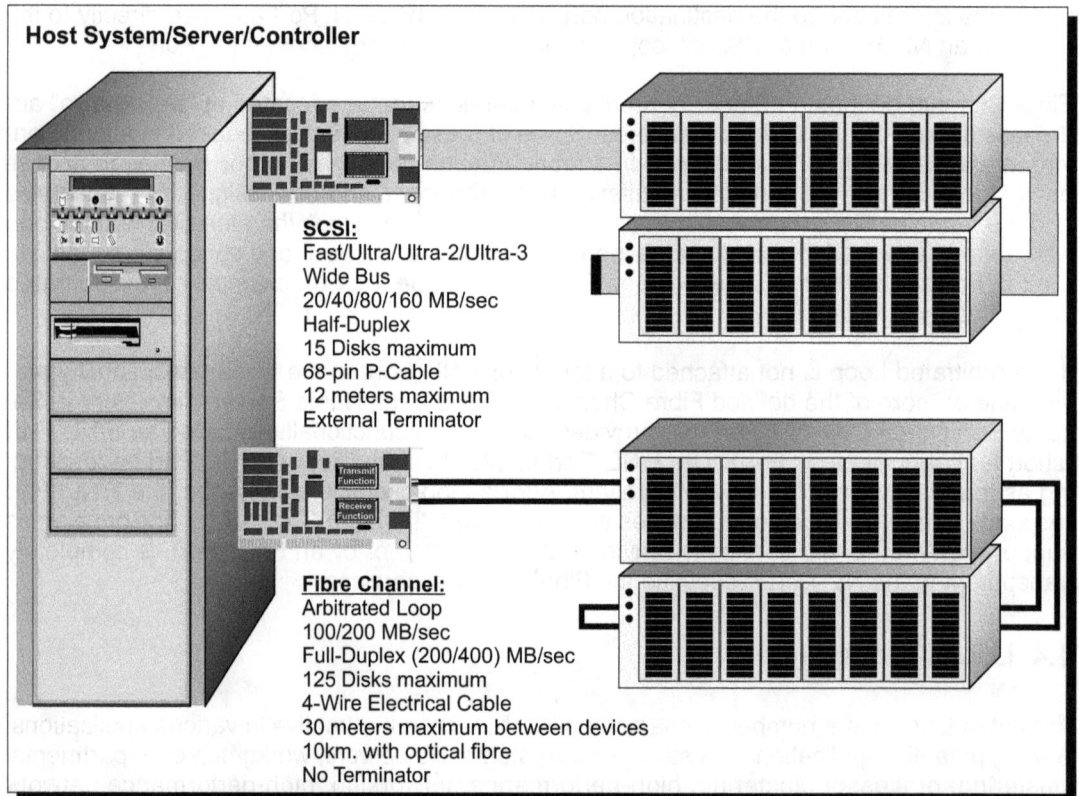

Host System/Server/Controller

SCSI:
Fast/Ultra/Ultra-2/Ultra-3
Wide Bus
20/40/80/160 MB/sec
Half-Duplex
15 Disks maximum
68-pin P-Cable
12 meters maximum
External Terminator

Fibre Channel:
Arbitrated Loop
100/200 MB/sec
Full-Duplex (200/400) MB/sec
125 Disks maximum
4-Wire Electrical Cable
30 meters maximum between devices
10km. with optical fibre
No Terminator

Figure 5. Disk Subsystem Example

The lower portion of Figure 5 shows a single Arbitrated Loop adapter attached to enclosures containing Fibre Channel disk drives. In this configuration, the adapter is capable of attaching

125 drives, more than eight times as many as can be attached to a SCSI wide parallel bus interface. The 100 megabyte per second bandwidth of the Fibre Channel link is significantly higher than that of a Fast/Wide SCSI interface. The Fibre Channel link transfers information in excess of 100 megabytes per second compared to a Fast/Wide bus speed of 20 megabytes per second, or Ultra SCSI's speed of 40 megabytes per second. Unlike the SCSI parallel bus, all transfers take place at the full link speed, not just the data transfer portion. Also, unlike a SCSI parallel bus, the Fibre Channel link is capable of full-duplex operation. This means that information can be transferred in both directions at the same time, providing a maximum bandwidth twice that of the link speed. Fibre Channel provides attachment capability of 125 drives with a bandwidth in excess of 200 megabytes per second through a single adapter using a simple four-wire interface (two differential pairs, one for transmitting, the second for receiving).

The advantages of Fibre Channel become even more apparent when contemplating large configurations. For example, consider the case of a one-terabyte storage subsystem using SCSI parallel busses as shown in Figure 6.

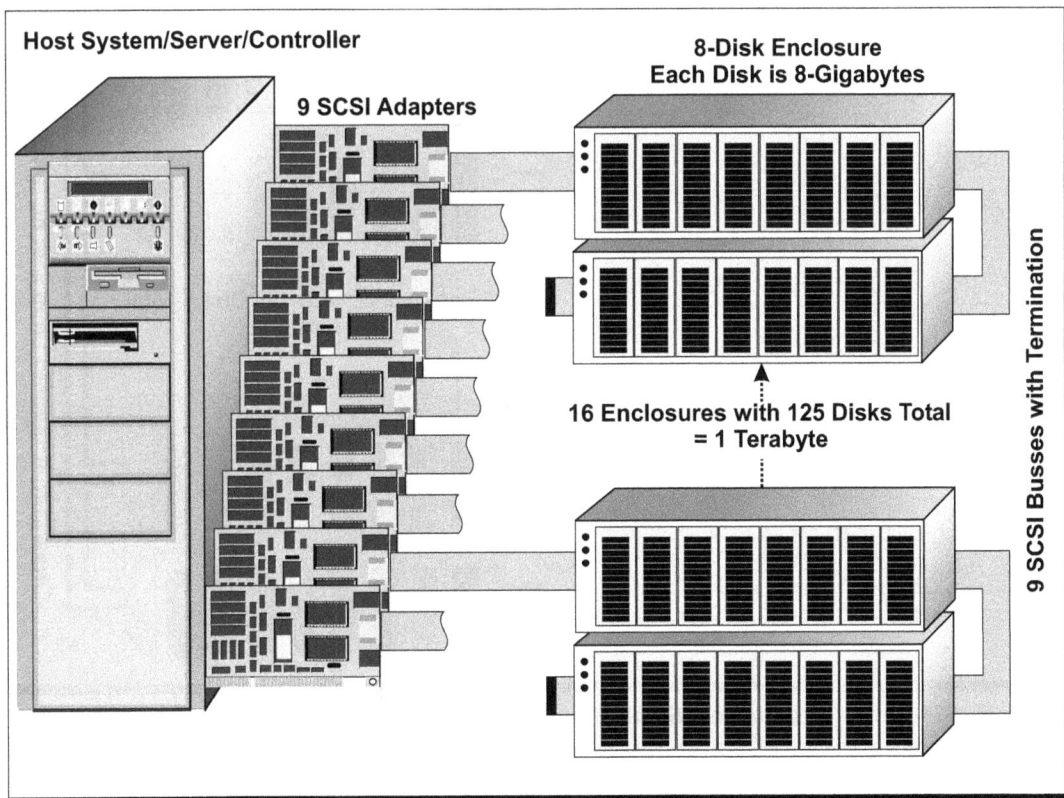

Figure 6. 1-Terabyte SCSI Disk Subsystem

To achieve a one-terabyte capacity using 8-Gigabyte disk drives, 125 disks drives are required. If this configuration is assembled using wide SCSI parallel bus interfaces, each initiator can attach a maximum of 15 drives. To support the 125 disk drives needed, nine initiators and their associated 68-pin cabling and terminators are required. Housing this many initiators may require more than one enclosure to provide the required physical space, power, and cooling. It is easy to see how the cost of this configuration can mount rapidly.

By using an Arbitrated Loop, each adapter can attach up to 125 disk drives. This allows the entire 1-Terabyte of storage to be accessed through a single Fibre Channel adapter and 4-wire interface as shown in Figure 7. The Fibre Channel configuration provides the same storage capacity while using 8 fewer adapters in the server. In addition, only a single slot is required for the adapter and the need for a second enclosure disappears. The amount of power required is reduced, cabling is simpler and less expensive, and no separate termination is required.

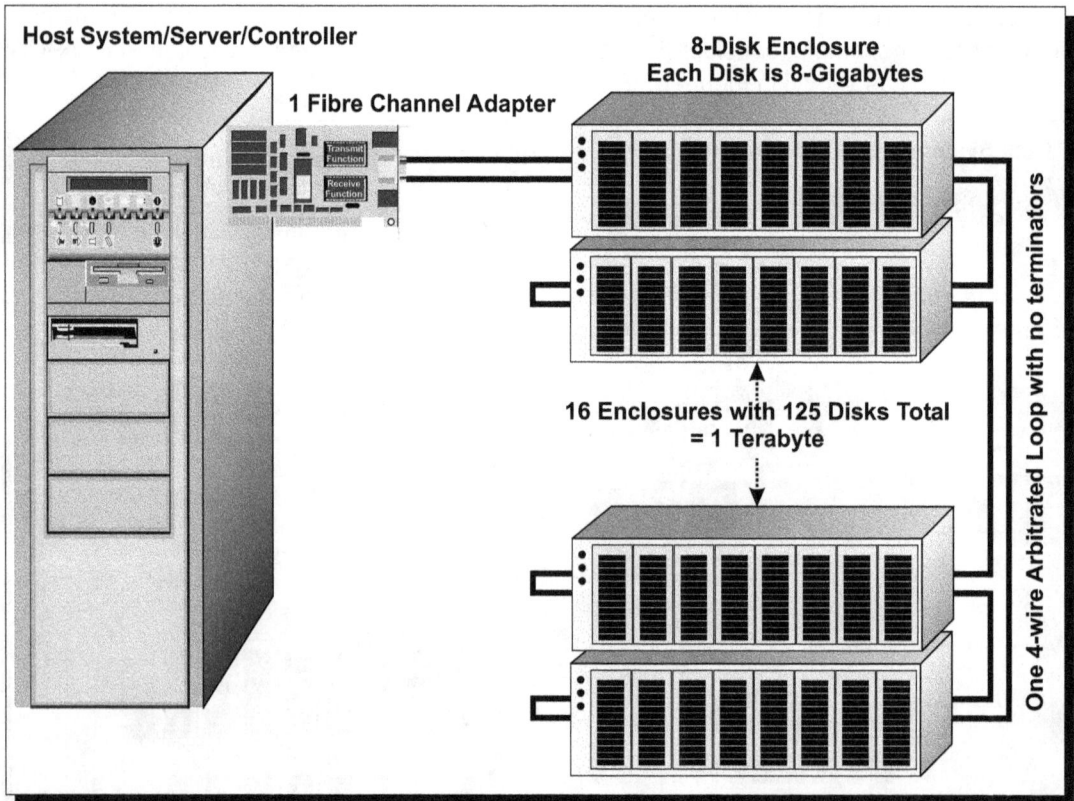

Figure 7. 1-Terabyte Fibre Channel Subsystem

Nine fast/wide SCSI initiators are capable of a maximum instantaneous bandwidth of 180 megabytes per second. The one Arbitrated Loop adapter is capable of 100 megabytes per second transmit and 100 megabytes per second receive for a total potential of 200 megabytes per second. Unlike parallel SCSI busses, the full Fibre Channel bandwidth is available for all phases of the operation, not just the data phase. Of course, as is the case with all bandwidth comparisons, many factors affect the actual performance achieved by different configurations which is usually less than the instantaneous rates. The chapter titled *Performance* on page 229 examines these factors and provides a basis for estimating loop performance.

1.4.2 Arbitrated Loop File Server

The traditional approach to building a file server is to connect a number of disk drives to the server using one or more SCSI parallel busses and provide the client interface using a standard network interface such as Ethernet. An example of this type of server configuration is shown in Figure 8.

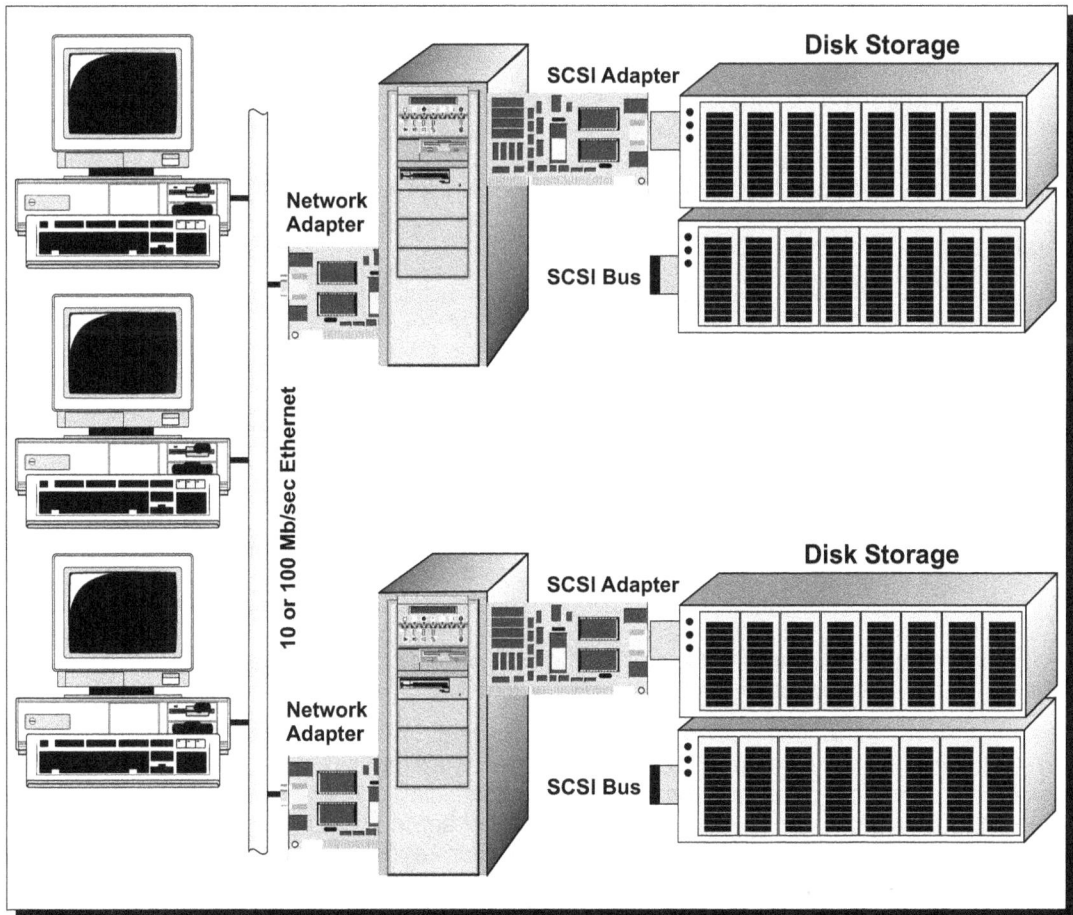

Figure 8. Legacy Network File Server

This approach has two significant shortcomings. The first is that the network interface is too slow for many applications that transfer large amounts of data. This requires users to have local disk storage to hold programs and frequently accessed data.

A standard 10 megabit per second Ethernet provides a maximum throughput of approximately one megabyte per second with typical throughputs somewhat less. This means that approximately 30 seconds are required to transfer a full page (8.5" x 11") 24-bit graphic image such as might be used in a publishing application.

While the new 100 megabit per second Ethernet is 10 times as fast, it is still too slow for many data intensive applications, especially when multiple users are sharing the same network segment.

A second shortcoming of the traditional configuration is that as the amount of disk storage increases, the number of SCSI initiators and, perhaps servers, increases to support the increased capacity. The need to use different adapter types (Ethernet and SCSI) and multiples of each adds to the total cost of this approach.

If the Fibre Channel disk subsystem shown in Figure 7 on page 10 is used as the basis for a file server, both shortcomings can be alleviated. An example of using a single Arbitrated Loop to provide both the device and client attachments is shown in Figure 9 on page 13. This approach has the dual advantages of higher bandwidths for both the clients and storage combined with the ability to attach a larger number of devices than is possible on a single SCSI parallel bus.

All ports on the loop now share the high performance of the loop. The workstations can still communicate with the file server using a network protocol such as TCP/IP or the encapsulation of the logical portion of existing network protocols such as Ethernet. When this is done, Fibre Channel simply appears to the user as a much higher performance physical layer. When clients access the file server, or communicate with other workstations on the loop, the communications takes place at 1,062.5 megabits per second, rather than the 10 or 100 megabits per second associated with typical networks. In some cases, access to the network-attached disk drives may be faster than accessing the workstation's own disks.

The file server processes client requests and accesses the disk storage to read or write the desired information. In this case, the file server uses the SCSI-3 Fibre Channel Protocol (FCP) to access the disk devices. Both the network traffic (TCP/IP or Link Encapsulation of a standard network protocol) and the file server's SCSI-3 FCP protocol share the same loop, as well as the same adapter in the file server. The file server no longer requires separate adapters to service its clients and access the disk devices, one Fibre Channel adapter can do both.

The basic loop configuration shown in Figure 9 on page 13 can be expanded by connecting the Arbitrated Loop to a fabric switch via an FL_Port. When this is done, the workstations and file server can communicate with other devices accessible via the fabric. When the same loop is going to be used for both client and device traffic, some way of logically isolating the two types of traffic is essential. The disk drives may need to remain private to the file server. Client activity may need to be restricted to requests made to the file server. Conversely, disk traffic should be limited to file server access only. The file server, on the other hand needs to communicate with both the clients and disk drives.

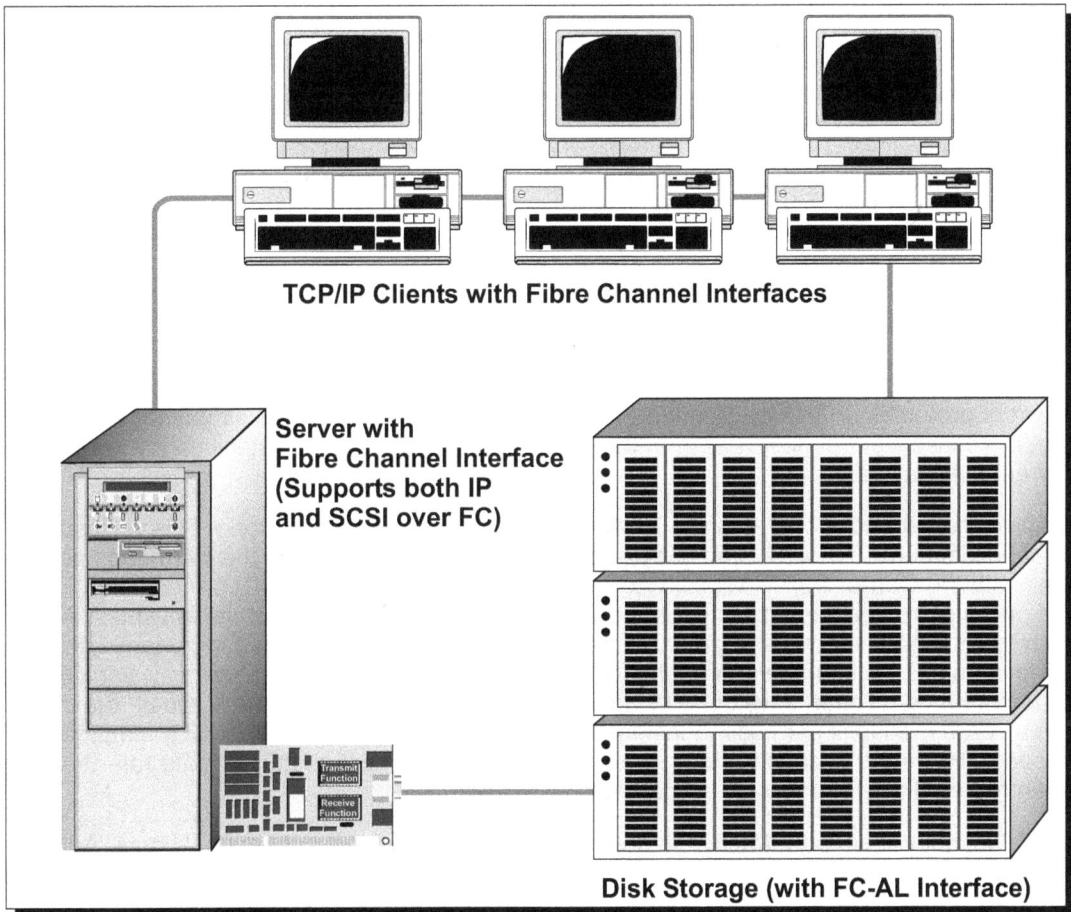

TCP/IP Clients with Fibre Channel Interfaces

Server with Fibre Channel Interface (Supports both IP and SCSI over FC)

Disk Storage (with FC-AL Interface)

Figure 9. Arbitrated Loop Network File Server

The Arbitrated Loop provides this capability by partitioning the address space on the loop into private ports and public ports. Private ports are limited to communication with other ports on the same loop, while public ports can communicate with ports on the loop and, via the FL_Port, with ports outside the loop. Ports outside the loop can only communicate with the public ports on the loop. Therefore, a single loop can have a public file server able to access both the external clients and private ports on the loop, while the external clients are unable to access the private disks directly.

If the file server is a Network File Server, it needs to support the appropriate network protocol such as TCP/IP or another network protocol. On the other hand, the disk drives probably recognize only the SCSI-3 FCP protocol. The file server can take advantage of Fibre Channel's multi-protocol architecture and communicate to the clients using TCP/IP while at the same time using the SCSI-3 FCP protocol to access the disk drives. Both can occur simultaneously through the same port, which supports multiple protocols.

The file server can communicate with its clients using either the TCP/IP or SCSI-3 FCP protocols and with the private disk drives using the SCSI-3 FCP protocol. Public operations via the fabric may use Class-1 or Class-2 service to provide the required delivery confirmation, if desired. Operations with the private disk drives on the loop may use Class-3 service because it is simpler and has less overhead than Class-1 or Class-2. In this configuration, the file server may be supporting multiple protocols (TCP/IP and SCSI-3 FCP) and different classes of service (Class-1 or Class-2 and Class-3) simultaneously.

1.4.3 High-Performance Network Replacement

Fibre Channel offers an attractive high-performance physical interface for transporting existing network protocols. In this application Fibre Channel can be viewed as simply an alternative Media Access Control (MAC) layer in the network protocol stack, but significantly faster than current MAC layers.

Ethernet, for example, operates at 10 megabits or 100 megabits per second. This corresponds to approximately 1.25 or 12.5 megabytes per second maximum. When the overheads associated with the Carrier Sense Multiple Access/Collision Detect (CSMA/CD) protocol and Ethernet packets are considered, actual throughput may fall to about 60% of these values. As the activity on a given network segment increases the CSMA/CD overhead increases because more collisions occur in the shared media resulting in increased packet retransmission.Gigabit Ethernet has also been developed using common Fibre Channel hardware (albeit, the clocks run at 1250 megabits per second instead of the Fibre Channel speed of 1062.5 megabits per second). However, because of the Ethernet overhead, the best sustained data rate that has been reported at this time is 30 megabytes per second.

Fibre Channel offers an attractive, high-speed alternative to conventional networks. An Arbitrated Loop is capable of achieving throughputs of approximately 90 megabytes per second when using large transfer sizes. Smaller transfer sizes provide less throughput because the overhead associated with the loop protocols remains the same. For selected applications, Fibre Channel can provide throughput orders of magnitude greater than current networks.

In many ways, a network based on Arbitrated Loop is similar to a token ring or Fiber Distributed Data Interface (FDDI) network, only with different low-level MAC layer protocols and speeds. A number of workstations are attached to the loop creating a basic network segment. As the configuration grows, an FL_Port can be added to allow multiple loops to interconnect. This has the advantage that, in a well-planned configuration, most of the traffic stays on the same loop, with the FL_Port providing access to external ports as needed.

Existing legacy networks are likely to remain in service for some time and it is essential that any new Fibre Channel segments can operate with other networks such as Ethernet and TCP/IP. This is accomplished by using routers to connect the two different networks. In the example in Figure 10 on page 15, an Arbitrated Loop is internetworked with an Ethernet segment by using a router to accomplish the connection.

As with all loop and ring topologies, consideration must be given to maintaining the loop's integrity when ports are removed, powered off, or fail. The traditional network solution is to use a device called a hub which automatically senses when an individual port is not operational and shunts or bypasses the loop around that port. When hubs are used, the loop physically has the appearance of a "star" configuration, but in fact a loop exists within the hub. Because hubs receive and redrive the signals to individual ports, each port can be separated from the hub by the maximum link distance allowed for the media type chosen. Hubs also provide a convenient point to mix optical and copper media types because hubs can typically be configured with a mixture of both optical and copper ports.

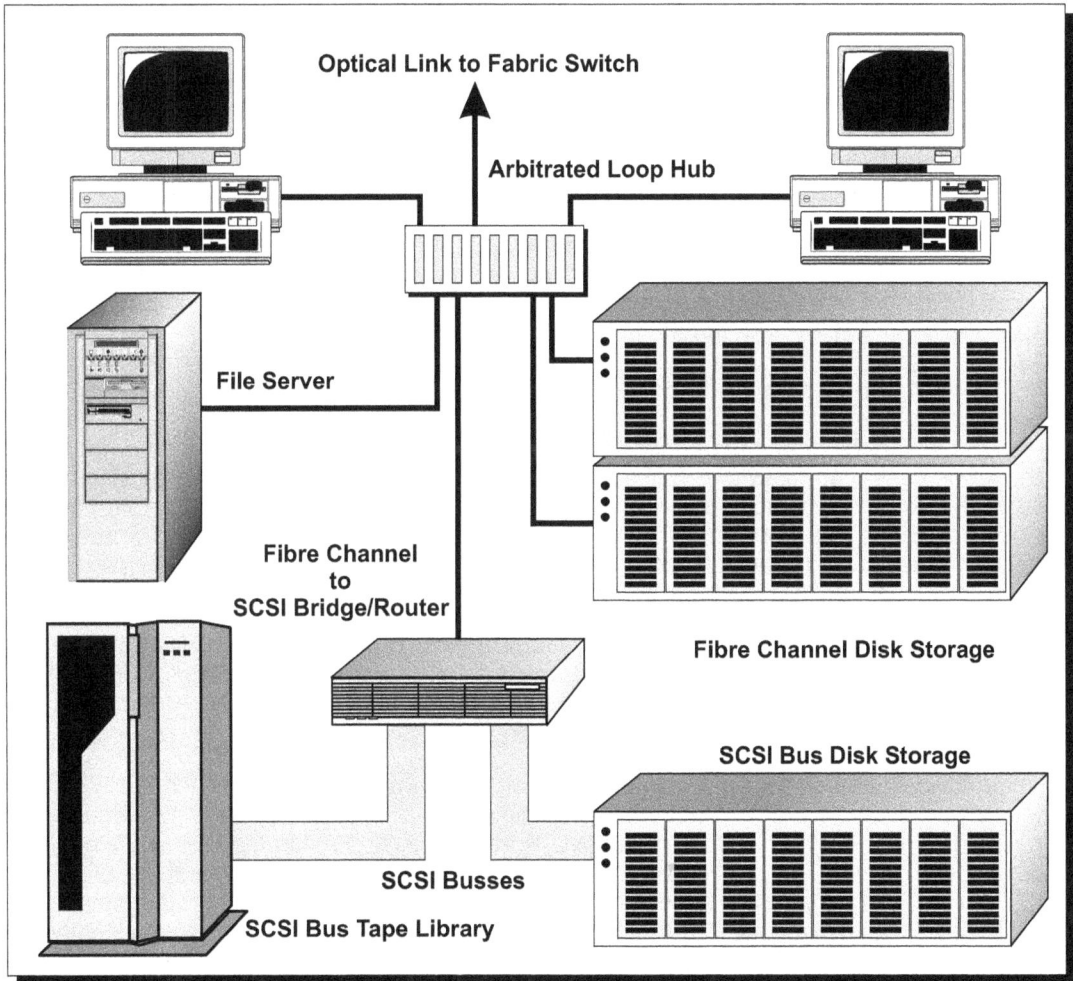

Figure 10. Arbitrated Loop With Hub

1.4.4 Workgroup or Departmental Clustering

Figure 10 illustrates how a hub can be used in an Arbitrated Loop serving as both a high-performance network and storage interface in a departmental cluster. In this example, each workstation is connected to a single loop with a Fibre Channel adapter (high-availability applications may use multiple adapters and redundant loops). Each uses the adapter for both storage access to the file server and network communication with other workstations. Communication between workstations and with the file server use the TCP/IP protocol while communications between the file server and its devices use the SCSI-3 FCP protocol. Communications with nodes external to the loop occur through the FL_Port, then via the fabric to the ultimate destination or to existing networks through the router.

Existing Ethernet, Token Ring, and FDDI network segments can be integrated in the configuration through the use of routers permitting existing networks and new Fibre Channel based networks to interoperate. Fibre Channel's physical media choices provide options that support distances of up to 50 kilometers per link. This allows Fibre Channel links to support multiple building campus environments making it ideal as a high-performance backbone.

When longer distances are required, the Fibre Channel domain can be expanded by using common carrier facilities and a high-performance interconnection such as ATM/SONET operating at 155 or 622 megabits per second or faster. This permits Fibre Channel configurations to span the continent, or even the globe.

1.4.5 Using Arbitrated Loops and Fabric Together

One of the factors hindering the adoption of switched fabrics has been the relatively high cost of the fabric itself. Fabric switches, like all current high-speed serial switches, tend to be expensive due to the technology involved and the limited manufacturing volumes. Even though the original prices of $2,000 to $3,000 per port have dropped to around $800 at this time, switched fabric are still relatively expensive. This price range is typical of high-speed serial switches and is not unique to Fibre Channel.

Arbitrated Loop offers a unique cost-effective alternative to switched fabrics for some applications by allowing large configurations to be created using smaller fabric switches. For example, if one wanted to connect 1024 ports using a switched fabric, 1024 switch ports would be required at cost of $800 per port, for a total fabric cost of approximately $800,000 dollars.

An alternative approach might use a 16-port fabric switch with each port attached to an Arbitrated Loop containing 64 NL_Ports. In this configuration, the $800 cost of each fabric switch port is effectively amortized across the 64 NL_Ports on each attached loop resulting in a connection cost of just $12.50 per NL_Port. The total cost for the 16-port fabric in this case is just $12,800. Figure 11 on page 17 shows an example of a multiple loop configuration attached to a small fabric. In this example, four Arbitrated Loops are attached to a fabric. Nodes located on loop 1 can communicate directly with other nodes on loop 1 as well as those nodes attached to the fabric switch or located on other loops attached to the fabric switch. This allows individual loops to provide direct connectivity for up to 126 ports while using the fabric to enable larger configurations as the application requires.

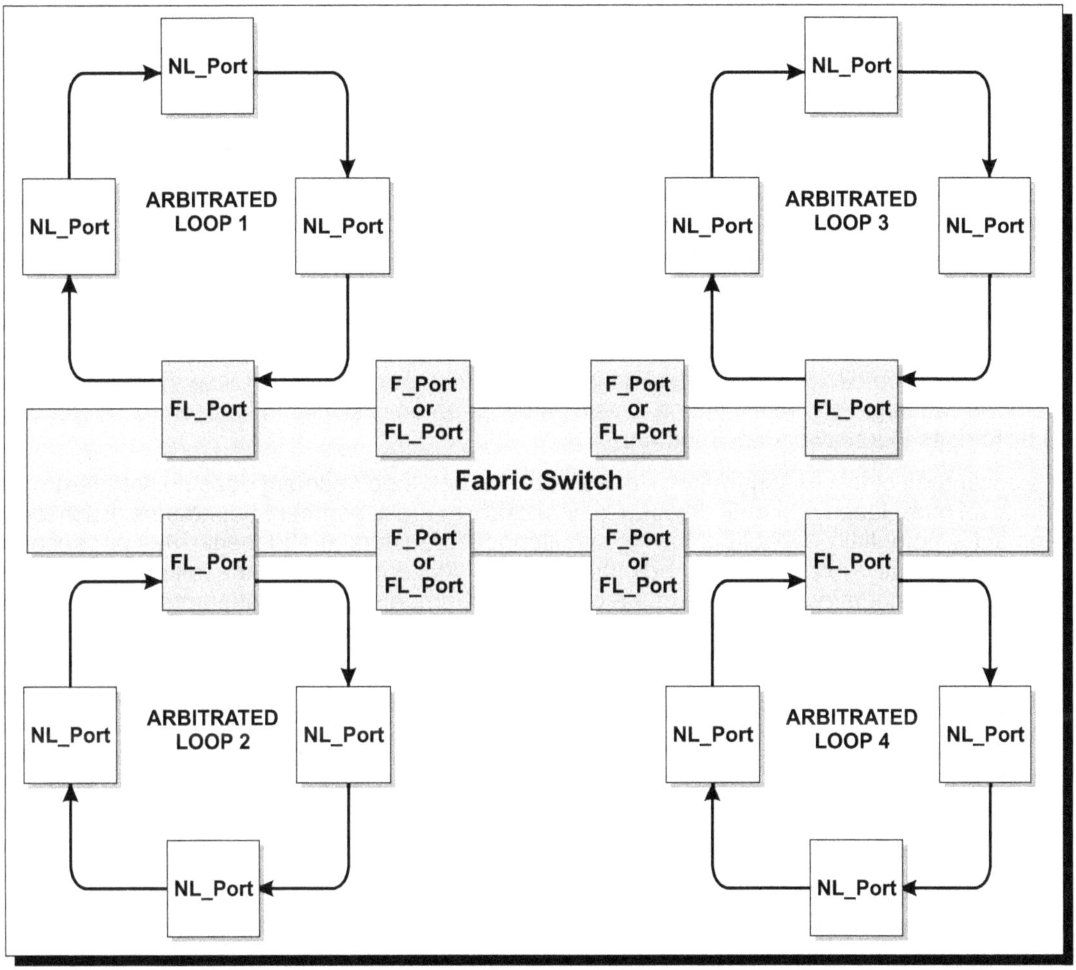

Figure 11. Multiple Loops Attached to a Fabric Switch

The reduced cost achieved by combining loops and fabrics has its trade-offs. Whereas a 1024-port fabric is theoretically capable of supporting 512 concurrent transfers with an aggregate throughput of 102.4 gigabytes per second, the multiple loop configuration with a 16-port fabric is only capable of supporting 8 off-loop connections (1.6 gigabytes per second), or 16 on-loop connections (3.2 gigabytes per second). Combining the two topologies presents intriguing possibilities for balancing cost and bandwidth by varying the number of fabric ports, loops, and ports per loop.

1.4.6 Multiple Arbitrated Loops With Hub

Another approach to creating loop-based configurations is shown in Figure 12 on page 19. In this example, a special hub (sometimes called a switching hub) connects multiple loop segments together while providing independent operations within each loop segment. If the total number of ports on all loop segments does not exceed the Arbitrated Loop's addressing capabilities, this can be done transparently to the ports.

When a port needs to communicate with another port, it arbitrates for access to its local loop. When it wins arbitration, the port attempts to establish a loop circuit with the destination port. If the destination port is on the same loop segment, the hub simply acts as a repeater.

If the destination port is not located on the local loop segment, the hub intercepts the request to establish the loop circuit, acquires access to the proper destination loop segment, and establishes the loop circuit with the destination port on that loop segment. Once this is done, the two ports can begin communications. This type of operation is similar in function to that provided by bridges in a network environment.

The advantage of this configuration is that activity on one loop segment does not interfere with activity on other loop segments unless it is necessary to cross segment boundaries. Each loop segment is potentially capable of having simultaneous transfers at 100 megabytes per second (200 MB/sec. full duplex). Another advantage of this configuration is that a failure in one loop segment does not affect operation of the other loop segments. If a port attempts to establish a loop circuit with a port on a failed loop segment, the hub simply bypasses the faulty segment.

The concept of interconnecting multiple loop segments can be extended to allow configurations consisting of more than 126 NL_Ports. To accomplish this, new loop protocols are needed to allow for the increased addressability. This can be done by extensions of the existing protocol with new ordered sets. These extensions are being discussed as additions to a future version of the Arbitrated Loop standard. In one proposal, the process of establishing a loop circuit with the destination becomes a two-step operation; the first step identifies the correct destination loop, the second establishes the loop circuit with the correct port on that loop.

The hub example shown in Figure 12 on page 19 uses a loop as its internal interconnection structure. This has the effect of allowing only a single connection between only two of the attached loops at any time. This is not a concern if most activity remains on the local loops but may become a factor if significant activity crosses loop boundaries.

The goal of using a hub-based approach is to allow larger, or more efficient, configurations to be created without incurring the cost of a fabric switch. The tradeoff is that the hub does not provide the addressability, nor the same simultaneous connection and bandwidth capabilities that are provided by a true switched fabric.

1.4.7 Fibre Channel as a Device Interface

Several of the earlier examples used the Arbitrated Loop as a device interface. Using Fibre Channel as a device interface was not practical prior to Arbitrated Loop except in specialized applications. Building a storage subsystem around a switched fabric currently can't be justified based on the cost of the fabric in all but the most unusual circumstances. Arbitrated Loop brings the cost of Fibre Channel connectivity down to the level where it is competitive with oth-

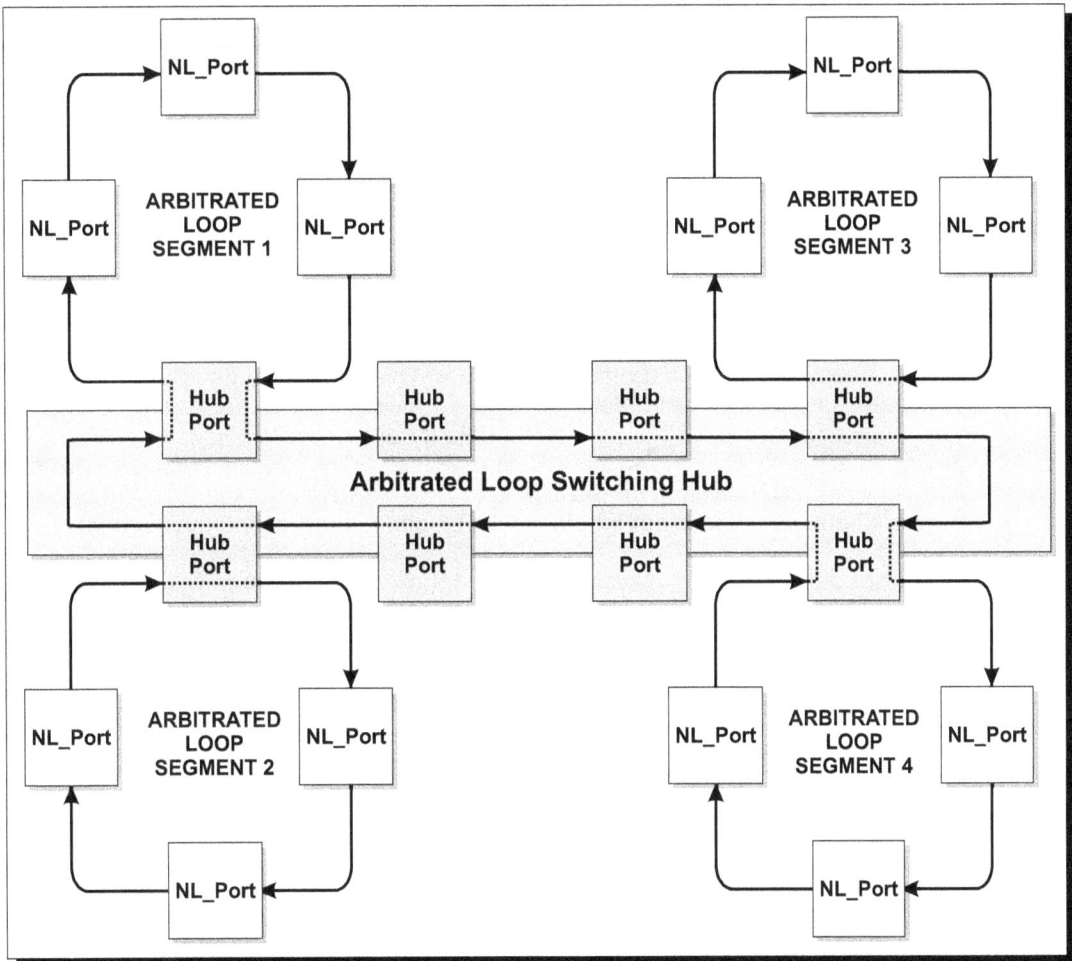

Figure 12. Multiple Loops Attached to a "Smart" Hub

er device interfaces such as differential SCSI. Fibre Channel's high bandwidth and the loop's low cost connectivity make an attractive combination. Sharing a high-speed loop among a number of lower-speed devices provides a more cost-effective solution than multiple low-speed interfaces. The key to overall subsystem performance lies in efficient use of the loop.

Disk Drives. Modern disk drives are capable of reading or writing disk data at speeds between 20 and 30 megabytes per second. As read/write head and recording channel technology advances, this number will continue to increase.

Current high-performance disk drives normally contain a cache memory used to improve the drive's performance. The amount of cache memory used varies but typically falls in the range of 256 kilobytes to 1 or 2 megabytes. The cache is used to store data that was pre-read from the disk in anticipation of future read commands. Efficient cache designs can achieve hit ratios of 50% to 80%. When a read operation retrieves data from the cache, the drive is able to transfer that data immediately without accessing the disk. This results in a very efficient transfer with the data rate being limited only by the cache speed and interface bandwidth.

Cache memory may also be used during write operations. When a write command is received, a portion of the cache memory is allocated to hold the write data. As data is transferred from the interface, it is temporarily stored in the cache allowing the transfer to take place at interface speeds. Status for the command can be sent at the end of the transfer into the cache (write back caching) or when the data has been actually written to the disk (write through caching).

By designing the cache to support Fibre Channel's link speeds, the entire transfer of data to or from the device cache can occur in a high-speed burst. This allows the device to transfer its data and free up the interface for other devices. When a device requires the interface, it establishes a loop circuit and transfers all or part of the data for one or more commands. Many devices can share the same loop by multiplexing their operations. The optimal number of devices depends upon several factors which are discussed in *Performance* on page 229, but typically ranges between 32 and 96 devices per interface with 62 being a representative number.

Tape Drives. Tape device designs have taken two dramatically different directions. At one end of the spectrum are relatively low-cost designs with data transfer rates ranging from a few hundred kilobytes per second up to 1 or 2 megabytes per second. At the other end of the spectrum are high-performance devices capable of sustaining raw data transfer rates of 15 to 30 megabytes per second. Many of these devices incorporate data compression technologies capable of providing typical compression ratios of 1.5x to 3x. This results in interface data rates of 22.5 to 90 megabytes per second. For this type of device, Fibre Channel's high bandwidth offers a natural speed match.

Most modern high-performance tape devices incorporate buffering to allow the device to stream extended bursts of data to or from the tape. Once tape motion is started, it is desirable to read or write as much data as possible without having to stop tape motion. To avoid the mechanical latencies associated with starting and stopping the tape, the interface must be capable of equaling or exceeding the device's data rate. When the interface has enough bandwidth, multiple tape devices can share a single interface by bursting their data transfers.

Printers. Printers are frequently overlooked when discussing high-performance peripherals. While the familiar parallel printer port is sufficient for personal printers, workgroup or high-volume printers may have requirements that can tax the capabilities of even Fibre Channel. As printer speeds increase to meet the needs of 'print on demand' or fully customized high volume color printing, Fibre Channel begins to offer an attractive option.

Consider the case of a 90 page per minute 300 dpi full-color printer. Each 8.5" by 11" page is 2550 pixels wide by 3300 pixels high for a total of 7.65 million pixels per page. For full color reproduction, each pixel typically consists of 24 bits (3 bytes) of color information, for a total of 22.95 million bytes per page. A 90 page per minute printer requires 2.065 gigabytes per minute, or 34.4 megabytes per second.

1.5 Chapter Summary

Arbitrated Loop

- Third Fibre Channel topology
- Fills gap between point-to-point and switched fabric
- Point-to-point is too limited
- Fabric is too expensive ($800 per port)
- Need something to replace Fast/Wide SCSI
- Can also be used as a high-performance network

Arbitrated Loop Goals

- Provide low-cost connectivity without a fabric
- Performance and connectivity 5x-10x SCSI
- Backward compatibility with non-loop environments
- Loop ports must self discover the environment
  - No switches or jumpers
- Original goal: simple addition to normal port
- Complement switched fabrics by lowering the per-port cost of attachment

What Is Arbitrated Loop?

- Loop (or ring) topology with up to 127 ports
- Routing function distributed to each port
  - Different than fabric with its centralized routing
- The loop is a blocking topology
  - Only one circuit at any point in time
  - Fabric allows multiple concurrent operations
- Loop bandwidth is shared by all ports
- Loops can be attached to fabrics to create larger configurations

Loop Basics

- Transmit and receive fibres are separated
- Transmitter of one port connects to receiver input of next port
- Information travels around the loop in a single direction
- All ports operate at the same link rate
  - 1,062.5 megabaud or 2,125 megabaud
- Each port contains a repeater function
  - Repeater does not buffer frames
  - Operates on a transmission word basis

Loop Protocols

- All ports share the loop
- A port must arbitrate before it can use the loop
- When it wins arbitration, it establishes a loop circuit with another port
- The two ports have full use of the loop
  - Full bandwidth
  - Full-duplex transmission, if desired
- When done, the loop circuit is closed
- Loop is then available for next user

Fibre Channel Compatibility

- Arbitrated Loop is one of the Fibre Channel topologies, not a new architecture
- Supports all Fibre Channel speeds
  - With restriction that all ports must operate at the same speed
- Supports all Fibre Channel media types
- Supports all Fibre Channel classes of service
  - Class-1, Class-2, Class-3, Class-4, etc.
- Supports all protocols mapped to Fibre Channel
  - SCSI-FCP, TCP/IP, FICON®, etc.

Port Types

- Each loop-capable port has an "L" in its port type
  - NL_Port: loop-capable node port
  - FL_Port: loop-capable fabric port
  - F/NL_Port: NL_Port that provides Fibre Channel services in absence of a fabric
- Non loop-capable ports
  - N_Port: node port
  - F_Port: fabric port
  - E_Port: expansion port used to connect fabric switches

Loop Applications

- Storage subsystem
- File server
- Network file server
- Workgroup cluster
- Diskless workstation
- Network backbone
- High-performance network
- Device interface

1-Terabyte SCSI Disk Subsystem

- 8 Gigabyte disk drives
- 125 disk drives in 16 enclosures
- 15 drives per fast/wide interface
- 9 initiators, interfaces, terminators
- May require 2 enclosures to house the initiators
- Power, cooling, etc. for 9 initiators

1-Terabyte Fibre Channel Disk Subsystem

- 8 Gigabyte disk drives
- 125 disk drives in 16 enclosures
- 125 drives per Arbitrated Loop
- 1 adapter, 4-wire interface, no terminators
- 1 slot in one enclosure
- 200 MB/sec maximum bandwidth (full-duplex)
  - 400 MB/sec with 2,125 megabaud rate

Traditional File Server

- SCSI parallel bus to disk drives
  - 20 MB/sec fast/wide (160 mbits/sec)
  - 40 MB/sec Ultra wide (320 mbits/sec)
  - 80 MB/sec Ultra-2 wide (640 mbits/sec)
  - 160 MB/sec Ultra-3 wide (1280 mbits/sec)
  - One or more SCSI adapter cards
- Ethernet to clients
  - 10 Mbits/sec or 100 Mbits/sec
  - Approximately one to 10 MB/sec
- Network is too slow for some applications
  - Storing programs on server

Workgroup Clustering

- Use Arbitrated Loop for two protocols
  - Network connection
  - Peripheral attachment
- Higher performance for both
- Single Fibre Channel adapter in workstation
- Network access is as fast as local peripheral access facilitating:
  - Remote program loading
  - Data intensive applications

Diskless Workstation

- With a high-speed connection why have local disk storage?
  - Network the workstations and store data on servers
  - Performance equivalent to local storage
- Single Fibre Channel adapter replaces
  - Local disk
  - SCSI adapter
  - Network adapter
- Facilitates centralized backup/data management

Multiple Loops With Fabric

- Connect multiple Arbitrated Loops to a fabric
  - Growth path for loop configurations
  - Create larger configurations than possible with a loop alone
- Amortize cost of fabric across the loop ports
- 1,024 port configuration
  - 16-port fabric
  - 16 Arbitrated Loops with 64 ports per loop
  - Each fabric port supports 64 loop ports

2. Loop Concepts

In point-to-point and switched fabric topologies, a port has direct access to the physical interface to send frames whenever it wishes. While the actual transmission of frames may be restrained by the availability of credit, no other constraint prevents a port from being able to send frames. In an Arbitrated Loop environment, the physical interface is shared by all ports on the loop. The primary function of the Arbitrated Loop standard is to define the mechanisms and protocols required to allow multiple ports to operate together on the same loop.

Arbitrated Loop draws upon concepts borrowed from both the point-to-point and fabric topologies, while introducing several new concepts not present in those topologies. Among the key features are:

- Every loop-capable port (L_Port) includes a repeater function which allows loop traffic to flow through that port on route to another port on the loop.

- Loop operations are controlled using loop-specific protocols implemented with new Arbitrated Loop specific ordered sets.

- A Loop Port State Machine (LPSM) in each loop-capable port controls the operation of the loop protocols.

- L_Ports have a one-byte address called the Arbitrated Loop Physical Address (AL_PA).

- Ports on an Arbitrated Loop may be either participating or non-participating in loop operations.

- Loops may be either public (FL_Port present) or private (no FL_Port present), and ports on a loop may also be either public (FLOGI with fabric) or private (no FLOGI).

- A port bypass circuit which allows nonfunctional ports to be bypassed.

Arbitrated Loop introduces a level of functionality that is logically located between Fibre Channel's FC-0 (physical interface, serialization, and deserialization) and FC-1 (8B/10B encode and decode, Ordered Set generation and recognition) levels and the frame transmission and reception function (Fibre Channel's FC-2 level) as shown in Figure 13 on page 26.

When no loop circuit exists, the Loop Port State Machine (LPSM) retransmits all received transmission words other than selected fill words (e.g., those that were removed for clock elasticity). In effect, the LPSM is acting as a repeater. When a loop circuit exists, the LPSM logically connects the FC-2 function to the FC-0 and FC-1 functions thereby conditioning the port for frame transmission and reception. All non-fill words received are routed to the FC-2, while received fill words are processed by the LPSM itself.

The following sections provide an overview of these concepts and how they affect loop operations.

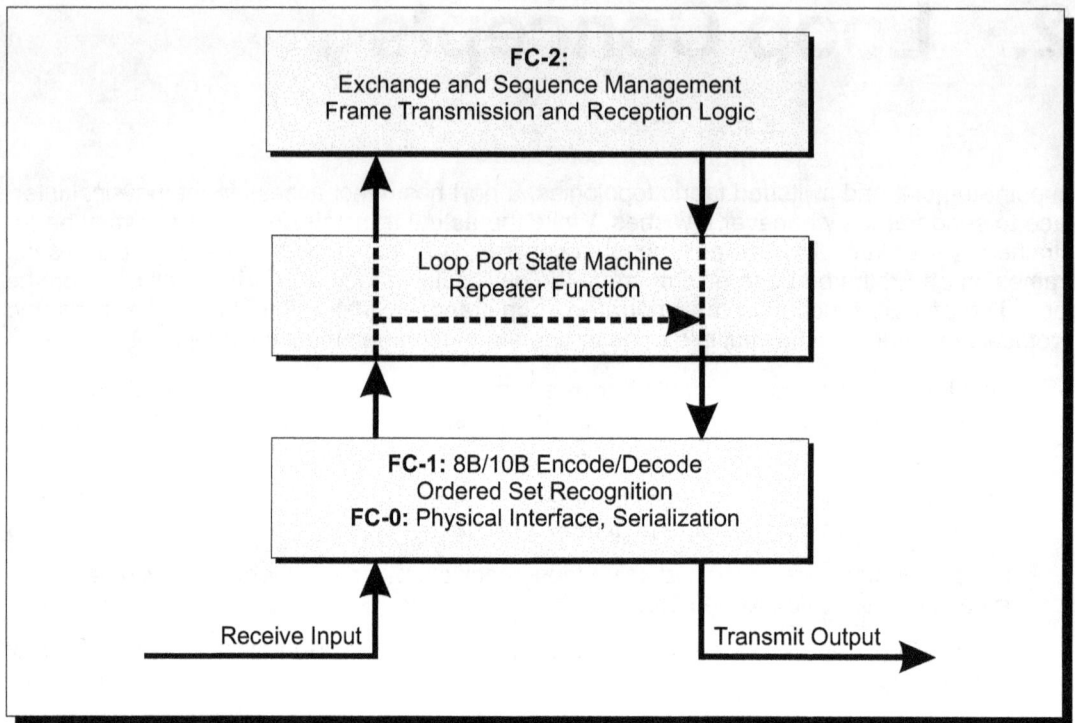

```
┌─────────────────────────────────────────────┐
│                  FC-2:                        │
│      Exchange and Sequence Management         │
│      Frame Transmission and Reception Logic   │
└─────────────────────────────────────────────┘

┌─────────────────────────────────────────────┐
│           Loop Port State Machine             │
│              Repeater Function                │
└─────────────────────────────────────────────┘

┌─────────────────────────────────────────────┐
│       FC-1: 8B/10B Encode/Decode              │
│            Ordered Set Recognition            │
│     FC-0: Physical Interface, Serialization   │
└─────────────────────────────────────────────┘

     Receive Input              Transmit Output
```

Figure 13. Loop Port State Machine Location

2.1 Repeater Function

Each LPSM contains a repeater function allowing it to retransmit received information. This function allows information to flow from one port, and through intermediate ports, until it arrives at its final destination. The repeater function does not buffer frames. Rather, it operates selectively on a transmission word-by-transmission word basis. Each received transmission word is examined and a decision made as to whether that word is repeated or not.

Some received words are not retransmitted. Several loop protocols employ the concept of fill word substitution. This procedure allows a loop port to replace a received fill word with a different fill word. The process is described in *Fill Word Substitution* on page 109.

The Loop Port State Machine (LPSM) is also responsible for performing the low-level loop protocols, including the repeater function and fill word substitution. For more information about this, refer to the chapter titled *Loop Port State Machine* on page 59.

2.1.1 Synchronous Transmitter/Receiver

Fibre Channel ports consist of independent transmitter and receiver functions. To process the received data stream, a portion of the receive function derives its clock from the incoming data stream. A synchronous repeater can obtain its transmit clock from a global clock provided to all ports on the loop or by using the receiver's Phase Locked Loop (PLL) synchronized to the received data stream. The PLL provides the clock used to sample the received data stream and deserialize the data. Once the data is deserialized, the receiver function can continue to use the PLL as a clock, or switch to an internal clock.

The transmitter function can either use the PLL clock in the receiver function or an independent transmit clock. If the receiver's PLL clock is used as the transmit clock, the output data stream is transmitted at exactly the same bit rate as the received data. While the transmit and received bits may be separated in time, the two functions are synchronous with each other. An example of a synchronous transmitter/receiver implementation is shown in Figure 14.

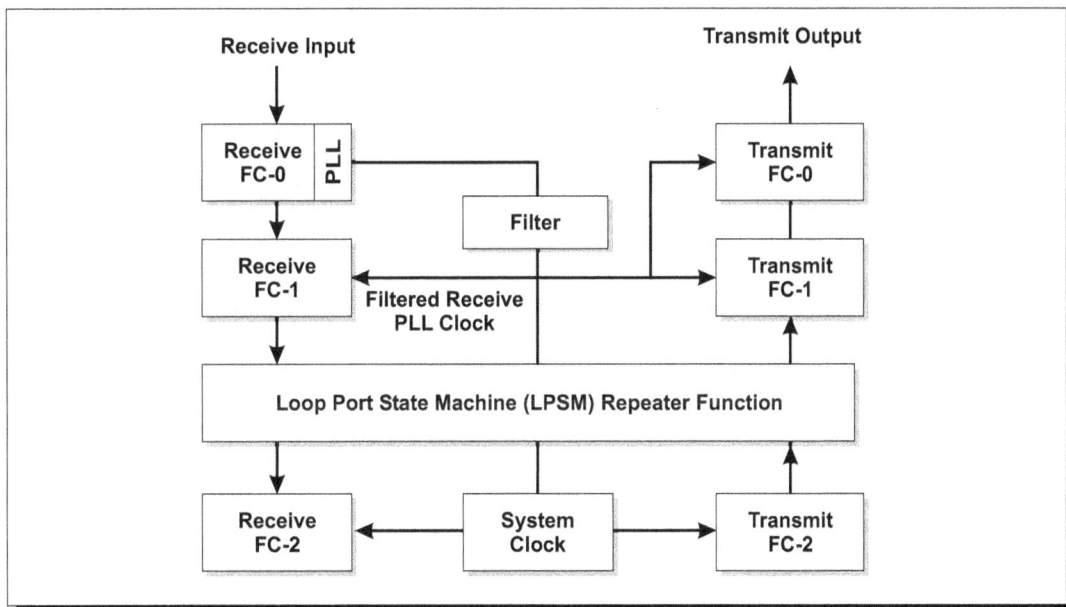

Figure 14. Synchronous Transmitter/Receiver

Even though the transmitter and receiver are operating synchronously, other areas of the port may use a different clock for their internal operations. For example, the frame reception and buffer functions may use a clock associated with the device or system bus.

2.1.2 Asynchronous Transmitter/Receiver and Clock Elasticity

If an independent transmit clock is used, the rate at which bits are received may differ from the rate at which bits are transmitted. The receiver still uses a PLL to deserialize the data, but the transmitter is now operating *asynchronously* to the receiver. An example of an asynchronous implementation is shown in Figure 15 on page 28.

One consequence of asynchronous operation is that the bit rate of the received data stream may differ from that of the transmit data stream. This is not a problem when the received infor-

---

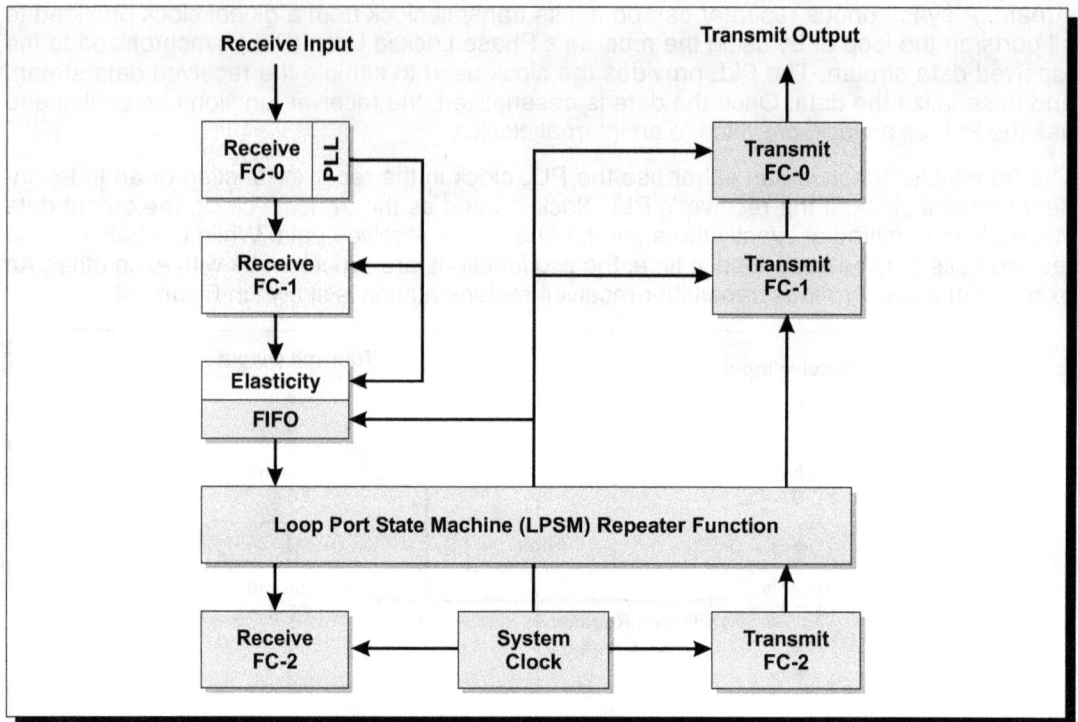

Figure 15. Asynchronous Transmitter/Receiver

In the figure:

- Receive Input → Receive FC-0 (with PLL)
- Transmit Output ← Transmit FC-0
- Receive FC-1
- Transmit FC-1
- Elasticity FIFO
- Loop Port State Machine (LPSM) Repeater Function
- Receive FC-2 ← System Clock → Transmit FC-2

mation is being processed by the port, but it does become a possible problem when the received information is being retransmitted as shown in Figure 16 on page 29. In this situation, the tolerances permitted in the transmit and receive rates can become a problem.

Each Fibre Channel transmitter clocks the transmit data with a tolerance of +/- 100 parts per million (.01%). A transmitter operating at the fast end of the tolerance range transmits bits at a rate of 1,062,606,250 bits per second (106,250 bits per second fast) while a transmitter operating at the slow end of the tolerance range transmits bits at a rate of 1,062,393,750 bits per second (106,250 bits per second slow). The maximum difference between any two transmitters is therefore 212,500 bits per second.

If the repeater function in the port is receiving bits at the fast end of the tolerance and transmitting bits at the nominal link rate, it is receiving 106,250 bits more per second than it is able to retransmit. Even worse, if the port is receiving bits at the fast end of the tolerance range and transmitting at the slow end of the tolerance range, the repeater function is receiving 212,500 bits per second more than it is transmitting. Without some mechanism to alleviate this speed mismatch, the repeater function falls farther behind as time progresses.

If the opposite tolerance conditions occur, the repeater function transmits 212,500 more bits per second than it receives. In this case, the repeater function must create new transmission words of its own because occasions may occur when a transmission word is required, but no received transmission word is available.

Under the worst case tolerances permitted by the Fibre Channel standard, 40-bits of difference accumulate after 200,000 data bits. This corresponds to a clock-induced difference of one word every 5,000 transmission words. Stated differently, this amounts to one transmission word after approximately 9 full-sized frames.

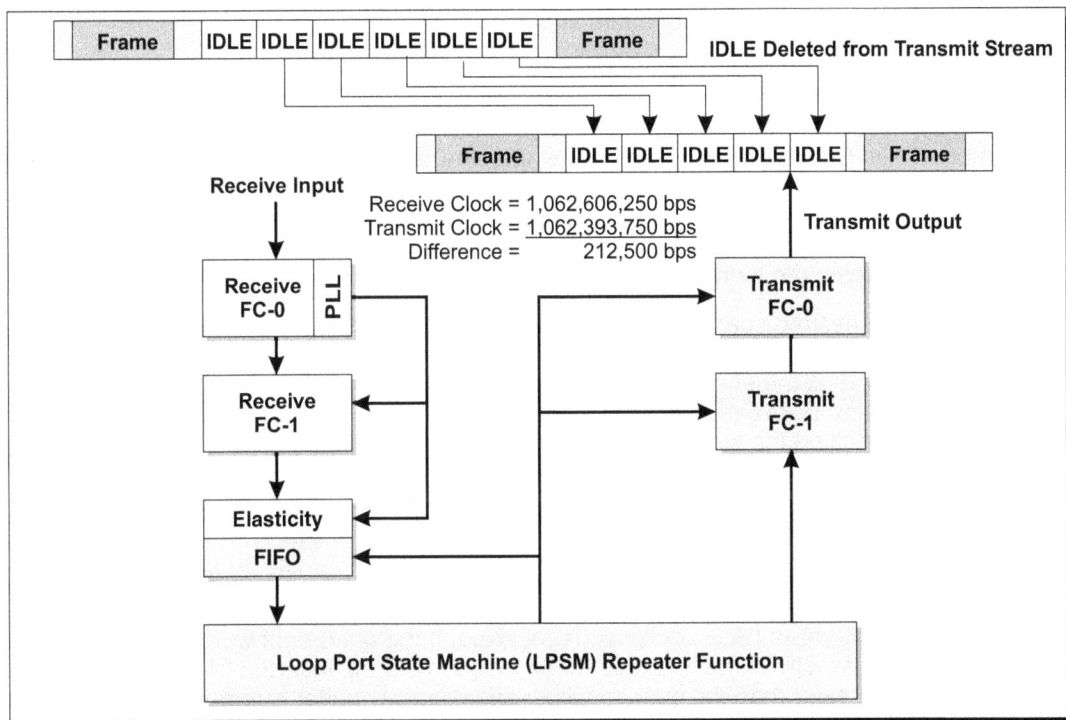

Figure 16. Clock Tolerance and Fill Word Deletion

The Fibre Channel standard provides a solution to this problem by allowing the fabric to insert or delete IDLEs between frames to compensate for the clock differences. To ensure an adequate number of IDLEs for the deletion process, the standard requires that a minimum of six primitive signals be transmitted between frames. This ensures that at least five IDLEs are present between frames (the sixth primitive signal may be an R_RDY). Whenever the clock tolerances cause the repeater function to fall more than a word behind the transmit function, the fabric can delete one of the IDLEs to catch up. If the clock tolerances require the insertion of a transmission word, the fabric can insert one or more IDLEs. These two capabilities allow the fabric to insert or delete IDLEs as needed to compensate for the clock tolerances between the receive input and transmit output.

Arbitrated Loop adopts a similar approach for managing clock tolerances associated with the transmitters on a loop. The problem of retransmitting received data is compounded in a loop environment because most of the ports are acting as repeaters at any point in time. Arbitrated Loop expands the number of ordered sets that may appear between frames and categorizes some of them as *'Fill Words'* (words that fill the space between frames but do not carry information meaningful to the FC-2 level). Prior to Arbitrated Loop, the only fill word was the IDLE primitive signal. Just as the fabric is allowed to insert or delete IDLEs between frames, loop-capable ports are allowed to insert or delete fill words to compensate for the clock differences between the received and transmitted data streams.

Insertion or deletion of fill words is performed by a clock elasticity function. The purpose of the clock elasticity circuit is to keep the inter-frame gap at a predetermined number of transmission words by inserting or deleting elasticity buffers into the loop as required. If the inter-frame gap is shorter than the desired number of fill words, the clock elasticity circuit inserts an additional fill word elasticity buffer into the loop to accommodate the inserted fill word. In effect, the loop has been lengthened to hold the added fill word. If the inter-frame gap is longer than the desired number of fill words, the clock elasticity circuit removes an elasticity buffer which has the effect of shortening the loop and deleting one fill word.

If, for example, the desired spacing between frames is six words and the clock elasticity circuit detects a spacing of five words between frames, the circuit adds one elasticity buffer to insert a fill word. This action has the effect of making the loop one transmission word longer than it was before. If the spacing between frames is seven fill words, the circuit removes one elasticity buffer, effectively making the loop one transmission word shorter. By constantly attempting to maintain the spacing between frames at six words, the elasticity circuit ensures that sufficient fill words are available to the next port in the loop. An example of a clock elasticity circuit is shown in Figure 17 on page 31.

The elasticity circuit works by determining whether the number of fill words between frames exceeds the desired size. The determination begins when the first fill word is detected and ends when a start-of-frame (SOF) delimiter is received. If the number of words is less than the desired value, an elasticity buffer is added to the loop to hold the inserted fill word. If the number of fill words is greater than the desired value, one elasticity buffer is removed from the loop to shorten the loop and delete a fill word.

The Fibre Channel and Arbitrated Loop standards both require that each non-fill word primitive signal (such as R_RDY) be preceded and followed by a minimum of two fill words. The elasticity circuit maintains this positioning by delaying fill word deletion until the third consecutive occurrence of a fill word has been recognized. This ensures that at least two consecutive occurrences of a fill word always remain.

2.2 Loop Circuits

Before a port can send frames to another port in an Arbitrated Loop environment, a loop circuit must be established. The Arbitrated Loop standard defines loop-level protocols which allow a port to gain access to the loop and establish, manage, and terminate loop circuits. Loop circuits can operate in either a 'point-to-point' like manner or in 'replicate mode' depending upon

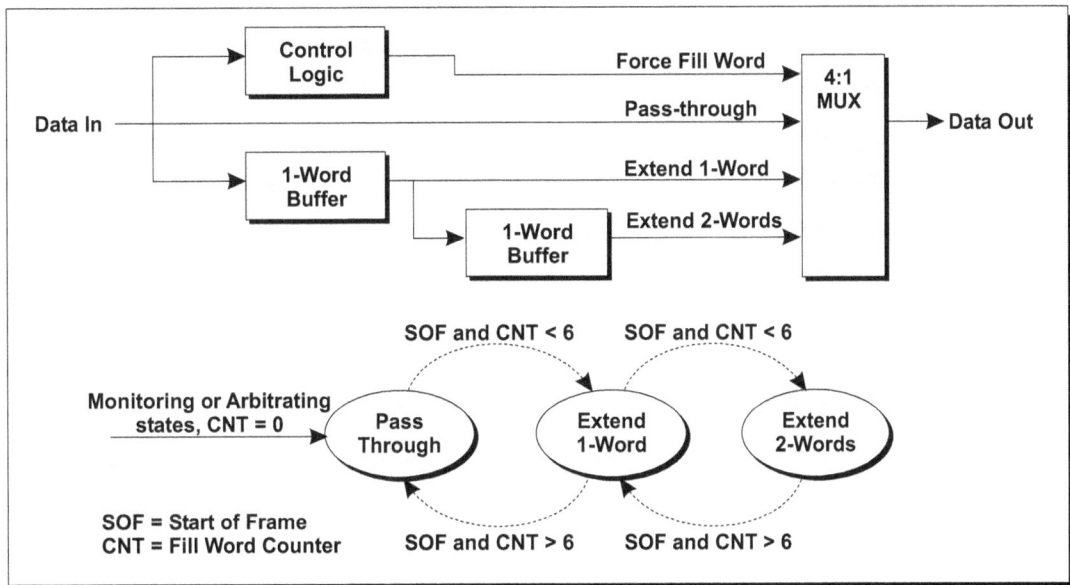

Figure 17. Clock Elasticity Circuit

the protocol used to establish the loop circuit. The protocol associated with opening loop circuits, and the options available, are described in *Opening a Loop Circuit* on page 151.

2.2.1 Point-to-Point Circuit

When a 'point-to-point' loop circuit is established with another port, those two ports can send and receive frames with each other. All of the other ports on the loop are acting as repeaters and retransmitting information. This results in a logical point-to-point like connection which appears to have a number of repeaters in each leg of the circuit. While the loop circuit is open, either full-duplex or half-duplex operation is possible between the two ports depending upon the protocol used to open the loop circuit. Full-duplex operation allows both ports to send and receive frames, while a half-duplex circuit limits data frame transmission to the port that established the loop circuit (i.e., only acknowledge, busy, and reject frames may be transmitted by the other port). When frame transmission is complete, the loop circuit is closed and the loop becomes available for use by other ports.

Point-to-point loop circuits are dynamic and have many characteristics similar to Class-1 while open. They provide full bandwidth and in-order and guaranteed latency for all frames for the duration of the loop circuit. They are opened as needed and may be closed when the ports are unable to make efficient use of the loop. A single operation, such as a command, may require multiple loop circuits. A typical SCSI-3 FCP operation may use one loop circuit to send a command to the target, one or more loop circuits to send data, and perhaps a final loop circuit to send status at the end of the command. Loop circuits do not necessarily correspond to Fibre Channel sequences or exchanges. Multiple loop circuits may be used to send a single se-

---

quence, or multiple sequences may be sent during a single loop circuit. The design of the ports involved determine how much, and what, information is sent during a single loop circuit.

2.2.2 Replicate Mode

Replicate mode does not establish a point-to-point like connection, but rather is used to create a broadcast or multicast environment. When a port is opened in replicate mode, it conditions its frame reception logic enabling it to receive frames but continues to retransmit received information (effectively, copying all non-fill words to FC-2).

Because the port is retransmitting received information, that information propagates around the loop and may be received by other ports that have also been opened in replicate mode. While in this mode, a port is not able to originate information of its own, including flow control signals, because its transmit output is committed to replicating the received information. This behavior is consistent with the normal behavior associated with broadcasting of information. Replicate mode is discussed in more detail in *Open Replicate (OPNr)* on page 152.

2.3 Loop Protocols

Arbitrated Loop ports use a series of loop-specific protocols to control loop operations. These protocols facilitate loop initialization, arbitration, opening and closing loop circuits, and providing access fairness for the ports on the loop. The loop protocols are similar to those used by the parallel SCSI interface. Although the actual mechanism is much different, the steps involved are similar.

Before a port can access the loop, it must first arbitrate. Once the port has won arbitration, it can then open (select) a destination port. The process of opening a destination port establishes a loop circuit which allows the two ports to send and receive information with each other. When the ports have finished communication, the loop circuit is closed (disconnection), and the loop is relinquished (bus free). The loop is then available for use by other ports.

The steps necessary to perform the loop protocols are implemented by a Loop State Machine present in each port. The signalling required by each protocol is accomplished using new loop-specific ordered sets.

2.3.1 Loop Initialization

Loop initialization is used to initialize the loop, assign addresses to the ports on the loop, and provide notification that the configuration may have changed.

Loop initialization can occur at any time. Loop initialization occurs whenever a new port is added to the loop, a loop failure is detected, or a port suspects that another port on the loop may be hung. If loop initialization occurs while operations are in progress, those operations are temporarily suspended while the initialization is performed. Normally, loop initialization does not perform a reset operation. This allows suspended operations to resume once the initialization is complete.

Addresses are assigned during Loop Initialization. The assignment mechanism does not require any address switches or jumpers on the ports, although it does support such address as-

---

signments if desired. If no addresses are assigned by switches or jumpers, the loop initialization process dynamically assigns address.

The entire Loop Initialization process is described in detail in the chapter titled *Loop Initialization* on page 67.

2.3.2 Arbitration Protocol

The loop is a resource shared by all ports, so a mechanism is needed to control access to the loop and ensure that information sent from one port does not interfere with information from a different port.

The arbitration protocol provides this mechanism by ensuring that only one port owns the loop at any time. Before a port can establish a loop circuit with another port and begin frame transmission, it must arbitrate for access to the loop and win arbitration. If more than one port requires access to the loop at the same time, each port arbitrates and the protocol determines which port wins arbitration. Ports that fail to win arbitration continue to arbitrate to win arbitration after the current loop circuit closes.

2.3.3 Access Fairness Protocol

The arbitration protocol resolves simultaneous arbitration requests based on each port's loop address. Each address has an associated fixed priority that determines which port wins arbitration. If the higher-priority ports were allowed to arbitrate whenever they wanted, lower-priority ports might not be able to gain access to the loop at all (especially with 127 ports all trying to access the loop). Without some compensating mechanism, ports with higher-priority addresses could completely shut out (or starve) lower-priority ports.

To prevent this problem, Arbitrated Loop provides an *access fairness* protocol. Access fairness is used when multiple ports are arbitrating simultaneously for use of the loop. The access fairness protocol establishes an access fairness window during the period when multiple ports are arbitrating. During the access fairness window, each port observing access fairness is limited to winning arbitration one time. Once a port has won arbitration, it must wait until a new access fairness window begins before it can arbitrate again. When all ports that are arbitrating during the current window have won arbitration, the access fairness window is reset and ports that were waiting can begin arbitrating if they require the loop.

Observing access fairness is optional (although highly recommended). Ports that observe access fairness are called *fair* ports and those that don't are called *unfair* ports. The decision of whether to be a fair or an unfair port is left to the system designer and may be fixed or dynamically changeable, depending on the workload. Some applications may benefit by allowing one or more ports to be unfair while requiring the remainder to observe access fairness.

The fabric's FL_Port has permission to be unfair to forward fabric traffic onto a loop as rapidly as possible and avoid fabric congestion. Certain NL_Ports, such as an initiator in a disk subsystem may choose to be unfair to enhance the performance. Most designs that support both fair and unfair behavior allow the firmware to control fairness as conditions require. This allows a port to observe fairness except in times of peak workload when occasional unfair behavior may be used to improve performance.

Arbitration and access fairness are explained more fully in the chapter titled *Arbitration and Fairness* on page 109.

2.3.4 Opening a Loop Circuit Protocol

Once a port has won arbitration, it uses the open protocol to establish a loop circuit with another port. This protocol conditions the two ports for frame transmission and reception with each other. Other ports on the loop are either idle and monitoring the loop, or require accesses of their own and are arbitrating for access once the current loop circuit is closed. In either case, the other ports are retransmitting the frames and control information between the two ports involved in the loop circuit.

After the loop circuit has been established, the loop exhibits many of the characteristics of a point-to-point connection. Only the two ports in the loop circuit are able to originate frame transmission. Information sent from the transmit output of each port in the circuit flows through the intervening ports (acting as repeaters) until it reaches the receive input of the destination. The other ports are not conditioned for frame reception and do not examine the frames that are retransmitted.

As in the case in a normal point-to-point connection, the two ports involved in the loop circuit can transmit and receive information in full-duplex mode.

The opening protocol is examined in the chapter titled *Opening a Loop Circuit* on page 151.

2.3.5 Closing a Loop Circuit Protocol

When the ports have completed their frame transmission, the closing protocol is used to end the loop circuit and make the loop available for use by other ports. The point at which the closing protocol is invoked is determined by the design of the ports. Loop circuits are required to transmit frames, but the loop circuit may be relinquished before all of the frames associated with a sequence or exchange have been sent. This might occur if the port is unable to refill the transmit buffers fast enough to sustain uninterrupted frame transmission.

Assume that a port on a 100 megabyte per second loop is sending information retrieved from a 25 megabyte per second memory. It reads data from the memory and stores it temporarily in one or more transmit buffers capable of sending the data at the full link speed of 100 megabytes per second. As each frame is sent, the corresponding transmit buffer is empty and the port attempts to refill it from the memory. Because the Fibre Channel link is much faster than the memory, the port is not able to keep up and eventually all of the transmit buffers may become empty. When that occurs, the port does not have any information available to send on the link.

The port could wait until one or more transmit buffers had been refilled, then resume frame transmission. The time spent waiting for the transmit buffers to refill is idle time on the loop because no information is being sent. This causes a degradation in the loop's performance if the idle time is significant. In the case of the 25 megabyte per second memory, loop performance is reduced to the speed of the memory and it would be more efficient to relinquish the loop while refilling the buffers, then reacquire the loop when there is more information to send.

2.3.6 Transfer Protocol

The transfer protocol is used to improve the efficiency of the loop under certain circumstances. Transfer allows the current owner of the loop (the port that won arbitration) to close the current loop circuit without relinquishing control of the loop. Once the current circuit is closed, the port can use the open protocol to establish a new loop circuit with a second port.

This allows ports with frames for multiple destinations to transmit those frames in a succession of loop circuits, all occurring during a single loop ownership.

One use of the transfer protocol is to facilitate the operation of an FL_Port attached to the loop. By using transfer, the FL_Port could rapidly transmit data to multiple ports without having to relinquish control of the loop between each destination port. This helps prevent congestion in the fabric switch due to a backlog of traffic destined for the loop.

Using the transfer protocol while other ports are arbitrating is unfair behavior because each transfer is equivalent to a new loop circuit. However, it is up to the system designer to decide if the unfair behavior is advantageous from a system performance standpoint.

2.4 Addressing

The Fibre Channel standard defines a 24-bit port address used to route frames in a fabric environment. Every frame carries a 24-bit destination address (D_ID) and a 24-bit source address (S_ID) in the frame header. Several loop operations use an abbreviated addressing form called the Arbitrated Loop Physical Address (AL_PA). This is a single byte address corresponding to the 8 least significant bits of the 24-bit address.

In environments consisting of Arbitrated Loops attached to fabrics, the uppermost 16 bits (bits 23-8) of the address identify a specific loop (actually the FL_Port to which that loop attaches) and the lower eight bits (bits 7-0) identify a specific port on that loop. This relationship is shown in Figure 18.

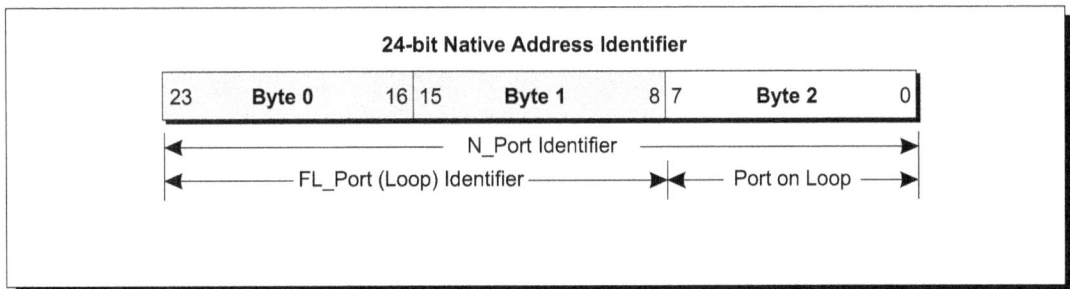

24-bit Native Address Identifier

| 23 | Byte 0 | 16 | 15 | Byte 1 | 8 | 7 | Byte 2 | 0 |

N_Port Identifier

FL_Port (Loop) Identifier — Port on Loop

Figure 18. Loop Addressing

2.4.1 Arbitrated Loop Physical Address

The Arbitrated Loop uses several ordered sets to perform the loop-related protocols. As a result, some of the loop protocols operate concurrent with frame transmission by occupying the space between frames. Prior to the development of Arbitrated Loop, the only ordered sets normally found between the end of one frame and the start of the next frame were IDLE and Receiver Ready (R_RDY). IDLE is transmitted when a port does not have anything else to send. The requirement for a minimum of six ordered sets between frames allows the fabric to compensate for transmit clock tolerances between ports in switches and repeaters (see *Asynchronous Transmitter/Receiver and Clock Elasticity* on page 27), while the R_RDY implements the buffer-to-buffer flow control.

Arbitrated Loop adds several new primitive signals and primitive sequences for the purposes of initialization, arbitration, opening and closing loop circuits, and other functions. Primitive signals consist of a single 40-bit ordered set and are normally used to communicate events. Primitive sequences require at least three consecutive occurrences of the same 40-bit ordered set before they are recognized. Primitive sequences are normally used to communicate states and during the time where the link may be unstable.

The first character of all ordered sets is a K28.5 special character. The presence of K28.5 is what indicates that the transmission word is an ordered set rather than a data word. The remaining characters of the ordered set define the function of the ordered set. Many of the loop-specific ordered sets use the second character to define the function, leaving the third and fourth characters to specify destination and source ports. To accommodate two port addresses, a shortened form of the normal 24-bit port address is used in those ordered sets which need to identify one or more ports. This short address form is called the Arbitrated Loop Physical Address, or AL_PA.

An AL_PA can be associated with either a destination port or a source port. Most of the time it is not necessary to differentiate destination from source and the term AL_PA is used. When it is necessary to identify a destination port, the term AL_PD is used, and when a source port is being identified, the term AL_PS is used.

The ordered sets added to support the Arbitrated Loop are listed in *'Primitive Signals',* on page 51, and *'Primitive Sequences',* on page 54.

2.4.2 NL_Port Limit

Power on, and the end-of-frame (EOF) delimiter forces the running disparity negative. The subsequent start-of-frame (SOF) delimiter requires the running disparity to be negative. The Fibre Channel standard requires that negative running disparity is maintained at the end of each transmission word occurring in the interval from the end of one frame until the start of the next frame. Because ordered sets between frames begin and end with negative running disparity, the ordered set must contain an equal number of one bits and zero bits.

When ordered sets are used to communicate two variable values in the third and fourth characters, certain combinations of characters result in incorrect running disparity at the end of the ordered set. Table 2 on page 37 lists the ending running disparity for all possible combinations of neutral disparity and non-neutral disparity characters in the third and fourth positions.

Combining a neutral disparity character and a non-neutral disparity character in the third and fourth character positions results in a disparity error at the end of the ordered set. If both characters are neutral, or both are non-neutral the disparity is correct. To maintain correct running disparity at the end of the ordered sets, the combinations of characters must be restricted.

Ordered Set									Ending Disparity
RD	Char 1	RD	Char 2	RD	Char 3	RD	Char 4	RD	
-	K28.5	+	Function	-	Positive	+	Negative	-	OK
-	K28.5	+	Function	-	Positive	+	Neutral	+	Incorrect
-	K28.5	+	Function	-	Neutral	-	Positive	+	Incorrect
-	K28.5	+	Function	-	Neutral	-	Neutral	-	OK

Table 2. AL_PA Disparity Problem

There are 134 neutral disparity characters in the 8B/10B encoding and 122 non-neutral disparity characters. To have the greatest number of available AL_PA values, only the neutral disparity characters are used for AL_PA values.

When multiple ports arbitrate simultaneously for access to the loop, some means of tie-breaking is needed. This is accomplished by assigning priorities to the AL_PA values. Table 3 lists the neutral disparity characters with assigned usage and order of priority, where applicable.

Character	Assigned to:	Priority
x'00'	AL_PA value for FL_Port (may be used by F/NL port when no FL_Port present)	Highest
x'01' - - - x'EF'	AL_PA values available for NL_Ports (126 values)	
x'F0'	Special ARB value used for Access Fairness Used during Loop Initialization	
x'F7' and x'F8'	Used during initialization in the LIP primitive sequence	
x'F9' through x'FE'	Reserved (3 neutral disparity values)	
x'FF'	Special ARB value for EMI and RFI reduction Used as a special character in OPNr and to address all ports	Lowest

Table 3. Neutral Disparity Character Usage

Neutral disparity characters are distributed irregularly throughout the range of x'00' through x'FF' and, consequently, the allowable AL_PA values are not consecutive. A summary of AL_PA values is shown in Table 4 on page 38. The Loop ID shown in the table is used to designate a preferred AL_PA value is set by a switch, jumpers, backplane wiring or other means.

AL_PA=x'00' is reserved for the FL_Port. If no FL_Port is present, AL_PA=x'00' may be used by an F/NL_Port on the loop. The remaining 126 AL_PA values are available for use by NL_Ports on the loop. This limits the maximum active loop configuration to 1 FL_Port (or F/NL_Port) and 126 NL_Ports.

Arbitrated Loop Physical Addresses								
AL_PA	**Loop ID**		**AL_PA**	**Loop ID**		**AL_PA**	**Loop ID**	
(hex)	(hex)	(decimal)	(hex)	(hex)	(decimal)	(hex)	(hex)	(decimal)
EF	00	0	A3	2B	43	4D	56	86
E8	01	1	9F	2C	44	4C	57	87
E4	02	2	9E	2D	45	4B	58	88
E2	03	3	9D	2E	46	4A	59	89
E1	04	4	9B	2F	47	49	5A	90
E0	05	5	98	30	48	47	5B	91
DC	06	6	97	31	49	46	5C	92
DA	07	7	90	32	50	45	5D	93
D9	08	8	8F	33	51	43	5E	94
D6	09	9	88	34	52	3C	5F	95
D5	0A	10	84	35	53	3A	60	96
D4	0B	11	82	36	54	39	61	97
D3	0C	12	81	37	55	36	62	98
D2	0D	13	80	38	56	35	63	99
D1	0E	14	7C	39	57	34	64	100
CE	0F	15	7A	3A	58	33	65	101
CD	10	16	79	3B	59	32	66	102
CC	11	17	76	3C	60	31	67	103
CB	12	18	75	3D	61	2E	68	104
CA	13	19	74	3E	62	2D	69	105
C9	14	20	73	3F	63	2C	6A	106
C7	15	21	72	40	64	2B	6B	107
C6	16	22	71	41	65	2A	6C	108
C5	17	23	6E	42	66	29	6D	109
C3	18	24	6D	43	67	27	6E	110
BC	19	25	6C	44	68	26	6F	111
BA	1A	26	6B	45	69	25	70	112
B9	1B	27	6A	46	70	23	71	113
B6	1C	28	69	47	71	1F	72	114
B5	1D	29	67	48	72	1E	73	115
B4	1E	30	66	49	73	1D	74	116
B3	1F	31	65	4A	74	1B	75	117
B2	20	32	63	4B	75	18	76	118
B1	21	33	5C	4C	76	17	77	119
AE	22	34	5A	4D	77	10	78	120
AD	23	35	59	4E	78	0F	79	121
AC	24	36	56	4F	79	08	7A	122
AB	25	37	55	50	80	04	7B	123
AA	26	38	54	51	81	02	7C	124
A9	27	39	53	52	82	01	7D	125
A7	28	40	52	53	83	00	7E	126
A6	29	41	51	54	84	—	7F	127
A5	2A	42	4E	55	85			

Table 4. Arbitrated Loop Physical Addresses

2.5 Participating and Nonparticipating Ports

During the loop initialization process a unique AL_PA value is normally assigned each port on the loop. When a port has a valid AL_PA it can participate in loop operations. It is possible to configure a loop with more ports than there are AL_PA values. When this happens, one or more ports are not able to acquire an AL_PA value and enter the nonparticipating mode. Ports in the nonparticipating mode act as repeaters for all loop traffic and cannot arbitrate or originate information onto the loop because they lack an AL_PA. These ports may only be communicated with using certain ordered sets when an AL_PA=x'FF' (i.e., broadcast) is used.

A loop may be configured with nonparticipating ports to provide a 'hot standby' capability in the event of failures on the loop. For example, a loop may have with two FL_Ports, even though only one can acquire an AL_PA and participate in loop operations. The other FL_Port enters the nonparticipating mode and acts as a repeater. If the primary FL_Port fails, it can be bypassed allowing the alternate port to acquire AL_PA=x'00' in the subsequent loop initialization.

The same strategy can be applied to the NL_Ports. An example might be a large storage array with 128 disk devices and a SCSI initiator attached to the loop. During Loop Initialization, the SCSI initiator and 125 of the disk drives acquire an AL_PA while the other 3 disk drives enter the nonparticipating mode. If one of the active drives fails, it can be bypassed and one of the spare drives can acquire the relinquished AL_PA during the subsequent loop initialization.

2.6 FL_Port Support

Arbitrated Loop supports the attachment of a fabric through a single active (participating) FL_Port which, by definition, may only exist at AL_PA=x'00.' If more than one FL_Port is present, one FL_Port acquires AL_PA=x'00'; any additional FL_Port(s) enter the nonparticipating mode. Limiting the support for fabric attachment to a single FL_Port was an intentional decision by the loop architects. There were a number of reasons to impose this limit, some of which are discussed in the following paragraphs.

When a port on the loop wishes to send frames to a destination port that is not on the loop, it establishes a loop circuit with the FL_Port and sends those frames to the FL_Port. The FL_Port introduces the frames into the switched fabric which routes them to their final destination. If more than one FL_Port were active on the loop, each NL_Port would need a routing table specifying which FL_Port should be used to access each N_Port or external NL_Port accessible via the fabric. This would add an unacceptable burden to each port that was not required in a normal fabric environment.

An even more undesirable situation can arise when two different fabrics are connected to the same loop. In this case, the two different fabrics become a new single fabric joined by the Arbitrated Loop. The two fabrics now need to coordinate their formerly independent activities and resolve their address spaces into a new single address space. If this isn't done, it is possible for the same 24-bit addresses to exist in each of the fabrics creating the possibility that a port could receive frames from two different fabric-attached ports, both having the same address.

Arbitrated Loop was never intended to act as a bridge between fabrics and the only way to prevent this was to limit the loop to a single participating FL_Port.

2.7 Public and Private Loops and Ports

The Arbitrated Loop provides considerable configuration flexibility to meet the needs of different applications. Loops can be configured as a stand-alone environment, or attached to a fabric. Ports on the loop can login with the fabric and communicate with other ports attached to the fabric, or they can remain independent of the fabric.

2.7.1 Private and Public Loops

A private loop is a loop without an active FL_Port. In a private loop, information can only be sent to other ports located on the same loop. There is no external, public access to the loop.

Some private loops may contain NL_Ports that act as agents or proxies for remote ports. When this occurs, remote ports may have access to ports on the loop through the proxy port even though they are not physically attached to the loop. Many Fibre Channel fabrics provide this type of port behavior which is variously referred to as Emulated Private Loop mode, Translative mode, or Stealth mode. In this case, a port in the fabric is acting as an NL_Port on behalf of one or more remote clients. Since this port is acting as an NL_Port, not an FL_Port, this is by definition a private loop. It is important to keep in mind that the term 'Private Loop' refers to the absence of an FL_Port, not the absence of remote access to the loop.

A public loop is a loop that has an active FL_Port. It is considered public because ports outside the loop may use the FL_Port to send and receive information with ports on the loop.

If a port attached to the fabric wishes to send information to a port on a public loop (although the fact that the destination port is on a loop is transparent to the sending port), it uses the same protocol as it would normally use to communicate with any another fabric attached port. The sending port transmits one or more frames to the fabric and the fabric assumes the responsibility for delivering those frames to the correct destination port.

When a frame has traveled through the fabric and arrives at the FL_Port, the FL_Port arbitrates for access to the loop. When the FL_Port wins arbitration, it opens the port identified by the destination address in the frame header. Once the port is opened, one or more frames may be sent to that port, subject to end-to-end and buffer-to-buffer credit rules. If the fabric has frames originating from more than one source for the same destination port on the loop, those frames may be sent while the destination port is opened. This is the only time a port can receive frames from multiple source ports (frame multiplexing) during a single loop circuit (a port could receive frames for different operations, or even from different upper level protocols during any loop circuit).

If the frames are out of order when they arrive at the FL_Port, the FL_Port delivers them to the port out of order. This is the only time that a port can receive frames that are out of order because all frame transmission on the loop itself ensures in-order frame delivery.

When a port wishes to send frames to ports that are external to the loop and are accessible via the fabric, the port arbitrates for access to the loop. When it wins arbitration, it opens the FL_Port and sends the frames to the FL_Port. The FL_Port forwards the frames to the appropriate fabric-attached destination port based on the destination address in the frame header. This frame transmission is subject to normal End-to-End and Buffer-to-Buffer credit rules.

If the port has frames for more than one fabric-attached destination port, it may be able to send them during a single loop circuit if allowed by the class of service in use. The fabric examines the destination address in the frame header of each frame and routes it to the proper destination. This allows a port to send frames to more than one destination (frame multiplexing) within a single loop circuit.

2.7.2 Public and Private Ports

Ports on a loop may be either public or private, even if that loop has an active FL_Port and is a public loop. Public ports login with the fabric and communicate with other fabric-attached ports via the FL_Port. Public ports may also communicate with other public or private ports on the same loop.

Public ports must support all of the requirements associated with normal fabric operations such as proper handling of fabric busy and fabric reject conditions, frame multiplexing (sending and receiving frames with different destinations concurrently), and potential out-of-order frame delivery. The following list summarizes some of the required behaviors:

- Public ports must initiate FLOGI to log in with the fabric. A port that does so is, by definition, a public port.

- Public ports must accept the address assigned by the fabric during FLOGI. The fabric will assign the most-significant 16-bits (normally the FL_Port's address) concatenated to the AL_PA acquired by the port during loop initialization.

- Public ports must qualify other ports using their full 24-bit address identifiers. Private ports may use only the least-significant byte (the AL_PA) in building port-related structures.

- Public ports need to consider the larger address space provided by the fabric. This may affect the manner in which data structures associated with other ports are designed.

- Public ports must recognize x'00 00 AL_PA' in addition to their public address identifier. This allows private ports to initiate communications with public ports (private ports have no way to know the upper 16-bits of a public port's address).

- Public ports need to incorporate logic to determine whether the destination port is located on the same loop or not. If the port is on the same loop, it is opened directly. If the port is external to the loop, a circuit must be opened with the FL_Port prior to frame transmission.

- When a public port has a circuit open with the FL_Port it can send frames to different fabric-attached ports during a single circuit. It may also receive frames from multiple fabric-attached ports during single loop circuit. Private ports only communicate with one other port during any loop circuit and cannot multiplex frames to or from different ports.

- If the fabric does not preserve frame delivery order, frames may be received out-of-order by a public port—there is no requirement that the FL_Port sort frames before placing them on the loop. Private ports always receive frames in-order.

- If a public port is using any class of service other than Class-3, it may receive F_BSY or F_RJT in response to frames it sends.

- Public ports must recognize and process (but not originate) the Fabric Address Notification (FAN) extended link service. FAN is sent by the FL_Port following loop initialization to provide a mechanism by which public ports can verify that they are still connected to the same FL_Port and fabric prior to resuming normal operations.

- Public ports must register with the Name Server to be visible to other fabric-attached ports. This involves logging in with the Name Server at well-known address x'FF FF FC' and registering the appropriate information. Communication with the name server uses the Fibre Channel Common Transport (FC-CT) protocol as defined in the Fibre Channel Generic Services standard.

- Public ports may need to query the Name Server to identify other public ports available for communications. Private ports may use the initialization loop map or scan the loop to identify other ports available for communications.

- Public ports may want to register to receive Registered State Change Notification (RSCN) extended link services. To receive these notifications, the port must register with the Fabric Controller at well-known address x'FF FF FD' using the State Change Registration (SCR) extended link service.

Private ports only communicate with other ports on the same loop. They do not login with the fabric and their presence is not known to the fabric. Private port implementations may be simpler than public ports because they do not have to support fabric-related operations.

Public and private ports may be mixed on the same loop and communicate with one another. For example, a single loop can consist of a public file server and its private disks. The public file server processes client requests received from the fabric via the FL_Port as well as communicating with the private disks. The private disks cannot be accessed from the fabric, nor can they send frames to the fabric.

Public and private ports on a loop are partitioned into two separate address spaces defined by the upper 16 bits of the 24-bit port address (i.e., if the upper 16 bits are = x'0000,' the port is private, otherwise, it is public). The FL_Port is responsible for ensuring that the private address space is isolated from the fabric, preventing fabric-attached ports from accessing private ports on the loop.

2.8 Classes of Service

Arbitrated Loop supports all classes of service defined by the Fibre Channel standard, although the dynamics of each class may differ from the other topologies.

Class-1 provides a dedicated connection between a pair of ports with confirmed delivery or notification of nondelivery. When operating in a loop environment, the loop circuit must be established between the pair of ports before the Class-1 connection is established, and the Class-1 connection must be ended before the loop circuit is closed. To ensure that the Class-1 connection is removed, only the port that receives the end-of-frame disconnect terminate (EOFdt) is permitted to initiate the closing protocol signalling the end of the loop circuit.

Class-2 provides a frame switched service with confirmed delivery or notification of nondelivery. Because the loop operates by creating dynamic loop circuits, frame transmission cannot

---

begin until a loop circuit is established with the recipient port. This is different than Class-2 operation in a non-loop environment, where the port can transmit frames at any time credit permits. On a loop, the loop circuit is established, one or more frames are sent, then the loop circuit is ended. While the loop circuit is established, frames may be sent between the port involved in the loop circuit, but no others. The only exception to this is when the loop circuit is established with the FL_Port. In this case the port can send frames to different destination ports and receive frames from different source ports provided they are all accessible via the FL_Port.

The acknowledge, busy, and reject responses associated with Class-2 may either be transmitted during the same loop circuit as was used to send the associated frames, or these responses may be sent in a separate, subsequent loop circuit.

Class-3 provides a frame switched service similar to Class-2 but without notification of frame delivery or non-delivery. As with Class-2, a loop circuit must be established prior to frame transmission and the loop circuit is ended when frame transmission is completed. Class-3 operation reduces the amount of loop traffic because no acknowledge, busy, or reject frames are transmitted. This may reduce the number of arbitration cycles and improves loop performance.

Class-4 provides a fractional bandwidth service with confirmed delivery or notification of non-delivery. Usually, this class of service is managed by the fabric. In the absence of a fabric, it is possible to provide class 4 behavior with an F/NL_Port and through special management of the ports.

2.9 Chapter Summary

Key Arbitrated Loop Concepts

- Each loop port includes a repeater function
- Loop operations are controlled using loop-specific protocols
- A Loop Port State Machine (LPSM) controls the loop protocols
- Loop ports have a one-byte address called the AL_PA
- Ports are either participating or nonparticipating
- Loops may be either public or private (FL_Port)
- Ports may be either public or private (FLOGI)
- Non-functional ports can be bypassed

Repeater Function

- Repeater operates on a transmission word basis
  - Port does not buffer frames for other ports
  - Port does not interpret frames unless it is in loop circuit
- Not all transmission words are repeated
  - Fill words may be discarded
  - Different words may be transmitted in place of a fill word
- Loop Port State Machine (LPSM) controls the repeater

Repeater Clocking

- Synchronous repeater
  - Transmit and receive use same clocks
  - Clock derived from receive PLL
  - One bit transmitted for each bit received
- Asynchronous repeater
  - Transmit and receive use different clocks
  - Transmit clock controlled by crystal oscillator
  - Number of bits transmitted and received may differ
  - Requires clock elasticity circuit

Clock Elasticity

- Separate clock sources for transmit and receive data
  - Clock tolerance of +/- 100 ppm
  - +/-106,250 bits per second
- If receive data is fast
  - Repeater discards a fill word when 40 bits have accumulated
  - Every 9 frames worst case
- If receive data is slow
  - Repeater inserts a fill word when needed

Loop Protocols

- Manage Arbitrated Loop operations
- Use new loop-specific ordered sets
- Controlled by the loop state machine
- Loop protocols are used for:
  - Loop initialization
  - Arbitration
  - Access fairness
  - Opening a loop circuit
  - Closing a loop circuit
  - Transferring a loop circuit

Loop Initialization

- Temporarily suspends loop operations
- Assigns loop addresses (AL_PAs)
- Builds a positional map of the loop
  - Optional in FC-AL-1
- Provides notification to other ports
  - When the configuration changes
  - When a loop failure is detected
- Not a reset!
  - Activity resumes after initialization

Arbitration

- All ports share the loop
- No master to control loop access
  - Control is distributed
- Ports must arbitrate before opening a loop circuit
  - Prevents multiple ports from sending frames at the same time
  - AL_PA priority used to resolve simultaneous requests

Access Fairness

- Each AL_PA has an associated priority
- If ports arbitrated whenever they wished
  - High-priority ports could lock out low-priority ports
- Access fairness offsets the AL_PA priority
  - Restricts when a port can arbitrate
- Access fairness, not time fairness!

Opening a Loop Circuit

- After a port wins arbitration, it opens a loop circuit
  - Prepares the ports for frame transmission and reception
- Circuit can be either full-duplex or half-duplex
  - Full-duplex allows two-way data frame transmission
  - Half-duplex is one-way
- Replicate mode allows broadcast and multicast
  - Port replicates received frames
  - Frames processed if port recognizes D_ID, otherwise discarded

Closing a Loop Circuit

- Circuit closed when frame transmission is complete
- Either port can initiate the protocol
- Both ports must send a close to end circuit
  - Both closes can be sent simultaneously
- Loop is then available for other ports

Transferring a Loop Circuit

- Function available to arbitration winner
- Allows closing first loop circuit and opening a second without re-arbitrating
  - No equivalent SCSI bus function
- Improves performance in some applications
  - FL_Port: off-load fabric traffic to multiple loop ports
  - Initiator: operate with multiple targets
- No externally observable protocol - all within port

Loop Addressing

- Frames on the loop carry a full 24-bit address in the header
  - Frames on loop same as elsewhere
- Many of the loop protocols use ordered sets
- Need to identify one or two ports
- Ordered set only has 2 characters for addresses
- Shortened address used in ordered sets
  - Called the AL_PA
  - Corresponds to third byte of the 24-bit address

Allowable AL_PA Values

- Link maintains negative running disparity between frames
- Ordered sets must follow this rule
- 1st and 2nd characters selected to force negative disparity
  - K28.5 and function byte
- 3rd and 4th characters may be AL_PA values
- Allowing any character combination may result in disparity errors
  - Ordered set must contain an equal number of ones and zeros

AL_PA and Disparity

- Must allow any combination of AL_PA values
  - Used in 3rd and 4th characters of ordered set
- Certain disparity combinations cause link errors
  - Neutral disparity and non-neutral disparity combination
  - Both neutral or both non-neutral are OK
- More neutral disparity than non-neutral
  - AL_PA values are restricted to neutral disparity characters

AL_PA and Flag Values

- There are 134 neutral disparity characters
- Assigned as follows:
  - x'00' is reserved for the FL_Port
  - x'01' through x'EF' are available for NL_Ports
  - x'FF' is used to address all ports
  - x'F0' used for access fairness and initialization
  - x'F7' and x'F8' used during initialization
  - x'FF' is used in ARBf and OPNr
- 1 FL_Port and 126 NL_Ports per loop

Participating/Nonparticipating

- AL_PA values are assigned during initialization
  - Each port receives a unique AL_PA
- No way to limit the number of ports on a loop
- If there are more ports than AL_PA values
  - One or more ports is unable to acquire an AL_PA
  - A port without an AL_PA enters the nonparticipating mode
  - Repeats loop traffic but can't arbitrate or participate in loop circuits

Nonparticipating Ports

- Nonparticipating ports may exist intentionally
- To provide redundancy
  - Two FL_Ports on the same loop
- To provide hot spares
  - Multiple disk drives
- When a failure occurs, bypass the failed port
  - Its AL_PA becomes available during initialization
  - One of the spares acquires the AL_PA

FL_Port Support

- Loop is restricted to a single participating FL_Port
  - Always exists at AL_PA = x'00'
- If multiple FL_Ports are present
  - One acquires AL_PA = x'00', the other becomes nonparticipating
- When a loop port communicates with ports external to the loop
  - Opens a circuit with the FL_Port
  - Sends frames via the FL_Port into the fabric
  - Fabric routes the frames to their final destination

Why Only One FL_Port?

- Multiple fabrics connected to a loop become one larger fabric
  - Single larger address space
  - Loop is the bridging connection
  - All fabric-to-fabric traffic flows through the loop
  - Loop port needs to know which FL_Port to open for every destination
- If multiple fabrics remain separate
  - No coordination of address spaces
  - Duplicate addresses could exist
  - Loop port wouldn't know which fabric a frame came from

Public and Private Loops

- Public loops contain a participating FL_Port
  - Loop ports can send frames to external ports via the FL_Port
  - External ports can send frames to loop ports via the FL_Port
- Private loops do not contain a participating FL_Port
  - Loop ports can only send or receive frames with other ports on the same loop
- Some fabrics mask their presence
  - Provide switch ports that act as NL_Ports on behalf of remote clients

Public and Private Ports

- Ports can be either public or private, even if the loop is public
- Public ports login with the fabric (FLOGI)
  - Can send and receive frames with external ports via the FL_Port
  - May encounter fabric busy and fabric reject conditions
  - May receive out-of-order frames
  - May send or receive frames from any fabric attached port during a single loop circuit
- Private ports do not login with the fabric
  - Can only send or receive frames from ports on the loop
  - Frames are always received in order

Address Space Partitioning

- Public and private ports exist in separate address spaces
  - Public ports are part of the fabric's address space
  - Private ports are not
- Public port addresses are 'xxxx'+AL_PA
  - 'xxxx' is nonzero and the same for all public ports on the loop
  - 'xxxx' is really a loop identifier
- Private port addresses are '0000'+AL_PA
  - Fabric will not deliver frames from a private port
  - Fabric will not forward frames to a private port

Classes of Service

- Loop supports all classes of service
- Class-1
  - Dedicated connection with confirmation
  - Connection ends prior to closing loop circuit
- Class-2
  - Connectionless service with confirmation
- Class-3
  - Connectionless service without confirmation
- Class-4
  - Fractional bandwidth with confirmation
  - Requires a bandwidth manager

3. Ordered Sets

Fibre Channel Arbitrated Loop adds several new loop-specific ordered sets to implement the loop protocols. These are in addition to the existing ordered sets previously defined by the Fibre Channel standard.

Primitive signals are normally used to indicate events or actions. For example, the OPN ordered sets are used to signal the recipient to prepare for frame reception, and perhaps, frame transmission.

Primitive sequences are used to indicate states or conditions and are normally transmitted continuously until something causes the current state to change. Many of the loop protocols require that a specific primitive sequence be transmitted continuously until it has travelled completely around the loop and is received by the original sender.

3.1 Transmission Word Relationship

Figure 19 organizes the ordered sets in a form that illustrates the relationship of the various transmission words.

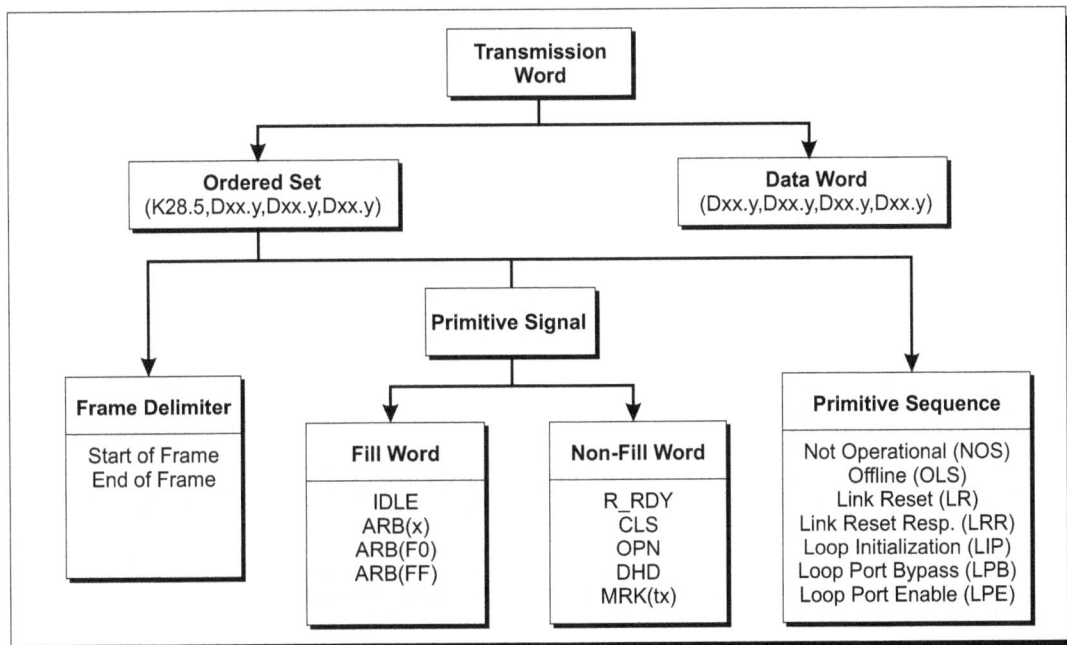

Figure 19. Transmission Word Hierarchy

3.2 Frame Delimiters

Arbitrated Loop does not add any new frame delimiter ordered sets. Table 5 summarizes the frame delimiters defined by both the Fibre Channel and Arbitrated Loop standards.

Frame Delimiter	Abbr.	RD	Ordered Set				Doc.
SOF Connect Class-1	SOFc1	Neg.	K28.5	D21.5	D23.0	D23.0	FC-PH
SOF Initiate Class-1	SOFi1	Neg.	K28.5	D21.5	D23.2	D23.2	FC-PH
SOF Normal Class-1	SOFn1	Neg.	K28.5	D21.5	D23.1	D23.1	FC-PH
SOF Initiate Class-2	SOFi2	Neg.	K28.5	D21.5	D21.2	D21.2	FC-PH
SOF Normal Class-2	SOFn2	Neg.	K28.5	D21.5	D21.1	D21.1	FC-PH
SOF Initiate Class-3	SOFi3	Neg.	K28.5	D21.5	D22.2	D22.2	FC-PH
SOF Normal Class-3	SOFn3	Neg.	K28.5	D21.5	D22.1	D22.1	FC-PH
SOF Activate Class-4	SOFc4	Neg	K28.5	D21.5	D25.0	D25.0	FC-PH2
SOF Initiate Class-4	SOFi4	Neg	K28.5	D21.5	D25.2	D25.2	FC-PH2
SOF Normal Class-4	SOFn4	Neg	K28.5	D21.5	D25.1	D25.1	FC-PH2
SOF Fabric	SOFf	Neg	K28.5	D21.5	D24.2	D24.2	FC-PH
SOF Initiate Loop (same as SOFi3)	SOFiL	Neg.	K28.5	D21.5	D22.2	D22.2	FC-AL
EOF Normal	EOFn	Neg.	K28.5	D21.4	D21.6	D21.6	FC-PH
		Pos.	K28.5	D21.5	D21.6	D21.6	
EOF Terminate	EOFt	Neg.	K28.5	D21.4	D21.3	D21.3	FC-PH
		Pos.	K28.5	D21.5	D21.3	D21.3	
EOF Disconnect Terminate (Class-1) EOF Deactivate Terminate (Class-4)	EOFdt	Neg.	K28.5	D21.4	D21.4	D21.4	FC-PH
		Pos.	K28.5	D21.5	D21.4	D21.4	FC-PH2
EOF Abort	EOFa	Neg.	K28.5	D21.4	D21.7	D21.7	FC-PH
		Pos.	K28.5	D21.5	D21.7	D21.7	
EOF Normal Invalid	EOFni	Neg.	K28.5	D10.4	D21.6	D21.6	FC-PH
		Pos.	K28.5	D10.5	D21.6	D21.6	
EOF Disconnect Terminate Invalid (Class-1) EOF Deactivate Terminate Invalid (Class-4)	EOFdti	Neg.	K28.5	D10.4	D21.4	D21.4	FC-PH
		Pos.	K28.5	D10.5	D21.4	D21.4	FC-PH2
EOF Remove Terminate (Class-4)	EOFrt	Neg.	K28.5	D21.4	D25.4	D25.4	FC-PH2
		Pos.	K28.5	D21.5	D25.4	D25.4	
EOF Remove Terminate Invalid (Class-4)	EOFrti	Neg.	K28.5	D10.4	D25.4	D25.4	FC-PH2
		Pos.	K28.5	D10.5	D25.4	D25.4	

Table 5. Frame Delimiters

Running disparity (RD) is forced negative by the EOF delimiter, and remains negative after each ordered set until transmission of the next SOF delimiter. Because the running disparity of the information within the frame is variable, two different EOF delimiters are used depending upon the running disparity of the frame's content. If the running disparity following transmission of the CRC is negative, the EOF delimiter preceded by 'Neg.' in the RD column is used. If the running disparity following transmission of the CRC is positive, the EOF delimiter preceded by 'Pos.' in the RD column is used. This results in the running disparity always being negative following transmission of the EOF delimiter.

3.3 Primitive Signals

Table 6 on page 51 lists the primitive signals used in an Arbitrated Loop environment. This list also contains the primitive signals defined by the Fibre Channel standard (FC-PH) that are used during Arbitrated Loop operations.

Primitive Signal	Abbr.	Ordered Set			Doc.
Arbitrate	ARB(x)	K28.5	D20.4	AL_PA AL_PA	FC-AL
Arbitrate (Fairness and Initialization Signal)	ARB(F0)	K28.5	D20.4	D16.7 D16.7	FC-AL
Arbitrate (Alternative to IDLE)	ARB(FF)	K28.5	D20.4	D31.7 D31.7	FC-AL2
Clock Synchronization X	SYNx	K28.5	D31.3	CS_X CS_X'	FC-PH3
Clock Synchronization Y	SYNy	K28.5	D31.5	CS_Y CS_Y'	FC-PH3
Clock Synchronization Z	SYNz	K28.5	D31.6	CS_Z CS_Z'	FC-PH3
Close	CLS	K28.5	D05.4	D21.5 D21.5	FC-AL
Dynamic Half-Duplex	DHD	K28.5	D10.4	D21.5 D21.5	FC-AL2
IDLE	IDLE	K28.5	D21.4	D21.5 D21.5	FC-PH
Mark	MRK(tx)	K28.5	D31.2	MK_TP AL_PS	FC-AL
Open Full-Duplex (Point-to-point)	OPN(yx)	K28.5	D17.4	AL_PD AL_PS	FC-AL
Open Half-Duplex (Point-to-point)	OPN(yy)	K28.5	D17.4	AL_PD AL_PD	FC-AL
Open Broadcast Replicate	OPN(fr)	K28.5	D17.4	D31.7 D31.7	FC-AL
Open Selective Replicate	OPN(yr)	K28.5	D17.4	AL_PD D31.7	FC-AL
Receiver Ready	R_RDY	K28.5	D21.4	D10.2 D10.2	FC-PH
Virtual Circuit Ready (Class-4 flow control)	VC_RDY	K28.5	D21.7	VC_ID VC_ID	FC-PH2

Table 6. Primitive Signals

The notation used in this table and throughout the rest of the text follows the form shown in the abbreviation (Abbr.) column of the table. Each primitive signal is identified by its function followed by applicable variable values. For example, ARB(x) means an arbitration primitive with both AL_PA values set to the value of 'x'. OPN(yx) means an OPN primitive with the AL_PD set to the value of 'y' and the AL_PS set to the value of 'x'.

3.3.1 Arbitration (ARB)

The arbitration ordered sets are used to indicate that a loop port requires access to the loop and to manage the access fairness mechanism. All ARBs are fill words and subject to fill word substitution or clock elasticity deletion and insertion.

ARB(x). This ordered set is used by a port in the Arbitrating state to indicate that it is arbitrating for access to the loop. A port in the Arbitrating state substitutes its ARB(x) for every IDLE and lower priority ARB received.

ARB(F0). ARB(F0) is used during loop initialization and by the access fairness protocol. During loop initialization, ARB(F0) signals loop ports that an temporary Loop Initialization Master has been selected and the LISM phase of initialization is complete.

During access fairness processing this ordered set is transmitted by the current arbitration winner to determine if any loop ports are arbitrating. If any port is arbitrating, that port substitutes its own ARB(x) for the received ARB(F0). If no loop port is arbitrating, the ARB(F0) propagates around the loop and is received by the current arbitration winner. This indicates the access fairness window has ended.

ARB(FF). FC-AL2 added this form of the ARB as an alternative to IDLE. This was done to reduce the emitted electromagnetic interference produced by the high number of transitions present in the IDLE. Once a port in the Monitoring state has transmitted the required minimum number of IDLEs, it may switch to sending ARB(FF) instead of IDLE.

3.3.2 Clock Synchronization (SYNx, SYNy, SYNz)

The use of these ordered sets for point-to-point and switched fabric configurations is defined by FC-PH3. No usage is defined for Arbitrated Loop environments.

3.3.3 Close (CLS)

The CLS ordered set is sent by a loop port to begin the process of closing the current loop circuit. No address is associated with the CLS and it is recognized by any port that is in an appropriate state.

3.3.4 Dynamic Half-Duplex (DHD)

The DHD ordered set was added by FC-AL2 and indicates that the port sending the DHD has no more device data frames to send. Once a port sends the DHD, it is not permitted to send any additional device data frames, although it can send R_RDYs and link control frames (ACKs, BSYs, and RJTs), if appropriate for the class of service. DHD may only be used if a full-duplex circuit exists. There are two principal applications of DHD.

The first use of DHD is between full-duplex ports. One of the problems with full duplex operation is deciding when to close the current loop circuit. If a port completes its frame transmission and sends a CLS, it is unable to send any subsequent responses to received frames. This prevents the port from sending R_RDYs or ACKs to replenish the buffer-to-buffer or end-to-end credit. Without being able to replenish the credit, frame transmission will exhaust the available credit and force the loop circuit to be closed, even if there is more information to send. By sending DHD instead of CLS, the loop port can signal that it has no further device data frames to send. This allows the other port to complete frame transmission (while still receiving R_RDYs or ACKs) before closing the loop circuit.

Another potential use of DHD is to cause a change of direction when operating with a loop port capable of data transfer in one direction only. When operating in this manner, the open origina-tor defaults to frame transmit mode while the open recipient defaults to frame receive mode. Prior to inclusion of the DHD ordered set, the only way to initiate a change of direction so that the open recipient could send frames was to close the current loop circuit, then arbitrate and establish a new loop circuit. With DHD, the open originator can send the DHD to indicate that it has completed device data frame transmission. This allows the open recipient to change its di-rection of frame processing without the hazard of unexpected device data frames arriving. In this fashion, a pair of ports, one or both of which are half-duplex can send and receive a series of frames while maintaining half-duplex at any point in time.

If a loop port transmits DHD and immediately receives CLS, the other loop port has no frames to transmit and the loop circuit must be closed. Use of the DHD during loop closing is dis-cussed in greater detail in *Using Dynamic Half Duplex During Close* on page 169.

3.3.5 IDLE

IDLE has the same meaning in an Arbitrated Loop environment as it does in the other Fibre Channel topologies. It is transmitted by a port when it does not have other information to trans-mit, or as dictated by the Loop Port State Machine (see *Loop Port State Machine* on page 59).

3.3.6 Open Point-to-Point (OPNy)

The OPNy ordered set is used by the open originator to establish a point-to-point like circuit with another loop port. It has two forms, the OPN(yx), which indicates that the open originator is capable of operating full-duplex and the OPN(yy), which indicates that the open originator is specifying that the loop circuit shall operate in half-duplex mode only. In half-duplex mode, the open originator assumes the role of sending device data frames, while the open recipient as-sumes the role of receiving device data frames.

While operating in Class-1 or Class-2, the open originator must be capable of processing Link Control frames regardless of the OPNy used.

3.3.7 Open Replicate (OPNr)

The OPNr is used to set replicate mode in one or more loop ports. The OPN(yr) sets replicate mode in the specified port with AL_PA=y, while OPN(fr) sets replicate mode in all ports on the loop.

When replicate mode is set, a port repeats and replicates to FC-2 all non-fill words. FC-2 ex-amines the D_ID of the received frame to determine if the frame should be processed. This mode facilitates multicast and broadcast operations in an Arbitrated Loop topology. Replicate mode is discussed in further detail in *Open Replicate (OPNr)* on page 152.

3.3.8 Receiver Ready (R_RDY)

Receiver ready (R_RDY) is used to grant buffer-to-buffer credit to a port. During frame transmission, it indicates that the receiver has emptied a receive buffer and is capable of receiving another frame. When the alternate buffer-to-buffer credit management model is used, R_RDY is also used to dynamically signal the availability of receive buffers when a loop circuit is opened. This use of R_RDY provides a credit granting service similar to that provided during login, but on a dynamic basis. Loop operations allow ports to use either method to communicate buffer-to-buffer credit (see *Buffer-to-Buffer Flow Control* on page 136).

3.3.9 Virtual Circuit Ready (VC_RDY)

VC_RDY provides buffer-to-buffer flow control signaling for Class-4 virtual circuits.

3.4 Primitive Sequences

In addition to the primitive signals, a number of primitive sequences were defined for loop initialization and to control an optional port bypass circuit. As with all primitive sequences, a minimum of three consecutive occurrences of the same ordered set is required before a primitive sequence is recognized and action is taken. Table 7 on page 54 lists both the Fibre Channel and Arbitrated Loop primitive sequences.

Primitive Sequence	Abbr.	Ordered Set			Doc.
Link_Reset	LR	K28.5	D9.2 D31.5	D9.2	FC-PH
Link_Reset_Response	LRR	K28.5	D21.1 D31.5	D9.2	FC-PH
Loop Initialization (no valid AL_PA)	LIP(F7,F7)	K28.5	D21.0 D23.7	D23.7	FC-AL
Loop Initialization (loop failure, no valid AL_PA)	LIP(F8,F7)	K28.5	D21.0 D24.7	D23.7	FC-AL
Loop Initialization (valid AL_PA)	LIP(F7,x)	K28.5	D21.0 D23.7	AL_PS	FC-AL
Loop Initialization (loop failure, valid AL_PA)	LIP(F8,x)	K28.5	D21.0 D24.7	AL_PS	FC-AL
Loop Initialization (selective reset AL_PD)	LIP(yx)	K28.5	D21.0 AL_PD	AL_PS	FC-AL
Loop Initialization (reset all)	LIP(fx)	K28.5	D21.0 D31.7	AL_PS	FC-AL
Loop Port Bypass	LPB(yx)	K28.5	D9.0 AL_PD	AL_PS	FC-AL
Loop Port Bypass All	LPB(fx)	K28.5	D9.0 D31.7	AL_PS	FC-AL
Loop Port Enable	LPE(yx)	K28.5	D5.0 AL_PD	AL_PS	FC-AL
Loop Port Enable All	LPE(fx)	K28.5	D5.0 D31.7	AL_PS	FC-AL
Not_Operational	NOS	K28.5	D21.2 D31.5	D5.2	FC-PH
Offline	OLS	K28.5	D21.1 D10.4	D21.2	FC-PH

Table 7. Primitive Sequences

3.4.1 Link Reset (LR) and Link Reset Response (LRR)

These FC-PH defined primitive sequences are used to abnormally end a Class-1 connection and reset the receiving port. Use of Link Reset and Link Reset Response is defined by FC-PH. The Loop Port State Machine recognizes these primitive sequences while in selected states to support the associated protocols should the loop port receive one of these sequences while participating in a Class-1 connection.

3.4.2 Loop Initialization (LIP)

Five forms of the LIP sequence allow the loop port in the initializing process to indicate the reason for loop initialization, the AL_PA of the initializing loop port (if it has one), and, in the case of the Selective Reset LIP, the loop port to be reset.

Initialization LIP(F7,F7). LIP(F7,F7) indicates that the loop port in the initializing process is requesting loop initialization but does not currently have a valid AL_PA. This could result from a device being powered on, hot plugged into the loop, or when a nonparticipating loop port without an AL_PA is attempting to become participating and needs to acquire an AL_PA to do so.

Initialization LIP(F7,x). LIP(F7,AL_PS) indicates that the loop port identified by the AL_PS value is requesting loop initialization. This LIP may be used if the loop port detects a performance degradation, arbitration wait time-out, or for another unspecified reason.

Loop Failure LIP(F8,F7). LIP(F8,F7) indicates that the loop port in the initializing process is requesting loop initialization due to a loop failure. The loop port does not currently have a valid AL_PA and uses x'F7' instead. This LIP could occur if a nonparticipating loop port without an AL_PA detects a loop failure, or a loop port in the process of acquiring an AL_PA detects a loop failure.

Loop Failure LIP(F8,x). LIP(F8,AL_PS) indicates that the loop port identified by the AL_PS value has detected a loop failure. This LIP may occur when a loop interconnection has failed, a loop port has failed, a loop port has been powered off or removed from the loop when no bypass circuit is present, or if the bypass circuit itself fails.

Selective Reset LIP(yx). LIP(AL_PD,AL_PS) is used to perform a vendor-specific reset at the loop port specified by the AL_PD value. All loop ports other than the one identified by the AL_PD value treat this as a normal LIP and do not perform a reset. The AL_PS value identifies the loop port that originated the request.

The extent of the Selective Reset LIP is defined by each protocol or application depending upon the information associated with that environment (e.g., the PLDA profile states that it is a power-on reset).

The selective reset LIP might be used during error recovery procedures to reset a device in a questionable or hung state.

Selective Reset LIP(fx). LIP(x'FF',AL_PS) is used to perform a vendor-specific reset at all loop ports except the loop port identified by the AL_PS value. The AL_PS value identifies the loop port that originated the request.

The extent of the Selective Reset LIP is defined by each protocol or application depending upon the information associated with that environment (e.g., the PLDA profile states that it is a power-on reset).

This selective reset LIP might be used during error recovery procedures to reset all loop ports that are in a questionable or hung state; this is the only means to reset loop ports that do not have an AL_PA.

3.4.3 Loop Port Bypass Primitive Sequences

The loop port bypass primitive sequences are used to set and reset the Repeat variable in the Loop Port State Machine. When this variable is set, the LPSM retransmits received transmission words and does not attempt to arbitrate or participate in loop circuits. Some implementations may use the state of this variable to control an optional port bypass circuit to electrically bypass the loop port.

The loop port bypass primitive sequences are normally transmitted continuously by the originating port until they are received by that port. This indicates that the sequence has travelled completely around the loop. Loop port bypass primitive sequences are removed from the loop by the originating port.

Loop Port Bypass LPB(yx)/LPB(fx). When recognized, this primitive sequence causes the designated port y or all ports to set the Repeat variable and optionally activate a control line to an external port bypass circuit, if present.

Loop Port Enable LPE(yx)/LPE(fx). When recognized, this primitive sequence causes the designated port y or all ports to reset the Repeat variable and optionally deactivate a control line to an external port bypass circuit, if present.

3.4.4 Not Operational (NOS) and Offline (OLS)

These Fibre Channel standard defines the Not Operational and Offline primitive sequences link initialization in a point-to-point or fabric-attached link. The Loop Port State Machine recognizes these primitive sequences while in selected states to support the associated protocols should the loop port receive one of these sequences.

3.5 Chapter Summary

Loop Specific Ordered Sets

- Arbitrated loop adds several new Ordered Sets to implement the loop protocols
  - Arbitration for access to the loop
  - Opening a Loop Circuit
  - Closing a Loop Circuit
  - Managing a half-duplex circuit
  - Initializing the loop
  - Controlling an optional Port Bypass Circuit

Arbitration Ordered Sets

- ARB(x)
  - Used by a port in the Arbitrating state to indicate it is arbitrating for access to the loop
- ARB(F0)
  - Used during loop initialization and by the access fairness protocol
- ARB(FF)
  - May be used as an alternative to IDLE once 6 IDLEs have been sent (FC-AL2)

Open Ordered Sets

- "Point-to-Point" Open
  - Creates a point-to-point like circuit between two ports
  - OPN(yx)
    - Opens port 'y' full-duplex from port 'x'
  - OPN(yy)
    - Opens port 'y' half-duplex
    - Port 'y' can only originate Link Control frames (e.g., ACK)
- Replicate Mode
  - Port receives and replicates frames around loop
  - OPN(yr) - open port 'y' in replicate mode
  - OPN(fr) - open all ports in replicate mode

Close Ordered Set

- Close (CLS) closes the current loop circuit
  - Port sends a CLS to indicate that it is done originating FC-2 level information (frames and R_RDY)
  - When a port receives a CLS, it knows that the other port is done originating FC-2 level information
  - Loop circuit is closed at a port when that port has both sent and received a CLS
- CLS resets replicate mode
  - A single CLS resets replicate mode (closes) all loop ports
- CLS signals the end of loop initialization

Dynamic Half Duplex

- Dynamic Half Duplex (DHD) is used to manage loop circuits
  - New addition in FC-AL2
- Indicates that the Arbitration winner is done sending frames
  - Allows a full-duplex port to signal that it has no more frames to send
  - Open recipient can then initiate a CLS if nothing to send

Loop Initialization

- Primitive Sequence used to begin loop initialization
- Indicates reason for initialization
  - Port attempting to acquire an AL_PA - LIP(f7,x)
  - Arbitration wait timeout - LIP(f7,x)
  - Loop failure detected - LIP(f8,x)
  - Port is resetting another port - LIP(AL_PD,x)
- Indicates AL_PA or originating port (if available)
  - Port uses x'F7' if no AL_PA
- May also be used to reset another port

Loop Port Bypass Controls

- Loop Port Bypass (LPB)
  - Causes a port to become bypassed
  - Port continues to monitor its receive fibre but otherwise acts as a repeater
  - May activate an optional bypass circuit
- Loop Port Enable (LPE)
  - Causes a port to become enabled
  - Deactivates the bypass circuit, if present

4. Loop Port State Machine

The Loop Port State Machine (LPSM) defines the behavior required for a port to operate on the arbitrated loop. The Arbitrated Loop standard presents a detailed model of the functionality required of the Loop Port State Machine. This book uses that model as a basis for presenting the various states and their operation. The reader should bear in mind that specific implementations may differ from the model described.

To facilitate cross-referencing to the model given in the Arbitrated Loop standard, all LPSM states maintain naming conventions similar to those used in the standard and are followed by the word 'state.'

4.1 Loop Port State Machine Overview

The LPSM controls the initialization, arbitration, opening, data transfer, and closing protocols of the loop. Figure 20 on page 60 illustrates the states and major transitions between states. Detailed descriptions of the individual states can be found in *LPSM State Tables* on page 321.

The basic (nonreplicate mode) operation of the LPSM is as follows:

1. When a loop port is first initialized it begins the loop initialization process. If the loop initialization process fails to detect an operational loop, the LPSM goes to the Old-Port state, if supported, and behaves as a normal N_Port or F_Port. If the initialization process detects an operational loop, the port performs the balance of the loop initialization process. In most designs, the initialization process is performed by firmware.

2. At the end of the loop initialization process, the loop is filled with IDLE ordered sets and all LPSMs are in the Monitoring state. LPSMs in the Monitoring state are idle and functioning as repeaters for loop traffic.

3. When a loop port requires access to the loop, its LPSM enters the Arbitrating state and begins arbitrating for access to the loop. When the LPSM wins arbitration, it goes to the Arbitration Won state, sends an OPN (either full-duplex or half-duplex) to select the desired destination loop port, and enters the Open state. While in the Open state, the port's FC-2 function is logically connected to the loop so frames can be sent and received (see Figure 21 on page 62). The port in the Open state is commonly referred to as the open originator.

4. When the destination port receives the OPN(yy) or OPN(yx), it enters the Opened state completing the loop circuit. While in the Opened state, the port's FC-2 function is logically connected to the loop establishing a loop circuit between the two ports (see Figure 21 on page 62). Once the loop circuit is established, the two ports can begin frame transmission with each other subject to the applicable flow control rules. The port in the Opened state is commonly referred to as the open recipient.

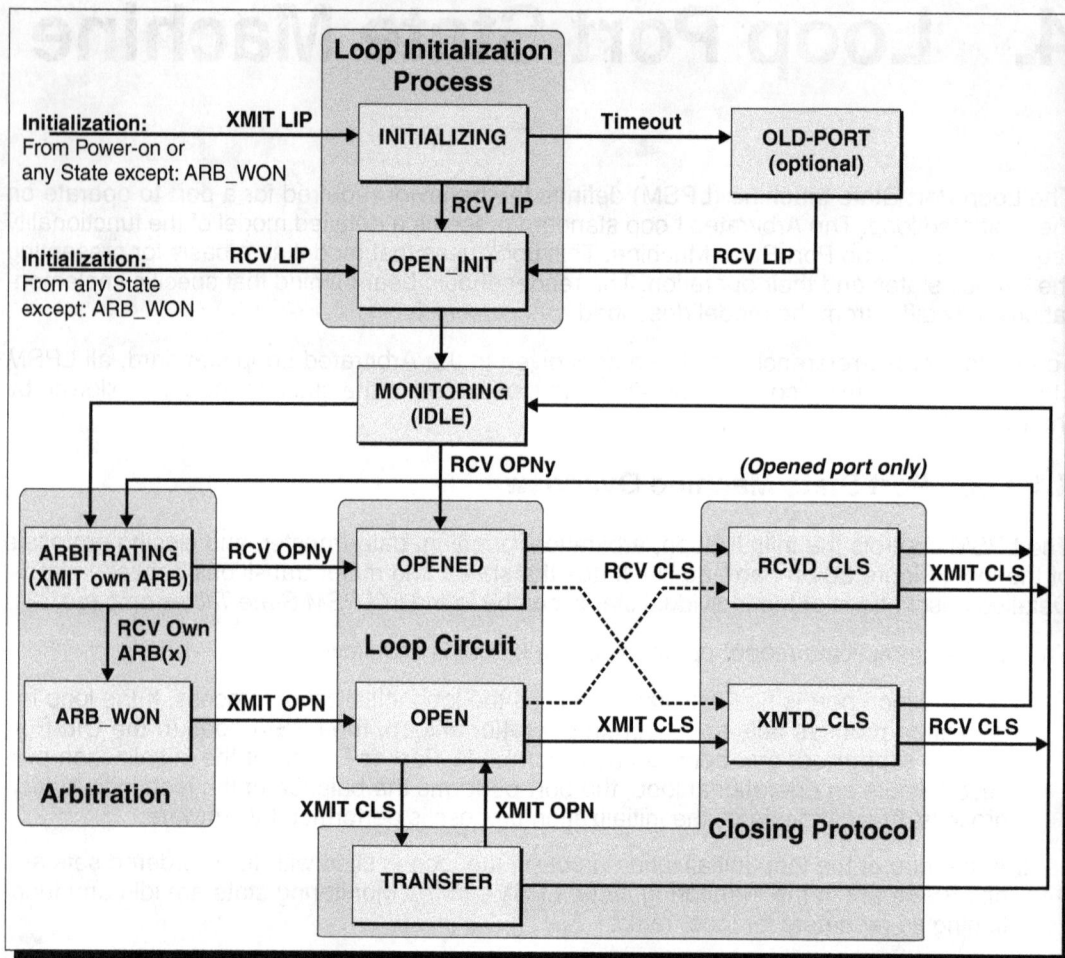

Figure 20. Loop Port State Machine (LPSM)

5. When either of the two ports has completed frame transmission and wishes to end the loop circuit, it sends a CLS and enters the Transmitted Close state. Once a port transmits a CLS, it is not allowed to send any further frames or R_RDYs (used for flow control) and the FC-2 transmit function is now logically disconnected from the loop (see Figure 21 on page 62).

6. When the other port receives the CLS, it enters the Received Close state. The port may be in the middle of frame transmission when it receives the CLS and it is allowed to continue to send frames and R_RDYs (although there is no value in sending R_RDYs) as long as it has frames to send and the flow control rules permit. In the Received Close state, the port's FC-2 receive function is logically disconnected from the loop. When the port has nothing further to send, it sends a CLS of its own and enters the Monitoring

state where both the FC-2 receive and transmit functions are logically disconnected from the loop.

7. When the port in the Transmitted Close state receives the CLS, it also enters the Monitoring state and logically disconnects its FC-2 receive function from the loop. At this point, the loop is available for use by other ports.

8. If the port that was in the Arbitrating state receives an OPN prior to winning arbitration (i.e., some other port won arbitration first), it enters the Opened state as described in step 4 earlier and the operation continues as described earlier. If the port still needs to arbitrate after the loop circuit is closed, it returns to the Arbitrating state and resumes arbitration.

9. The port that wins arbitration controls the loop and enters the Open state. When the port in the Open state wishes to close the loop circuit, it has an option not available to the port in the Opened state. It may enter the Transfer state when the CLS is sent rather than the Transmitted Close state. When the other port closes its half of the loop circuit, the port in the Transfer state can send a new OPN to establish another loop circuit and reenters the Open state. This allows a port to sequentially establish and end loop circuits with a series of ports without the overhead associated with arbitrating for each loop circuit.

Figure 21 on page 62 illustrates the relationship of LPSM states to the logical connection between the loop port's FC-2 and FC-0/FC-1 functions. While this example shows the LPSM between the FC-1 and FC-2 levels, actual designs may also choose to implement this function between the FC-0 and FC-1 levels in which case the LPSM works with the encoded transmission words.

4.1.1 Loop Port State Machine Control Variables

In addition to the states in the LPSM defined by the FC-AL standard, there are several variables used to control or modify the operation of the LPSM and its associated port. These variables are set and reset as the result of ordered sets received from the loop, conditions detected within the LPSM, or L_Port controls originating in the port or its firmware. Figure 22 on page 63 shows the L_Port control inputs and control variable outputs of the LPSM.

Access. The access variable is used to control when the LPSM is allowed to arbitrate for access to the loop. When access is true, the port is allowed to arbitrate and when access is false a fair port will not arbitrate. A port that is not observing access fairness may arbitrate regardless of the state of access. Details describing when this variable is set and reset are described in *Access Fairness* on page 125.

Alternate BB_Credit. The alternate BB_Credit variable is used to control whether a port uses the normal Fibre Channel defined BB_Credit management rules, or the alternate BB_Credit management rules defined for Arbitrated Loop operations.

When alternate BB_Credit is true, the port uses the alternate BB_Credit model for buffer-to-buffer flow control. The alternate BB_Credit model is the default mode of operation in a loop environment and is described in *Granting a Login BB_Credit Value Equal to Zero* on page 140.

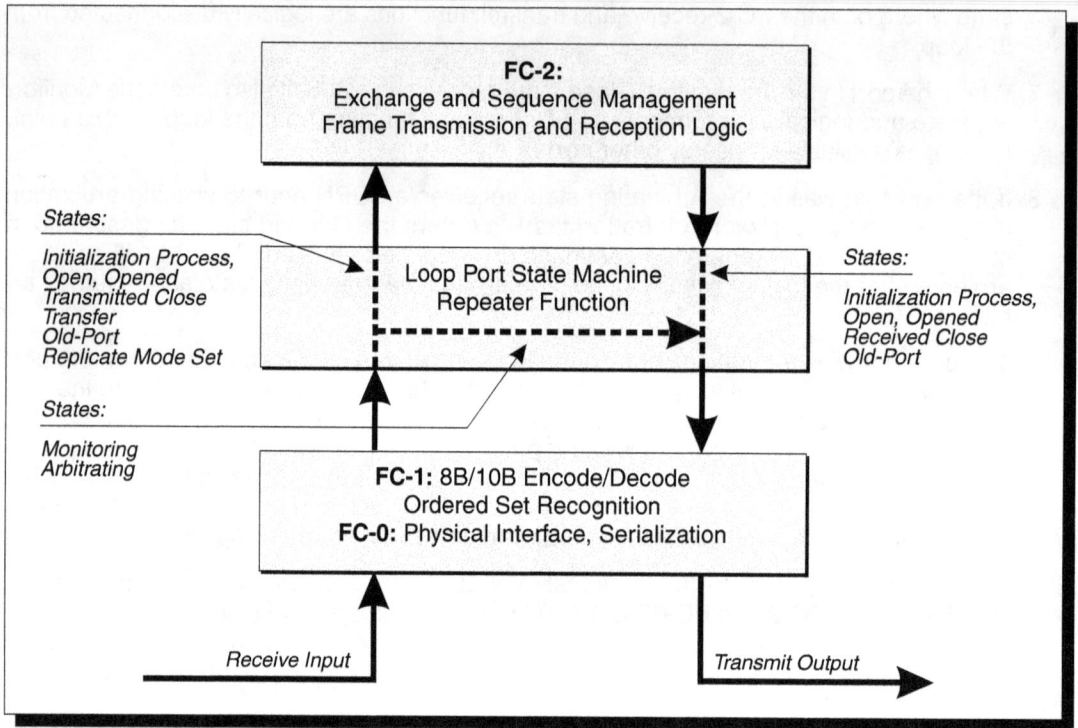

Figure 21. FC-2 Logical Connections

When the port is operating in a point-to-point or fabric environment, alternate BB_Credit is set to false, and normal BB_Credit flow control as described in the Fibre Channel standard (FC-PH) is used.

ARB_Won. When Arb_Won is true, this loop port has won arbitration and is the loop owner for the current loop circuit. Arb_Won is set when a loop port wins arbitration and provides memory of that fact while in the Open, Transfer, Transmitted Close, and Received Close states. Arb_Won controls the propagation of ARBs, determines if the port is responsible for the management of access fairness, and is a required condition to enter the Transfer state.

Duplex. Duplex remembers whether the opened port received a full-duplex OPN(yx) or a half-duplex OPN(yy). When Duplex is true, the port was opened in full-duplex mode, when Duplex is false, the port was opened in half-duplex mode. Duplex is not used by the LPSM, but may be required by full-duplex designs to signal the frame transmission logic to limit the operation to half-duplex mode for the current loop circuit. Examples of full-duplex and half-duplex designs are given in *Full-Duplex Operation* on page 190 and *Half-Duplex Operation* on page 197.

Bypass. When Bypass is true, the port activates the control signal to an optional external bypass function and retransmits all received transmission words. The port does not originate any transmission words of its own on the loop (except, perhaps, as required by the elasticity func-

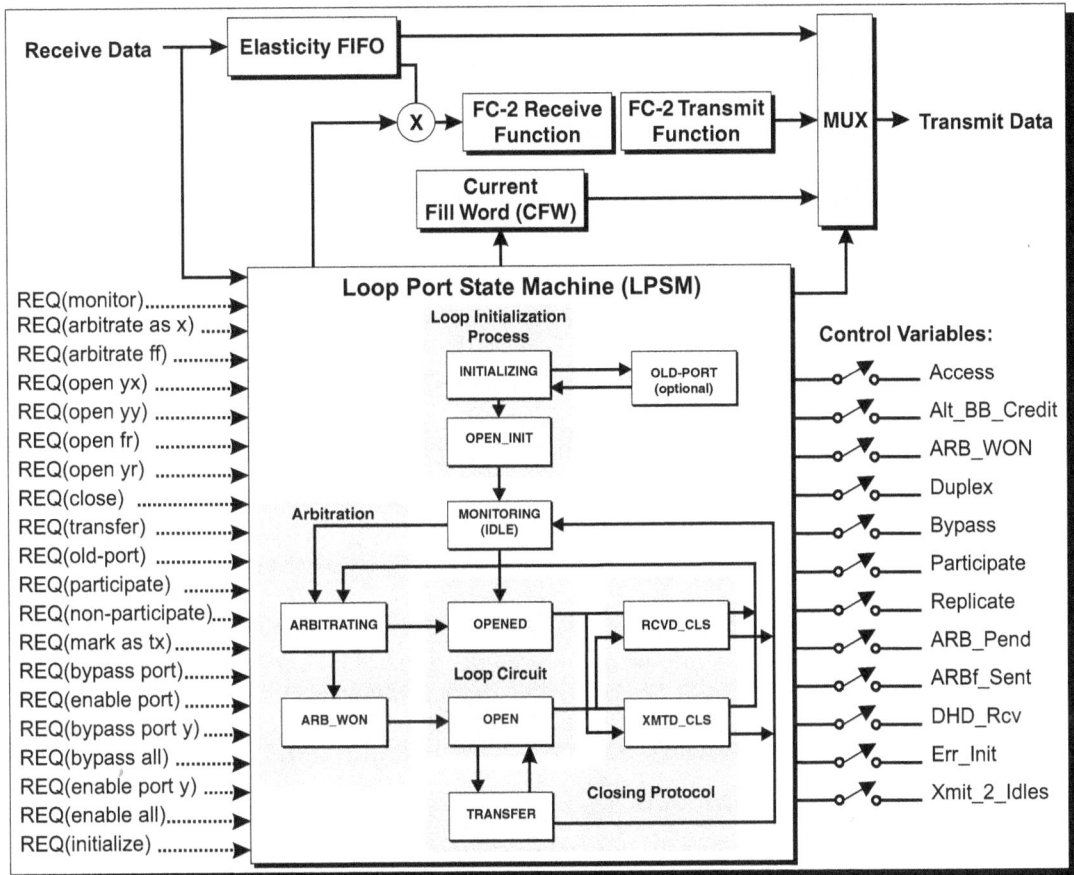

Figure 22. Loop Port State Machine (LPSM) Inputs and Outputs

tion). While Bypass is active, the loop port monitors the receive input for ordered sets that affect the Bypass condition. These include LPE(fx), LPE(yx) where y equals the AL_PA of the loop port, and LIP.

The operation of the external bypass circuit is discussed in *Port Bypassing* on page 282 which discusses its use in high-availability loop applications.

Participate. When participate is true, the port is allowed to participate in loop operations. When false, the port is in the nonparticipating mode and isn't allowed to participate in loop operations. These modes are described in *Participating and Nonparticipating Ports* on page 39.

Replicate. When replicate is true, the port follows the behavior defined for replicate mode as described in *Open Replicate (OPNr)* on page 152.

ARB_Pend. ARB_Pend is used by the LPSM to remember that it was arbitrating when opened and wishes to continue arbitrating during and after the current loop circuit.

ARBf_Sent. ARBf_Sent is used to remember that the LPSM has been requested to set its current fill word to ARB(FF).

DHD_Rcv. DHD_Rcv is used by the open recipient to remember that a DHD ordered set has been received. If the open recipient has frames to sent to the open originator, it should send those frames as soon as possible. If the open recipient does not have frames for the open originator, it should transmit a CLS to begin the closing protocol.

Err_Init. Err_Init is used during loop initialization to prevent initialization from being attempted when the probability of success is low. If Err_Init=true and LIP(F8) is received, initialization may be deferred.

Repeat. Repeat is used to remember that the LPSM has been directed to repeat most received transmission words. Repeat is true when (Participate=false or Bypass=true). Repeat is false when (Participate=true and Bypass=false).

Xmit_2_IDLEs. Xmit_2_IDLEs remembers that ARB(F0) has been received and the LPSM is not allowed to modify its current fill word until at least two IDLEs have been transmitted.

4.1.2 Current Fill Word (CFW)

All loop-capable ports contain a one-word memory used to hold a variable called the Current Fill Word (CFW) that is sent on the port's transmit output whenever a fill word is needed. The value contained in the current fill word is updated based upon loop operations and may contain an IDLE, ARB(F0), ARB(x) for another port, or this port's own ARB(x).

4.1.3 L_Port State Machine Controls

The Arbitrated Loop standard identifies a number of inputs used to control the Loop Port State Machine. These inputs may occur as a result of firmware controls or hardware conditions.

REQ(monitor)	The LPSM is requested to enter the Monitoring state
REQ(arbitrate as x)	The LPSM is requested to arbitrate using AL_PA=(x)
REQ(open yx)	The LPSM is requested to send a full-duplex open to port (y) from port (x)
REQ(open yy)	The LPSM is requested to send a half-duplex open to port (y)
REQ(open fr)	The LPSM is requested to send a broadcast open replicate
REQ(open yr)	The LPSM is requested to send a selective open replicate to port (y)
REQ(close)	The LPSM is requested to send a close
REQ(transfer)	The LPSM is requested to send a CLS and enter the Transfer state
REQ(old-port)	The LPSM is requested to enter the Old-Port state
REQ(participating)	The LPSM is to enter participating mode
REQ(non-participating)	The LPSM is to enter nonparticipating mode
REQ(mark as tx)	The LPSM is to transmit a Mark(tx) at the next appropriate Fill Word

REQ(bypass port)	The LPSM is requested to set Bypass mode
REQ(enable port)	The LPSM is requested to reset Bypass mode
REQ(bypass port y)	The LPSM is requested to transmit the LPB(yx) primitive sequence
REQ(bypass all)	The LPSM is requested to transmit the LPB(fx) primitive sequence
REQ(enable port y)	The LPSM is requested to transmit the LPE(yx) primitive sequence
REQ(enable all)	The LPSM is requested to transmit the LPE(fx) primitive sequence
REQ(initialize)	The LPSM is requested to enter the Initializing state

4.1.4 Invalid Transmission Words

As part of the repeater function, loop ports are capable of retransmitting received transmission words. It is possible that the port will receive invalid transmission characters or words on its input if errors occur on the link. Invalid transmission words are not retransmitted as this could cause the error to propagate around the entire loop. The action taken upon reception of an invalid character or transmission word depends upon the current state of the LPSM.

- When the LPSM is in the Monitoring, Arbitrating, Transmitted Close, or Transfer state and an invalid Transmission Character, misplaced Special Character, or incorrect running disparity at an Ordered Set is detected, the port substitutes its Current Fill Word.

- When the LPSM is in any other state, it passes the received word to the FC-2 receive function for processing. For information regarding how specific errors are handled, refer to ANSI X3.230, Fibre Channel Physical and Signalling (FC-PH), clause 24.3.5 and clause 29. These two clauses discuss sequence management and error detection/recovery respectively.

If the error occurs within a frame, the substitution of the Current Fill Word causes an invalid frame error being detected at the destination port (any ordered set ends a frame). The normal Fibre Channel processing at a port receiving an invalid frame is to discard the frame.

An Arbitrated Loop port is not required to log errors that are detected when retransmitting received transmission words. However, while the standard does not require logging these errors, fault isolation and error analysis may be significantly enhanced if the port logs the errors, even when retransmitting received words.

4.2 Chapter Summary

Loop Port State Machine (LPSM)

- Every loop-capable port contains a LPSM
- The LPSM controls
  - The repeater function
  - The loop protocols
- The L_Port controls make requests to the LPSM
- The LPSM uses several variables in addition to the states
  - Remember conditions not appropriate for states
- Arbitrated Loop standard contains a set of state transition tables
  - Defining the behavior of the LPSM

L_Port Controls

- The L_Port makes requests to the LPSM to:
  - Begin the initialization process
  - Enter participating or nonparticipating mode
  - Manage loop circuits by arbitrating, or transmitting an OPN or CLS
  - Transmit the port bypass control sequences
  - Control the local port bypass circuit

LPSM Variables

- Each LPSM contains several control variables
  - **Access** defines when a fair port can arbitrate
  - **Alternate BB_Credit** controls the buffer-to-buffer credit operation
  - **ARB_Won** indicates this LPSM won arbitration
  - **Duplex** is set when a full-duplex OPN is received
  - **Bypass** controls a Port Bypass Circuit (PBC)
  - **Participate** indicates that the LPSM has a valid AL_PA
  - **Replicate** indicates the LPSM is in replicate mode

LPSM Variables

- **ARB_Pend** indicates the LPSM will continue arbitrating during the current loop circuit
- **ARBf_Sent** indicates the LPSM has been requested to set its current fill word to ARB(FF)
- **DHD_Rcv** is used to remember that a DHD ordered set has been received
- **Err_Init** is used to prevent loop initialization when the probability of success is low
- **Repeat** indicates the LPSM has been directed to repeat most received words
- **Xmit_2_IDLEs** indicates ARB(F0) has been received and the LPSM must send at least two IDLEs before changing its CFW

Current Fill Word (CFW)

- The CFW is transmitted when a fill word is required
- Updated by LPSM as loop protocols execute
- If a frame is received, it may be replaced by multiple CFWs
  - Port is part of a loop circuit and has nothing to send
- May contain IDLE, ARB(x), ARB(F0), ARB(FF)
  - ARB(x) may be for a different port
  - Other port is arbitrating, CFW is set to that port's ARB(x)

Invalid Transmission Word

- If an invalid transmission word is detected
- The invalid word is replaced by the Current Fill Word in the following states:
  - Monitoring, Arbitrating, Transmitted Close, Transfer
- The error is passed to the FC-2 in the:
  - Open, Opened, Received Close, Old-Port states
- In the Initialization process the action taken depends on when the error occurs
  - LIP may be transmitted, or
  - The error may be passed to the FC-2

5. Loop Initialization

Loop initialization is used to initialize the loop prior to beginning loop operations or when configuration changes are detected. The primary functions performed by loop initialization are:

- Temporarily suspend loop operations and set the Loop Port State Machine (LPSM) in all loop ports to a known state (Open-Init state)
- Determine if loop capable ports are connected to an operational loop environment
- Manage the assignment of AL_PA values
- Provide notification of possible configuration changes
- Provide notification of loop failures or potential hang conditions
- Return all loop ports to the Monitoring state

Loop initialization does not cause a reset action unless specifically requested by a reset LIP. This allows initialization to occur on an active loop because it temporarily suspends any operations in progress, performs loop initialization, then allows resumption of the suspended operations.

The Loop Initialization Primitive (LIP) sequence and a series of loop initialization frames are used to accomplish loop initialization. Some portions of loop initialization are performed by the LPSM while other portions may be performed by either the Fibre Channel protocol chip or under firmware or software control.

Any port on the loop is capable of starting loop initialization by entering the Initializing state and transmitting one of the LIP sequences. The port may be unable to coordinate transmission of the LIP sequence with current loop traffic. If the initializing port begins transmission of the LIP while frames are being sent on the loop, it is possible that one or more frames may be corrupted. If this occurs, normal error recovery will be required upon completion of loop initialization to recover from the error. This is discussed further in the section titled *Minimizing Loop Disruption During Initialization* on page 86

When the LIP sequence is recognized by the next port on the loop, that port enters the Open-Init state and retransmits at least 12 of the received LIP. This process continues around the loop, with each port entering the Open-Init state and retransmitting LIP until a LIP sequence is recognized by the original port in the Initializing state. When this occurs, that loop port enters the Open-Init state as well. Loop initialization conditions all of the loop ports to send and receive initialization frames as shown in Figure 23 on page 68.

All of the ports are now in the Open-Init state and normal loop operations have been suspended. Because normal loop initialization does not perform a reset, the suspended operations may be resumed once loop initialization is complete.

Arbitrated Loop does not have a permanent loop master. Initialization requires that one port assume the role of Loop Initialization Master to manage loop initialization and generate a se-

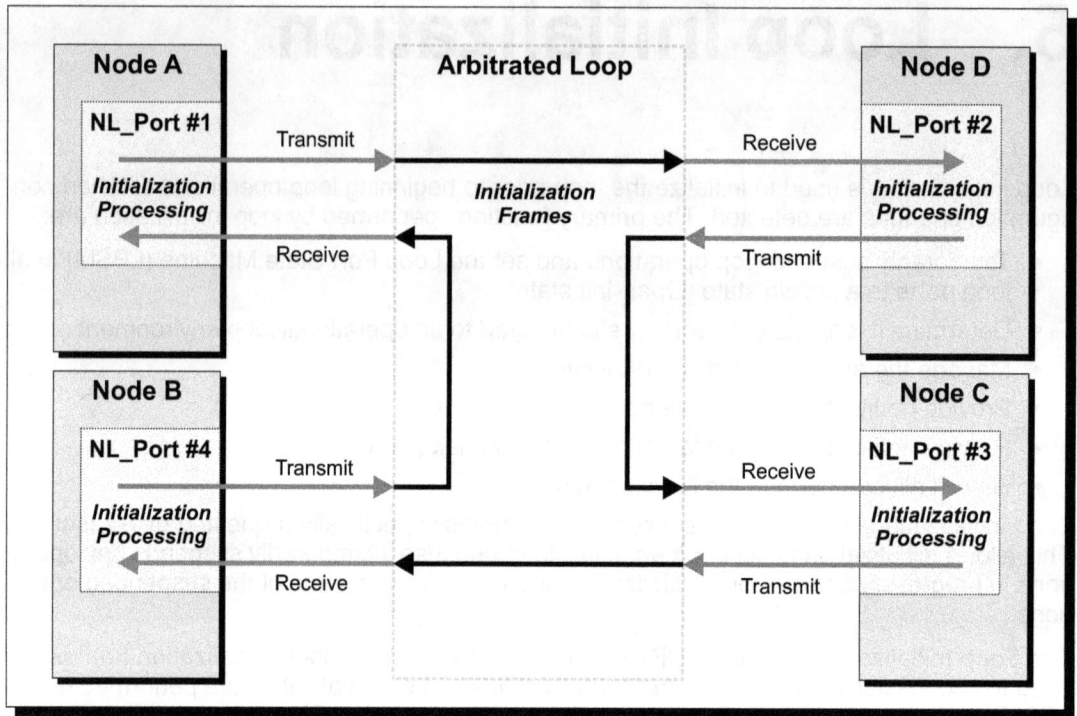

Figure 23. Open-Initialize Condition

ries of initialization frames. The frames are used to perform the AL_PA assignment and build a positional map of the loop.

The process used to determine the Loop Initialization Master is called the Loop Initialization Select Master (LISM) procedure and is shown in detail in Figure 26 on page 73. If an FL_Port is present on the loop, it will become the Loop Initialization Master, otherwise, the NL_Port with the lowest Port_Name will become the Loop Initialization Master. It is not required that every port be capable of being the Loop Initialization Master. However, at least one port must be capable or loop initialization cannot complete.

Following the LISM procedure, the loop master transmits a series of four AL_PA assignment frames which each port processes and retransmits to the next port on the loop. The AL_PA assignment process provides a four-tier hierarchy of addresses to allow a precedence of AL_PA assignments.

After the four AL_PA assignment frames have been processed, the loop master may initiate a position mapping operation. This step requires a frame data field size of 132 bytes and may not be supported by some FC-AL-1 ports. If any port is not capable of performing the positional mapping operation, it notifies the loop master during the last step of the AL_PA assignment operation that the position mapping steps should not be performed.

The positional mapping process consists of two steps. In the first step, the Loop Initialization Master transmits a frame used to collect the AL_PA values associated with each port on the loop. As each port receives the frame, it stores its AL_PA value in the next position in the positional map and retransmits the updated frame. When the frame has propagated completely around the loop and is received by the loop master, it contains a complete map of all of the ports on the loop. The Loop Initialization Master transmits the completed map so that all ports have an opportunity to capture the completed positional map.

The final action taken by the loop master is to transmit CLS. The CLS causes all ports to exit the Open-Init state and enter the Monitoring state where they are ready to resume normal operations. A simplified flowchart of the initialization process is shown in Figure 24 on page 70.

5.1 Reasons for Initialization

There are several events that may cause a port to begin loop initialization. Some of the more common ones are described in the following paragraphs.

Power On/Power On Reset. If a port was powered on or received an equivalent reset, it may need to acquire an AL_PA and notify the other ports on the loop that the configuration has changed.

The Arbitrated Loop standard cannot define whether a port retains or loses its AL_PA after it has been powered off (this is implementation specific). In most implementations, the AL_PA is lost when the port is powered off, and a new AL_PA must be acquired whenever the port is powered on. In addition to managing the AL_PA assignment, the loop initialization serves as notification that the configuration may have changed so that appropriate actions can be taken.

The port sends the LIP(F7,F7) sequence to begin loop initialization. This initialization sequence indicates that the originating port does not have an AL_PA because the AL_PS field is set to x'F7' and loop initialization is not due to a loop failure because the AL_PD is not x'F8'.

Enter Participating Mode. When a port in the nonparticipating mode wishes to begin participating, it begins loop initialization to acquire an AL_PA and notify other ports on the loop that the configuration has changed. If the port is successful in acquiring an AL_PA during loop initialization, it can begin normal loop operations when loop initialization is complete.

A port which has no AL_PA uses the LIP(F7,F7) sequence to begin loop initialization because it does not have a valid AL_PA to use in the AL_PS field.

If the port is not successful in acquiring an AL_PA (i.e., all AL_PAs have been assigned), it remains in nonparticipating mode. The port can attempt to enter participating mode after an implementation dependent timeout, or during the next loop initialization.

Leave Participating Mode. When a port in the participating mode wishes to transition to nonparticipating mode, it begins loop initialization to relinquish its AL_PA and notify other ports on the loop that the configuration has changed.

The port uses the LIP(F7,AL_PS) sequence to begin loop initialization and then does not set an AL_PA bit during loop initialization. This allows another port to take over the released AL_PA.

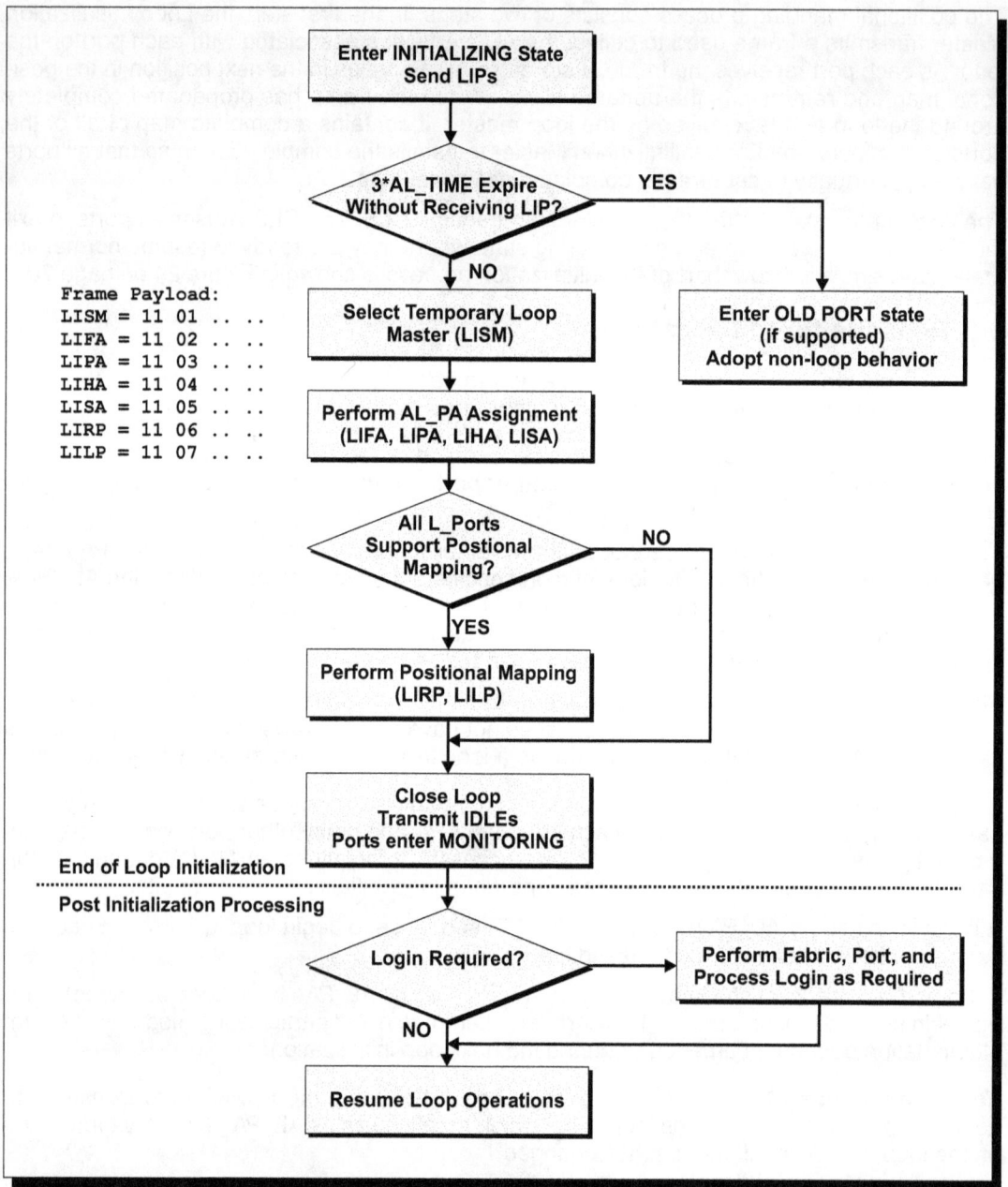

Figure 24. Loop Initialization (Simplified)

Frame Payload:
```
LISM = 11 01 .. ..
LIFA = 11 02 .. ..
LIPA = 11 03 .. ..
LIHA = 11 04 .. ..
LISA = 11 05 .. ..
LIRP = 11 06 .. ..
LILP = 11 07 .. ..
```

Loop Failure. A port may begin loop initialization as the result of detecting a loop failure on its receive input. Initialization serves to notify other ports of the failure condition and to determine if the loop is still operational.

A loop failure could be detected because a port on the loop has failed, been powered off, or the physical connection between a transmitter and receiver is broken. Normally, activating the port bypass circuit does not result in a loop failure.

When loop initialization is being performed due to a loop failure, either the LIP(F8,F7) or LIP(F8,AL_PS) sequence is sent. A value of x'F8' in the AL_PD position indicates that a loop failure is being reported at the port with the AL_PA value AL_PS. If the originating port does not have an AL_PA, it uses the value of x'F7' as its AL_PA.

The AL_PS value allows the position of the failure to be determined to facilitate diagnostic or maintenance activities. For loops with port bypass circuits, the AL_PS value indicates the port, or ports, requiring activation of the port bypass circuit. The failure is located in the upstream transmitter, the interconnecting link, or port bypass circuits, or the reporting port's receiver. Figure 25 on page 71 illustrates how the LIP(F8,AL_PS) can be used to identify the failing link.

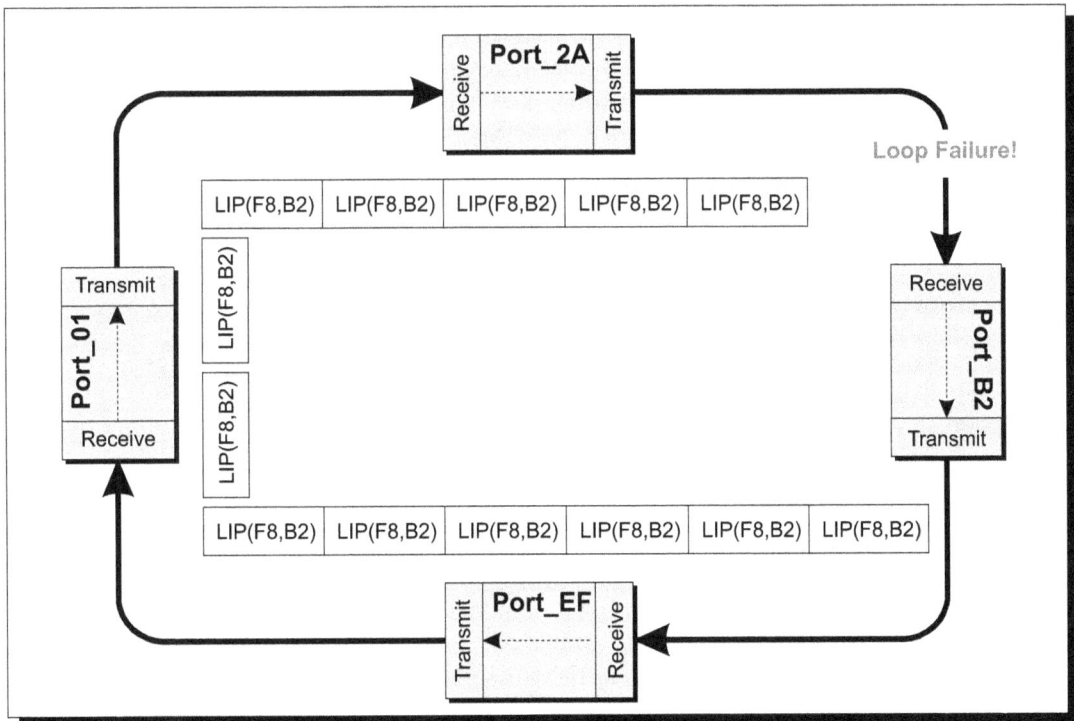

Figure 25. Using LIP to Determine the Point of a Loop Failure

Arbitration Wait Timeout. If a port is not successful in winning arbitration within LP_TOV (i.e., two seconds), it may be an indication of excessive unfairness or a potentially hung port.

The port may use loop initialization in an attempt to force an unfair or hung port off the loop when this occurs. The port can then attempt to access the loop following successful completion of loop initialization.

The port originating loop initialization uses the LIP(F7,AL_PA) sequence to trigger the loop initialization. The AL_PA value identifies which port on the loop began loop initialization.

Using initialization in an attempt to resolve arbitration wait problems caused by excessive activity due to an overloaded or saturated loop will only aggravate the situation. Loop initialization requires loop time that could otherwise be used for servicing requests. The time required by loop initialization only adds to the other ports' arbitration wait time, and could ultimately result in thrashing. For this reason, this use of loop initialization should be used carefully.

Selective Reset LIP. Loop initialization does not normally result in a reset to the port. However, the selective reset form of the LIP causes the designated port on the loop to perform a vendor unique reset. This is useful when it is necessary to reset a specific port. Generally, the selective reset LIP performs the equivalent of a power-on reset. The selective reset form of the LIP may be used during error recovery or reconfiguration procedures.

A port that wishes to issue the selective reset LIP to another port uses the LIP(AL_PD,AL_PS) primitive sequence. The AL_PD field contains the AL_PA of the port being reset and the AL_PS field contains the AL_PA of the port issuing the reset. LIP(FF,AL_PS) may be used to reset all ports on the loop except the issuing port identified by the AL_PS value. This reset should be used as a last resort to restore a defective loop.

5.2 Loop Initialization Select Master (LISM) Procedure

Loop initialization requires a temporary Loop Initialization Master which originates a number of initialization frames on the loop. If there are one or more FL_Ports on the loop, the FL_Port with the lowest Port_Name will become the temporary master and the other FL_Ports will ultimately enter the nonparticipating mode. If no FL_Ports are present on the loop, the NL_Port with the lowest Port_Name will become the Loop Initialization Master.The process of selecting the Loop Initialization Master is called the Loop Initialization Select Master (LISM) procedure and begins as each port enters the Open-Init state. A flowchart of the complete LISM process is shown in Figure 26 on page 73.

The reason for selecting the FL_Port as the first choice for the Loop Initialization Master is that every fabric element is assumed to have an associated element controller present and the element controller can manage loop initialization. The fabric element also has more knowledge of the overall configuration than is available to the ports and may have information indicating whether the ports must re-login following the loop initialization. This could occur if the fabric configuration has changed and the upper 16 bits of the native address identifiers are no longer the same (the fabric assigns the upper 16 address bits to public NL_Ports during fabric login).

When each port enters the Open-Init state, it transmits at least 12 LIPs of the same type as received, then ignores all LIPs for AL_Time. All FL_Ports assume an initial AL_PA value of x'00' and all NL_Ports assume an initial AL_PA value of x'EF'. Each port then begins transmitting a special initialization frame called the LISM frame. The LISM frame identifies the port type and contains the Port_Name. The format of the LISM frame is shown in Figure 27 on page 74.

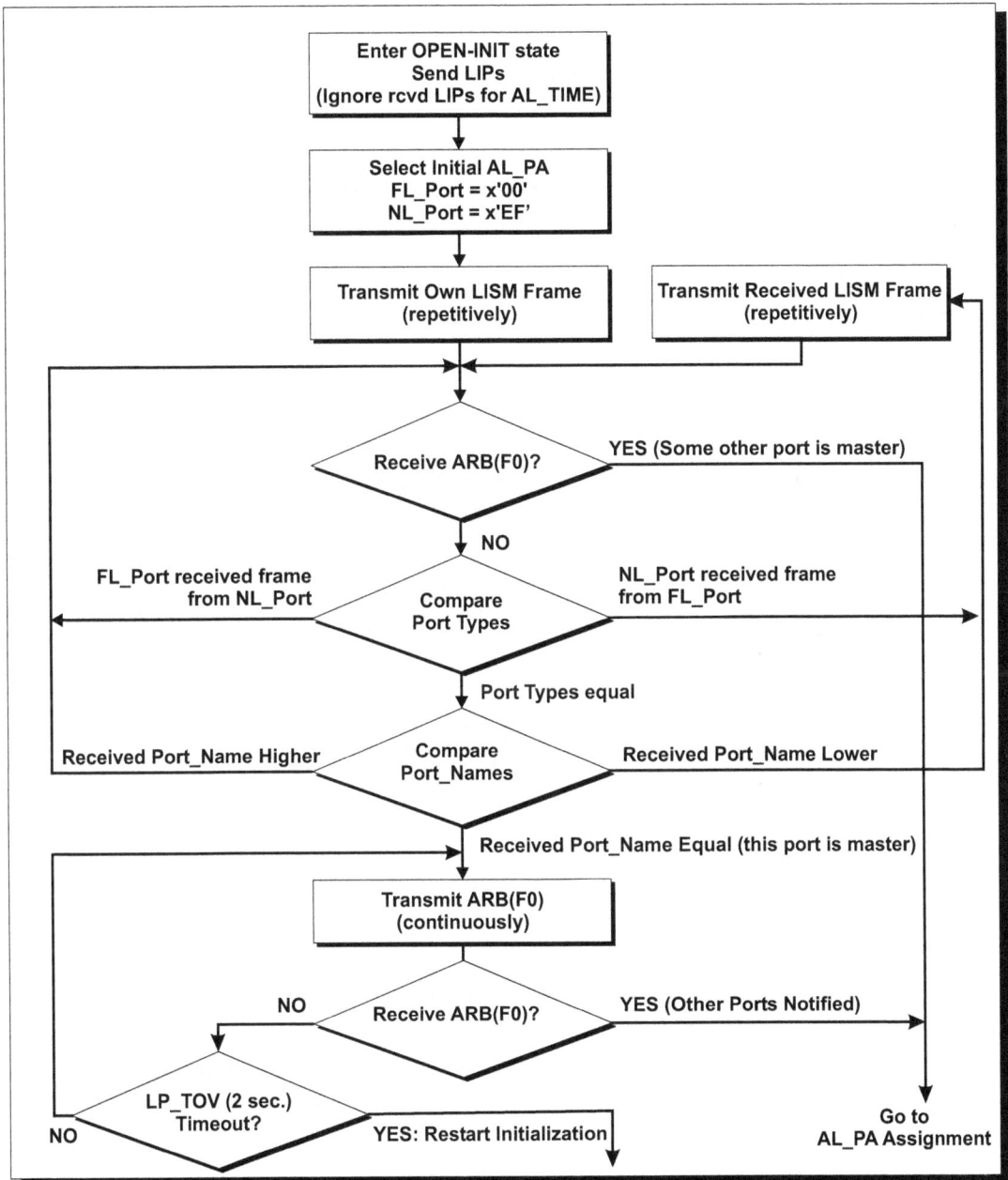

Figure 26. Loop Initialization Select Master Procedure

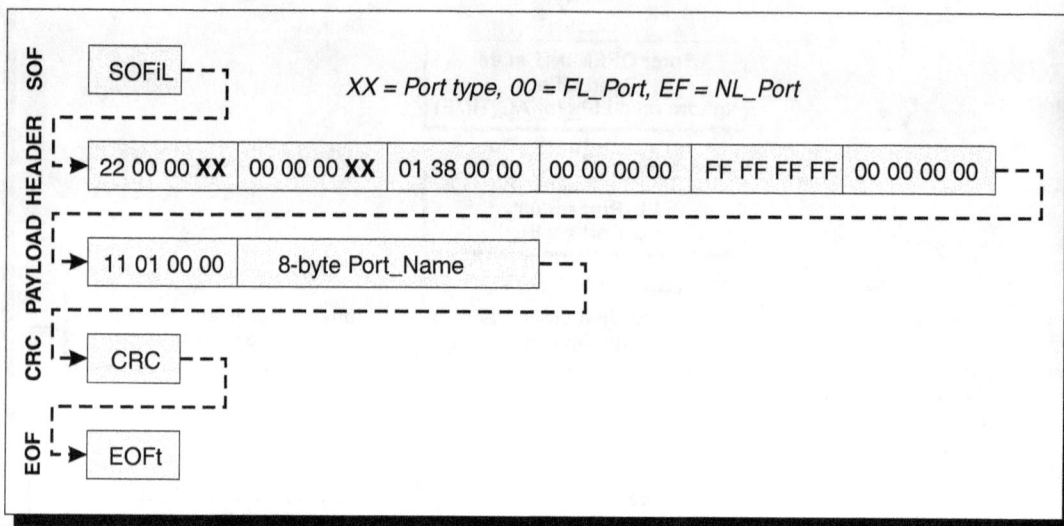

Figure 27. LISM Frame Format

All loop initialization frames are structured as Extended Link service frames to facilitate processing by the normal port hardware and firmware facilities. As with all Extended Link service frames, the first word of the payload contains the Extended Link service request or reply in the first byte. For loop initialization, this byte is always set to x'11'.

The remaining three bytes in the first word of the payload are request or reply parameters. Arbitrated Loop initialization frames use the second byte to indicate the initialization step associated with a given frame. LISM is the first step of loop initialization using initialization frames so the first word of the payload is set to x'11 01 00 00' (the last two bytes are used as flag bits and will be discussed later).

The value in the least significant byte of both the Destination_ID (D_ID) and Source_ID (S_ID) fields of the frame header are used to identify which type of port transmitted this frame. This byte is set to x'00' by an FL_Port and x'EF' by an NL_Port. An analyzer trace of the LISM frame is shown in Figure 28 on page 75.

LISM frame transmission is repetitive and not subject to normal flow control. Even though the SOFiL frame delimiter uses the same ordered set as the SOFi3, it does not indicate Class-3 service during initialization because no flow control is used.

When each port receives a properly formatted LISM frame it compares the port type received as indicated by the least significant byte of the D_ID and S_ID fields of the header with its own port type. If an FL_Port receives a LISM frame from an NL_Port it discards the received frame and continues to transmit its own frame. If an NL_Port receives a LISM frame from an FL_Port, it stops transmitting its frame and retransmits the received FL_Port's frame.

If the port type indicated by the D_ID and S_ID fields in the received LISM frame is the same as that of the receiving port, the Port_Names are compared. If the Port_Name in the received frame is algebraically higher than the receiver's Port_Name, the port discards the received

Chapter 5. Loop Initialization

```
0006E6:Idle 119.6 us              |Idle 119.6 us
0006E8:Idle 480 ns                |   SOFi3    480 ns
0006E9:    .                      |    R_CTL:22    D_ID:0000EF
0006EA:    .                      |                S_ID:0000EF
0006EB:    .                      |    Type:01         F_CTL:380000
0006EC:    .                      |    Seq:00, DF_CTL:00, CNT:0000
0006ED:    .                      |    OX_ID:FFFF RX_ID:FFFF
0006EE:    .                      |    Parameter:00000000
0006EF:    .    1st Word of payload indicates initialization step ──▶ Payload:12($C) Bytes
0006F0:    .                      ▶ 11 01 00 00 21 00 00 20
0006F1:    .                      |    37 00 3B 9E
0006F2:    .        Address fields indicate port type    CRC:362EF78B
0006F3:    .                      |   EOFt
0006F4:Idle 113.8 us              |Idle 113.9 us
0006F6:   SOFi3    480 ns         |Idle 480 ns
0006F7:    R_CTL:22    D_ID:0000EF|    .
0006F8:                S_ID:0000EF|    .
0006F9:    Type:01         F_CTL:380000|    .
0006FA:    Seq:00, DF_CTL:00, CNT:0000|    .
0006FB:    OX_ID:FFFF RX_ID:FFFF  |    .
0006FC:    Parameter:00000000     |    .
0006FD:        Payload:12($C) Bytes|    .
0006FE:        11 01 00 00 20 00 00 00 ◀──── World_Wide Port_Name ────
0006FF:        D1 19 F3 F9        |    .
000700:    CRC:0A2E8AB6           |    .
000701:    EOFt                   |    .
000702:Idle 5.2 us               |Idle 5.1 us
```

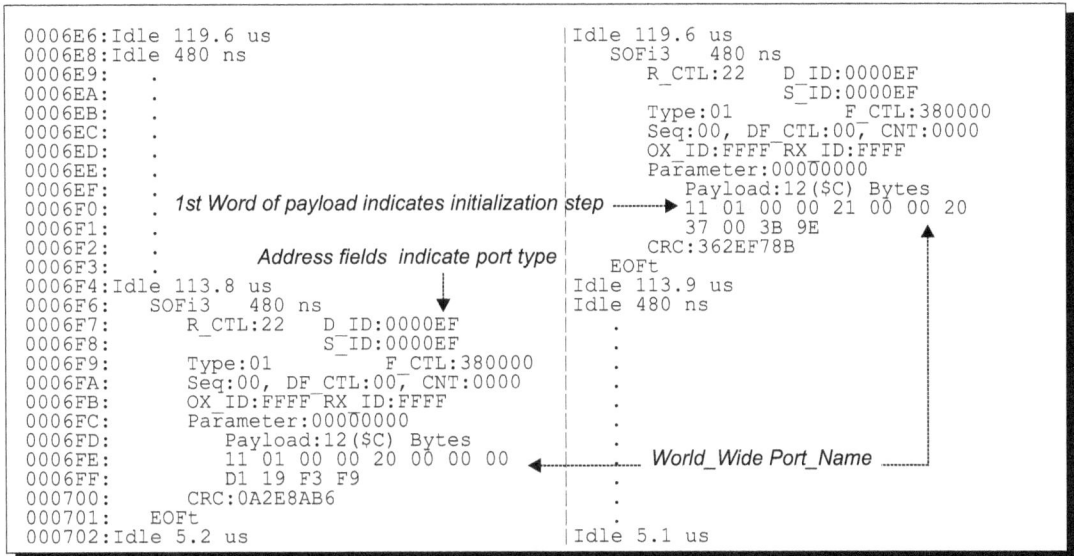

Figure 28. LISM Frame Trace

frame and continues to transmit its LISM frame. Otherwise, the port stops originating its LISM frame and begins transmitting the received frame. Once a port has retransmitted another port's frame it should not transmit its own frame again unless loop initialization is restarted.

Eventually, one of the ports will receive its own LISM frame. When this occurs, that port's frame has propagated completely around the loop and that port becomes the Loop Initialization Master. It then begins transmitting ARB(F0) continuously to inform the other ports that the LISM procedure has been completed and a Loop Initialization Master has been selected.

As each port receives ARB(F0), it stops transmitting LISM frames and prepares for the AL_PA assignment phase of initialization. Each port retransmits ARB(F0) which eventually propagates around the loop and is received by the Loop Initialization Master. At this point, the Loop Initialization Master has been selected, all other ports have been notified, and all LISM frames have been purged from the loop in preparation for AL_PA assignment.

If a Loop Initialization Master is not selected within the LP_TOV timeout value, or the ARB(F0) is not received by the Loop Initialization Master within LP_TOV, loop initialization is restarted.

5.2.1 Avoidance of Loop Master

Some configurations may not want to leave selection of the Loop Initialization Master up to the relationship of the Port_Names. For example, a SCSI disk subsystem (without an FL_Port on the loop) may want to have the SCSI initiator become the Loop Initialization Master in all cases. Because Port_Names are assigned by each port's manufacturer, it is not always possible to ensure that the SCSI initiator will have the lowest Port_Name.

Avoidance of Loop Master   75

One approach to ensure that specific port becomes the Loop Initialization Master is for the SCSI target ports to always forward any received LISM frame. As long as the SCSI initiator (or FL_Port) originates LISM frames and the targets retransmit those frames, the SCSI initiator (or FL_Port) will always receive its LISM frame and become the Loop Initialization Master.

5.3 AL_PA Assignment

Assignment of AL_PA values is one of the principal functions of loop initialization. The Arbitrated Loop architecture allows all addresses to be assigned dynamically by loop initialization removing any requirement to manually set addresses. This is consistent with the Fibre Channel philosophy of allowing the topology to control the address assignment.

Some applications, however, may require or prefer predefined addresses. Storage subsystems or system implementations with fixed configuration tables may need to know the address associated with a specific port. Allowing the topology to assign addresses dynamically may not be the best approach in these cases. Recognizing the special needs of these applications, loop initialization allows ports to attempt to acquire a *hard address* set by address switches, jumpers, backplane wiring or other means.

Because initialization may occur at any time, it is possible that the loop was functioning and ports had operations in progress with other ports when loop initialization occurred. Those operations could be with other ports on the loop, as well as ports accessible via the fabric. Because loop initialization manages AL_PA assignment, it is important to retain the same AL_PA values during subsequent loop initializations.

If conflicts arise for a specific AL_PA value, loop initialization provides a mechanism for determining which port acquires the contested AL_PA. This is done by dividing the AL_PA assignment into a four-step procedure and assigning AL_PA values according to the potential scope of that port's operations. The steps involved in the AL_PA assignment process are illustrated in Figure 29 on page 77.

5.3.1 AL_PA Bit Map

There are 127 AL_PA values possible on an Arbitrated Loop (one for the FL_Port and 126 for the NL_Ports). To identify which AL_PA values have been taken, a 128-bit (four word) map is used. Except for the L_bit, each bit in the AL_PA map corresponds to a specific AL_PA. The correspondence between bits in the map and AL_PA values is shown in Table 8 on page 78.

When an AL_PA is available, the corresponding bit in the map is set to '0'. When the AL_PA is assigned, the bit is changed to a '1' and the AL_PA is no longer available. During the AL_PA assignment procedure, the bit map is transmitted in a frame from port to port around the loop. Before a port can acquire an AL_PA value, it must first examine the bit corresponding to that value. If the bit is '0', the AL_PA is available and the port can claim that AL_PA by setting the bit to '1'. If the bit corresponding to a hard-assigned AL_PA is set to '1' when the port attempts to acquire that address, some other port has already claimed the AL_PA and the port will have to take a soft-assigned AL_PA instead. In this way, address conflicts are avoided because once the bit corresponding to a specific AL_PA is set to '1', no other port can use that AL_PA.

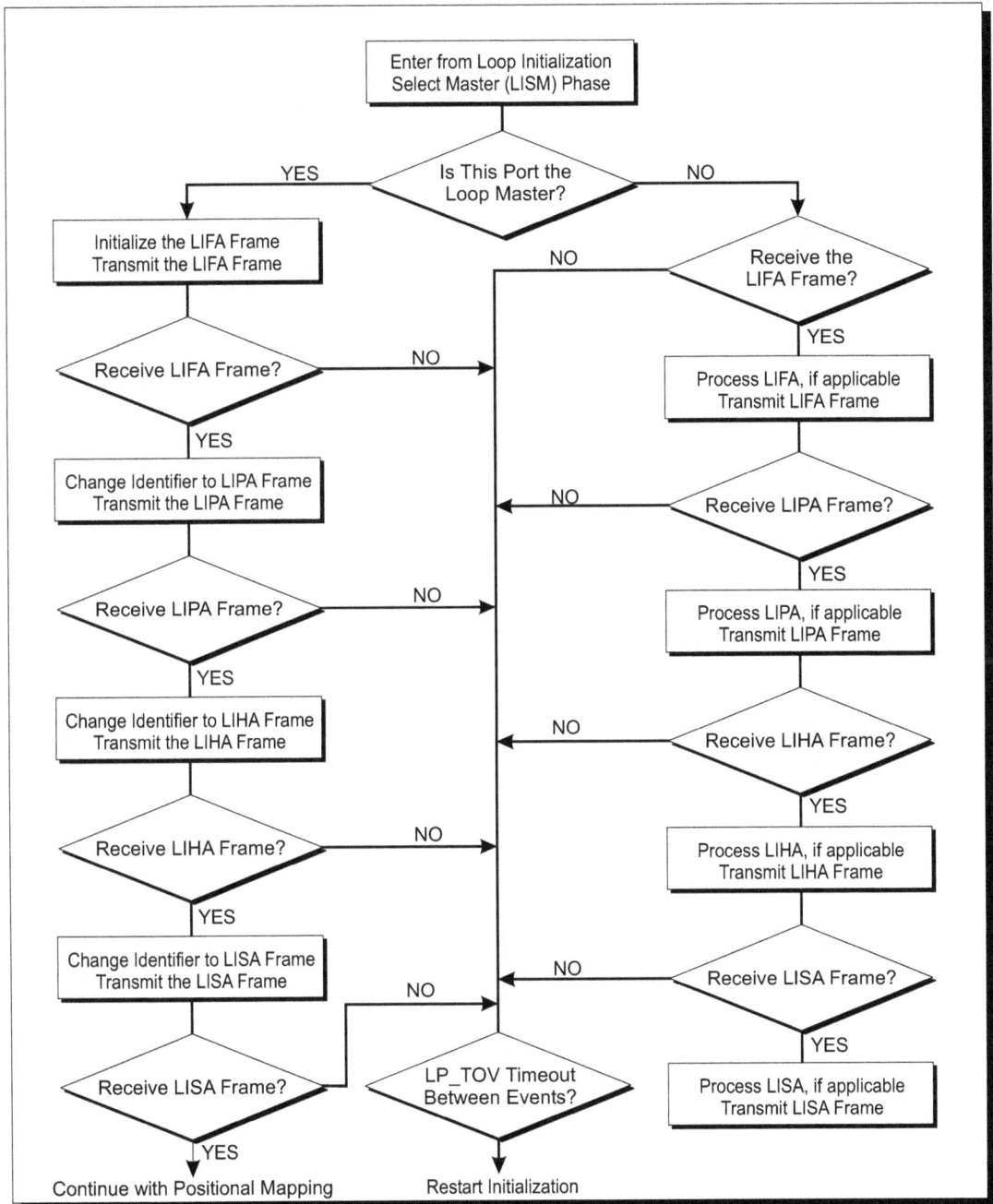

Figure 29. Loop Initialization AL_PA Assignment

AL_PA Bit Map							
Word 0		Word 1		Word 2		Word 3	
Bit	AL_PA	Bit	AL_PA	Bit	AL_PA	Bit	AL_PA
31	L_bit	31	3C	31	73	31	B3
30	00	30	43	30	74	30	B4
29	01	29	45	29	75	29	B5
28	02	28	46	28	76	28	B6
27	04	27	47	27	79	27	B9
26	08	26	49	26	7A	26	BA
25	0F	25	4A	25	7C	25	BC
24	10	24	4B	24	80	24	C3
23	17	23	4C	23	81	23	C5
22	18	22	4D	22	82	22	C6
21	1B	21	4E	21	84	21	C7
20	1D	20	51	20	88	20	C9
19	1E	19	52	19	8F	19	CA
18	1F	18	53	18	90	18	CB
17	23	17	54	17	97	17	CC
16	25	16	55	16	98	16	CD
15	26	15	56	15	9B	15	CE
14	27	14	59	14	9D	14	D1
13	29	13	5A	13	9E	13	D2
12	2A	12	5C	12	9F	12	D3
11	2B	11	63	11	A3	11	D4
10	2C	10	65	10	A5	10	D5
9	2D	9	66	9	A6	9	D6
8	2E	8	67	8	A7	8	D9
7	31	7	69	7	A9	7	DA
6	32	6	6A	6	AA	6	DC
5	33	5	6B	5	AB	5	E0
4	34	4	6C	4	AC	4	E1
3	35	3	6D	3	AD	3	E2
2	36	2	6E	2	AE	2	E4
1	39	1	71	1	B1	1	E8
0	3A	0	72	0	B2	0	EF

Table 8. AL_PA Bit Map

Word 0, bit 31 is designated the login-required bit (L_bit). This bit is only set by an FL_Port or F/NL_Port to indicate that the configuration has potentially changed and all ports are required to perform a fabric login again. If the native address of the port changes in any way during initialization, that port is implicitly logged out with all other ports and a port login is required to re-establish a session. The format of the AL_PA addressing frames is shown in Figure 30.

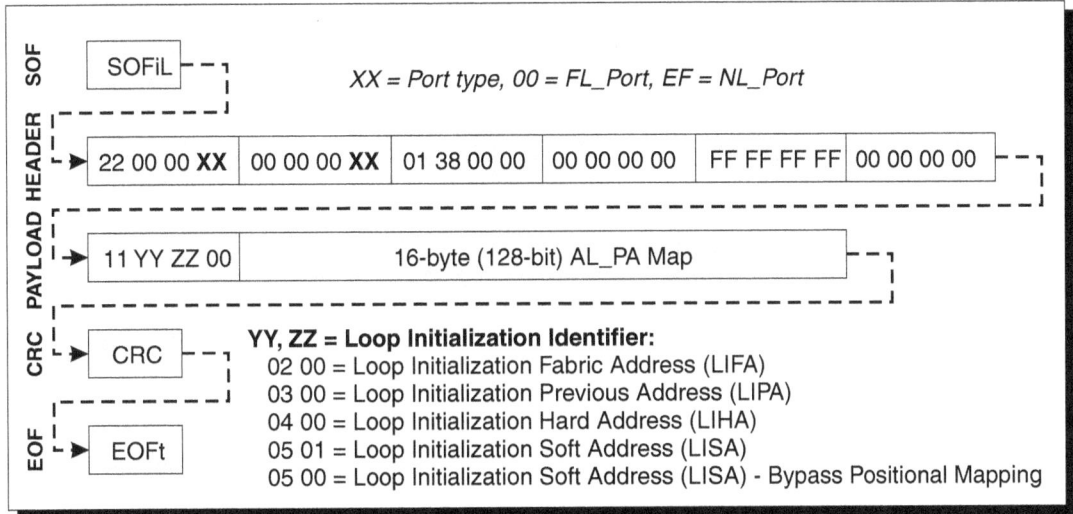

Figure 30. LIFA/LIPA/LIHA/LISA Frame Formats

5.3.2 Loop Initialization Fabric Address (LIFA)

The first step of the AL_PA assignment process allows public ports that had successfully logged-in with the fabric to reclaim the AL_PA they had been using immediately prior to loop initialization.These ports may be engaged in active operations and maintaining the same AL_PA is essential to resuming those operations upon completion of loop initialization. The first step of the AL_PA addressing operation allows ports that had fabric-assigned addresses to reclaim those AL_PA values

The Loop Initialization Master initializes the AL_PA bit map to all '0's and builds the LIFA frame with the initialized bit map in the second through the fifth word of the payload. The first word of the payload contains the loop initialization identifier which is set to x'11 02 00 00' to indicate that this is the LIFA frame.

If the Loop Initialization Master had a fabric-assigned AL_PA prior to loop initialization (this includes the FL_Port), it sets the bit corresponding to that AL_PA (thereby reclaiming that AL_PA) and transmits the frame to the next port. Unlike the LISM operation, the LIFA and remaining initialization frames are transmitted only once because the state of every port on the loop is known and a receive buffer should be available.

If the next port on the loop had a fabric-assigned AL_PA prior to this initialization (i.e., it is a public port and had previously completed FLOGI), it examines the bit corresponding to that

AL_PA. If the bit is '0', the port sets it to '1' and reclaims the AL_PA. If the bit was already set to '1', some other port has claimed that AL_PA and the port will have to wait and take a soft-assigned address. This should not normally happen, but could occur if two formerly separate loops were connected to form a new single loop. If the port did not have a fabric-assigned AL_PA, it leaves the AL_PA map unchanged. The port calculates a new CRC, if required, and retransmits the frame.

This process continues until every port on the loop has processed the LIFA frame and it is received by the Loop Initialization Master. At this point, all of the fabric-assigned AL_PA values have been reclaimed when possible.

If the Loop Initialization Master receives any improperly formatted frame or fails to receive the LIFA frame within LP_TOV it goes to the Initializing state and restarts loop initialization.

5.3.3 Loop Initialization Previous Address (LIPA)

After public ports logged in with the fabric have reclaimed their fabric-assigned AL_PA values, the next group of AL_PA values assigned are for other NL_Ports, that had an AL_PA value immediately prior to this loop initialization. These ports may be engaged in active operations and maintaining the same AL_PA is essential to resuming those operations upon completion of loop initialization. Consequently, the second step of the AL_PA addressing operation allows ports that had previously-assigned addresses to reclaim those AL_PA values.

When the Loop Initialization Master receives the LIFA frame, the LIFA step is complete. It changes the loop initialization identifier in the first word of the payload from LIFA to LIPA (x'11 03 00 00') to indicate this is the Loop Initialization Previously Assigned step, but otherwise leaves the payload unchanged.

Each port, starting with the Loop Initialization Master determines if it had a non-fabric assigned AL_PA prior to initialization. If so, it examines the bit corresponding to that AL_PA in the LIPA frame payload. If the bit is '0', the port sets it to '1' and reclaims the AL_PA. If the bit is already set to '1', some other port has claimed that AL_PA and the port will have to wait and take a soft-assigned address. As mentioned earlier during the LIFA discussion, the only time that a previously assigned AL_PA value is not available is if two formerly separate loops have been connected, or a malfunction has occurred in one of the ports. If the port did not have a previously-assigned AL_PA, it leaves the AL_PA map unchanged. The port calculates a new CRC, if required, and retransmits the frame.

An analyzer trace of the LIPA frame is shown in Figure 31 on page 81. In this example, no AL_PAs are claimed in the first frame and AL_PA x'E8' is claimed in the second frame.

This process continues until every port on the loop has processed the frame and it is received by the Loop Initialization Master. At this point, all of the previously assigned AL_PA values have been reclaimed when possible.

If the Loop Initialization Master receives any improperly formatted frame or fails to receive the LIPA frame within LP_TOV it goes to the Initializing state and restarts loop initialization.

```
000742:Idle 6.1 us                            |Idle 6.1 us
000744:    SOFi3    560 ns                     |Idle 560 ns
000745:        R_CTL:22    D_ID:0000EF         | .
000746:                    S_ID:0000EF         | .
000747:        Type:01          F_CTL:380000   | .
000748:        Seq:00, DF_CTL:00, CNT:0000     | .
000749:        OX_ID:FFFF RX_ID:FFFF           |....... 1st Word of payload indicates initialization step
00074A:        Parameter:00000000             | ·   (Step 3 = LIPA)
00074B:            Payload:20($14) Bytes       | ·
00074C:            11 03 00 00 00 00 00 00  ◄  |....... 128-bit AL_PA map (no AL_PAs taken yet)
00074D:            00 00 00 00 00 00 00 00     | .
00074D:            00 00 00 00                 | .
00074E:        CRC:70F7CBFB                    | .
00074F:    EOFt                                | .
000750:Idle 189.0 us                          |Idle 188.9 us
000752:Idle 560 ns                            |    SOFi3    560 ns
000753:    .                                   |        R_CTL:22    D_ID:0000EF
000754:    .                                   |                    S_ID:0000EF
000755:    .                                   |        Type:01          F_CTL:380000
000756:    .                                   |        Seq:00, DF_CTL:00, CNT:0000
000757:    .                                   |        OX_ID:FFFF RX_ID:FFFF
000758:    .                                   |        Parameter:00000000
000759:    .                                   |            Payload:20($14) Bytes
00075A:    .                                   |            11 03 00 00 00 00 00 00
00075B:    .  128-bit AL_PA map (AL_PA x'E8' taken) |  00 00 00 00 00 00 00 00
00075B:    .                                   |            00 00 00 02
00075D:    .                                   |        CRC:5C96C515
00075E:    .                                   |    EOFt
00075F:Idle 6.2 us                            |Idle 6.2 us
```

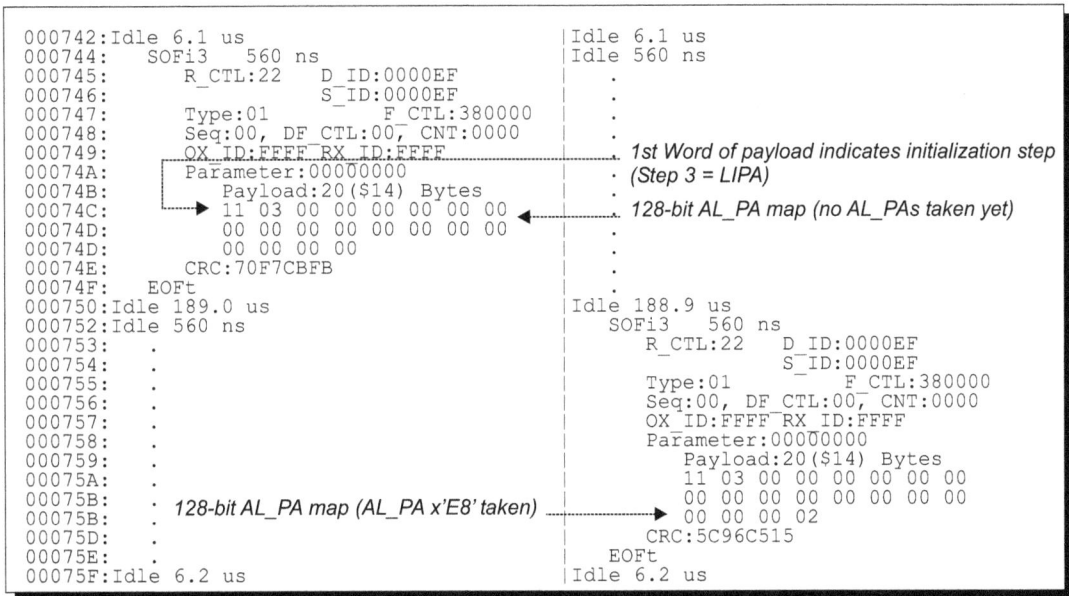

Figure 31. LIPA Frame Trace

5.3.4 Loop Initialization Hard Address (LIHA)

If a port did not have an AL_PA prior to this loop initialization (it was powered off, or nonparticipating) but does have a preferred AL_PA value set by switches, jumpers, backplane wiring, or some other method, the port can attempt to acquire that AL_PA in the third step of the AL_PA process. This allows products such as storage subsystems to assign hard-wired addresses to simplify configurations or problem analysis.

When the Loop Initialization Master receives the LIPA frame, the LIPA step is complete. It changes the loop initialization identifier in word 0 of the payload from LIPA to LIHA (x'11 04 00 00') to indicate this is the Loop Initialization Hard Assigned addressing step, but otherwise leaves the payload unchanged.

Each port, starting with the Loop Initialization Master, that did not have an AL_PA prior to this initialization, but does have a hard-assigned AL_PA, examines the bit corresponding to that AL_PA in the LIHA frame payload. If the bit is '0', the port sets it to '1' and claims that hard-assigned AL_PA. If the bit was already set to '1', some other port has claimed that AL_PA and the port will have to wait and take a soft-assigned address. If the port does not have a hard-assigned AL_PA, it leaves the AL_PA map unchanged. The port calculates the new frame CRC, if required, and retransmits the frame.

This process continues until every port on the loop has processed the frame and it is received by the Loop Initialization Master. At this point, all possible hard-assigned AL_PA values have been claimed.

If the Loop Initialization Master receives any improperly formatted frame or fails to receive the LIHA frame within LP_TOV it goes to the Initializing state and restarts loop initialization.

5.3.5 Loop Initialization Soft Address (LISA)

If a port did not acquire an AL_PA in any of the prior three steps, it may select the first available AL_PA in the fourth and final step and use that *soft assigned* AL_PA.

When the Loop Initialization Master receives the LIHA frame, the LIHA step is complete. The Loop Initialization Master changes the identifier in word 0 of the payload from LIHA to LISA (x'11 05 01 00' or x'11 05 00 00' to indicate that it supports or does not support the loop position mapping, respectively) to indicate this is the Loop Initialization Soft Assigned step, and leaves the AL_PA bit map unchanged.

Each port, starting with the Loop Initialization Master that does not yet have an AL_PA, scans the AL_PA bit map to find the first available AL_PA. When it finds a '0' bit, the port sets it to '1' and claims that soft-assigned AL_PA (although not required, 'first available' means soft addresses should be claimed in order of descending AL_PA priority. See *AL_PA Order on the Loop* on page 127).

If the port is unable to perform the loop positional mapping steps which follow AL_PA assignment, it sets the third byte of the loop initialization identifier in the first word of the frame payload to x'00'. This will be interpreted by the Loop Initialization Master as an indication that the positional mapping steps should be bypassed. The port then calculates the new LISA frame CRC, if required, and retransmits the frame.

If the port is scanning for a soft-assigned AL_PA and finds that all bits in the AL_PA bit map are set to '1', there are no AL_PA values available. In this case, the port retransmits the received frame and enters the nonparticipating mode. This situation could occur if the loop contains more than one FL_Port (only one FL_Port is allowed at AL_PA=x'00') or more than 126 NL_Ports.

If the Loop Initialization Master receives any improperly formatted frame or fails to receive the LISA frame within LP_TOV it goes to the Initializing state and restarts loop initialization.

5.3.6 Soft-Address Order

During the LISA step, the port selects an AL_PA by examining the AL_PA bit map in the received frame. Normally, the AL_PA values would be assigned starting at the most significant bit of the AL_PA map and proceeding towards the least significant bit (logically proceeding left to right). This approach provides the optimal ordering of AL_PA values around the loop (optimal ordering is discussed later in the section titled *AL_PA Order on the Loop* on page 127).

Some implementations using soft addresses have suggested that SCSI initiators examine the bit map starting at the most significant bit and proceed towards the least significant bit while the SCSI targets do just the opposite. This allows the initiators to acquire the higher priority AL_PA values with the targets acquiring the lower priority AL_PA values. This technique has an undesirable consequence in that it yields a non-optimal AL_PA ordering for the SCSI targets and may result in increased overhead when the targets arbitrate for access to the loop.

A preferred approach would be to have a range of AL_PA values corresponding to the most significant bits of the AL_PA bit map reserved for the initiators (highest priority AL_PA values) with the targets assigning soft addresses beginning at the end of the reserved range and proceeding from higher priority to lower priority AL_PA values). For example, if an implementation allowed up to 15 initiators on a loop, AL_PA bit map word 0, bits 30 through 16 could be reserved for the initiators. Targets could start allocating AL_PA values at word 0, bit 15 and proceed through word 0, bit 0 in order. This would avoid the AL_PA ordering problem while still allowing the initiators to acquire high-priority AL_PA values.

The discussion on priority is not as important in Arbitrated Loop as it is on other interfaces because when the fairness algorithm is adhered to, all ports get equal access to the loop no matter what their AL_PA value is.

5.4 Building a Positional Map of the Loop

When the Loop Initialization Master receives the LISA frame, the AL_PA assignment operation is complete. Every port on the loop either acquired a unique AL_PA or entered the nonparticipating mode.

Although AL_PA values have been assigned, only the Loop Initialization Master is guaranteed to know all of the AL_PA values and no specific position information of any specific AL_PA has been provided. If AL_PA values have been assigned in the LISA step, their positions may be completely arbitrary. What is needed is a mechanism to build a position map of the loop to facilitate configuration management or problem analysis.

This procedure was added when some early implementations could not support it. All new implementations require this procedure. Those early implementations set byte 2 of the loop initialization identifier to x'00' during the LISA sequence to indicate nonsupport of the positional mapping process. At the end of the LISA sequence, the Loop Initialization Master examines the loop initialization identifier to determine if the positional mapping steps should be performed. If the identifier is x'11 05 01 00' positional mapping is performed, if it is x'11 05 00 00' the positional mapping procedure is bypassed and the Loop Initialization Master ends the initialization process by transmitting CLS.

5.4.1 Loop Initialization Report Position (LIRP)

The first step of the mapping process is to build a map of the AL_PA values according to their positions on the loop relative to the Loop Initialization Master. The Loop Initialization Master begins the procedure by transmitting a Loop Initialization Report Position (LIRP) frame.

The LIRP frame payload consists of the 1-word loop initialization identifier x'11 06 00 00'), a 1-byte offset, and up to 127 AL_PA entries. The loop master initializes the LIRP frame payload by setting the offset to x'01', storing its own AL_PA at offset 1 into the AL_PA map and storing x'FF' in all remaining positions of the AL_PA map (x'FF' is used to avoid any potential ambiguity with valid AL_PA values). The format of the LIRP and LILP frames is shown in Figure 32.

The frame is transmitted to the next participating port on the loop which increments the offset value and stores its AL_PA at that location in the AL_PA positional map. The CRC is recalculated and the frame transmitted to the next port on the loop. Nonparticipating ports merely re-

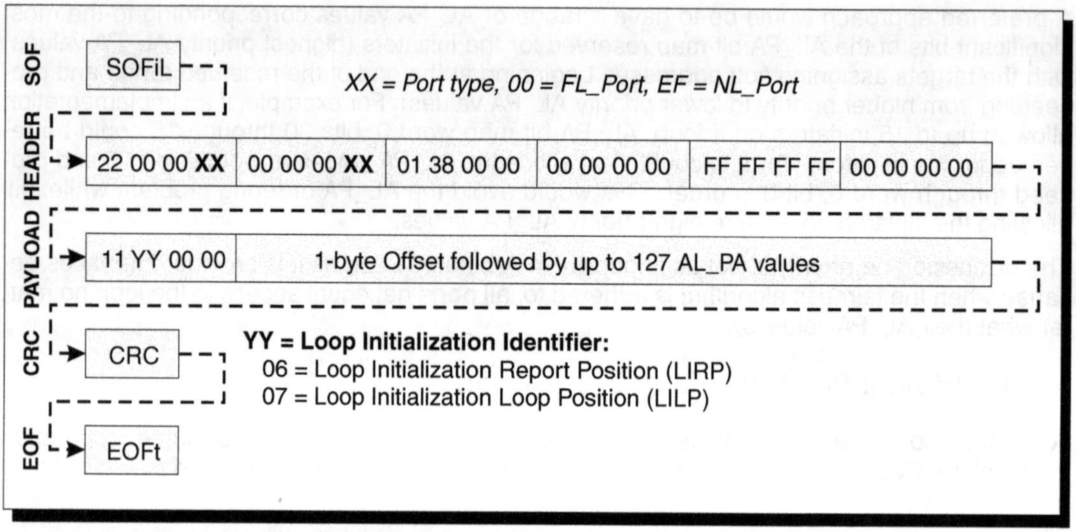

Figure 32. LIRP/LILP Frame Formats

transmit this frame. This process continues until the LIRP frame has been processed by every port on the loop and reaches the Loop Initialization Master. An analyzer trace of the LIRP frame with two entries in the map is shown in Figure 33.

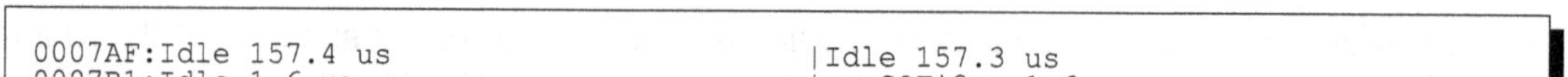

```
0007AF:Idle 157.4 us                                    |Idle 157.3 us
0007B1:Idle 1.6 us                                      |  SOFi3   1.6 us
0007B2:   .                                             |  R_CTL:22    D_ID:0000EF
0007B3:   .                                             |             S_ID:0000EF
0007B4:   .                                             |  Type:01        F_CTL:380000
0007B5:   .                                             |  Seq:00, DF_CTL:00, CNT:0000
0007B6:   .                                             |  OX_ID:FFFF RX_ID:FFFF
0007B7:   .                                             |  Parameter:00000000
0007B8:   .                                             |       Payload:132($84) Bytes
0007B9:   .    1st Word of payload indicates initialization step ----▶ 11 06 00 00 02 01 E8 FF
0007BA:   .    (Step 6 = LIRP)                          |  FF FF FF FF FF FF FF FF
0007BB:   .                                             |  FF FF FF FF FF FF FF FF
0007BB:   .                                             |  FF FF FF FF FF FF FF FF
0007BB:   .                                             |  FF FF FF FF FF FF FF FF
0007BB:   .                                             |  FF FF FF FF FF FF FF FF
0007BB:   .    128-byte AL_PA list. 1st byte is number  |  FF FF FF FF FF FF FF FF
0007BB:   .    of ports on the loop followed by a list of    FF FF FF FF FF FF FF FF
0007BB:   .    AL_PA values starting with the Loop  ----▶  FF FF FF FF FF FF FF FF
0007BB:   .    Initialization Master. Unused positions  |  FF FF FF FF FF FF FF FF
0007BB:   .    are initialized to x'FF'.                |  FF FF FF FF FF FF FF FF
0007BB:   .                                             |  FF FF FF FF FF FF FF FF
0007BB:   .                                             |  FF FF FF FF FF FF FF FF
0007BB:   .                                             |  FF FF FF FF FF FF FF FF
0007BB:   .                                             |  FF FF FF FF FF FF FF FF
0007BB:   .                                             |  FF FF FF FF
0007BC:   .                                             |       CRC:435F59C6
0007BD:   .                                             |  EOFt
0007BE:Idle 12.9 us                                     |Idle 12.9 us
```

Figure 33. LIRP Frame Trace

If the loop contains nonparticipating or bypassed ports, their presence is not indicated in the LIRP frame which may reduce the usefulness of the positional mapping.

If the Loop Initialization Master receives any improperly formatted frame or fails to receive the LIRP frame within LP_TOV it goes to the Initializing state and restarts loop initialization.

5.4.2 Loop Initialization Loop Position (LILP)

When the Loop Initialization Master receives the LIRP frame, it changes the loop initialization identifier to indicate that this is the LILP step (x'11 07 00 00') and retransmits the fully completed positional map. This allows any interested port to capture the AL_PA positional map for subsequent use.

If the Loop Initialization Master receives any improperly formatted frame or fails to receive the LILP frame within LP_TOV it goes to the Initializing state and restarts loop initialization from the beginning.

5.5 Closing the Loop Initialization Process

When the LILP frame is received by the Loop Initialization Master (or if positional mapping was not performed), loop initialization is complete. The Loop Initialization Master transmits a single CLS. The CLS propagates around the loop causing the LPSM in each port to make the transition to the Monitoring state.

Upon entry to the Monitoring state, the ports are now ready to resume the operations suspended (if any) by loop initialization and can begin arbitrating for access to the loop to transmit and receive frames.

5.6 Post Loop Initialization Processing

Upon completion of the loop initialization, a port that does not yet have a 24-bit native address identifier initially assumes a value with the upper 16 bits equal to zeros and the lower 8 bits set to the AL_PA acquired during loop initialization.

Public ports that have not previously logged-in with the fabric perform a fabric login and acquire a full 24-bit address from the fabric login server. Public ports also login with the fabric if the 'login required' bit was set during processing of the AL_PA assignment frames.

The upper 16 bits of a fabric-assigned address are nonzero and are the same for all ports on the loop. In effect, the upper 16 bits provide a loop identifier (i.e., all public ports have the same upper 16 bits). The lower 8 bits of the fabric-assigned address are equal to the AL_PA acquired during initialization. If, for any reason, the lower 8 bits of the fabric-assigned address do not match the AL_PA acquired during initialization, the port restarts loop initialization and subsequently acquires the AL_PA assigned by the fabric during the LIFA step.

If there is no FL_Port or N/FL_Port present, the attempt to open the FL_Port fails and the public port keeps the 24-bit address with the upper 16 bits equal to zeros.

Private ports do not attempt a fabric login and simply keep the 24-bit address with the upper 16 bits equal to zeros.

Public ports on a public loop acquire 24-bit addresses where the upper 16 bits are nonzero and the same for all public ports on the loop. Private ports (and public ports on private loops) acquire 24-bit addresses where the upper 16 bits are zeros. This partitions the address space on the loop in a public partition and a private partition. The fabric is responsible for ensuring that frames to or from the private ports are confined to the loop and excluded from the fabric.

Ports can locate the other ports on the loop by examining the LILP frame, if the mapping steps were done, or attempting to open a loop circuit with each possible AL_PA (see *Opening a Loop Circuit* on page 151 for a description of how loop circuits are opened and *Open Failures* on page 158 for techniques to determine if the open failed.)

Before ports can perform operations other than Link Services, a Port_Login (PLOGI) is transmitted to establish a session. If the port is a public port the D_ID of this PLOGI consists of the common loop identifier and the AL_PA in the lower 8 bits. The receiving port, whether public or private, must accept this D_ID for the PLOGI. If the port is a private port the D_ID of this PLOGI consists of the upper 16 bits of zero and the AL_PA in the lower 8 bits. The receiving port, whether public or private, must accept this D_ID for the PLOGI. After PLOGI, only the correct 24 bit address should be used

5.7 Minimizing the Impact of Initialization

There are two key considerations associated with loop initialization. The first is to quantify the time required for loop initialization and how that affects loop throughput or operations. The second is to examine what can be done to minimize the impact of the loop initialization on operations in progress.

Because initialization can be expected to be infrequent in normal operations, why be concerned with how long it takes? In many cases, this is true. However, certain applications are not able to tolerate an interruption to data delivery, no matter how infrequent. For example, real time applications or video servers may demand sustained performance at a predictable and reliable throughput.

5.7.1 Minimizing Loop Disruption During Initialization

Because the beginning of initialization is not required to be synchronized to other loop operations, it is possible for the LIP primitive sequence to corrupt one or more frames. This could result in temporary errors and their associated recovery actions. If the beginning of initialization could be timed to occur when the loop is quiesced, this problem would not occur. The question is: How can initialization be synchronized?

If loop initialization is being performed as a result of a loop failure, the concern about disrupting loop traffic is irrelevant because the failure is disruptive by itself. On the other hand, if loop initialization is the result of a port being powered up or added to the loop, there is a very real potential for causing temporary errors.

The question of minimizing loop disruption is tied to the service philosophy associated with the loop or product containing the loop. If the loop can be quiesced, either manually or under program control, initialization can be performed non disruptively. All that is required to quiesce the loop is for a port to win arbitration, send and OPN to itself, then begin loop initialization.

If the port being powered up or added to the loop could win arbitration, it could ensure that no other activity was in progress when loop initialization began. The problem is that the port needs to initialize to acquire an AL_PA so it can begin arbitrating. In environments where all of the AL_PA values are hard assigned by switches or jumpers, the port can assume that its hard assigned AL_PA is not being used and use that AL_PA to arbitrate for access to the loop. When it wins arbitration, the port can begin loop initialization to notify other ports of the configuration change and ensure that the assumed AL_PA is indeed valid.

What can be done when the AL_PA values are not assigned by switches or jumpers? For ports that do not have a means to arbitrate, one approach might be to wait for another port to start the initialization process. This could be an implementation choice where designated ports periodically perform loop initialization to allow new ports join the loop when the loop is quiesced. Another means is being considered with the use of MRKtx where t is a request for a port to arbitrate and when it wins, to initialize the loop; x would be x'F7' to indicate that the source has no AL_PA. If the MRKtx returns to the originator the port may wait for LP_TOV and then transmit LIP without regard to quiescing the loop. If the MRKtx does not return to the originator, another port captured the MRKtx and may initialize the loop or the MRKtx was discarded. MRKtx could be transmitted every AL_Time until the MRKtx is returned or a LIP sequence is received.

5.8 Multiple Ports Initializing

It is possible for multiple ports to begin loop initialization simultaneously, or for one or more ports to begin loop initialization before a previous loop initialization has completed. For example, a disk subsystem which sequences power to the disk drives may experience loop initialization as each disk becomes operational. When this occurs, loop initialization may occur many times, until the last port's initialization completes.

When a port in the Initializing state transmits a LIP sequence and waits for 3 AL_Times for a LIP to be received (45 ms. by default). If any LIP is received during this time, the LPSM enters the Open-Init state and continues loop initialization. It is not necessary for the received LIP to be the same as the one that was originally sent. Figure 34 on page 88 illustrates a case where Port_01 is sending LIP(F7,F7) while at the same time Port_B2 is transmitting LIP(F8,B2).

As each port recognizes LIP, it enters the Open-Init state, transmits at least 12 LIPs of the same type as received and then begins transmitting the LISM sequence. During this time up to AL_Time, received LIPs are ignored to prevent continuous LIP circulation on the loop if multiple ports are sending LIP simultaneously.

In the example in Figure 34 on page 88, Port_B2 enters the Open-Init state when it recognizes the LIP(F7,F7) from Port_01 and Port_01 enters the Open-Init state when it recognizes the LIP(F8,B2) from Port_B2. Port_2A and Port_EF received different LIPs, but both entered the Open-Init state and passed the received LIP on.

This procedure allows multiple loop initializations to begin simultaneously with all ports successfully entering the Open-Init state. Because a port in the Initializing state removes any received LIPs from the loop, it prevents potentially endless circulation of LIPs, but may prevent some ports from recognizing all of the reasons for the current loop initialization (e.g., Port_2A does not know that Port_B2 has detected a loop failure).

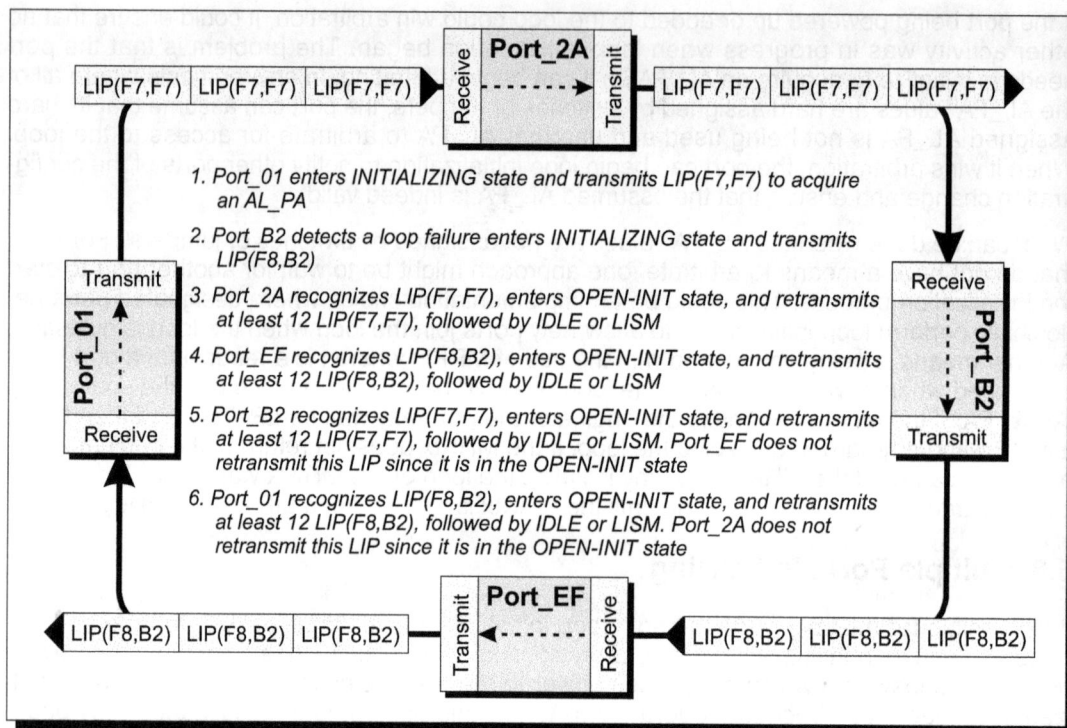

```
LIP(F7,F7) | LIP(F7,F7) | LIP(F7,F7)     Receive   Port_2A   Transmit     LIP(F7,F7) | LIP(F7,F7) | LIP(F7,F7)
```

Transmit
Port_01
Receive

1. Port_01 enters INITIALIZING state and transmits LIP(F7,F7) to acquire an AL_PA

2. Port_B2 detects a loop failure enters INITIALIZING state and transmits LIP(F8,B2)

3. Port_2A recognizes LIP(F7,F7), enters OPEN-INIT state, and retransmits at least 12 LIP(F7,F7), followed by IDLE or LISM

4. Port_EF recognizes LIP(F8,B2), enters OPEN-INIT state, and retransmits at least 12 LIP(F8,B2), followed by IDLE or LISM

5. Port_B2 recognizes LIP(F7,F7), enters OPEN-INIT state, and retransmits at least 12 LIP(F7,F7), followed by IDLE or LISM. Port_EF does not retransmit this LIP since it is in the OPEN-INIT state

6. Port_01 recognizes LIP(F8,B2), enters OPEN-INIT state, and retransmits at least 12 LIP(F8,B2), followed by IDLE or LISM. Port_2A does not retransmit this LIP since it is in the OPEN-INIT state

Receive
Port_B2
Transmit

```
LIP(F8,B2) | LIP(F8,B2) | LIP(F8,B2)     Transmit   Port_EF   Receive     LIP(F8,B2) | LIP(F8,B2) | LIP(F8,B2)
```

Figure 34. Multiple Loop Ports Initializing

5.9 Initializing State

When a port wishes to begin loop initialization, it signals the LPSM to enter the Initializing state and transmit a LIP sequence. Recognition of the LIP causes the next port on the loop to enter the Open-Init state and transmit at least 12 LIPs of the same type as received. This process repeats port-by-port around the loop until the port in the Initializing state recognizes a LIP sequence on its receive input and also enters the Open-Init state (the received LIP may be different than the one that was transmitted if multiple ports are initializing). At this point, loop operations have been suspended and all ports are in the Open-Init state.

If the port in the Initializing state fails to recognize a valid LIP sequence after transmitting LIPs for 3 AL_Times, (45 ms. by default), the port may assume that it is not operating in a functional loop environment and enter the Old-Port state. This may be done automatically by the LPSM, or by asserting the REQ(old-port) L_Port control *(line 36: 'REQ(old-port)', on page 347)*. While in the Old-Port state the port behaves as an F_Port or N_Port rather than a loop port. This mechanism allows a loop-capable port to interoperate with an F_Port or N_Port which do not recognize or retransmit the LIP primitive.

In some implementations, such as a peripheral subsystem, a designated port may try to recover from the condition where loop initialization fails to complete successfully by attempting to bypass the failing port using the LPB primitive sequence. In this case, the REQ(bypass loop port y) control *(line 41: 'REQ(bypass L_Port y)', on page 347)* may be used to signal the LPSM to transmit the LPB(yx) sequence. The AL_PA value for the port may be obtained from a prior loop configuration map, or simply by attempting all AL_PA values except that of the port itself. If the LPB(yx) (where x = the AL_PA of this port) is not received within 2 AL_Times, the loop is still not operational and it may be necessary to try bypassing a different port until the correct one is located. When the failing port has been identified, any functional ports which had been bypassed can be re-enabled *(line 44: 'REQ(enable L_Port y)', on page 347)* and initialization can continue by reentering the Initializing state *(line 24: 'LPB(yx) of LPB(fx)', on page 347)* and transmitting LIPs which should now propagate around the loop successfully. If this procedure fails, it is possible that the port which is causing the failure does not have an AL_PA (i.e., non-participating). In this case, a REQ(bypass all) control *(line 42: 'REQ(bypass all)', on page 347)* can be used to bypass all ports.

5.9.1 Initializing State Entry Actions

Upon entry to the Initializing state, the Bypass variable is reset to allow ports that had been bypassed earlier to attempt to rejoin loop operations.

A LIP sequences is sent multiple times because individual LIP ordered sets may be deleted by the clock elasticity circuit in other ports on the loop. Also, ports in the open, opened, received close, transmitted close, and transfer states do not retransmit the first two LIP ordered sets (the LIP is not recognized as a valid primitive sequence until the third consecutive occurrence of the ordered set, the first two occurrences are processed as 'other ordered sets').

The port continues to transmit LIP for up to 3 AL_Time periods or until it recognizes a LIP sequence on its receive input. The LPSM state machine transmits LIP in place of each received transmission word except the LPB/LPE primitive sequences.

5.9.2 Received Errors and Elasticity in Initializing State

No interpretation of received characters is performed until it is determined that the received character is a valid transmission character.

If a temporary Loss of Sync occurs *(line 1: 'Loss of Synchronization', on page 346)*, a Loop Failure is detected *(line 2: 'Loop Failure', on page 346)*, an invalid transmission word is received *(line 3: 'Invalid Transmission Word', on page 346)* or a running disparity error is detected *(line 4: 'Running Disparity Error at Ordered Set', on page 346)*, the received word is discarded.

Elasticity words are not applicable in this state *(line 5: 'Elasticity Word Required', on page 346)* because the port is open. However, if an LPB or LPE sequence is recognized, the port transmits that sequence instead of LIPs for as long as the LPB or LPE sequence is recognized.

If a valid data word is received *(line 6: 'Valid Data Word', on page 346)*, the received word is discarded, as is every other received word except LIP and the LPB/LPE primitive sequences.

5.9.3 Initialization and Loop Bypass in Initializing State

The normal exit from the Initializing state occurs when LIP is recognized *(line 23: 'LIP', on page 346)* and the LPSM makes the transition to the Open-Init state.

While in the Initializing state, the port continues to process loop bypass primitive sequences.

If LPB(yx) or LPB(fx) is recognized *(line 24: 'LPB(yx) of LPB(fx)', on page 347)* the LPSM examines both the AL_PD and AL_PS fields (the y and x values respectively)

- If 'x' equals the AL_PA of this port, the LPB(yx) is replaced by LIP. This is the port that originally sent the LPB(yx) and is responsible for removing it from the loop.

- If 'y' equals the AL_PA of this port, the LPSM sets the Bypass variable and enters the Monitoring state. This port has been bypassed by another port on the loop.

- If 'y' equals x'FF', the LPSM sets the Bypass variable and enters the Monitoring state. This port has been bypassed by another port on the loop. The LPB(fx) will be retransmitted in the Monitoring state.

- If 'y' does not equal the AL_PA of this port, the LPB(yx) is retransmitted

If LPE(yx) or LPE(fx) is recognized *(line 25: 'LPE(yx) or LPE(fx)', on page 347)*, the LPSM examines the AL_PS field to determine if this was the port that originally transmitted the LPE. If so, the LPE is discarded and replaced by a LIP. Otherwise, the LPE is retransmitted.

If at any time REQ(bypass L_Port) is active while in the Initializing state *(line 40: 'REQ(bypass L_Port)', on page 347)*, the LPSM state machine sets the Bypass variable, activates the bypass circuit (if present), and enters the Monitoring state.

5.9.4 Processing Other Valid Ordered Sets in Initializing State

If any other valid ordered set is received *(line 26: 'Other Ordered Set', on page 347)*, it is discarded and the port continues to transmit LIPs. As mentioned earlier, this includes the first two ordered sets of a primitive sequence because the primitive sequence is not recognized until the third consecutive occurrence of the ordered set.

5.10 Old-Port State

The Old-Port state is an optional state depending on the implementation. The state is entered when the LPSM is unsuccessful in propagating a LIP or LPB(yx) around the loop within 3 AL_Times. This could occur because the port is connected to an N_Port or F_Port, and although proper bit and word synchronization ordered sets are received, the transmitted LIP or LPB(yx) are not.

Ports that are not loop capable do not recognize the loop-specific ordered sets and discard them. As a result, a port in the Initializing state never sees its LIP or LPB(yx), times out, enters the Old-Port state, and adopts nonloop behavior.

While in the Old-Port state, all primitive signals and primitive sequences defined by FC-PH have their defined meanings. No fill word substitution occurs.

Arbitration, opening, and closing are not performed in this state. All loop-specific ordered sets are ignored with the exception of LIP. If LIP is recognized, the LPSM enters the Open-Init state.

The alternate BB_Credit management mode is reset, causing the BB_Credit flow control to function in accordance with the normal Fibre Channel FC-PH model. An initial BB_Credit of one is assumed to allow the port to perform fabric and/or N_Port login.

5.10.1 Old-Port State Entry Actions

Upon entry to the Old-Port state, the alternate BB_Credit management mode is reset, the available BB_Credit is set one, and the current fill word is set to IDLE. The current fill word is not affected by any input conditions while in the Old-Port state.

5.10.2 Error Inputs, Elasticity Words, Received Data Words

Normal Fibre Channel FC-PH rules apply for all received transmission word error conditions except loop failure.

If a loop failure is detected *(line 2: 'Loop Failure', on page 351)* or REQ(initialize) is active *(line 46: 'REQ(initialize)', on page 352)*, the LPSM enters the Initializing state.

Elasticity words are not applicable in this state *(line 5: 'Elasticity Word Required', on page 351)* because received transmission words are not retransmitted.

5.10.3 Re-Initialization

If LIP is recognized *(line 23: 'LIP', on page 352)*, the port implicitly logs out with the other port and enters the Open-Init state.

5.10.4 Processing Other Valid Ordered Sets in Old-Port State

If any other valid ordered set is received, it is processed as defined by the Fibre Channel standard for point-to-point and fabric environments.

5.11 Open Initializing (Open-Init) State

The Open-Init state is used to perform loop initialization. While in this state, initialization frames are transmitted and received to identify a Loop Initialization Master and assign AL_PA values. Entry to this state assumes the port is in a loop environment, and consequently the alternate BB_Credit management mode is set and the available BB_Credit is set to zero.

Upon entry to the Open-Init state, the port transmits at least 12 LIPs of the same type as received and then continuously transmits the Loop Initialization Select Master (LISM) frame. Any received LIPs are ignored for AL_Time.

The LISM frames are used to select a Loop Initialization Master which is responsible for originating the subsequent initialization sequences. When the Loop Initialization Master has been selected, it transmits an ARB(F0) to notify all ports to stop transmitting LISM frames. The Loop Initialization Master is responsible for originating the loop initialization frames required during loop initialization. Other ports receive, process, and retransmit the frames originated by the Loop Initialization Master.

While in the Open-Init state, frame transmission reverts to Class-3 behavior without flow control. If an R_RDY is received it is ignored and discarded.

While in the Open-Init state, the Loop Initialization Master is responsible to correctly transmit and process ARB(F0) and CLS.

5.11.1 Open-Init State Entry Actions

Upon entry to the Open-Init state, alternate BB_Credit mode is set, available BB_Credit is set to zero, and the current fill word is set to IDLE. The current fill word is not affected by any input conditions while in the Open-Init state.

The port transmits at least 12 LIPs of the same type as received. All received LIPs are ignored for AL_Time.

5.11.2 Received Errors, Elasticity Words, Received Data Words

If a temporary loss of synchronization occurs (line 1: 'Loss of Synchronization', on page 348), the LPSM transmits IDLEs until synchronization is regained.

If synchronization is not re-acquired within R_T_TOV (100 msec) a loop failure is detected (line 2: 'Loop Failure', on page 348) and the LPSM enters the Initializing state to begin a loop initialization to notify other ports of the failure. The LIP used in this case is LIP(F8,F7) or LIP(F8,AL_PS) depending upon whether the port currently has a valid AL_PA.

If an invalid transmission word (line 3: 'Invalid Transmission Word', on page 348) or an ordered set with incorrect running disparity (line 4: 'Running Disparity Error at Ordered Set', on page 348) is received, it is discarded.

Elasticity words are not applicable in this state (line 5: 'Elasticity Word Required', on page 348) because received transmission words are not retransmitted (see Error Inputs, Elasticity Words, Received Data Words on page 91).

5.11.3 Arbitration and Access Fairness in Open-Init State

No arbitration occurs while in the Open-Init state (see Loop Initialization Select Master (LISM) Procedure on page 72). If an ARB(x) is received (line 13: 'ARB(x)', on page 348), it is discarded and the current fill word transmitted in its place.

5.11.4 Frame Transmission and Closing

No OPN primitive signal is required to prepare the ports for frame transmission and reception in the Open-Init state as this state implicitly opens all ports.

After the initial LIPs have been sent, each port begins repetitively transmitting LISM frames. When a Loop Initialization Master has been determined, it transmits ARB(F0) to notify the other ports to stop LISM transmission. The means by which the LPSM is instructed to transmit ARB(F0) is not identified because this depends upon the specific implementation. ARB(F0) is transmitted continuously until it is received by the Loop Initialization Master (line 12: 'ARB(F0)', on page 348) to purge all LISM frames from the loop and prepares the other ports to receive the remaining initialization sequences.

Once the LISM process has been completed, the Loop Initialization Master transmits a series of AL_PA assignment and positional mapping frames (see *AL_PA Assignment* on page 76 and *Building a Positional Map of the Loop* on page 83).

When the AL_PA assignment and configuration mapping sequences are complete, the temporary master transmits a CLS to signal the end of the initialization process. When the CLS is received by the other ports *(line 16: 'CLS', on page 349)*, they retransmit the CLS at the next appropriate fill word and enter the Monitoring state. When the CLS has propagated completely around the loop and is received by the Loop Initialization Master *(line 16: 'CLS', on page 349)*, the Loop Initialization Master enters the Monitoring state, discards the CLS, and relinquishes its Loop Initialization Master responsibility.

The only valid start-of-frame delimiter *(line 7: 'Start of Frame (SOF)', on page 346)* while in the Open-Init state is SOFiL (same as the SOFi3). The only valid end-of-frame delimiter *(line 8: 'End of Frame (EOF)', on page 346)* is EOFt. Although the frames with the appropriate delimiters are defined, many implementations check only the D_ID, S_ID, payload, and CRC.

5.11.5 Initialization and Loop Bypass While in Open-Init State

If the LIP primitive sequence is recognized *(line 23: 'LIP', on page 349)*, the LPSM reenters the Open-Init state and performs the entry actions again. This could occur if a second port begins initializing while loop initialization is underway.

The port can also request initialization by asserting the REQ(initialize) input to the state machine *(line 46: 'REQ(initialize)', on page 350)* which causes the LPSM to enter the Initializing state. In this case, the port is responsible for determining the LIP to be sent.

If the port no longer requires access to the loop it asserts the REQ(nonparticipate) L_Port control *(line 38: 'REQ(nonparticipate)', on page 349)* and the LPSM enters the Monitoring state.

If the LPB(yx) primitive sequence is recognized and y equals the AL_PA of the port *(line 24: 'LPB(yx) or LPB(fx)', on page 349)* or REQ(bypass L_Port) is active *(line 40: 'REQ(bypass L_Port)', on page 349)*, the Bypass variable is set and the LPSM enters the Monitoring state.

5.11.6 Processing Other Valid Ordered Sets in Open-Init State

The only valid ordered sets not explicitly listed in Table 38 on page 348 that are processed while in the Open-Init state are SOFiL and EOF. Other valid ordered sets are ignored.

5.12 Loop Initialization Trace

A trace of the entire loop initialization process is shown beginning in Figure 35 on page 94. This portion of the trace illustrates the LIP transmission and select Loop Initialization Master (LISM) portions of the initialization process. The end of this phase is signalled by use of the ARB(F0) ordered set.

The LIFA and LIPA AL_PA acquisition frames are shown in Figure 36 on page 95. These two addressing steps are for ports with AL_PAs prior to this initialization to reclaim their AL_PA, if possible. Public ports reclaim their AL_PA in step x'02', private ports reclaim their AL_PA in step x'03'.

```
000003:LIP    (No valid Port Addr)      |Idle 280 ns
000005:       .                         |LIP   (No valid Port Addr)
000007:Idle 224.2 us                    |     .
000009:Idle 16.0 ms                     |Idle 16.0 ms
0006E6:Idle 119.6 us                    |Idle 119.6 us
0006E8:Idle 480 ns                      |   SOFi3    480 ns
0006E9:       .                         |      R_CTL:22    D_ID:0000EF
0006EA:       .                         |                 S_ID:0000EF
0006EB:       .                         |      Type:01        F_CTL:380000
0006EC:       .                         |      Seq:00, DF_CTL:00, CNT:0000
0006ED:       .                         |      OX_ID:FFFF RX_ID:FFFF
0006EE:       .                         |      Parameter:00000000
0006EF:       .                         |         Payload:12($C) Bytes
0006F0:       .                         |         11 01 00 00 21 00 00 20
0006F1:       .                         |         37 00 3B 9E
0006F2:       .                         |      CRC:362EF78B
0006F3:       .                         |   EOFt
0006F4:Idle 113.8 us                    |Idle 113.9 us
0006F6:   SOFi3    480 ns               |Idle 480 ns
0006F7:      R_CTL:22    D_ID:0000EF     |     .
0006F8:                 S_ID:0000EF      |     .
0006F9:      Type:01        F_CTL:380000 |     .
0006FA:      Seq:00, DF_CTL:00, CNT:0000 |     .
0006FB:      OX_ID:FFFF RX_ID:FFFF       |     .
0006FC:      Parameter:00000000          |     .
0006FD:         Payload:12($C) Bytes     |     .
0006FE:         11 01 00 00 20 00 00 00  |     .
0006FF:         D1 19 F3 F9              |     .
000700:      CRC:0A2E8AB6                |     .
000701:   EOFt                          |     .
000702:Idle 5.2 us                      |Idle 5.1 us
000704:Idle 480 ns                      |   SOFi3    480 ns
000705:       .                         |      R_CTL:22    D_ID:0000EF
000706:       .                         |                 S_ID:0000EF
000707:       .                         |      Type:01        F_CTL:380000
000708:       .                         |      Seq:00, DF_CTL:00, CNT:0000
000709:       .                         |      OX_ID:FFFF RX_ID:FFFF
00070A:       .                         |      Parameter:00000000
00070B:       .                         |         Payload:12($C) Bytes
00070C:       .                         |         11 01 00 00 21 00 00 20
00070D:       .                         |         37 00 3B 9E
00070E:       .                         |      CRC:362EF78B
00070F:       .                         |   EOFt
000710:Idle 223.9 us                    |Idle 224.0 us
000712:Idle 480 ns                      |   SOFi3    480 ns
000713:       .                         |      R_CTL:22    D_ID:0000EF
000714:       .                         |                 S_ID:0000EF
000715:       .                         |      Type:01        F_CTL:380000
000716:       .                         |      Seq:00, DF_CTL:00, CNT:0000
000717:       .                         |      OX_ID:FFFF RX_ID:FFFF
000718:       .                         |      Parameter:00000000
000719:       .                         |         Payload:12($C) Bytes
00071A:       .                         |         11 01 00 00 20 00 00 00
00071B:       .                         |         D1 19 F3 F9
00071C:       .                         |      CRC:0A2E8AB6
00071D:       .                         |   EOFt
00071E:Idle 9.1 us                      |Idle 9.2 us
000720:ARBx  Port F0                    |Idle 66.1 us
000722:       .                         |ARBx  Port F0
```

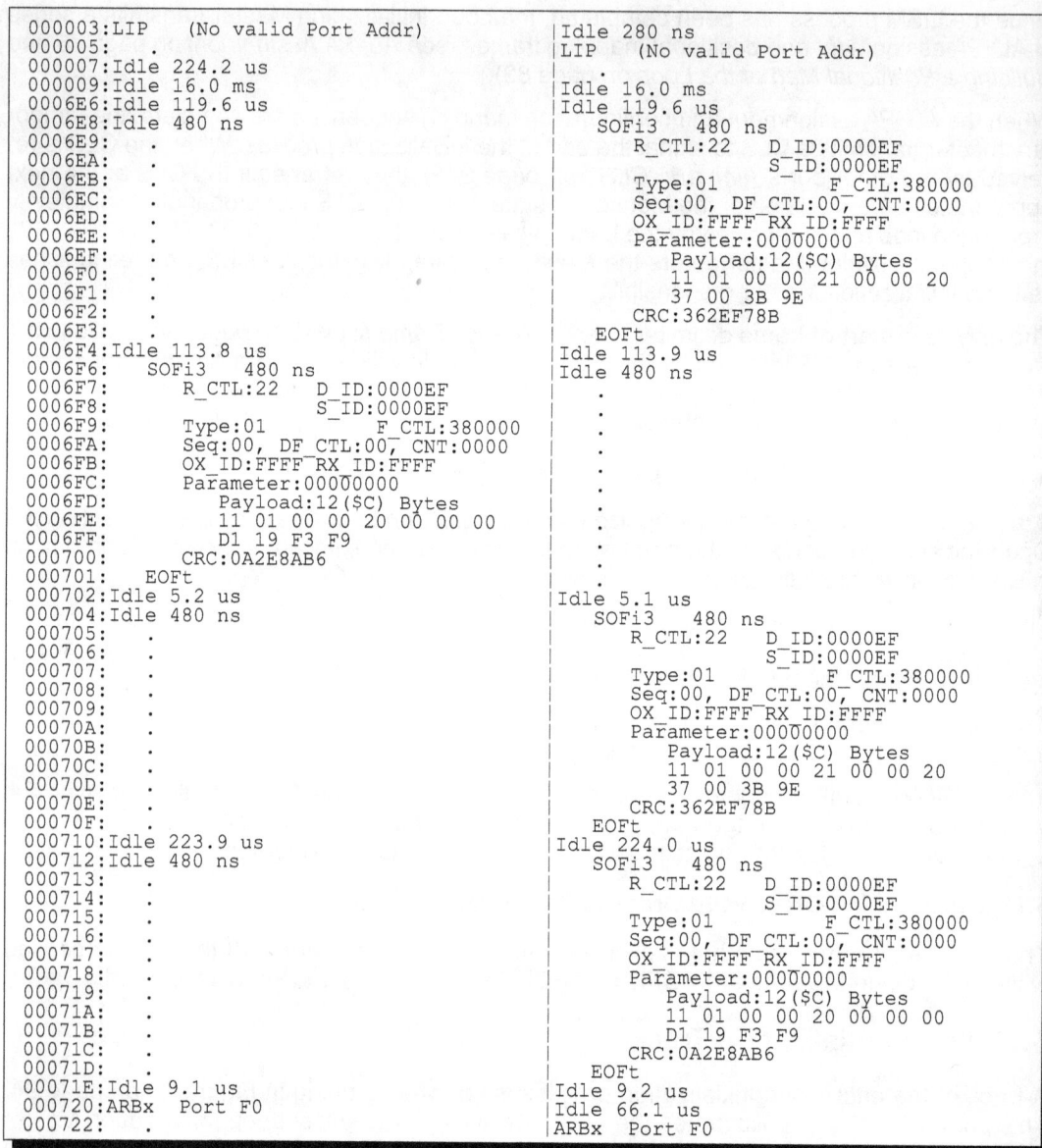

Figure 35. Loop Initialization Trace (Part 1 - LISM)

The LIHA and LISA AL_PA acquisition frames are shown in Figure 37 on page 96. These two steps are for ports without AL_PAs to acquire one. Ports with a hard-assigned AL_PA can attempt to acquire that AL_PA in step x'04' and ports without an AL_PA preference can acquire any available AL_PA in step x'05'.

```
000724:Idle 4.2 us                              |   .
000726:    SOFi3    560 ns                       |   .
000727:       R_CTL:22    D_ID:0000EF            |   .
000728:                   S_ID:0000EF            |   .
000729:       Type:01         F_CTL:380000       |   .
00072A:       Seq:00, DF_CTL:00, CNT:0000        |   .
00072B:       OX_ID:FFFF RX_ID:FFFF              |   .
00072C:       Parameter:00000000                 |   .
00072D:          Payload:20($14) Bytes           |   .
00072E:          11 02 00 00 00 00 00 00         |   .
00072F:          00 00 00 00 00 00 00 00         |   .
00072F:          00 00 00 00                     |   .
000730:       CRC:2877292C                       |   .
000731:    EOFt                                  |   .
000732:Idle 86.4 us                             |   .
000734:Idle 72.3 us                             |Idle 72.3 us
000736:Idle 560 ns                              |    SOFi3    560 ns
000737:    .                                     |       R_CTL:22    D_ID:0000EF
000738:    .                                     |                   S_ID:0000EF
000739:    .                                     |       Type:01         F_CTL:380000
00073A:    .                                     |       Seq:00, DF_CTL:00, CNT:0000
00073B:    .                                     |       OX_ID:FFFF RX_ID:FFFF
00073C:    .                                     |       Parameter:00000000
00073D:    .                                     |          Payload:20($14) Bytes
00073E:    .                                     |          11 02 00 00 00 00 00 00
00073F:    .                                     |          00 00 00 00 00 00 00 00
00073F:    .                                     |          00 00 00 00
000740:    .                                     |       CRC:2877292C
000741:    .                                     |    EOFt
000742:Idle 6.1 us                              |Idle 6.1 us
000744:    SOFi3    560 ns                       |Idle 560 ns
000745:       R_CTL:22    D_ID:0000EF            |   .
000746:                   S_ID:0000EF            |   .
000747:       Type:01         F_CTL:380000       |   .
000748:       Seq:00, DF_CTL:00, CNT:0000        |   .
000749:       OX_ID:FFFF RX_ID:FFFF              |   .
00074A:       Parameter:00000000                 |   .
00074B:          Payload:20($14) Bytes           |   .
00074C:          11 03 00 00 00 00 00 00         |   .
00074D:          00 00 00 00 00 00 00 00         |   .
00074D:          00 00 00 00                     |   .
00074E:       CRC:70F7CBFB                       |   .
00074F:    EOFt                                  |   .
000750:Idle 189.0 us                            |Idle 188.9 us
000752:Idle 560 ns                              |    SOFi3    560 ns
000753:    .                                     |       R_CTL:22    D_ID:0000EF
000754:    .                                     |                   S_ID:0000EF
000755:    .                                     |       Type:01         F_CTL:380000
000756:    .                                     |       Seq:00, DF_CTL:00, CNT:0000
000757:    .                                     |       OX_ID:FFFF RX_ID:FFFF
000758:    .                                     |       Parameter:00000000
000759:    .                                     |          Payload:20($14) Bytes
00075A:    .                                     |          11 03 00 00 00 00 00 00
00075B:    .                                     |          00 00 00 00 00 00 00 00
00075B:    .                                     |          00 00 00 02
00075D:    .                                     |       CRC:5C96C515
00075E:    .                                     |    EOFt
00075F:Idle 6.2 us                              |Idle 6.2 us
```

Figure 36. Loop Initialization Trace (Part 2 - LIFA/LIPA)

Building the positional map occurs in step x'06' using the LIRP frame. In this step ports increment the offset in word 1 of the payload and write their AL_PA at that position in the map. This step provides a count of the number of ports on the loop and their position relative to the Loop Initialization Master. The LIRP frame is shown in Figure 38 on page 97.

```
000761:    SOFi3    560 ns                        |Idle 520 ns
000762:       R_CTL:22    D_ID:0000EF             | .
000763:                   S_ID:0000EF             | .
000764:       Type:01           F_CTL:380000      | .
000765:       Seq:00, DF_CTL:00, CNT:0000         | .
000766:       OX_ID:FFFF RX_ID:FFFF               | .
000767:       Parameter:00000000                  | .
000768:          Payload:20($14) Bytes            | .
000769:          11 04 00 00 00 00 00 00          | .
00076A:          00 00 00 00 00 00 00 00          | .
00076A:          00 00 00 02                      | .
00076C:       CRC:171DFB5F                        | .
00076D:    EOFt                                   |
00076E:Idle 161.8 us                              |Idle 161.8 us
000771:    .                                      |    SOFi3    560 ns
000772:Idle 520 ns                                |       R_CTL:22    D_ID:0000EF
000773:    .                                      |                   S_ID:0000EF
000774:    .                                      |       Type:01           F_CTL:380000
000775:    .                                      |       Seq:00, DF_CTL:00, CNT:0000
000776:    .                                      |       OX_ID:FFFF RX_ID:FFFF
000777:    .                                      |       Parameter:00000000
000778:    .                                      |          Payload:20($14) Bytes
000779:    .                                      |          11 04 00 00 00 00 00 00
00077A:    .                                      |          00 00 00 00 00 00 00 00
00077A:    .                                      |          00 00 00 02
00077C:    .                                      |       CRC:171DFB5F
00077D:    .                                      |    EOFt
00077E:Idle 6.7 us                                |Idle 6.7 us
000781:    SOFi3    560 ns                        |
000782:       R_CTL:22    D_ID:0000EF             |Idle 520 ns
000783:                   S_ID:0000EF             | .
000784:       Type:01           F_CTL:380000      | .
000785:       Seq:00, DF_CTL:00, CNT:0000         | .
000786:       OX_ID:FFFF RX_ID:FFFF               | .
000787:       Parameter:00000000                  | .
000788:          Payload:20($14) Bytes            | .
000789:          11 05 01 00 20 00 00 00          | .
00078A:          00 00 00 00 00 00 00 00          | .
00078B:          00 00 00 02                      | .
00078D:       CRC:D3507470                        | .
00078E:    EOFt                                   |
00078F:Idle 167.2 us                              |Idle 167.1 us
000792:Idle 560 ns                                |    SOFi3    560 ns
000793:    .                                      |       R_CTL:22    D_ID:0000EF
000794:    .                                      |                   S_ID:0000EF
000795:    .                                      |       Type:01           F_CTL:380000
000796:    .                                      |       Seq:00, DF_CTL:00, CNT:0000
000797:    .                                      |       OX_ID:FFFF RX_ID:FFFF
000798:    .                                      |       Parameter:00000000
000799:    .                                      |          Payload:20($14) Bytes
00079A:    .                                      |          11 05 01 00 20 00 00 00
00079B:    .                                      |          00 00 00 00 00 00 00 00
00079C:    .                                      |          00 00 00 02
00079E:    .                                      |       CRC:D3507470
00079F:    .                                      |    EOFt
0007A0:Idle 11.8 us                               |Idle 11.8 us
```

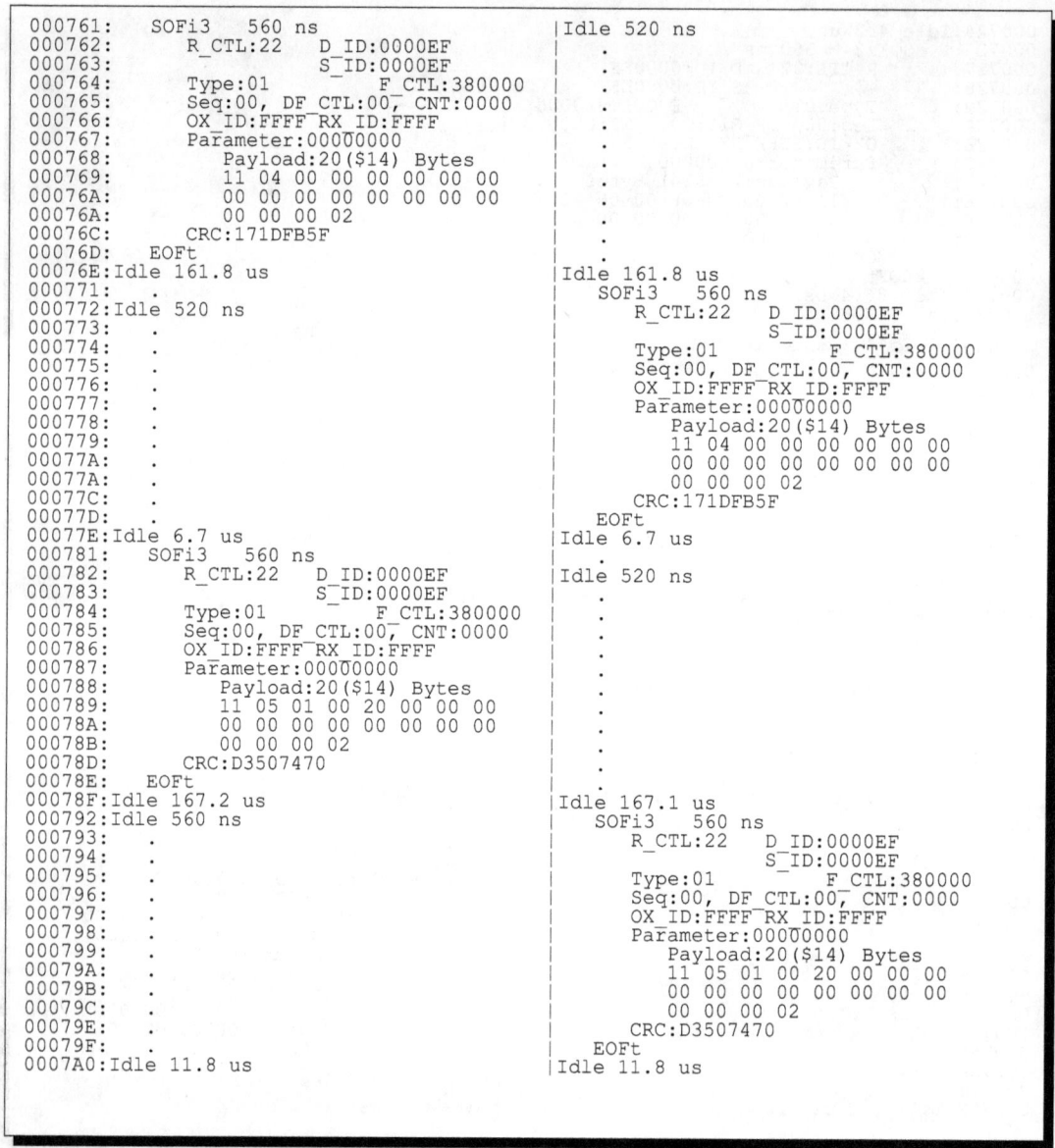

Figure 37. Loop Initialization Trace (Part 2 - LIHA/LISA)

The final phase of loop initialization is to send the completed positional map around the loop. This is performed using the LILP frame. When this frame is received by the Loop Initialization Master, a CLS is transmitted signalling the end of loop initialization as shown in Figure 39 on page 98.

```
0007A2:    SOFi3   1.6 us                    |Idle 1.6 us
0007A3:      R_CTL:22    D_ID:0000EF          | .
0007A4:                 S_ID:0000EF          | .
0007A5:      Type:01       F_CTL:380000      | .
0007A6:      Seq:00, DF_CTL:00, CNT:0000     | .
0007A7:      OX_ID:FFFF RX_ID:FFFF           | .
0007A8:      Parameter:00000000              | .
0007A9:        Payload:132($84) Bytes        | .
0007AA:        11 06 00 00 01 01 FF FF       | .
0007AB:        FF FF FF FF FF FF FF FF       | .
0007AC:        FF FF FF FF FF FF FF FF       | .
0007AC:        FF FF FF FF FF FF FF FF       | .
0007AC:        FF FF FF FF FF FF FF FF       | .
0007AC:        FF FF FF FF FF FF FF FF       | .
0007AC:        FF FF FF FF FF FF FF FF       | .
0007AC:        FF FF FF FF FF FF FF FF       | .
0007AC:        FF FF FF FF FF FF FF FF       | .
0007AC:        FF FF FF FF FF FF FF FF       | .
0007AC:        FF FF FF FF FF FF FF FF       | .
0007AC:        FF FF FF FF FF FF FF FF       | .
0007AC:        FF FF FF FF FF FF FF FF       | .
0007AC:        FF FF FF FF FF FF FF FF       | .
0007AC:        FF FF FF FF FF FF FF FF       | .
0007AC:        FF FF FF FF FF FF FF FF       | .
0007AC:        FF FF FF FF                   | .
0007AD:      CRC:A13604EA                    | .
0007AE:    EOFt                              | .
0007AF:Idle 157.4 us                         |Idle 157.3 us
0007B1:Idle 1.6 us                           |    SOFi3   1.6 us
0007B2:    .                                 |      R_CTL:22    D_ID:0000EF
0007B3:    .                                 |                 S_ID:0000EF
0007B4:    .                                 |      Type:01       F_CTL:380000
0007B5:    .                                 |      Seq:00, DF_CTL:00, CNT:0000
0007B6:    .                                 |      OX_ID:FFFF RX_ID:FFFF
0007B7:    .                                 |      Parameter:00000000
0007B8:    .                                 |        Payload:132($84) Bytes
0007B9:    .                                 |        11 06 00 00 02 01 E8 FF
0007BA:    .                                 |        FF FF FF FF FF FF FF FF
0007BB:    .                                 |        FF FF FF FF FF FF FF FF
0007BB:    .                                 |        FF FF FF FF FF FF FF FF
0007BB:    .                                 |        FF FF FF FF FF FF FF FF
0007BB:    .                                 |        FF FF FF FF FF FF FF FF
0007BB:    .                                 |        FF FF FF FF FF FF FF FF
0007BB:    .                                 |        FF FF FF FF FF FF FF FF
0007BB:    .                                 |        FF FF FF FF FF FF FF FF
0007BB:    .                                 |        FF FF FF FF FF FF FF FF
0007BB:    .                                 |        FF FF FF FF FF FF FF FF
0007BB:    .                                 |        FF FF FF FF FF FF FF FF
0007BB:    .                                 |        FF FF FF FF FF FF FF FF
0007BB:    .                                 |        FF FF FF FF FF FF FF FF
0007BB:    .                                 |        FF FF FF FF FF FF FF FF
0007BB:    .                                 |        FF FF FF FF FF FF FF FF
0007BC:    .                                 |        FF FF FF FF
0007BD:    .                                 |      CRC:435F59C6
0007BE:Idle 12.9 us                          |    EOFt
                                             |Idle 12.9 us
```

Figure 38. Loop Initialization Trace (Part 4 - LIRP)

```
0007C0:    SOFi3    1.6 us              |Idle 1.6 us
0007C1:        R_CTL:22    D_ID:0000EF  | .
0007C2:                    S_ID:0000EF  | .
0007C3:        Type:01        F_CTL:380000 | .
0007C4:        Seq:00, DF_CTL:00, CNT:0000 | .
0007C5:        OX_ID:FFFF RX_ID:FFFF    | .
0007C6:        Parameter:00000000       | .
0007C7:            Payload:132($84) Bytes | .
0007C8:            11 07 00 00 02 01 E8 FF | .
0007C9:            FF FF FF FF FF FF FF FF | .
0007CA:            FF FF FF FF FF FF FF FF | .
0007CA:            FF FF FF FF FF FF FF FF | .
0007CA:            FF FF FF FF FF FF FF FF | .
0007CA:            FF FF FF FF FF FF FF FF | .
0007CA:            FF FF FF FF FF FF FF FF | .
0007CA:            FF FF FF FF FF FF FF FF | .
0007CA:            FF FF FF FF FF FF FF FF | .
0007CA:            FF FF FF FF FF FF FF FF | .
0007CA:            FF FF FF FF FF FF FF FF | .
0007CA:            FF FF FF FF FF FF FF FF | .
0007CA:            FF FF FF FF FF FF FF FF | .
0007CA:            FF FF FF FF FF FF FF FF | .
0007CA:            FF FF FF FF FF FF FF FF | .
0007CA:            FF FF FF FF            | .
0007CB:        CRC:CCFEBDA4              | .
0007CC:    EOFt                          | .
0007CD:Idle 121.0 us                    |Idle 121.0 us
0007CF:Idle 1.6 us                      |    SOFi3    1.6 us
0007D0:    .                            |        R_CTL:22    D_ID:0000EF
0007D1:    .                            |                    S_ID:0000EF
0007D2:    .                            |        Type:01        F_CTL:380000
0007D3:    .                            |        Seq:00, DF_CTL:00, CNT:0000
0007D4:    .                            |        OX_ID:FFFF RX_ID:FFFF
0007D5:    .                            |        Parameter:00000000
0007D6:    .                            |            Payload:132($84) Bytes
0007D7:    .                            |            11 07 00 00 02 01 E8 FF
0007D8:    .                            |            FF FF FF FF FF FF FF FF
0007D9:    .                            |            FF FF FF FF FF FF FF FF
0007D9:    .                            |            FF FF FF FF FF FF FF FF
0007D9:    .                            |            FF FF FF FF FF FF FF FF
0007D9:    .                            |            FF FF FF FF FF FF FF FF
0007D9:    .                            |            FF FF FF FF FF FF FF FF
0007D9:    .                            |            FF FF FF FF FF FF FF FF
0007D9:    .                            |            FF FF FF FF FF FF FF FF
0007D9:    .                            |            FF FF FF FF FF FF FF FF
0007D9:    .                            |            FF FF FF FF FF FF FF FF
0007D9:    .                            |            FF FF FF FF FF FF FF FF
0007D9:    .                            |            FF FF FF FF FF FF FF FF
0007D9:    .                            |            FF FF FF FF FF FF FF FF
0007DA:    .                            |            FF FF FF FF
0007DB:    .                            |        CRC:CCFEBDA4
0007DC:Idle 2.8 us                      |    EOFt
0007DE:CLS                              |Idle 2.8 us
0007DF:Idle 360 ns                      |Idle 40 ns
0007E1:Idle 40 ns                       |Idle 320 ns
                                        |CLS
```

Figure 39. Loop Initialization Trace (Part 4 - LILP)

5.13 Chapter Summary

Loop Initialization Sequence

- A port begins loop initialization by transmitting LIP
- Loop activity is suspended
- All ports enter the Open-Init state
- A Loop Initialization Master is selected
- AL_PA assignment occurs
- If supported, a positional map of the loop is built
- All ports return to the Monitoring state and loop operations resume

Causes of Initialization

- Power on or power-on-reset of a port
  - The port does not have an AL_PA and needs to acquire one
- Port attempting to change participating/nonparticipating mode
- Loop failure
  - The port has detected a loop failure and is providing notification
- Arbitration wait timeout
  - The port's arbitration wait timer has expired
- Selective reset LIP

Initialization Disruption

- Initialization is not necessarily synchronized to loop activity
- LIP may occur at any time
  - LIP may corrupt one or more frames
  - If so, normal error recovery is invoked after initialization
- Steps can be taken to minimize the possibility of errors
  - Synchronizing initialization to loop activity
  - Selected port periodically transmits LIP

LIP Primitive Sequences

- LIP(F7,F7) - port does not have a valid AL_PA
- LIP (F8,F7) - port has detected a loop failure and does not have a valid AL_PA
- LIP(F7,AL_PS) - port AL_PS has encountered an arbitration wait timeout or the port is requesting initialization for another, unspecified reason
- LIP(F8,AL_PS) - port AL_PS has detected a loop failure
- LIP(AL_PD,AL_PS) - port AL_PS is issuing a selective reset to port AL_PD
- LIP(f,AL_PS) - port AL_PS is issuing a reset to all other ports

Old-Port State

- After the Initializing port transmits LIPs, it starts a timer
- If LIP is not recognized within 3 AL_Times, the LPSM enters the Old-Port state (if supported)
  - In the Old-Port state, the port adopts nonloop behavior
  - The port is attached to an N_Port or F_Port, or,
  - The loop is not operational
- Non-loop ports don't recognize loop specific ordered sets and discard them

Select Loop Initialization Master

- Next step is to select a Loop Initialization Master
- If an FL_Port is present it becomes the Loop Initialization Master
- If multiple FL_Ports, the one with the lowest Port_Name becomes master
- If no FL_Port is present,
  - The NL_Port with the lowest Port_Name becomes master
- How is all this determined?

LISM Sequence

- Each port begins transmitting the LISM frame
  - Frame contains the port type and Port_Name
- Each port examines the received frame
- Port stops transmitting its own frame and starts transmitting the received frame if
  - An NL_Port receives a frame from an FL_Port, or
  - The port types match and the Port_Name in the received frame is lower, or
- If a port receives its own frame it is the Loop Initialization Master
  - Transmits ARB(F0) to signal other ports to stop transmitting LISM frame

AL_PA Assignment

- AL_PAs are assigned in four steps
  - Each step is for a specific category of AL_PA values
  - Allows for an AL_PA hierarchy
- The Loop Initialization Master transmits a series of 4 frame types
  - LIFA - reclaim fabric-assigned AL_PA values
  - LIPA - reclaim previously-assigned AL_PA values
  - LIHA - acquire hard-assigned AL_PA values
  - LISA - acquire soft-assigned AL_PA values
- After each frame travels completely around the loop, the Loop Initialization Master steps to the next type

AL_PA Frame Payload

- Consists of an identifier and a 128-bit AL_PA map
  - Each bit corresponds to a specific AL_PA
  - All bits are initially set to '0'
  - When an AL_PA value is taken, the corresponding bit is set to '1'
- AL_PA bit map is cumulative as frame is transmitted around the loop
- When arrives at Loop Initialization Master, only the type is changed
  - Payload containing the AL_PA map is cumulative

Positional Mapping

- Optional step to build an position map of the loop by AL_PA values
- May not be supported by all ports
  - Requires frame payload of 132 bytes
  - Late addition to the standard
- If not supported by all ports, it is skipped
  - LISA frame indicates if all ports support
- Two steps in the mapping process
  - LIRP - report loop position
  - LILP - transmit completed positional map

Ending Initialization

- The Loop Initialization Master transmits a CLS
- CLS travels around the loop
  - Causes all ports to enter the Monitoring state
  - Ends the role of the Loop Initialization Master
- Normal loop operations can resume
- Some technical reports require post-initialization processing
  - Target authentication to verify configuration
  - Public ports wait for FAN ELS
  - Private ports wait for ADISC or PDISC ELS from SCSI initiator

24-Bit Port Address

- Ports without a 24-bit native address initially use the value x'0000'+AL_PA
- Public ports attempt a fabric login
- If an FL_Port is present, the port receives an address of the form 'xxxx'+AL_PA
  - Where 'xxxx' is not equal to x'0000' and is the same for all public NL_Ports on the loop
  - If no FL_Port is present, the login fails and the port keeps the address x'0000'+AL_PA
- Private ports do not attempt a fabric login and use address x'0000'+AL_PA

Minimizing Loop Disruption

- Errors may occur if LIP is transmitted when loop is open
- Challenge is to synchronize the LIP with loop activity
- A port can suspend loop activity by winning arbitration
  - OPN is sent to itself
- Initialization can begin without hazard of causing frame errors
- How can this be accomplished?

Assuming a Hard AL_PA

- Another approach is to assume that a hard-assigned AL_PA value is currently unused
  - Hard-assigned AL_PA is set by switches or jumpers
- Port uses that AL_PA to win arbitration
- Then begins loop initialization
  - Initialization is synchronized to the loop so no errors occur
  - Initialization confirms the hard-assigned AL_PA is valid
  - Proposal to enable this behavior via mode pages for SCSI devices only

Designated Port Signals

- This approach lets a designated port signal when initialization should occur
  - Could be the initiator
  - Designated port arbitrates periodically
  - The sole purpose is to send a unique signal
  - No activity is occurring on the loop when the signal is sent
- L_Ports recognize the signal and begin initialization
- One possible implementation:
  - Use MRK(tx) signal with a known value for "t"

6. Monitoring State

The Monitoring state is the main repeat state of the Loop Port State Machine. While in this state, the LPSM is repeating all non-fill words and is monitoring the loop for an OPN addressed to the port, one of the LIP initialization primitive sequences, the LPB/LPE port bypass/enable primitive sequences, or an L_Port control request to arbitrate, initialize, change the participating/nonparticipating mode, or activate/deactivate the port bypass circuit.

If the LPSM is in participating mode, it monitors received transmission words for certain ordered sets that result in modification of the current fill word (CFW) or one or more of the L_Port control variables. Unless replicate mode is set, the loop port is not conditioned for frame reception and not aware that frames may have been forwarded.

6.1 Loop State Machine Operation

The following sections describe the operation of the LPSM while in the Monitoring state.

6.1.1 Entry Actions

When a loop port enters the Monitoring state, the ARB_Won and Duplex variables are reset. This is the normal reset for these LPSM variables if Monitoring state was entered from either the Transmitted Close or Received Close states.

Replicate mode is reset as a general cleanup action because replicate mode should not be active upon entry to the Monitoring state.

The Access and Bypass variables and current fill word are unchanged by entry into the Monitoring state.

6.1.2 Received Errors

No interpretation of received characters is performed until it is determined that the received character is a valid transmission character.

If an invalid transmission character is received *(line 3: 'Invalid Transmission Character or Word', on page 323)*, the current fill word is transmitted in place of the invalid transmission word. This action may seem strange at first, but the objective is to count the error where it was first detected and not propagate it further. If the current fill word replaces an ordered set, that error will be detected in another manner; if the current fill word replaces a data word, the frame is abnormally terminated by the ordered set and discarded by the recipient.

If a temporary loss of synchronization occurs *(line 1: 'Loss of Synchronization', on page 323)* for less than the receiver-transmitter timeout value (R_T_TOV, or 100 msec. per FC-PH), the LPSM transmits IDLEs or the current fill word until synchronization is regained. Loss of synchronization requires a minimum of 5 consecutive invalid transmission words to be detected, and may require more if valid transmission words occur intermixed with the invalid transmission words. Invalid transmission characters encountered prior to detection of the loss of synchronization are replaced by the current fill word.

If synchronization is not reacquired within R_T_TOV, a loop failure is detected. If this occurs and the Bypass variable is not set *(line 2: 'Loop Failure', on page 323)*, the LPSM enters the Initializing state. If a loop failure is detected and the Bypass variable is set, no action is taken.

If an ordered set with incorrect running disparity *(line 4: 'Running Disparity Error at Ordered Set', on page 323)* is received, it is discarded and the current fill word is substituted.

If an elasticity word is required *(line 5: 'Elasticity Word Required', on page 323)*, the current fill word is used.

6.1.3 Port Bypass Operation

If the Bypass variable is set, the LPSM responds only to LPE(fx) or LPE(yx) sequences if the AL_PD (f or y fields, respectively) in the third character of the ordered set is x'FF' or equals the AL_PA of the port. This allows a loop port with the Bypass variable set to recognize the bypass enabling sequences and enable the port on the loop, if appropriate.

If the LPB(fx) or LPB(yx) primitive sequence *(line 21: 'LPB(yx) or LPB(fx)', on page 325)* or the LPE(yx) or LPE(fx) sequence *(line 22: 'LPE(yx) or LPE(fx)', on page 325)* is recognized and the AL_PS (x value in the fourth character of the LPB ordered set) equals the AL_PA of this port, the LPB or LPE ordered set is discarded and the current fill word is substituted (this loop port was the original sender of the LPB or LPE sequence).

If the LPB(fx) or LPB(yx) primitive sequence is recognized that did not originate in this loop port *(line 21: 'LPB(yx) or LPB(fx)', on page 325)* and the AL_PD value (y in the third character of the L equals the AL_PA of the port, the LPSM sets the Bypass variable and activates the port bypass circuit, if present.

If the LPE(fx) or LPE(yx) sequence that did not originate in this loop port *(line 22: 'LPE(yx) or LPE(fx)', on page 325)* is recognized and the AL_PD (y value in the third character of the LPE) is hex 'FF' or equals the AL_PA of the port, the LPSM resets the Bypass variable and deactivates the port bypass circuit, if present.

If this loop port was neither the originator nor intended recipient of the LPB or LPE, the ordered set is retransmitted.

If REQ(bypass L_Port) is active *(line 38: 'REQ(bypass L_Port)', on page 326)*, the LPSM sets the Bypass variable and activates the port bypass circuit, if present.

6.1.4 Participating/Nonparticipating Mode Behavior

If the LPSM is in nonparticipating mode, it retransmits all received transmission words on the loop. It is not permitted to participate in further loop operations until the REQ(initialize) or REQ(participating) L_Port control is asserted and loop initialization is performed. If it is necessary to delete a word for clock elasticity purposes, a fill word or word from a primitive sequence may be deleted following normal clock elasticity deletion rules as described in *Asynchronous Transmitter/Receiver and Clock Elasticity* on page 27.

If LIP is recognized and the Bypass variable is set *(line 20: 'LIP', on page 325)*, the LPSM enters nonparticipating mode, relinquishes its AL_PA, and retransmits the LIP. This forces bypassed ports to relinquish their AL_PA during loop initialization making those AL_PA values available for other ports.

The loop port can request the LPSM enter nonparticipating mode by asserting the REQ(nonparticipate) input *(line 36: 'REQ(nonparticipate)', on page 326)*. This causes the LPSM to relinquish its AL_PA, transmit a single sequence of at least 12 LIPs (LIP F7,F7) to trigger loop initialization, and enter the nonparticipating mode. Loop initialization allows another loop port which may have been in nonparticipating mode because it was unable to acquire an AL_PA to attempt to acquire the relinquished AL_PA.

If REQ(participating) *(line 35: 'REQ(participating)', on page 326)* or REQ(initialize) *(line 44: 'REQ(initialize)', on page 326)* is active, the LPSM sets participating mode and enters the Initializing state to begin a loop initialization. During that initialization, the loop port can attempt to acquire an AL_PA and join loop operations.

6.1.5 Processing Arbitration and Access Fairness

When the loop port requires access to the loop, it requests the LPSM to arbitrate by activating the L_Port control REQ(arbitrate as x). This could be done by either the hardware or firmware associated with the port, depending upon the implementation. Before the LPSM can arbitrate for access to the loop, a number of conditions must be met. First, there must be no higher priority conditions present at the port. The LPSM state tables are intended to be processed from top to bottom. If an earlier condition is active, the loop port may not begin arbitrating even if the L_Port request is active. If no higher priority conditions exist, and the Bypass variable is not set (indicating that the loop port is not bypassed), the LPSM has a valid AL_PA and is in participating mode, and the access variable is set *(line 25: 'REQ(arb own AL_PA)', on page 325)*, the LPSM enters the Arbitrating state.

If an IDLE is received *(line 9: 'IDLE', on page 323)*, the access fairness window has ended. The current fill word is set to IDLE and the access variable is set allowing the loop port to begin arbitrating again after at least two IDLEs has been transmitted (see *Access Fairness* on page 125).

If ARB(F0) is received *(line 13: 'ARB(F0)', on page 324)*, the current fill word is examined.

- If the current fill word is IDLE, the current fill word is not changed. This is done to remove any orphaned ARB(F0)'s from the loop. It also has the effect of ending the access fairness window if a temporary loss of synchronization occurs at an upstream port.
- If the current fill word is not IDLE, the current fill word is set to ARB(F0).

If ARB(x) is received *(line 14: 'ARB(x)', on page 324)*, the AL_PA value contained in the third and fourth characters of the ARB(x) ordered set is examined. Individual loop port designs may choose to examine either of the characters in making the following tests, however it is recommended that the fourth character be used. This is consistent with the normal interpretation of the fourth character as being the AL_PS of the originating loop port.

- If 'x' value in the received ARB(x) equals the AL_PA of this port, the current fill word is unchanged. This situation should not occur, as one or more ARBs associated with this

---

loop port are circulating on the loop even though the loop port is not arbitrating. Because the current fill word was not changed upon entry to the Monitoring state it could be an ARB(x), ARB(F0), ARB(FF), or IDLE. A footnote in the FC-AL document indicates that this may be altered in a future FC-AL standard to read "...the current fill word is set to IDLE." This would purge the orphaned ARBs from the loop, but could have the undesired effect of prematurely resetting the access fairness window.

- If 'x' does not equal the AL_PA of this port, the current fill word is set to ARB(x). A different loop port on the loop is arbitrating and this port's fill word is updated to reflect the other port's ARB(x) primitive.

6.1.6 Processing OPN(yx), OPN(yy), and CLS

If an OPNy is received *(line 16: 'OPN(yx) or OPN(yy)', on page 324)*, the loop port examines the third character to determine if the open is directed to this port. If an OPN(yx) full-duplex open or OPN(yy) half-duplex open is received and the AL_PD (the y value in the third character) is equal to the AL_PA of this port, the LPSM enters the Opened state. Another loop port won arbitration and has opened this loop port to begin communications. If the AL_PD in the OPN does not equal the AL_PA of this port, the OPN is retransmitted as it is intended for a different port.

If a CLS is received *(line 17: 'CLS', on page 324)* it is retransmitted. This loop port is not open and the close is intended for a different port. If replicate mode is set, it is reset ending replicate mode in this port, if it was active.

6.1.7 Replicate Mode

If an OPN(fr) or OPN(yr) is received *(line 15: 'OPN(fr) or OPN(yr)', on page 324)* the LPSM examines the AL_PD value in the third character of the OPNr.

- If OPN(fr) (AL_PD = x'FF') is received, the LPSM sets replicate mode. A different loop port has won arbitration is using the broadcast replicate OPN to set replicate mode in all NL_Ports on the loop (the FL_Port never enters replicate mode).

- If an OPN(yr) is received where the AL_PD value in the third character is equal to the AL_PA of this port, the LPSM sets replicate mode. A different loop port has won arbitration and is using the selective replicate OPN to set replicate mode in this port.

In either case, the OPNr ordered set is retransmitted, even if it was addressed to this port. The loop port that originated the OPNr will remove it from the loop after it has propagated completely around the loop.

6.1.8 Processing MRK(tx)

If a MRK(tx) is received *(line 19: 'MRK(tx)', on page 324)* and the MK_TP and AL_PS match expected values, the action or notification associated with the MRK(tx) is performed (this is not shown on the state table because the action to be performed is undefined by the standard). If this was the loop port that originally transmitted the MRK(tx) (the AL_PS equals the AL_PA of this port) the MRK(tx) is removed from the loop. Otherwise, it is retransmitted.

If the L_Port control REQ(mark as tx) input is active *(line 37: 'REQ(mark as tx)', on page 326)*, the LPSM transmits a single MRK(tx) in place of the next appropriate fill word (that is, it must be preceded and followed by at least two fill words) unless the REQ(mark as tx) input is removed before the MRK(tx) is transmitted.

6.1.9 Processing Other Transmission Words

If any valid ordered set not specifically identified by the state table is received, it is retransmitted. This allows the LPSM to forward ordered sets which may be added in future versions of the standard for compatibility purposes.

If a valid data word is received it is retransmitted. No evaluation is made as to whether the data word occurred within frame boundaries. In the Monitoring state, the loop port is not conditioned for frame reception unless replicate mode is set.

6.2 Chapter Summary

Monitoring State

- Idle state for the LPSM
- Arb_won, replicate, and duplex are reset on entry to Monitoring state
- Port is waiting
  - For a request by the loop port to arbitrate
  - To receive an OPN addressed to the port
- Received transmission words are retransmitted
  - Fill words may be inserted or deleted for clock elasticity
- Port is not conditioned for frame reception unless replicate mode is set

Arbitration Request

- If the loop port requests arbitration, the LPSM may enter the Arbitrating state
  - If the LPSM is in participating mode and
  - Bypass is not set and
  - Access is set (the loop port is not waiting due to access fairness)
- Otherwise, the loop port is not allowed to arbitrate

OPN Received

- If an OPN(yy) or OPN(yx) addressed to this loop port is received
  - Duplex is set for an OPN(yx)
  - The loop port enters the Opened state
- If an OPN(yr) addressed to this loop port or an OPN(fr) is received
  - The loop port remains in the Monitoring state
  - Replicate mode is set
  - The frame reception logic is enabled
  - Only frames with a 24-bit address recognized by the loop port are processed

7. Arbitration and Fairness

Arbitration is the process that allows a port to gain access to the Arbitrated Loop. If ports were allowed to send information whenever they wanted, data from one port might interfere with data from another port, causing errors. To prevent this from occurring, all ports must successfully win arbitration before they transmit frames or R_RDYs of their own on the loop (except when in the Open-Init state). In this respect, arbitration for the loop is similar to the arbitration cycle on a parallel SCSI bus, although the actual mechanism is much different.

When multiple ports arbitrate at the same time, some means is required to resolve the simultaneous requests and allow one port to exclusively win arbitration. This is done by allowing the port with a lower value AL_PA to have priority over ports with higher AL_PA values. This type of prioritizing based on the AL_PA could result in higher-priority ports monopolizing the loop (as can occur with the SCSI bus), while the lower-priority ports are unable to gain access. To ensure that every port has an opportunity to use the loop, an access fairness mechanism is incorporated into the arbitration protocol.

Access fairness is a required behavior implemented by the Arbitrated Loop protocols; the use of it, however, is optional. When a port observes the access fairness rules, it is called a fair port. When it does not follow the access fairness rules, it is called an unfair port. Access fairness defines an interval during which a fair port is allowed to win arbitration only once. This interval is called the access fairness window. When a port is observing access fairness, it does not attempt to arbitrate again until the access fairness window has been reset. After a port has won arbitration, and subsequently relinquished control of the loop, it waits while other arbitrating ports take their turns. When all of the ports arbitrating for the loop have had a turn, the access fairness window is reset and the fair ports that are waiting may begin to arbitrate again.

Access fairness ensures that every port that wants access to the loop is able to win arbitration within the access fairness window. It does not set any limit on the length of time that a port can hold the loop once it has won arbitration so access fairness does not imply time fairness. The Fibre Channel standard does not impose any time constraint on the duration of a Class-1 connection; the Arbitrated Loop wanted to support all classes of service defined by FC-PH.

Arbitration and access fairness comprise one of the more sophisticated and easily misunderstood aspects of Arbitrated Loop. The original loop architects faced a challenging problem in defining an arbitration mechanism that allows multiple ports to share a single loop interconnect without frame collisions or the requirement to designate one of the ports as a loop master.

7.1 Fill Word Substitution

The basic concept underlying the arbitration process is *fill word substitution*. This process allows a port to remove a received fill word from the loop and transmit a different fill word in its place. Figure 40 on page 110 shows an example of fill word substitution.

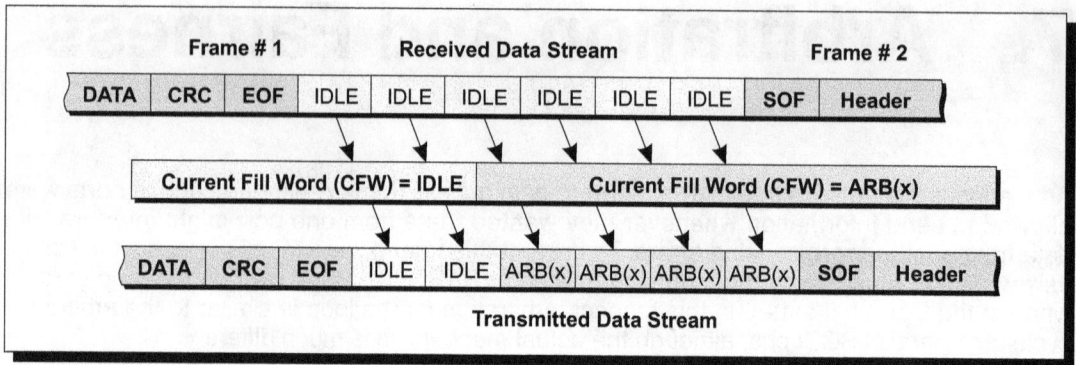

Figure 40. Fill Word Substitution

The term fill word substitution is somewhat of a misnomer because ports never truly repeat a received fill word. Instead, the received fill word is examined to determine if the current fill word should be updated, then the received word is discarded. Whenever the transmit function requires a fill word, it uses the value contained in the current fill word. In the example shown in Figure 40, the received data stream consists of two frames separated by six fill words. This is the minimum number of transmission words a sender must insert between frames. In the example, the port starts arbitrating after the second IDLE is received. The current fill word is changed from IDLE to ARB(x). Once the current fill word is updated, the port begins transmitting ARB(x) as its fill word rather than IDLE, substituting its ARB(x) for the IDLE.

Figure 41 on page 111 is an example of the logic associated with the processing of fill words. The current fill word is one of the potential transmit sources. Other sources include the repeater FIFO, frame transmission logic, and ordered set generator. The current fill word may be set with either fill words from the receiver function or internally generated fill words such as IDLE, ARB(x), ARB(F0), or ARB(FF). Whenever a fill word is required by the transmit function, the content of the current fill word register is gated through the multiplexer to the transmitter, and then onto the link.

One final item deserves discussion before leaving the topic of fill word substitution. Each port is always transmitting information to the downstream port's receiver. Ports in the Monitoring state are normally repeating received information with the possible exception of performing fill word substitution. Active ports, however, may be removing information from the loop. Whenever a port removes information from the loop, it must transmit something to fill the space left by the information removed—that something is the current fill word.

When a port is receiving a frame, it must transmit something to fill the space left by the received frame. It may transmit a frame of its own, primitive signals such as R_RDY or CLS, primitive sequences, or its current fill word. If the port's current fill word is equal to the ARB(x) of an upstream port, the port fills the space left by the received frames with ARB(x) for another port. While this may seem strange at first look, it is logically consistent with the arbitration process in which ARB(x) primitive signal replaces all fill words.

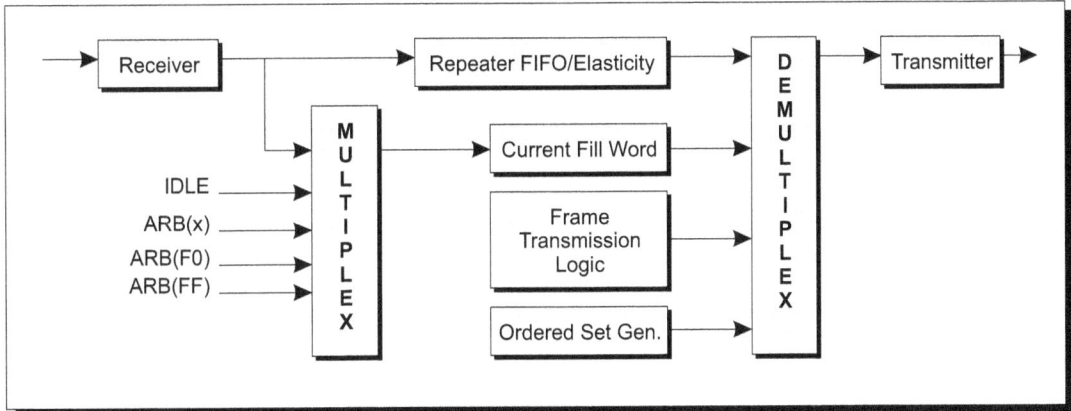

Figure 41. Fill Word Substitution Logic

7.2 The Arbitration Process

Following initialization, each port is in the Monitoring state, and no ports are arbitrating. When a port needs access to the loop, it arbitrates by substituting its ARB(x) for each IDLE and lower-priority ARB(x) received. The third and fourth characters in the ARB(x) are set to the AL_PA value of the arbitrating port.

When an ARB(x) is received by an arbitrating port, the AL_PA value in the ARB(x) is compared to the port's AL_PA. If the AL_PA values match, the port has won arbitration. The port must examine both the third or fourth character of the ARB(x) to determine whether a match has occurred.

Immediately upon winning arbitration, the port changes its current fill word to ARB(F0). All received ARB(x) primitive signals are discarded preventing any other port from receiving its own ARB(x) and winning arbitration. Whenever a fill word is needed, for example to replace the discarded ARB(x), the current fill word (either ARB(F0) or IDLE) is used as will be discussed later in *Access Fairness* on page 125.

The ARB(F0) allows the port which won arbitration to discover that it is the last port in the access fairness window. If any other port is arbitrating, the ARB(F0) is replaced by that port's own ARB(x) because the ARB(F0) is lower priority than the AL_PA value of any port. As long as another port is arbitrating, the ARB(F0) does not return to the current arbitration winner. As long as ARB(x) is received, the current fill word remains ARB(F0). Once the arbitration winner relinquishes the loop, the current fill word is changed to the received ARB(x) to allow the next port to win arbitration.

If no other port is arbitrating, ARB(F0) will be received by the current arbitration winner. The arbitration winner then changes its current fill word to IDLE. Changing the current fill word to IDLE is the signal for all ports that the access fairness window has been reset. It is possible for the ARB(F0) to completely circle the loop and be replaced by IDLEs before any frame has been sent.

This ARB(F0) and IDLE behavior is used in the access fairness mechanism to detect when other ports are arbitrating as described in detail in *Access Fairness* on page 125. The arbitration and access fairness process is summarized in the flow chart in Figure 42.

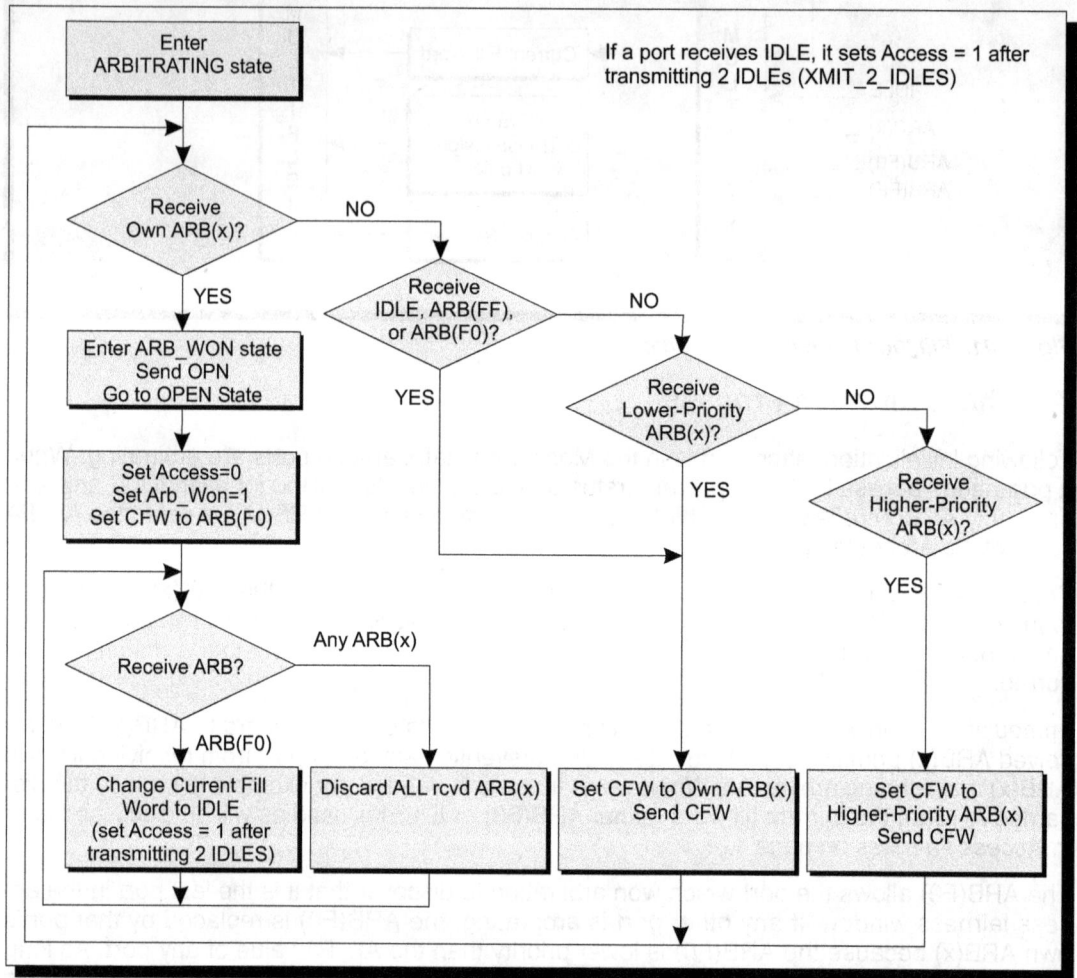

Figure 42. Arbitration and Access Fairness Flowchart

A port requiring access to the loop continues to arbitrate even if a different port has won arbitration. While the two ports in the loop circuit may be sending and receiving frames, the frames are separated by fill words and other ordered sets.

When the arbitration winner completes frame transmission and is ready to relinquish the loop, it enters the Monitoring state and sets its current fill word from the received data stream allowing any pending ARB(x) to pass so that the next highest priority port wins arbitration.

7.2.1 What Initiates Arbitration?

Arbitration normally occurs whenever a port has one or more frames to send on the loop and is only incidentally related to an FC-4 operations. A port may also arbitrate to perform control functions such as loop initialization, controlling the port bypass circuits, or sending a MRK(tx) signal.

A single FC-4 operation may be separated into multiple loop circuits, each requiring a separate arbitration. For example, a SCSI initiator arbitrates to send a write command to a target. Once the command is sent, the loop circuit may be closed so it is available for other ports to use (if no other port is arbitrating, the loop circuit may be held open indefinitely). If the loop circuit was closed, when the target is ready for the data it arbitrates to send a transfer ready request to the initiator and may close the loop circuit. When the initiator is ready to send the data, it arbitrates (if the loop circuit was closed) and sends some or all of the data. If there's a large amount of data to send, the target may break the data transfer up into multiple SCSI bursts and close the loop circuit between each SCSI burst. When the data transfer is complete, the target arbitrates to send the command response to the initiator.

The cycle of arbitration, opening the loop circuit, frame transmission and reception, and closing the loop circuit may occur one or more times per SCSI command. Each cycle is called a *loop tenancy*, and the period of time that a port retains access to the loop is called the *loop tenancy time*.

Loop tenancy time has a direct effect on the overall performance of the loop. If a port maintains a loop tenancy when it does not have information to send, other ports are prevented from using the loop and performance may suffer. On the other hand, if a port relinquishes the loop too often it may require more loop tenancies to complete operations. In this case, performance suffers due to the increased number of arbitration, opening, and closing cycles. The chapter titled *Performance* on page 229 explores the relationship of loop tenancy to performance in greater detail.

In most cases, arbitration is initiated automatically by the hardware in accordance with decisions made by the designer. The algorithms used to initiate arbitration may vary among designs, but some general observations apply to all designs.

The loop hardware normally arbitrates whenever it has one or more frames to send. If a single-frame sequence (such as a SCSI FCP_CMND frame) is pending, the port must arbitrate and send the sequence because subsequent actions may be dependent upon that sequence. If the port waited until more frames were available for transmission, the command might never be sent and the operation could not proceed to the next step.

During data sequences, it may be advantageous for the hardware to delay arbitration until it has a predetermined minimum number of data frames available to send, or it has reached the end of the data sequence. By waiting until there are multiple frames to send, each loop tenancy can transfer more data and improve overall throughput.

In some special cases, arbitration may result directly from actions initiated by the firmware. For example, an implementation may arbitrate before sending the port bypass primitive sequences. This might be done to ensure that the loop is in a known state when the port bypass primitive sequence is sent.

7.3 Arbitration Scenarios

The following sections present different arbitration scenarios which illustrate the basic operation of the arbitration process.

7.3.1 Single Port Arbitrating

Figure 43 on page 115 is an example of the arbitration protocol when a single port is arbitrating. Initially, the loop is assumed to be filled with IDLEs. This would be the case whenever there is no loop activity. Port_01 begins arbitrating by transmitting an ARB(01) for every received IDLE. The loop fills up with ARB(01) as the IDLEs are replaced. When the first ARB(01) is received by Port_01, it wins arbitration, enters the Arbitration Won state, transmits an OPN to open a loop circuit and goes to the Open state. Upon entry to the Open state, the LPSM changes its current fill word to ARB(F0), and discards any received ARB(x). This prevents any other port from winning arbitration because no other port is able to receive its own ARB(x).

Table 9 on page 114 illustrates an alternative method of viewing the loop activity through the use of a table showing the step-by-step output at each port on the loop.

While the figures and table might seem to imply synchronous activity, each port on the loop is acting asynchronously and independently of the other ports. The actual time when a fill word arrives at one port and the current fill word is updated is completely independent of other ports. Also, due to clock elasticity requirements, the number of fill words transmitted does not necessarily equal the number of fill words received. Each port discards received fill words and transmits new ones, based on the current fill word, as required. This is necessary due to minute differences between the receive and transmit clock rates (see *Asynchronous Transmitter/Receiver and Clock Elasticity* on page 27).

7.3.2 Multiple Ports Arbitrating

When multiple ports arbitrate simultaneously, each transmits its own ARB(x) in place of every IDLE and lower-priority ARB(x) it receives. Because multiple ports may be performing fill word substitution simultaneously, the current fill word at different points on the loop may be different. An example of multiple ports arbitrating is shown graphically in Figure 44 on page 118, with a more detailed table representation of the same operation provided by Table 10 on page 120.

In this second example, Port_01 and Port_B2 begin arbitrating at the same time. Port_01 transmits its own ARB(01) for every IDLE and lower-priority ARB(x) it receives and Port_B2 transmits its own ARB(B2) for every IDLE and lower-priority ARB(x) it receives.

Port_2A receives the ARB(01) and updates its current fill word to ARB(01). Whenever Port_2A requires a fill word, ARB(01) is used. Because there is no other loop activity at this time, Port_2A transmits ARB(01) for every word.

Port_EF receives the ARB(B2) and updates its current fill word to ARB(B2). Whenever Port_EF requires a fill word, ARB(B2) is used. Because there is no other loop activity at this time, Port_EF transmits ARB(B2) for every word.

Port_01 compares the AL_PA of the received ARB(B2) with its own AL_PA. AL_PA=B2 is lower priority than AL_PA=01 so Port_01 discards the ARB(B2) and continues to send ARB(01).

---

1. The loop is initially filled with IDLEs as the result of no activity. 2. Each port is in the Monitoring state waiting to arbitrate or be opened by another port. 3. Because no activity is occurring, the current fill word at all ports is IDLE. 4. Received IDLEs are discarded and the current fill word is transmitted in their place.	Step 1
1. Port_01 begins arbitrating for access to the loop. 2. Port_01 changes its CFW from IDLE to ARB(01). 3. Port_01 transmits ARB(01) when a fill word is required.	Step 2
1. ARB(01) is received by the next port which updates its current fill word to ARB(01). 2. Whenever a fill word is required, the ARB(01) is transmitted. Because there is no other activity on the loop, ARB(01) is transmitted. 3. Discarding received fill words and transmitting the current fill word allows the port to compensate for clock differences between the received data stream and transmit data stream.	Step 3

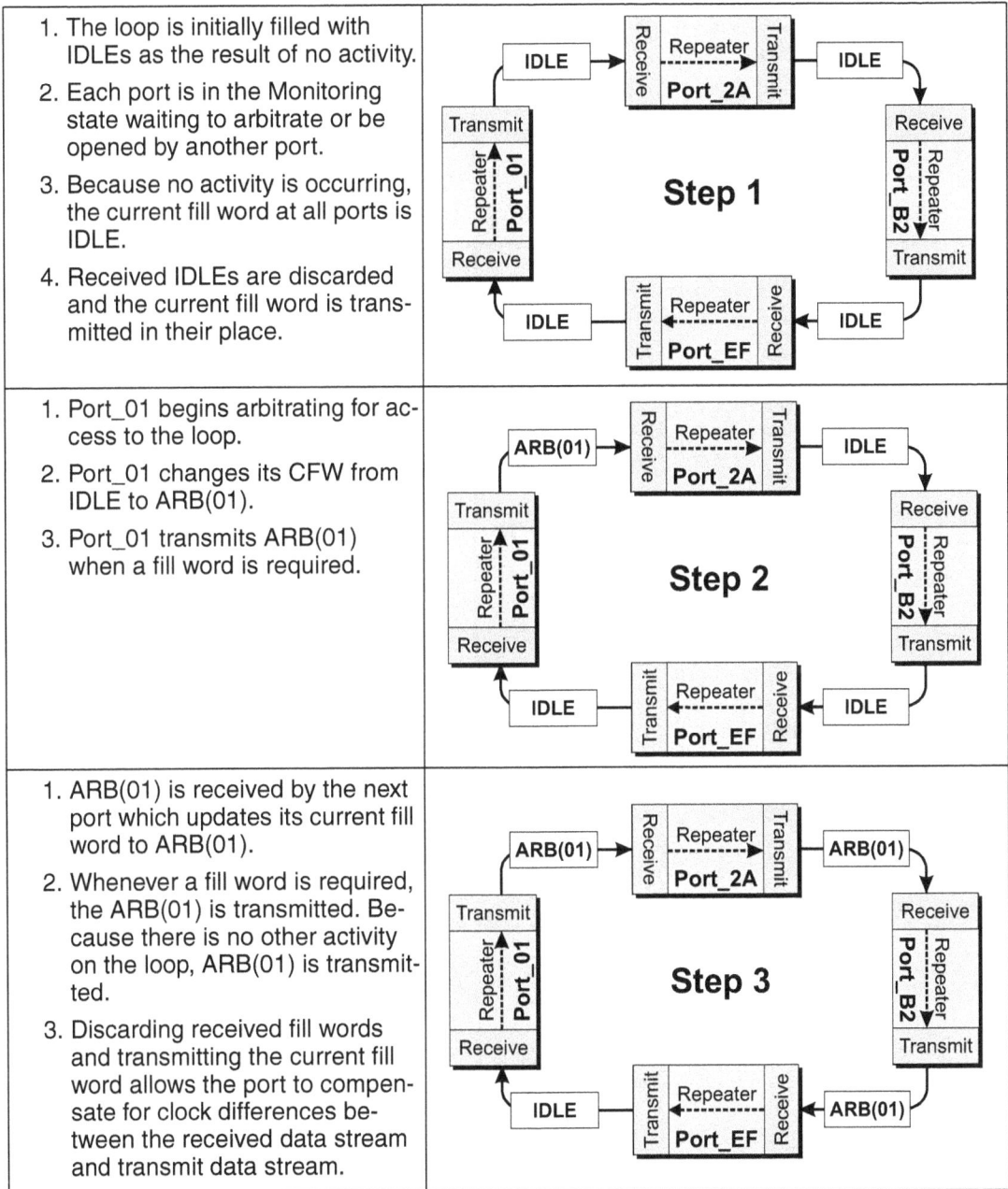

Figure 43. Single Port Arbitration (Part 1 of 2)

1. When Port_01 receives its own ARB(01), it wins arbitration.

2. Port_01 sends an OPN to open a loop circuit and changes its current fill word to ARB(F0).

3. Port_01 discards any received ARB(x). This prevents any other port from winning arbitration because that port's ARB(x) never makes it around the loop.

Step 4

1. As each port receives the ARB(F0) it updates its current fill word to ARB(F0), and then transmits ARB(F0) whenever a fill word is required.

2. Assuming that no other port is arbitrating, ARB(F0) travels completely around the loop.

3. When ARB(F0) is received by Port_01 (the winner of arbitration in this example), the CFW in Port_01 is changed to IDLE.

Step 5

1. Each port receives the IDLE, and updates its current fill word to IDLE.

2. Assuming that no other port is arbitrating, the IDLEs travel completely around the loop.

3. As long as Port_01 owns the loop, it discards any received IDLE or ARB(x) and continues to send its CFW (i.e., IDLE) as its fill word when necessary. Discarding the received ARB(x) prevents any other port from winning arbitration.

Step 6

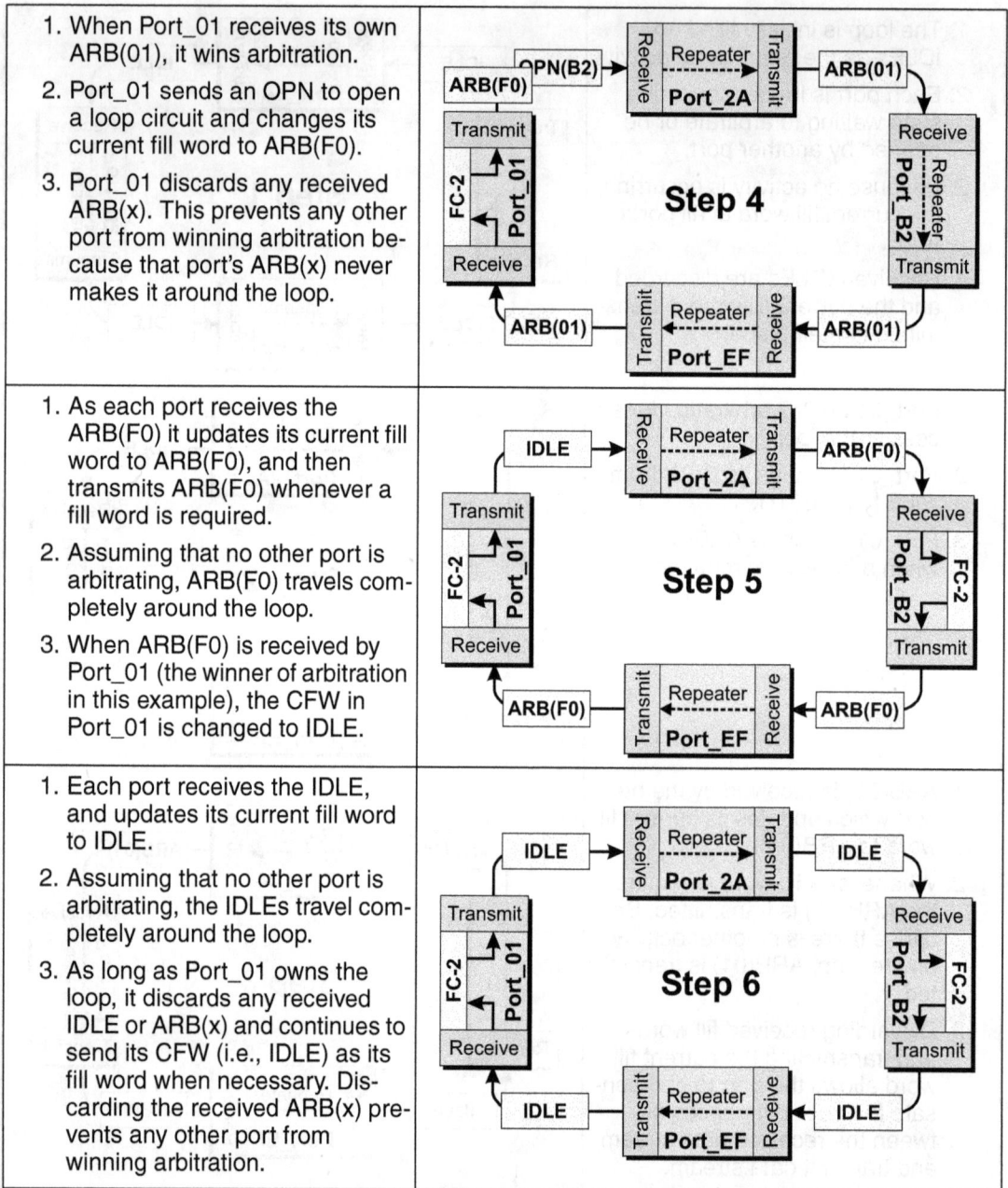

Figure 43. Single Port Arbitration (Part 2 of 2)

Chapter 7. Arbitration and Fairness

Step	Description	Port_01	Port_2A	Port_B2	Port_EF
1.	Loop is idle	IDLE	IDLE	IDLE	IDLE
2.	Port_01 starts arbitrating; changes CFW to ARB(01)	ARB(01)	IDLE	IDLE	IDLE
3.	Port_2A updates its CFW and propagates ARB(01)	ARB(01)	ARB(01)	IDLE	IDLE
4.	Port_B2 updates its CFW and propagates ARB(01)	ARB(01)	ARB(01)	ARB(01)	IDLE
5.	Port_EF updates its CFW and propagates ARB(01)	ARB(01)	ARB(01)	ARB(01)	ARB(01)
6.	Port_01 wins arbitration; transmits OPN to Port_EF Port_01 changes CFW to ARB(F0)	OPN(EF)	ARB(01)	ARB(01)	ARB(01)
7.	Port_01 transmits CFW (when nothing else to send) Port_2A retransmits the OPN	ARB(F0)	OPN(EF)	ARB(01)	ARB(01)
8.	Port_2A updates its CFW and propagates ARB(F0) Port_B2 retransmits the OPN	ARB(F0)	ARB(F0)	OPN(EF)	ARB(01)
9.	Port_B2 updates its CFW and propagates ARB(F0) Port_EF recognizes the OPN and removes it	ARB(F0)	ARB(F0)	ARB(F0)	ARB(01)
10.	Port_EF updates its CFW and propagates ARB(F0)	ARB(F0)	ARB(F0)	ARB(F0)	ARB(F0)
11.	Port_01 receives ARB(F0); changes its CFW to IDLE	IDLE	ARB(F0)	ARB(F0)	ARB(F0)
12.	Port_2A updates its CFW and propagates IDLE	IDLE	IDLE	ARB(F0)	ARB(F0)
13.	Port_B2 updates its CFW and propagates IDLE	IDLE	IDLE	IDLE	ARB(F0)
14.	Port_EF updates its CFW and propagates IDLE	IDLE	IDLE	IDLE	IDLE

Table 9. Single Port Arbitrating

Port_B2 compares the AL_PA of the received ARB(01) with its own AL_PA. AL_PA=1 is higher priority than AL_PA=B2 so Port_B2 updates its current fill word to ARB(01) and begins transmitting ARB(01) whenever a fill word is needed. Port_B2 is still in the Arbitrating state, it just can not transmit its ARB(B2) at this time.

When Port_01 receives the ARB(01), it wins arbitration, opens a loop circuit, immediately changes its current fill word to ARB(F0), and discards any received ARB(x). When Port_B2 receives the ARB(F0), it changes its current fill word back to ARB(B2) and begins transmitting its arbitration request. Port_B2 cannot win arbitration, however, until Port_01 relinquishes control of the loop and allows the ARB(B2) to pass.

7.3.3 Lower-Priority Port Wins Arbitration

This example illustrates what happens when a higher-priority port begins arbitrating after allowing a single ARB(x) from a lower-priority port to pass. The scenario is illustrated graphically in Figure 45 on page 121, and in table form in Table 11 on page 123.

In this example, Port_B2 begins arbitrating by replacing every received IDLE and lower-priority ARB(x) with ARB(B2). The ARB(B2) travels through Port_EF and is received by Port_01 which updates its current fill word to ARB(B2). Port_01 transmits a single instance of the ARB(B2) fill

1. Port_01 begins arbitrating for access to the loop. It does this by replacing every IDLE and lower-priority ARB(x) received with ARB(01).

2. Port_B2 begins arbitrating for access to the loop. It does this by replacing every IDLE and lower-priority ARB(x) received with ARB(B2).

1. The ARB(01) travels around the loop to Port_2A which updates its current fill word to ARB(01), transmitting the ARB(01) whenever a fill word is needed.

2. The ARB(B2) travels around the loop to Port_EF which updates its current fill word to ARB(B2), transmitting the ARB(B2) whenever a fill word is needed.

1. When Port_B2 receives ARB(01) it changes its current fill word to ARB(01) because ARB(01) has higher priority (AL_PA is lower numerically).

2. When Port_01 receives ARB(B2) it replaces the ARB(B2) with ARB(01).

3. Because Port_B2's ARB(B2)s are replace by Port_01, Port_B2 doesn't receive its own ARB(B2) and cannot win arbitration at this time.

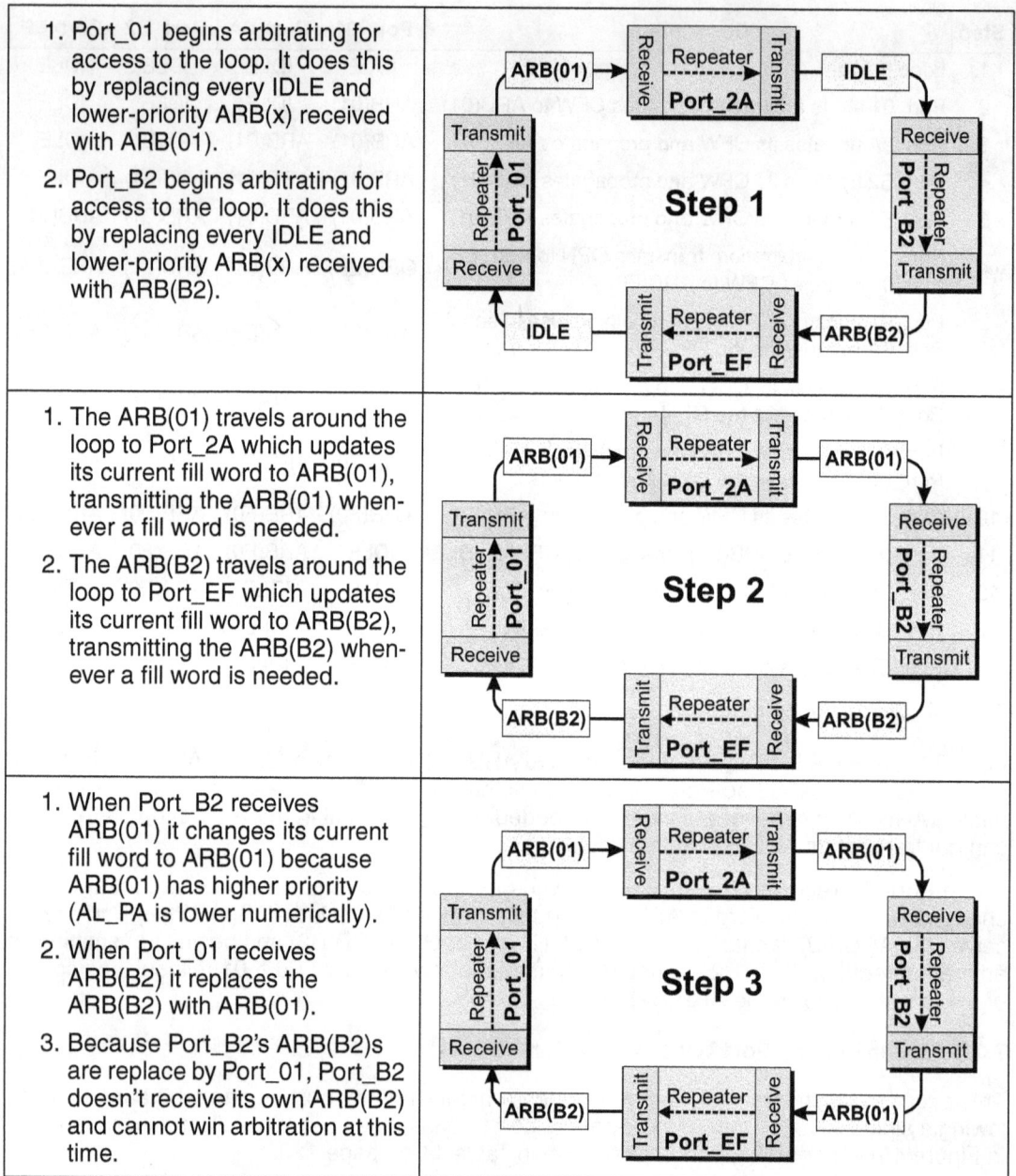

Figure 44. Multiple Port Arbitration (Part 1 of 2)

Step 4

1. The ARB(01) is received by Port_01 which wins arbitration.

2. Immediately upon winning arbitration, Port_01 opens its loop circuit, updates its current fill word to ARB(F0) and begins transmitting ARB(F0) whenever a fill word is required.

3. Port_B2 is still in the Arbitrating state, it just can't transmit its ARB(B2) because all received fill words are ARB(01) which has higher priority.

Step 5

1. Port_2A recognizes the OPN with its AL_PA and goes to the Opened state.

2. Port_2A receives ARB(F0) and updates its current fill word to ARB(F0) which is used whenever a fill word is required.

3. Port_B2 replaces the lower-priority ARB(F0) and transmits ARB(B2).

Step 6

1. Port_EF updates its current fill word to ARB(B2) and passes it on to Port_01.

2. Port_01 transmits ARB(F0) when a fill word is required.

3. Port_B2 continues to replace every received ARB(F0) with ARB(B2). Port_01 discards all received ARB(x) ordered sets.

4. When Port_01 relinquishes control of the loop, it changes its current fill word to ARB(B2) allowing Port_B2 to win arbitration.

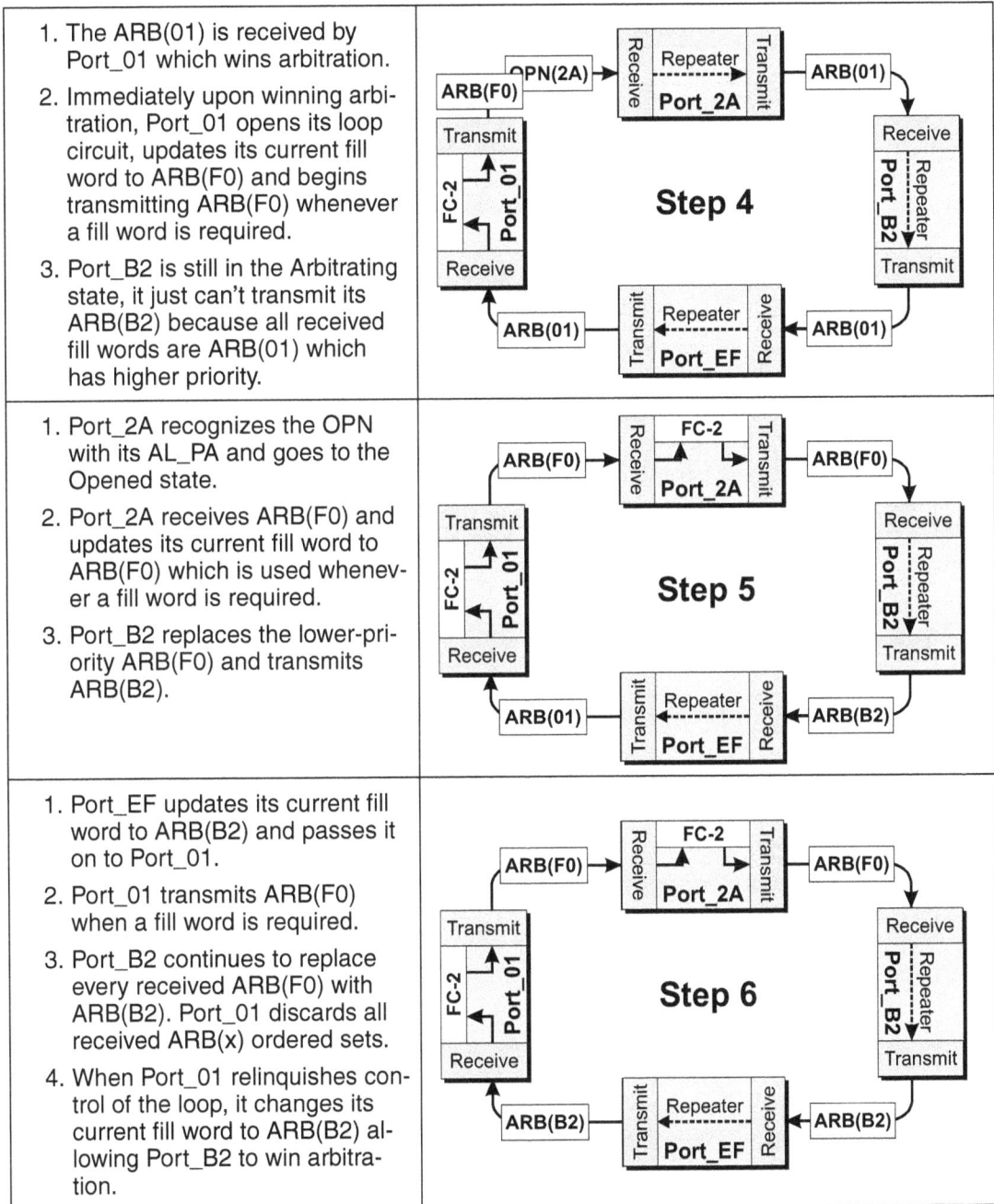

Figure 44. Multiple Port Arbitration (Part 2 of 2)

Step	Description	Port_01	Port_2A	Port_B2	Port_EF
1.	Loop is idle	IDLE	IDLE	IDLE	IDLE
2.	Port_01 and Port_B2 start arbitrating simultaneously	ARB(01)	IDLE	ARB(B2)	IDLE
3.	Port_2A and Port_EF propagate the received ARB(x)	ARB(01)	ARB(01)	ARB(B2)	ARB(B2)
4.	Port_01 substitutes its ARB(01) for the ARB(B2) Port_B2 updates its CFW and propagates ARB(01)	ARB(01)	ARB(01)	ARB(01)	ARB(B2)
5.	Port_EF updates its CFW and propagates ARB(01)	ARB(01)	ARB(01)	ARB(01)	ARB(01)
6.	Port_01 wins arbitration; transmits OPN to Port_EF Port_01 changes CFW to ARB(F0)	OPN(EF)	ARB(01)	ARB(01)	ARB(01)
7.	Port_01 transmits CFW (when nothing else to send) Port_2A retransmits the OPN	ARB(F0)	OPN(EF)	ARB(01)	ARB(01)
8.	Port_2A updates its CFW and propagates ARB(F0) Port_B2 retransmits the OPN	ARB(F0)	ARB(F0)	OPN(EF)	ARB(01)
9.	Port_B2 substitutes its ARB(B2) for the ARB(F0) Port_EF recognizes the OPN and removes it	ARB(F0)	ARB(F0)	ARB(B2)	ARB(01)
10.	Port_EF updates its CFW and propagates ARB(B2)	ARB(F0)	ARB(F0)	ARB(B2)	ARB(B2)
11.	Port_01 does not update its CFW. The loop stays in this state until Port_01 releases the loop.	ARB(F0)	ARB(F0)	ARB(B2)	ARB(B2)
12.	Port_01 relinquishes the loop; updates its CFW and propagates ARB(B2)	ARB(B2)	ARB(F0)	ARB(B2)	ARB(B2)
13.	Port_2A updates its CFW and propagates ARB(B2)	ARB(B2)	ARB(B2)	ARB(B2)	ARB(B2)
14.	Port_B2 wins arbitration; transmits OPN to Port_2A Port_B2 changes CFW to ARB(F0)	ARB(B2)	ARB(B2)	OPN(2A)	ARB(B2)
15.	Port_B2 transmits CFW (when nothing else to send) Port_EF retransmits the OPN	ARB(B2)	ARB(B2)	ARB(F0)	OPN(2A)
16.	Port_EF updates its CFW and propagates ARB(F0) Port_01 retransmits the OPN	OPN(2A)	ARB(B2)	ARB(F0)	ARB(F0)
17.	Port_2A recognizes the OPN and removes it	ARB(F0)	ARB(B2)	ARB(F0)	ARB(F0)
18.	Port_2A updates its CFW and propagates (ARB(F0)	ARB(F0)	ARB(F0)	ARB(F0)	ARB(F0)
19.	Port_B2 changes its current fill word to IDLE	ARB(F0)	ARB(F0)	IDLE	ARB(F0)
20.	Port_EF updates its CFW and propagates IDLE	ARB(F0)	ARB(F0)	IDLE	IDLE
21.	Port_01 updates its CFW and propagates IDLE	IDLE	ARB(F0)	IDLE	IDLE
22.	Port_2A updates its CFW and propagates IDLE	IDLE	IDLE	IDLE	IDLE

Table 10. Multiple Ports Arbitrating

1. Port_B2 begins arbitrating for the loop by changing its current fill word to ARB(B2).

2. Each received IDLE and lower-priority ARB(x) is discarded by Port_B2 and the ARB(B2) is substituted in its place.

1. The ARB(B2) propagates around the loop to Port_EF.

2. Port_EF changes its current fill word to ARB(B2) and transmits the ARB(B2) whenever a fill word is needed.

1. The ARB(B2) propagates around the loop to Port_01.

2. Port_01 changes its current fill word to ARB(B2) and transmits the ARB(B2) whenever a fill word is needed. In this case, only one ARB(B2) is transmitted.

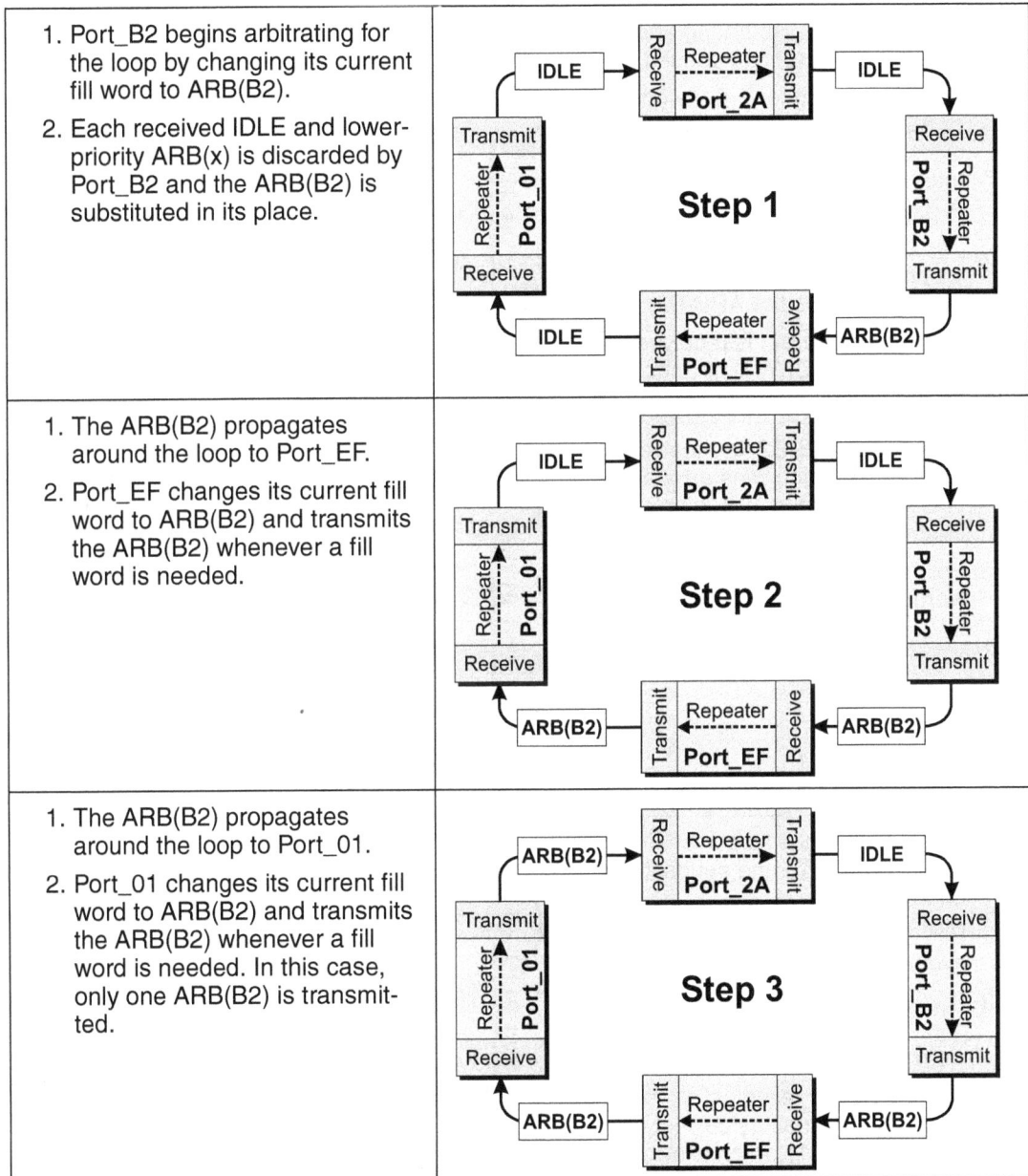

Figure 45. Lower Priority Port Wins (Part 1 of 2)

1. Port_01 begins arbitrating after a single ARB(B2) has passed.

2. Port_01 has higher priority (lower AL_PA) than Port_B2 and discards ARB(B2) and substitutes its own ARB(01) for each ARB(B2).

3. The single ARB(B2) travels around the loop to Port_2A. Port_2A passes the ARB(B2).

4. When the ARB(01) is received at Port_2A its CFW is changed from ARB(B2) to ARB(01)

Step 4

1. The single ARB(B2) is received by Port_B2 which wins arbitration and immediately begins discarding any received ARB(x).

2. Port_B2 changes its current fill word to ARB(F0)

Step 5

1. Port_EF changes its current fill word to ARB(F0) and sends it on to Port_01

2. Port_01 substitutes ARB(01) for every ARB(F0) it receives.

3. Port_B2 discards the ARB(01) and sends ARB(F0) as its fill word.

4. When Port_B2 relinquishes the loop, it will change its current fill word to ARB(01) which allows Port_01 to win arbitration and repeat the whole cycle.

Step 6

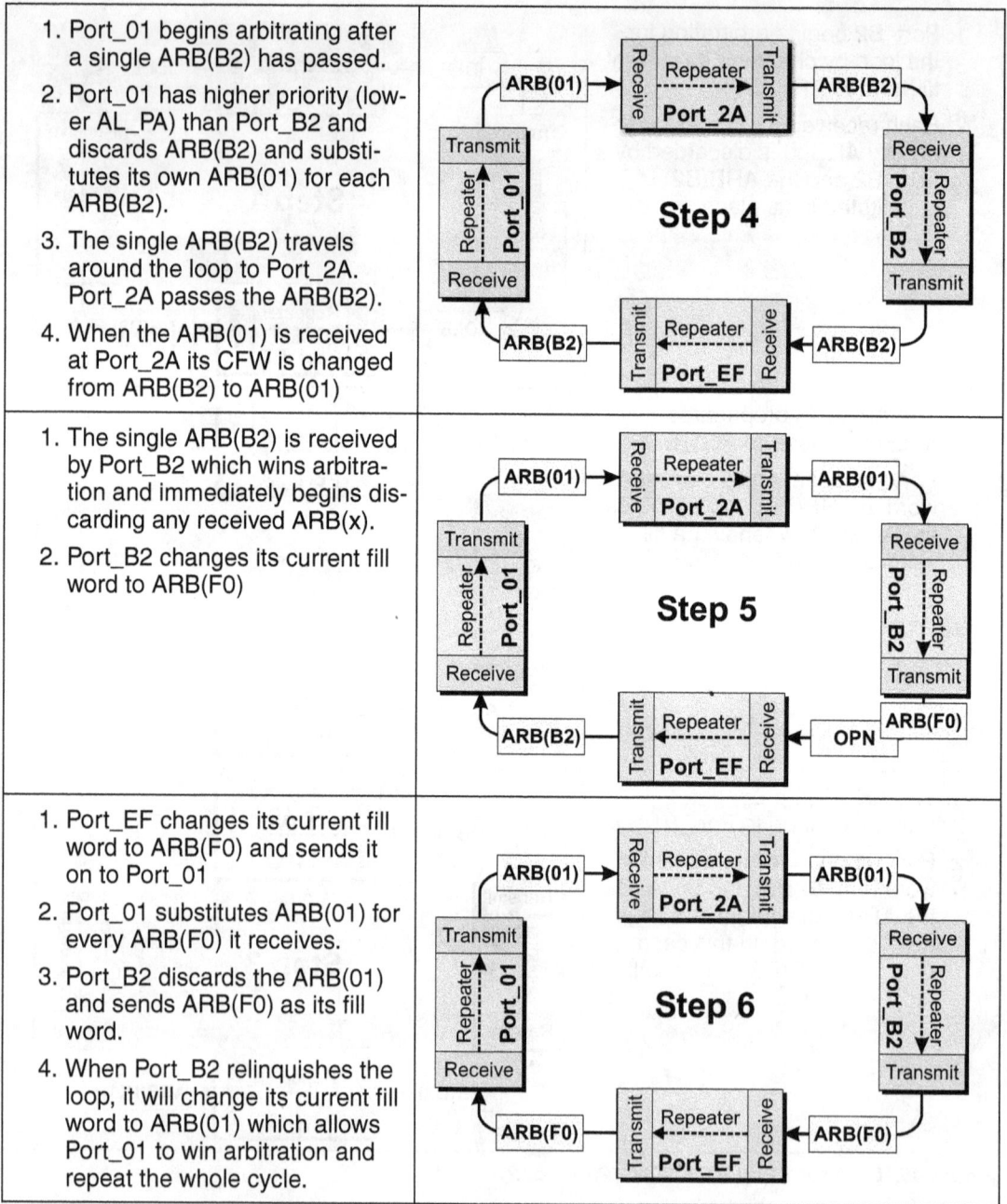

Figure 45. Lower Priority Port Wins (Part 2 of 2)

Step	Description	Port_01	Port_2A	Port_B2	Port_EF
1.	Loop is idle	IDLE	IDLE	IDLE	IDLE
2.	Port_B2 begins arbitrating	IDLE	IDLE	ARB(B2)	IDLE
3.	Port_EF propagates the received ARB(B2)	IDLE	IDLE	ARB(B2)	ARB(B2)
4.	Port_01 propagates a single ARB(B2)	ARB(B2)	IDLE	ARB(B2)	ARB(B2)
5.	Port_01 begins arbitrating Port_2A propagates the single ARB(B2)	ARB(01)	ARB(B2)	ARB(B2)	ARB(B2)
6.	Port_B2 wins arbitration; transmits OPN to Port_EF Port_B2 changes its CFW to ARB(F0) Port_2A propagates the ARB(01)	ARB(01)	ARB(01)	OPN(EF)	ARB(B2)
7.	Port_B2 transmits its CFW Port_EF recognizes the OPN and removes it	ARB(01)	ARB(01)	ARB(F0)	ARB(B2)
8.	Port_EF updates its CFW and propagates ARB(F0)	ARB(01)	ARB(01)	ARB(F0)	ARB(F0)
9.	Port_B2 discards ARB(01) and sends ARB(F0). The loop stays in this state until Port_B2 releases the loop	ARB(01)	ARB(01)	ARB(F0)	ARB(F0)
10.	Port_B2 finishes with loop and allows ARB(01) to pass	ARB(01)	ARB(01)	ARB(01)	ARB(F0)
11.	Port_EF propagates ARB(01)	ARB(01)	ARB(01)	ARB(01)	ARB(01)
12.	Port_01 wins arbitration, transmits OPN to Port_B2 Port_01 changes CFW to ARB(F0)	OPN(B2)	ARB(01)	ARB(01)	ARB(01)
13.	Port_01 transmits CFW (when nothing else to send) Port_2A retransmits the OPN	ARB(F0)	OPN(B2)	ARB(01)	ARB(01)
14.	Port_2A updates its CFW and propagates ARB(F0) Port_B2 recognizes the OPN and removes it	ARB(F0)	ARB(F0)	ARB(01)	ARB(01)
15.	Port_B2 updates its CFW and propagates ARB(F0)	ARB(F0)	ARB(F0)	ARB(F0)	ARB(01)
16.	Port_EF updates its CFW and propagates ARB(F0)	ARB(F0)	ARB(F0)	ARB(F0)	ARB(F0)
17.	Port_01 changes its current fill word to IDLE	IDLE	ARB(F0)	ARB(F0)	ARB(F0)
18.	Port_2A propagates the IDLE	IDLE	IDLE	ARB(F0)	ARB(F0)
19.	Port_B2 propagates the IDLE	IDLE	IDLE	IDLE	ARB(F0)
20.	Port_EF propagates the IDLE	IDLE	IDLE	IDLE	IDLE

Table 11. Lower Priority Port Wins Arbitration

word, then begins arbitrating. Port_01 changes the current fill word from ARB(B2) to ARB(01) and begins to transmit ARB(01) when a fill word is required.

The single ARB(B2) travels around the loop followed by multiple ARB(01)s as it passes through Port_2A and eventually reaches Port_B2.

When Port_B2 sees its own ARB(B2) it wins arbitration and immediately changes its current fill word to ARB(F0), thereby discarding the received ARB(01)s and keeping Port_01 from winning arbitration. When Port_B2 relinquishes control of the loop, Port_B2 changes the current fill word to ARB(01) which then travels around the loop allowing Port_01 to win arbitration.

Because fill words may be inserted or deleted by ports as part of the clock elasticity function, it is possible for the single ARB(B2) to be deleted by Port_2A. If this should occur, Port_B2 does not win arbitration because it didn't receive its ARB(B2). Instead, Port_2A propagates ARB(01) to Port_B2. Port_B2 updates its current fill word to ARB(01) because AL_PA=01 is higher priority than AL_PA=B2. The ARB(01)s travel around the loop and Port_01 wins arbitration. When Port_01 wins arbitration, it changes its current fill word to ARB(F0) allowing Port_B2 to again transmit its ARB(B2). Port_B2 can not win arbitration until Port_01 relinquishes the loop and allows the ARB(B2) to pass.

7.4 Withdrawn Arbitration

Once a port begins arbitrating, there is no method defined by the Arbitrated Loop standard to allow that port to withdraw the arbitration request. The need to withdraw an arbitration request may occur on a multiple ported node if the node arbitrates on multiple ports simultaneously and uses the first port that wins arbitration. The reason for not allowing a port to withdraw its arbitration request is to guarantee that the access fairness is reset correctly.

Examination of the LPSM state table reveals that the only exit from the Arbitrating state is to win arbitration *(line 12: 'ARB(x) or ARB(F0) or ARB(FF)', on page 328)*, receive an OPNy for that port *(line 14: 'OPN(yx) or OPN(yy)', on page 328)*, to be bypassed *(line 19: 'LPB(yx)', on page 328)* or *(line 35: 'REQ(bypass L_Port)', on page 329)*, or begin loop initialization *(line 41: 'REQ(initialize)', on page 329)*. None of these provides a clean method of withdrawing the request.

Rather, the LPSM continues to arbitrate until it wins arbitration and then it must transmit OPN. If the LPSM no longer requires access to the loop, it may transmit OPNy to itself and continue to the Open state; transmit CLS to itself and go to the Transmitted Close state; and, when the CLS is received, return to the Monitoring state. Between the transmission of the OPNy and receiving the CLS, the access fairness window continues to be processed correctly.

It is also possible for a port to begin the arbitration process and subsequently withdraw its request due to error conditions. If this occurs, one or more ARB(x) ordered sets for that port may be in transit in the loop. To prevent endless circulation of the ARB(x), a port that is not in the Arbitrating state discards any received ARB(x) if the AL_PA matches that port's AL_PA.

If a port begins the arbitration process and is subsequently removed without causing a loop interruption (for example, an active hub maintains loop integrity), it is possible for one or more ARB(x) ordered sets for that port to be in transit on the loop. If a higher priority AL_PA begins arbitrating, it discards the circulating ARB(x) and the loop returns to the correct condition.

If the loop happens to be completely full of ARB(x) ordered sets for the removed port, it is impossible for lower priority ports to win arbitration. In this case, one or more ports eventually times out and causes a loop initialization which purges any orphaned ARB(x) ordered sets from the loop.

7.5 Access Fairness

The Arbitrated Loop standard assigns a priority to each AL_PA such that lower numerical values have priority over higher numerical values. Left unchecked, this could result in ports with higher-priority AL_PA values monopolizing the loop and starving ports with lower-priority AL_PA values. Access fairness counteracts the AL_PA priority to ensure that every port has an equal opportunity to access the loop.

Access fairness dictates that once a port has won arbitration, it does not arbitrate again until all other ports that are arbitrating have won arbitration. A port that follows the access fairness protocol is called a *fair port*. A port that does not follow the access fairness protocol is called an *unfair port*. The decision to use access fairness is optional and left up to each individual port. A specific port may choose to always be fair, always be unfair, or dynamically switch between being fair and unfair.

The FL_Port always has permission to be unfair because traffic for ports on the loop may be backing up in the fabric. If the FL_Port had to be fair, it is possible that the entire fabric could become congested as the result of activity taking place on the loop. By choosing to be unfair, and by virtue of having the highest-priority AL_PA (x'00'), the FL_Port always wins during the next arbitration cycle. This allows the FL_Port to forward traffic to ports as rapidly as possible.

One might make a similar argument for a SCSI initiator in a disk subsystem to be an unfair port. The initiator may have tasks for multiple targets in its queues and waiting for a fair access to the loop could cause the initiator to become congested. By assigning the initiator a high-priority AL_PA value and choosing to be unfair may improve overall performance.

SCSI targets may also use unfair access to lower latency for some commands. SCSI devices are not given special privilege, just commonsense use. Excessive use of unfair behavior may result in loop initialization by a port unable to gain access to the loop within an LP_TOV (2 seconds) time period.

Any port may selectively choose to be fair or unfair. In many implementations, the decision to be fair or unfair is controlled by the firmware and can be altered dynamically as conditions dictate. This allows a port to be fair during periods of normal activity, but switch to unfair behavior during periods of peak activity.

Access fairness does not imply time fairness. Once a port has won arbitration, it may keep the loop for as long as it requires. The Arbitrated Loop standard does not specify a maximum time the loop may be held, although some applications such as the Private Loop Direct Attach Technical Report define a maximum arbitration wait time (AW_TOV) of 1 second for that environment. However, every port which wins arbitration, when it receives ARB(x) from another port must realize that if that port does not win arbitration within LP_TOV, it may initialize the loop (a port is either 'hogging' the loop bandwidth or may be unable to get off the loop - in either case, the LIP process should stabilize the loop).

7.5.1 Access Fairness Window

Access fairness applies within a time interval called the access fairness window. The window begins when the first port wins arbitration and ends when an arbitration winner discovers that it is the last arbitrating port.

Each fair port must remember that it has won arbitration during the current window and not arbitrate again until the window has ended. This is done with a control variable called Access. When Access is set, the port may arbitrate for the loop. When Access is not set, the port can not arbitrate. When a port is observing access fairness, Access is reset when that port wins arbitration. Access is subsequently set when the access fairness window ends.

The task of managing the access fairness window and notifying all ports that the window has ended is the responsibility of the current arbitration winner. If the access fairness window has not ended when the current arbitration winner relinquishes the loop, management of the access fairness window is passed to the next winner of arbitration.

The current arbitration winner uses the ARB(F0) fill word to detect if any port on the loop is arbitrating. If any port is arbitrating, that port substitutes its own ARB(x) for the ARB(F0) and ARB(F0) is not received by the current arbitration winner. The current arbitration winner continues to send ARB(F0) as its fill word until it travels completely around the loop or the port relinquishes control of the loop.

If the current arbitration winner receives an ARB(F0), it indicates that for at least one cycle around the loop no other port was arbitrating. This marks the end of the current access fairness window. At this point, fair ports that are waiting (their Access variable is reset) need to be notified so that they can begin arbitrating if they so desire. This notification is provided by changing the current fill word at the arbitration winner from ARB(F0) to IDLE.

When a port receives an IDLE, it sets the Access variable and transmits at least two IDLEs before changing the current fill word. Once the Access variable is set, the port can begin arbitrating if it needs access to the loop. The use of IDLE to signal the end of the fairness window works because there are no IDLEs on the loop from the time that the first port won arbitration until the access fairness window ends. All IDLEs have been discarded and replaced by either ARB(x) or ARB(F0).

7.5.2 Making the Decision to Be Unfair

Access Fairness is an optional behavior. Ports may choose to be fair, unfair, or dynamically switch between being fair and unfair. This raises the question of when a port should be fair and when it is appropriate to be unfair. The Arbitrated Loop standard left this decision open so that individual implementations could select the mode of operation that was best for their particular applications.

If the operation of the overall loop is improved by unfair port behavior, then it makes sense to allow that behavior. One example may be a loop with one or more SCSI initiators and a number of disk devices. Overall performance may be improved if the SCSI initiators are allowed to be unfair while the disk devices are restricted to being fair.

The transfer function allows a port to close one loop circuit and open another without relinquishing control of the loop and rearbitrating (see *Using Transfer* on page 179). This operation is inherently unfair if it is used when other ports are arbitrating because using the transfer function allows a port to establish a series of loop circuits during a single loop tenancy.

Excessive unfair behavior or use of the transfer function may lead to timeout conditions for some ports or operations. If this occurs, a loop initialization may occur which negates any benefits derived from unfair behavior.

7.6 Using AL_PA and Fairness to Set Priority

The Arbitrated Loop standard does not provide any specific mechanisms to assign priority to ports other than through the hard assignment of AL_PA values. This combined with unfair behavior allows selected ports to have priority access to the loop.

If the ports requiring priority access to the loop are assigned higher-priority AL_PA values, they normally win arbitration before lower-priority AL_PA values (see *Lower-Priority Port Wins Arbitration* on page 117 for the exception). In a disk subsystem, for example, the SCSI initiator(s) could be assigned AL_PA values starting at x'01' while the disk devices are assigned lower-priority (higher numerically) AL_PA values. This would allow the initiator to win arbitration should it and one or more disk drives arbitrate at the same time. When this is done, it is still important to maintain the optimal ordering of AL_PA values on the loop.

If a port follows the fairness rules, it only arbitrates once per access fairness window. In a fully populated loop, this could mean that the port would get one access to the loop, then potentially have to wait for each of the 125 other ports and the FL_Port to access the loop. The initiator can avoid this wait by choosing to be unfair and arbitrating whenever it has traffic for another port.

Alternatively, if there is one initiator and multiple targets on the loop, as each target opens the initiator this gives the initiator one access per target per access fairness window if full-duplex opens are used. In this case, special priority is not necessary.

7.7 AL_PA Order on the Loop

The order of AL_PA values around the loop has an effect on the time required for the next port to win arbitration when multiple ports are arbitrating for access to the loop. For best performance, the AL_PA values should be arranged in descending priority (increasing AL_PA value) in the direction of information flow.

Two examples help illustrate why the order of AL_PA values is significant. Both examples assume that Port_01 has won arbitration and Port_2A is arbitrating for access to the loop. Port_2A transmits its ARB(2A) for each fill word received while Port_01 discards each received ARB(2A) and substitutes ARB(F0). When Port_01 relinquishes control of the loop, it allows the ARB(2A) to pass and Port_2A wins arbitration.

In the first example, shown in Figure 46 on page 128, the AL_PA values are not optimally ordered. When Port_01 relinquishes control of the loop, the ARB(2A) is allowed to pass. Due to the order of AL_PA assignment, the ARB(2A) must propagate completely around the loop before Port_2A wins arbitration. Contrast this with the next example which illustrates the optimal order.

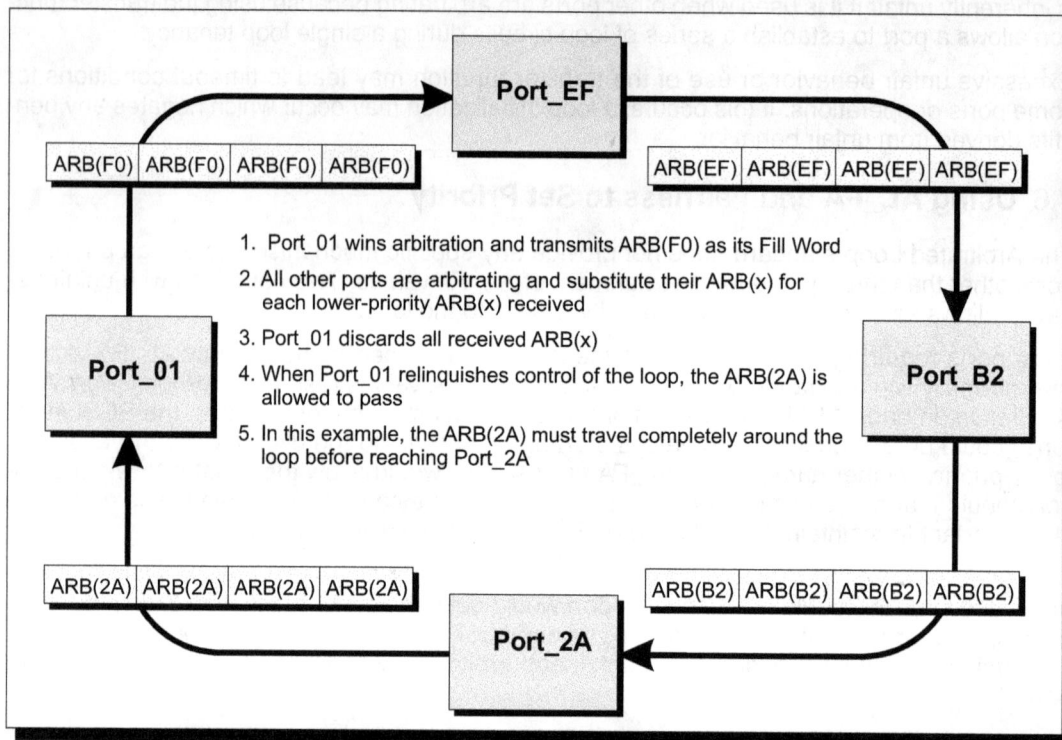

Figure 46. Non-Optimal AL_PA Ordering

Optimal ordering of the AL_PA values is shown in Figure 47 on page 129. Now, when Port_01 relinquishes control of the loop, the ARB(2A) only has to propagate to the next port to reach Port_2A. This represents a substantial savings in time required to win arbitration compared to the non-optimal case and can significantly improve loop performance, especially in loops with a large number of ports.

The use of hard-assigned AL_PA values may contribute to non-optimal ordering if the AL_PA values are assigned incorrectly. Soft-assigned AL_PA values naturally result in optimal ordering when the LISA processing is done correctly (that is, the AL_PA value chosen is the most significant available bit in the bit map).

7.8 LPSM Arbitrating State

In the Arbitrating state, the LPSM is retransmitting non-fill word traffic and waiting to win arbitration or be opened by another port.

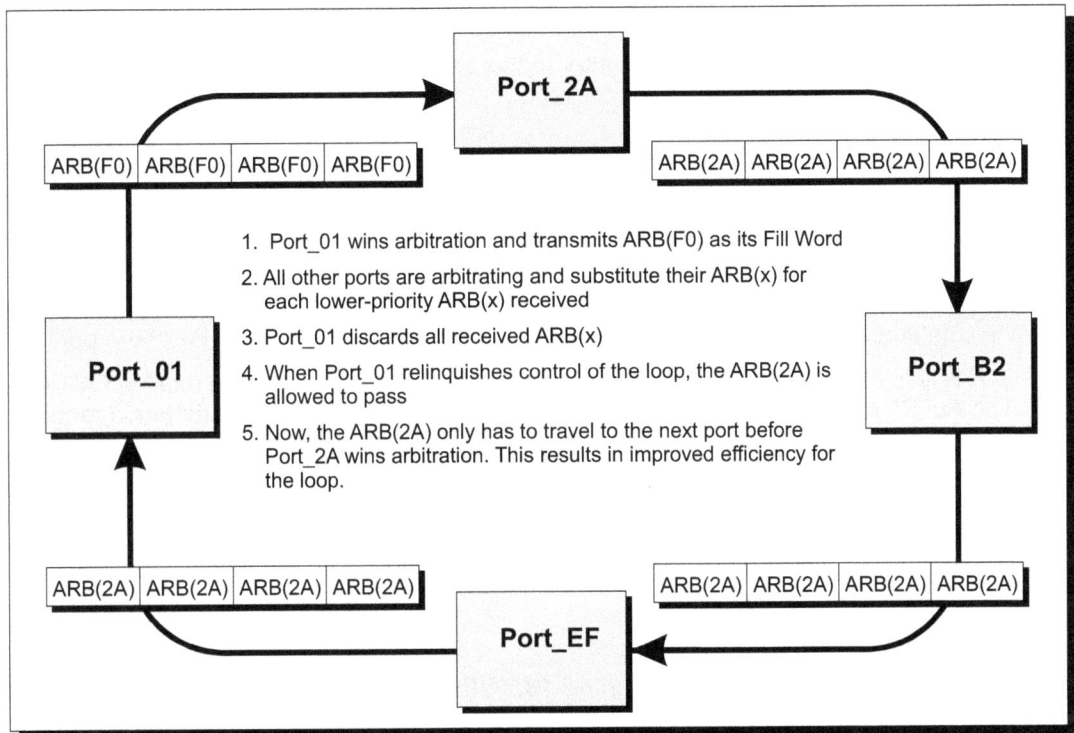

Figure 47. Optimal AL_PA Ordering

A port arbitrates by substituting its own ARB(x) for every IDLE and lower-priority ARB(x) received. If an ARB(x) is received where 'x' equals the AL_PA of the port, the port has won arbitration and enters the Arbitration Won state. If a higher-priority ARB(x) is received, the port sets its current fill word equal to the received ARB(x) and discontinues substituting its own ARB(x).

Once the LPSM has transmitted its own ARB(x), it is not allowed to retransmit a lower-priority ARB(x), even if the port no longer requires access to the loop. Instead, it continues to arbitrate until it has won arbitration. The port then transmits an OPN(yy) to itself, then closes the loop. This is done to correctly process the access fairness protocol.

Unless replicate mode has been set, the port is not conditioned for frame reception and does not detect the fact that frames may have been received and retransmitted.

The following sections describe the LPSM actions taken as the result of selected input stimuli. Numbered items in the descriptions refer to numbered events in the left column of *'Arbitrating State',* on page 327.

7.8.1 Entry Actions

No special processing is required upon entry to this state and the LPSM control variables are unchanged; only Duplex and ARB_Won are reset.

7.8.2 Arbitration and Access Fairness

If an IDLE is received *(line 9: 'IDLE', on page 327)*, the current fill word is set to ARB(x) where 'x' equals the AL_PA of the port and is duplicated in both the third and fourth characters of the ARB(x) ordered set.

If an ARB(x) is received *(line 12: 'ARB(x) or ARB(F0) or ARB(FF)', on page 328)*, the AL_PD ('x' value contained in the third and fourth character) is compared to the AL_PA of the port.

- If 'x' is less than the AL_PA of this port, the current fill word is set to the received ARB(x). The AL_PA of the received ARB(x) has higher priority than this port's arbitration request.

- If 'x' is greater than the AL_PA of this port, the current fill word is set to ARB(x) where 'x' equals the AL_PA of this port. This port's arbitration request has higher priority than the received port's arbitration request.

- If 'x' equals the AL_PA of the port, this port has won arbitration and the LPSM enters the Arbitration Won state.

7.8.3 Opening a Loop Circuit

If an OPN(yx) or OPN(yy) is received *(line 14: 'OPN(yx) or OPN(yy)', on page 328)*, the AL_PD (y value in the third character) is examined to determine if the open is addressed to this port. If the fourth character of the OPN ordered set is equal to x'FF', then an OPN Replicate has been received (OPNr).

- If 'y' equals the AL_PA of this port and the fourth character is not x'FF', the LPSM enters the Opened state. Another port on the loop has won arbitration and wishes to begin communication with this port.

- If 'y' does not equal the AL_PA of this port and the fourth character is not x'FF', the OPNy is for a different port and is retransmitted.

7.8.4 Replicate Mode

If an OPN Replicate (OPNr) is received *(line 13: 'OPN(fr) or OPN(yr)', on page 328)*, the AL_PD (third character) is examined to determine if the OPNr is addressed to this port.

- If an OPN(fr) (f=x'FF') is received, the LPSM sets replicate mode. A different port has won arbitration is using the broadcast replicate OPN to set replicate mode in all NL_Ports on the loop.

- If an OPN(yr) is received where 'y' equals the AL_PA of this port, the LPSM sets replicate mode. A different port has won arbitration and is setting replicate mode in this port.

In either case, the OPNr is retransmitted and eventually propagates around the loop until it reaches the original sender at which point it is discarded.

If a CLS is received *(line 15: 'CLS', on page 328)* and replicate mode is set, replicate mode is reset. The CLS is retransmitted in all cases.

7.8.5 Processing MRK(tx)

If a MRK(tx) is received *(line 17: 'MRK(tx)', on page 328)* and the MK_TP and AL_PS match expected values, the action or notification associated with the MRK(tx) is performed (this action is not shown on the state table). If this was the port that originally transmitted the MRK(tx) (x=AL_PA), the MRK(tx) is discarded and the current fill word substituted in its place, otherwise the MRK(tx) is retransmitted.

If the REQ(mark as tx) input is active *(line 34: 'REQ(mark as tx)', on page 329)*, the LPSM transmits a single MRK(tx) at the next appropriate fill word unless the REQ(mark as tx) input is removed before the MRK(tx) is transmitted. The next appropriate fill word occurs when the MRK(tx) is preceded and followed by two fill words.

7.8.6 Initialization and Loop Bypass

If a loop failure is detected *(line 2: 'Loop Failure', on page 327)* or the loop port requests initialization by asserting the REQ(initialize) input *(line 41: 'REQ(initialize)', on page 329)*, the LPSM enters the Initializing state.

If the LIP primitive sequence is recognized, the LPSM enters the Open-Init state *(line 18: 'LIP', on page 328)*.

If the LPB(yx) primitive sequence is recognized and 'y' equals the AL_PA of the port *(line 19: 'LPB(yx)', on page 328)* or REQ(bypass L_Port) is active *(line 36: 'REQ(bypass L_Port y)', on page 329)*, the LP_Bypass variable is set and the LPSM enters the Monitoring state.

If REQ(bypass port) is active *(line 35: 'REQ(bypass L_Port)', on page 329)*, the LPSM activates the port bypass circuit (if present), sets the LP_Bypass variable, and enters the Monitoring state.

7.8.7 Other Valid Ordered Sets

If any other valid ordered set is received, it is retransmitted *(line 21: 'Other Ordered Set', on page 328)*.

7.9 LPSM Arbitration Won State

When an arbitrating port wins arbitration it enters the Arbitration Won state. This is an immediate state (i.e., no transmission words are received while in this state). The LPSM only decides on which OPN should be sent or whether to initialize the loop.

7.9.1 Entry Actions

No special processing is required upon entry to this state and the LPSM control variables are unchanged.

7.9.2 Opening or Closing the Loop Circuit

If the port still requires access to the loop when it wins arbitration, one of the L_Port open-type control inputs is active. If a point-to-point open is requested, then *(line 25: 'REQ(open yx)', on page 331)* or *(line 26: 'REQ(open yy)', on page 331)* is active. If an open replicate is requested, then *(line 27: 'REQ(open fr)', on page 331)* or *(line 28: 'REQ(open yr)', on page 331)* is active. The LPSM transmits the corresponding OPN and enters the Open state. If none of the open requests is active and the request to send a CLS is not active, the LPSM transmits the current fill word (ARB(F0).

If the port no longer requires access to the loop, the REQ(close) L_Port control is active *(line 29: 'REQ(close)', on page 331)*, the LPSM transmits an OPNy to itself and enters the Open state. This could occur if a multiple ported node attached to multiple loops was simultaneously arbitrating for access on more than one loop, won arbitration on a different loop first, and no longer needs access via this port. Some true multiple ported devices may be capable of supporting operations on both ports concurrently and may send an OPN on more than one port. The REQ(close) L_Port control in the Open state *(line 29: 'REQ(close)', on page 333)* would cause the port to close the circuit which it just created with itself; but, it continues to manage the access fairness window during this time.

7.10 Chapter Summary

Arbitration

- Ports must arbitrate for access to the loop
- When a port wins arbitration, it opens a loop circuit
  - Frame transmission occurs during the loop circuit
- If ports transmitted whenever they had data, frames from one port could interfere with frames from another
- Arbitration resolves simultaneous requests
  - AL_PA values are prioritized

Access Fairness

- Ports with higher-priority AL_PA values could lock out lower-priority ports
  - When they arbitrate, they always win
  - Lower-priority ports might never win arbitration
- Access fairness limits how often a port can arbitrate
- Access fairness ensures that each arbitrating port can access the loop
- Access fairness does not mean time fairness
  - Does not limit how long a port uses the loop
- Observing access fairness is optional, but highly recommended

Fairness Window

- Fairness applies within an access fairness window
  - Window begins when the first port wins arbitration
  - Ends when a port discovers that it was the last arbitrating port
  - IDLE resets the fairness window
- Fair ports can only arbitrate once per window
  - After winning arbitration, they wait for the end of the window before arbitrating again
- Unfair ports can arbitrate at any time

Fill Word Substitution

- Arbitration protocol uses the concept of fill word substitution
  - Allows a port to discard a received fill word and transmit a different one in its place
  - Does not affect other transmission words
- Fill words do not carry information meaningful for the FC-2 level
  - IDLE, ARB(x), ARB(F0), ARB(FF)
- Fill words are transmitted when there is nothing else to transmit

Arbitration Process

- When a port is arbitrating it enters the Arbitrating state
- The CFW is updated to the port's ARB(x) if the port receives:
  - IDLE, ARB(F0), or ARB(FF)
  - A lower-priority ARB(x) (higher value AL_PA)
- Other transmission words are retransmitted
- Arbitration occurs even if a loop circuit exists between another pair of ports
  - During the fill word interval between frames
- Once a port starts arbitrating it
  - Must continue arbitrating until it wins or the loop is initialized, or
  - May withdraw arbitration if it is opened

Arbitration Won

- When a port receives its own ARB(x), it wins arbitration and enters the Arbitration Won state
- Immediately sends an OPN and goes to the Open state
- The arbitration winner changes its CFW to ARB(F0)
  - if another port is arbitrating it substitutes its ARB(x) for the ARB(F0)
  - If not, the ARB(F0) travels around the loop
- If the arbitration winner receives ARB(F0), it changes its fill word to IDLE

Opening a Loop Circuit

- If the port requires the loop when it wins arbitration,
  - It sends an OPN and
  - Enters the Open state
- If the port does not require the loop when it wins arbitration
  - It sends OPN(yy) to itself
  - Enters the Open state
  - Sends a CLS
  - Enters the Transmitted Close state
  - Receives the CLS and enters Monitoring state
  - For example, a dual ported node that won arbitration on the other port

Prioritizing Ports

- AL_PA values and fairness can be used to assign port priorities
- Lower AL_PA values win arbitration over higher values first within each access fairness window
  - Assign SCSI initiators high-priority AL_PA values
  - Assign SCSI targets lower-priority AL_PA values
- Allow ports to be unfair when system behavior dictates

AL_PA Order

- The AL_PA assignment order on the loop is important for optimal performance
  - AL_PA values should be in order of decreasing priority
  - Minimizes the time required to win arbitration when the loop is busy
  - ARB(x) travels the minimum distance to next winner
- Non-optimal order causes ARB(x) to travel further
- Assigning initiators from x'01' up and targets from x'EF' down may not be optimal

---

8. Flow Control

Fibre channel's flow control mechanisms prevent a transmitter from overrunning a receiver's buffering capabilities by preventing the transmission of frames when no receive buffers are available. FC-PH defines two levels of flow control—a link-level mechanism called *buffer-to-buffer* flow control, and a port-level mechanism called *end-to-end* flow control. Both types of flow control use a credit management scheme in their operation.

Credit is advance permission granted to send one or more frames. As long as the proper type of available credit for each class of service is greater than zero, a port can send frames. Each frame sent reduces the available credit by one, each flow control response received replenishes the available credit. Larger credit values allow the transmitter to stream multiple frames while waiting for responses from the receiver. The optimal credit value is one that allows the transmitter to stream frames uninterrupted with the responses arriving just before the credit is exhausted. The exact values depend upon the distance between the ports and frame processing overhead at the receiving port.

Both types of credit are granted by a port during the login process. In FC-PH, an initial credit of one is assumed prior to login so that the ports can begin communication and perform the login process. In an Arbitrated Loop topology, an initial credit of zero is assumed for buffer-to-buffer credit and permission to send frames prior to login is controlled by sending one or more R_RDYs. An NL_Port discovers which topology it is in during loop initialization.

The different Fibre Channel classes of service use the two types of credit differently as shown in Table 12.

Frame Being Transmitted	Subject to End-to-End Credit?	Subject to Buffer-to-Buffer Credit?
Class-1 frame with SOFc1	Yes	Yes
Class-1 frame with SOFi1, SOFn1	Yes	No
Class-2 frame	Yes	Yes
Class-3 frame (normal)	No	Yes
Class-3 frame (replicate mode)	No	No
Loop initialization sequence frame	No	No
Link control frame (Ack, Busy, Reject)	No	Yes
Responses to above frames	Acknowledge, Busy, Reject Link Control Frame	Receiver ready (R_RDY) primitive signal

Table 12. Class Specific Flow Control Characteristics

8.1 End-to-End Flow Control

End-to-end flow provides confirmation of frame delivery or notification of non deliverability of frames in Class-1 and Class-2. Class-3 is an unacknowledged service which does not provide delivery confirmation or participate in end-to-end flow control. As its name implies, end-to-end flow control manages the flow of frames from a source port to a destination port. Initial permission to send frames to a particular destination port is given during the PLOGI port login process when the two ports grant end-to-end credit (EE_Credit) to each other.

A port using a class of service subject to end-to-end flow control is required to maintain separate login and available EE_Credit values for each other node port that it is logged in with. When frame transmission is to take place with a destination node port, the available EE_Credit value for that port is retrieved and, if the value is nonzero, one or more frames may be sent based on that credit. The available EE_Credit for that specific destination node port is decremented for each frame sent and incremented for each end-to-end flow control response received. If the available EE_Credit for a specific node port is zero, frame transmission with that destination node port is suspended until the available EE_Credit is nonzero.

Exhausting the available EE_Credit for one node port does not affect the ability of a port to send frames to a different node port for which the available EE_Credit is greater than zero. Each port's available EE_Credit is managed independently of the available EE_Credit for other ports.

Transmission of some types of frames is also subject to the availability of buffer-to-buffer credit (BB_Credit). Before a port can transmit an SOFc1 Class-1 frame, any Class-2 frame, or a link control frame, the port must have an available BB_Credit greater than zero.

Because the end-to-end flow control responses are link control frames, they follow all of the normal rules governing frame transmission. link control frames can only be sent when a loop circuit exists with the destination port. If no such circuit currently exists, the sending port must arbitrate, win arbitration, and open the destination port prior to sending a link control frame.

End-to-end responses may be sent during a different loop circuit than was used for the original frame. A port may send one or more frames during a given loop circuit and close the loop circuit before the responses are received.

Ports that use end-to-end flow control in an Arbitrated Loop topology may encounter conditions where they are unable to immediately transmit the link control response frames and must buffer them for later transmission just like other frames.

8.2 Buffer-to-Buffer Flow Control

Buffer-to-buffer flow control shares many conceptual similarities with the end-to-end flow control mechanism. Both end-to-end and buffer-to-buffer flow control use a credit mechanism to regulate the transmission of frames. Both grant an initial credit value during login. Both require that their respective available credit values be nonzero to transmit a frame. Both decrement the available credit for each applicable frame sent and increment the available credit for each response received. Beyond these similarities lie a number of significant difference as will be seen shortly.

Buffer-to-buffer flow control manages the flow of Class-1 SOFc1, Class-2 and Class-3 frames (see Table 12 on page 135) from the sender of a frame to the frame recipient. The port that is the frame recipient varies depending upon the topology, as shown in Table 13.

BB_Credit Characteristics	Topology		
	Point-to-Point	Fabric	Arbitrated Loop
Controls frame flow with	N_Port at opposite end of the link	F_Port at opposite end of the link	Other loop port in current loop circuit
When BB_Credit is granted	N_Port login (PLOGI)	Fabric login (FLOGI)	N_Port and/or fabric Login (PLOGI/FLOGI)
			Dynamically, when loop circuit opened
Minimum BB_Credit value granted	1	1	0
BB_Credit value used	Value granted during N_Port login	Value granted during F_Port login	From 0 to actual value granted during login
Number of login BB_Credit values	1	1	0 or 1 per loop port (126 ports maximum)
Number of available BB_Credit counts	1	1	1
Available credit set from login credit	At N_Port login (PLOGI)	At Fabric login (FLOGI)	When loop circuit opened

Table 13. Buffer-to-Buffer Flow Control Characteristics

In the point-to-point topology, the frame recipient is the N_Port at the opposite end of the link. In the fabric topology, it is the F_Port at the opposite end of the link. In either topology, the same frame recipient is always at the other end of an individual link and a single login BB_Credit value and available BB_Credit counter is sufficient.

The Arbitrated Loop topology operates differently than either of the other topologies and necessitates some changes in the buffer-to-buffer credit mechanism to accommodate those differences. The following sections discuss the differences and the operation of the BB_Credit mechanism in a loop environment.

8.2.1 What Makes a Loop Different?

The Arbitrated Loop is different form the other topologies because dynamic loop circuits may be established and relinquished with numerous other ports over a period of time. Each time a loop circuit is established, the loop port may be communicating with a different set of receive buffers in the destination port. The dynamic nature of these circuits means that while point-to-point and fabric always have the same set of receive buffers present at the other end of a link, an Arbitrated Loop does not. Each loop circuit potentially connects a transmitter to a different set of receive buffers.

When a port sends a frame, it uses one of the available receive buffers at the destination port. For each frame sent, the available buffer-to-buffer Credit (BB_Credit) is reduced by one. For each R_RDY primitive signal received, the available BB_Credit is incremented by one. If the available BB_Credit reaches zero, the transmitting port is not permitted to send additional frames until the credit is replenished.

Because the R_RDY does not contain any addressing or port identification information it is only meaningful in relationship to the current loop circuit. In the point-to-point and fabric topologies, there is only a single long-lived circuit corresponding to the physical link. In these topologies, the logical circuit and physical circuit have a one-to-one correspondence as long as the link is connected and operational. The BB_Credit in these topologies can be managed with a single login BB_Credit value and available BB_Credit counter.

In the Arbitrated Loop topology, a single physical interconnect (the loop) is now capable of supporting a number of dynamic logical circuits between different pairs of loop ports. To manage the login BB_Credit value for each port in this topology requires that a loop port remember the value granted during login and then use that value to initialize the available BB_Credit counter when a loop circuit is opened with that port. The need to manage login BB_Credit values for each loop port introduces complexity that was not acceptable to some cost-sensitive designs.

The loop environment also forces a reexamination of the meaning of the login BB_Credit value. In the point-to-point and fabric topologies, the login BB_Credit establishes the initial available BB_Credit which is then used to control subsequent frame transmission. The same set of receive buffers is always at the other end of the link and the number of available receive buffers is always known. In the loop topology, neither port has knowledge of the number of available receive buffers in the other port. All of the receive buffers may be available, or a prior loop circuit may have used some or all of the available receive buffers.

These, and other considerations, have led to the adoption of an *alternate BB_Credit management* model used in the Arbitrated Loop. This model enhances the basic Fibre Channel BB_Credit model by providing a number of extensions tailored to the unique characteristics of the loop topology. Support for the alternate BB_Credit management model is mandatory in loop environments. The key highlights of this model are:

- The login BB_Credit granted by a loop port may be zero or nonzero.

- The login BB_Credit remembered and used by a loop port may be any value from zero to the actual value granted by the other loop port.

- The login BB_Credit granted by a port is used to set the available BB_Credit whenever a loop circuit is opened (if the login BB_Credit value for that loop port was remembered).

- BB_Credit is always signalled dynamically by both ports when a loop circuit is opened by sending one R_RDY for each available receive buffer. This is done to accommodate those ports that either granted a login BB_Credit of zero, or did not remember a nonzero login BB_Credit value.

- Because BB_Credit is communicated both by port login and dynamic signalling, loop ports must discard as many R_RDYs as the remembered login BB_Credit value to prevent double crediting.
- If a loop circuit is closed before all owed R_RDYs have been sent, any outstanding R_RDYs are not sent.

Because the FC-PH BB_Credit model and the Arbitrated Loop alternate BB_Credit management model are incompatible, a port indicates that the alternate model is being used by setting word 1, bit 27 of the fabric and N_Port login common service parameters to designate that the port is using the 'alternate BB_Credit management' mechanism.

During loop initialization, the defaults for the alternate BB_Credit management bit and the BB_Credit value are set by the Loop Port State Machine (LPSM). If the state machine enters the Old-Port state, the alternate BB_Credit management bit is set to zero indicating normal BB_Credit management and the available BB_Credit value is set to one. If the state machine enters the Open-Init state, the alternate BB_Credit management bit is set to one indicating alternate BB_Credit management and the available BB_Credit value is set to zero.

8.2.2 Granting Login BB_Credit

Advance information about receive buffer availability is communicated during the N_Port or fabric login process. However, in an Arbitrated Loop topology, the login BB_Credit is interpreted to mean the number of receive buffers that a port guarantees to have available at the next open regardless of prior loop activity.

Part of this guarantee is to make Class 3 frame transmission more reliable. For the other classes of service, a busy could be returned if a port is found not to have a receive buffer available. However, some implementations who are using Class 3 require reliable transmission; therefore, the login BB_Credit is a guarantee that those buffers will be available whenever a port sends frames to that port.

Login BB_Credit is only useful for the port which transmits the OPN. A BB_Credit of greater than zero allows frame transmission without a handshake from the receiving port. During the time that the port is arbitrating, there is ample time to decide what the appropriate BB_Credit should be for the other port. The port which receives the OPN is in a maximum surprise mode (i.e., OPN is received and the port must make decisions at hardware speeds). This port does not use login BB_Credit for transmitting any frames; it completely relies on the R_RDYs which the other port sends. The port which sends the OPN must send at least one RDY (to allow the other port to return a busy or reject for certain classes of service), but normally sends one RDY for each frame buffer that it has available at the moment.

Each time a loop circuit is opened, the login BB_Credit value for the appropriate port is retrieved and used to initialize the available BB_Credit value used to manage the flow of frames with the destination port. The login BB_Credit value represents the number of frames that may be transmitted after the OPN and prior to receiving any R_RDYs from the receiving port.

Available BB_Credit is decremented as frames are transmitted and incremented as R_RDYs are received during the loop circuit. If the available BB_Credit is exhausted and reaches zero, frame transmission is suspended until one or more R_RDYs are received. The login BB_Credit

---

value is a constant granted during NL_Port or fabric login and is not altered by the process of frame transmission. Its sole purpose is to initialize the available BB_Credit when a loop circuit is established.

Regardless of the login BB_Credit value for the current port, the available BB_Credit is set to zero when each loop circuit is closed because it has no significance while the loop circuit is closed or for the next loop circuit.

Granting a Login BB_Credit Value Equal to Zero. Ensuring the availability of one or more frame buffers at each loop opening is not an easy task. The alternate BB_Credit management model allows a loop port to grant a login BB_Credit value of zero. This relieves the port of having to guarantee the availability of receive buffers by preventing the transmitting port from sending any frames when the loop circuit is initially opened. For frame transmission to occur, the receiving port dynamically indicates the availability of receive buffers by sending one or more R_RDYs when each loop circuit is opened.

Each R_RDY sent indicates the availability of one receive buffer at the receiving port. The actual number of R_RDYs sent is implementation dependent and may or may not represent the total number of available receive buffers. The port receiving the R_RDYs increments its available BB_Credit by one for each R_RDY received and can transmit frames and decrement the available BB_Credit for each frame sent as long as the available BB_Credit is greater than zero. Using this option of granting a login BB_Credit of zero simplifies the design of the receiver, but incurs a performance penalty opening every loop circuit because frame transmission is delayed waiting for the initial R_RDY to be received.

If no receive buffers are available when the loop circuit is opened, no R_RDYs are sent and the loop circuit can be closed immediately. Under these circumstances, the CLS indicates that frame transmission must occur during a subsequent loop circuit and represents an implied busy. An example of this behavior is shown in Figure 48 on page 141. In this example, Port_01 opens Port_E8 three times and receives an immediate CLS in response. This behavior could occur numerous times before the open recipient is able to receive frames and is not considered to be an error.

8.2.3 Managing Nonzero Login BB_Credit

Ports that indicate nonzero BB_Credit during login must ensure that they have at least the granted number of receive buffers available on each open. If this is not done, the port may not have enough receive buffers to hold the inbound frames that are sent immediately after the loop circuit is opened. If no receive buffer is available when a frame is received from the link, the frame will be lost, and the sequence fails. In the case of the present Fibre Channel Protocol for SCSI-3, a sequence failure may result in termination of an entire exchange.

The problem of ensuring adequate receive buffer availability is complicated by the fact that a loop port can be opened immediately after closure of the prior loop circuit. The open can originate from any other port on the loop.

Consider the case where a SCSI initiator grants a login BB_Credit of two to each of 125 SCSI targets on the same loop. It is possible that each of the SCSI targets will win arbitration, open the SCSI initiator, immediately send two frames based upon the login BB_Credit value, and

```
003D43:Idle 61.9 us                              |Idle  62.2 us
003D45:ARBx  Port 01                             |   .
003D48:     .                                    |ARBx   Port 01
003D4A:ARBx  Port F0                             |   .
003D4B:OPN   Full Duplex, Ports E8,01 ·······    |   .
003D4C:ARBx  Port F0                             |   .
003D4E:R RDY 40 ns                               |   .
003D4F:ARBx  Port F0                             |ARBx   Port F0
003D52:Idle 360 ns                          ·····|CLS
003D53:     .                                    |ARBx   Port F0
003D56:Idle 120 ns                               |Idle  160 ns
003D58:CLS  ◄·······                             |Idle  40 ns
003D59:Idle 40 ns                                |Idle  40 ns
003D5A:ARBx  Port 01                             |Idle  280 ns
003D5C:     .                                    |ARBx   Port 01
003D5E:ARBx  Port F0                             |   .
003D5F:OPN   Full Duplex, Ports E8,01 ·······    |   .
003D60:ARBx  Port F0                             |   .
003D62:R RDY 40 ns                               |   .
003D63:ARBx  Port F0                             |ARBx   Port F0
003D66:Idle 360 ns                          ·····|CLS
003D67:     .                                    |ARBx   Port F0
003D6A:Idle 120 ns                               |Idle  160 ns
003D6C:CLS  ◄·······                             |Idle  40 ns
003D6D:Idle 40 ns                                |Idle  40 ns
003D6E:ARBx  Port 01                             |Idle  280 ns
003D70:     .                                    |ARBx   Port 01
003D72:ARBx  Port F0                             |   .
003D73:OPN   Full Duplex, Ports E8,01 ·······    |   .
003D74:ARBx  Port F0                             |   .
003D76:R RDY 40 ns                               |   .
003D77:ARBx  Port F0                             |ARBx   Port F0
003D7A:Idle 360 ns                          ·····|CLS
003D7B:     .                                    |ARBx   Port F0
003D7E:Idle 120 ns                               |Idle  160 ns
003D80:CLS  ◄·······                             |Idle  40 ns
003D81:Idle 40 ns                                |Idle  40 ns
```

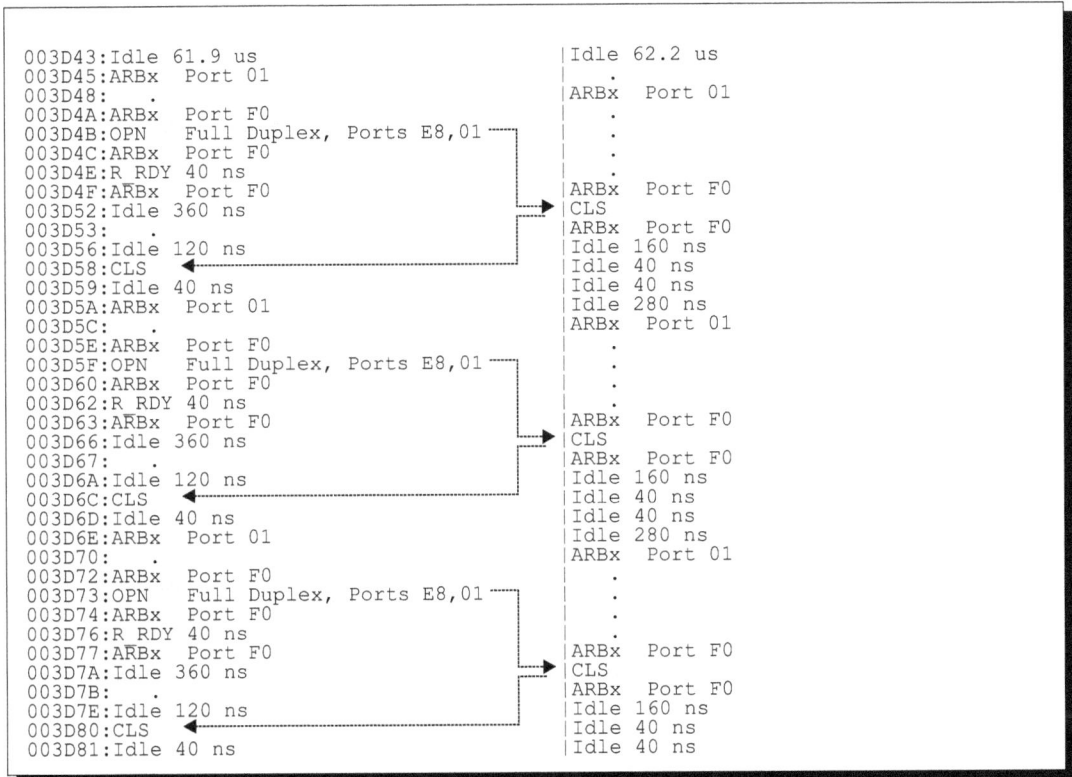

Figure 48. Busy Port Responding to OPN with Immediate CLS

close the loop allowing the next SCSI target to repeat the process. In this case, the SCSI initiator could receive 250 frames in rapid succession without the opportunity to limit frame transmission through the normal flow control mechanisms.

A second example illustrates an additional difficulty associated with nonzero login BB_Credit. A SCSI target is logged in with a single SCSI initiator and grants a login BB_Credit of two to that SCSI initiator. The initiator begins a 128-frame data transfer to the target by opening the loop circuit and immediately sending two frames based upon the login BB_Credit granted. The initiator then closes the target and immediately reopens it (which restores the login BB_Credit) and sends another two frames. If the initiator continues this process, it could legitimately send all 128 frames without the target having an opportunity to limit the frame transmission.

Once a port grants nonzero login BB_Credit, it is essentially unable to control the initial burst of frames following each open. No matter how many receive buffers the port has, it is always possible to construct scenarios, such as the two above, that exhaust the available buffers. With this in mind, what can be done to allow a port to extend nonzero login BB_Credit and still have a reasonable receive buffer implementation?

One strategy is to have a design capable of emptying receive buffers as fast as the Fibre Channel link can fill them. A simple ping-pong arrangement alternating between two receive buffers allows the Fibre Channel link to fill one receive buffer while the port is emptying the other. When the link buffer is full and the port buffer is empty, their functions swap allowing the link to begin filling the empty buffer and the port to begin emptying the full buffer. Graphics devices, processors, solid state disks, and similar devices may be able to operate in this mode due to their high-internal bandwidths.

Port designs that have assured access to high-speed memory can support extended periods of frame transmission by emptying receive buffers into the high-speed memory. The memory can be viewed as an extension of the receive buffers, and as long as memory space is available, receive buffers can be emptied as fast as the link can fill them and a simple ping-pong arrangement will suffice. This type of implementation may assemble one or more complete sequences in the high-speed memory, then transfer the completed sequence from the high-speed memory making space available for additional sequences. If receive buffers are being transferred to the high-speed memory simultaneously with data being transferred from the memory, the total memory bandwidth must be at least twice that of the Fibre Channel link.

Designs that access slow-speed memory or arbitrate for access to off-chip memory may need to manage nonzero login BB_Credit using only the resources available in the Fibre Channel receive function itself. This is due to the fact that access to the resources necessary to empty the receive buffers may not be available immediately causing delays in emptying the receive buffers.

Designs that implement dedicated single-frame sequence buffers in addition to data buffers need to base their login BB_Credit on the minimum quantity of the two types of buffers because there is no way to anticipate which type of frame will be received next.

One method of ensuring that the required number of receive buffers are available at the next open is to delay closing the loop until the necessary buffers are available to handle an immediate, subsequent OPN.

The following rules prevent a port from sending a CLS when insufficient receive buffers are available, and allow it to send a CLS as soon as a sufficient number of receive buffers are available.

- The open initiator may send a CLS at any time, provided that it delays returning to the Monitoring state until it has at least (maximum login BB_Credit granted to any loop port) of receive buffers available.

- If the open recipient has received a full-duplex OPN(yx), it is not allowed to transmit a CLS, unless it has at least (login BB_Credit of OPN initiator + maximum login BB_Credit value granted to any loop port) of receive buffers available.

- If the open recipient has received a half-duplex OPN(yy), it is not allowed to transmit a CLS unless it has at least (2 x maximum login BB_Credit granted to any loop port) of receive buffers available.

- If the port has sent one or more R_RDYs and a CLS has not been received, it is not allowed to transmit a CLS unless it has at least (number of R_RDYs sent - number of frames received + maximum login BB_Credit granted to any loop port) of receive buffers available.

- If the port has received a CLS, it may transmit a CLS once it has at least (maximum login BB_Credit granted to any loop port) of receive buffers available.

The need to delay closing the loop circuit due to insufficient receive buffers can be alleviated somewhat by incorporating more buffers than are made available during login. This reduces the frequency of delaying the close, but cannot remove it entirely.

8.2.4 Remembering Login BB_Credit Received

In the point-to-point and fabric topologies, a port only has to manage a single login BB_Credit value because the port at the opposite end of the link is fixed. Due to the loop's dynamic point-to-point like behavior, a port may have to maintain separate login BB_Credit values for each other port on the loop because the port may be involved in a loop circuit with each other port on the loop over a period of time. Login with each of the other ports normally occurs prior to beginning communications, and each grants its own port-specific login BB_Credit value. What was a single login BB_Credit value in the point-to-point and fabric topologies now becomes up to 126 different login BB_Credit values, one for each other loop port.

One simplification of login BB_Credit provided by the alternate BB_Credit management model allows a loop port to either remember the actual login BB_Credit value that was received during login, or any lesser value, including zero. If a loop port chooses to use a single value of zero login BB_Credit for all other loop ports, it is not necessary to remember any values granted during login.

Designs seeking to take advantage of the login BB_Credit value may need to remember a login value for each other port on the loop (potentially up to 126 other loop ports), then restore the value for a specific port when a loop circuit is opened with that loop port. A loop port is not required to remember the actual login BB_Credit value, but may choose to remember any value from zero to the actual login BB_Credit value.

Remembering a lesser value may simplify the design of the loop port. For example, a loop port may choose to implement a single bit to indicate whether the login BB_Credit value granted by a specific loop port was zero, or greater than zero. If the login BB_Credit value was zero, the loop port must wait for an R_RDY before sending a frame. Otherwise, a single frame can be sent based upon the fact that the login BB_Credit was greater than zero. This could allow a design to send single-frame sequences more efficiently than one that treats all login BB_Credit values as zero.

8.2.5 Signalling Available BB_Credit with R_RDY

All loop ports using the alternate BB_Credit management mechanism send R_RDYs when the loop circuit is opened to indicate the current availability of receive buffers. If the loop port gave a nonzero login BB_Credit value, it must send at least one R_RDY for each login BB_Credit granted. Sending R_RDYs is necessary because the other loop port in the loop circuit may be waiting for the R_RDYs to begin frame transmission (neither loop port in the loop circuit knows whether the other loop port remembers the login BB_Credit values or assumes zero and waits for the R_RDYs).

Using both a login BB_Credit value and dynamic signalling with R_RDY results in duplicate communication of available buffers for those ports that remember a login BB_Credit value greater than zero. This necessitates discarding one or more received R_RDYs to prevent double crediting of the BB_Credit when a loop circuit is opened.

Discarding Initial R_RDYs. Loop ports that use nonzero login BB_Credit values for the other loop port in the circuit can begin sending frames immediately after the OPN. The transmitting port could experience ambiguity as to whether the received R_RDY indicates receive buffer availability or the buffer associated with the transmitted frame has been emptied. This could lead to incorrect management of the available BB_Credit as shown in Figure 49. In this example, the following events occur:

1. Port_1 logs in with Port_2 and Port_2 grants a login BB_Credit value of two.

2. Some time later Port_1 opens Port_2, sets the available BB_Credit to two based upon the login BB_Credit granted by Port_2.

3. Port_1 sends two frames and decrements its available BB_Credit to zero.

4. When Port_2 receives the open, it sends two R_RDYs to indicate that two receive buffers are available.

5. Port_1 receives the two R_RDYs and increments its available BB_Credit to two.

6. As Port_2 empties the receive buffers associated with Port_1's frames it sends two R_RDYs indicating the receive buffers have been emptied.

7. Port_1 receives the two R_RDYs and increments its available BB_Credit to four which is incorrect because it does not reflect the true number of receive buffers available at Port_2!

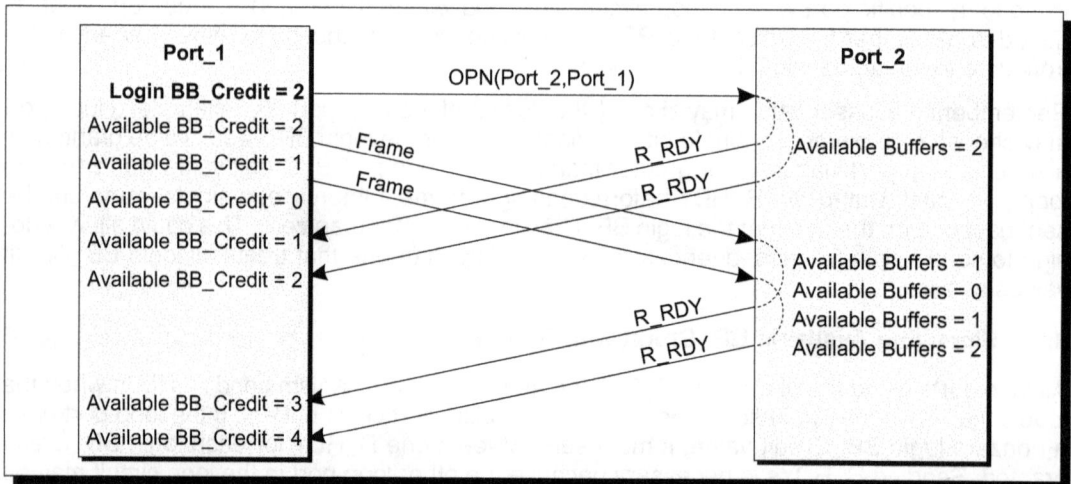

Figure 49. Incorrect Crediting of R_RDY

The problem of double crediting the R_RDYs is corrected by observing the following rule:

"Ports that use a nonzero login BB_Credit shall discard one received R_RDY until the number of R_RDYs discarded equals the number of frames sent based on the login BB_Credit value."

Once the requisite number of R_RDYs have been discarded the available BB_Credit is managed normally and decremented for each frame sent and incremented for each R_RDY received. The value of the available BB_Credit may even increment past the login BB_Credit used.

The example shown in Figure 50 illustrates correct discarding of initial R_RDYs and proper operation of the available BB_Credit. In this scenario, the following events occur:

1. Port_1 logs in with Port_2 and Port_2 grants a BB_Credit of two.

2. Some time later Port_1 opens Port_2, sets the available BB_Credit to two based upon the Login BB_Credit granted by Port_2.

3. Port_1 sends two frames and decrements its available BB_Credit to zero.

4. When Port_2 receives the open, it sends two R_RDYs to indicate that two receive buffers are available.

5. Port_1 discards one R_RDY for each frame sent until the number of R_RDYs discarded equals the number of frames that were sent based on the login BB_Credit (two in this case).

6. As Port_2 empties the receive buffers associated with Port_1's frames it sends two R_RDYs indicating the receive buffers have been emptied.

7. Port_1 receives the two R_RDYs and increments its available BB_Credit to two which is correct and reflects the correct number of receive buffers available at Port_2.

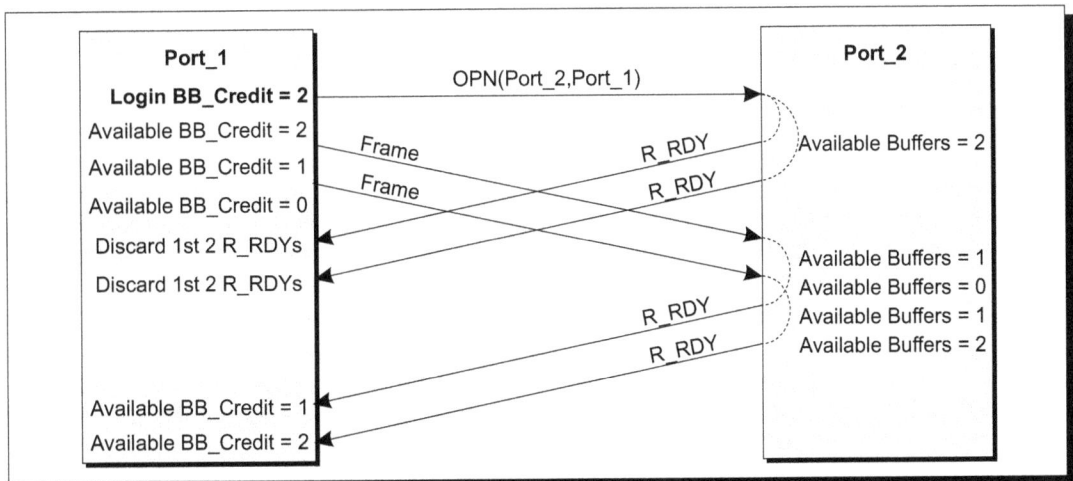

Figure 50. Correct Crediting of R_RDY

The same process of discarding R_RDYs functions correctly if the number of available buffers at the receiver is greater than the login BB_Credit retained by the transmitting port. In this last example, the transmitting port uses a single bit to remember whether the open recipient granted zero or nonzero BB_Credit during login. If the login BB_Credit value was zero, the port sets the nonzero login bit to zero and waits for one or more R_RDYs before beginning frame transmission. If the login BB_Credit was nonzero, the port sets the nonzero bit to one and assumes a default login BB_Credit of one regardless of the actual BB_Credit granted (this is a conservative approach, but works correctly).

When the loop circuit is opened, if the nonzero BB_Credit bit is set, the available BB_Credit is set to one, the port can send a single frame immediately and set a *discard R_RDY* indication. When the first R_RDY is received, it is discarded and the *discard R_RDY* indicator is reset. From this point on, normal flow occurs using the available BB_Credit. Consider the following case which is illustrated in Figure 51 on page 147:

1. Port_1 logs in with Port_2 and Port_2 grants a BB_Credit of three. Port_1 uses a single bit to manage the login BB_Credit. This bit simply indicates whether the login BB_Credit was zero or nonzero.

2. Some time later Port_1 opens Port_2, sets the available BB_Credit to one based upon the fact the Port_2 granted a nonzero login credit.

3. Port_1 sends one frame and decrements its available BB_Credit to zero.

4. When Port_2 receives the open, it sends three R_RDYs to indicate that three receive buffers are available.

5. Port_1 discards one R_RDY based on the *discard R_RDY* bit and increments its available BB_Credit to two based upon the remaining R_RDYs.

6. As Port_2 empties the receive buffer associated with Port_1's frame it sends one R_RDY to indicate that the receive buffer has been emptied.

7. Port_1 receives the R_RDY and increments its available BB_Credit to three which correctly reflects the number of receive buffers available at Port_2.

8.2.6 BB_Credit When a Loop Circuit Is Closed

When a loop circuit is closed, a decision must be made about any outstanding R_RDYs. Some implementations keep the loop circuit open until all outstanding R_RDYs had been sent. This approach balances the number of frames sent and R_RDYs received, but would require that the loop circuit remain open until the loop port empties its receive buffers and sends the associated R_RDYs. This represents nonproductive overhead on the loop because other ports are prevented from using the loop until the current loop circuit is closed.

Most implementations avoid the overhead associated with emptying receive buffers by allowing a loop circuit to be closed without waiting for the receive buffers to be emptied and the associated R_RDYs sent. The loop circuit is closed earlier, allowing the loop to be available for immediate use by other ports.

By allowing the loop circuit to close before all owed R_RDYs have been sent, the number of frames sent and R_RDYs received may or may not necessarily balance. Once the loop circuit

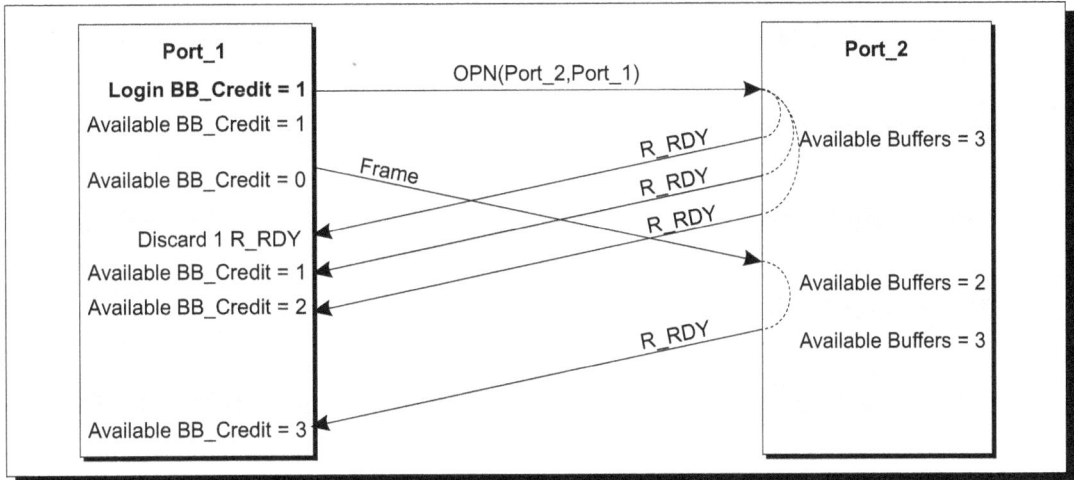

Figure 51. Remembered BB_Credit Less Than Login Credit

is closed, the receiving port cannot send R_RDYs as it empties its receive buffers because a new loop circuit between other ports may have been established by then and the R_RDYs would interfere with the new loop circuit (R_RDYs do not carry any address information and, therefore, cannot be associated with a specific port or operation).

8.3 Chapter Summary

Flow Control

- Two types of flow control credit
  - Link level called Buffer-to-Buffer flow control (uses BB_Credit)
  - Source to destination flow control called End-to-End flow control (uses EE_Credit)
- Both used to pace the transmission of frames
  - Prevents a transmitter from overrunning the receiver's buffers
- A Port must have permission before it can send frames
  - That permission is called available credit

Credit

- Buffer-to-Buffer credit is granted during:
  - Fabric login (FLOGI) with an F_Port / FL_Port
  - Port login (PLOGI) with other N_Ports (Point-to-Point only)
  - Port login (PLOGI) with other NL_Ports on the same loop
- End-to-End credit granted during PLOGI
- Each frame sent decrements the corresponding available credit(s)
  - When the applicable available credit is zero, no frames can be sent
- Responses replenish the available credit allowing additional frames to be sent

Buffer-to-Buffer Credit

- Buffer-to-buffer flow control paces frame transmission on a link
- Each frame sent decrements the available BB_Credit value
- Each R_RDY received increments the available BB_Credit value
- BB_Credit is used for:
  - Class-1 connect frame (SOFc1)
  - Class-2
  - Class-3

BB_Credit Assumptions

- FC-PH assumes that the same port is always at the end of each link
  - A single Login BB_Credit is received
  - A single available BB_Credit count is used
- For each frame sent, one R_RDY is received
- The number of frames sent and R_RDYs received always balance over time
- The number of available buffers at the receive end of the link is always known
  - This port is the only consumer of those buffers

BB_Credit on the Loop

- BB_Credit operates differently on the loop
- Loop circuits look like dynamic 'point-to-point' connections
  - During each loop circuit, a port may be connected to a different destination
  - Each destination has its own set of receive buffers
  - The state of the receive buffers prior to opening a loop circuit is unknown
- This is different than point-to-point and fabric
  - Led to development of the 'Alternate BB_Credit Model'

Login BB_Credit

- When a port grants a Login BB_Credit value it is granting permission to send frames
  - Permission is granted in advance by login
  - Called look-ahead flow control
- The port guarantees it has that many receive buffers available
  - In point-to-point and fabric this also represents the initial available credit value
- In Arbitrated Loop, the Login BB_Credit value represents the credit available at each open
  - Regardless of previous activity, the port guarantees to have that many buffers available

---

Login BB_Credit Values

- In point-to-point and fabric a single login BB_Credit value is used
- In Arbitrated Loop, multiple login BB_Credit values are required
  - One for each logged-in NL_Port (potentially up to 125 other NL_Ports)
  - One for the FL_Port
- When a loop circuit is established, the login BB_Credit value for that port is used to
  - Initialize the available BB_Credit credit count
  - Which controls frame transmission
- This significantly complicates the design

Zero Login BB_Credit

- Some designs wanted a simpler approach
  - Maintaining 126 login BB_Credit values is not simple
  - Guaranteeing buffer availability is not easy
- Led to the Alternate BB_Credit model
  - Allows a single available BB_Credit counter
  - Allows a port to grant zero login BB_Credit
  - Allows a port to assume the login BB_Credit is zero
  - Ports signal the number of available buffers at OPN time with R_RDYs
  - Zero BB_Credit incurs a delay because a frame can't be sent until R_RDY is received

Nonzero Login BB_Credit

- High-performance designs want to avoid the delay waiting for an R_RDY
- Use a nonzero login BB_Credit value by:
  - Storing the login BB_Credit granted by each port
  - Using a single bit per port that indicates a login BB_Credit value of at least 1
- This allows frame transmission to begin immediately after each OPN
  - Based on the login BB_Credit
  - Saves latency on the loop and improves performance

Mixing the Two Approaches

- Some ports on the loop may implement zero login BB_Credit
  - Grant zero login BB_Credit, and/or
  - Assume zero login BB_Credit, even if the other port granted a nonzero value
- Others may implement nonzero login BB_Credit
  - Grant login BB_Credit greater than zero
  - Remember login BB_Credit granted by other ports
- The two approaches need to interoperate with each other

Advising Credit with R_RDY

- When the loop circuit is opened, each port notifies the other of the availability of receive buffers
- Sends one R_RDY for each available buffer
  - Port doesn't know if the other port stored the login BB_Credit or not
  - If the other port doesn't store login BB_Credit, it can't send frames until an R_RDY is received, even if login BB_Credit was granted
- If no receive buffers are available, a port sends an immediate CLS
  - Only allowed for those ports that granted zero login BB_Credit

R_RDY Management

- Ports that store nonzero login BB_Credit values
  - Set the available BB_Credit from the stored login BB_Credit
  - May begin frame transmission based on available credit
- The other port is sending R_RDYs advising the number of receive buffers
  - The R_RDYs and frames pass in the loop
- To avoid double-crediting,
  - A port must discard R_RDYs until the number discarded equals the login BB_Credit value used

---

Unbalanced BB_Credit

- Close the loop circuit as soon as frame transmission is complete
  - Don't wait for the R_RDYs
  - No wasted time on the loop
- Once CLS is sent, outstanding R_RDYs are not transmitted
  - A new loop circuit may already be established
  - The R_RDYs would interfere with that circuit
- Available BB_Credit is set to zero when the loop is closed
  - It will be re-established on the next loop circuit

Guaranteeing BB_Credit

- Providing a Login BB_Credit value greater than zero is not easy
- Here are some approaches:
- Have more receive buffers available than granted during login
  - Withold R_RDYs as needed to ensure the buffers are available
- Use a design which empties receive buffers at the link rate
  - The link can never overrun the available buffers
- Delay closing the loop until the required number of buffers are available
  - Potential performance impact at closing time

End-to-End Credit

- Used for Classes 1, 2, and 4
  - Doesn't apply when ACK-0 is used
- EE_Credit does not apply to Class-3
- Functions the same in all topologies
- For each logged in N*_Port, whether on or off the loop
  - One login EE_Credit value
  - One available EE_Credit value

Lost Credit Recovery

- Lost BB_Credit is recovered automatically on the loop
  - Whenever a loop circuit is opened
  - Available BB_Credit is set to Login BB_Credit
  - Dynamic R_RDY signalling indicates additional buffers
- Lost EE_Credit recovered by normal mechanisms
  - History bit in ACK recovers lost ACKs
- Spurious R_RDYs may cause frame loss due to lack of receive buffer

9.   Opening a Loop Circuit

After a loop port has successfully won arbitration, it must select a destination port prior to sending frames to that port. This selection process is called *opening* the destination port and it uses one of the open (OPN) primitive signals. There are two types of opens, open point-to-point and open replicate. The two types use a total of four different ordered sets defined by the Arbitrated Loop standard (see Table 6 on page 51 for a definition of the OPN ordered sets).

Open point-to-point uses the OPN(yx) or OPN(yy) primitive signal (referred to generically as OPNy) to establish a logical point-to-point like circuit between a pair of loop ports. In this mode, frames may be sent and received between the two loop ports, while all other loop ports on the loop are acting as repeaters for all non-fill words. The receiving loop port removes all frames and selected ordered sets received from the loop. Point-to-point mode provides support for normal port-to-port communications.

Open replicate uses the OPN(yr) or OPN(fr) ordered set (referred to generically as OPN(r)) to condition one or more loop ports for frame reception. However, in replicate mode, received frames and ordered sets are not removed from the loop, but instead are replicated and sent around the loop until they reach the original sending loop port which removes them from the loop. Replicate mode supports multicast (information sent to multiple loop ports) and broadcast (information sent to all loop ports) operations.

An OPN ordered set (regardless of its form) must be preceded and followed by a minimum of two fill words. Because the arbitration winner had been sending ARB(x) prior to winning arbitration (and ARB(x) is a fill word), it sends OPN immediately upon winning arbitration.

9.1 Open Point-to-Point (OPNy)

A loop port that wins arbitration and wishes to establish a logical point-to-point circuit sends an OPNy (this loop port is called the open originator) and enters the Open state. The loop port that receives the OPNy (called the open recipient) enters the Opened state completing the logical circuit. All other ports on the loop are in either the Monitoring or Arbitrating states and acting as repeaters for all non-fill words.

The two forms of the OPNy allow the open originator to signal the open recipient whether the loop circuit is full-duplex or half-duplex.

9.1.1 Full-Duplex Open - OPN(yx)

The full-duplex OPN(yx) is used when the open originator wishes to begin two-way frame transmission with the open recipient. Full-duplex operation allows both loop ports to transmit frames simultaneously. This provides maximum utilization of the loop's bandwidth because the total information flow can equal twice the link bandwidth.

The open originator sets its available BB_Credit to the login BB_Credit value that it is using for the open recipient (which may be zero). If Class-1 or Class-2 is being used, the available EE_Credit value is restored from the saved value for the open recipient. If the applicable credit values allow, the open originator may begin sending frames as soon as two fill words have been sent following transmission of the OPN(yx). If the available BB_Credit value is zero (i.e., the login BB_Credit value used was zero), the open originator must wait for one or more R_RDYs from the open recipient before beginning frame transmission.

When the open recipient receives the OPN(yx), it sets its available BB_Credit to zero and transmits frames based on received R_RDYs only. If Class-1 or Class-2 is being used, the available EE_Credit value is restored from the saved value for the open originator. Once the available credit is non zero, the open recipient may begin sending frames.

There is no need to wait for confirmation that the OPN was received. In fact, there is no direct confirmation that the open recipient did in fact recognize the OPN and enter the Opened state. This can only be determined after the fact, although receipt of the OPN can be inferred if the open originator receives one or more R_RDYs. Allowing frame transmission to begin without requiring confirmation from the open recipient improves the performance of the loop. If the open originator had to wait for a response from the open recipient, it would add a minimum of one loop's delay to each open (the time for the OPN to reach the destination loop port plus the time for the response to be returned).

The opening process is logically equivalent to the SCSI bus selection or reselection process in that the pair of ports are conditioned to send and receive frames with each other. An example of a full-duplex open and subsequent frame transmission is shown in Figure 52 on page 153.

9.1.2 Half-Duplex Open - OPN(yy)

OPN(yy) is the half-duplex form of the OPNy and is used when the open originator wishes to send frames to the open recipient while preventing the open recipient from sending any FC-4 device data frames (link control frames such as Acknowledge, Busy, or Reject are allowed for the appropriate class of service).

The half-duplex open is used in those cases where the open originator is not able to support a full-duplex operation. Some implementations may not be capable of supporting sending and receiving FC-4 device data frames at the same time. Supporting only half-duplex operation offers one path to simplifying the design, although with a potential sacrifice in performance.

The open originator that sends a half-duplex open followed by Class-1 or Class-2 frames needs to send R_RDYs after the OPN to allow the open recipient to respond with link control frames for the class of service.

9.2 Open Replicate (OPNr)

Replicate mode is used to implement a dynamic multicast and broadcast capabilities in an Arbitrated Loop environment.

A loop port that wins arbitration and wishes to create a multicast or broadcast environment, transmits one of the OPNr primitive signals (this loop port is called the open originator) and enters the Open state. The two open replicate ordered sets cause the recipient loop port to set

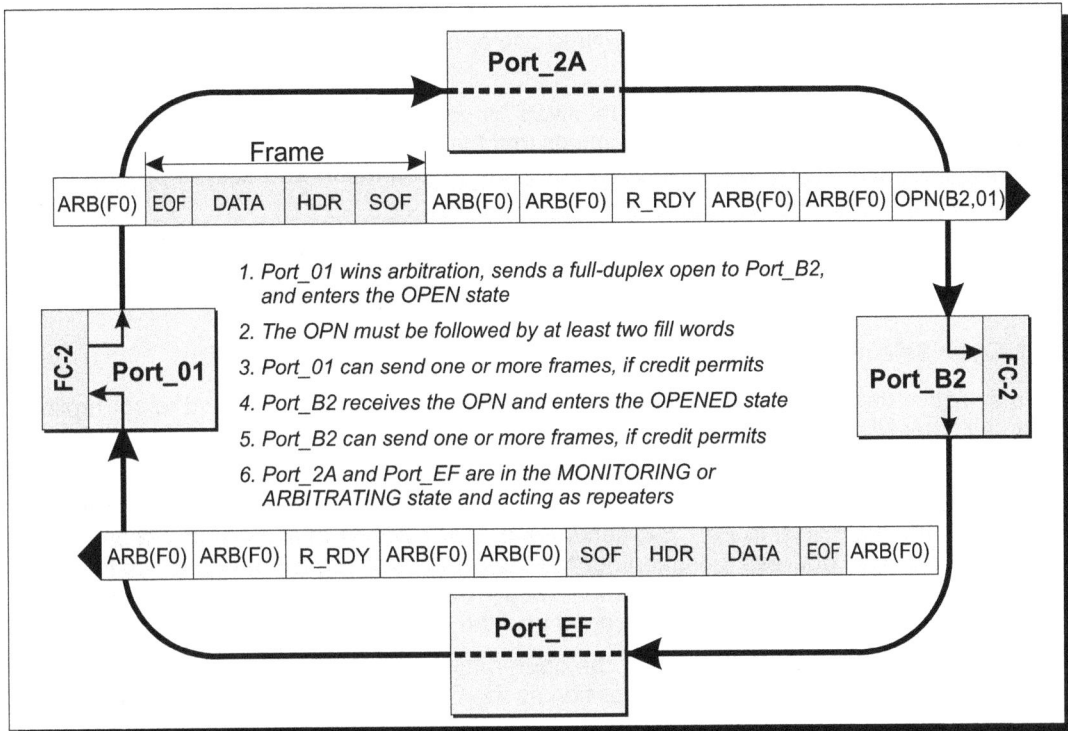

Figure 52. Full-Duplex Open (OPN(yx))

replicate mode. When replicate mode is set, the loop port replicates (retransmits) received information on its transmit output and processes received frames if the loop port recognizes the destination address in the frame header (destination address processing is done at the FC-2 level, the LPSM just delivers the frame). All received information is replicated with the possible exception of received fill words.

Replicate mode is not a state in the LPSM, but rather a mode of operation in the Monitoring and Arbitrating states. The open recipient sets replicate mode upon receipt of an appropriate Open Replicate (OPN(yr) or OPN(fr)) ordered set and resets it when a CLS is received.

If the loop port is in the Arbitrating state and replicate mode is set, it continues to arbitrate and perform normal fill word substitution.

Only the open originator may originate frames in replicate mode. Frame delivery is restricted to Class-3 service without buffer-to-buffer or end-to-end flow control. No confirmation of delivery nor notification of nondelivery is possible in the current loop circuit because the transmit function of each loop port with replicate mode set is dedicated to replicating the received data. Loop ports with replicate mode set are not permitted to originate R_RDYs for flow control purposes. It is the responsibility of the sending port to pace the frame transmission appropriately.

The FL_Port cannot be opened in replicate mode and replicated frames are never passed into the Fabric. The FL_Port may transmit OPNr to one or more NL_Ports on the loop to communicate with multiple ports.

NL_Ports with replicate mode set pass received frames to the loop port's FC-2 level function for possible processing. If the FC-2 determines that the destination address in the frame header is one that it recognizes (i.e., its native or an alias destination address), it processes the frame, otherwise the frame is ignored by that loop port.

Because frames and transmission words (other than fill words) are not removed from the loop by NL_Ports with replicate mode set, they ultimately arrive back at the open originator which is in the Open state and consequently removes all transmission words.

9.2.1 Open Selective Replicate - OPN(yr)

Open selective replicate causes the loop port designated by the AL_PD field to set replicate mode. All other NL_Ports ignore and retransmit the OPN(yr).

Multiple OPN(yr) ordered sets can be issued by the open originator during a single loop tenancy. The open originator could issue an OPN(yr) to Port_EF, send one or more frames to Port_EF, issue an OPN(yr) to Port_B2, send one or more frames to either Port_B2 or Port_EF by using their native address identifiers, or to both ports by addressing the frames to a common alias recognized by both ports (e.g., x'FF FF FF', the well-known broadcast address). Additional NL_Ports could be selectively opened until the group was as large as desired.

When frame transmission is completed, the open originator sends a CLS which causes each NL_Port to reset replicate mode in succession as the CLS is replicated around the loop.

9.2.2 Open Broadcast Replicate - OPN(fr)

The open broadcast replicate causes all NL_Ports on the loop to set replicate mode. This is a convenient way of conditioning all NL_Ports on the loop to examine any received frames and process them if they recognize the destination address in the frame header.

9.2.3 Use of Alias Addresses

The real potential of replicate mode is realized when the ports support an alias address. In addition to the normal 24-bit native address identifier recognized by a loop port, the alias address provides an alternate address also recognized as valid by that loop port. Alias addressing allows one or more ports opened in replicate mode to receive and process the same frames. By defining a common alias address and sending frames to that alias address, the open originator can broadcast or multicast information to multiple ports.

9.2.4 Example of Replicate Operation

Figure 53 on page 155 illustrates the use of open replicate. Assume that Port_01 wins arbitration and all NL_Ports on the loop recognize a common 24-bit alias address in addition to their native 24-bit address identifier in the Destination_ID (D_ID) field of the frame header.

Port_01 begins by transmitting OPN(yr) to Port_EF. Port_EF sets replicate mode and retransmits the OPNr which is returned to the open originator (Port_01). After transmitting a minimum

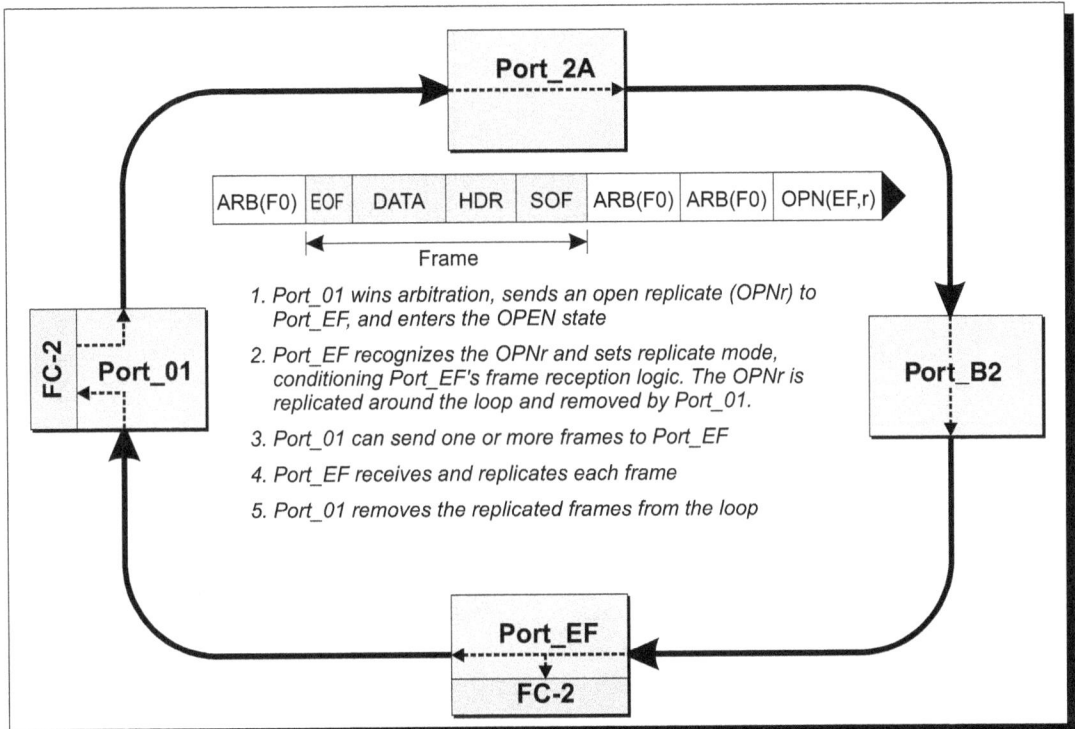

Figure 53. Open Replicate (OPNr), Part 1

The figure contains a frame sequence: ARB(F0) | EOF | DATA | HDR | SOF | ARB(F0) | ARB(F0) | OPN(EF,r) with "Frame" spanning DATA-HDR-SOF.

1. Port_01 wins arbitration, sends an open replicate (OPNr) to Port_EF, and enters the OPEN state

2. Port_EF recognizes the OPNr and sets replicate mode, conditioning Port_EF's frame reception logic. The OPNr is replicated around the loop and removed by Port_01.

3. Port_01 can send one or more frames to Port_EF

4. Port_EF receives and replicates each frame

5. Port_01 removes the replicated frames from the loop

of two fill words following the OPNr, Port_01 can send one or more frames to Port_EF using either Port_EF's native address identifier or an alias address identifier recognized by Port_EF.

The replicate operation continues in Figure 54 on page 156 with Port_01 sending an OPN(yr) to Port_B2 causing Port_B2 to also set replicate mode. At this point, both Port_B2 and Port_EF have replicate mode set and their frame reception logic enabled. Port_01 can now send frames to Port_B2 by using Port_B2's native address identifier, to Port_EF by using Port_EF's native address identifier, or both ports by using a common alias address identifier.

Frames transmitted while in this mode flow around the loop until they arrive at Port_01 (the open originator) which discards them. When Port_01 is finished with frame transmission, it transmits CLS and enters the Transmitted Close or Transfer state. The CLS causes each loop port on the loop to reset replicate mode as the CLS propagates around the loop. When the CLS arrives at Port_01, it causes Port_01 to go from the Transmitted Close state to the Monitoring state, or from the Transfer state to the Open state.

9.2.5 Applications of Replicate Mode

Two obvious applications of replicate mode present themselves when the Arbitrated Loop is considered for use as a high-speed network. Many existing network protocols rely on multicast

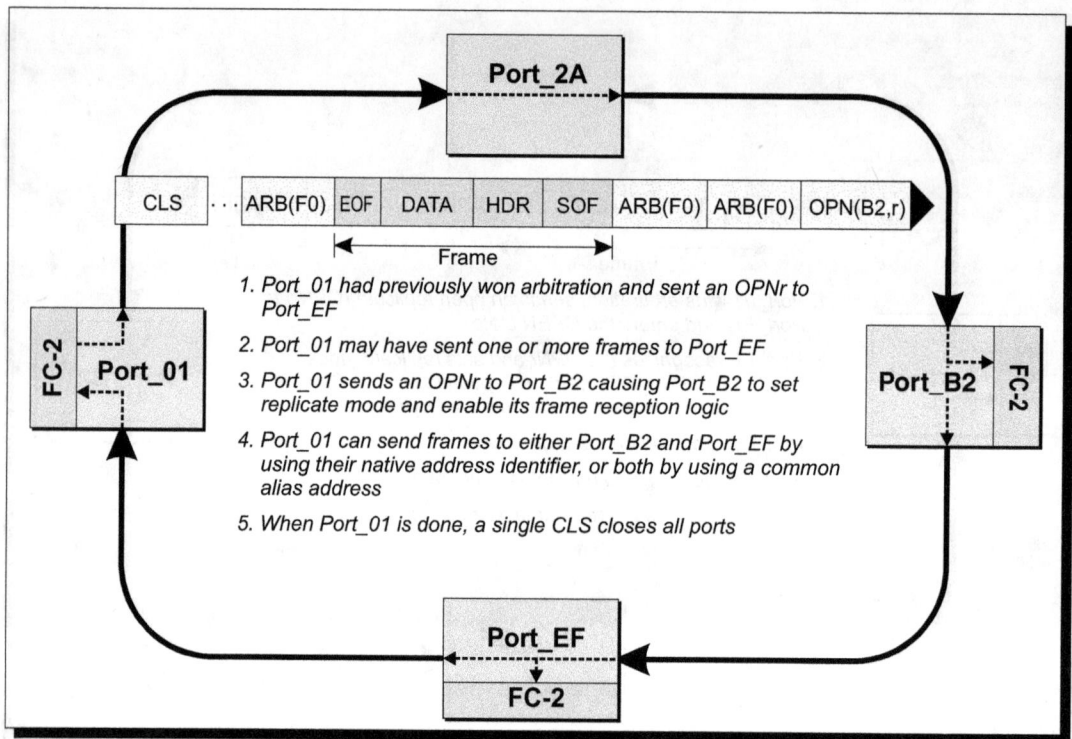

```
                        ┌──────────────┐
                        │   Port_2A    │
                        └──────────────┘

┌─────┐     ┌──────┬────┬──────┬─────┬─────┬───────┬───────┬──────────┐
│ CLS │ ··· │ARB(F0)│EOF│ DATA │ HDR │ SOF │ARB(F0)│ARB(F0)│ OPN(B2,r)│
└─────┘     └──────┴────┴──────┴─────┴─────┴───────┴───────┴──────────┘
                        |◄─── Frame ───►|
```

1. *Port_01 had previously won arbitration and sent an OPNr to Port_EF*

2. *Port_01 may have sent one or more frames to Port_EF*

3. *Port_01 sends an OPNr to Port_B2 causing Port_B2 to set replicate mode and enable its frame reception logic*

4. *Port_01 can send frames to either Port_B2 and Port_EF by using their native address identifier, or both by using a common alias address*

5. *When Port_01 is done, a single CLS closes all ports*

Figure 54. Open Replicate (OPNr), Part 2

or broadcast capabilities which can be provided on the loop by using replicate mode. The selective replicate operation is a dynamic operation (i.e., no login to the multicast server at well-known address x'FF FF F5' is needed) on the loop; it allows the open originator to dynamically select the recipient(s).

Other, less apparent applications for replicate mode also exist.

One proposed application consists of a number of distributed database query servers located on the loop. The loop port initiating the database query uses the OPN(yr) to set replicate mode in the desired subset of query servers. The query itself is then multicast to the open ports using a common alias address identifier. Once the query has been sent, the loop is closed and each server processes the query against its portion of the database. When each has completed its query processing, each arbitrates for the loop and reports the results of its portion of the query. By multicasting the query, the operation is more efficient than would be the case if the query were sent individually to each query server one loop circuit at a time.

Another potential application is disk mirroring. The file server uses the OPN(yr) to set replicate mode in the two disk devices which are mirrors. The write command and associated data are sent to a common alias address identifier recognized by both disks. Following transmission of the data, the open originator closes the loop. As each disk completes the write, each arbitrates for the loop and returns its command status.

Open replicate offers the potential to implement new applications that are not possible with traditional storage interfaces such as the SCSI parallel bus. Because this is a radical departure from normal SCSI operations, it may take some time for these applications to fully develop.

Open Replicate Failure. If an NL_Port wins arbitration and replicate mode is still active (i.e., the open originator which placed the loop port(s) into replicate mode disappeared from the loop before it could transmit CLS), several loop ports may be replicating frames. Of course frames that are not recognized by a loop port which has replicate mode active, are discarded and only the frames which the two ports of the loop circuit are transmitting are received by each loop port respectively. Eventually, when one of these loop ports transmits CLS, the replicate mode will be reset by all loopports.

9.3 Selecting the Destination Port

Before a loop port can send an open, it must determine the correct AL_PA to use in the OPN ordered set. The principal decision that must be made is whether the intended destination port is on the same loop as the open originator or is external to the loop (i.e., it must be accessed via the fabric).

Three simple tests will determine if the destination port is on the same loop:

- If the upper 16 bits of the destination address field (D_ID) in the frame header are all zeros, the destination port is a private port and must be on the same loop.
- If the upper 16 bits of the source address field (S_ID) in the frame header are all zeros, the source port is a private port and can only communicate with other ports on the same loop.
- If the upper 16 bits of the destination address field (D_ID) in the frame header are the same as the upper 16 bits of the source address field (S_ID) in the frame header, either both ports are private and therefore must be on the same loop, or both ports are public and attached to the same FL_Port.

If none of these conditions are true, the destination port is not on the same loop and must be accessed via the FL_Port.

9.3.1 Opening a Port on the Same Loop

To open a loop port on the same loop, the open originator inserts the AL_PD of the intended destination loop port in the AL_PD field of the OPN. The AL_PD is obtained from the low-order 8 bits of the destination address in the frame header. Other than selecting the type of OPN desired (half-duplex, full-duplex, open replicate or not), this processing may be done entirely by hardware for performance reasons.

9.3.2 Opening a Port off the Loop

To send frames to a port that is not on the same loop, the open originator inserts the AL_PD of the FL_Port (x'00') in the AL_PD field of the OPN. The FL_Port is opened, frames are sent to the FL_Port, and the fabric forwards them to their ultimate destination using the destination address field in the frame header.

While the open originator has the FL_Port open, it can send frames to multiple destination ports located off the loop and accessible via the FL_Port. Except when in replicate mode, this is the only time that a loop port can multiplex frames being sent to multiple destination ports.

9.3.3 FL_Port Open Behavior

When the FL_Port receives a frame delivered to it by the fabric, it verifies that the upper 16 bits of the destination address identifier (D_ID) in the frame header match the upper 16 bits of the FL_Port's address (if not the same, the frame has been misrouted). The FL_Port arbitrates for access to the loop, and, upon winning arbitration opens the destination NL_Port. The AL_PD field of the OPN is set to the lower 8 bits of the destination address field (D_ID) of the frame header. Once the appropriate OPN has been sent, the FL_Port may send one or more frames to the loop port based on available credit.

9.4 Open Failures

If a loop port is not opened prior to frame transmission, frames simply circle the loop. Ports that are in the Monitoring or Arbitrating states only look for loop-specific ordered sets and are not aware that frames may be retransmitted (unless replicate mode is set).

It is possible for frame transmission to begin without the intended destination loop port being open. This could occur if the open recipient fails to recognize the OPN (it has been bypassed or removed from the loop), or the OPN is corrupted by a link error prior to reaching the open recipient.

If the OPN travels around the loop and returns to the open originator, the open originator may detect the received OPN and report an error at that time. However, the LPSM as described in the Arbitrated Loop standard does not require checking for this condition and waits for subsequent actions to detect the error.

When frame transmission takes place following the failed OPN, any frames that were sent circle the loop, and ultimately return to the open originator. When the loop port examines the Destination_ID field in the frame header, it detects that the frame has been delivered to the wrong destination. At this point, there are three possible courses of action that the loop port can take:

1. Examine the Source_ID field of the frame header to determine that it sent the frame and if so, it discards the frame.

2. If operating in Class-1 or Class-2, blindly send a Port_Reject with a reason code of *invalid Destination_ID*. This action is identical to the behavior that would be followed if the port were operating in a fabric environment and received a misrouted frame. The Port_Reject travels around the loop and is received by the open originator (i.e., the port sends a Port_Reject to itself). However, no response is generated for this frame.

3. If operating in Class-3, the frame is discarded without notification and the sequence eventually times out causing error recovery to be invoked.

Regardless of which action is taken, the error condition is detected and the appropriate error recovery process can be initiated. Note that as a result of this error, a configuration change has been detected. Because the loop port still owns the loop, this would be a good time to initialize the loop to inform all other loop ports of the configuration change.

9.5 Open State

The Open state is entered after the LPSM has arbitrated, won arbitration, and transmitted one of the OPN primitive signals. The LPSM sets the ARB_Won variable to indicate that this loop port won arbitration and is the current owner of the loop. ARB_Won is used later in the Transmitted Close and Received Close states to control the propagation of received ARB(x) ordered sets and manage the access fairness protocol. If the loop port is observing access fairness, the Access variable is reset to prevent the loop port from arbitrating in the future until the access fairness window has ended. If the loop port is not observing Access fairness, the Access variable remains set allowing the loop port to arbitrate after the current loop circuit without waiting for the end of the access fairness window.

The Open state conditions the loop port to begin frame transmission and, potentially, frame reception. Frame reception may occur unless prevented by either of the following conditions:

- Credit is withheld preventing the open recipient from sending any frames
- A half-duplex OPN(yy) was sent and operations are restricted to Class-3 only

If an OPNy was sent, the open recipient enters the Opened state, prepares for frame reception, and optionally, frame transmission. If an OPNr was sent, the open recipient sets replicate mode and prepares for frame reception only.

Public loops introduce the possibility that the destination port is not located on the same loop. If this is the case, the FL_Port is opened and frames are sent via the FL_Port and fabric to the ultimate destination. The decision to open the FL_Port rather than an NL_Port is based upon the 16 most significant bits of the Destination_ID field in the frame header (see *Selecting the Destination Port* on page 157).

While a loop circuit is open, Class-1, Class-2, and Class-3 operations are allowed. If Class-1 is used, the Class-1 connection must end before the loop circuit is closed. There is no requirement to wait for outstanding ACKs in Class-2 prior to closing the loop circuit—they can be sent during a subsequent loop circuit. Class-1 and Class-2 operations use normal end-to-end flow control as defined by FC-PH with all frame transmission subject to the availability of EE_Credit. Frame transmission in Class-2, Class-3, and the SOFC1 frame in Class-1 is subject to buffer-to-buffer flow control.

9.5.1 Entry Actions and Flow Control

Following transmission of the OPN, the open originator sends at least 6 fill words (or 5 fill words and one R_RDY) before transmitting the first frame. The loop port transmits one R_RDY for each frame that it is willing to receive. If using Class 3 with a half-duplex open, no R_RDYs are required; in all other cases, at least one R_RDY must be sent for each frame to allow the recipient to return link control frames.

Placement of the R_RDY follows normal FC-PH requirements in that each R_RDY must be preceded and followed by at least two fill words. For example, a loop port willing to receive a single frame can send any of the following ordered set sequences after the OPN:

- CFW, CFW, **R_RDY**, CFW, CFW, CFW, ... FRAME
- CFW, CFW, CFW, **R_RDY**, CFW, CFW, ... FRAME
- CFW, CFW, CFW, CFW, CFW, CFW, ... FRAME, CFW, CFW, **R_RDY**, CFW, CFW, etc.

Once the six initial words (which may include an R_RDY) are sent, frame transmission can begin subject to the applicable buffer-to-buffer and end-to-end flow control mechanisms. The alternate BB_Credit management model is used to manage buffer-to-buffer flow control on an Arbitrated Loop. This model states that the login BB_Credit (which may be zero) is used to set the available BB_Credit for the open originator of every loop circuit and that a loop port will transmit one R_RDY for each frame it is willing to receive. A loop port may choose to use any value between zero and the actual value granted during the login process for the login BB_Credit. Details of the alternate BB_Credit management model are described in *Buffer-to-Buffer Flow Control* on page 136.

If the available BB_Credit is greater than zero, frame transmission can begin immediately after the initial six words have been sent. If the available BB_Credit is zero, the loop port must wait until one or more R_RDYs have been received before beginning frame transmission. Some implementations may choose to remember a login BB_Credit of zero for all destination ports and wait for one or more R_RDYs to be received prior to beginning frame transmission to simplify their designs (although this behavior has an adverse effect on loop performance).

9.5.2 Arbitration and Access Fairness

In the Open state, the LPSM is responsible for managing arbitration and access fairness.

To prevent other ports from winning arbitration, all received ARB(x) ordered sets are discarded *(line 13: 'ARB(x)', on page 332)*. This prevents other arbitrating ports from winning arbitration because they do not receive their ARB(x).

The LPSM initially uses ARB(F0) as its current fill word (set upon entry to the Open state). If any other port is arbitrating, that port replaces the ARB(F0) with its own ARB(x). If no ports are arbitrating, the ARB(F0) circles the loop and is received by the port in the Open state. This marks the end of the access fairness window. The LPSM changes its current fill word to IDLE *(line 12: 'ARB(F0)', on page 332)*. IDLE is the signal to all ports that a new access fairness window has begun. Fair ports set their Access variable allowing them to begin arbitrating, if access to the loop is required.

9.5.3 Closing the Loop Circuit

If a CLS is received *(line 16: 'CLS', on page 332)*, the LPSM enters the Received Close state.

If the L_Port control REQ(close) is active *(line 29: 'REQ(close)', on page 333)*, a CLS is sent at the next appropriate fill word and the LPSM enters the Transmitted Close state. The next appropriate fill word may not be the next fill word transmitted due to the requirement to follow a frame or an R_RDY with at least two fill words. Transmission of the CLS while a Class-1 connection is active is described in *Class-1 Operations* on page 161.

The loop port may decide to close the loop circuit for a number of reasons. The most common is that there are no more frames to be sent to the current destination loop port. Either all of the frames have been sent or the loop port's transmit buffers are empty and need to be refilled before further frame transmission can occur. See *Frame Transmission* on page 183 for additional information on loop circuit operations during frame transmission.

The loop port may also close the loop because it needs to open another loop port (see *Transfer* on page 161), is making the transition to the nonparticipating mode, or the loop port has detected that another loop port is arbitrating and is closing the current loop circuit to allow the other loop port access to the loop.

9.5.4 Class-1 Operations

If a Class-1 connection exists, the loop port is responsible for removing the Class-1 connection prior to transmitting the CLS. The connection is considered removed upon receipt of a frame with an EOFdt or EOFdti end-of-frame delimiter and only the loop port that receives these EOF delimiters may transmit the CLS.

9.5.5 Processing MRK(tx)

The MRK(tx) is not retransmitted by the LPSM in this state (the loop port may request the LPSM to transmit a MRK(tx) which looks like the received MRK(tx). MRK(tx) is examined to see if it should be acted upon. If a MRK(tx) is received and the MK_TP and AL_PS match expected values, the action identified is performed (not shown on the state table).

If the REQ(mark as tx) input is active *(line 35: 'REQ(mark as tx)', on page 333)*, the LPSM transmits a single MRK(tx) at the next appropriate fill word unless the REQ(mark as tx) input is removed before the MRK(tx) is transmitted.

9.5.6 Replicate Mode

If Replicate is true, the only transmission words processed are IDLE, ARB(F0), CLS and any primitive sequence. All other transmission words, including received frames are discarded (the loop port in the Open state removes all transmission words from the loop).

If replicate mode is set and REQ(open yr) is active *(line 28: 'REQ(open yr)', on page 333)*, the LPSM transmits one selective open replicate (OPN(yr)) at the next appropriate fill word. If the loop port wishes to transmit additional OPN(yr) signals, it must deassert, then reassert the REQ(open yr) control input.

9.5.7 Transfer

If the Access variable is set (implying a fair loop port; unfair loop ports ignore Access) and the loop port wishes to end the current loop circuit and establish a new one, it asserts the REQ(transfer) input *(line 31: 'REQ(transfer)', on page 333)* causing the LPSM to transmit a CLS at the next appropriate fill word. Once the CLS is sent, the LPSM enters the Transfer state and waits for a CLS before opening the new loop circuit (see *Using Transfer* on page 179).

9.5.8 Initialization and Loop Bypass

If a loop failure is detected *(line 2: 'Loop Failure', on page 332)* or the loop port requests initialization by asserting the REQ(initialize) input *(line 42: 'REQ(initialize)', on page 334)*, the LPSM enters the Initializing state.

If the LPB(yx) primitive sequence is recognized and 'y' equals the AL_PA of the loop port *(line 20: 'LPB(yx) or LPB(fx)', on page 333)* or REQ(bypass L_Port) is active *(line 36: 'REQ(bypass L_Port)', on page 333)*, the Bypass variable is set and the LPSM enters the Monitoring state.

If the loop port is requesting the transmission of the LPB(yx), LPE(fx), or LPE(yx) primitive sequences *(line 37: 'REQ(bypass L_Port y)', on page 333)*, *(line 41: 'REQ(enable all)', on page 334)*, and *(line 40: 'REQ(enable L_Port y)', on page 334)* respectively, the LPSM will begin transmission of the requested sequence at the next fill word (i.e., not in the middle of a frame) and continue transmission until the sequence has propagated around the loop and is recognized at the receive input of the originating loop port. The loop port is responsible for ensuring that these controls are only asserted when appropriate.

9.5.9 Other Valid Ordered Sets

If any other valid ordered set is received, it is processed in accordance with normal FC-PH rules *(line 22: 'Other Ordered Set', on page 333)*.

9.6 Opened State

The Opened state is entered when a loop port in the Monitoring or Arbitrating states receives an OPNy with the AL_PD field equal to the AL_PA value currently assigned to that loop port. If an OPN(yx) was received, the Duplex variable is set and the loop port is conditioned for full-duplex frame transmission and reception. If OPN(yy) was received, the Duplex variable is reset and the loop port is conditioned for frame reception and link control frame transmission only (e.g., ACKs).

> NOTE – OPN(yy) prevents link control frame transmission in the Opened state until the first frame is received because the identity of the open originator is not known until a frame is received. Normally, this is not a problem because the link control frame is related to the received frame.

Upon receipt of the OPN, the open recipient sends at least 6 fill words (or 5 fill words and an R_RDY) before transmitting the first frame. The loop port transmits one R_RDY for each frame it is willing to receive. If it is not ready to receive frames immediately, it must send a CLS to indicate that it is busy (this is only allowed if the port granted a login BB_Credit of zero).

Placement of the R_RDY follows normal FC-PH requirements in that each R_RDY must be preceded and followed by at least two fill words (in FC-PH, the only fill word is IDLE). For example, a loop port willing to receive a single frame can send any of the following primitive signal sequences after the OPN:

- CFW, CFW, **R_RDY**, CFW, CFW, CFW, ... FRAME
- CFW, CFW, CFW, **R_RDY**, CFW, CFW, ... FRAME
- etc.

Once the six initial fill words (which must include an R_RDY) are sent, frame transmission can begin subject to the applicable buffer-to-buffer and end-to-end flow control mechanisms. The alternate BB_Credit management model is used to manage buffer-to-buffer flow control on an Arbitrated Loop. This model states that the login BB_Credit (which may be zero) is used to set the available BB_Credit for every loop circuit and that a loop port will transmit an R_RDY for each frame it is willing to receive. A loop port in the Opened state must transmit at least as many R_RDYs as the login BB_Credit it granted during the login process. The alternate BB_Credit management model is described in *Buffer-to-Buffer Flow Control* on page 136.

Once available BB_Credit is greater than zero (i.e., the open recipient has received one or more R_RDYs), frame transmission can begin after the initial six fill words have been sent.

9.6.1 Arbitration and Access Fairness

If an ARB(x) is received *(line 13: 'ARB(x)', on page 336)* and 'x' is equal to the AL_PA of this loop port, the ARB(x) is discarded to purge the ARB(x) from the loop (this loop port is currently not arbitrating). This condition should not occur; it implies two arbitration winners or an upstream loop port is using the wrong AL_PA and indicates a protocol error has occurred.

If 'x' is not equal to the AL_PA of this loop port *(line 13: 'ARB(x)', on page 336)*, the current fill word is set to the value of the received ARB(x) which could be an ARB(F0). The LPSM effectively retransmits the other loop port's ARB(x) whenever a fill word is needed. When the loop port receives a frame, it removes the frame from the loop and if the loop port has nothing else to send, the current fill word is transmitted, effectively replacing the frame. This is normal behavior when operating in point-to-point mode.

If IDLE is received *(line 9: 'IDLE', on page 335)*, the current fill word is set to IDLE and the Access variable is set. After transmitting two IDLEs, the LPSM may begin arbitrating once the current circuit is closed. A future version of the standard may allow the open recipient to arbitrate in the Opened, Transmitted Close, or Received Close states (The change would require a modified REQ(arb own AL_PA) line in the state tables like in the Monitoring state *(line 25: 'REQ(arb own AL_PA)', on page 325)*. The modification would be to set ARB_Pend and remain in the current state.) This change would allow the opened port to begin arbitrating early.

9.6.2 Closing the Loop Circuit

If a CLS is received *(line 16: 'CLS', on page 336)*, the LPSM enters the Received Close state.

If the L_Port control REQ(close) is active *(line 29: 'REQ(close)', on page 336)*, a CLS is sent at the next appropriate fill word and the LPSM enters the Transmitted Close state. The next appropriate fill word may not be the next fill word sent due to the requirement to follow a frame or R_RDY with at least two fill words. Transmission of the CLS during Class-1 operations is subject to removal of the Class-1 connection as is described *Class-1 Operations* on page 161.

The loop port may decide to close the loop circuit for a number of reasons. The most common is that there are no more frames to be sent to the current destination loop port. Either all of the frames have been sent or the loop port's transmit buffers are empty and need to be refilled before further frame transmission can occur. See *Frame Transmission* on page 183 for additional information on loop circuit operations during frame transmission.

The loop port may also close the current loop circuit because it wishes to communicate with a different loop port and needs to establish a different loop circuit to do so.

9.6.3 Processing MRK(tx)

If a MRK(tx) is received *(line 18: 'MRK(tx)', on page 336)* and the MK_TP and AL_PS match expected values, the specified action is performed (not shown on the state table). The MRK(tx) is not retransmitted in this state by the LPSM (although a REQ(mark as tx) may originate a MRK(tx) that looks like the one that was received).

If the REQ(mark as tx) input is active *(line 35: 'REQ(mark as tx)', on page 337)*, the LPSM transmits a single MRK(tx) at the next appropriate fill word unless the REQ(mark as tx) input is removed before the MRK(tx) is transmitted.

9.6.4 Initialization and Loop Bypass

If a loop failure is detected *(line 2: 'Loop Failure', on page 335)* or the loop port requests initialization by asserting the REQ(initialize) input *(line 42: 'REQ(initialize)', on page 337)*, the LPSM enters the Initializing state.

If the LPB(yx) primitive sequence is recognized and y equals the AL_PA of the loop port *(line 20: 'LPB(yx) or LPB(fx)', on page 336)* or REQ(bypass L_Port) is active *(line 36: 'REQ(bypass L_Port)', on page 337)*, Bypass is set to true and the LPSM enters the Monitoring state.

9.6.5 Other Valid Ordered Sets

If any other valid ordered set is received, it is processed in accordance with normal FC-PH rules *(line 22: 'Other Ordered Set', on page 336)*.

9.7 Chapter Summary

Open Point-to-Point Protocol (OPNy)

- The port that wins arbitration and sends an OPNy enters the Open state
  - Prepares the port for frame transmission and reception
- The port that receives the OPNy enters the Opened state
  - Prepares the port for frame reception and transmission
- Now have a loop circuit between the ports
- Other ports are in the Monitoring or Arbitrating states and act as repeaters

Full/Half-Duplex OPNy

- Open can be full-duplex or half-duplex
- Full-duplex allows both data frame transmission and reception
  - Uses the OPN(yx) ordered set
- Half-duplex restricts open recipient to transmitting Link Control frames only
  - Uses the OPN(yy) ordered set
  - Cannot transmit device data frames
  - Used by designs that can't support simultaneous device data frame transmission and reception

Selecting the Destination Port

- The AL_PA for the OPNy can be determined from the frame header
- If the port is on the same loop, the AL_PA specified by the lower 8 bits of the destination address is opened
  - If the upper 16 bits of the source address are equal to x'0000', or
  - If the upper 16 bits of the destination address are equal to x'0000', or
  - The upper 16 bits of the destination and source addresses are equal
- Otherwise, the FL_Port at AL_PA x'00' is opened

Arbitrating While Opened

- The open recipient may arbitrate while opened
- May have been arbitrating prior to being opened
  - Current circuit doesn't satisfy the port's needs
  - If port is satisfied, can stop arbitrating when opened
- May start arbitrating while opened
  - Just as any other port may start arbitrating
- Ensures the opened port has fair access to the loop

Open Failures

- Errors may cause the open to fail
  - OPN ordered set is corrupted
  - Invalid destination AL_PA used
  - Destination loop port is not functional
- OPNy may circle the loop and be received by the sender
- Frames may also circle the loop and be received by the sending loop port
  - If so, the D_ID in the frame header is incorrect
  - The loop port can check the S_ID to determine if it sent the frame
  - Or, send a P_RJT to itself (except Class-3)

Open Failure Recovery

- What indicates an possible OPN failure?
  - No R_RDY, CLS, or own OPN received
- What action to take?
  - Send OPN again? Won't stimulate Opened port to send R_RDYs
  - Send CLS? If no port Opened, get own CLS back. If other port opened, starts normal close
  - Send LIP? Only as a last recourse!

10. Closing the Loop Circuit

When a port involved in a loop circuit completes its transmission of frames, does not want to receive any more frames, or wishes to communicate with a different port, it may send a CLS to begin the process of closing the current loop circuit. After a port transmits a CLS, it normally enters the Transmitted Close state and waits for the other port in the loop circuit to complete the closing protocol (the open originator may also enter the Transfer state as described in *Using Transfer* on page 169). While in the Transmitted Close or Transfer state, the port is not permitted to send any additional frames or flow control signals (e.g., R_RDY). In effect, the transmit function of its FC-2 is disconnected from the loop.

The port that receives a CLS enters the Received Close state. While in this state, the port can continue to send frames and R_RDYs (R_RDYs are not used for anything by the recipient) to the other port in the Transmitted Close or Transfer state for as long as it has frames to send and the proper credit to do so. Because the port in the Received Close state will not receive any more frames or R_RDYs, it can logically disconnect its FC-2 receive input from the loop.

Either port in the current loop circuit may transmit a CLS when it is ready to close the loop circuit. This may result in both ports sending a CLS and entering the Transmitted Close state simultaneously. The asynchronous nature of the closing protocol requires that the loop state machine be capable of correctly processing a received CLS concurrently with transmitting one.

When a port in the Transmitted Close state receives a CLS, the port closes its half of the loop and enters the Monitoring state if ARB_Pend is not set or the Arbitrating state if ARB_Pend is set. The open initiator may delay entry to the Monitoring state until it has sufficient receive buffers available to satisfy the largest login BB_Credit value that it granted to any other port. The open recipient does not have this option because it is not in control of the loop once the CLS has been sent (even if the open recipient should delay closing its half of the loop, another port may have already won arbitration and be in the process of opening a new loop circuit with this port).

When a port in the Transfer state receives a CLS, it normally sends an OPN (to replace the received CLS) to establish a new loop circuit and enters the Open state which logically reconnects its FC-2 transmit and receive functions to the loop. If the port no longer requires the loop, it may enter the Monitoring state and allow a different port to win arbitration.

When a port in the Received Close state has completed frame transmission, it may send a CLS once it has sufficient receive buffers available to satisfy the largest login BB_Credit value that it granted to any other port. After sending the CLS, the port closes its half of the loop circuit and enters the Monitoring state if ARB_Pend is not set or the Arbitrating state if ARB_Pend is set.

An example of the normal close protocol is shown in Figure 55 on page 168.

1. A loop circuit had been previously established between Port_01 and Port_B2 allowing frame transmission between the two ports.	**Existing Loop Circuit**
1. Port_01 sends a CLS to signal it is done with this circuit and enters the Transmitted Close state. 2. While in the Transmitted Close state Port_01 cannot send any more FC-2 related information (frames, R_RDYs, DHD). 3. Port_B2 receives the close and goes to the Received Close state. 4. Port_B2 may continue to send more frames as long as it has frames to send and credit	**Port_01 Closes**
1. When Port_B2 completes frame transmission or exhausts its credit, it sends a CLS and enters the Monitoring state. The loop circuit is now closed at Port_B2. 2. Port_01 receives the CLS and enters the Monitoring state ending the loop circuit at Port_01. 3. Both ports have returned to the Monitoring state and the loop is idle.	**Port_B2 Closes**

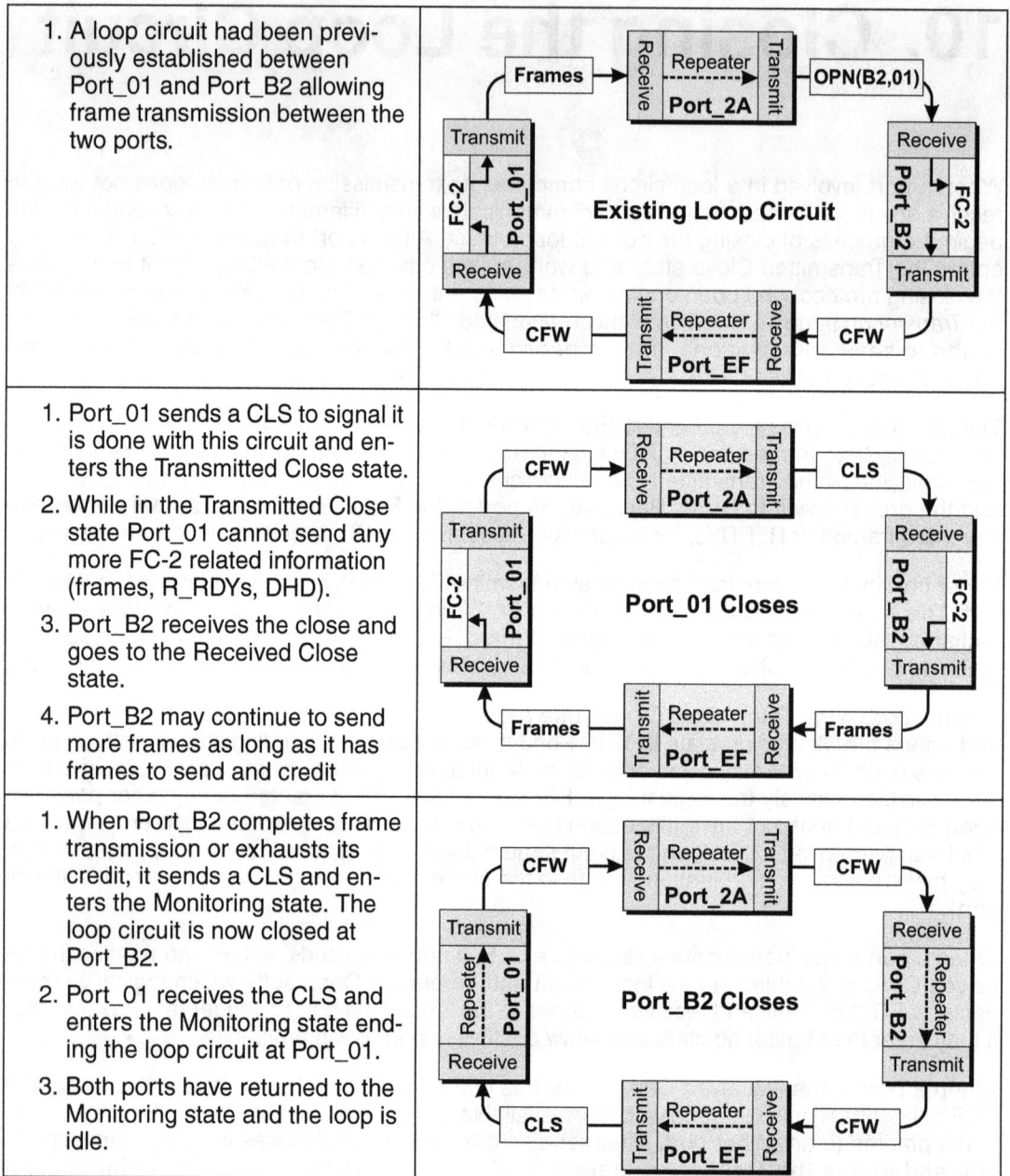

Figure 55. Close Protocol

10.1 Using Dynamic Half Duplex During Close

One of the difficulties that may arise when using full-duplex operation is deciding when to close the loop circuit. In a full-duplex environment, how does either port decide to close the current loop circuit because neither has knowledge of whether the other port has frames to send? Some implementations simply assume that the open originator closes the loop circuit when it no longer has any frames to send to the current open recipient.

This could lead to less than optimal utilization of the loop. Once a port has sent a CLS to begin the closing process it enters the Transmitted Close or Transfer state. If the other port begins sending frames, the port in the Transmitted Close or Transfer state is unable to send R_RDYs or ACKs to replenish BB_Credit and EE_Credit at the other port. The act of sending the CLS has ensured that the loop circuit will have to be closed once the available credit is exhausted.

If the port sends DHD (Dynamic Half Duplex) rather than CLS, it remains in the Open or Opened state, but inhibits device data frame transmission (R_RDYs and ACKs, BSY, and RJT may continue to be sent). DHD provides a signal to the open recipient that the open originator has no more device data frames to transmit during this loop circuit and that normally, the DHD recipient should initiate closing the loop circuit unless it has frames to send.

If the DHD recipient has frames to send, it can send them and still receive R_RDYs or ACKs from the DHD originator. When the DHD recipient has completed frame transmission, it sends a CLS to begin closing the loop circuit. When the DHD originator receives the CLS, it sends CLS and ends the loop circuit.

Use of the DHD does not add significantly to the loop protocol overhead (approximately one word delay). Assume that the open originator sends the DHD to the open recipient. The open recipient completes its frame transmission, sends a CLS, and enters the Transmitted Close state. When the open originator receives the CLS, it enters the Received Close state, trans-mits a CLS of its own, enters the Monitoring state and allows any received ARBs to pass. The ARB(x) of the next port immediately follows the CLS (it may be the next transmission word). When the open recipient receives the CLS, it enters the Monitoring state closing the loop cir-cuit at that port.

It is interesting to note that the next port may receive its own ARB(x) before the CLS is re-ceived by the open recipient. This does not cause a problem because the CLS will be ahead of any activity initiated by the new arbitration winner. An example of the use of DHD is shown in Figure 57 on page 173.

10.2 Using Transfer

The Transfer state enables the arbitration winner to close the current loop circuit at the open recipient to establish a new loop circuit with the same or a different port without relinquishing control of the loop. This allows a port with frames for multiple ports to transmit that traffic with-out incurring the overhead associated with additional arbitration cycles.

Transfer may be used to improve the performance of the FL_Port when forwarding fabric traffic to multiple destinations on the loop. Requiring the FL_Port to re-arbitrate for each destination wastes loop time because the FL_Port would normally win arbitration anyhow as it has the

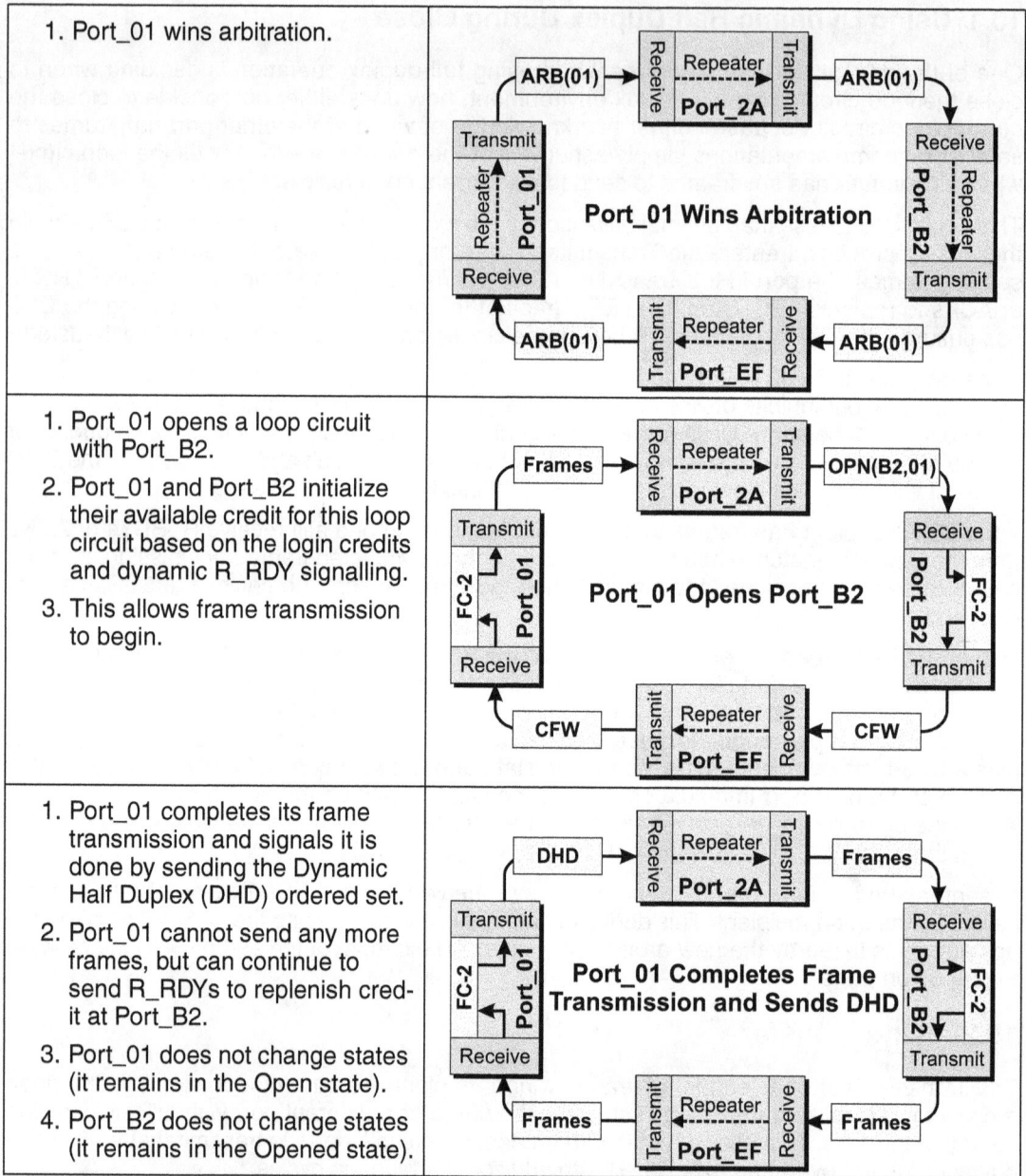

1. Port_01 wins arbitration.	**Port_01 Wins Arbitration**
1. Port_01 opens a loop circuit with Port_B2. 2. Port_01 and Port_B2 initialize their available credit for this loop circuit based on the login credits and dynamic R_RDY signalling. 3. This allows frame transmission to begin.	**Port_01 Opens Port_B2**
1. Port_01 completes its frame transmission and signals it is done by sending the Dynamic Half Duplex (DHD) ordered set. 2. Port_01 cannot send any more frames, but can continue to send R_RDYs to replenish credit at Port_B2. 3. Port_01 does not change states (it remains in the Open state). 4. Port_B2 does not change states (it remains in the Opened state).	**Port_01 Completes Frame Transmission and Sends DHD**

Figure 56. Dynamic Half-Duplex Operation (Part 1 of 2)

1. Port_B2 continues frame transmission for as long as it has frames to send.

2. Port_01 continues to replenishes credit by sending R_RDYs.

R_RDY → Receive / Repeater / Transmit / Port_2A → R_RDY	
Transmit / FC-2 / Port_01 / Receive	**Port_B2 sends frames, Port_01 sends R_RDYs**	Receive / Port_B2 / FC-2 / Transmit
Frame ← Transmit / Repeater / Receive / Port_EF ← Frame	

---

1. Port_B2 completes its frame transmission, transmits CLS and enters the Transmitted Close state.

2. Port_01 receives the CLS and enters the Received Close state.

CFW → Receive / Repeater / Transmit / Port_2A → CFW	
Transmit / FC-2 / Port_01 / Receive	**Port_B2 Closes**	Receive / Port_B2 / FC-2 / Transmit
CLS ← Transmit / Repeater / Receive / Port_EF ← CFW	

---

1. When Port_01 is ready to relinquish control of the loop it transmits CLS and enters the Monitoring state.

2. Once Port_01 enters the Monitoring state it allows any received ARB(x) to pass. This allows some other port to win arbitration immediately after the CLS.

3. When Port_B2 receives the CLS, it also enters the Monitoring state completing the closing protocol.

CFW → Receive / Repeater / Transmit / Port_2A → CLS	
Transmit / Repeater / Port_01 / Receive	**Port_01 Closes**	Receive / Port_B2 / Repeater / Transmit
CFW ← Transmit / Repeater / Receive / Port_EF ← CFW	

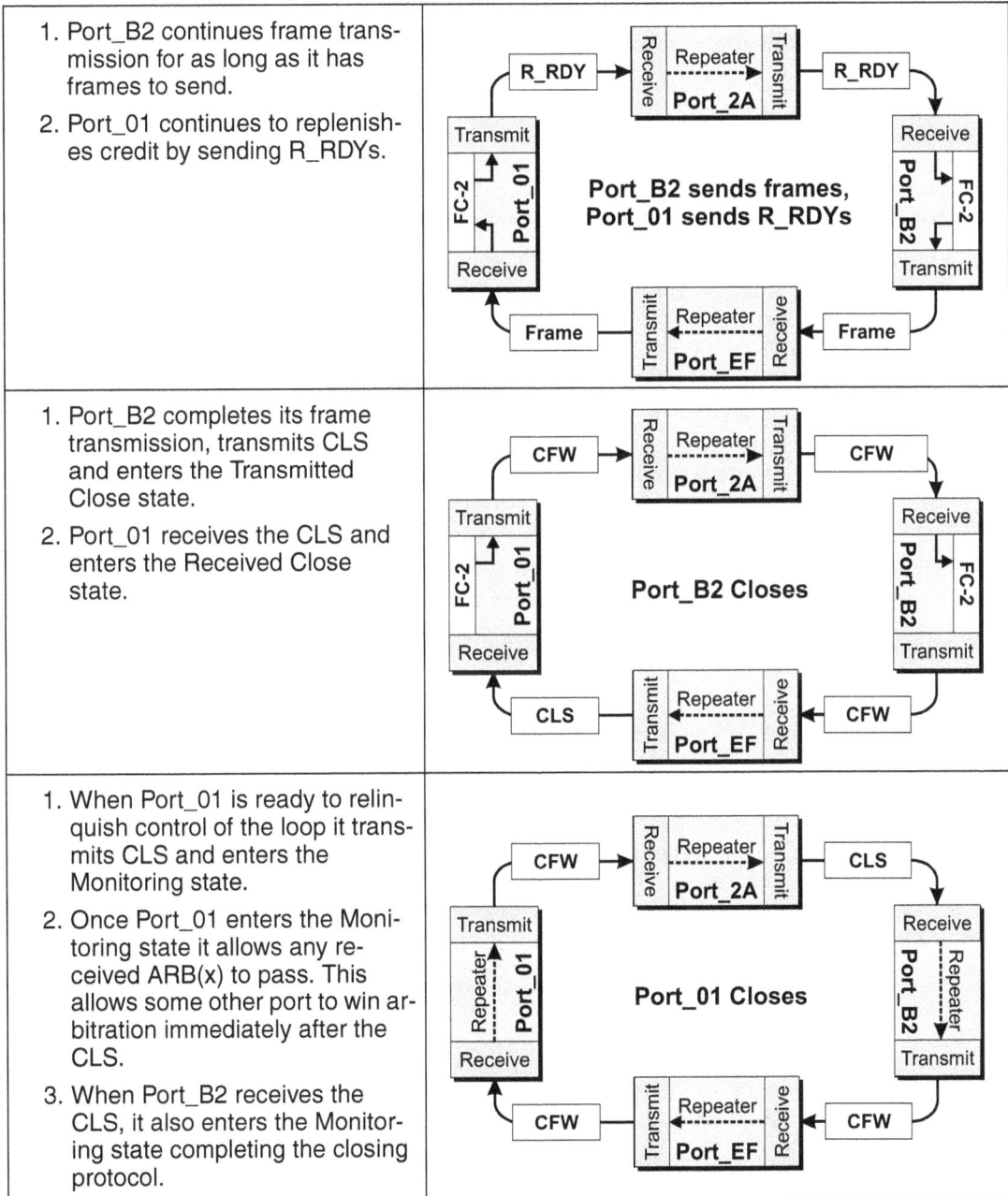

Figure 56. Dynamic Half-Duplex Operation (Part 2 of 2)

highest-priority AL_PA and is permitted to be unfair. A SCSI initiator may also be able to take advantage of transfer to improve its access to the attached targets.

When a port completes transmission with the open recipient and is using transfer, it sends a CLS and enters the Transfer state (normally, it would have entered the Transmitted Close state). When the open recipient receives the CLS, it enters the Received Close state and completes any frame transmission in progress, eventually transmits a CLS, and enters the Monitoring or Arbitrating state. The port in the Received Close state is not aware that transfer is being used because this appears to be a normal close operation from the perspective of that port.

When the port in the Transfer state receives the CLS the other port has closed its half of the loop. The port in the Transfer state may send an OPN to establish a new loop circuit and enter the Open state. The new loop circuit can be with a different port on the loop, or same port that it just closed. If the port in the Transfer state no longer requires the loop when the CLS is received, it enters the Monitoring state and closes its half of the loop circuit. An example of the transfer operation is shown in Figure 57 on page 173.

While in the Transfer state, the port continues to operate on the loop but, with the exception of MRK(tx), does not retransmit received transmission words. The port does not retransmit received LPB and LPE primitive sequences, but does process a received LPB primitive sequence, if appropriate.

The transfer process can continue indefinitely with the arbitration winner (the ARB_Won variable is set) opening and closing a succession of ports. In fact, some applications propose using a single arbitration cycle to allow an initiator to acquire control of the loop with all subsequent operations performed using transfer. This mode of operation is described in the next section.

Using transfer when another port is arbitrating is inherently unfair, and a fair port will not normally use transfer under these conditions.

10.2.1 Single-Arbitration Operation

One mode of operation that has been discussed for selected applications is based upon a designated master port (such as a SCSI initiator) arbitrating once and never relinquishing control of the loop after winning arbitration. Rather, it uses transfer, selectively opening and closing other ports as required.

The benefit of this mode of operation is that it avoids the overhead associated with arbitration. In the case of an idle loop, winning arbitration requires that the ARB(x) travel completely around the loop. Excessive arbitration can take a significant amount of time on a loop with many ports and represents nonproductive overhead. As the number of ports arbitrating for access to the loop increases, the time for subsequent ports to win arbitration decreases and the time saved may be less significant.

A master port, retaining control of the loop, can either poll the other ports or monitor its received input to determine if another port is arbitrating. If some other port is arbitrating, the master may use transfer to open that port. Because in this example all ports communicate only with the master, the only reason for the port to be arbitrating is to send information to the mas-

1. Port_01 wins arbitration	**Port_01 Wins Arbitration** ARB(01) — Port_2A (Receive / Repeater / Transmit) — ARB(01) — Port_B2 (Receive / Repeater / Transmit) — ARB(01) — Port_EF (Transmit / Repeater / Receive) — ARB(01) — Port_01 (Transmit / Repeater / Receive)
1. Port_01 sends an OPN to Port_B2 to establish the first loop circuit and enters the Open state. 2. Port_B2 receives the OPN and enters the Opened state completing the loop circuit. 3. Port_01 and Port_B2 can send and receive frames with each other.	**Port_01 Opens Port_B2** Frames — Port_2A (Receive / Repeater / Transmit) — OPN(B2,01) — Port_B2 (Receive / FC-2 / Transmit) — CFW — Port_EF (Transmit / Repeater / Receive) — CFW — Port_01 (Transmit / FC-2 / Receive)
1. Port_01 sends a CLS to Port_B2 and enters the Transfer state (normally Port_01 would have entered the Transmitted Close state). 2. Port_B2 completes its frame transmission, sends a CLS, and returns to the Monitoring state. 3. Port_01 is in the Transfer state, still owns the loop, and is preventing other ports from winning arbitration.	**Port_01 Closes, Port_B2 Closes** CFW — Port_2A (Receive / Repeater / Transmit) — CLS — Port_B2 (Receive / Repeater / Transmit) — CFW — Port_EF (Transmit / Repeater / Receive) — CLS — Port_01 (Transmit / FC-2 / Receive)

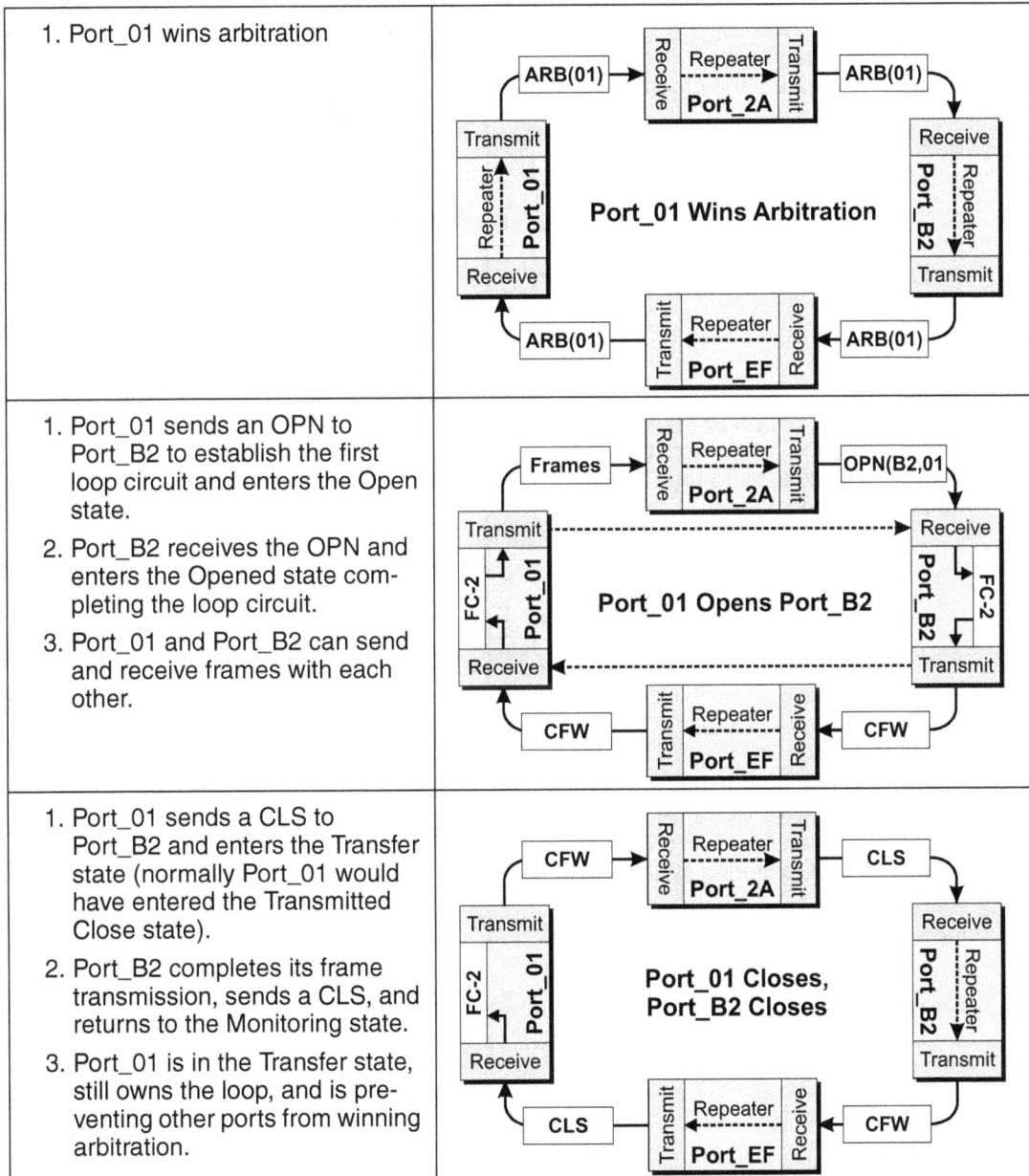

Figure 57. Transfer Operation (Part 1 of 2)

1. When Port_01 receives the CLS, it sends an OPN to Port_EF and enters the Open state. 2. Port_EF receives the OPN and enters the Opened state completing the new loop circuit. 3. Port_01 and Port_EF can send and receive frames with each other.	**Port_01 Opens Port_EF**
1. Port_01 sends a CLS to Port_EF and this time enters the Transmitted Close state (no transfer is taking place).	**Port_01 Closes**
1. Port_EF completes its frame transmission sends a CLS and returns to the Monitoring state. 2. When Port_01 receives the CLS it enters the Monitoring state. 3. The loop is now free and available for use by other ports.	**Port_EF Closes**

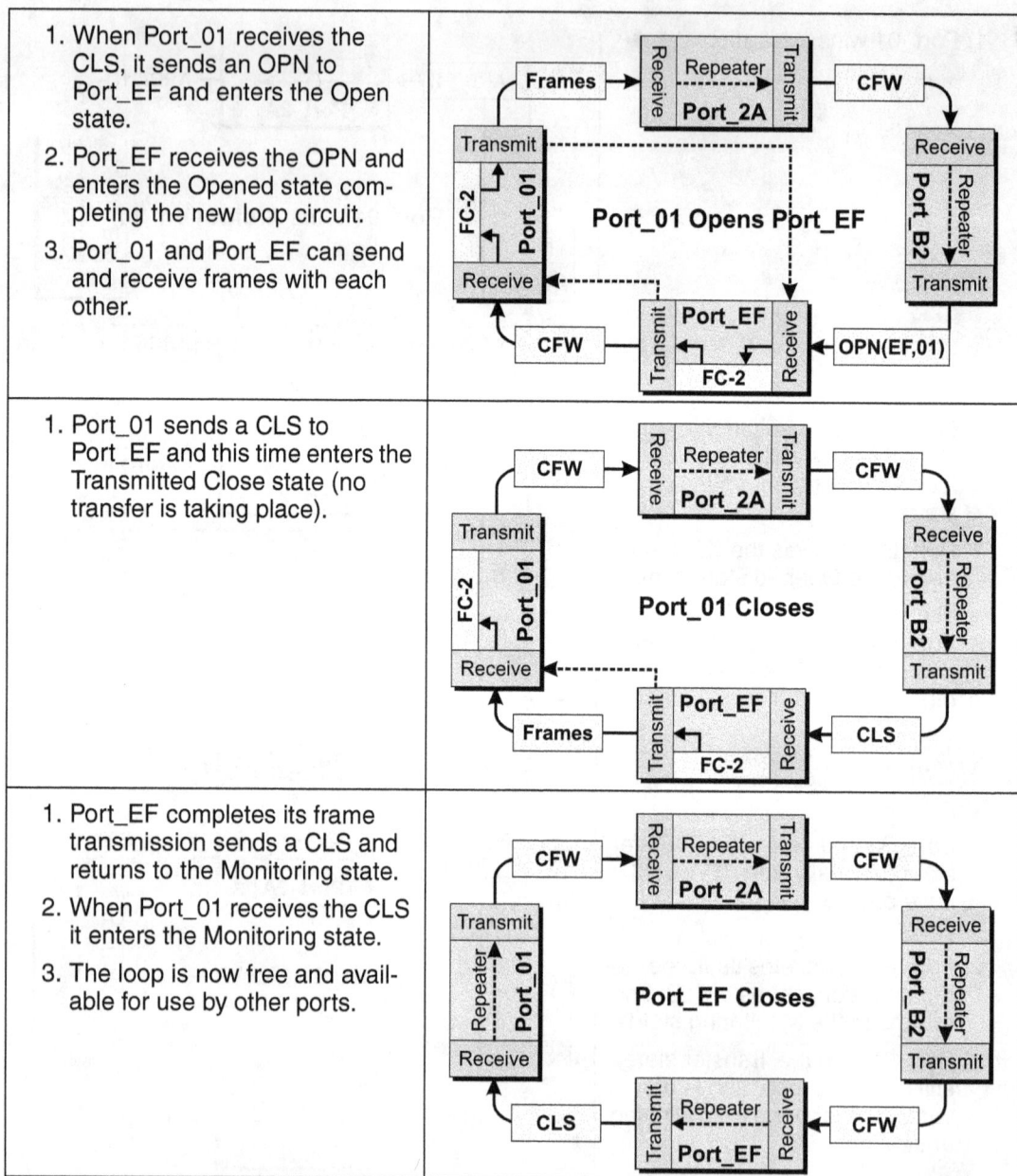

Figure 57. Transfer Operation (Part 2 of 2)

ter. Once the port is opened in full-duplex mode, it can send its traffic to the master and withdraw its arbitration request.

Access fairness is still observed even though only one port ever wins arbitration. The other ports arbitrate and withdraw their requests when they are opened and are able to transmit the frames that they would have transmitted had they won arbitration. These ports never win arbitration, but because they had access to the loop, their Access variable is reset and they cannot arbitrate again until the fairness window has been reset.

An example of an application that may benefit from this mode of operation is a single initiator disk subsystem such as a disk array controller. In this configuration all of the traffic is from the initiator to the disk drives, or from a disk drive to the initiator. In this application, the initiator would arbitrate and win arbitration only once, and then use Transfer state for all subsequent disk drive operations.

Another example might be where a number of workstations (i.e., NL_Ports) are attached to an FL_Port and all frame traffic is between the workstations and ports not on the loop. In this case the FL_Port would arbitrate and win arbitration only once, and then use the Transfer state for all subsequent workstation traffic on and off the loop.

Both of these example indicate that the configuration is known and the decision is made to operate in this manner outside the architecture. These configurations work because the frame traffic is assumed to be between the master port and the other ports on the loop (i.e., the other ports never communicate with each other and only communicate with the master port. A proposal had been made to use an ARB(yx) which would identify the arbitrating port as well as the port which will receive the OPN. If the would be open recipient already is currently in the Transfer or Open state, it can use the above procedure. If it is not the correct port, it would go to the Monitoring state to allow the other port to win arbitration. This would allow considerable flexibility, but for the time being, the standards committee has not accepted the ARB(yx).

The chapter titled *Performance* on page 229 provides techniques and guidelines for assessing loop performance that enable the reader to assess whether this mode of operation could benefit a particular application.

10.3 Transmitted Close State

The process of closing the loop circuit begins when one of the ports transmits a CLS and enters the Transmitted Close state. While in this state, the LPSM continues to process received transmission words, but the only transmission words that may be sent are the current fill word and MRK(tx).

A port normally does not wait until its receive buffers are emptied and the corresponding R_RDYs sent before closing the loop circuit, although it may delay sending the CLS to meet the login BB_Credit obligations. Once the CLS has been sent, the LPSM is prohibited from sending R_RDY because a new loop circuit may have already been established.

When a port in the Transmitted Close state receives a CLS it ends the loop circuit and if the ARB_Pend variable is set, enters the arbitrating state; if the ARB_Pend variable is not set, it enters the Monitoring state. If the ARB_Won variable is set, it may delay entry to the Monitoring state to meet the login BB_Credit obligations.

10.3.1 Arbitration and Access Fairness

Arbitration by other ports and access fairness continue to operate while in the Transmitted Close state. The port that won arbitration (ARB_Won variable is set) still has the responsibility of preventing other ports from winning arbitration and managing access fairness.

If the ARB_Won variable is set, this port is the owner of the current loop circuit and is responsible for preventing other ports from winning arbitration and managing access fairness.

- The LPSM discards all received ARB(x) ordered sets *(line 13: 'ARB(x)', on page 339)* and substitutes its current fill word in their place. Other ports are prevented from winning arbitration because their ARB(x) is unable to propagate around the loop.

- The LPSM continues the access fairness management. The LPSM initially transmitted ARB(F0) as its current fill word to determine if any other ports were arbitrating. If any port is arbitrating, that port will remove the ARB(F0) and substitute its own ARB(x). If no ports are arbitrating, the ARB(F0) will circle the loop and is received by the port in the Transmitted Close state. This marks the end of the access fairness window. The LPSM changes its current fill word to IDLE *(line 12: 'ARB(F0)', on page 338)* to notify the other ports on the loop to set their Access variables. This enables fair ports that have been waiting to begin arbitrating again, if required.

If the ARB_Won variable is not set, this port is not the owner of the current loop circuit and it continues to manage the fill word as it did prior to receiving the OPN.

- If the ARB_Pend variable is not set and an ARB(x) is received where 'x' does not equal the AL_PA of this port, its current fill word is set to the value of the received ARB(x) allowing it to propagate.

- If the ARB_Pend variable is set (i.e., the port had been arbitrating when it received the OPN), the LPSM continues to arbitrate per normal arbitration rules.

If IDLE is received *(line 9: 'IDLE', on page 338)*, its current fill word is set to IDLE and the Access variable is set allowing the LPSM to arbitrate once the current circuit is closed (a port cannot begin to arbitrate while it is in the Transmitted Close state even though it may have the REQ(arbitrate as x) input active).

10.3.2 Closing the Loop Circuit

When CLS is received *(line 16: 'CLS', on page 339)*, the LPSM ends the loop circuit and if ARB_Pend is set, enters the Arbitrating state; if ARB_Pend is not set, it enters the Monitoring state. logically disconnecting the FC-2 receive input and transmit output from the loop.

10.3.3 Processing MRK(tx)

If a MRK(tx) is received *(line 18: 'MRK(tx)', on page 339)* and the MK_TP and AL_PS match the expected values, the action or notification associated with the MRK(tx) is performed (not shown on the state table). If this was the port that originally transmitted the MRK(tx) (x = AL_PA), the MRK(tx) is discarded, otherwise the received MRK(tx) is retransmitted.

If the REQ(mark as tx) input is active *(line 35: 'REQ(mark as tx)', on page 340)*, the LPSM transmits a single MRK(tx) at the next appropriate fill word unless the REQ(mark as tx) input is removed before the MRK(tx) is transmitted.

10.3.4 Initialization and Loop Bypass

If a loop failure is detected *(line 2: 'Loop Failure', on page 338)* or the port requests initialization by asserting the REQ(initialize) input (line 42), the LPSM enters the Initializing state.

If a LIP primitive sequence is recognized, the LPSM enters the Open-Init state *(line 19: 'LIP', on page 339)*.

If the LPB(yx) is recognized and y equals the AL_PA of the port *(line 20: 'LPB(yx) or LPB(fx)', on page 339)* or REQ(bypass L_Port) is active *(line 36: 'REQ(bypass L_Port)', on page 340)*, the LP_Bypass variable is set and the LPSM enters the Monitoring state.

10.3.5 Other Valid Ordered Sets

If any other valid ordered set is received, it is discarded and the current fill word is transmitted in its place

10.4 Received Close State

The Received Close state is entered when a port in the Open state or Opened state receives a CLS indicating that the other port has begun the process of closing the current loop circuit. While in the Received Close state, a port may continue to send frames as long as it has frames to send and available BB_Credit or EE_Credit.

R_RDYs may be transmitted while in the Received Close state, although doing so is somewhat irrelevant because the other port is already in the Transmitted Close state and unable to take advantage of the R_RDYs to send additional frames.

When a port in the Received Close state transmits a CLS it ends the loop circuit and if the ARB_Pend variable is set, enters the Arbitrating state; if the ARB_Pend variable is not set, it enters the Monitoring state. If the ARB_Won variable is set, it may delay entry to the Monitoring state to meet the login BB_Credit obligations.

10.4.1 Arbitration and Access Fairness

Arbitration by other ports and access fairness continue to operate while in the Received Close state. The port that won arbitration (ARB_Won variable is set) still has the responsibility of preventing other ports from winning arbitration and managing access fairness.

If the ARB_Won variable is set, this port is the owner of the current loop circuit and is responsible for preventing other ports from winning arbitration and managing access fairness.

- The LPSM discards all received ARB(x) ordered sets *(line 13: 'ARB(x)', on page 342)* and substitutes its current fill word in their place. Other ports are prevented from winning arbitration because their ARB(x) is unable to propagate around the loop.
- The LPSM continues the access fairness management. The LPSM initially transmitted ARB(F0) as its current fill word to determine if any other ports were arbitrating. If any port

is arbitrating, that port will remove the ARB(F0) and substitute its own ARB(x). If no ports are arbitrating, the ARB(F0) will circle the loop and is received by the port in the Transmitted Close state. This marks the end of the access fairness window. The LPSM changes its current fill word to IDLE *(line 12: 'ARB(F0)', on page 338)* to notify the other ports on the loop to set their Access variables. This enables fair ports that have been waiting to begin arbitrating again, if required.

If the ARB_Won variable is not set, this port is not the owner of the current loop circuit and it continues to manage the fill word as it did prior to receiving the OPN.

- If the ARB_Pend variable is not set and an ARB(x) is received where 'x' does not equal the AL_PA of this port, its current fill word is set to the value of the received ARB(x) allowing it to propagate.

- If the ARB_Pend variable is set (i.e., the port had been arbitrating when it received the OPN), the LPSM continues to arbitrate per normal arbitration rules.

If IDLE is received *(line 9: 'IDLE', on page 341)*, the current fill word is set to IDLE and the Access variable is set to allow the LPSM to arbitrate once the current circuit is closed (a port cannot begin arbitrating while it is in the Received Close state even though it may have the REQ(arbitrate as x) input active).

10.4.2 Closing the Loop Circuit

When the L_Port control REQ(close) is active *(line 29: 'REQ(close)', on page 343)* a CLS is sent at the next appropriate fill word. Once the CLS is sent, the LPSM ends the loop circuit and if ARB_Pend is set, enters the Arbitrating state; if ARB_Pend is not set, it enters the Monitoring state logically disconnecting the FC-2 receive input and transmit output from the loop.

10.4.3 Processing MRK(tx)

If a MRK(tx) is received and the MK_TP and AL_PS match the expected values, the action or notification associated with the MRK(tx) is performed (not shown on the state table). The received MRK(tx) is not retransmitted by the LPSM.

If the REQ(mark as tx) input is active *(line 35: 'REQ(mark as tx)', on page 343)*, the LPSM transmits a single MRK(tx) at the next appropriate fill word unless the REQ(mark as tx) input is removed before the MRK(tx) is transmitted

10.4.4 Initialization and Loop Bypass

If a loop failure is detected *(line 2: 'Loop Failure', on page 341)* or the port requests initialization by asserting the REQ(initialize) input *(line 42: 'REQ(initialize)', on page 343)*, the LPSM enters the Initializing state.

If the LIP primitive sequence is recognized, the LPSM enters the Open-Init state *(line 19: 'LIP', on page 342)*.

If the LPB(yx) is recognized and 'y' equals the AL_PA of the port *(line 20: 'LPB(yx) or LPB(fx)', on page 342)* or REQ(bypass L_Port) is active *(line 36: 'REQ(bypass L_Port)', on page 343)*, the LP_Bypass variable is set and the LPSM enters the Monitoring state.

10.4.5 Other Valid Ordered Sets

If any other valid ordered set is received, it is processed in accordance with normal Fibre Channel FC-PH rules.

10.5 Transfer State

The Transfer state may be entered from the Open state only. The normal exit from the Transfer state is to the Open or Monitoring state. It is possible that a future version of the Arbitrated Loop standard will remove the Transfer state and allow the arbitration winner to return to the Open state from either the Received Close or Transmitted Close states. This is especially useful when DHD is used because the normal procedure is as follows:

- the open originator sends DHD to indicate it has finished sending device data frames.
- the open recipient normally sends CLS when it has no other frames to send.
- the open originator enters the Received Close state (even though it had wanted to use the Transfer state); the only exit for this port is to the Monitoring state.

10.5.1 Arbitration and Access Fairness

Arbitration by other ports and access fairness continue to operate while in the Transfer state and the port is responsible for managing access fairness and preventing other ports from winning arbitration.

The LPSM prevents other ports from winning arbitration by discarding all received ARB(x) primitives *(line 13: 'ARB(x)', on page 344)* and substituting its current fill word in their place. Other ports are prevented from winning arbitration because their ARB(x) is unable to propagate around the loop.

The LPSM continues the access fairness management uninterrupted from the Open state. The LPSM initially transmitted ARB(F0) as its current fill word in the Open state to determine if any other ports were arbitrating. If any port is arbitrating, that port will remove the ARB(F0) and substitute its own ARB(x). If no ports are arbitrating, the ARB(F0) will propagate around the loop. This marks the end of the access fairness window. The LPSM changes its current fill word to IDLE *(line 12: 'ARB(F0)', on page 344)* to notify the other ports on the loop to set their Access variables. This notifies fair ports that have been waiting to arbitrate that they may begin arbitrating again, if necessary.

If IDLE is received *(line 9: 'IDLE', on page 344)*, the current fill word is set to IDLE and the Access variable is set to allow the LPSM to arbitrate once the current circuit is closed (a port can't arbitrate while it is in the Transfer state even if the REQ(arbitrate as x) input is active).

10.5.2 Closing the Loop Circuit

When a CLS is received *(line 16: 'CLS', on page 344)*, the LPSM knows that the loop circuit is closed at the other port involved in the prior loop circuit and:

- if REQ(monitor) input is active when the CLS is received *(line 22: 'REQ(monitor)', on page 345)*, the LPSM enters the Monitoring state.

- if REQ(open yx), REQ(open yy), REQ(open fr), or REQ(open yr) is active when CLS is received *(line 24: 'REQ(open yx)', on page 345)*, *(line 25: 'REQ(open yy)', on page 345)*, *(line 26: 'REQ(open fr)', on page 345)*, *(line 27: 'REQ(open yr)', on page 345)*, the LPSM transmits the appropriate OPN and enters the Open state to begin a new loop circuit.

- If none of the above inputs are active, the LPSM remains in the Transfer state and retains control of the loop (no other ports are allowed to win arbitration).

10.5.3 Processing MRK(tx)

If a MRK(tx) is received *(line 17: 'MRK(tx)', on page 344)* and the MK_TP and AL_PS match the expected values, the action or notification associated with the MRK(tx) is performed (not shown on the state table). If this was the port that originally transmitted the MRK(tx) (x = AL_PA), the MRK(tx) is discarded, otherwise it is retransmitted.

If the REQ(mark as tx) input is active *(line 33: 'REQ(mark as tx)', on page 345)*, the LPSM transmits a single MRK(tx) at the next appropriate fill word unless the REQ(mark as tx) input is removed before the MRK(tx) is transmitted.

10.5.4 Initialization and Loop Bypass

If a loop failure is detected *(line 2: 'Loop Failure', on page 344)* or the port requests initialization by asserting the REQ(initialize) input *(line 40: 'REQ(initialize)', on page 345)*, the LPSM enters the Initializing state.

If a LIP primitive sequence is recognized, the LPSM enters the Open-Init state *(line 18: 'LIP', on page 345)*.

If the LPB(yx) primitive sequence is recognized and 'y' equals the AL_PA of the port *(line 19: 'LPB(yx) or LPB(fx)', on page 345)* or REQ(bypass L_Port) is active *(line 34: 'REQ(bypass L_Port)', on page 345)*, the LP_Bypass variable is set and the LPSM enters the Monitoring state.

10.5.5 Other Valid Ordered Sets

If any other valid ordered set is received, it is replaced by the current fill word.

10.6 Chapter Summary

Transmitted/Transfer Close State

- When a port completes frame transmission, it transmits a CLS
  - Either port can send a CLS
  - Both can send a CLS simultaneously
- The port that sends a CLS enters the Transmitted Close (or Transfer) state
  - Once the CLS is sent, no frames or R_RDYs can be sent
  - Waits for CLS from the other port
- When the port receives a CLS it enters the Monitoring (or Open) or Arbitrating state

Received Close State

- The port that receives a CLS enters the Received Close state
  - The port can continue to send frames as long as it has the appropriate credit
  - The other port will not send any more frames or R_RDYs
- Eventually the port completes frame transmission and sends a CLS of its own
- And, enters the Monitoring or Arbitrating state

BB_Credit at Close

- The port needs to have enough receive buffers to satisfy login BB_Credit when the loop is closed
- The open recipient may need to wait for the CLS (or DHD) to know that no more frames are on the way
  - If the required number of buffers are available, send a CLS
  - If not, wait until they are, then send a CLS
- The open originator can send a CLS (or DHD) when it has finished frame transmission
  - When a CLS is received, check the number of available buffers
  - If the required number of buffers are available, relinquish the loop
  - If not, wait until they are, then relinquish the loop

Transfer

- Transfer allows the arbitration winner to create new loop circuits without re-arbitrating
  - Open originator completes device date frame transmission to the first port
  - Transmits CLS to close the current loop circuit
  - Receives CLS and transmits OPN to create a new loop circuit without arbitrating
- May repeat the process indefinitely
- If other ports are arbitrating,
  - Multiple loop circuits in a single access fairness window is unfair behavior

Transfer Restrictions

- Transfer is only available to the arbitration winner
  - It controls the loop
- And, only if it sends CLS before receiving one
  - If the port receives a CLS, it enters the received close state rather than transfer state
  - This could be changed in the LPSM without adverse affects
- No external indication that transfer is occurring

Use of Transfer

- May improve efficiency of the loop
  - Allows frames for multiple destinations to be delivered efficiently
  - Removes the overhead associated with multiple arbitration cycles
  - Prevents fabric congestion
- Potential application:
  - Arbitrate once, then use transfer to open other ports
  - May improve performance by reducing arbitration overhead

Close Protocol Failures

- Close protocol may fail
- Open originator sends CLS, never receives CLS
  - Did other port receive the CLS?
  - If yes, other port's CLS was lost and port is in the Monitoring state
  - If no, other port is still in Opened state
  - Send CLS again?
- Open recipient sends CLS, never receives CLS
  - Open recipient can never resend CLS
  - Loop circuit may already be closed
  - New port may have won arbitration and opened a new loop circuit
  - Only recourse is to wait (or LIP)

11. Frame Transmission

After a port has won arbitration and opened the desired destination port using an OPN ordered set, frame transmission can begin subject to availability of the appropriate credit. The two ports are in the Open and Opened state, respectively. All other ports are in the Monitoring or Arbitrating states and act as repeaters for all non-fill word traffic. Ports in the Arbitrating state may also be performing fill word substitution on the fill words that occur between any frames passed through each arbitrating port.

Transmission of frames is subject to the appropriate class specific end-to-end and buffer-to-buffer flow control rules and the type of OPN used. As mentioned earlier, loop initialization and replicate mode do not use flow control.

Frame transmission may occur in either half-duplex mode or full-duplex mode as determined by the OPN ordered set used and the capabilities of the ports. When half-duplex operation is used, device data frames may be sent from the open originator to the open recipient only with the corresponding class specific link control response frames sent in the opposite direction. During full-duplex operation, device data frames and link control response frames may be sent in both directions simultaneously, taking full advantage of the loop's capabilities.

When frame transmission is completed, the loop circuit should be closed if other ports are arbitrating to allow them to win arbitration and send frames of their own.

11.1 General Design Considerations

Several key decisions face fibre channel designers, whether the design is intended for point-to-point, Arbitrated Loop, or switched fabric.

One is how to manage the control aspects associated with the port. Due to the nature of fibre channel operations, it is likely that many designs will delegate some of the port's control functions to a microprocessor. This microprocessor related functionality may be physically part of the adapter or port itself, or the design may rely on the host system's processor (typically as part of a host device driver). For example, a SCSI host bus adapter may contain an on-board processor, or the host system's processor may provide the port control via driver firmware. Device implementations (such as a disk device) may use a single processor to control both the fibre channel port and device operations.

Different implementations distribute the responsibility for control between the hardware and firmware in varying degrees. Some designs may assign more function to the microprocessor to reduce the amount of hardware required and reduce costs, while others may incorporate additional hardware functionality to enhance performance.

One aspect of controlling a fibre channel port is how the port manages switching from one exchange to another (i.e., context switching or task switching). Fibre channel by its nature leads to the potential for high degrees of fast context switching.

During Class-2 or Class-3 operations in a switched fabric environment, it is possible that every received frame may be part of a different operation for a different sending port. Realizing the maximum potential of this frame multiplexing capability may require the port to perform a context switch for each received frame. In Arbitrated Loop environments without an FL_Port, all of the frames received during a single loop circuit originate from the same sending port, but individual frames during that loop circuit may be associated with different operations or different processes behind that port. When an FL_Port is involved in the operation, frame multiplexing may occur, just as in a normal fabric environment.

As an example, a SCSI initiator may open a loop circuit with a SCSI target. During that loop circuit, the initiator may send one or more FCP_CMND information units, as well as all or part of data sequences associated with the prior or current commands. The receiving port may need to process an FCP_CMND followed by some or all of a data sequence for an entirely different operation. The time required to perform the context switching between these exchanges of information units may be manifested as idle time on the loop resulting in reduced loop throughput. Task switching implemented in hardware is generally faster and may provide improved performance when compared to designs that do the task switching in firmware.

Another key decision is how to provide the buffer memory required during the transmission and reception of sequences. How much buffering should be provided, whether the buffering is part the port or located externally, and the DMA mechanisms used to access the memory are all considerations facing the designer.

Closely related to the buffer memory implementation is the decision regarding support of full or half-duplex operation. Full-duplex operation requires independent data handling capabilities for transmitting and receiving data and may require multi-ported memory, multiple DMA capabilities, and higher memory bandwidth. A full-duplex design operating with 100 megabyte per second fibre channel links (106.25 megabyte per second instantaneous data rate) may require up to 425 megabytes per second of memory bandwidth (106.25 MB/s each for the link transmit and receive functions, plus 106.25 MB/s each for the system write and read interfaces). A half-duplex design operating in Class-1 or Class-2 requires enough bandwidth and controls to support the data transfer in one direction simultaneously with link control frame transmission in the opposite direction.

There are numerous possible approaches to building fibre channel ports. Each implementation attempts to achieve an optimal balance of cost, complexity, and performance for the intended market. There is no single design that provides the right answer for all applications. The following sections examine the basic transmit and receive functions and examine different approaches to port design and memory options. The following examples are intended to illustrate basic data transfer approaches and none of the examples include flow control details, microprocessors, or other functionality that may be required.

11.2 Basic Transmit Operation

A typical fibre channel transmitter function contains one or more transmit buffers used to hold frames prior to transmission. These transmit buffers may be located in the fibre channel transmit function itself, or in external memory. Data is taken from a transmit buffer, encoded, and serialized for transmission. Once transmission for a particular frame begins, that frame must be sent in its entirety at full link speed without interruption (although a frame may be ended early using the computed CRC and appropriate EOF). Fibre channel also permits a port to abort a frame (using the EOFa delimiter), but this is seldom used.

Figure 58 is a high-level block diagram of a hypothetical fibre channel transmitter function. Many of the details required by a practical implementation are omitted from this figure for the sake of clarity. In this example, the data to be transmitted resides in the sequence memory. Before the first frame can be transmitted, the frame header must be initialized, the transmit DMA address and data lengths set, and various control facilities (not shown) set to specify the frame data field size and other required control information. Once this initial setup is completed the hardware is instructed to begin frame transmission for the sequence.

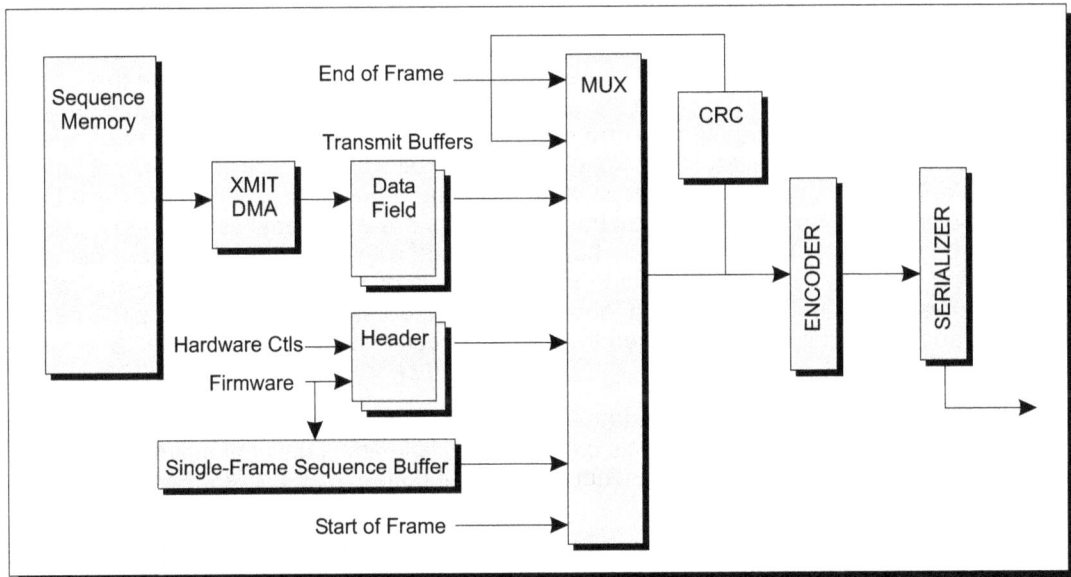

Figure 58. Basic Frame Transmit Function

The transmit DMA begins filling the first transmit buffer with data from the sequence memory. If additional frames are required to complete the sequence, the transmit DMA checks to see if there is an available transmit buffer. If so, the transmit DMA continues to fill the next transmit buffer. As long as there is additional data to transfer, the DMA continues to fill available transmit buffers. If all of the available transmit buffers are full, the DMA waits until one or more transmit buffers becomes available.

When the first transmit buffer is full, an indication is set notifying the LPSM that one or more frames are available for transmission. This causes the LPSM to begin arbitrating for access to the loop. When the LPSM wins arbitration, the appropriate OPN is sent to the open recipient. The AL_PA fields in the OPN can be extracted from the Destination and Source ID fields in the frame header. Also required is an indication of whether the open should be a full-duplex open OPN(yx) or a half-duplex open OPN(yy). This information may be provided by either the firmware or hardware based on the desired operation and the port's capabilities. After the OPN is sent followed by the initial six fill words, including an optional R_RDY (see *'Granting a Login BB_Credit Value Equal to Zero' on page 140*) frame transmission can begin subject to available credit.

Each frame is processed by sending the appropriate start-of-frame delimiter followed by the frame header, frame data field (including any optional headers), CRC, and the appropriate end-of-frame delimiter. In multi-frame sequences, the SEQ_CNT and relative offset (if applicable) are updated prior to transmission of each frame in the sequence. As frames are sent and the associated transmit buffer emptied, the transmit DMA can begin refilling the buffer with additional transmit data. Refilling empty transmit buffers occurs simultaneously with the transmission of data from other transmit buffers.

If the fibre channel link is able to accept frames faster than the transmit DMA can refill empty transmit buffers, it is possible for all of the transmit buffers to become empty. Once this occurs further frame transmission is limited to the transmit DMA's rate. If the port maintains the loop circuit while operating in this manner, the entire loop bandwidth is reduced to the transmit DMA's rate. To avoid this, the port may close the loop circuit when all available transmit buffers are empty and establish a new loop circuit later, after one or more transmit buffers have been refilled. Closing the loop circuit when all transmit buffers are empty makes the loop available for other ports use, but may incur the overhead associated with closing the loop, re-arbitrating, and opening the loop circuit. Establishing loop circuits is overhead. If no port is arbitrating, there is no value in closing an existing loop circuit, even if it is not operating at peak performance. If another port is arbitrating, then the current circuit should be closed to allow another port to transmit frames.

Some designs may open a loop circuit, transmit as many frames as they have transmit buffers, and then close the loop circuit. This cycle can occur multiple times until the entire sequence is transmitted. For example, a design with four 2k transmit buffers may break a 64k transfer into eight loop circuits of four frames each.

In FCP applications, the FCP_CMND, FCP_XFER_RDY, and FCP_RSP normally consist of a single-frame sequence and may be handled by a special single-frame sequence buffer (the FCP_RSP could consist of more than one frame if the sense data causes the information unit to require two frames. Some profiles restrict the amount of sense information to ensure that the FCP_RSP is a single-frame sequence.) Single-frame sequences handled in this manner may be created directly by the hardware (as might be the case for the FCP_XFER_RDY, or good status reported in the FCP_RSP), or rely on firmware to create the payload (for example the FCP_CMND, or FCP_RSP for error or exception conditions).

Some designs take advantage of this fact and dedicate one or more transmit buffers for sending single-frame sequences. This allows the data for the entire sequence to be assembled directly in the transmit buffer without involving the transmit DMA in the operation. This is shown by the block contained in the dotted lines in Figure 58 on page 185.

When a single-frame sequence is sent, the frame is assembled in the single-frame sequence buffer and the hardware is instructed to send the frame. As before, the appropriate start-of-frame delimiter is sent, then the contents of the single-frame sequence buffer (which contains both the frame header and data field), followed by the hardware generated CRC, and finally the appropriate end-of-frame delimiter.

One last approach eliminates separate transmit buffers by sending frames directly from the sequence memory, perhaps via a small FIFO (first-in first-out buffer). This is only possible when the frame transmission logic has guaranteed access to the sequence memory. An example of this approach is shown in Figure 59 on page 187. Note that this approach requires any optional headers to be imbedded within the payload (e.g., fibre channel Link Encapsulation, FC-LE, which is used to transport network protocols over fibre channel).

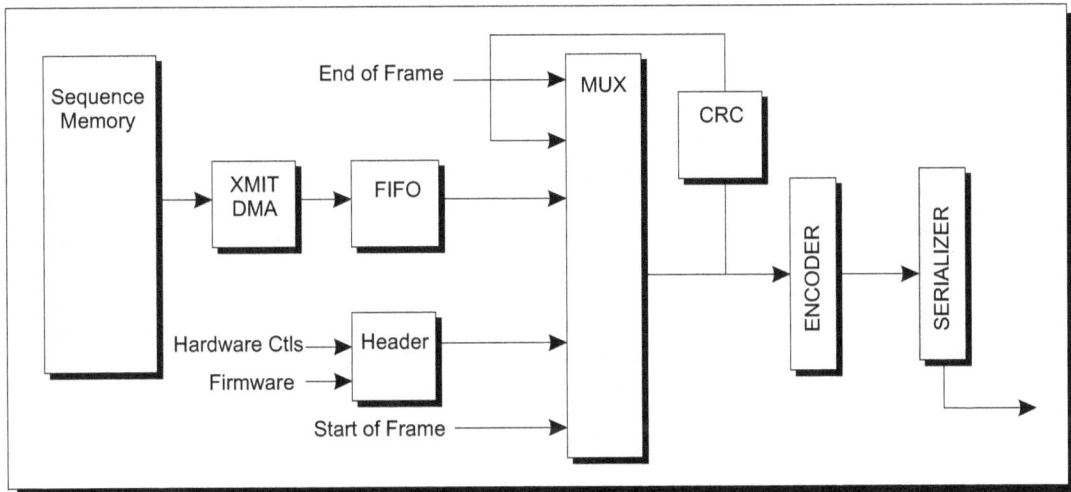

Figure 59. Transmitting Directly From Sequence Memory

Data to be transmitted is stored in the sequence memory, the header and transmit DMA are initialized to begin transmission. Once the appropriate start-of-frame and frame header are sent, the transmit DMA supplies the data field (including any optional headers). When the data field has been transmitted, the CRC is sent followed by the appropriate end-of-frame delimiter. If additional frames remain to be sent for this sequence, the appropriate frame header fields are updated and, if the available credits allow, transmission of the next frame begins. This process repeats until the entire sequence has been sent. If the frame transmission logic is unable to obtain data at the time it is required for transmission, frame transmission fails and the frame is terminated with an EOFa or a shorter frame could be transmitted. A small amount of FIFO buffering may be provided between the DMA and frame transmission logic to prevent this from happening.

Whichever approach is taken for frame transmission, once the final frame of the sequence has been sent and the appropriate Acknowledge frame received (if any), the transmit function can indicate that sequence delivery is complete.

11.3 Basic Receive Operation

The process of receiving frames is almost the reverse of transmitting with two significant exceptions: the receiving port lacks advance knowledge of the next operation for which a frame is received, and the receiving port is responsible for managing the flow of frames from the transmitter to ensure that there is always a receive buffer available to hold the next frame.

Unless the frame reception is part of a current established loop circuit, the first indication of impending frame reception is receipt of an OPN addressed to that port. The OPN(yx) indicates that full-duplex operation may be used while the OPN(yy) restricts the loop circuit to half-duplex operation. If full-duplex operation is indicated, and available credit allows, the port may begin sending any transmit frames outstanding for the port issuing the open. Even though a full-duplex OPN was received, there is no obligation on the open recipient to operate in a full-duplex manner. This allows a port capable of full-duplex operations to issue the OPN(yx) without knowing if the open recipient is capable of full-duplex operations. If the open recipient is capable and has device data frames to send, it can do so in full-duplex mode. If the open recipient is only capable of half-duplex operations, it simply does not originate any device data frames during this loop circuit even though it may originate link control frames, if appropriate. If half-duplex operation is indicated, the port is only permitted to send link control frames and R_RDYs in response to frames received.

The OPN is normally followed by at least six fill words, one or more R_RDYs (see the *'Buffer-to-Buffer Flow Control' on page 136*), and one or more frames if allowed by the flow control mechanism (i.e., login BB_Credit is greater than zero).

Figure 60 illustrates a high-level block diagram of a hypothetical fibre channel receive function. As was the case with the transmitter function discussed earlier, many details have been omitted from this figure for the sake of clarity.

Receive buffers are used to hold frames received from the link. These receive buffers may be located in the fibre channel receive function itself, or in external memory. Data is received from the link, deserialized, decoded, placed into a receive buffer, and then stored into the sequence reassembly memory. Because a frame may be received at any time flow control permits, the receiver must be prepared to begin frame reception whenever a start-of-frame delimiter is detected. According the fibre channel rules, this should never occur unless there is a receive buffer available to receive the frame (unless replicate mode is being used or this is the LISM sequence of loop initialization).

In this example, the received data is ultimately placed in the sequence memory. When a frame is received, the frame header and optional headers may be analyzed to determine if the frame belongs to an existing sequence. If so, the context for that sequence is restored (receive DMA address, remaining count, and other controls) so that frame processing for that sequence can continue.

If the received frame is not part of the current operation, a check is made to determine if the frame is for another operation already in progress. If so, the context of the current operation is saved and the context of the operation associated with the new frame is restored. The fibre channel Originator Exchange_ID combined with the Source_ID or the receiving port may have a local variable called the Responder Exchange_ID may be used as an index to locate the

---

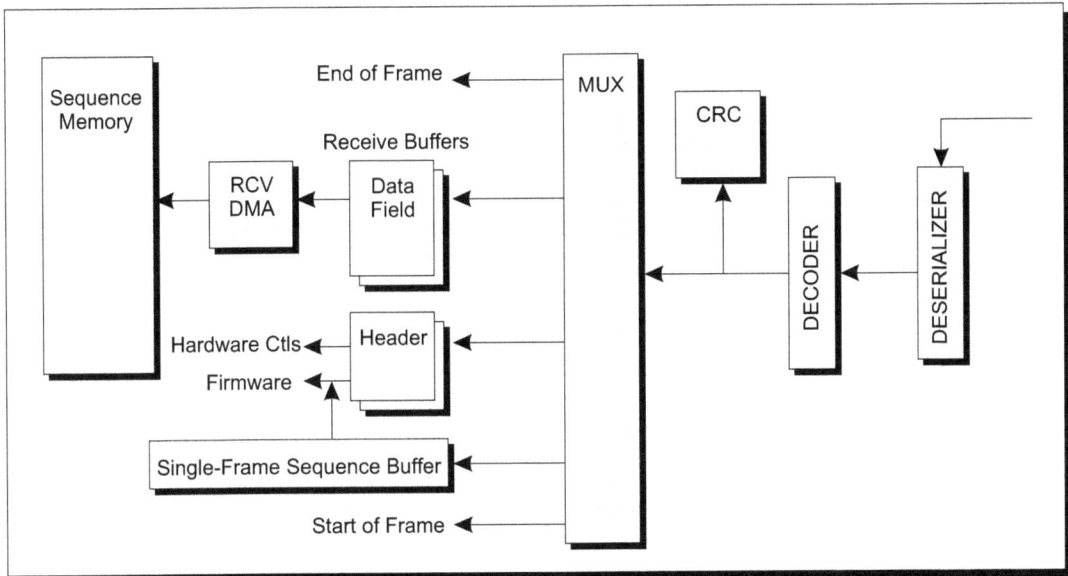

Figure 60. Basic Frame Receive Function

context of the resumed operation. The context of the receive DMA is part of the saved context information enabling the DMA to resume data transfer for the restored operation. The exchange context information may reside in a reserved portion of the sequence memory, or in other memory, not shown in the figure.

If the received frame is for a new operation, context information for the new operation needs to be initialized and memory allocated in the sequence memory before the frame can be stored. Once this initial setup for the new sequence is completed the receive DMA is instructed to process the frames for that sequence. As frames are received, they are placed into one of the available receive buffers. When a receive buffer is full and the frame validity confirmed, the receive DMA may begin transferring the data field into the sequence memory. After all of the data for a given receive buffer has been transferred, an R_RDY is sent to the transmitter indicating that a receive buffer has been emptied (for the first Class-1 frame, all Class-2 and Class-3 frames only).

As long as there is one or more filled receive buffers for the current sequence, the receive DMA continues to transfer data from the receive buffers to the sequence memory. If all of the receive buffers are empty, the DMA waits until one or more receive buffers is filled. As frames are received and the associated receive buffer is filled, the receive DMA can begin emptying the buffer. Emptying full receive buffers occurs simultaneously with the reception of frames into other receive buffers.

If the receive DMA is unable to keep up with the rate of frame reception, all of the available receive buffers may eventually fill up and the flow control mechanism prevents the sender from transmitting any more frames until a receive buffer is available. This can occur if the bandwidth of the memory is less than the fibre channel link rate, or if the memory is shared or located external to the port.

For example, if the memory bandwidth is 25 MB/s, the fibre channel link rate is 100 MB/s, and the receiver has four buffers available, all of the receive buffers may fill before the first buffer can be emptied to the external sequence memory.

If sequences are stored in system memory and accessed via a system bus such as PCI, accesses to the sequence memory by the fibre channel port may be temporarily blocked by other activity on the system bus. These blockages and the effective bandwidth of the system bus may limit the receiver's ability to sustain the full data rate of the fibre channel link.

If the loop circuit remains open under these conditions, the entire loop bandwidth is reduced to the receiver's DMA or memory access rate. To avoid this, the transmitting port may decide to close the loop circuit when it appears that all available receive buffers are full (i.e., credit is exhausted) and open a new loop circuit again later with the expectation that one or more receive buffers will have been emptied in the interim. This makes the loop available for other ports use, but does incur the overhead associated with closing the loop, rearbitrating, and reopening the loop. Establishing loop circuits is overhead. If no port is arbitrating, there is no value in closing an existing loop circuit, even if it is not operating at peak performance. If another port is arbitrating, then the current circuit should be closed to allow another port to transmit frames.

Some designs may dedicate one or more receive buffers for receiving single-frame sequences. This allows the data for the entire sequence to be processed directly from the receive buffer without involving the receive DMA in the operation. Figure 60 on page 189 shows single-frame sequence buffer in dotted lines.

Because all non-data sequences in FCP can normally be transmitted as single-frame sequences, the receiver can examine the R_CTL and TYPE fields of the frame header to determine if the frame should be placed into a single-frame sequence buffer, or processed by the receive DMA. This allows the FCP_CMND, FCP_XFER_RDY, and FCP_RSP sequences to normally be handled by a single-frame sequence buffer.

Designs that utilize single-frame sequence buffers may process the contents of the frame in hardware (e.g., the FCP_XFER_RDY), or notify the firmware via an interrupt or other mechanism (e.g., FCP_CMND and FCP_RSP).

In some applications, it may be possible to eliminate the receive buffers altogether and move the frames directly into the sequence memory as is shown in Figure 61. If no separate receive buffers are used, inbound frames are routed directly to the sequence memory. Header information may optionally be split off and processed separately by the hardware or firmware.

11.4 Full-Duplex Operation

Full-duplex operation allows a fibre channel port to take maximum advantage of fibre channel's full-duplex capability by simultaneously sending and receiving frames. Use of full-duplex can potentially double the link data rate allowing 100 MB/s links to achieve a throughput of 200 MB/s (100 MB/s transmit and 100 MB/s receive). Perhaps even more important in an Arbitrat-

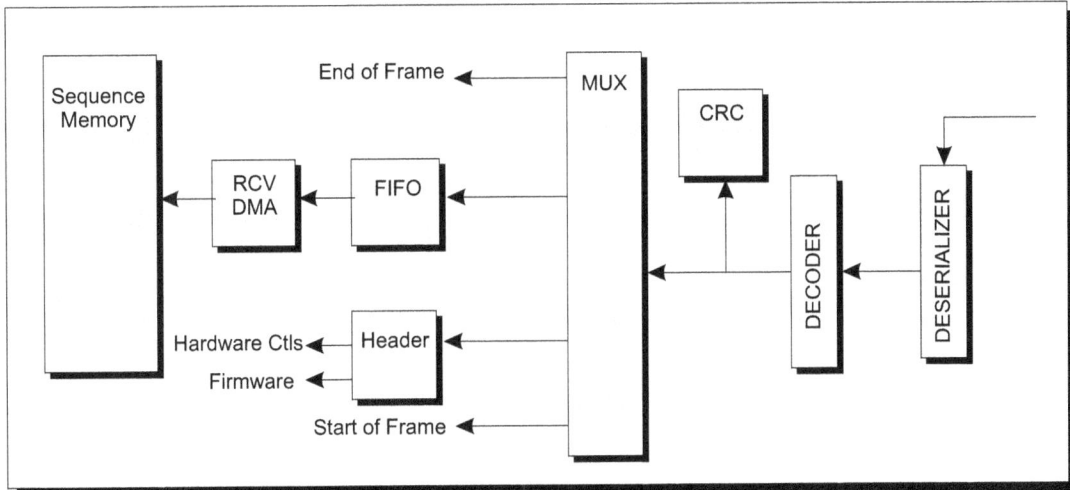

Figure 61. Receiving Directly Into Sequence Memory

ed Loop environment is that the use of full-duplex operation can reduce the number of loop tenancies significantly and improve the overall efficiency of the loop.

Examination of the SCSI-3 FCP protocol reveals that individual SCSI tasks always operate in half-duplex mode (i.e., each SCSI-3 FCP exchange is half-duplex). First the FCP_CMND is sent from the SCSI initiator to the target. Then the FCP_XFER_RDY (optional on both reads and writes) is sent from the target to the initiator. Next an FCP_DATA in or out sequence is sent if appropriate for the command. Finally, the FCP_RSP is sent from the target to the initiator indicating that the task is complete. Overlapping the information units for one task is not permitted and, therefore, individual tasks are unable to take advantage of fibre channel's full-duplex capabilities.

When command queueing is supported between a SCSI initiator and target, full-duplex operation is possible by overlapping the transfer of information for different exchanges (i.e., SCSI tasks). For example, an FCP_CMND can be sent from a SCSI initiator to a target while the target is sending an FCP_XFER_RDY, FCP_DATA, or FCP_RSP for a previous command.

Table 14 provides a matrix illustrating the sequences sent from a SCSI target to the initiator while the columns list sequences sent from the SCSI initiator to the target. Each intersection identifies a potential opportunity for full-duplex transfers to occur for different tasks. Because some designs handle single-frame sequences differently than data transfers, the table also identifies those information units that normally consist of a single frame. This may be helpful in some cases where a design is only capable of supporting half-duplex transfer of the data in or data out, but may be able to support full-duplex operations involving single-frame sequences.

Even those devices not normally thought of as full-duplex may benefit from designs capable of supporting full-duplex operations. For example, while disk drives cannot read and write to the disk at the same time, the addition of caching memory creates the potential for full-duplex operations. This means that a disk drive could conceivably be transferring read data for one com-

SCSI Target	SCSI Initiator	
	FCP_CMND (Single-frame)	Data Out (Multi-frame)
FCP_XFER_RDY (Single-frame)	Single frame sequence, Single frame sequence	Write DMA, Single frame sequence
Data In (Multi-frame)	Read DMA, Single frame sequence	Read DMA and Write DMA both
FCP_RSP (Single-frame)	Single frame sequence, Single frame sequence	Write DMA, Single frame sequence

Table 14. FCP Protocol Full-Duplex Combinations

mand while simultaneously transferring write data for another. Both transfers could take place using the drive's cache memory with the actual disk accesses occurring only as required.

Each port involved in a loop circuit has full control over whether it allows full-duplex operations or not. The open initiator may restrict the operation of the open recipient through its selection of which OPN is sent. If the open initiator desires full-duplex operation, it sends the full-duplex OPN(yx) open; otherwise, it sends the half-duplex OPN(yy) open. Each port paces frame transmission by the other through the flow control mechanisms.

When a port receives an OPNy, it assumes that the open initiator has one or more frames to send. If the open recipient does not desire full-duplex operation, it simply refrains from sending any data frames of its own, even if a full-duplex OPN(yx) is received.

11.4.1 Full-Duplex Port With On-Board Memory

If the basic transmit and receive functions discussed earlier are combined as shown in Figure 62 on page 193, the result is a port capable of full-duplex operation. In host adapter applications, data is transferred between system memory and the port via a system specific bus, such as PCI. In imbedded applications, there may or may not be an equivalent to the system bus. If not, the fibre channel design may interface to one or more device specific interfaces.

In this example, a single sequence memory is used to hold the data associated with both transmit and receive operations. The sequence memory is accessed by independent transmit and receive DMAs permitting the simultaneous transfer of received data into the memory and transmit data out of the memory. Using a shared memory allows the available storage to be dynamically allocated between receive and transmit operations permitting more efficient usage of the memory. However, shared memory designs place rather stringent demands on the memory to sustain the aggregate bandwidth required by both the transmit and receive functions. In a 100 megabyte per second implementation operating full-duplex, the bandwidth required just to support one full-duplex fibre channel port may be in excess of 200 megabytes per second.

In addition to supporting the fibre channel port, the memory must also support accesses by the host system or device. This places additional demand on the memory bandwidth resulting in a total memory bandwidth requirement greater than 400 megabytes per second to support full-speed simultaneous transfers.

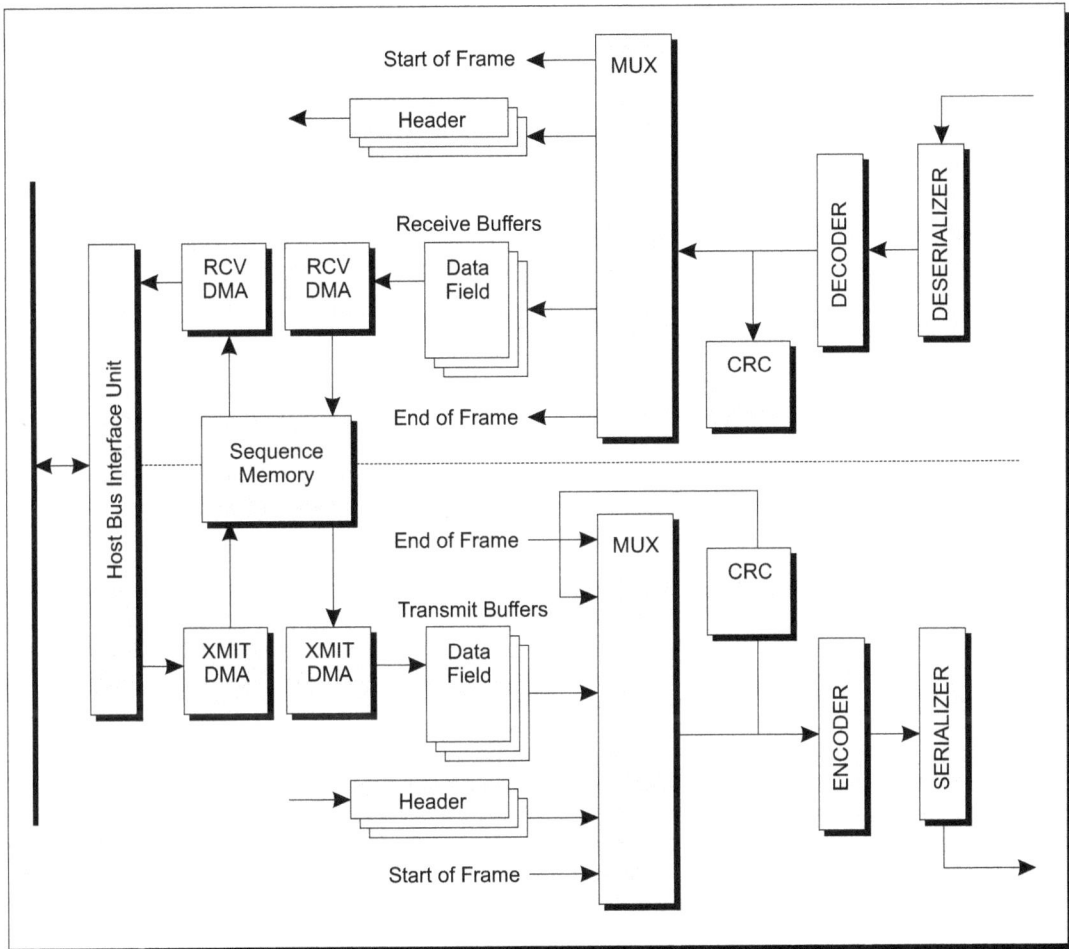

Figure 62. Full-Duplex Port With On-Board Memory

Each function that accesses the memory may require its own DMA capability to manage the transfer of data into or out of the memory. In the example shown, there are four DMA functions to support concurrent accesses by all of the memory users. One is used to control the transfer of received link data into the memory, the second to control the transfer of link transmit data from the memory, the third to control the transfer of received data from the memory to the system bus, and the fourth to control the transfer of data from the system bus to the memory. It is possible that this approach could be simplified by using a single DMA function to control the transfer of system data to and from the memory.

Full-duplex operations may also place severe demands on the system bus. To sustain full link speeds, the system bus bandwidth must equal or exceed the link rates. In full-duplex operation, this can be greater than 206 megabytes per second. A large number of systems today are implementing the PCI bus as their primary system bus. A 32-bit wide PCI bus operating at 33 Mhz. (30 nsec. bus cycle time) is capable of bursting at 132 MB/s with a sustained throughput of approximately 70 megabytes per second. This data rate is barely sufficient for supporting half-duplex operation on a full-speed fibre channel link. A 64-bit wide PCI bus operating at 33 Mhz. is capable of bursting data at 264 megabytes per second (with a data rate of perhaps 140 to 160 megabytes per second) and offers a better match for a single full-duplex fibre channel port.

The requirements on the system bus become even more apparent when one considers that some systems plan to implement multiple fibre channel ports per card!

11.4.2 Full-Duplex Port With External Memory

Incorporating the sequence memory as part of the port may add significant cost to the design. One alternative is to use the system memory (or device cache) to hold the transmit and receive sequences. An example of this is shown in Figure 63. In this example, received frames are transferred directly from the receive buffers into system memory. No sequence memory is provided as part of the port resulting in a simpler design with reassembly of received sequences performed in system memory as each frame is processed.

Some designs may allocate buffer space to hold the entire sequence when the operation is initiated. Others may manage system memory by creating a dynamic pool of available memory buffers and allowing the port to use buffers from the pool as required. Dynamic buffer pools allows efficient use to be made of the available memory space, but may lead to complications when reassembling sequences received out of order.

As frames are received, buffers are drawn from the pool. As long as frames are received in order, an ordered linked list can be created connecting all of the buffers used. When an out of order frame is received, there is no straightforward way to incorporate it in the linked list because it doesn't have a predecessor to link to the prior frame at this time. One approach to handling this is to terminate the current linked list and start a new one every time an out of order condition occurs. At the end of the sequence, the hardware provides the firmware with pointers to all of the fragments and lets the firmware perform the final sequence reassembly.

Alternatively, if one links the frame header information this is not a problem, where the frame header information points to the payload. For SCSI-3 FCP information units T8-T11 and I6-I7, this approach must be used because there are two different information categories used in the R_CTL field of the frame headers within the sequence.

If the received frame is not part of the current sequence context, the current sequence context is saved and the context associated with the received frame is restored or created. In designs with external memory, the sequence context is generally stored in a reserved portion of the system memory. To permit relocation of the context information in system memory the system normally supplies a pointer to the base of the sequence context and the port calculates the location of the context for a specific sequence. One way to perform this calculation is for the exchange originator to use the OX_ID field and the exchange responder to use the RX_ID field as an index into the context table.

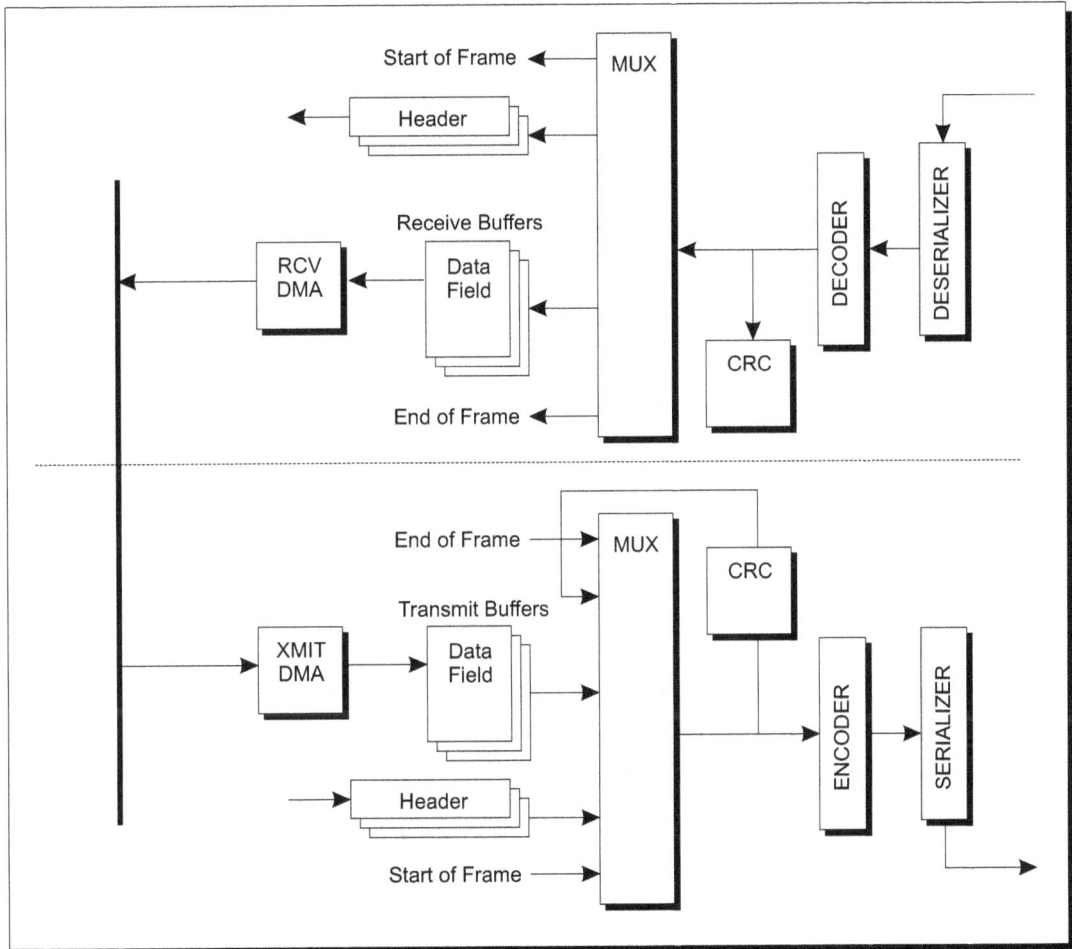

Figure 63. Full-Duplex Port With External Memory

During transmit operations, the system stores the transmit data field in a buffer located in system memory, initializes the frame header and transmit DMA (direct memory access function), and instructs the transmit DMA to begin filling the frame buffers. From this point on, operation is identical to that described earlier for ports with on-board memory.

One significant operational difference that occurs when the memory holding transmit and receive sequences is accessed via a system bus is that latency may be experienced in access to the system bus. This is especially true in systems with a high-level of activity on the system bus. The presence of transmit and receive buffers in the port helps mask normal system bus delays, but throughput is still dependent upon system bus performance.

11.4.3 Full-Duplex Port With No Frame Buffers

Combining the two earlier figures illustrating frame transmission and reception directly from sequence memory produces a design such as the one shown in Figure 64 on page 196.

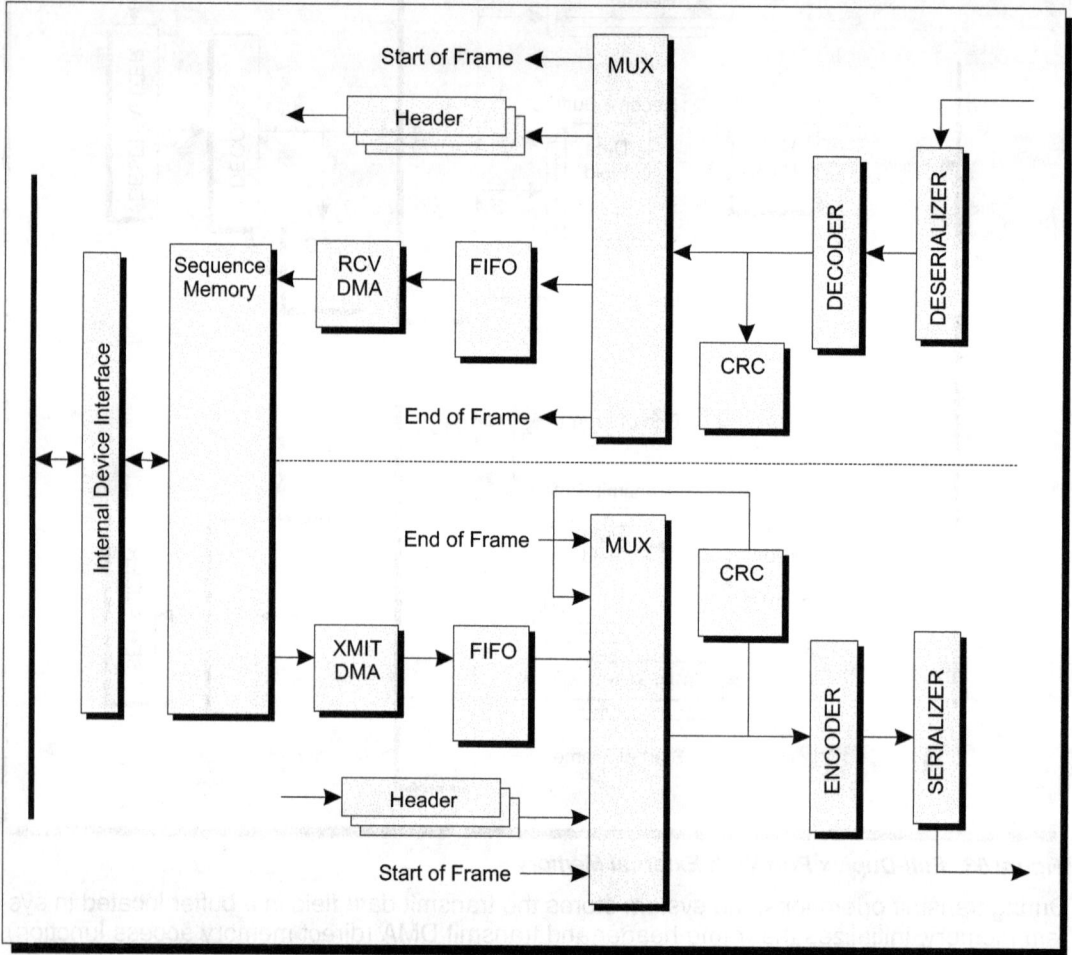

Figure 64. Full-Duplex Port With No Frame Buffers

To support full-duplex operations, this design must guarantee full link bandwidth to the transmit and receive functions. If the receive function is unable to obtain access to the sequence memory when required, one or more words in the frame may be lost causing the frame to be corrupted and the CRC check fails. This causes the frame to be discarded and results in a sequence delivery failure. In the case of SCSI-3 FCP, that results in an aborted task.

If the transmit function is unable to obtain access to the memory when required, the current frame may have to be aborted (terminated with an end-of-frame abort delimiter). Receiving ports ignore aborted frames so this action should have no effect on the receiver. If the transmitter is able to back up and restart transmission for the aborted frame, a successful recovery may occur.

The internal device bus may have another time critical user of the sequence memory. If the device is a disk drive and write data is being transferred from the sequence memory to the disk, failure to obtain the data within the required time may result in a failed write. If a read is in progress and the read data is unable to be stored in the sequence memory, an overrun condition occurs and the sector read fails.

Access controls to the common sequence memory need to ensure that each function receives the required access to the memory, both in terms of overall bandwidth and latency. This can be done through a time slice mechanism which guarantees access or a priority scheme giving highest priority to received frames, with lower priority to the transmit and device functions because they can be retried. One example of a priority scheme is:

1. Frame receive function
2. Frame transmit function
3. High-priority device functions
4. Low-priority device functions

11.5 Half-Duplex Operation

All of the examples in the full-duplex section can be simplified for half-duplex operation by removing that part of the design not required in a half-duplex environment. The following sections take two of the full-duplex designs presented earlier and illustrate half-duplex variations of those designs. In some cases (e.g., Class-3 operations on an Arbitrated Loop) it may be possible to remove one complete set of DMA and buffering capabilities because true half-duplex operation can be enforced.

11.5.1 Half-Duplex Port With External Memory

For example, if the port with external memory shown in Figure 63 on page 195 is simplified to support only half-duplex operations, the resulting design may be similar to that shown in Figure 65 on page 198.

This design has a single set of frame buffers that are used for both transmit and receive frames and a single DMA to the system bus. When the port has information to send, it arbitrates for the loop, and when it wins arbitration, sends an OPN(yy) to the destination port, and transfers data from the sequence buffers located in system memory to one of the available frame buffers. When one or more frame buffers is filled, data transmission begins.

Because the frame buffers and DMA are committed to the transmit operation, this design is not able to receive frames while it is conditioned for transmission. This may prevent its use in a Class-1 or Class-2 environment because there is no way to receive the link control response frames during the same loop circuit. If this design were intended for use in a Class-1 or Class-

---

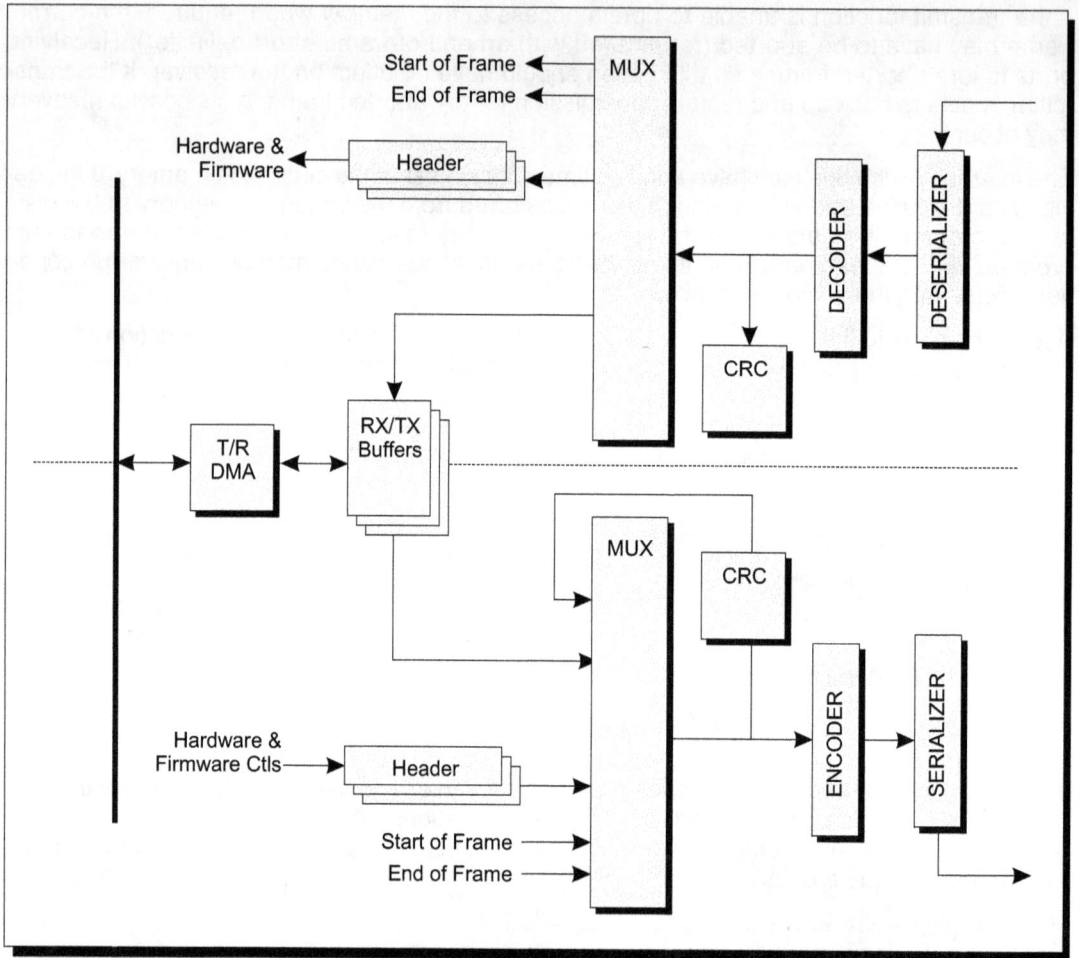

Figure 65. Half-Duplex Port With External Memory

2 environment, it would have to incorporate receive buffering to hold the link control frames received in response to frames. In Class-3, no ACKs are sent so that buffering is not required.

If the port receives an OPNy (either full-duplex or half-duplex) it initializes the frame buffers and DMA for frame reception. Received frames are held in the frame buffers and then transferred to system memory via the system bus. In the Opened state, the port is not able to originate any frames of its own because the DMA and frame buffers are committed to the receive operation. Whether the received OPN is full-duplex or half-duplex is immaterial because the port itself only operates in half-duplex mode. If the port needs to send a frame, it waits for the current loop circuit to close, then arbitrates to send the frame(s) in a separate loop circuit.

This leads to an interesting problem. Even though a design may be intended for a Class-3 only environment, it still needs to generate the appropriate responses to any Class-1 or Class-2 frames received (with the correct frame delimiters). Therefore, if a Class-1 frame is received and Class-1 is not supported, a Port_Reject link control frame is required. The only way to send the response is to wait for the current loop circuit to close, arbitrate, and then send the link control response during a new loop circuit.

11.5.2 Half-Duplex Port With No Frame Buffers

The final example, shown in Figure 66 on page 199, takes the design from Figure 64 on page 196 and simplifies it to support only half-duplex operations.

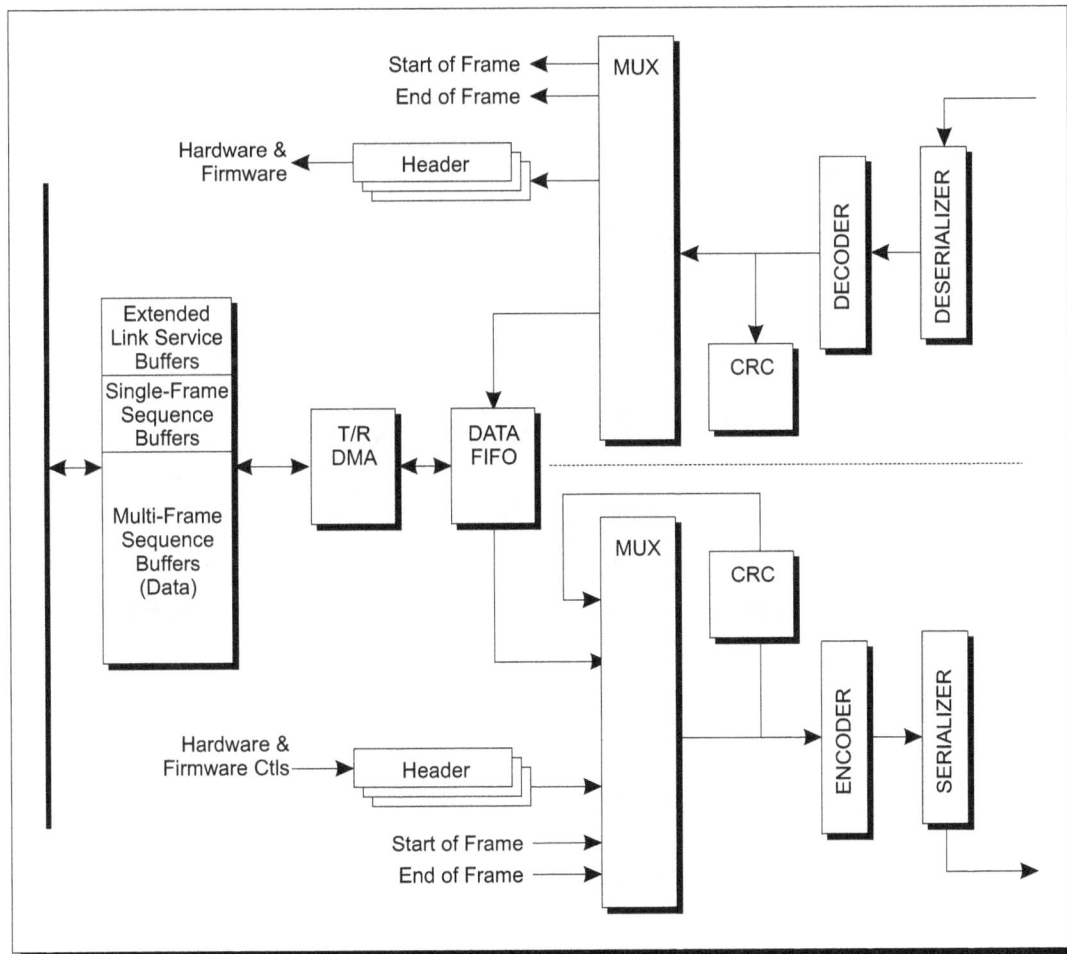

Figure 66. Half-Duplex Port With No Frame Buffers

This figure also shows one possible partitioning of the sequence memory into separate single-frame sequence buffers, fibre channel extended link services buffers, and data frame buffer areas. When a frame is received, the receiving logic examines the R_CTL and TYPE fields in the frame header to determine where the frame should be stored.

If this design is used in a SCSI target device and the R_CTL and TYPE fields indicate that this is a SCSI FCP device data frame and the information category is 6 (FCP_CMND) the frame is stored in a single-frame sequence buffer, the buffer pointer is updated in case additional FCP_CMND sequences are received, and the firmware is notified.

If the R_CTL field indicates that this is a device data frame, the TYPE field is equal to SCSI FCP, and the information category is 1 (FCP_DATA) the frame is stored in the data portion of the memory. By limiting the number of FCP_XFER_RDYs outstanding at any point in time to no more than one, only one data transfer is possible, so the data frame must be part of that transfer.

If the R_CTL bits indicate that this is an extended link service frame, it is routed to the extended link service section of the buffer, the buffer pointer is updated in case additional extended link service frames are received, and the firmware is notified.

This relatively simple design may suited for devices that implement one upper level protocol and require compact and cost effective solutions. As long as data buffer space is available, it can support extended bursts of frames at full fibre channel link rates in one direction. Limiting the design to half-duplex simplifies the logic required and reduces the potential memory bandwidth by half compared to a full-duplex implementation.

While there are potential savings, the designer should be cautioned that excessive reliance on the characteristics of one upper level protocol may lead to a design that is not capable of supporting a different upper level protocol without significant change. Also, relying on an anticipated normal behavior may result in interoperability problems when encountering a design that complies with the applicable fibre channel standards but doesn't exhibit the expected behavior. For example, it is widely assumed that the FCP_RSP sequence will consist of a single frame, and in fact the Private Loop Direct Attach profile enforces this assumption. However, some devices in the future may generate FCP_RSP sequences that consist of more than one frame. If this occurs, designs built around the assumption of a single-frame FCP_RSP sequence may not be able to accept a longer sequence. Finally, reliance on the characteristics of a particular topology may lead to a design that is not capable of operating in the other fibre channel topologies.

11.6 Chapter Summary

Key Questions

- Fibre channel ports probably require processor support
- Where is the processor located?
  - On an adapter card?
  - Does the design use the system or device processor?
- Where is the memory used to assemble sequences located?
  - On an adapter card?
  - Use the system or device memory?
- How is the FC-2 function distributed between the hardware and firmware/software?

Context Switching

- How does a port manage context switching?
- Consecutive frames may be associated with different operations
- Some frame types may arrive as rapidly as one per microsecond
  - If the context switch is done in software, performance may suffer
- What happens when a sequence being transmitted stalls (e.g., the available credit is exhausted)?
  - Wait for the credit to be replenished?, or
  - Switch to a different port that has credit available?

Full or Half Duplex?

- Full-duplex designs are capable of transmitting and receiving frames simultaneously
  - Potentially doubles the bandwidth
  - 100 MB/sec transmit and 100 MB/sec receive
- Requires at least 2 DMA functions
  - One for the transmit data
  - One for the receive data
- If both paths share the same memory, the memory bandwidth is doubled
- Half-duplex simplifies the design
  - One DMA and half the memory bandwidth

Protocol Assists

- Fibre channel chips may provide assist functions for certain protocols
  - SCSI and perhaps FC-LE or IP
- This improves performance by reducing the amount of firmware intervention
- More hardware is required, however
  - Adds to the complexity of the design
  - Adds to the cost

Basic Transmit Operation

- Transmit data is stored in sequence memory
- Firmware initializes the XMIT_DMA
- The XMIT_DMA transfers the data from the memory into transmit buffers
- When one or more frames are ready for transmission the LPSM is requested to arbitrate
- When the LPSM wins arbitration, an OPN is sent to the destination port
- Frame transmission can begin, subject to flow control rules

Frame Transmission

- When a frame data field is filled, the frame is sent by sequentially transmitting the:
  - Start-of-frame
  - Frame header
  - Data field
  - Calculated CRC
  - End-of-Frame
- Once the frame is sent, the transmit buffer is marked empty
- This allows the XMIT DMA to begin refilling the data field

Transmit Buffers

- Transmit buffers are refilled as soon as possible
- Frame transmission overlaps refilling empty buffers
- Ideally, one or more buffers is always ready for transmission
  - Prevents waiting for a buffer to fill
  - Which would reduce performance
- If the memory speed is less than the link speed the buffers will empty
  - Must decide whether to close the loop circuit, or
  - Keep the loop circuit while the buffers are re-filling

When to Arbitrate?

- Designer has to decide when to arbitrate
  - As soon as the XMIT DMA is started
  - When the first frame buffer is full, or
  - When a minimum threshold of full buffers is reached
- Some time is required to win arbitration
  - Filling the transmit buffers could overlap arbitration time for improved performance
- However, the port could be opened by a different device than anticipated
  - The transmit buffers might have to be flushed, or,
  - Run half-duplex and hold the XMIT data?

Basic Receive Operation

- Information is received from the link and stored in receive buffers
- When the first frame of a sequence is received, the receive DMA is initialized
- When each receive buffer is full, it is transferred to sequence memory
- If all of the available receive buffers fill, frame transmission must be stopped
  - This is done by a flow control mechanism
  - When one or more buffers becomes available, transmission can resume

Sample Implementations

- Full-Duplex designs
  - On-board sequence memory
  - External sequence memory
  - Design with no transmit or receive buffers
- Half-Duplex designs
  - On-board sequence memory
  - External sequence memory
  - Design with no transmit or receive buffers

12. SCSI-3 FCP Commands

This chapter describes the Fibre Channel Protocol (FCP) for SCSI-3 information units and associated frames used to send those information units. It then examines a number of different command scenarios performed in an Arbitrated Loop environment to illustrate how the various information units and loop protocols are used to perform a complete SCSI command.

12.1 FCP Use of the Exchange

The Fibre Channel Protocol for SCSI-3 standard defines a direct correspondence between the SCSI task and the Fibre Channel exchange. Therefore, a Fibre Channel exchange corresponds to a single command or group of linked commands.

12.2 FCP Information Units

The FCP mapping of SCSI-3 to fibre channel defines a number of information units that are exchanged between a SCSI initiator and a target. Each information unit corresponds to one fibre channel sequence. All of the sequences except the FCP_DATA normally fit within a single fibre channel frame. The number of frames required for the data sequence depends on the amount of data being transferred during that sequence and the data field size of the frames used.

In some situations, it may be possible for the FCP_RSP sequence to require multiple frames to accommodate the SCSI autosense data. This could occur if the amount of sense data results in a sequence size larger than the frame data field size (this could occur if the frame data field size is less than 512 bytes).

12.2.1 Command Information Unit (FCP_CMND)

The FCP_CMND information unit defines the data structure containing the SCSI Command Descriptor Block (CDB) and other command related information. The format of the FCP_CMND information unit is illustrated in Figure 67 on page 204.

The FCP_LUN field contains the eight-byte expanded Logical Unit Number (LUN) introduced by SCSI-3. For those devices which report their device type as controller in their inquiry data, the format of this field is defined by the SCSI-3 Storage Controller Commands (SCC) document. Other device types position the LUN in byte 1 of the FCP_LUN field as shown in Figure 67 on page 204.

The FCP_CNTL field contains the task attributes (queue type), task management flags (specifying a task management function to be performed), and the execution management flags (read or write data will be transferred).

The FCP_CDB is a 16-byte field containing the SCSI CDB starting in byte 0. When a six, ten, or twelve byte CDB is used, the unused bytes in the FCP_CDB field are undefined, but still present. For long CDBs, bytes beyond 16 follow the FCP_DL field.

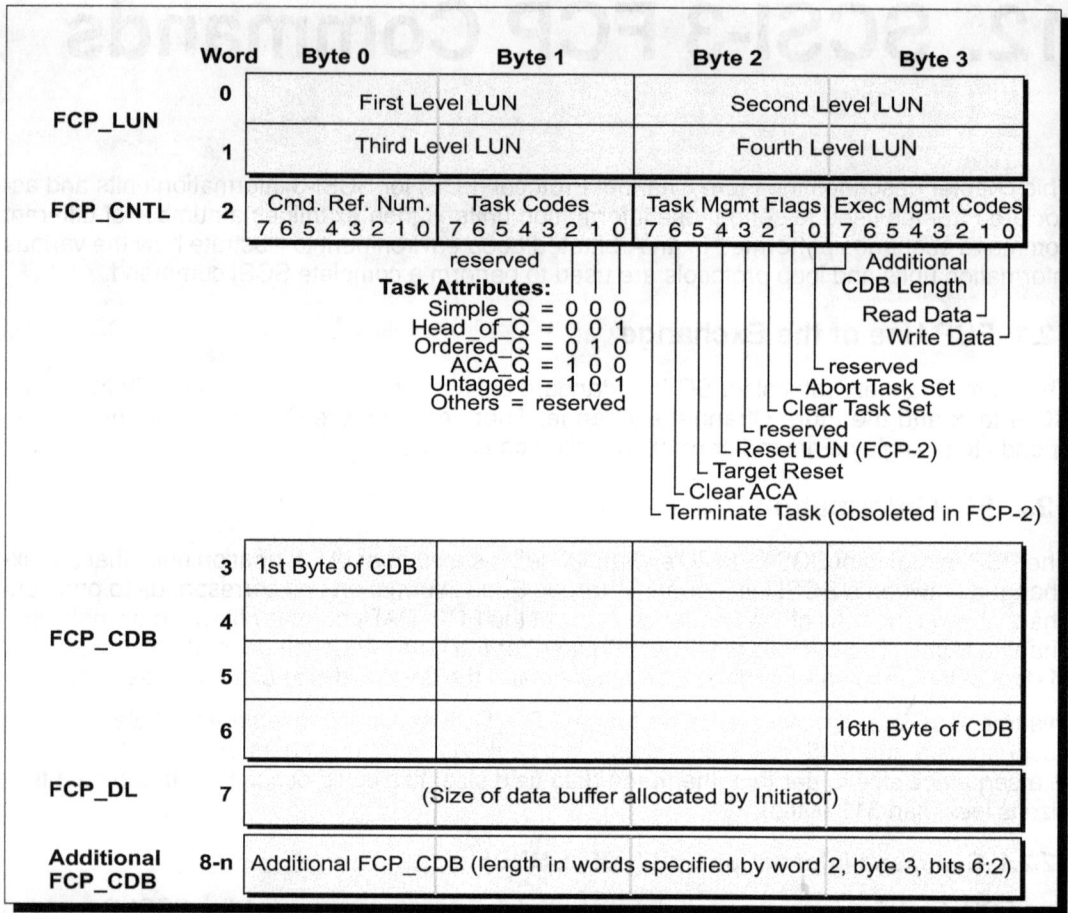

Figure 67. FCP_CMND Information Unit

The FCP_DL field contains the number of data bytes (command parameter data, command response data, or logical data) that are expected to be transferred by this command. Failure to transfer the specified number of bytes is not necessarily an error because this may be normal behavior for some commands and some devices.

12.2.2 Transfer Ready Information Unit (FCP_XFER_RDY)

The FCP_XFER_RDY information unit contains the relative offset and length of the following data sequence. The format of the FCP_XFER_RDY data structure is defined by the FCP standard and is shown in Figure 68 on page 205.

The DATA_RO field specifies the offset of the first byte of the FCP_DATA information unit that follows. It specifies the lowest offset value of any byte of the FCP_DATA information unit (if relative offset is not used or continuous relative offset is used the first frame of the FCP_DATA in-

Word	Byte 0	Byte 1	Byte 2	Byte 3
0		DATA_RO		
1		BURST_LEN		
2		reserved		

Figure 68. FCP_XFER_RDY Information Unit

formation unit carries data for this relative offset. If random relative offset is used, that is not necessarily the case.).

The BURST_LEN field specifies the exact length of the FCP_DATA information unit that follows. This value cannot exceed the value of the Maximum Burst Size field in the SCSI disconnect-reconnect mode page. If the actual number of bytes transferred by the subsequent FCP_DATA information unit does not match this value, the RSP_CODE in the FCP_RSP information unit is set to x'01'.

12.2.3 Data Information Unit (FCP_DATA)

Some SCSI commands transfer data between an initiator and a target. The data may be sent as a single FCP_DATA information unit, or broken up into multiple information units. This is analogous to the transfer of data in multiple bursts across the SCSI parallel bus interface.

A SCSI command may result in the transfer of one of three different types of data. The Fibre Channel Protocol for SCSI does not distinguish between these data types. The data types are:

- Command parameter data (e.g., data associated with a Mode Select or Format Unit command)
- Command response data (e.g., data associated with a Mode Sense or Inquiry command)
- Logical data (e.g., data associated with a read or write command)

There is no structure to the FCP_DATA information unit, it is simply the data associated with the command transferred as a sequence of one or more frames.

12.2.4 Response Information Unit (FCP_RSP)

The FCP_RSP information unit defines the data structure containing the SCSI status byte, SCSI autosense, and FCP response code and is used to signal the completion of a SCSI command or task management function. The format of the FCP_RSP information unit is defined by the FCP standard and is illustrated in Figure 69 on page 206.

The FCP_RSP is normally the last sequence of an exchange (the exception occurs when command linking is used). The FCP_RSP is normally a single-frame sequence, however, it may require multiple frames when SCSI autosense data causes the size of the FCP_RSP to exceed that which can be carried in a single frame.

	Word	Byte 0	Byte 1	Byte 2	Byte 3
reserved	0				
reserved	1				
FCP_STATUS	2	reserved 7 6 5 4 3 2 1 0	reserved 7 6 5 4 3 2 1 0	Validity Flags 7 6 5 4 3 2 1 0	SCSI Status byte 7 6 5 4 3 2 1 0

reserved
FCP_CONF_REQ. ⌐
FCP_RESID_UNDER ⌐
FCP_RESID_OVER ⌐
FCP_SNS_LEN_VALID ⌐
FCP_RSP_LEN_VALID ⌐

	Word				
FCP_RESID	3				
FCP_SNS_LEN	4				
FCP_RSP_LEN	5	(Defined by FCP to be 0, 4, or 8 bytes)			

00 = No Failure or Task Management function complete
01 = FCP_DATA length different than BURST_LEN
02 = FCP_CMND Fields Invalid
03 = FCP_DATA RO mismatch with FCP_XFER_RDY DATA_RO
04 = Task Management Function Not Supported
05 = Task Management Function Failed
06-FF = reserved

	Word	Byte 0	Byte 1	Byte 2	Byte 3
FCP_RSP_INFO	6	reserved	reserved	reserved	RSP_CODE
	7	reserved	reserved	reserved	reserved
FCP_SNS_INFO		(Variable length as defined by FCP_SNS_LEN)			

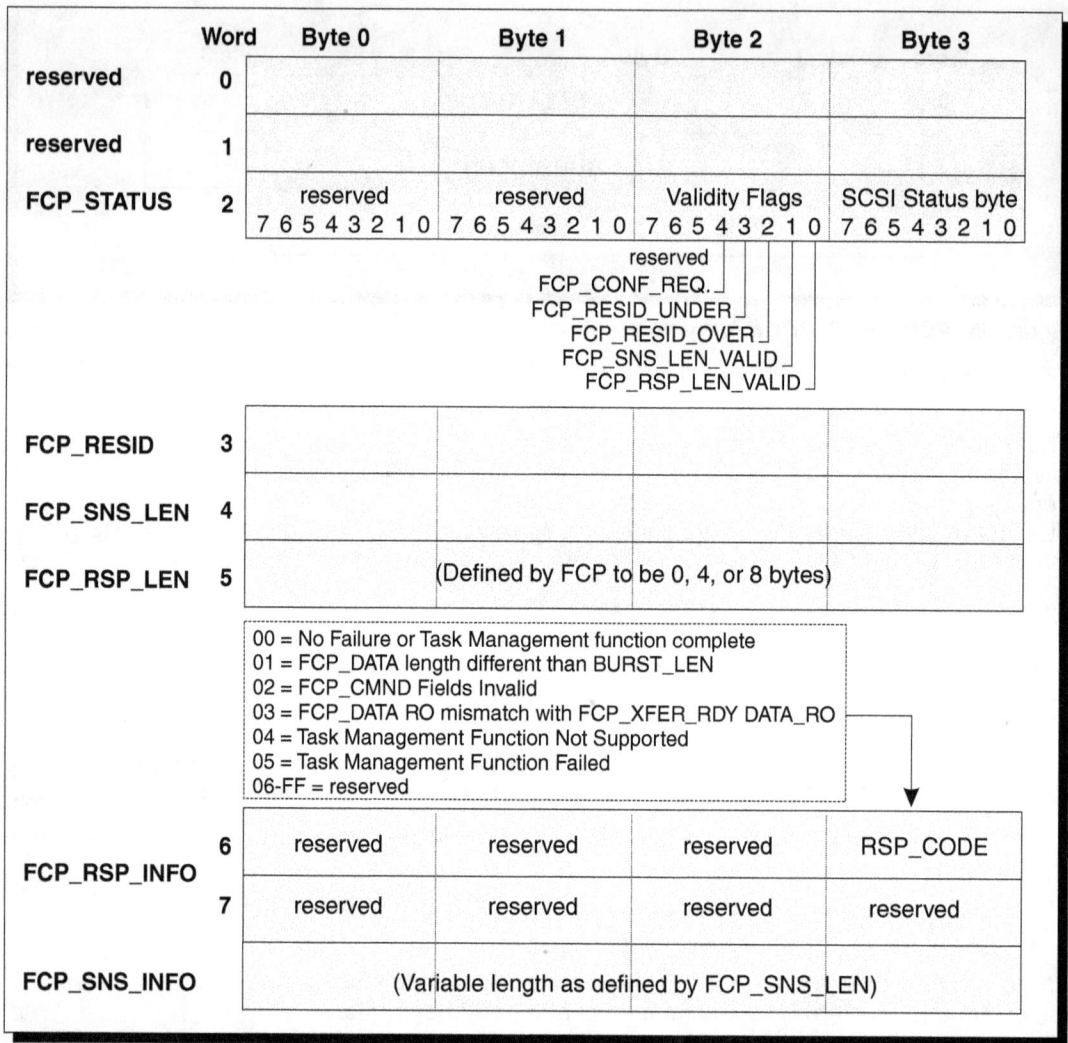

Figure 69. FCP_RSP Information Unit

The FCP_STATUS field contains validity bits indicating which other fields contain valid information and the SCSI status byte.

FCP_CONF_REQ. This bit indicates the target is requesting an FCP_CONF information unit in response to this FCP_RSP. FCP_CONF is a sequence consisting of a single frame with no payload. The information category is set to Solicited Control (x'3') and the Last Sequence bit is set to end the exchange.

FCP_RESID_UNDER. This bit indicates the FCP_RESID field is valid and the data transfer did not fill the buffer to the expected displacement as indicated by the FCP_DL field in the FCP_CMND information unit. The value of FCP_RESID is equal to:

FCP_RESID = FCP_DL - (highest offset of any byte transmitted)

A condition of FCP_RESID_UNDER may not be an error for some devices and commands.

If either the FCP_RESID_UNDER or the FCP_RESID_OVER bit is set to a one, the FCP_RESID field contains a count of the number of residual data bytes which were not transferred in the FCP_DATA information units for this command. Upon successful completion of a command, the residual value is normally zero and the FCP_RESID value is not valid. Devices having indeterminate data lengths may have a nonzero residual byte count after completing valid operations. Targets are not required to verify that the data length implied by the contents of the CDB will create an overrun or underrun before beginning execution of a command.

If the FCP_RESID_UNDER and the FCP_RESID_OVER bits are set zero, the FCP_RESID field is not meaningful and may have any value.

FCP_RESID_OVER. This bit indicates the FCP_RESID field is valid and the transfer was truncated because the data transfer required by the SCSI command extended beyond the displacement value of FCP_DL. Those bytes that could be transferred without violating the FCP_DL value may be transferred. The FCP_RESID is a number equal to:

FCP_RESID = (Transfer length required by command) - FCP_DL

If a condition of FCP_RESID_OVER is detected, the termination state of the SCSI command is not certain. Data may or may not have been transferred and the SCSI status byte may or may not provide correct command completion information.

FCP_RSP_LEN_VALID. This bit indicates the FCP_RSP_LEN field is valid and contains the count of bytes in the FCP_RSP_INFO field.

FCP_SNS_LEN_VALID. This bit indicates the FCP_SNS_LEN field is valid and contains the count of bytes in the FCP_SNS_INFO field.

The SCSI status byte contains the status as defined by the SCSI architecture.

FCP_RSP_INFO. This field provides task or task management response information that cannot be communicated through the SCSI status byte or sense information. It is used to provide information about the FCP information unit, data transfer consistency, or response to a Task Management request. The Fibre Channel Protocol for SCSI standard defines this as a variable length field width of zero, four, or eight bytes with other values reserved for possible future standardization. The convention being adopted by the disk drive community is that this field will be either zero or eight bytes in length with the one-byte response code in byte 3 (byte 0 is the most significant byte of the word). The actual length of the response information is indicated in the FCP_RSP_LEN field.

Using an eight byte FCP_RSP_INFO field results in a normal response frame payload of 32-bytes (eight words) plus any associated autosense data.

FCP_SNS_INFO. This field contains the SCSI sense information. The length of the sense information field is indicated in the FCP_SNS_LEN field and is less than or equal to 255 bytes. Some profiles may restrict the number of sense bytes to ensure that the entire FCP_RSP fits within a single 128-byte frame. As an example, the Private Loop Direct Attach Technical Report restricts the sense data to 78 bytes or less to allow the entire response frame to fit within a single 128-byte frame.

12.3 Class-3 FCP Frames

This section illustrates the format of frames used to carry the FCP information units when Class-3 operation is used.

12.3.1 Class-3 FCP Command Frame

The FCP_CMND information unit is normally sent as a single-frame sequence which is the first sequence of an exchange (T1 information unit). When linking is used (T3 information unit) or when a *Terminate Task* task management function is being issued (the Terminate Task function is being obsoleted by the FCP-2 standard) the FCP_CMND information unit may occur within the middle of an existing exchange. The only difference between the T1 and T3 information units is whether the *first sequence of exchange* bit in the F_CTL field of the frame header is set or not. A trace of a typical Class-3 FCP command frame is shown in Figure 70.

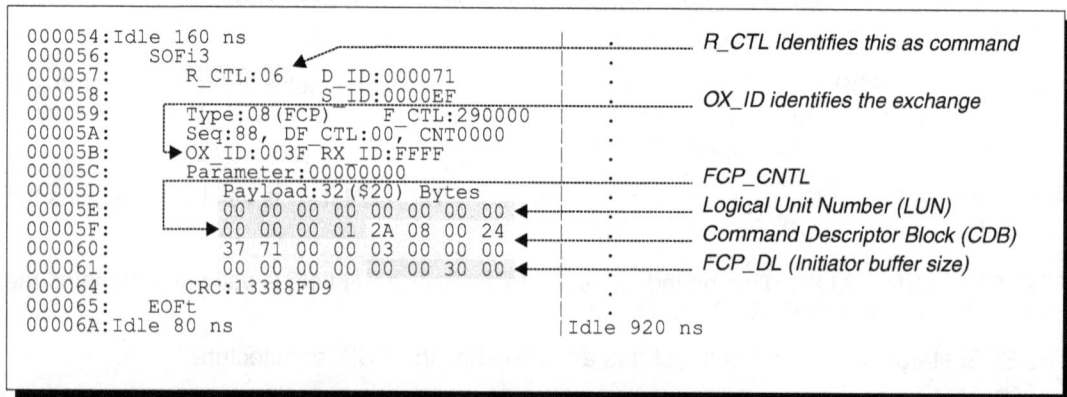

```
000054:Idle 160 ns                                    .        R_CTL Identifies this as command
000056:    SOFi3                                       .
000057:       R_CTL:06    D_ID:000071                  .
000058:                   S_ID:0000EF                  .        OX_ID identifies the exchange
000059:       Type:08(FCP)     F_CTL:290000            .
00005A:       Seq:88, DF_CTL:00, CNT0000               .
00005B:     OX_ID:003F RX_ID:FFFF                      .
00005C:       Parameter:00000000                       .        FCP_CNTL
00005D:          Payload:32 ($20) Bytes                .
00005E:          00 00 00 00 00 00 00 00  ◄──────────  .        Logical Unit Number (LUN)
00005F:          00 00 00 01 2A 08 00 24  ◄──────────  .        Command Descriptor Block (CDB)
000060:          37 71 00 00 03 00 00 00  ◄──────────  .
000061:          00 00 00 00 00 00 30 00  ◄──────────  .        FCP_DL (Initiator buffer size)
000064:       CRC:13388FD9                             .
000065:    EOFt                                        .
00006A:Idle 80 ns                               |Idle 920 ns
```

Figure 70. Class-3 FCP Command Frame

The FCP standard states that relative offset in the parameter field is not meaningful for the FCP_CMND information unit. The preferred implementation is to set the *relative offset present* bit in the F_CTL field (bit 3) to a zero indicating that the relative offset is not present.

12.3.2 Class-3 FCP Transfer Ready Frame

The FCP transfer ready information unit is normally a single-frame sequence sent by the target in response to a data transfer command to indicate that the target is ready to send or receive a data sequence. Use of the transfer ready is optional in the SCSI-3 FCP mapping and is negotiated during the FCP process login (PRLI) process. Normally, in the case of disk type devices, transfer ready is used on write-type commands and disabled (not used) on read-type commands. All of the examples shown later follow this convention.

The DATA_RO relative offset field establishes the base address for the following data sequence and the Burst_Len field specifies the number of bytes in the data sequence. An FCP_XFER_RDY sent to request write data transfers Sequence Initiative (bit 16 in the F_CTL field), while the FCP_XFER_RDY preceding read data does not. Other than this, frames for the two information units are identical.

As was the case for the FCP_CMND information unit, the FCP standard states that the relative offset in the parameter field is not meaningful for the FCP_XFER_RDY information unit. The preferred implementation is to set the relative offset present bit in the F_CTL field (bit 3) to a zero indicating that the relative offset is not present. As an alternative, the relative offset present bit may be set to a one and the parameter field set to all zeros.

A trace of a Class-3 FCP_XFER_RDY frame is shown in Figure 71.

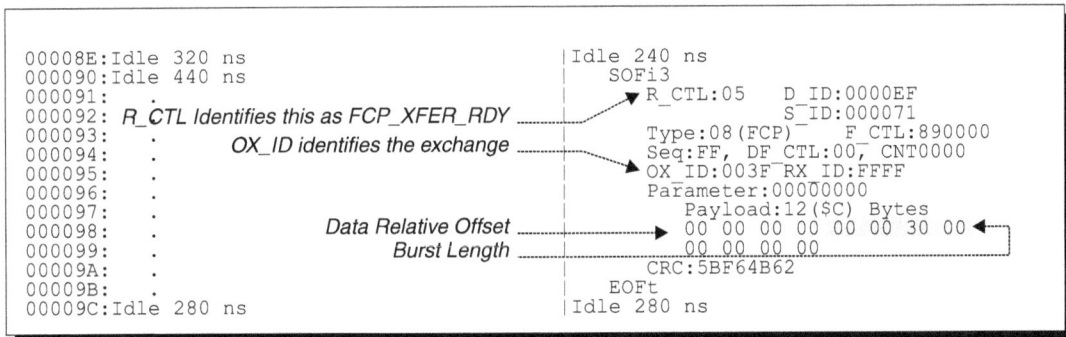

```
00008E:Idle 320 ns                             |Idle 240 ns
000090:Idle 440 ns                             |   SOFi3
000091:     .                                  |   R_CTL:05    D_ID:0000EF
000092:  R_CTL Identifies this as FCP_XFER_RDY ...........|              S_ID:000071
000093:     .                                  |   Type:08(FCP)    F_CTL:890000
000094:          OX_ID identifies the exchange .........  Seq:FF, DF_CTL:00, CNT0000
000095:     .                                  |   OX_ID:003F RX_ID:FFFF
000096:     .                                  |   Parameter:00000000
000097:     .                                  |        Payload:12($C) Bytes
000098:     .          Data Relative Offset ............▶ 00 00 00 00 00 00 30 00 ◀
000099:     .              Burst Length ..........|        00 00 00 00
00009A:     .                                  |   CRC:5BF64B62
00009B:     .                                  |   EOFt
00009C:Idle 280 ns                             |Idle 280 ns
```

Figure 71. Class-3 FCP Transfer Ready Frame

12.3.3 Class-3 FCP_DATA Frame

The FCP_DATA sequence, when used, consists of one or more data frames. Each data frame within a data sequence contains the same SEQ_ID value. The SEQ_CNT increases by one for each frame sent within the sequence. The parameter field in the header of each data frame may contain the relative offset of the data in the payload in that frame.

While the Fibre Channel standard allows variable size data fields for frames within a data sequence, at least one early implementation requires that all frames within a data sequence are the same size except for the last frame of the sequence. This simplifies the sequence reassembly for that recipient port. Because there is no way to negotiate or communicate this constraint via FC-PH mechanisms, interoperability could present a potential problem if this restriction is not observed.

FC-PH only allows the presence of fill bytes in the last frame of a sequence. This raises an interesting question about which frame is the last frame of the sequence in the context of the fill bytes. If random relative offset is not used, then the frame with the End_Sequence bit set (Class-1, 2, or 4) or EOFt delimiter (Class-3) is the last data frame of the sequence and may contain fill bytes. If random relative offset is used, then the frame with the EOFt is the last frame of the sequence transmitted, but may not represent the frame with the highest relative offset which is where the fill bytes should logically exist.

The position of a data frame within the sequence dictates which frame delimiters are used. Table 15 on page 210 summarizes the correct Class-3 frame delimiter usage for sequences with different numbers of frames.

Data Sequence	First Frame of Sequence	Middle Frames of Sequence	Last Frame of Sequence
Single frame data sequence	SOFi3, EOFt		
Two frame data sequence	SOFi3, EOFn		SOFn3, EOFt
Three or greater frame data sequence	SOFi3, EOFn	SOFn3, EOFn	SOFn3, EOFt

Table 15. Data Sequence Frame Delimiters for Class-3

Each data frame must correctly reflect the appropriate settings of appropriate F_CTL bits depending on the operation being performed and position of the frame within the sequence. A trace of an FCP data frame is shown in Figure 72.

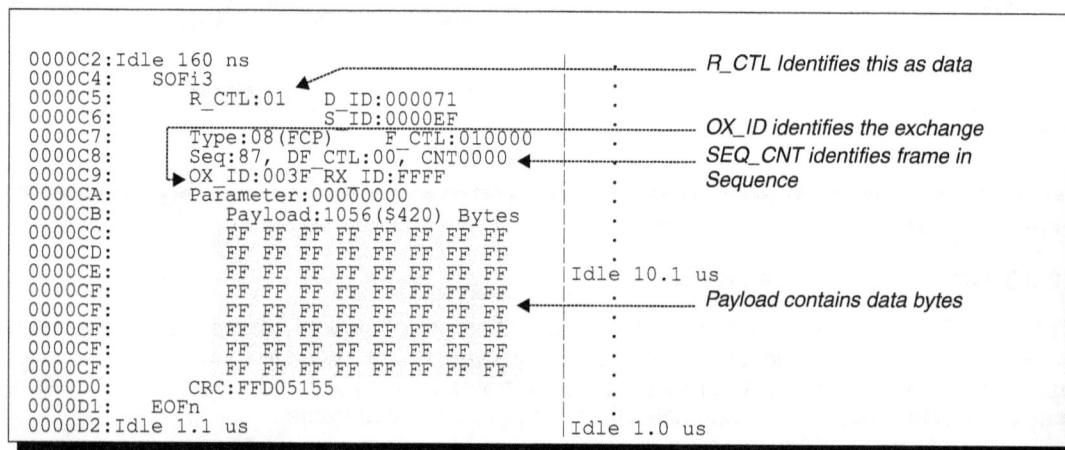

```
0000C2:Idle 160 ns                                      R_CTL Identifies this as data
0000C4:    SOFi3
0000C5:      R_CTL:01    D_ID:000071
0000C6:                  S_ID:0000EF
0000C7:      Type:08(FCP)    F_CTL:010000                OX_ID identifies the exchange
0000C8:      Seq:87, DF_CTL:00, CNT0000                  SEQ_CNT identifies frame in
0000C9:      OX_ID:003F RX_ID:FFFF                       Sequence
0000CA:      Parameter:00000000
0000CB:      Payload:1056($420) Bytes
0000CC:        FF FF FF FF FF FF FF FF
0000CD:        FF FF FF FF FF FF FF FF
0000CE:        FF FF FF FF FF FF FF FF     |Idle 10.1 us
0000CF:        FF FF FF FF FF FF FF FF
0000CF:        FF FF FF FF FF FF FF FF                   Payload contains data bytes
0000CF:        FF FF FF FF FF FF FF FF
0000CF:        FF FF FF FF FF FF FF FF
0000CF:        FF FF FF FF FF FF FF FF
0000D0:      CRC:FFD05155
0000D1:    EOFn
0000D2:Idle 1.1 us                         |Idle 1.0 us
```

Figure 72. Class-3 FCP Data Frame

Because data sequences can be sent by either the exchange originator or responder, the Exchange Context (bit 23) in the F_CTL field of the frame header must be set accordingly.

Write-type operations normally transfer sequence initiative at the end of each data sequence while read-type commands do not. The *sequence initiative* bit (bit 16) in the F_CTL field of the frame header is set to indicate when sequence initiative is being transferred. The sequence initiative bit is only meaningful on the last frame of the sequence, but may be set earlier by some designs. When the sequence initiative bit is set prior to the last frame of the sequence, there may be a temptation to use this as an early indicator of the intent to transfer the initiative at the end of the sequence. However, if this is done, it should be remembered that the sequence initiator could change the setting of the sequence initiative on the last frame.

The End_Sequence (bit 19) in the F_CTL field of the frame header is set on the last data frame of each sequence.

12.3.4 Class-3 FCP_RSP Frame

The FCP_RSP is sent to indicate completion of a command or task management request. This is normally a single-frame sequence, although it may require more than one frame in some circumstances. The FCP_RSP is the last information unit of an exchange (I4) unless linking is used or an FCP_CONF is being requested (I5). The difference between the two cases is the setting of the *last sequence of exchange* bit in the F_CTL field of the frame header.

As was the case for the FCP_CMND and FCP_RSP information units, the FCP standard states that the relative offset in the parameter field is not meaningful for the FCP_RSP information unit. The preferred implementation is to set the relative offset present bit in the F_CTL field (bit 3) to a zero indicating that the relative offset is not present. As an alternative, the relative offset present bit may be set to a one and the parameter field set to all zeros.

An analyzer trace of a single frame Class-3 FCP response frame is shown in Figure 73.

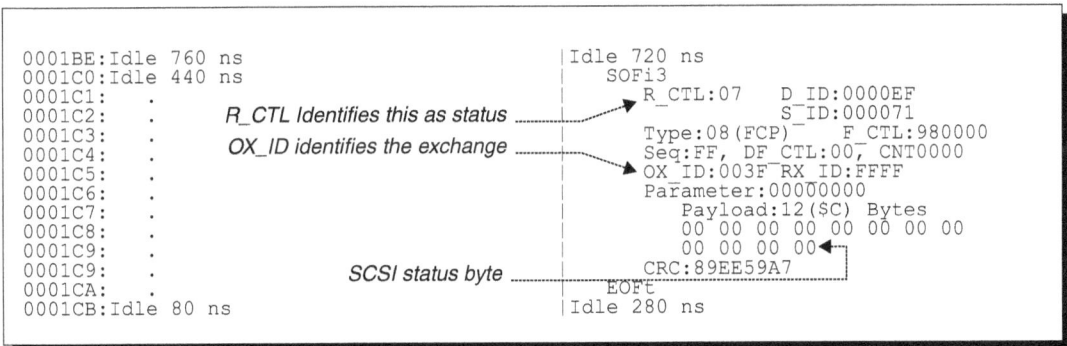

```
0001BE:Idle 760 ns                              |Idle 720 ns
0001C0:Idle 440 ns                              |  SOFi3
0001C1:   .                                     |   ► R_CTL:07    D_ID:0000EF
0001C2:   .      R_CTL Identifies this as status|----┘        S_ID:000071
0001C3:   .                                     |     Type:08(FCP)    F_CTL:980000
0001C4:   .      OX_ID identifies the exchange  |·····Seq:FF, DF_CTL:00, CNT0000
0001C5:   .                                     |  ► OX_ID:003F RX_ID:FFFF
0001C6:   .                                     |     Parameter:00000000
0001C7:   .                                     |         Payload:12($C) Bytes
0001C8:   .                                     |         00 00 00 00 00 00 00 00
0001C9:   .                                     |         00 00 00 00◄--
0001C9:   .      SCSI status byte  ·············|·····CRC:89EE59A7
0001CA:   .                                     |  EOFt
0001CB:Idle 80 ns                               |Idle 280 ns
```

Figure 73. Class-3 FCP Response Frame

12.4 Loop Tenancies

When a port wins arbitration, it begins a loop tenancy. This tenancy persists until that port returns to the Monitoring state and allows another port to win arbitration. During this loop tenancy, one or more loop circuits may be opened and closed. Unless the Transfer state is used, each loop tenancy is used to establish a single loop circuit.

Once the various information units and associated sequences have been defined, the next step is to determine how those information units are transferred using the Arbitrated Loop. Will all information units for a given command be transferred during a single loop circuit or will a given command be spread across multiple loop circuits, each of which may transfer one or more information units? For implementations that only support half-duplex operation, some of the choices are made automatically because those designs may require a new loop circuit to change the direction of frame transmission (see the Dynamic Half Duplex description *Dynamic Half-Duplex (DHD)* on page 52).

As an example, an FCP write-type command normally transfers at least four information units, changing the direction of information flow after each. A half-duplex design unable to change direction within a loop circuit requires at least four circuits to accommodate the direction changes, while a full-duplex design may be able to transfer multiple information units during the same loop circuit.

Another implementation decision to be made is the number of concurrent exchanges and sequences that a design is capable of supporting. Most designs will support multiple concurrent exchanges to facilitate behaviors such as command queueing. If this is the case, a design must be able to accommodate the transfer of information units for different operations during the same loop circuit. For example, a SCSI initiator may send multiple FCP_CMNDs during a single loop circuit. As long as the direction of frame transmission is the same, half-duplex designs can support this type of operation, while full-duplex designs may support the transfer of information units for different operations in both directions during the same loop circuit.

Before each loop tenancy begins, the port wishing to transmit one or more information units must arbitrate for access to the loop. After the port wins arbitration, it sends an OPN to establish a loop circuit with the open recipient. Once the loop circuit has been established, and as credit allows, one or more frames can be sent. There is no direct relationship to the information units that are transmitted during a loop tendency (i.e., there is no requirement that all of an information unit is transmitted within the same loop tendency as long as other timing constraints for fibre channel are met). However, normally, a complete information unit is typically transmitted during one loop tendency.

If the login BB_Credit value is zero, the open originator must wait for one or more R_RDYs indicating that the open recipient is ready to receive one or more frames. After the first R_RDY is received, the open originator can send the initial frame for that loop circuit. As additional R_RDYs are received, the port can send additional frames, if desired (the operation may not allow multiple frames to be sent, however, the open originator may be able perform an opportunistic transfer and send frames for a different operation). If the login BB_Credit value is greater than zero, the open originator can begin frame transmission based upon that credit value provided that at least two fill words have been sent after the OPN.

If the open originator does not have any more frames to send to the open recipient, it may send a CLS provided that at least two fill words have been sent after the last frame. When the open recipient receives the CLS, it completes its frame transmission, if any, and responds by sending a CLS of its own, ending the loop circuit.

There are many ways to map the basic SCSI-3 FCP information units to loop circuits. The following examples show some of the possibilities. These examples all illustrate a single loop circuit per loop tenancy. This is typical of current fibre channel operations, although some implementations may use the Transfer state to provide multiple loop circuits per tenancy. Also, while not shown in these examples illustrating loop tenancies, information units for different exchanges can frequently be transferred during the same loop circuit, either in half-duplex or full-duplex mode as supported by the ports. For simplicity, the examples show transfers for one exchange at a time only.

12.5 FCP Control Command Scenarios

Control type commands such as Test Unit Ready and Start-Stop Unit consist of the FCP_CMND and FCP_RSP information units. These can be transferred using a separate loop circuit for each as shown by example 1 in Figure 74 on page 213, or both information units can be transferred during the same loop circuit as shown by example 2. If the command requires significant time to complete, or the ports are only capable of half-duplex operation, example 1 may be used. If the command is an immediate command and the ports are capable of full-duplex operation (or the Dynamic Half Duplex ordered set is used) then example 2 may be used.

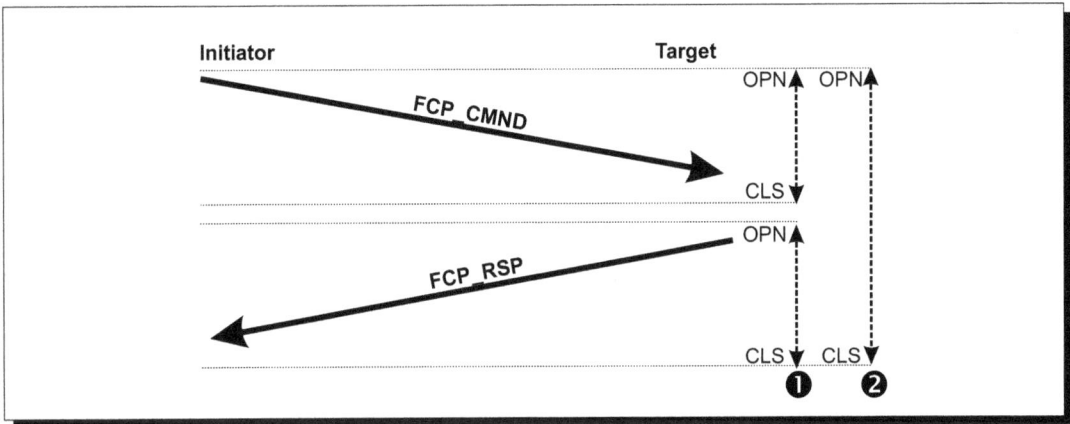

Figure 74. Control Command Loop Tenancies

An example of a control type command is shown in Figure 75 on page 214. In this Class-3, half-duplex, login BB_Credit=0 example, the command uses two loop tenancies; one for the FCP_CMND, and a second for the FCP_RSP. Between these two tenancies, the loop is available for use by other ports. Although the example uses two loop tenancies, some immediate control type commands (i.e., those that are completed within a short time) may be executed in a single circuit by designs capable of supporting full-duplex operation or support the Dynamic Half Duplex (DHD) ordered set.

The operation begins when the initiator prepares the FCP_CMND, arbitrates for access to the loop (in the Arbitrating state) and wins arbitration (Arbitration Won state). It then sends an OPNy to open the target and enters the Open state. The OPNy is followed by (a minimum of) two current fill words, one or more R_RDYs (each of which must be preceded and followed by a minimum of two fill words - note that one R_RDY takes no bandwidth because it replaces a fill word) to advise the target that the initiator has receive buffer(s) available, followed by current fill words. One R_RDY must be sent for each frame that the open originator transmits to allow the open recipient to transmit link continue frames (e.g., ACKs), if any. The open recipient can only transmit frames based on the number of R_RDYs which the open initiator transmits (i.e., the open recipient does not use login BB_Credit). This is normal operation of the alternate BB_Credit management model on the Arbitrated Loop.

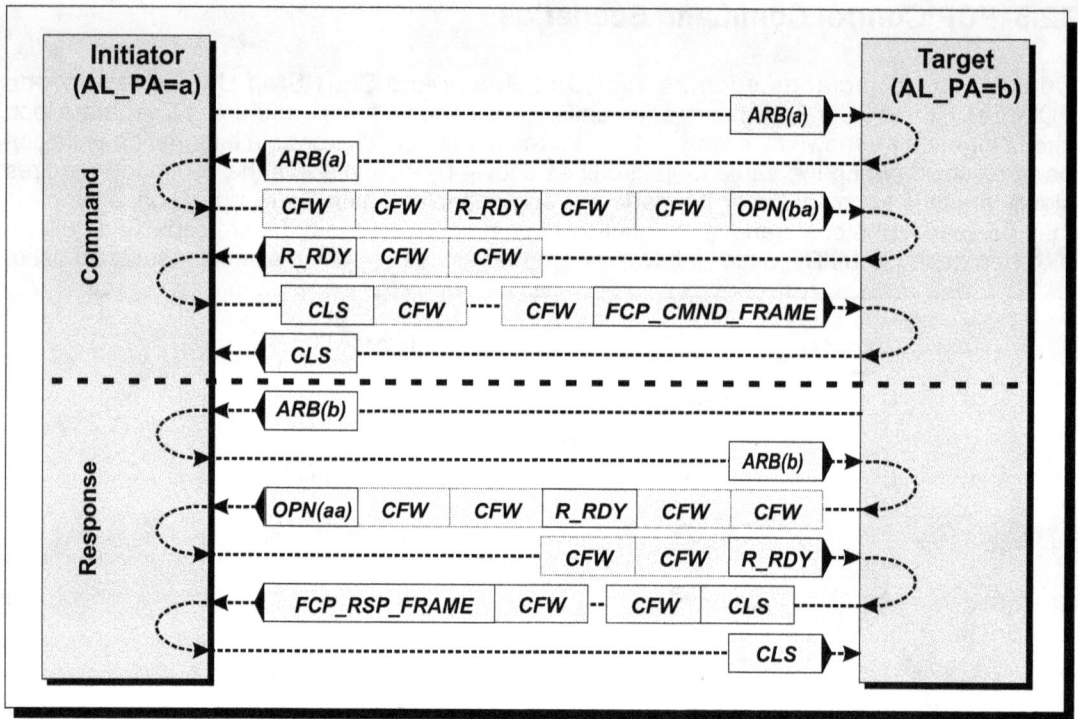

Figure 75. Control Command BB_Credit = 0

When the target receives the OPN, it leaves the Monitoring or Arbitrating state and enters the Opened state. Upon entry to the Opened state, the target sends a minimum of two current fill words, and one R_RDY for each available receive buffer (each R_RDY must be preceded and followed by a minimum of two fill words). If the open recipient granted a login BB_Credit of zero during login and is unable to accept frames at this time, it must send an immediate CLS to close the loop circuit. This convention is interpreted as meaning that the open recipient is busy and the open originator should retry the operation later (the FC-AL protocols do not provide for a 'no-longer busy' indication).

This implied busy is useful to make Class-3 more reliable on a loop. When the open originator transmits the OPN, it expects one of the following events within AL_TIME:

1. an R_RDY to indicate that the recipient has at least one receive buffer available.

2. a CLS to indicate that the port is present, but unable to receive a frame at this time (i.e., busy).

3. the OPNy which indicates that the port at AL_PA=y is not available on the loop.

Assuming the initiator receives at least one R_RDY from the target, it increments its available BB_Credit value by the number of R_RDYs received minus the login BB_Credit value used. This allows the initiator to send the FCP_CMND, which is followed by a minimum of two fill words (some designs may transmit six fill words rather than two) and a CLS (if there are no more frames for the target). After sending the CLS, the initiator enters the Transmitted Close state and continues to send fill words.

The target receives the FCP_CMND, two or more fill words, and CLS and enters the Received Close state. If the target has no frames to send to the initiator, or is operating in half-duplex mode, it transmits a CLS and enters the Monitoring state. The loop circuit is now closed at the target. Because the command sequence is complete, the command information unit is passed to the appropriate logical unit which processes the command while the port is off the loop.

When the initiator receives the CLS (and transfer is not being used), it enters the Monitoring state and closes the loop circuit at its end making the loop available for use by other ports.

When the target has completed processing the command and prepared the FCP_RSP, it arbitrates for access to the loop (in the Arbitrating state). When it wins arbitration (and enters the Arbitration Won state), the target transmits an OPNy to the initiator (and enters the Open state) to establish the loop circuit. Upon entry to the Open state, the target transmits a minimum of two current fill words, one R_RDY for each available receive buffer (each R_RDY must be preceded and followed by a minimum of two fill words), followed by current fill words.

The initiator receives the OPN and enters the Opened state. It transmits a minimum of two fill words, one R_RDY for each available receive buffer (each R_RDY must be preceded and followed by a minimum of two fill words), followed by current fill words.

When the target receives the R_RDYs in excess of the login BB_Credit value used, it increments its available BB_Credit value by one for each R_RDY. This allows it to transmit the FCP_RSP, followed by a minimum of two fill words, a CLS, and then enter the Transmitted Close state.

The initiator receives the FCP_RSP followed by the CLS, and enters the Received Close state. The initiator transmits a CLS and enters the Monitoring state. The loop circuit is now closed at the initiator end of the loop. The port passes the FCP_RSP information unit to the upper level protocol for processing.

When the target receives the CLS, it transitions from the Transmitted Close state to the Monitoring state and ends the loop circuit.

12.6 Write-Type Command Scenarios

The basic FCP write operation is used for all SCSI commands that transfer either command parameter data or logical data to a logical unit. Write-type commands such as Write, Mode Select, and Format Unit normally use all four FCP information units. Figure 76 on page 216 illustrates some common usage of loop tenancies during FCP write-type commands. Some of these loop circuit examples can be performed using half-duplex operations, while others require full-duplex capabilities (or use of the Dynamic Half Duplex ordered set).

A typical SCSI-3 FCP write-type command consists of the FCP_CMND, FCP_XFER_RDY, FCP_DATA, and FCP_RSP. In a four-tenancy operation, each information unit sequence is a separate loop tenancy as shown by example 2 in Figure 76. In this example, and the others, it is possible for the FCP_DATA sequence to be split across multiple loop tenancies. That is, a loop tenancy could be closed before the entire sequence of frames has been sent and then the sequence completed in a subsequent loop tenancy.

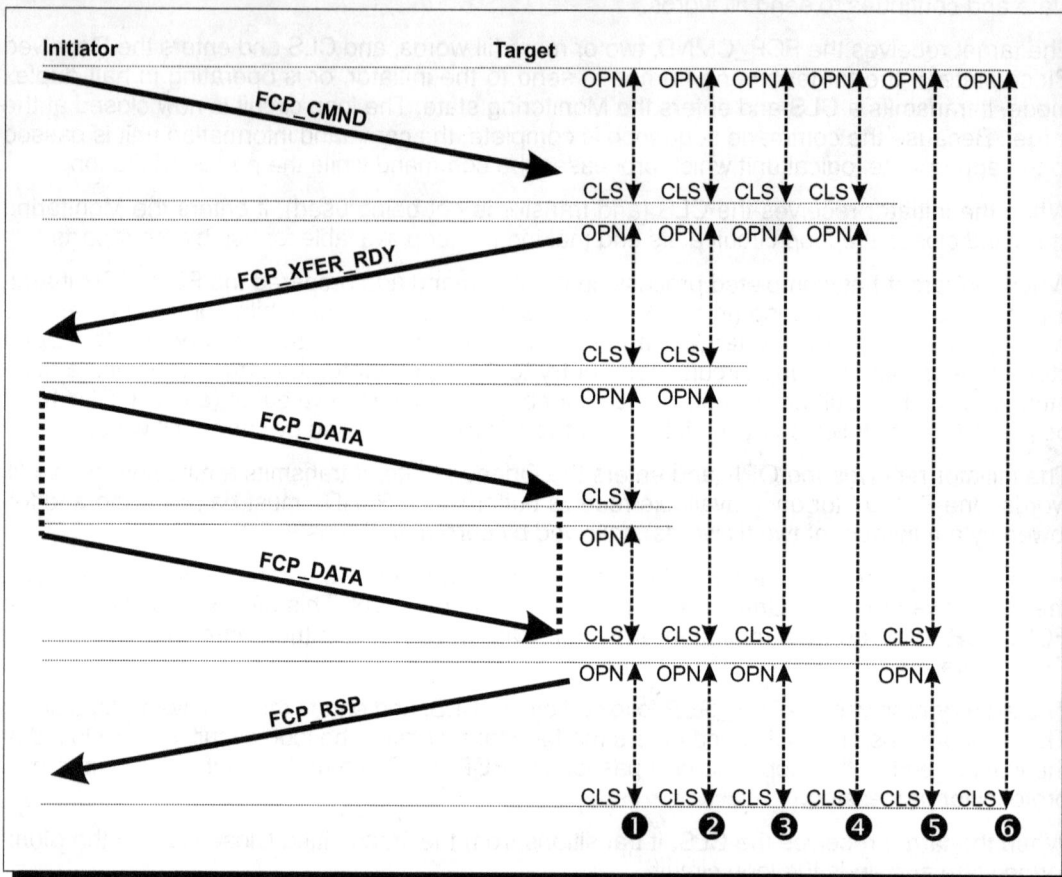

Initiator   Target

FCP_CMND

OPN OPN OPN OPN OPN OPN

CLS CLS CLS CLS

FCP_XFER_RDY

OPN OPN OPN OPN

CLS CLS

FCP_DATA

OPN OPN

CLS

OPN

FCP_DATA

CLS CLS CLS CLS

OPN OPN OPN OPN

FCP_RSP

CLS CLS CLS CLS CLS CLS

❶ ❷ ❸ ❹ ❺ ❻

Figure 76. Write Command Loop Tenancies

It is also possible a target may break the data transfer up into multiple bursts as is done today with data transfers on the SCSI parallel bus. When this is done, multiple FCP_XFER_RDY and FCP_DATA sequences may occur with each FCP_DATA sequence corresponding to a SCSI burst. As is the case with all data transfers, the SCSI target controls the data transfer. During write-type commands, the target determines the FCP_DATA sequence size and number of sequences through the FCP_XFER_RDY information unit. The amount of data requested by the transfer ready information unit should not exceed the *'maximum burst size* parameter from the *disconnect-reconnect* mode page reported during a Mode Sense command.

In one approach to a three-tenancy design, the FCP_XFER_RDY and FCP_DATA are transferred during a single loop tenancy as shown by example 3 in Figure 76 (this requires full-duplex operation or use of DHD).

There are a couple of possible ways that two-tenancy operations may occur. When using buffered or cached writes, it is possible to combine the FCP_XFER_RDY, write FCP_DATA, and FCP_RSP into a single loop tenancy as shown by example 4. Another possibility is to combine the FCP_CMND, FCP_XFER_RDY, and write FCP_DATA into a single loop tenancy as shown by example 5. The FCP_RESP is sent during a second tenancy after the write data has been written to the media. Both of these operations require full-duplex or use of DHD.

The last example is the single-tenancy write-type command shown by example 6. In this example, the entire operation is completed during a single loop tenancy.

The examples in this section illustrate how FCP write-type commands behave when using different numbers of tenancies and login BB_Credit values of both zero and nonzero. All examples show a single command using half-duplex, Class-3 operations for simplicity. Real world operations should take advantage of each loop circuit and transfer as much information for each port as is possible (e.g., multiple commands, or combinations of commands and data for different tasks). As a result, these simplified examples illustrate basic operation, but do not show the full potential of the Arbitrated Loop.

12.6.1 Four Tenancy Write, BB_Credit = Zero

This is the most common first-generation implementation of a write-type command. Four loop tenancies are used, one for each information unit used in the exchange. An example of this operation is illustrated in Figure 77 on page 218. This example corresponds to example 2 in Figure 76 on page 216.

This mode of operation may be used by some half-duplex designs that require closing the current loop circuit before changing the direction of frame transmission or reception. Due to the number of loop tenancies associated with this mode of operation and the use of zero login BB_Credit, this example has more inherent overhead than the other options.

If one counts the maximum number of loop round trips (the worst case time required for a signal to travel to the other port and a response to return) required during each Sequence of the operation, a rough estimate of the performance can be obtained. The command Sequence requires three loop round trips: one to win arbitration, one to send the OPN and receive the R_RDY, and one to send the command frame, send the CLS, and receive the CLS from the target. Each of the other Sequences of the command also require three round trips, for a total of 12 loop round trips per command.

Normally, the entire data sequence is sent during a single loop circuit, although this is not mandatory. A design may split the sequence across multiple loop tenancies as shown by example 1 in Figure 76 on page 216. This may be done to match loop circuits to internal buffering capabilities of the port. For example, a design may limit the number of data frames per loop circuit to four 2,048 byte frames to match its internal buffers. This allows a maximum of 8,192 bytes to be transferred per loop circuit. A 64k-byte operation would require eight tenancies under these conditions, each of which has four frames transmitted during each loop circuit.

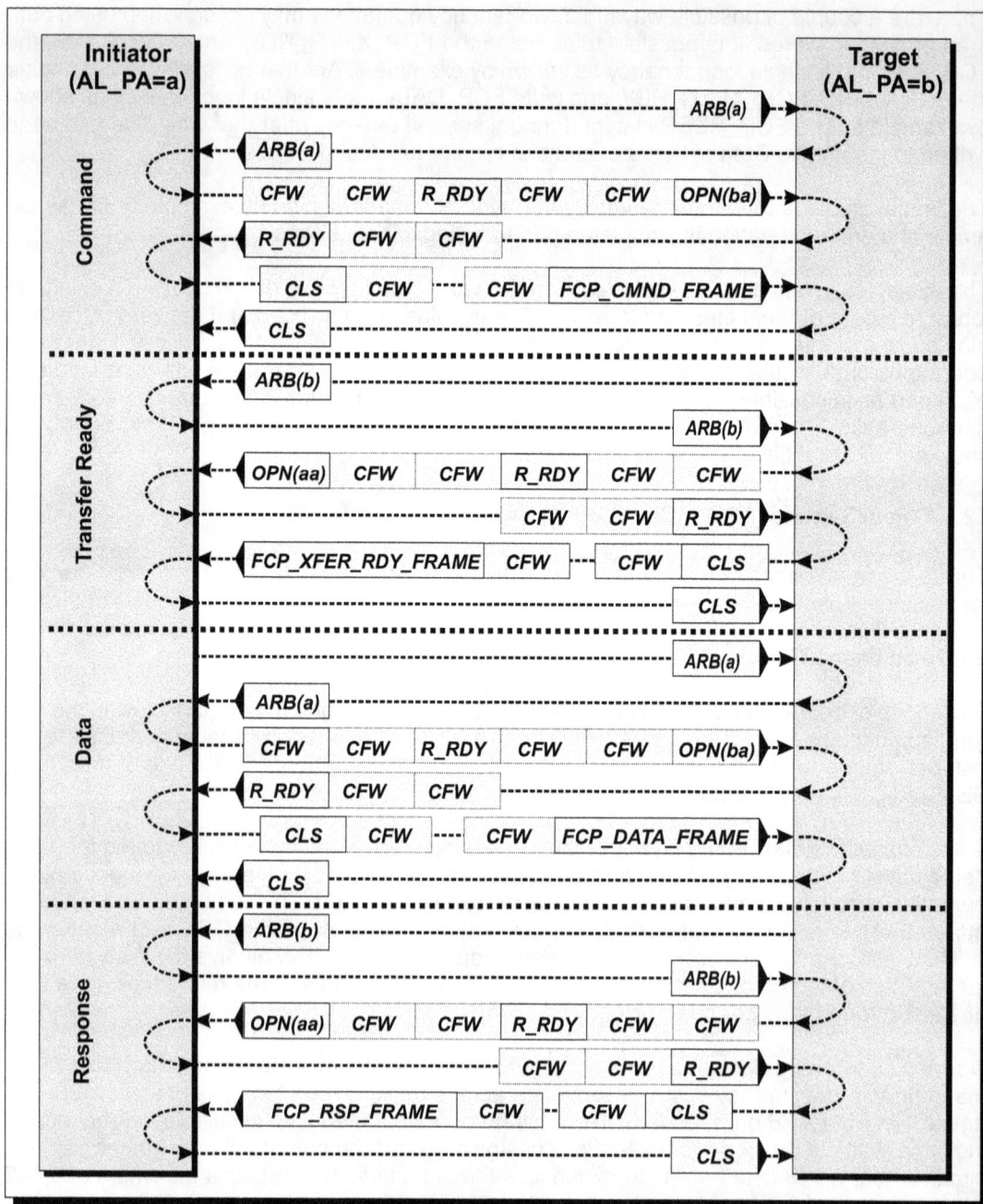

Figure 77. Write Command, 4-Tenancy, BB_Credit = 0

12.6.2 Four Tenancy Write, BB_Credit > Zero

When a login BB_Credit value greater than zero is used, the efficiency of the operation may significantly improved because frame transmission can begin immediately after the OPN is sent (after the required two fill words). An example of this operation is illustrated in Figure 78 on page 220.

A login BB_Credit value of zero requires three loop round trips per loop tenancy, while a login BB_Credit value greater than zero removes the delay associated with waiting for the initial R_RDY response to the OPN. When a zero BB_Credit value is used, the open originator is unable to send the first frame until the open recipient sends an R_RDY indicating that a receive buffer is available. The time for the OPN to reach the open recipient and the R_RDY to return to the open originator is one complete loop time. Once an R_RDY is received, the first frame can be transmitted. On average, the frame requires one-half of a loop time to reach the destination port. It has taken a total of one and a half loop times from when arbitration was won until the first frame is delivered to the open recipient.

Using nonzero login BB_Credit allows the frame to follow the OPN without waiting for the R_RDY from the open recipient. In this instance only one-half of a loop time is needed for the frame to reach the destination port. This results in a savings of one complete round trip delay per loop tenancy. Instead of the 12 round trips required with a BB_Credit of zero, a nonzero BB_Credit reduces this to eight loop round trips. This results in a nearly 50% improvement in loop protocol efficiency.

12.6.3 Three Tenancy Write, BB_Credit = Zero

Loop performance can also be improved significantly by reducing the number of loop tenancies from the four used in the prior examples to three tenancies as shown in Figure 79 on page 221. This example corresponds to number 3 in Figure 76 on page 216.

In this example, the first loop tenancy is used to transfer the command from the initiator to the target. When this is complete, the loop circuit is closed while the target processes the command and prepares for the data transfer.

When the target is ready to begin the data transfer, it arbitrates for access to the loop, and upon winning arbitration establishes a loop circuit with the initiator. The target sends the FCP_XFER_RDY and waits for the initiator to begin the data transfer. If the initiator is not able to start the transfer immediately, loop time may be wasted waiting for the initiator to begin the transfer resulting is lost performance. The actual data transfer may occur in one loop tenancy, or, as was discussed in the prior examples, the data transfer may span multiple loop tenancies.

After the target has received the write data, it may close the loop circuit while the data is written to the medium and the response generated. After this has been completed, the target arbitrates for access to the loop, wins arbitration, opens the initiator and sends the response frame signalling completion of the command. The complete operation requires a total of three loop tenancies and nine loop round trips compared to the 12 loop round trips required by the four-tenancy operation.

Some applications may take this process one step further and reduce the number of loop tenancies to two. Devices that buffer the write data may generate the response when the data has

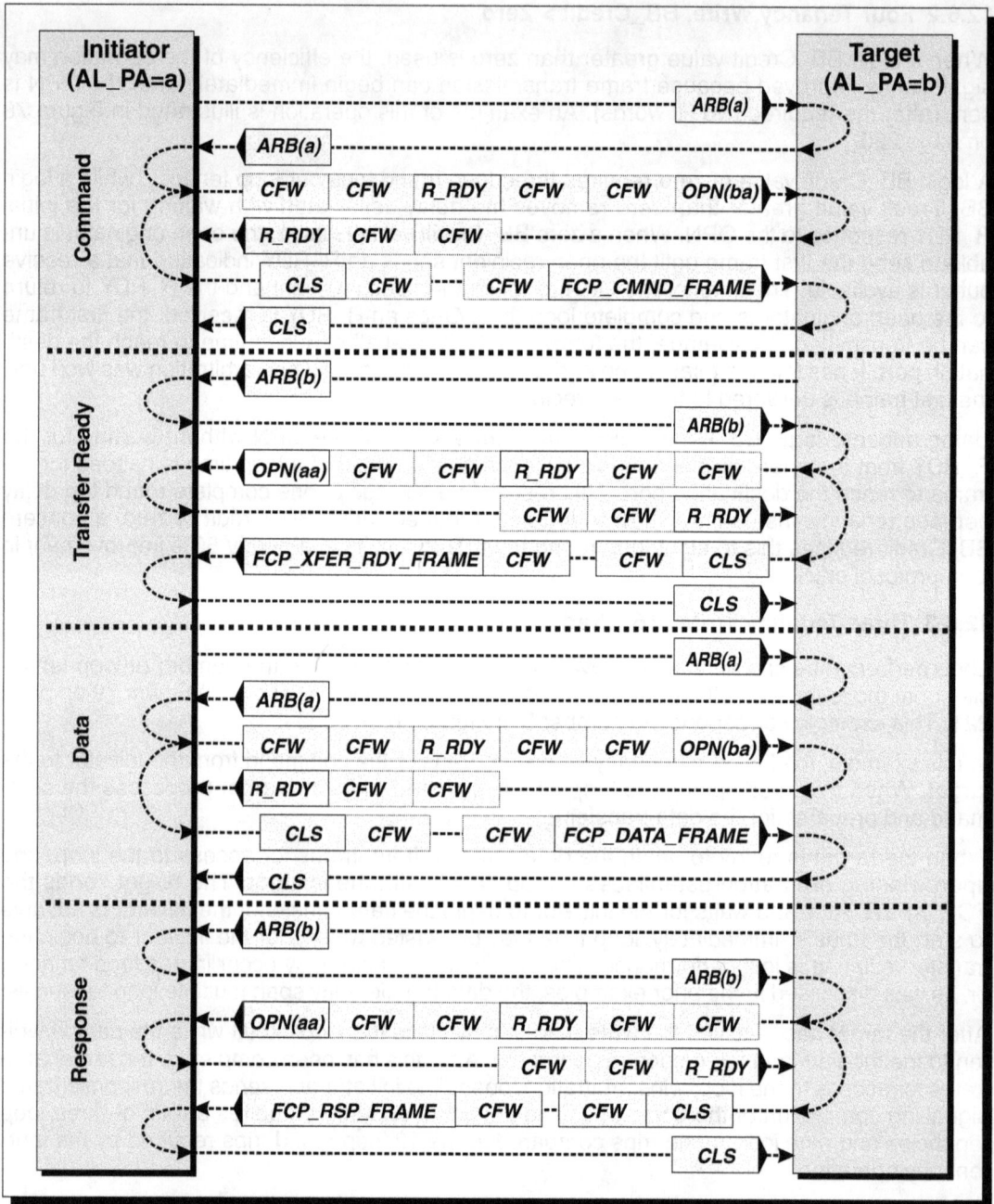

Figure 78. Write Command, 4-Tenancy, BB_Credit > 0

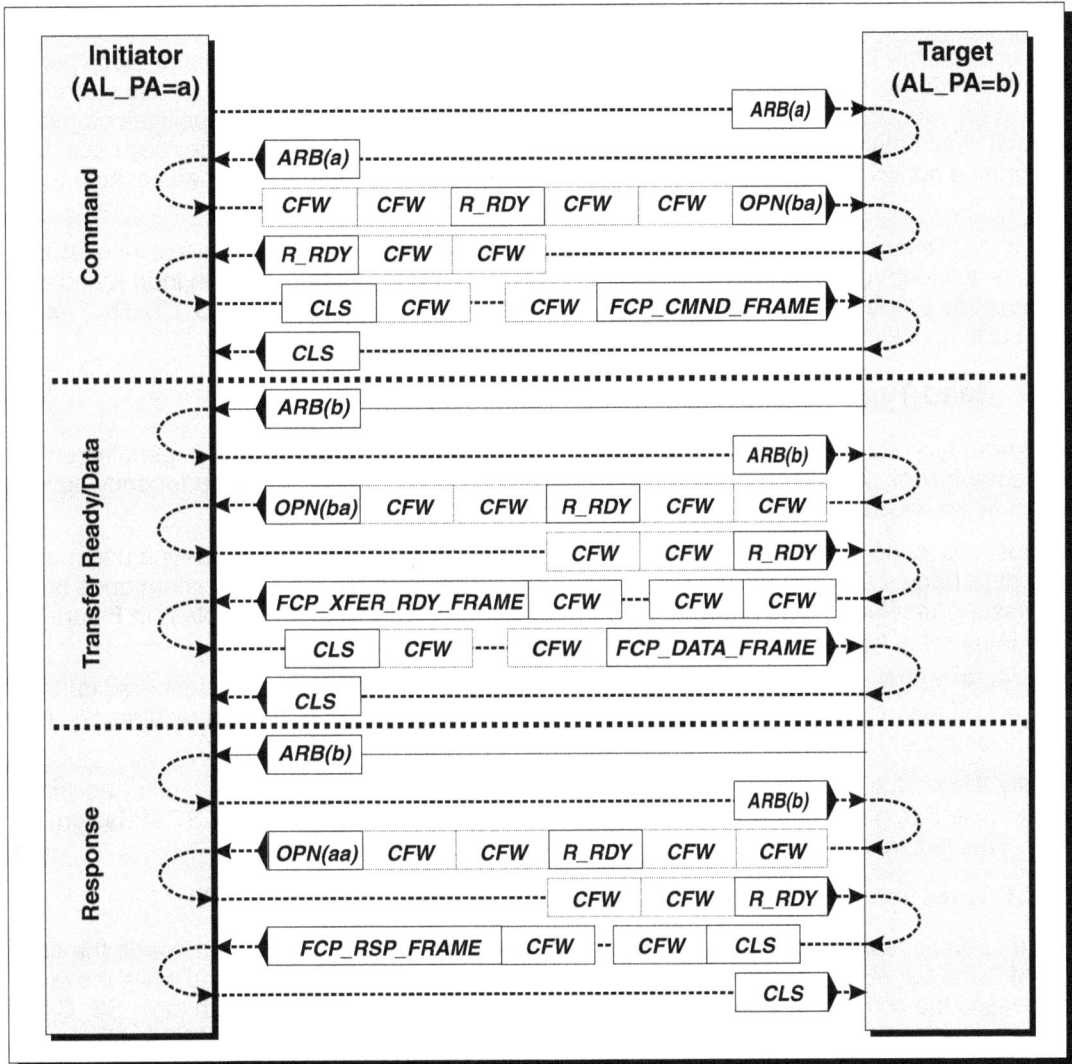

Figure 79. Write Command, 3-Tenancy, BB_Credit = 0

been successfully written to the buffer without waiting until the actual write to the medium has completed. In this mode of operation, the FCP_RSP can be sent immediately following validation of the data frames without requiring a separate loop tenancy to send the response. This results in total of seven loop round trips, or an additional savings of two round trips.

12.6.4 Three Tenancy Write, BB_Credit > Zero

When a nonzero login BB_Credit value is used in a three-tenancy write operation, loop performance is improved even more. See Figure 80 on page 223 for an example of this operation. This is probably the most efficient mode of operation for those devices or applications requiring that write data is written to the medium before status is reported. Some devices capable of performing nonvolatile buffered writes may improve this to two tenancies when caching is enabled.

Three loop tenancies are used to complete this operation with each tenancy requiring approximately two loop round trips to complete. The entire operation requires seven loop round trips as opposed to the 12 loop round trips required by the four-tenancy, login BB_Credit=0 example resulting in almost twice the loop protocol performance.

12.7 Read-Type Command Scenarios

FCP read-type commands may require one or more loop tenancies as well, depending on the implementations of the ports. Figure 81 on page 224 illustrates several loop tenancy options that may be encountered for read-type commands.

In most cases the FCP_XFER_RDY information unit is not used during read-type commands (the data frames are self defining and the FCP_XFER_RDY for read-type commands is not necessary) resulting in the basic three-tenancy operation shown by example 3 in Figure 81. This behavior is typical of first generation disk drives.

If the FCP_XFER_RDY (when used), read FCP_DATA, and FCP_RSP are transferred during a single loop tenancy as shown by example 4 in Figure 81, the read command requires two loop tenancies rather than three.

Finally, it is possible to combine all of the information units into a single loop tenancy as shown in example 5 (e.g., a read with a cache hit as is done in some parallel bus SCSI designs today). This requires full-duplex operation or use of the DHD ordered set.

12.7.1 Three Tenancy Read, BB_Credit = Zero

Read operations begin with a command sequence during which the initiator sends the command to the target. Following receipt of the command, the loop circuit is closed while the target processes the command. An example of a three tenancy read operation with login BB_Credit equals zero is shown in Figure 82 on page 225 and is equivalent to example 3 in Figure 81. This operation requires a total of nine loop round trips.

When the target is ready to perform the data transfer, it arbitrates for access to the loop, opens the initiator, and sends the data frame(s). The data sequence may be broken into multiple data sequences to match the burst size capabilities of the target. Further, each data sequence may be split over multiple loop tenancies when the amount of data exceeds the transmit or receive buffering capabilities of the target or initiator.

If the target is able to send the FCP_RSP immediately after the last data sequence (something that should be natural because if the target can send the last data byte, it knows the status of the operation), it may do so during the same loop tenancy. In this case, the read would require

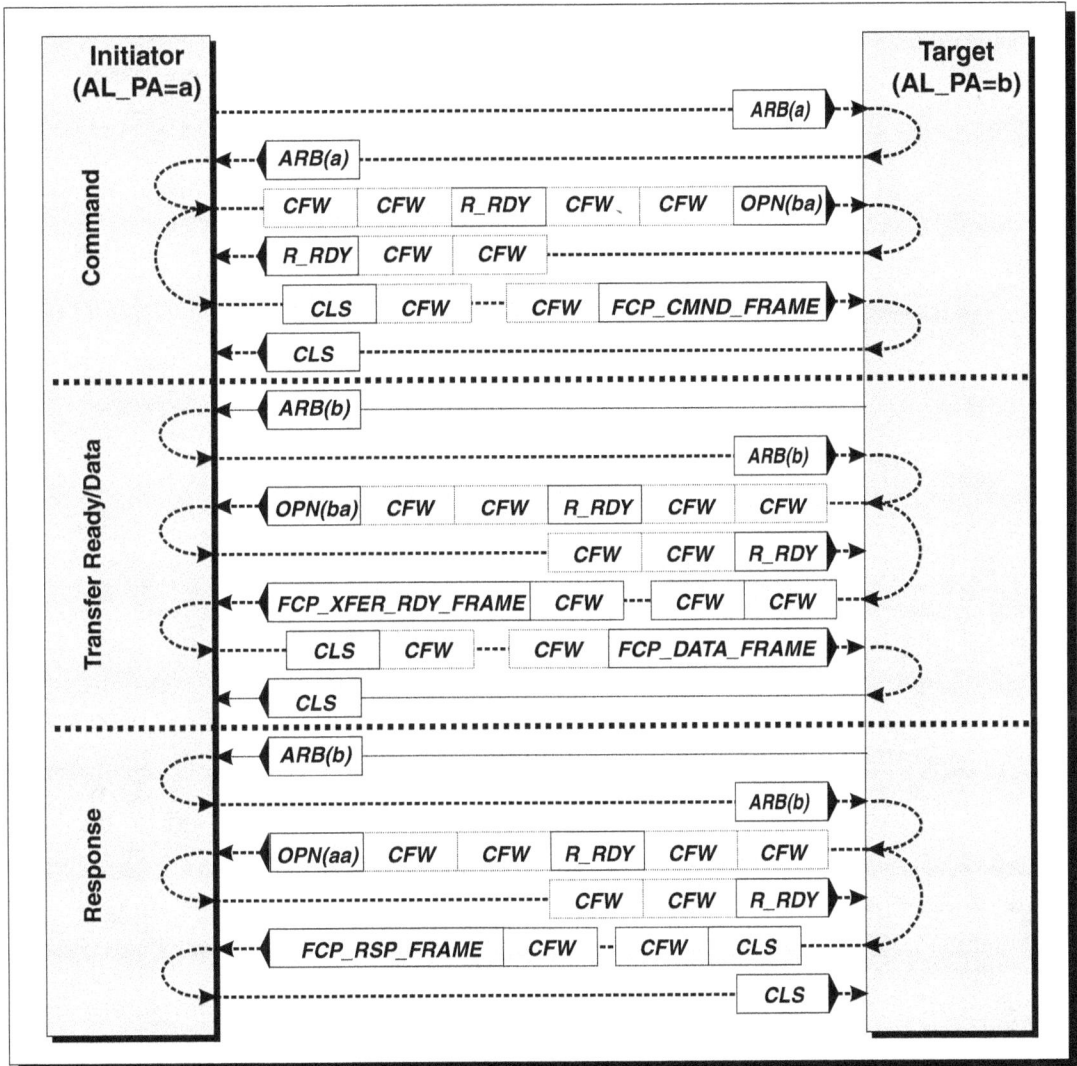

Figure 80. Write Command, 3-Tenancy, BB_Credit > 0

a minimum of two loop tenancies, one for the command and a second for the data and response. When the login BB_Credit is zero, each tenancy requires approximately three loop round trips, or a total of six loop round trips for the two loop tenancy case.

Some devices may be unable to send the FCP_RSP immediately and close the loop circuit while the response is generated. When the response is ready for transmission, the target arbitrates, wins arbitration, opens the initiator, and sends the response frame signalling the end of

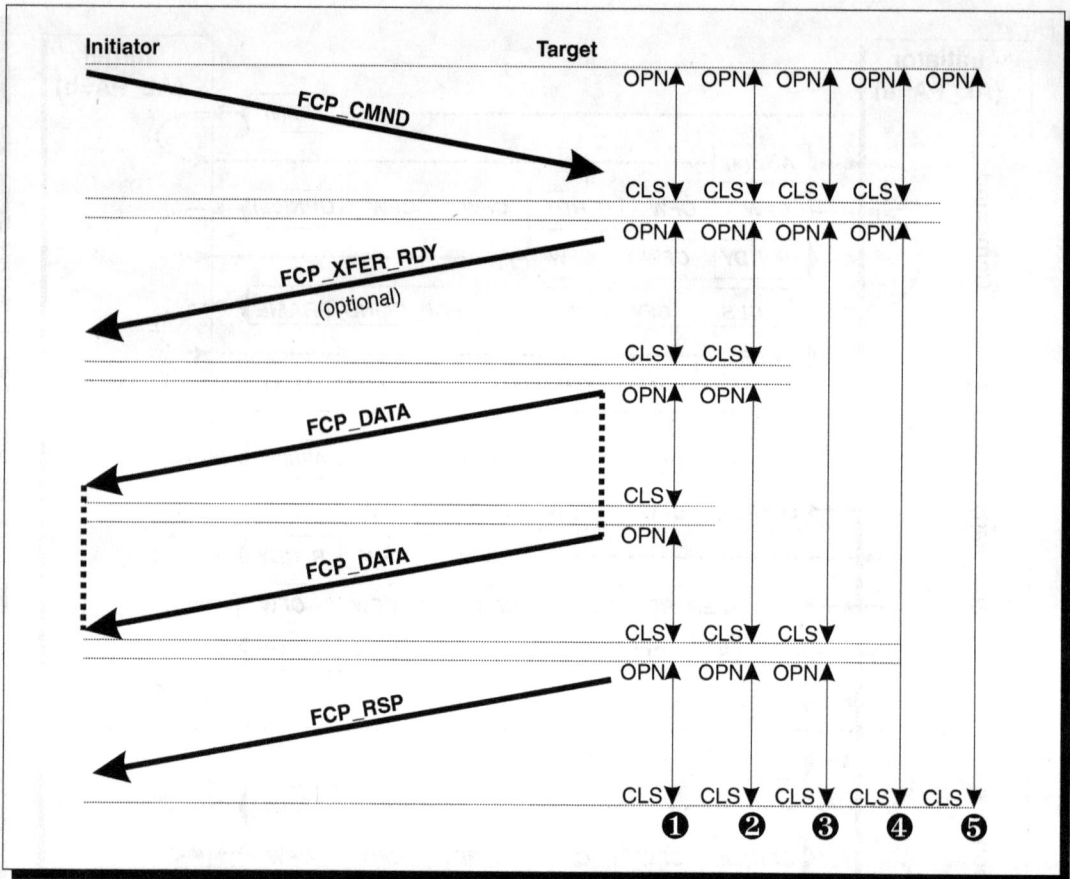

Figure 81. Read Command Loop Tenancies

the command. When this is done, three loop tenancies are required, each with three loop round trips, for a total of nine loop round trips.

12.7.2 Three Tenancy Read, BB_Credit > Zero

An example of a three tenancy read operation with login BB_Credit value greater than zero is shown in Figure 83 on page 226.

This case is similar to the prior read example, except that the open initiator port does not have to wait for an R_RDY from the open recipient before sending the first frame of each loop tenancy. This saves one loop round trip for each OPN and improves loop utilization.

Each loop tenancy requires two loop round trips for a total of six round trips versus the nine round trips required when the login BB_Credit was zero. This represents an improvement of almost 50% in loop protocol performance.

Chapter 12. SCSI-3 FCP Commands

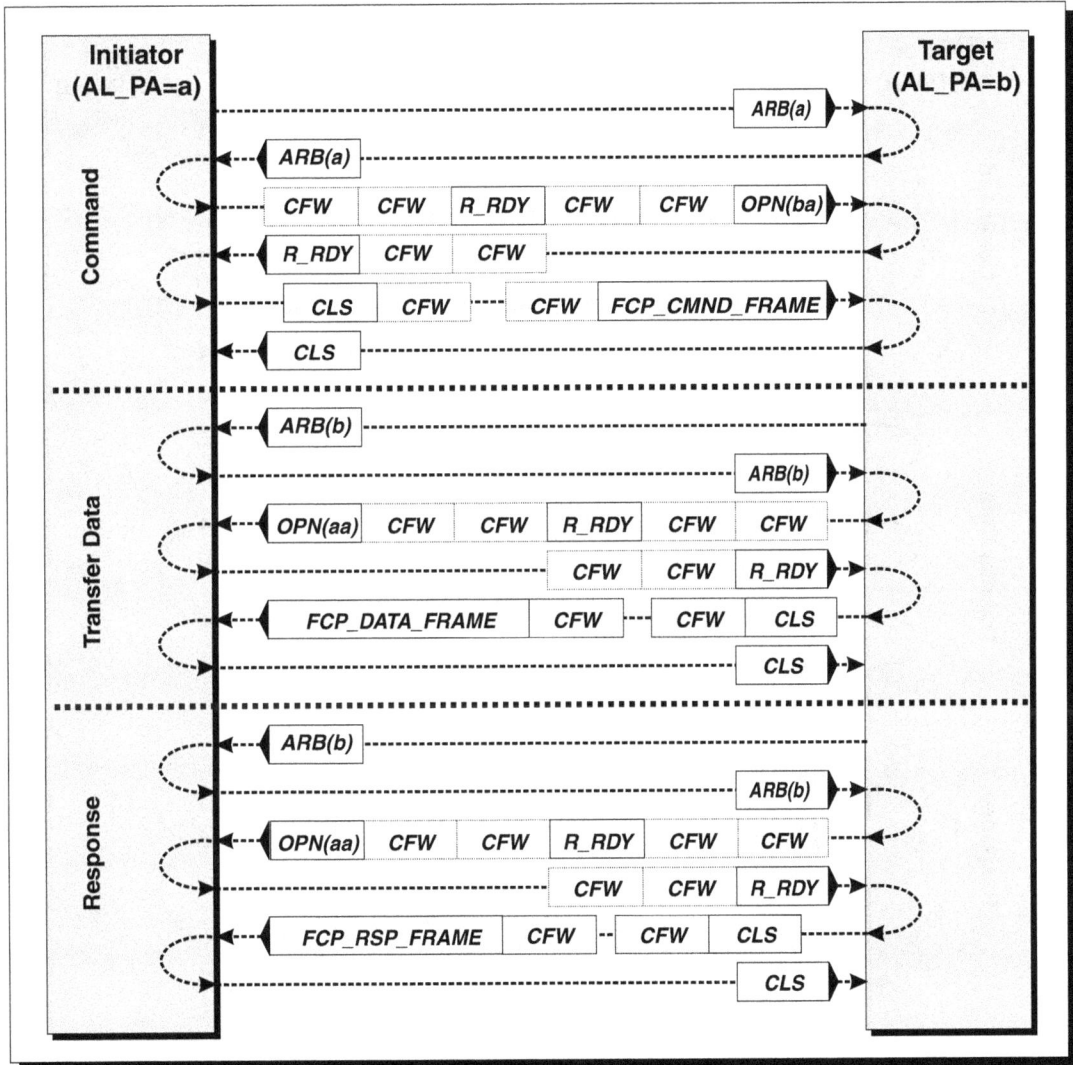

Figure 82. Read Command, 3-Tenancy. BB_Credit = 0

12.7.3 Two Tenancy Read, BB_Credit = Zero

One final example of a read-type operation is illustrated in Figure 84 on page 227. This corresponds to example 4 in Figure 81 on page 224.

This behavior is typical of what should be expected in Arbitrated Loop ports as they mature but don't implement command processing in hardware. In this example, the initiator sends the

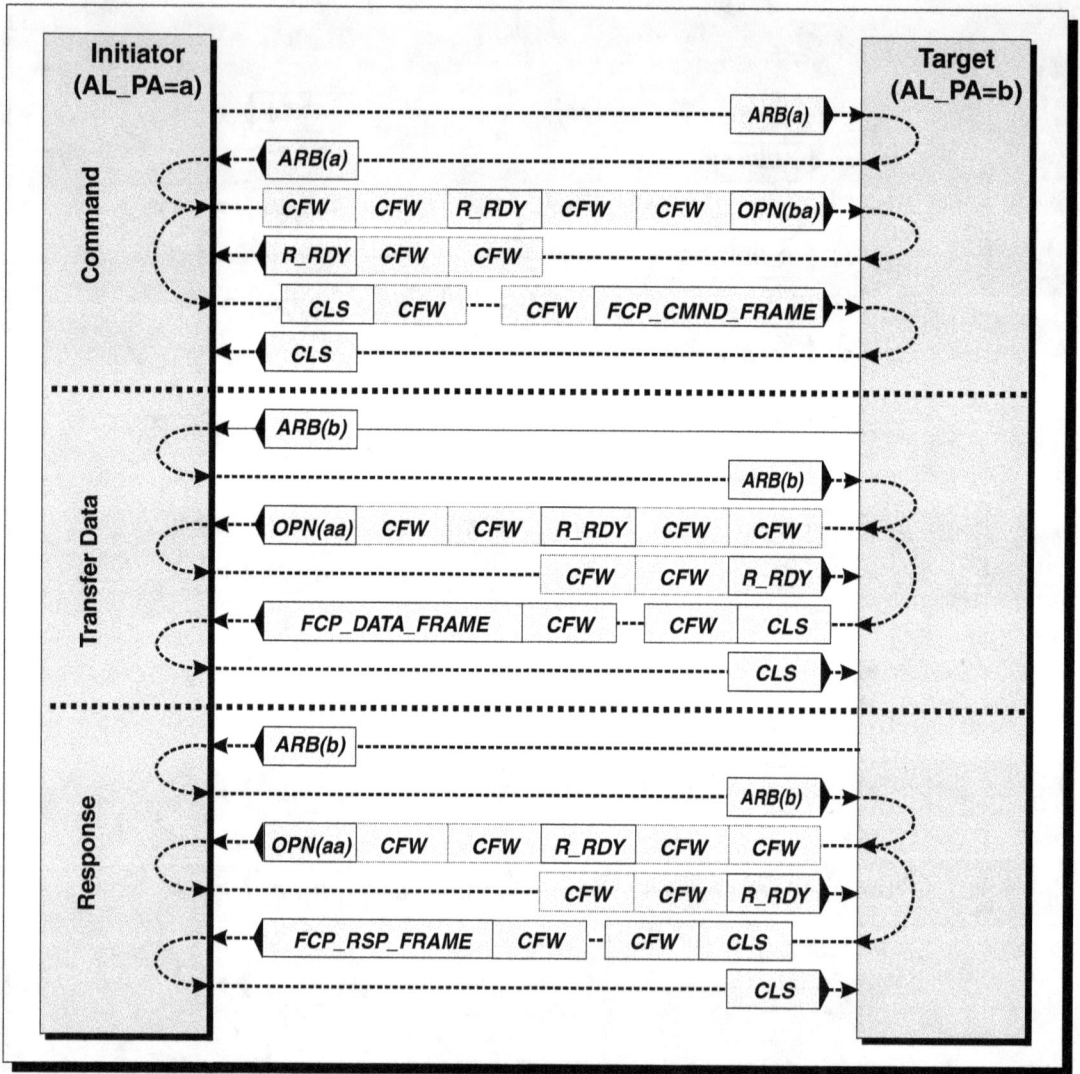

Figure 83. Read Command, 3-Tenancy, BB_Credit > 0

FCP_CMND during the first loop tenancy and the target sends the FCP_DATA sequence and FCP_RSP during a second loop tenancy.

12.8 Summary

All of the examples shown in this chapter illustrate half-duplex operation for simplicity (sometimes full-duplex capability or use of the DHD is required). Total performance is greatly en-

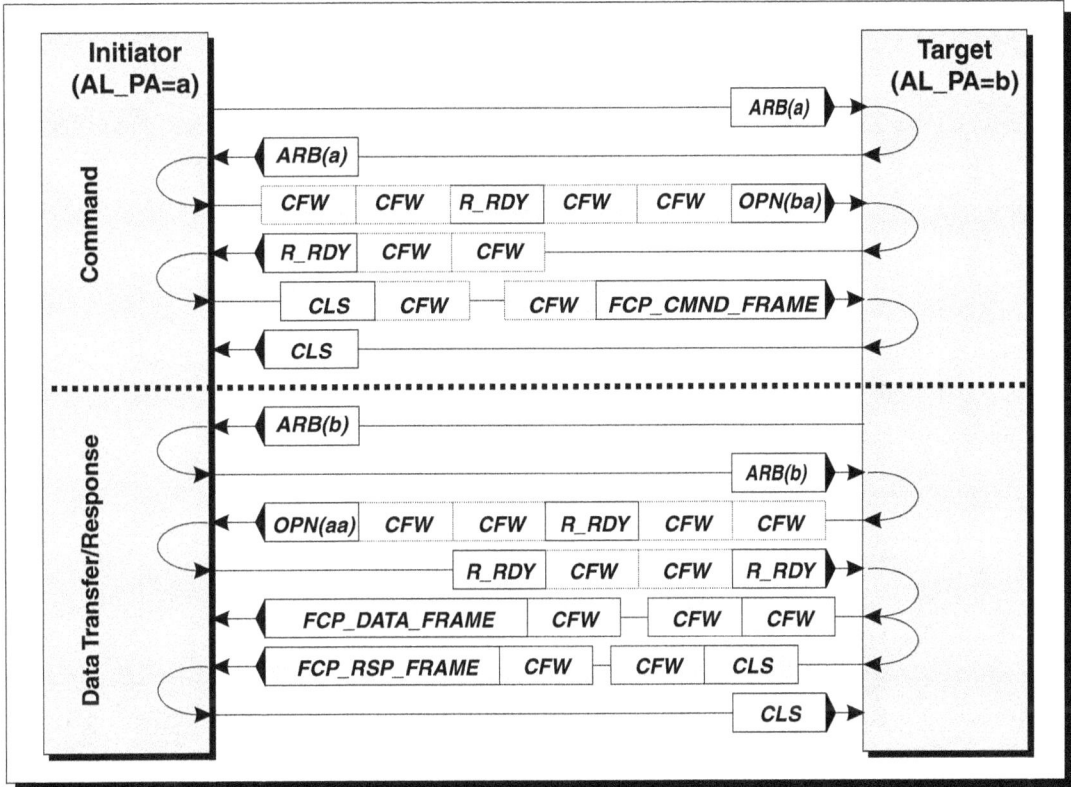

Figure 84. Read Command, 2-Tenancy, BB_Credit = 0

hanced by using true full duplex operation and login BB_Credit greater than zero as will be seen in the chapter titled *Performance* on page 229.

13. Performance

The performance of an Arbitrated Loop configuration depends upon the complex interaction of a number of different factors. Some of these factors are relatively simple to quantify, while others are highly dependent upon design choices made in a particular implementation and the nature of the workload. Understanding the dynamics of the loop protocols and their affect on performance is not a simple task. On a fully populated loop, there may be in excess of 100 ports arbitrating for access to the loop at random intervals with each using the loop for varying periods. Different designs may use the loop differently. Some may require four loop tenancies to complete a SCSI-3 write command, while others may require two. Some designs and applications may be able to transfer all of the data in a single loop tenancy while others may break the data into multiple loop tenancies.

This chapter provides some general thoughts and approaches to estimating loop behavior for a set of assumptions, and then applies standard queueing theory techniques to provide an estimate of overall loop performance.

13.1 Factors Affecting Loop Performance

Several factors are critical to understanding loop performance including the:

- Time required for a signal to travel completely around the loop. This is called the *loop round-trip time* and consists of two principal components:
  - Number of ports on the loop and the delay through each port, and
  - Time required for signals to travel from one port to another
- Time required to win arbitration after a previous loop circuit is closed
- Number of loop tenancies required to complete an operation
- Duration of each loop tenancy. The duration is affected by:
  - The loop round-trip time
  - Login buffer-to-buffer credit (login BB_Credit) value used
  - Amount of data transferred per loop tenancy
  - Frame data field size used during the each phase of an operation
- Number of information units transferred during each loop tenancy
- Use of full-duplex or half-duplex operation
- Number of simultaneous operations supported (i.e., command queueing)
- Utilization of opportunistic transfers. That is, the transfer of information for multiple operations during a single loop circuit

The following sections examine these factors and their influence on loop performance. Following the discussion of these key factors, examples of different command scenarios are used to analyze typical loop performance for a specific set of parameters.

13.1.1 Calculating the Loop Round-Trip Time

Loop round-trip time is the term used to describe the time required for a signal to travel completely around a loop. Loop round-trip time is significant because many of the loop protocols require all or part of a loop round-trip time to execute.

The following examples illustrate the relationship between loop round-trip time and the primary loop protocols.

- On an idle loop, the arbitration protocol requires that a port's ARB(x) travels completely around the loop for that port to win arbitration.

- One-half of a loop round-trip time, on average, is required for the OPN to reach the destination port. If the login BB_Credit value is zero, an additional one-half loop round-trip time is required, on average, for the R_RDY to be received by the open originator after the OPN is received by the open recipient. A final one-half loop round-trip time is required for the first frame to travel to the open recipient. A login BB_Credit of zero adds one additional full loop round-trip time to the overhead associated with each OPN.

- Closing the loop circuit requires one-half of a loop round-trip time for the CLS to reach the other port and one-half of a loop round-trip time for that other port's CLS to be returned.

There are two components to the loop round-trip time. The first is the amount of delay contributed by each port. The Arbitrated Loop standard permits a maximum delay of six transmission words through a port when the port is repeating information from its receive input to its transmit output. This delay provides the time required for the port to synchronize the received data stream to the port's internal clock, examine a received transmission word, decide how to process that word, and transmit the appropriate output word.

Six transmission words is a total of 240 bits (each transmission word is 40 bits). At 1.0625 gigabaud, each bit requires 0.941 nanoseconds to transmit. Multiplying 240 bits times 0.941 nanoseconds each results in a total time of 225.882 nanoseconds for six transmission words. This is the maximum delay permitted in a port while retransmitting information. If all of the ports on the loop contribute six words of delay to a signal travelling around the loop, the total delay introduced by all the ports is equal to the number of ports times 225.882 nanoseconds.

The second factor contributing to the loop round-trip time is the delay contributed by the copper or optical media used to interconnect the ports. Copper transmission lines typically specify the delay value as the *velocity factor*. The velocity factor is the ratio of the speed of light in a vacuum to the propagation speed of the electrical signal in the conductor. The actual value depends upon the characteristics of the transmission line and varies from 66% for some types of coaxial cable to 90% for open wire transmission lines. If one assumes a velocity factor of 67% for copper interfaces, approximately five nanoseconds are required for a signal to propagate through each meter of copper interconnection.

Optical media also introduces a transmission delay. The term used to describe this delay is called the *index of refraction*. Typical optical fibers have an index of refraction of approximately 1.50, meaning that the light takes 1.5 times as long to reach its destination when travelling through the optical fiber compared to the time required if the light were travelling in a vacuum. An optical fiber with an index of refraction of 1.5 requires approximately five nanoseconds for a signal to travel through each meter of the fiber. For example, it requires approximately 500 nanoseconds (or one-half of a microsecond) for a light pulse to travel through 100 meters of optical fiber.

Loop round-trip time can be estimated by totalling all of the delays incurred as a signal travels around the loop.The worksheet in Table 16 may be used to estimate the loop round-trip time for a loop operating at 1.0625 gigabaud with a six-word delay per port.

Variable	Time Per	Number	Total Time
Number of Ports on Loop	225.882 ns.		
Meters of Copper Medium	5 ns.		
Meters of Optical Medium	5 ns.		
Total			

Table 16. Loop Round-Trip Time Worksheet

Assume that the loop under consideration has 64 ports connected by a total of 40 meters of copper interconnect and 25 meters of optical cable (this might represent a typical disk sub-system). Table 17 illustrates how the loop round-trip time may be estimated for this loop.

Variable	Time Per	Number	Total Time
Number of Ports on Loop	225.882 ns.	64	14.456 usec.
Meters of Copper Medium	5 ns.	40	.200 usec.
Meters of Optical Medium	5 ns.	25	.125 usec.
Total			14.781 usec.

Table 17. Loop Round-Trip Time for a 64 Port Loop

The delay through the ports themselves makes up the major portion of the loop round-trip time when there are a large number of ports on the loop. This suggests that reducing the amount of delay per port presents a potential opportunity for improving loop performance. Even a one-word reduction can have a significant influence for large loops. Reducing the delay per port from six words to five words results in a delay of 188 nanoseconds per port rather than the 226 nanoseconds calculated earlier. Using the 64-port loop shown in Table 17, a six-word delay results in a total loop round-trip time of 14.781 microseconds while a five-word delay results in a total loop round-trip time of 12.372 microseconds, or an improvement of 2.409 microseconds (or nearly 16.3%) each time a signal has to travel around the loop. While this amount of time may not seem significant, a four-tenancy FCP write operation with a login BB_Credit value of zero may require as many as 12 loop round trips to complete. In this case, the total time saved by using a five-word delay per port would amount to 28.908 microseconds per command.

13.1.2 Arbitration Win Time

Before a port can begin frame transmission, it must win arbitration to establish a loop circuit. The time required for a port to win arbitration after the previous loop circuit closes depends on the loop round-trip time, the number of ports that are currently arbitrating, and the location of the next arbitration winner relative to the previous arbitration winner (i.e., how far does the ARB(x) have to travel before reaching the port that will win arbitration).

If the loop is idle and no other ports are arbitrating, the time required for a port to win arbitration is one loop round-trip time. This reflects the fact that the ARB(x) must travel completely around the loop for the port to win arbitration. A port on the example 64-port loop shown in Table 17 on page 231 requires 14.781 microseconds to win arbitration when the loop is idle.

When the loop is not idle, two things must occur before a port wins arbitration. First, the current arbitration winner and all higher priority ports must be serviced. Second, the ARB(x) has to propagate from the last arbitration winner to the port under consideration. The time that a port has to wait while the other ports are being serviced is examined later in the section titled *Arbitration Wait Time* on page 238.

The time for a port to win arbitration after the last higher priority port relinquishes the loop is simply the time required for the ARB(x) to travel from the port relinquishing the loop to the next arbitration winner. The average time required for this to occur can be estimated by dividing the loop round-trip time by the number of ports that are currently arbitrating (provided that the AL_PAs are ordered in descending order of priority). When multiple ports are arbitrating simultaneously, the highest priority ARB(x) normally will be present at the receive input of the current arbitration winner (lower priority ports have retransmitted the higher-priority ARB(x)). When the current loop circuit is closed, the arbitration winner simply allows the ARB(x) present at its input to pass. When the ARB(x) is received by the port that originated it, that port wins arbitration. If the AL_PA values on the loop are ordered in descending priority around the loop (increasing AL_PA value) the highest priority arbitrating port is the closest of all the arbitrating ports. The following formula can be used to estimate the average time required to win arbitration when the fibre distance between ports is constant.

$$\text{Arbitration Win Time} = \frac{\text{Loop Round-Trip Time}}{\text{Number of Arbitrating Ports+1}}$$

If the 64-port loop in Table 17 on page 231 is used as an example and 16 ports are currently arbitrating for access to the loop, the average time required for the next loop port to win arbitration once the loop circuit is closed is approximately the loop round-trip time of 14.781 microseconds divided by 17 (the number of loop ports that are currently arbitrating plus one).

If AL_PA values are not assigned in order of descending priority around the loop, the time required for the next port to win arbitration may be significantly increased. The importance of this was examined in *AL_PA Order on the Loop* on page 127. Also, this simplistic view of arbitra-

---

$$\text{Arbitration Win Time} = \frac{\text{Loop Time}}{\text{Number of Arbitrating Ports}}$$

$$= \frac{14781}{(17)}$$

$$\text{Arbitration Win Time} = 923.8 \text{ nanoseconds}$$

Figure 85. Arbitration Win Time Example

tion win time assumes a random distribution of arbitrating ports and provides an average number.

As mentioned earlier, the arbitration win time discussed in this section does not include the time that a port may wait while the current loop circuit is open. Nor does it consider the number of other ports that may win arbitration first. These times are examined in *Arbitration Wait Time* on page 238 and *Arbitration Queue Depth* on page 239.

13.2 Loop Tenancies

The number of loop tenancies has an important influence on the performance of an Arbitrated Loop configuration. This is due to the fact that a significant amount of overhead may be associated with establishing and ending each loop tenancy. Time is required to win arbitration, open the loop circuit, wait for one or more R_RDYs if the login BB_Credit is zero, transmit one or more frames, and close the loop circuit. The total amount of overhead is a function of the loop round-trip time and adversely affects performance by consuming loop time that could otherwise be used for transferring information.

Typically, the following actions and associated times are required for each loop tenancy when the login BB_Credit is zero:

- Win arbitration: one loop round-trip time on an idle loop (loop round-trip time divided by the number of arbitrating ports on a busy loop)
- Send the OPN and associated R_RDYs: one-half loop round-trip time (on average)
- Wait for the first R_RDY if the login BB_Credit is zero: one-half loop round-trip time (on average)
- Send one or more frames, and CLS: one-half loop round-trip time (on average)
- Destination port returns the CLS: one-half loop round-trip time (on average)

This requires a minimum of three complete loop round-trip times for each loop tenancy (assuming the login BB_Credit is zero). If the login BB_Credit is nonzero this time is reduced by one round trip because the first frame can follow immediately after the OPN without waiting for the first R_RDY.

The amount of time required for each loop tenancy can be determined by identifying all of the actions involved in that tenancy and the time required for each action. Each tenancy contains variable times consisting of the arbitration win time and loop round-trip time and constant times that are independent of the loop configuration (e.g., the time needed to transmit an

---

FCP_CMND frame or required ordered sets). Later examples examine the time required for each loop tenancy for the example 64-port loop.

13.3 Performance Estimation

Once the time to complete an entire operation has been determined, the performance, as measured by the *'Effective Data Rate'* (EDR), or *'Inputs/Outputs operations Per Second'* (IOPS) can be calculated.

13.3.1 Effective Data Rate

The Arbitrated Loop's effective data rate is simply the rate at which information can be delivered over the loop after all of the overheads associated with that delivery have been taken into consideration. The loop's effective data rate is always lower than the instantaneous data rate which is the peak bandwidth associated with data transmission. For example, the instantaneous data rate of a loop operating at 1,062.5 megabaud is 106.25 megabytes per second (1,062.5 megabaud divided by 10 bits per byte). After the overhead associated with the frame structure is taken into account, the actual rate is reduced to approximately 103 megabytes per second (for frames with a 2,048 byte data field) because the frame delimiters, header, CRC, and the IDLEs between frames consume 60 bytes of the available bandwidth.

This data rate is reduced even further when the upper-level protocol specific overheads are considered as some of the frames associated with an operation are used to carry the FCP_CMND, FCP_XFER_RDY, and FCP_RSP information associated with the command. These frames represent FCP protocol overhead because they do not carry read or write data.

Estimation of the effective data rate is simple once the total amount of loop time used by a command is known. The total time command time is based on the number of loop tenancies, time per tenancy, and number of data bytes transferred. The formula is simply the number of bytes transferred divided by the total amount of loop time needed to complete the command as shown in the following formula.

$$\text{Effective Data Rate}_{(\text{Megabytes per second})} = \frac{\text{Number of Bytes Transferred}}{\text{Total Command Time}_{(\text{Microseconds})}}$$

It should be observed that commands which transfer larger quantities of data provide a higher effective data rate than those which transfer smaller amounts of data. This is because all commands have a certain amount of fixed overhead which is independent of the actual amount of data transferred.

For example, if the amount of loop time required to complete a read or write command that transfers 4,096 bytes is 100 microseconds, the effective data rate can be calculated as shown in Figure 86 on page 235.

13.3.2 Input/Output Operations per Second

Some applications measure performance not in megabytes per second, but rather in terms of the number of input and output operations that can be performed per second (IOPS). Once the

$$\text{Effective Data Rate}_{\text{(Megabytes per second)}} = \frac{\text{Number of Bytes Transferred}}{\text{Total Command Time}_{\text{(Microseconds)}}}$$

$$= \frac{4096}{100}$$

$$\text{Effective Data Rate}_{\text{(megabytes per second)}} = 40.96 \text{ megabytes per second}$$

Figure 86. Effective Data Rate Example

time per operation is known, the number of IOPS can be determined by dividing the command time per operation into one second as shown in the following formula.

$$\text{Input/Output Operations Per Second (IOPS)} = \left(\frac{1}{\text{Total Command Time}_{\text{(Microseconds)}}}\right) \times 10^6$$

Continuing with the previous example of a command that transfers 4,096 bytes with an on-loop time of 100 microseconds produces an IOPS figure of 10,000 I/O operations per second as shown in Figure 87.

$$\text{Input/Output Operations Per Second (IOPS)} = \left(\frac{1}{\text{Total Command Time}_{\text{(Microseconds)}}}\right) \times 10^6$$

$$= \left(\frac{1}{100}\right) \times 10^6$$

$$\text{Input/Output Operations Per Second (IOPS)} = 10,000 \text{ IOPS per second}$$

Figure 87. IOPS Example

IOPS and effective data rate are different ways of expressing the same information using different terms. When the amount of time to complete an operation is known, the number of IOPS can be determined. When the number of IOPS and the amount of data transferred per I/O are known, the effective data rate can be determined.

Actual calculations of IOPS or effective data rates must state the type of operation or operations being performed and the amount of data transferred per command to provide meaningful information. Commands which transfer small amounts of data take less time to complete than commands which transfer larger amounts of data. Therefore, the number of IOPS is larger when transferring shorter blocks than when transferring larger blocks of data, while the effective data rate is usually less. In addition, the amount of time required to complete a write operation may be different than that required to complete a read operation. In many cases, a performance is expressed for a typical mix of read and write commands to simulate actual operations. To provide the most accurate indication of IOPS performance, the mix of reads and writes needs to be specified, along with the data block size or sizes used.

Performance estimating is always dependent upon defining the conditions and parameters used to arrive at a particular result. The arbitrated loop is no different in this respect.

13.4 Arbitration Wait Time

Estimating loop performance when a single port is using the loop is relatively straightforward. The time required to win arbitration is the time required for the ARB(x) ordered set to travel completely around the loop, or one loop round-trip time. When multiple ports are arbitrating at the same time it is necessary to apply basic queueing theory techniques to determine how long the average port must wait before winning arbitration.

13.4.1 Loop Utilization

When a port is performing an operation, it establishes a loop circuit and uses a portion of the loop's available bandwidth. For the duration of a loop circuit, other ports are unable to gain access to the loop and must wait. The Arbitrated Loop can be viewed as a serially reusable shared resource, providing a single service to all ports on the loop. That service is access to the loop, and is granted by a successful arbitration. Once arbitration is won by one port, the loop is busy and the other arbitrating ports are waiting in a queue to access the loop.

The loop has the potential to service many arbitration requests during a given period of time. Each arbitration request, and the associated loop tenancy, consume some of the loop's capacity. To calculate the loop's ability to service the ports it is necessary to calculate what is called the *service rate*. The service rate is the number of requests that the arbitrated loop can service in a period of time. It is simply one divided by the duration of the average loop tenancy as shown in the following formula for calculating the service rate:

$$\text{Service Rate} = \frac{1}{\textit{Duration} \text{ of average loop tenancy}}$$

The duration of an average loop tenancy is determined by adding up the loop tenancy times required to complete a single operation, such as a SCSI command, and dividing that total by the number of loop tenancies used. The average loop tenancy time includes the time required to win arbitration after the previous winner relinquishes the loop, open the destination port, transmit one or more frames, close the destination port, and receive the CLS back. The time includes the time required to transmit the signals, the time needed for those signals to travel around the loop, and the time required for the destination port to act on the received signal.

As the parameters associated with the loop tenancies change, the service rate changes. The service rate identifies the maximum capabilities of the loop for a given set of conditions. Different data transfer sizes, loop round-trip times, and the use of a zero or nonzero login BB_Credit values all affect the loop's service rate. The only method of establishing the service rate for a specific configuration is to calculate the average loop tenancy for that set of parameters, then calculate the associated service rate.

To simplify the calculations, it can be assumed that, on average, the other port is half way around the loop and the time from a sending port to a receiving port is one-half of the loop round-trip time.

The earlier example that transferred 4,096 bytes in four loop tenancies totalling 100 microseconds has an average tenancy duration of 25 microseconds. When this is used to calculate the service rate, a value of 40,000 tenancies per second is obtained as shown in Figure 88.

$$\text{Service Rate} = \left(\frac{1}{\text{Duration of average loop tenancy}_{(micro\, sec onds)}} \right) \times 10^6$$

$$= \left(\frac{1}{25 \text{ microseconds}} \right) \times 10^6$$

$$\text{Service Rate} = 40,000 \text{ tenancies per second}$$

Figure 88. Service Rate Example

This result is intuitive because it was earlier determined that the loop could achieve 10,000 IOPS and each I/O operation, in this example, requires four loop tenancies.

The service rate provides an indication of the capacity of the loop in terms of requests per unit of time. As requests are serviced, loop bandwidth is used. *Loop utilization* is the term use to describe how busy the loop is. The rate at which requests are made is called the *request rate*. In the case of an Arbitrated Loop, the request rate is the rate at which ports arbitrate for access to the loop. Loop utilization is the request rate divided by the loop's service rate.

$$Loop \text{ Utilization} = \frac{\text{Request Rate}}{\text{Service Rate}}$$

If ports are arbitrating for access to a loop which has a service rate of 40,000 tenancies per second at a rate of 20,000 requests per second, the loop utilization is 0.5, or 50%. Half of the capacity is used, the other half is still available. When the request rate equals the service rate, loop utilization is 1.0, or 100%, and the loop has reached saturation. If the request rate should attempt to exceed the service rate, the loop is unable to keep up with the requests. The request queue grows indefinitely until some other factor limits the requests. In the case of the Arbitrated Loop, the number of participating ports per loop and the fairness mechanism determine the maximum number, and rate, of requests.

It should be noted that the request rate is a function of the application using the loop, not the loop itself. The loop is providing a service, but some other entity is creating the work. Because the generation of requests is outside the loop, this represents another parameter which must be supplied to determine the loop's behavior. When the request rate is low (i.e., the loop is lightly utilized) contention for the loop is minimized and most of the time finds only a single port arbitrating. As the request rate goes up, the probability of contention for the loop increases. This means that individual ports wait longer for the prior ports to be serviced. It also means that more ports are attempting acquire the loop at any given point in time. Ultimately, when the loop reaches 100% utilization, every port is attempting to acquire the loop during each access fairness window.

13.4.2 Arbitration Wait Time

The time an average request spends waiting in the arbitration queue can be determined once the loop utilization is known (or a utilization is assumed). The formula for calculating the time waiting in the arbitration queue is given by the following formula:

$$\text{Time}_{queue} = \text{Time}_{\text{Average Tenancy}} \times \left(\frac{\text{Loop Utilization}}{(1 - \text{Loop Utilization})} \right)$$

As the loop utilization increases, the time in the queue increases at a non-linear rate. If the loop utilization is 0.5 (50%), the average time in the queue is equal to the average tenancy time. If the loop utilization increases to 75%, the average time in the queue increases to three times the average tenancy time. If the loop utilization increases to 90%, the average time in the queue increases to nine times the average loop tenancy as shown in Figure 89.

$$\text{Time}_{queue} = \text{Time}_{\text{Average Tenancy}} \times \left(\frac{\text{Loop Utilization}}{(1 - \text{Loop Utilization})} \right)$$

$$= 25 \times \left(\frac{0.9}{(1 - 0.9)} \right)$$

$$= 25 \times \frac{0.9}{0.1}$$

$$\text{Time}_{queue} = 225 \text{ microseconds}$$

Figure 89. Arbitration Wait Time for Example Loop with 90% Utilization

If the primary performance consideration is the number of input/output operations that can be performed per second (IOPS), then the response time, or latency, may not be a factor. But, if minimizing the time to perform an individual operation is important, the loop will have to be designed to provide the desired performance, or some other topology used.

One last observation before leaving the topic of arbitration wait time. As the loop utilization approaches 100%, the arbitration wait time increases dramatically. If a loop is operating in the region of high utilization, even small changes in the request rate can have a significant effect on the arbitration wait time. For example, increasing the loop utilization from 90% to 95% more than doubles the arbitration wait time.

The queue depth and time in the queue increase exponentially as the utilization increases as shown in Figure 90 on page 239. This characteristic makes the performance of a loop increasingly sensitive to small changes in activity as the utilization approaches 100%.

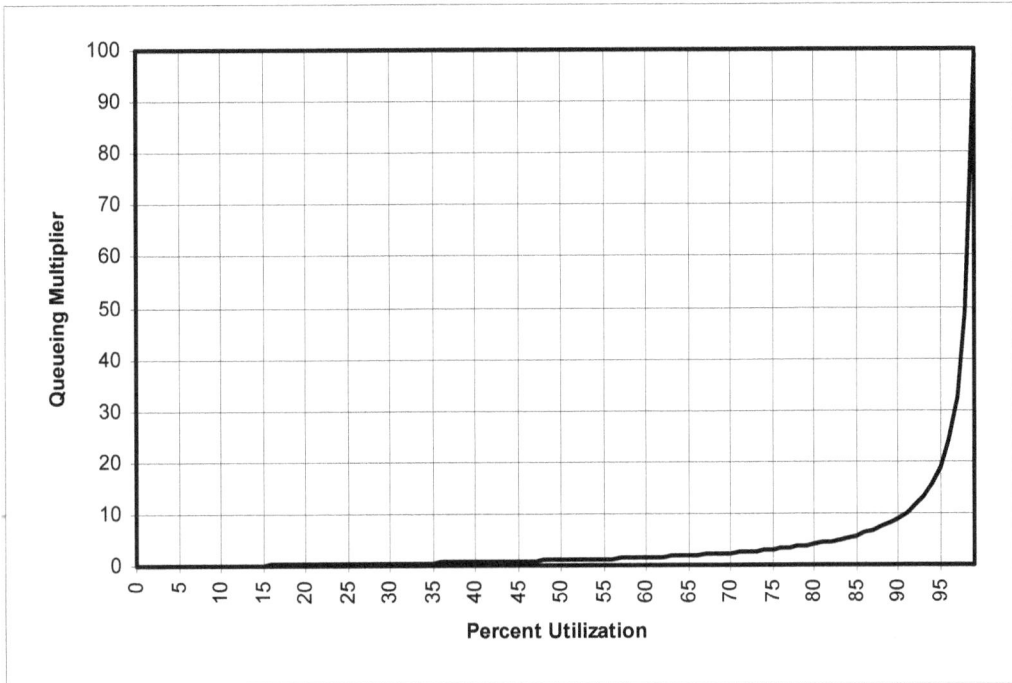

Figure 90. Queue Time vs. Utilization

13.4.3 Arbitration Queue Depth

The final element of the arbitration calculations is the arbitration queue depth, or the average number of ports that are arbitrating at time. The formula for calculating the number of ports in the arbitration queue is:

$$\text{Length}_{queue} = \text{Request Rate} \times \text{Time}_{queue}$$

If arbitration requests are occurring at the rate of 20,000 requests per second (50% utilization in the example), the time in the arbitration wait queue is 25 microseconds (or 0.000025 seconds). Using these numbers in the above formula gives the average number of ports that are arbitrating. Figure 91 on page 240 shows the calculation of the arbitration queue depth for the sample loop with 50% utilization.

If the loop utilization is increased to 90%, the time in the arbitration queue increases to 225 microseconds (or 0.000225 seconds). Recalculating the queue depth with these values produces the results shown in Figure 92 on page 240. This indicates that, on average, there will be 4.5 ports arbitrating and the average wait to win arbitration is 225 microseconds.

$$\text{Length}_{queue} = \text{Request Rate} \times \text{Time}_{queue}$$
$$= 20000 \times 0.000025$$
$$\text{Length}_{queue} = .5 \text{ ports}$$

Figure 91. Arbitration Queue Depth for 50% Loop Utilization

$$\text{Length}_{queue} = \text{Request Rate} \times \text{Time}_{queue}$$
$$= 20000 \times 0.000225$$
$$\text{Length}_{queue} = 4.5 \text{ ports}$$

Figure 92. Arbitration Queue Depth for 90% Loop Utilization

If these calculations are repeated for a loop utilization of 95%, the average wait time to win arbitration is 475 microseconds and, on average, 9.5 ports will be arbitrating.

With these basic performance estimating concepts in hand, the next section examines several SCSI FCP command scenarios to estimate the performance achieved by typical operations.

13.5 FCP Command Performance Examples

This section examines typical SCSI-3 FCP commands using several different sets of assumptions. This provides examples of the actions required to perform each step of an operation, the time required for different events, and an awareness of the effect of different loop configurations and design options. The examples are by no means exhaustive, but rather provide representative cases and are chosen to correspond to the command scenarios presented in *SCSI-3 FCP Commands* on page 203.

Following the command examples, the section titled *FCP Command Time Comparisons* on page 255 examines the performance behavior of each example and compares the resultant throughput and input/output operations per second values.

13.5.1 Four-Tenancy Write Command, BB_Credit = 0

A basic four-tenancy write command is shown in Table 18 on page 241. This example assumes that the login BB_Credit value used is zero and 8,192 bytes are transferred using four 2,048 byte frames. The loop round-trip time is based on the 64-port loop with 50 meters of copper medium and 25 meters of optical fibre discussed earlier (see Table 17 on page 231). This configuration was chosen as representative of a disk subsystem with the disk drives connected by copper backplane wiring and the attachment made to the file server with an optical cable. Because this represents a loop populated to one-half of the maximum number of ports, performance numbers reflect the overhead associated with an intermediate number of ports.

The timings used in this and later examples assume that only one port is arbitrating, so the time to win arbitration is one full loop round-trip time. The total time required to complete the four-tenancy, 8,192-byte write command with a buffer-to-buffer credit of zero on this 64-port example loop is 259.712 microseconds (see Table 18 on page 241).

Command	Initiator	Loop	Target	Start Time	End Time
Time to Win Arbitration		14,781		0	14,781
Send OPN Ordered Set	38			14,781	14,819
Loop Latency to Receive OPN		7,391		14,819	22,210
Send R_RDY Ordered Set			38	22,210	22,247
Wait for BB_Credit R_RDY		7,391		22,247	29,638
Send FCP Command Frame	866			29,638	30,504
Send CLS Ordered Set	38			30,504	30,542
Loop Latency to Receive CLS		7,391		30,542	37,932
Send CLS Ordered Set			38	37,932	37,970
Loop Latency to Receive CLS		7,391		37,970	45,361
Total for Command	**941**	**44,344**	**75**		**45,361**

Transfer Ready	Initiator	Loop	Target	Start Time	End Time
Time from last CLS to Win Arbitration		14,781		0	14,781
Send OPN Ordered Set			38	14,781	14,819
Loop Latency to Receive OPN		7,391		14,819	22,210
Send R_RDY Ordered Set	38			22,210	22,247
Wait for BB_Credit R_RDY		7,391		22,247	29,638
Send FCP XFER_RDY Frame			678	29,638	30,316
Send CLS			38	30,316	30,353
Latency to Receive XFER_RDY/CLS		7,391		30,353	37,744
Send CLS (ARB can follow immediately)	38			37,744	37,782
Loop Latency to Receive CLS		7,391		37,782	45,173
Total for Transfer Ready	**75**	**44,344**	**753**		**45,173**

Data Transfer (Number of bursts=1)	Initiator	Loop	Target	Start Time	End Time
Time from last CLS to Win Arbitration		14,781		0	14,781
Send OPN to Target	38			14,781	14,819
Loop Latency to Receive OPN		7,391		14,819	22,210
Send R_RDY Ordered Set			38	22,210	22,247
Wait for BB_Credit R_RDY		7,391		22,247	29,638
Send Burst of FCP Data Frame(s)	79,360			29,638	108,998
Send CLS at end of burst	38			108,998	109,036
Loop Latency to Receive CLS		7,391		109,036	116,427
Send CLS in Response			38	116,427	116,464
Loop Latency to Receive CLS		7,391		116,464	123,855
Total for Data Transfer	**79,435**	**44,344**	**75**		**123,855**

Status	Initiator	Loop	Target	Start Time	End Time
Time from last CLS to Win Arbitration		14,781		0	14,781
Send OPN Ordered Set			38	14,781	14,819
Loop Latency to Receive OPN		7,391		14,819	22,210
Send R_RDY Ordered Set	38			22,210	22,247
Wait for BB_Credit R_RDY		7,391		22,247	29,638
Send FCP Response Frame			828	29,638	30,466
Send CLS			38	30,466	30,504
Loop Latency to Receive CLS		7,391		30,504	37,895
Send Final CLS	38			37,895	37,932
Loop Latency to Receive CLS		7,391		37,932	45,323
Total for Status	**75**	**44,344**	**904**		**45,323**

Table 18. Four-Tenancy Write, 8192-Bytes, login BB_Credit = 0

The first loop tenancy is used to transfer the FCP_CMND sequence from the SCSI initiator to the target. The initiator LPSM enters the Arbitrating state and begins arbitrating for access to the loop. Upon winning arbitration, the initiator LPSM enters the Arbitration Won state, sends an OPN and enters the Open state. The OPN is followed by one or more R_RDYs indicating the number of receive buffers the initiator has available. As is always the case with OPN, R_RDY, and CLS, each must be preceded and followed by a minimum of two fill words. Because the login BB_Credit value used is zero in this example, the initiator must wait for an R_RDY from the target before sending the FCP_CMND (which is normally a single-frame sequence). The target receives the OPN, enters the Opened state and sends one or more R_RDYs. After the first R_RDY is received, the initiator sends the FCP_CMND Sequence, which consists of a single frame, followed by a minimum of two fill words and a CLS and enters the Transmitted Close state. Some implementations may transmit additional fill words in excess of the required minimum prior to sending the CLS. After the target receives the CLS, it enters the Received Close state, sends a CLS of its own, and enters the Monitoring state ending the loop circuit at the target's end. When the initiator receives the CLS, it relinquishes control of the loop and enters the Monitoring state, ending the first loop tenancy. The total time required for this loop tenancy is 45.361 microseconds in this example.

When the target is ready to begin the write data transfer it enters the Arbitrating state and arbitrates for access to the loop to send the FCP_XFER_RDY sequence. After winning arbitration (Arbitration Won state), the target sends an OPN to the SCSI initiator, enters the Open state, and may send one or more R_RDYs. When the initiator receives the OPN, it enters the Opened state and sends one or more R_RDYs to the target. After the target receives the first R_RDY, it can send the FCP_XFER_RDY Sequence (which normally consists of a single frame sequence). In this example, the target does not have additional frames for the SCSI initiator so it follows the frame with a minimum of two fill words, a CLS, and enters the Transmitted Close state. The initiator receives the CLS, enters the Received Close state, sends a CLS to the target and enters the Monitoring state. Once the target receives the CLS, it enters the Monitoring state ending the second loop tenancy. The total amount of time required for this loop tenancy is 45.173 microseconds in this example.

The initiator prepares for the data transfer requested by the target's FCP_XFER_RDY and when it is ready to begin the transfer, the SCSI initiator enters the Arbitrating state and arbitrates for access to the loop to send the requested data. When the SCSI initiator wins arbitration (Arbitration Won state), it sends an OPN to the target, enters the Open state and sends one or more R_RDYs. The target receives the OPN, enters the Opened state, and sends the initial R_RDYs to the initiator allowing frame transmission to begin. When the first R_RDY is received by the initiator, it sends the first data frame of the FCP_DATA sequence. If the target has additional receive buffers, it may send additional R_RDYs giving the SCSI initiator permission to send additional frames. These R_RDYs may overlap transmission of the first frame allowing the SCSI initiator to send the second frame immediately following completion of the first frame (separated by the required minimum of six fill words). After all data frames have been sent, the SCSI initiator sends a CLS to the target and enters the Transmitted Close state. The CLS may occur as soon as two fill words have been sent following the end-of-frame delimiter. When the target receives the CLS, it enters the Received Close state, transmits a CLS to the initiator, and enters the Monitoring state. The initiator receives the CLS and enters the Monitoring state ending the third loop tenancy. The total amount of time required for this loop tenancy is 123.855 microseconds in this example.

After the target has processed the write data, it enters the Arbitrating state and arbitrates for access to the loop to send the FCP_RSP sequence. Upon winning arbitration (Arbitration Won state), the target sends an OPN to the SCSI initiator, enters the Open state, and may send one or more R_RDYs. When the initiator receives the OPN, it enters the Opened state and sends one or more R_RDYs to the target. After the target receives the first R_RDY, it can send the FCP_RSP Sequence (which normally consists of a single frame). The target follows the frame with a minimum of two fill words, a CLS, and enters the Transmitted Close state. The initiator receives the CLS, enters the Received Close state, sends a CLS to the target and enters the Monitoring state. Once the target receives the CLS, it enters the Monitoring state ending the fourth and final loop tenancy of the command. The total time required for this loop tenancy is 45.323 microseconds in this example loop.

To calculate the effective data rate of the four-tenancy write command, the number of bytes transferred (8,192 in this example) is divided by the total loop time used by the entire operation (259.712 microseconds). This calculation reveals that the operation has an effective data rate of 31.54 megabytes per second as shown in Figure 93.

$$\text{Effective Data Rate}_{(\text{Megabytes per second})} = \frac{\text{Number of Bytes Transferred}}{\text{Total Command Time}_{(\text{Microseconds})}}$$

$$= \frac{8192}{259.712}$$

$$\text{Effective Data Rate}_{(\text{megabytes per second})} = 31.54 \text{ megabytes per second}$$

Figure 93. EDR: 4-Tenancy 8192-Byte Write, login BB_Credit Value Used = 0

If the number of I/O's per second is desired, this can be determined by dividing one by the total loop time used for the entire operation. In this example, the loop is capable of achieving 3,860 IOPS as shown in Figure 94.

$$\text{Input/Output Operations Per Second (IOPS)} = \left(\frac{1}{\text{Total Command Time}_{(\text{Microseconds})}}\right) \times 10^{6}$$

$$= \left(\frac{1}{259.712}\right) \times 10^{6}$$

$$\text{Input/Output Operations Per Second (IOPS)} = 3{,}850 \text{ IOPS per second}$$

Figure 94. IOPS: 4-Tenancy 8,192-Byte Write, login BB_Credit Value Used = 0

3,850 I/O's per second with four loop tenancies per I/O is 15,402 loop tenancies per second. This is the service rate of the loop under the set of parameters assumed for this command example. The calculation to determine the service rate is shown in Figure 95 on page 244.

$$\text{Service Rate} = \left(\frac{1}{\text{Duration of average loop tenancy}_{(micro\,seconds)}}\right) \times 10^6$$

$$= \left(\frac{1}{64.928\text{ microseconds}}\right) \times 10^6$$

$$\text{Service Rate} = 15,402\text{ tenancies per second}$$

Figure 95. Service Rate: 4-Tenancy 8,192-byte Write Command, BB_Credit = 0

Because the total on-loop time required to perform this command is 259.712 microseconds and four loop tenancies are used, the duration of the average loop tenancy is 64.928 microseconds. If arbitration requests are occurring at a rate of 7,701 requests per second, the loop utilization is 0.5 (or, 50%). In this case, the average time that a port would wait to win arbitration is 64.928 microseconds. The calculation of the arbitration wait time is shown in Figure 96. Because the loop is busy half of the time, the average wait time is equal to the average loop tenancy time.

$$\text{Time}_{queue} = \text{Time}_{Average\ Tenancy} \times \left(\frac{\text{Loop Utilization}}{(1 - \text{Loop Utilization})}\right)$$

$$= 64.928 \times \left(\frac{0.5}{(1 - 0.5)}\right)$$

$$= 64.928 \times \frac{0.5}{0.5}$$

$$\text{Time}_{queue} = 64.928\text{ microseconds}$$

Figure 96. Arbitration Wait Time for 50% Loop Utilization

At a request rate of 7,701 requests per second (50% utilization), the average time in the arbitration queue is 64.928 microseconds (0.000649 seconds) and the average number of ports that are arbitrating is 0.5 ports as shown in Figure 97.

$$\text{Length}_{queue} = \text{Request Rate} \times \text{Time}_{queue}$$

$$= 7,701 \times 0.000649$$

$$\text{Length}_{queue} = 0.5\text{ ports}$$

Figure 97. Arbitration Queue Depth for 50% Loop Utilization

If the request rate for this example increases to 13,862 requests per second (90% utilization), and the average loop tenancy remains at 64.928 microseconds, the average time that a port has to wait to win arbitration is 962.475 microseconds, or nine times as long as when the loop utilization was 50%. An example of how this value is calculated is shown in Figure 98 on page 245.

$$\text{Time}_{\text{queue}} = \text{Time}_{\text{Average Tenancy}} \times \left(\frac{\text{Loop Utilization}}{(1 - \text{Loop Utilization})} \right)$$

$$= 64.928 \times \left(\frac{0.9}{(1 - 0.9)} \right)$$

$$= 64.928 \times \frac{0.9}{0.1} = 64.928 \times 9$$

$$\text{Time}_{\text{queue}} = 584.352 \text{ microseconds}$$

Figure 98. Arbitration Wait Time for a Loop Utilization of 90%

At a request rate of 13,862 requests per second (90% utilization), the time in the queue is increased to 584.352 microseconds (0.000584 seconds) and the average number of ports that are arbitrating increases to 8.1 ports as shown in Figure 99.

$$\text{Length}_{\text{queue}} = \text{Request Rate} \times \text{Time}_{\text{queue}}$$

$$= 13,862 \times 0.000584$$

$$\text{Length}_{\text{queue}} = 8.1 \text{ ports}$$

Figure 99. Arbitration Queue Depth for 90% Loop Utilization

As mentioned earlier, as the loop utilization approaches 100%, the wait time increases at an exponential rate (see Figure 90 on page 239). For example, if the loop utilization increases to 0.95 (95%), the arbitration wait time increases to 1,233.632 microseconds, or 19 times as long as the wait time when the loop was 50% utilized. This calculation is shown in Figure 100.

$$\text{Time}_{\text{queue}} = \text{Time}_{\text{Average Tenancy}} \times \left(\frac{\text{Loop Utilization}}{(1 - \text{Loop Utilization})} \right)$$

$$= 64.928 \times \left(\frac{0.95}{(1 - 0.95)} \right)$$

$$= 64.928 \times \frac{0.95}{0.05} = 64.928 \times 19$$

$$\text{Time}_{\text{queue}} = 1,233.632 \text{ microseconds}$$

Figure 100. Arbitration Wait Time for a Loop Utilization of 95%

If the request rate increases to 14,632 arbitration requests per second (95% utilization), the time in the queue increases to 1,233.632 microseconds (.001234 seconds) and the number of ports that are arbitrating increases to 18.05 ports as shown in Figure 101 on page 246.

When the loop utilization is 1.0 (100%) the wait time is 63 ports times 64.928 microseconds per loop tenancy, or 4,090.464 microseconds (4.090 milliseconds) and the number of ports that are arbitrating is saturated at 63 ports.

$$\text{Length}_{\text{queue}} = \text{Request Rate} \times \text{Time}_{\text{queue}}$$
$$= 14,632 \times 0.001234$$
$$\text{Length}_{\text{queue}} = 18.05 \text{ ports}$$

Figure 101. Arbitration Queue Depth for 95% Loop Utilization

This example shows how the various performance characteristics of a sample loop can be estimated. If actual numbers are available, they can be used in the calculations rather than the assumed numbers used in this case.

A four-tenancy FCP write using a login BB_Credit of zero is typical of first generation Fibre Channel disk drives. The trade-offs between design simplicity and performance represent an emphasis on simplicity at the expense of potential performance. Consequently, the numbers in this example probably represent the low end of performance numbers that can be anticipated on an Arbitrated Loop. The following examples illustrate how different design choices can affect performance. As with the previous example, no attempt is made to quantify the benefits of full-duplex operation or command queueing. Both of these allow multiple operations to share a single loop tenancy and can significantly reduce the overhead and improve performance. Figure 102 on page 247 plots the performance of the example loop as the number of ports is varied from 2 to 126 ports.

Affect of Port Delay. Before leaving this example, a few words about the influence of the delay introduced by each port are in order. This example, and all of the remaining examples in this chapter, assume a six-word delay for each port on the loop. As was seen earlier, this delay is frequently the major contributor to loop overhead on loops with a large number of ports.

It is possible to reduce the delay per port to five words with careful attention to the timings involved. When this is done, the loop round-trip time is reduced and more of the loop's bandwidth is available for user data.

Reducing the delay per port to four words or less may not be possible with asynchronous retransmitter designs due to the necessity to align the transmit and receive data to different clocks. However, by using synchronous designs or a common global clock, it may be possible to reduce the delay to as little as two words per port.

Table 19 on page 247 illustrates the relationship between the delay per port and overall loop performance for this example loop of 64 ports performing 8kb write commands with a BB_Credit of zero.

It can be seen that reducing the delay per port can have a significant effect on performance, providing approximately a 10% improvement when the delay is reduced from six words to five, and potentially providing nearly an 80% improvement if the delay could be reduced to two words per port. Delay per port is just one of the factors the affect loop performance. In the following sections, the affect of loop tenancy and BB_Credit is examined.

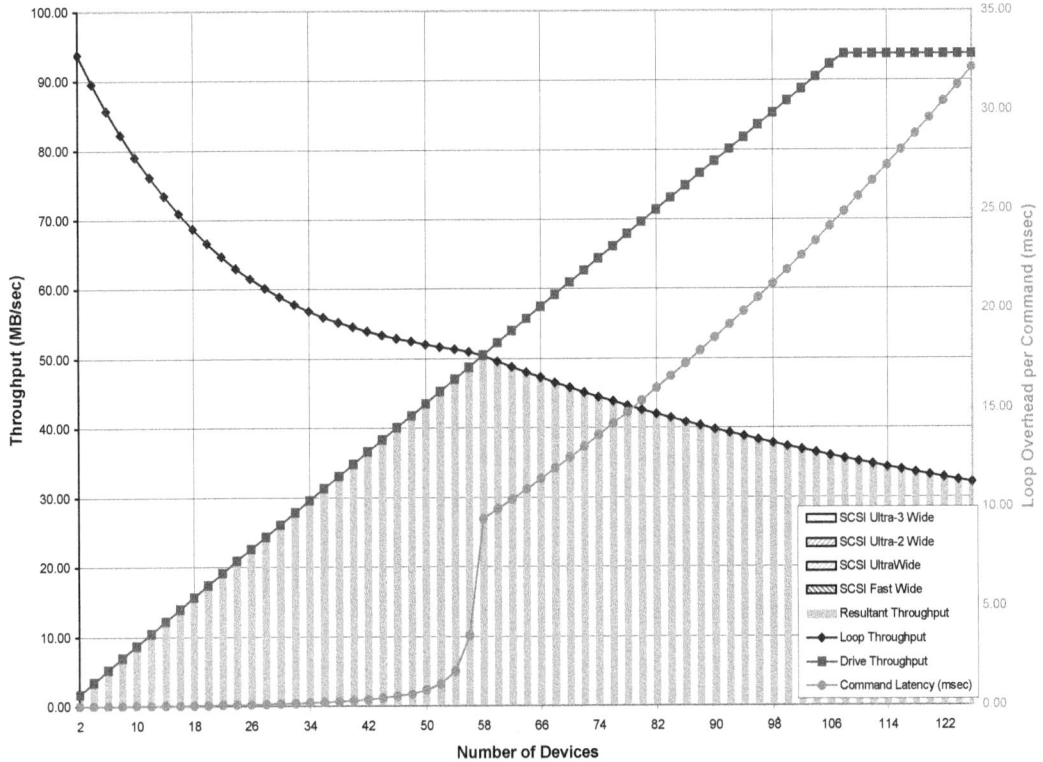

Fibre Channel Arbitrated Loop Performance Estimate

(Transfer size = 8,192 bytes: 6 Word delay, Half-Duplex, BB_Credit = Zero, 50% Reads / 50% Writes, 4 Write Tenancies, 2 Read Tenancies)

Figure 102. Loop Performance vs. Number of Ports

Delay per Port	Delay for 64 Ports	Effective Data Rate	I/O Per Second
6	14.456 usec.	31.54 MB/sec.	3,850
5	12.372 usec.	35.49 MB/sec.	4,333
4	9.963 usec.	40.58 MB/sec.	4,953
3	7.553 usec.	47.36 MB/sec.	5,781
2	5.144 usec.	56.87 MB/sec.	6,942

Table 19. Performance Versus Port Delay (4-Tenancy 8k Write)

13.5.2 Four Tenancy Write Command, BB_Credit > 0

If a write command is performed using four loop tenancies and a login BB_Credit value greater than zero, the operation looks like the example shown in Table 20 on page 250. This example is the same as the previous example with the exception of the login BB_Credit value used.

In this example, the duration of each loop tenancy is reduced by one full loop round-trip time when compared to using a login BB_Credit value of zero. This results because the open originator can begin frame transmission as early as two fill words after the OPN is sent based on the login BB_Credit value and does not have to wait for an R_RDY.

The total loop time required to complete this command is 201.038 microseconds distributed across four loop tenancies (see Table 20 on page 250). The effective data rate for this example is 40.75 megabytes per second as calculated in Figure 103 on page 251.

The number of I/O's per second for this example is 4,974 as shown in Figure 104 on page 251.

Simply by changing the login BB_Credit from zero as used in the previous example (*Four-Tenancy Write Command, BB_Credit = 0* on page 240) to greater than zero, the effective data rate is increased from 31.54 megabytes per second to 40.75 megabytes per second and the number of I/O's per second is increased from 3,860 to 4,974.

Supporting use of a login BB_Credit value greater than zero is not a trivial task in the design of a Fibre Channel port. However, as can be seen in this example, it does provide a significant improvement in performance that may well be worth the extra effort.

13.5.3 Three-Tenancy Write Command, BB_Credit > 0

If the FCP_XFER_RDY and FCP_DATA Sequences are combined into a single loop tenancy, performance can be improved even further because the overhead associated with one complete loop tenancy is removed. The example shown in Table 21 on page 252 illustrates this operation.

The total on-loop time required to complete this three-tenancy write command is 171.437 microseconds distributed across three loop tenancies. This provides an effective data rate of 47.78 megabytes per second as shown in Figure 105.

The number of IOPS for this command example is 5,833 as shown in Figure 106 on page 251.

Performing this command sequence requires that the ports either support full-duplex operation, or the ability to dynamically change the direction of half-duplex flow between the FCP_XFER_RDY and subsequent FCP_DATA sequences (as might be done by using the FC-AL-2 Dynamic Half Duplex ordered set). The example also assumes that the initiator is able to provide the requested data in minimal time (i.e., the data had been prefetched while the FCP_CMND was issued).

13.5.4 Three-Tenancy Read Command, BB_Credit = 0

A typical FCP read command consists of three loop tenancies, the FCP_CMND, FCP_DATA, and FCP_RSP Sequences (the FCP_XFER_RDY Sequence is generally disabled for read commands). An example of this type of command is shown in Table 22 on page 254.

The total time on-loop required to complete the command is 214.766 microseconds spread across three loop tenancies. This provides an effective data rate of 38.14 megabytes per second as shown in Figure 107.

Notice that the performance of a read command is higher than that of an equivalent write command (see *Four-Tenancy Write Command, BB_Credit = 0* on page 240). This is due to the use of three loop tenancies rather than four.

The number of I/O's per second for this command example is 4,666 as shown in Figure 108.

The next example examines the effect of using a login BB_Credit value greater than zero while performing the same FCP read command.

13.5.5 Three Tenancy Read Command, BB_Credit > 0

A typical read command consists of three tenancies, command, data, and response as shown in Table 23 on page 256. The login BB_Credit value used is greater than zero allowing frame transmission to begin as early as two fill words after the OPN is sent.

The total time on-loop required to complete the command is 170.533 microseconds spread across three loop tenancies. This behavior provides an effective data rate of 48.04 megabytes per second as shown in Figure 109.

The number of I/O's per second for this command example is 3,928 as shown in Figure 110.

Again, keep in mind that these examples do not illustrate the beneficial effects of transferring information for multiple commands during a loop tenancy and, therefore, tend to indicate the low end of the performance range.

13.5.6 Single Arbitration Operation With Transfer

Originally, it was envisioned that each port would arbitrate for access to the loop when it had information to send. This is the model used in the earlier examples where arbitration is an integral part of each loop tenancy. However, there is nothing that mandates this type of operation and a somewhat innovative approach has been proposed to reduce the overhead associated with arbitration. This proposal applies to configurations which have one dominant device and a number of slave devices. One example of this type of configuration would be a single initiator disk subsystem with a number of target devices (e.g., a disk array).

The proposal is that the initiator arbitrates once for control of the loop and never relinquishes the loop. Target devices can arbitrate, but their ARB(x) is not propagated by the initiator. The initiator can use the transfer function to establish a loop circuit with one of the targets, send one or more frames, and then close the loop circuit with that target and enter the Transfer state. When the initiator needs to communicate with another target, it sends an OPN to that port and establishes a new loop circuit. An example of this mode of operation applied to the four-tenancy write command with a login BB_Credit value of zero is shown in Table 24 on page 258.

Because the target devices are unable to win arbitration, the initiator is responsible for servicing target devices which require attention. Two approaches have been suggested that can be used to determine when a target needs servicing. The first is for the initiator to poll target de-

Command	Initiator	Loop	Target	Start Time	End Time
Time to Win Arbitration		14,781		0	14,781
Send OPN Ordered Set	38			14,781	14,819
Send two Fill Words	75			14,819	14,894
Send FCP Command Frame	866			14,894	15,760
Send two Fill Words	75			15,760	15,836
Send CLS Ordered Set	38			15,836	15,873
Loop Latency to Receive CLS		7,391		15,873	23,264
Send CLS Ordered Set			38	23,264	23,302
Loop Latency to Receive CLS		7,391		23,302	30,692
Total for Command	**1,092**	**29,563**	**38**		**30,692**
Transfer Ready	Initiator	Loop	Target	Start Time	End Time
Time from last CLS to Win Arbitration		14,781		0	14,781
Send OPN Ordered Set			38	14,781	14,819
Send two Fill Words			75	14,819	14,894
Send FCP XFER_RDY Frame			678	14,894	15,572
Send two Fill Words			75	15,572	15,647
Send CLS			38	15,572	15,685
Latency to Receive XFER_RDY/CLS		7,391		15,685	23,076
Send CLS (ARB can follow immediately)	38			23,076	23,113
Loop Latency to Receive CLS		7,391		23,113	30,504
Total for Transfer Ready	**38**	**29,563**	**904**		**30,504**
Data Transfer (Number of bursts=1)	Initiator	Loop	Target	Start Time	End Time
Time from last CLS to Win Arbitration		14,781		0	14,781
Send OPN to Target	38			14,781	14,819
Send two Fill Words	75			14,819	14,894
Send Burst of FCP Data Frame(s)	79,360			14,894	94,254
Send two Fill Words	75			94,254	94,330
Send CLS at end of burst	38			94,254	94,367
Loop Latency to Receive CLS		7,391		94,367	101,758
Send CLS in Response			38	101,758	101,796
Loop Latency to Receive CLS		7,391		101,796	109,186
Total for Data Transfer Phase	**79,586**	**29,563**	**38**		**109,186**
Status	Initiator	Loop	Target	Start Time	End Time
Time from last CLS to Win Arbitration		14,781		0	14,781
Send OPN Ordered Set			38	14,781	14,819
Send two Fill Words			75	14,819	14,894
Send FCP Response Frame			828	14,894	15,723
Send two Fill Words			75	15,723	15,798
Send CLS			38	15,723	15,836
Loop Latency to Receive CLS		7,391		15,836	23,226
Send Final CLS	38			23,226	23,264
Loop Latency to Receive CLS		7,391		23,264	30,655
Total for Status	**38**	**29,563**	**1,054**		**30,655**

Table 20. Four-Tenancy Write, 8192-Bytes, login BB_Credit > 0

$$\text{Effective Data Rate}_{(\text{Megabytes per second})} = \frac{\text{Number of Bytes Transferred}}{\text{Total Command Time}_{(\text{Microseconds})}}$$

$$= \frac{8192}{201.038}$$

$$\text{Effective Data Rate}_{(\text{megabytes per second})} = 40.75 \text{ megabytes per second}$$

Figure 103. EDR: 4-Tenancy 8192-Byte Write, login BB_Credit Value Used > 0

$$\text{Input/Output Operations Per Second (IOPS)} = \left(\frac{1}{\text{Total Command Time}_{(\text{Microseconds})}}\right) \times 10^6$$

$$= \left(\frac{1}{201.038}\right) \times 10^6$$

$$\text{Input/Output Operations Per Second (IOPS)} = 4,974 \text{ IOPS per second}$$

Figure 104. IOPS: 3-Tenancy 8,192-Byte Write, login BB_Credit Value Used > 0

$$\text{Effective Data Rate}_{(\text{Megabytes per second})} = \frac{\text{Number of Bytes Transferred}}{\text{Total Command Time}_{(\text{Microseconds})}}$$

$$= \frac{8192}{171.437}$$

$$\text{Effective Data Rate}_{(\text{megabytes per second})} = 47.78 \text{ megabytes per second}$$

Figure 105. EDR: 3-Tenancy 8192-Byte Write, login BB_Credit Value Used > 0

$$\text{Input/Output Operations Per Second (IOPS)} = \left(\frac{1}{\text{Total Command Time}_{(\text{Microseconds})}}\right) \times 10^6$$

$$= \left(\frac{1}{171.437}\right) \times 10^6$$

$$\text{Input/Output Operations Per Second (IOPS)} = 5,833 \text{ IOPS per second}$$

Figure 106. IOPS: 3-Tenancy 8,192-Byte Write, login BB_Credit Value Used > 0

vices for outstanding activity using an OPN(yx). The initiator opens each target and waits a predetermined time to see if the target sends any frames or closes the loop circuit. If the target does not send any frames, the initiator closes the loop circuit and moves on to the next device.

A second approach is for the initiator to detect that a target is arbitrating for access to the loop by recognizing the received ARB(x). In a loop with a single initiator and multiple targets, the targets may only communicate with the initiator. Therefore, the only port that the target could be attempting to establish a loop circuit with is the initiator itself. When an ARB(x) is received,

Command	Initiator	Loop	Target	Start Time	End Time
Time to Win Arbitration		14,781		0	14,781
Send OPN Ordered Set	38			14,781	14,819
Send two Fill Words	75			14,819	14,894
Send FCP Command Frame	866			14,894	15,760
Send two Fill Words	75			15,760	15,836
Send CLS Ordered Set	38			15,836	15,873
Loop Latency to Receive CLS		7,391		15,873	23,264
Send CLS Ordered Set			38	23,264	23,302
Loop Latency to Receive CLS		7,391		23,302	30,692
Total for Command	**1,092**	**29,563**	**38**		**30,692**

Transfer Ready	Initiator	Loop	Target	Start Time	End Time
Time from last CLS to Win Arbitration		14,781		0	14,781
Send OPN Ordered Set			38	14,781	14,819
Send two Fill Words	75			14,819	14,894
Send FCP XFER_RDY Frame			678	14,894	15,572
Send six Fill Words	226			15,572	15,798
Send Burst of FCP Data Frame(s)	79,360			15,798	95,158
Send two Fill Words	75			95,158	95,233
Send CLS	38			95,233	95,271
Loop Latency to Receive CLS		7,391		95,271	102,662
Send CLS in Response			38	102,662	102,699
Loop Latency to Receive CLS		7,391		102,699	110,090
Total for Command	**79,774**	**29,563**	**753**		**110,090**

Status	Initiator	Loop	Target	Start Time	End Time
Time from last CLS to Win Arbitration		14,781		0	14,781
Send OPN Ordered Set			38	14,781	14,819
Send two Fill Words			75	14,819	14,894
Send FCP Response Frame			828	14,894	15,723
Send two Fill Words			75	15,723	15,798
Send CLS			38	15,723	15,836
Loop Latency to Receive CLS		7,391		15,836	23,226
Send Final CLS	38			23,226	23,264
Loop Latency to Receive CLS		7,391		23,264	30,655
Total for Status	**38**	**29,563**	**1,054**		**30,655**

Table 21. Three-Tenancy Write, 8192-Bytes, login BB_Credit > 0

the initiator knows that the arbitrating port requires servicing. The initiator establishes a loop circuit with that port allowing the target to transfer its information.

There are several factors to be considered when this type of operation is contemplated.

Both of the above approaches require that the target device support usage of the full-duplex OPN(yx) because they must be able to transmit frames when they receive an OPN(yx). If a half-duplex target is opened, it will assume that frames are to follow and condition its FC-2 function for frame reception. This can be alleviated by use of the Dynamic Half Duplex (DHD) ordered set as follows. After the initiator sends the OPN and subsequent R_RDYs, it sends the

$$\text{Effective Data Rate}_{(\text{Megabytes per second})} = \frac{\text{Number of Bytes Transferred}}{\text{Total Command Time}_{(\text{Microseconds})}}$$

$$= \frac{8192}{214.766}$$

$$\text{Effective Data Rate}_{(\text{megabytes per second})} = 38.14 \text{ megabytes per second}$$

Figure 107. EDR: 3-Tenancy 8192-Byte Read, login BB_Credit Value Used = 0

$$\text{Input/Output Operations Per Second (IOPS)} = \left(\frac{1}{\text{Total Command Time}_{(\text{Microseconds})}}\right) \times 10^6$$

$$= \left(\frac{1}{214.766}\right) \times 10^6$$

$$\text{Input/Output Operations Per Second (IOPS)} = 4,666 \text{ IOPS per second}$$

Figure 108. IOPS: 3-Tenancy 8,192-Byte Read, login BB_Credit Value Used = 0

DHD. This informs the (half-duplex) target that no frames will be transmitted and that it is safe for the target to change its direction of operation to frame transmission. This allows the target to transfer one or more frames to the initiator. Use of the DHD does not prevent the initiator from sending one or more R_RDYs in response to the target's frames as the CLS would have done.

If the target sends a CLS prior to the initiator, the initiator may not able to enter the Transfer state. According to the Loop Port State Machine in the Arbitrated Loop standard, the initiator enters the Received Close state and is unable to use the transfer function. This can be alleviated by modifying the operation of the state machine to allow a port to enter the Transfer state, even if it has received a CLS from the other port (as if it had sent the CLS first). The next version of the Arbitrated Loop standard may move the transfer function to the Received Close and Transmitted Close states to allow the open originator to transfer whether it sent or received the first CLS.

Of course multiple target ports could require servicing simultaneously. Each port follows the normal arbitration rules and either transmits its own ARB(x) or retransmits a received ARB(x) if it has higher priority. When these target ports receive an OPN and are able to send frames to the correct destination, the ports reset the Access variable and will not re-arbitrate again until the fairness window has been reset. This assures that all ports obtain the same access to the loop as any other port (i.e., access fairness). The Loop Port State Machine does not show this behavior specifically because the only way that an arbitration request can be withdrawn is when the port realizes that another upstream port is arbitrating (i.e., it appears not to be the last arbitrating port in the fairness window). Because this procedure is a controlled environment (i.e., all ports are communicating with only one other port on the loop, these ports could be programmed to reset the Access variable (as if they had won arbitration), or the open originator could transmit a low-priority ARB(x) (e.g., x=x'FE' - which assumes that there is no

Command	Initiator	Loop	Target	Start Time	End Time
Time for Initiator to Win Arbitration		14,781		0	14,781
Send OPN Ordered Set	38			14,781	14,819
Loop Latency to Receive OPN		7,391		14,819	22,210
Send R_RDY Ordered Set			38	22,210	22,247
Wait for BB_Credit R_RDY		7,391		22,247	29,638
Send FCP Command Frame	866			29,638	30,504
Send CLS Ordered Set	38			30,504	30,542
Latency to deliver CLS		7,391		30,542	37,932
Send CLS Ordered Set			38	37,932	37,970
Latency to Receive CLS Ordered Set		7,391		37,970	45,361
Total for Command	**941**	**44,344**	**75**		**45,361**

Data Transfer	Initiator	Loop	Target	Start Time	End Time
Time for Target to Win Arbitration		14,781		0	14,781
Send OPN Ordered Set			38	14,781	14,819
Loop Latency to Receive OPN		7,391		14,819	22,210
Send R_RDY Ordered Set	38			22,210	22,247
Wait for BB_Credit R_RDY		7,391		22,247	29,638
Send Burst of FCP Data Frame(s)			79,360	29,638	108,998
Send CLS			38	108,998	109,036
Loop Latency to Receive CLS		7,391		109,036	116,427
Send Final CLS	38			116,427	116,464
Loop Latency to Receive CLS		7,391		116,464	123,855
Total for Data Transfer	**75**	**44,344**	**79,435**		**123,855**

Status	Initiator	Loop	Target	Start Time	End Time
Time for Target to Win Arbitration		14,781		0	14,781
Send OPN Ordered Set			38	14,781	14,819
Loop Latency to Receive OPN		7,391		14,819	22,210
Send R_RDY Ordered Set	38			22,210	22,247
Wait for BB_Credit R_RDY		7,391		22,247	29,638
Send FCP Response Frame			828	29,638	30,466
Send CLS			38	30,466	30,504
Loop Latency to Receive CLS		7,391		30,504	37,895
Send Final CLS	38			37,895	37,932
Loop Latency to Receive CLS		7,391		37,932	45,323
Total for Status	**75**	**44,344**	**904**		**45,323**

Table 22. Three-Tenancy Read, 8192-Bytes, login BB_Credit = 0

AL_PA=x'FE' on the loop) to guarantee that a port will withdraw its arbitration request because it assumes that another port is arbitrating). Now, if the open initiator receives the ARB(FE), it knows that there is no one arbitrating (at which time it would reset the access fairness window by transmitting IDLEs).

When multiple initiators exist on the same loop, the initiators must take turns winning arbitration according to some implementation defined algorithm (the initiators are usually high-priority and unfair). This allows each initiator to access the loop to send commands and service its de-

$$\text{Effective Data Rate}_{(\text{Megabytes per second})} = \frac{\text{Number of Bytes Transferred}}{\text{Total Command Time}_{(\text{Microseconds})}}$$

$$= \frac{8192}{170.533}$$

$$\text{Effective Data Rate}_{(\text{megabytes per second})} = 48.04 \text{ megabytes per second}$$

Figure 109. EDR: 3-Tenancy 8192-Byte Read, login BB_Credit Value Used > 0

$$\text{Input/Output Operations Per Second (IOPS)} = \left(\frac{1}{\text{Total Command Time}_{(\text{Microseconds})}}\right) \times 10^6$$

$$= \left(\frac{1}{170.533}\right) \times 10^6$$

$$\text{Input/Output Operations Per Second (IOPS)} = 5,864 \text{ IOPS per second}$$

Figure 110. IOPS: 3-Tenancy 8,192-Byte Read, login BB_Credit Value Used > 0

vices. A potential problem arises when a target arbitrates because it requires servicing and the wrong initiator currently owns the loop. If the initiator opens the target, the target sends a CLS because it does not have anything for that initiator and continues to arbitrate. One possible solution is for each initiator to maintain a list of target devices with outstanding activity for that initiator. That way, the initiator could match the received ARB(x) with its table and decide whether to open the target or relinquish the loop at the next opportunity. This allows the other initiator or the target to win arbitration. If the other initiator wins arbitration, it opens the target. If the target wins arbitration, it opens the initiator. In either case, a loop circuit is established between the correct initiator and target.

The performance benefits of this type of operation can be significant, especially when the loop is lightly utilized. When this is the case, one complete loop round-trip time is saved for each loop tenancy because the entire arbitration cycle is eliminated.

The total time on-loop required to complete the command is 200.586 microseconds spread across three loop tenancies. This provides an effective data rate of 40.84 megabytes per second as shown in Figure 111.

The number of I/O's per second for a four-tenancy write command that transfers 8,192 bytes and uses a login BB_Credit of zero is 4,985 as shown in Figure 112.

13.5.7 FCP Command Time Comparisons

The total amount of loop time required to perform a command can be determined by adding the times required for each individual loop tenancy of the command. This value is not the time required to complete the command but how much of the loop's time is used during command execution. Both the SCSI initiator and target contribute addition command overhead time, both on and off the loop. Command execution overhead which occurs while off the loop does not af-

Command	Initiator	Loop	Target	Start Time	End Time
Time for Initiator to Win Arbitration		14,781		0	14,781
Send OPN Ordered Set	38			14,781	14,819
Send two Fill Words	75			14,819	14,894
Send FCP Command Frame	866			14,894	15,760
Send two Fill Words	75			15,760	15,836
Send CLS Ordered Set	38			15,836	15,873
Latency to deliver CLS		7,391		15,873	23,264
Send CLS Ordered Set			38	23,264	23,302
Latency to Receive CLS Ordered Set		7,391		23,302	30,692
Total for Command	**1,092**	**29,563**	**38**		**30,692**

Data Transfer	Initiator	Loop	Target	Start Time	End Time
Time for Target to Win Arbitration		14,781		0	14,781
Send OPN Ordered Set			38	14,781	14,819
Send two Fill Words			75	14,819	14,894
Send Burst of FCP Data Frame(s)			79,360	14,894	94,254
Send two Fill Words			75	94,254	94,330
Send CLS			38	94,330	94,367
Loop Latency to Receive CLS		7,391		94,367	101,758
Send Final CLS	38			101,758	101,796
Loop Latency to Receive CLS		7,391		101,796	109,186
Total for Data Transfer	**38**	**29,563**	**79,586**		**109,186**

Status	Initiator	Loop	Target	Start Time	End Time
Time for Target to Win Arbitration		14,781		0	14,781
Send OPN Ordered Set			38	14,781	14,819
Send two Fill Words			75	14,819	14,894
Send FCP Response Frame			828	14,894	15,723
Send two Fill Words			75	15,723	15,798
Send CLS			38	15,798	15,836
Loop Latency to Receive CLS		7,391		15,836	23,226
Send Final CLS	38			23,226	23,264
Loop Latency to Receive CLS		7,391		23,264	30,655
Total for Status	**38**	**29,563**	**1,054**		**30,655**

Table 23. Three-Tenancy Read, 8192-Bytes, login BB_Credit > 0

fect loop performance, although it may affect the device's ability to sustain a desired performance level or response time. This time may be in the range of 100-500 microseconds per command in a typical target. Also, the device itself may contribute significant time if it needs to seek to the appropriate logical block before reading or writing the data.

Table 25 on page 259 summarizes the different 8,192 byte FCP command examples presented in the previous sections. It contains a comparison of the times required by each of the command examples and the resulting performance. This comparison quantifies the benefit associated with each step taken to improve loop performance. Using a login BB_Credit value greater than zero saves one loop round-trip time (14.781 microseconds in these examples) per loop tenancy and improves the performance by nearly 30% (+29% in the write example, +26%

in the read case). The three-tenancy FCP write example illustrates how full-duplex capability (or the ability to change direction in a half-duplex design) saves one additional complete loop tenancy by combining the FCP_XFER_RDY and FCP_DATA Sequences into a single loop tenancy and improves the performance by approximately +51% when combined with a login BB_Credit value greater than zero. This is a significant increase in loop performance that can be realistically achieved. Finally, using transfer in a single-arbitration mode provides approximately 29% better performance than the basic four-tenancy write operation and is comparable to the result obtained by using a login BB_Credit value greater than zero (which may be difficult to do in some designs).

It should be noted that FCP read commands provide somewhat higher performance than the equivalent write commands because reads normally eliminate the FCP_XFER_RDY information unit and its associated overhead.

13.6 Performance Summary

The examples in this chapter estimate the performance of FCP commands using a certain set of assumed parameters. Command operations on loops with different parameters will yield different performance results which can be estimated using the same techniques described in this chapter.

When it is necessary to estimate the performance of a loop under dynamic conditions, the number of interdependent variables makes an analytical solution difficult, if not impossible. In this case, it is often better to use a simulation model rather than attempt to calculate the performance. The Fibre Channel Industry Association (FCIA) and the Distributed Multimedia Research Center and Computer Science Department at the University of Minnesota have both done modeling studies of Arbitrated Loop performance under dynamic conditions. For further information, reference the appropriate reports listed in the *Bibliography* on page 377.

All of the estimates in this chapter reflect the behavior of an example loop performing one command at a time using half-duplex operation (with DHD in the case of the three-tenancy write command). As such, they produce performance estimates at the lower end of the range for a loop with the specified number of ports. There are a number of factors that contribute to the 'real world' performance of a loop exceeding these numbers. Among them are:

- As the number of ports arbitrating simultaneously increases, the time required for the next port to win arbitration after the current loop circuit is closed decreases. This means that a busy loop has less arbitration overhead than a loop with a single arbitrating port. For example, if the number of ports arbitrating in the four-tenancy write command with a login BB_Credit of zero (shown in *Four-Tenancy Write Command, BB_Credit = 0* on page 240) is increased from one to eight, the Effective Data Rate increases from 31.54 megabytes per second to 39.39 megabytes per second and the number of I/O per second increases from 3,860 to 4,808. This behavior provides a performance increase of +25%.

- When the effect of 'opportunistic transfers' and the transmission of information units for multiple commands during the same loop circuit are included, loop performance may nearly double when compared to the simple cases examined.

Command	Initiator	Loop	Target	Start Time	End Time
Time to Win Arbitration		0		0	0
Send OPN Ordered Set	38			0	38
Loop Latency to Receive OPN		7,391		38	7,428
Send R_RDY Ordered Set			38	7,428	7,466
Wait for BB_Credit R_RDY		7,391		7,466	14,857
Send FCP Command Frame	866			14,857	15,723
Send CLS Ordered Set	38			15,723	15,760
Loop Latency to Receive CLS		7,391		15,760	23,151
Send CLS Ordered Set			38	23,151	23,189
Loop Latency to Receive CLS		7,391		23,189	30,579
Total for Command	**941**	**29,563**	**75**		**30,579**

Transfer Ready	Initiator	Loop	Target	Start Time	End Time
Time from last CLS to Win Arbitration		0		0	0
Send OPN Ordered Set			38	0	38
Loop Latency to Receive OPN		7,391		38	7,428
Send R_RDY Ordered Set	38			7,428	7,466
Wait for BB_Credit R_RDY		7,391		7,466	14,857
Send FCP XFER_RDY Frame			678	14,857	15,534
Send CLS			38	15,534	15,572
Latency to Receive XFER_RDY/CLS		7,391		15,572	22,963
Send CLS (ARB can follow immediately)	38			22,963	23,000
Loop Latency to Receive CLS		7,391		23,000	30,391
Total for Transfer Ready	**75**	**29,563**	**753**		**30,391**

Data Transfer (Number of bursts=1)	Initiator	Loop	Target	Start Time	End Time
Time from last CLS to Win Arbitration		0		0	0
Send OPN to Target	38			0	38
Loop Latency to Receive OPN		7,391		38	7,428
Send R_RDY Ordered Set			38	7,428	7,466
Wait for BB_Credit R_RDY		7,391		7,466	14,857
Send Burst of FCP Data Frame(s)	79,360			14,857	94,217
Send CLS at end of burst	38			94,217	94,254
Loop Latency to Receive CLS		7,391		94,254	101,645
Send CLS in Response			38	101,645	101,683
Loop Latency to Receive CLS		7,391		101,683	109,073
Total for Data Transfer	**79,435**	**29,563**	**75**		**109,073**

Status	Initiator	Loop	Target	Start Time	End Time
Time from last CLS to Win Arbitration		0		0	0
Send OPN Ordered Set			38	0	38
Loop Latency to Receive OPN		7,391		38	7,428
Send R_RDY Ordered Set	38			7,428	7,466
Wait for BB_Credit R_RDY		7,391		7,466	14,857
Send FCP Response Frame			828	14,857	15,685
Send CLS			38	15,685	15,723
Loop Latency to Receive CLS		7,391		15,723	23,113
Send Final CLS	38			23,113	23,151
Loop Latency to Receive CLS		7,391		23,151	30,542
Total for Status	**75**	**29,563**	**904**		**30,542**

Table 24. Transfer Operation: Four-Tenancy Write Command, login BB_Credit = 0

$$\text{Effective Data Rate}_{(\text{Megabytes per second})} = \frac{\text{Number of Bytes Transferred}}{\text{Total Command Time}_{(\text{Microseconds})}}$$

$$= \frac{8192}{200.586}$$

$$\text{Effective Data Rate}_{(\text{megabytes per second})} = 40.84 \text{ megabytes per second}$$

Figure 111. EDR: 4-Tenancy Transfer 8192-Byte Write, login BB_Credit Value Used = 0

$$\text{Input/Output Operations Per Second (IOPS)} = \left(\frac{1}{\text{Total Command Time}_{(\text{Microseconds})}}\right) \times 10^6$$

$$= \left(\frac{1}{200.586}\right) \times 10^6$$

$$\text{Input/Output Operations Per Second (IOPS)} = 4{,}985 \text{ IOPS per second}$$

Figure 112. IOPS: 4-Tenancy Transfer 8,192-Byte Write, login BB_Credit Value Used = 0

	FCP Writes				FCP Reads	
Number of Tenancies	4	4	4/Transfer	3	3	3
login BB_Credit	= 0	> 0	= 0	> 0	= 0	> 0
Reference:	Table 18	Table 20	Table 24	Table 21	Table 22	Table 23
FCP_CMND time	45.361	30.692	30.579	30.692	45.361	30.692
FCP_XFER_RDY time	45.173	30.504	30.391	110.090	n/a	n/a
FCP_DATA time	123.855	109.186	109.073		123.855	109.186
FCP_RSP time	45.323	30.655	30.542	30.655	45.323	30.655
Total time	**259.712**	**201.038**	**200.586**	**171.437**	**214.539**	**170.533**
Megabytes per second	31.54	40.75	40.84	47.78	38.18	48.04
I/O's per second	3,850	4,974	4,985	5,833	4,661	5,864
Performance Improvement	Baseline	+29%	+29%	+51%	Baseline	+26%

Table 25. FCP Command Time Comparisons: 64-Port Loop

- Finally, the use of full-duplex operations may provide another significant increase in loop performance by reducing the number of loop circuits needed to complete an operation.

As implementations begin to take advantage of these types of behavior, one might anticipate that loop performance may easily reach four times the values calculated in this chapter.

13.7 Chapter Summary

Key Performance Factors

- Loop round-trip time (time required for a signal to travel around the loop)
  - Number of ports on the loop and the delay through each port
  - Time required for signals to travel between ports
- Number of loop tenancies to complete a command
- Number of round-trips per loop tenancy
- Login BB_Credit used
- Taking advantage of opportunistic transfers

Loop Round-Trip Time

- Each port is allowed a six-word delay
  - 225.8 nsec @ 1062.5 mbaud (100 MB/sec)
  - 112.9 nsec @ 2125 mbaud (200 MB/sec)
  - Hubs that retime the signal may add similar amount of delay
  - Port delay scales with signalling rate
- Time for signals to travel between ports
  - Use 5 nsec. per meter for estimating time
  - Propagation delay not dependent on signalling rate (speed of light)

Loop Tenancies

- Number of times loop is acquired during command
  - Includes arbitration, opening, and closing overheads
  - If Transfer is not used, each loop circuit = one loop tenancy
- Each tenancy may require two, or more, round trips
  - One to win arbitration (if loop is idle, less if loop is busy)
  - One to send CLS and receive CLS
  - Zero login BB_Credit adds a third round trip
- Minimizing tenancies improves performance
  - Full-duplex port designs
  - Use of Transfer

Half-Duplex Ports

- Half-duplex ports may require a new loop tenancy to change direction
  - Open originator sets up to transmit frames
  - Open recipient sets up to receive frames
  - Most half-duplex ports are not able to change direction during a loop circuit
- Results in more loop tenancies per command
  - Minimum of four per write command
  - Minimum of two per read command
- Less likelihood of opportunistic transfers
  - Limited to single direction opportunities

Login BB_Credit

- Zero login BB_Credit adds one round-trip per loop circuit
  - Wait for R_RDY in response to OPN before sending frame(s)
  - May have a severe impact on large loops
- Nonzero login BB_Credit may improve performance
  - Benefit is significant on large loops
  - Loops with a large number of ports
  - Loops that are physically large

Opportunistic Transfers

- Send frames whenever opportunities arise
  - Send multiple commands during one tenancy
  - Send data or status for multiple commands during same tenancy
  - Initiator opens target, target sends data or status for outstanding command
- Can reduce the number of tenancies required
  - Reduces loop overhead and improves performance
  - Opportunistic transfers can cut write command tenancies in half
- Generally requires that both ports are full-duplex

14. Errors

The Arbitrated Loop configuration introduces the potential for error conditions that do not occur in non-loop environments. In addition, loop ports are subject to the same types of errors that are found in point-to-point and fabric configurations. This chapter examines the errors that may occur and their affect on loop operations.

14.1 Loop Timers and Timeouts

The Arbitrated Loop standard defines two timers called Arbitrated Loop time (AL_Time) and Loop time-out value (LP_TOV). The default value for AL_Time is obtained by taking twice the largest possible time for a signal to propagate around the loop. This is twice 134 ports (maximum possible AL_PA values possible, even though only 127 are currently defined for ports) times the maximum six-word latency allowed per port, each connected by 10 kilometer links. The resultant value is 15 milliseconds. The default value for LP_TOV is set to 2 seconds. LP_TOV is used primarily to detect failures during loop initialization and access fairness.

The Fibre Channel standard also defines the value for the Receiver_Transmitter time-out value (R_T_TOV) used to detect loop failures. The default value for this timer is 100 milliseconds.

14.2 Link Errors

Link errors can occur during the ordered sets used to implement the loop protocols. Most link errors will result in an 8B/10B error manifested as either an invalid transmission character or running disparity error. Some link errors may result in a valid, but incorrect, character being decoded. Either of these conditions could result in an ordered set being unrecognizable by the receiving port. There is also a possibility that one ordered set could be transformed into a different, valid, ordered set or that an AL_PA value in the ordered set could be transformed into a different AL_PA value.

Frame delimiters and primitive signals such as R_RDY, ARB(x), ARB(yx), ARB(F0) ARB(FF), OPN, and CLS are more vulnerable to corruption due to link errors because they are processed upon receipt of a single occurrence. The potential for mis-interpretation of a primitive sequence is extremely low because three consecutive occurrences of the same ordered set are required before the primitive sequence is recognized.

14.2.1 Invalid Transmission Characters and Words

If an ordered set is corrupted in a manner that results in an invalid transmission character or word, it is processed in accordance with the LPSM table entries labeled *invalid transmission character* or *invalid transmission word*. The action taken depends on the current state of the LPSM receiving the corrupted transmission word.

If the LPSM receives an invalid transmission character while in the Monitoring or Arbitrating states, it substitutes the current fill word in its place. If this occurs in the middle of a frame, the receiving port will not find a valid frame (i.e., a K28.5 which is not an end-of-frame) and consequently, discards what it has received (the attempt is not to count an error twice and to isolate the path to where the error was detected). If the substitution occurs outside of a frame, it may replace a non-fill word primitive signal (thereby loosing information). The effect of lost ordered sets is discussed later.

When an invalid transmission word is received in the other states, the LPSM discards the received word and either transmits the current fill word or continues normal frame transmission.

14.2.2 Unrecognized Ordered Set

If the ordered set is corrupted and unrecognizable, it is processed in accordance with the entry in the LPSM tables labeled *Other O.S.* The action taken differs depending on the current state of the receiving LPSM(s) with the invalid ordered set either being retransmitted, the current fill word substituted for the received ordered set, or normal FC-2 frame transmission taking place. If the original ordered set was significant to loop operations, the original ordered set is lost as a result of the corruption. The effect of lost ordered sets is discussed later.

If the LPSM is in the Monitoring or Arbitrating states, an unrecognized ordered set is retransmitted. The unrecognized ordered set could potentially circulate on the loop repeatedly until one of the ports enters a state other than the Monitoring or Arbitrating state. The behavior allows a newer version of FC-AL to add new ordered sets (which would result in an unrecognized ordered set for previous generation ports, not due to corruption).

If the LPSM receives an unrecognized ordered set in the Transmitted Close or Transfer states, it discards the received ordered set and substitutes the current fill word.

If the LPSM receives an unrecognized ordered set while in the Open, Opened, Received Close, Open-Init, or Old-Port states, it processes it in accordance with normal Fibre Channel rules. That is, the ordered set is discarded and the port continues with normal FC-2 frame transmission or appropriate fill word or other ordered set transmission.

If the LPSM receives an unrecognized ordered set while in the Initializing state, it transmits LIP in place of the received ordered set. In this case, no harm is done as a result of the error, as LIP would normally be retransmitted in place of received ordered sets anyway.

14.3 Loop Protocol Errors

Loop protocol errors can occur as a result of lost ordered sets, incorrect ordered sets, or unexpected ordered sets. The errors can occur during any of the loop protocols, including arbitration, while opening or closing a loop circuit, and during frame transmission or initialization.

A lost ordered set is one that is never recognized by the intended recipient. It could have been corrupted due to a link error or never transmitted due to a failure in the sending port. Lost ordered sets result in an expected action never occurring, for example, a port fails to open because the OPN was lost.

An incorrect ordered set is one that has been corrupted such that it is recognized as a valid ordered set (i.e., there are no code violations and the disparity rules are met), but is not the one that was sent, or contains an AL_PA value other than what was sent. This type of error may result in an incorrect action occurring or the action occurring at the wrong port. For example, a corrupted OPN may result in the wrong port being opened or no port being opened.

The final category of errors occurs when a valid ordered set is received that is unexpected under the current conditions. For example, an OPN is received while a loop circuit already exists.

The following sections examine the effects of different types of errors that may occur during the loop protocols.

14.3.1 Arbitration Protocol Errors

Errors during the arbitration protocol may result in one or more ARB primitive signals being lost or corrupted.

Lost ARB(x). If one or more ARB(x) primitive signals is lost on the loop while a port is in the Arbitrating state, no harm is done because the arbitrating port transmits multiple occurrences of the ARB(x). If the first ARB(x) of a series is lost, the port simply has to wait until the next (non-corrupted) ARB(x) is received. If a later ARB(x) is lost there is no effect because the port will have already won arbitration.

A lost ARB(x) is not abnormal behavior because the elasticity smoothing buffer may delete an ARB(x) during normal operation. This is one of the reasons why an arbitrating port sends ARB(x) at every opportunity.

Orphaned ARB(x). If a port begins arbitration, transmits one or more ARB(x) ordered sets and then disappears from the loop due to a failure or being removed from the loop without causing a loop failure, the transmitted ARB(x) ordered sets are orphaned.

If the orphaned ARB(x) ordered sets are higher priority than any arbitrating port, the current fill word at each port is set to the orphaned ARB(x). The loop may fill with the orphaned ARB(x) because the port with the matching AL_PA is no longer present to win arbitration.

If a port with a lower-priority AL_PA begins arbitrating once this condition occurs, it can not win arbitration because it will always forward the orphaned ARB(x) instead of transmitting its own. However, if a port does not win arbitration within LP_TOV, an arbitration wait time-out occurs which would normally result in loop initialization (thereby, purging the orphaned ARB(x).

If a port with a higher-priority AL_PA begins arbitrating, it begins substituting its own ARB(x) for each occurrence of the orphaned ARB(x). This purges all orphaned ARB(x) ordered sets from the loop by the time the port wins arbitration.

If a loop circuit exists, the orphaned ARBs are also purged by the LPSM in the Open state.

Corrupted ARB(x). If an error causes an incorrect AL_PA value in the ARB(x), an error may or may not occur. The ARB(x) repeats the AL_PA value in the third and fourth characters of the ordered set to improve the reliability of the ARB(x) under error conditions. The Arbitrated Loop standard requires that both characters are identical, however, there are some known implementations which do not make this check. If the check is performed, the probability of incorrectly interpreting a corrupted ARB(x) is greatly reduced, if not, a degree of error protection is sacrificed.

The chance of both bytes being corrupted to the same character is extremely small. All of the AL_PA values are neutral disparity and corrupting both transmission characters to the same different valid neutral disparity transmission character would require changing both a one bit to a zero bit and a different zero bit to a one bit in both transmission characters. The probability of such an occurrence is extremely small.

A more likely scenario arises when a port in the Monitoring or Arbitrating states detects that both the third and fourth characters are invalid. Any transmission word where a code violation or a disparity error is detected or an ARB where the third and fourth characters are not identical (if checked), are replaced by the current fill word (which could be the correct ARB) to make sure that the error is detected as close as possible to the source and not propagated.

If an ARB(x) is corrupted such that it mimics a valid ARB(x), a number of possible outcomes may occur. If the port with the AL_PA corresponding to the corrupted AL_PA is in the Monitoring state, it discards the ARB(x) and substitutes its current fill word. This prevents the loop from filling up with the corrupted ARB(x). If the port is in the Arbitrating state, it may win arbitration early and attempt to open a destination port. This could occur when another port already owns the loop and has established a loop circuit.

If this occurs, the frames from the three or four ports may arrive at the wrong destination port. If this occurs, the destination port may detect an incorrect Destination_ID, discard the frame, and send a P_RJT, if appropriate for the class of service (the P_RJT may also go to an incorrect destination and is discarded). This continues until one of the ports initiates a close, at which time the loop circuit(s) will be progressively closed with the loop ultimately returning to the closed condition.

Unexpected ARB(x). If a port receives its own ARB(x) at an unexpected time, it may indicate that some other port's ARB(x) has been corrupted (or even that the port transmitted its own ARB(x) when it shouldn't have).

A port may legitimately receive its own ARB(x) while in the Open, Transmitted Close, and Transfer states. This occurs when the port wins arbitration and transitions to these states before all of the ARB(x) ordered sets have been purged from the loop.

If the port is in the Monitoring state, and receives its own ARB(x), it discards the received ARB(x) and transmits its current fill word instead. The port is not currently arbitrating, and the ARB(x) is not appropriate at this time.

If a port in the Opened state or Received Close state receives its own ARB(x), it is discarded and normal FC-2 frame transmission continues. Receipt of the ARB(x) in either of these states is indicative of a loop protocol error condition, such as a corrupted ARB(x).

Any ARB(x) received while in the Open-Init state is inappropriate. It is discarded and the current fill word may be transmitted in its place.

Lost ARB(F0). ARB(F0) is used during initialization and the access fairness protocol. During initialization, the temporary loop master transmits ARB(F0) to signal the other ports on the loop to stop transmitting the LISM frames and prepare to receive the LIFA frame. Because the loop master transmits ARB(F0) continuously until it receives ARB(F0) at its receive input, loss of one or more ARB(F0) ordered sets does not affect the operation.

During the access fairness protocol, the current arbitration winner begins transmitting ARB(F0) as its current fill word to determine if any other port is arbitrating. If another port is arbitrating, it substitutes its own ARB(x) for every received ARB(F0). If the arbitration winner receives an ARB(F0), it signals the end of the access fairness window by transmitting IDLEs. If one or more ARB(F0) signals are lost, the effect is to delay ending of the access fairness window until a valid ARB(F0) is received. This may have a slight influence on the duration of the window, but no error conditions should occur.

Corrupted ARB(F0). If ARB(F0) is corrupted, the result is that one or more ARB(F0) signals is lost. As described in the prior section, this does not normally cause a problem.

If the ARB(F0) is corrupted to a valid ARB(x), the result is the same as described earlier regarding the corruption of one ARB(x) into another.

14.3.2 Open Protocol Errors

The open protocol is subject to the same types of errors as may affect the ARB ordered sets. An OPN ordered set may be lost, corrupted, or occur at an unexpected time.

Lost OPN(yx) or OPN(yy). If an OPNy ordered set is lost or corrupted such that it is not recognizable as an OPNy, the intended destination port fails to enter the Opened state.

If the login BB_Credit value used for the open recipient is zero, the open originator is stalled waiting for one or more R_RDYs from the open recipient. The loop is unproductive and will remain so until the open originator times out (recommended timeout is AL_Time) and transmits a CLS, or one of the ports on the loop (which could include the open originator) times out and begins loop initialization.

If the login BB_Credit between the value used for the open recipient is nonzero, the open originator can begin frame transmission based on the available BB_Credit value. The frames will circle the loop and be received by the open originator. The open originator detects that the Destination_ID is incorrect and can determine that it sent the frames by examining the source ID in the frame header. In Class-1, Class-2, or Class-4, the port may also choose to send an P_RJT based upon the incorrect Destination_ID without checking the Source_ID. If it does so, the P_RJT frame is sent to itself providing the error indication.

If the CLS is sent before credit is exhausted, the loop circuit may close normally, although any transmitted frames are lost. If available BB_Credit is exhausted prior to sending CLS, the loop is unproductive as described earlier until a timeout occurs and the loop is closed or initialized.

Lost OPN(yr) or OPN(fr). If an open replicate is lost, the intended destination port(s) fails to set replicate mode. If selective replicate mode OPN(yr) is being used to build a group of ports, the group will be incomplete. The only indication of this occurrence is that the affected port may fail to provide some expected indication such as status that should be presented during a subsequent loop circuit.

If a broadcast open replicate OPN(fr) is lost, some or all of the intended ports may fail to set replicate mode. Ports that recognized the OPN(fr) set replicate mode while those that fail to recognize the OPN(fr) do not. The only indication of this occurrence is that one or more of the ports fail to perform some expected subsequent action.

The open originator can verify OPNr is correctly propagated around the loop by confirming that it receives OPNr at its receive input. If the open originator fails to detect each OPNr within one loop round-trip time (AL_Time, which has a default value of 15 ms.), it knows that the OPNr was corrupted and a reasonable action would be to transmit CLS to end this circuit. This check is not required by the Arbitrated Loop standard. The fact that the OPNr was received correctly at the originating port does not confirm that the intended port(s) actually set replicate mode.

The open originator can also confirm that frames were properly propagated around the loop in replicate mode through a similar process. Again, this checking is not required by the standard but may prove worthwhile when replicate mode is used.

Corrupted OPNy. It is possible for an error to cause one or both of the AL_PA fields in the OPN primitive to be corrupted. This could result in the open being directed to the wrong port (AL_PD in error), or having the appearance of coming from the wrong port (AL_PS in error), or a half-duplex OPN(yy) being converted into a full-duplex OPN(yx) or vice versa.

Opening the wrong port results in frame delivery to the incorrect destination. When the port validates the Destination_ID field in the frame header, it finds that the frame has been mis-routed. In Class-1, Class-2, or Class-4, the port discards the frame and sends a port reject response with an invalid D_ID indication. Receipt of the P_RJT response results in a sequence delivery failure and the attendant error recovery process.

In Class-3 service, a frame with an incorrect Destination_ID is discarded without notification. The sequence initiator (or upper level protocol) times out and the sequence fails. In no case should a port operate on the incorrectly routed frame.

If the AL_PS field is corrupted of a full-duplex OPN(yx), the open recipient may send one or more frames to the apparent open originator. In this case, the earlier situation is reversed but the Destination_ID is still incorrect for the receiving port with the same results.

If a half-duplex OPN(yy) is corrupted into a full-duplex OPN(yx) either the AL_PD or AL_PS characters, or both, may be incorrect. If the AL_PD character was corrupted, the wrong port will open in full-duplex mode. Frame transmission may occur, but the Destination_ID fields in the frame headers will be incorrect as discussed previously. If the AL_PS field was corrupted, the open recipient may begin frame transmission to the wrong port, but again the Destination_ID field in the frame header will lead to the error detection at the receiver. This could be significant for Class-3 SCSI FCP operations where the FCP_RSP could be misrouted without any indication to the target.

If the open recipient begins full-duplex operation when the open originator is only capable of half-duplex operation, it is possible that one or more frames will be discarded due to the lack of receive buffers. However, the lost frames are either coming from the wrong port (if the AL_PD was corrupted), or intended for the wrong destination (if the AL_PS of the OPN was corrupted). In either case, a sequence error occurs and sequence or exchange error recovery will be required. Again, use of Class-3 may result in the sequence initiator believing that a sequence was delivered, when it fact it was not. Class-1, Class-2, and Class-4 provide a positive indication of sequence delivery to the sequence recipient through use of the Acknowledge response, or failure to receive an Acknowledge.

Unexpected OPN. It is possible for a port to receive an OPN when it does not expect to receive one. This may indicate a failure in the loop protocols or a port malfunction.

An LPSM in the Open, Transmitted Close, or Transfer states may correctly receive the same OPN it transmitted upon entry to the Open state. This could occur if the destination port failed to recognize the OPN, the intended destination port is not operational, the open was addressed to a nonexistent port, or the OPN was addressed to itself. In Open state case, frame transmission should not be attempted unless the OPN was addressed to itself, because the loop circuit was not established (frame transmission is not allowed in the other listed states although one or more frames may have been transmitted before entering that state).

If frames have been transmitted, the frames will, in all probability, circle the loop and return to the sending port. When the Destination_ID of the received frame is checked, it reveals that the frame was not delivered to the correct destination port. The frame is discarded and a P_RJT may be sent, if appropriate for the class of service in use.

If the LPSM receives an OPN while in the opened, received close, or Open-Init states, the OPN is ignored and normal frame or ordered set transmission continues. Receipt of the OPN is indicative of a loop protocol failure, perhaps indicating that a third port has erroneously entered the Open state. This could occur if an ARB(F0) were corrupted into a valid ARB(x) that duplicated the ARB(x) of a port in the Arbitrating state located downstream from the current arbitration winner. Because the unexpected OPN is not retransmitted, no new loop circuit is established (the fact that the OPN was received indicates that it did not reach its intended destination port).

With three ports open on the loop, frames sent by two of the ports will arrive at the wrong destination. This is detected by examination of the Destination_ID of the received frames.

14.3.3 Close Protocol Errors

Errors during the closing protocol are generally more straight forward because the CLS ordered set is not address specific. If the CLS is corrupted, it is unrecognizable and the CLS is lost. It is also possible for a loop circuit to be closed prematurely due to a malfunction in one of the ports on the loop.

If a CLS is lost or corrupted, the loop circuit may fail to close correctly. Assume, for example, that the open originator sends a CLS that is lost due to an error. If the open recipient waits to receive the CLS before sending one of its own, the loop is hung until one of the ports on the loop times out and begins loop initialization. After transmitting a CLS, the Arbitrated Loop standard requires that a CLS should be received within LP_TOV; if it is not, loop initialization is used to re-establish loop integrity.

If the open originator sends a CLS that is lost due to an error, the open originator enters the Transmitted Close state while the open recipient remains in the Opened state. When the open recipient sends a CLS (before the open originator times out with LP_TOV), it enters the Transmitted Close state. The open originator receives the CLS, enters the Monitoring state and closes its half of the loop circuit but does not retransmit the CLS. The loop is now available for another port to win arbitration even though the open recipient has not closed its half of the loop circuit and is still in the Transmitted Close state (If the ARB_Won variable is not set, the LPSM allows them to pass, as in this example). This scenario is shown in Figure 113 on page 269.

When the next port wins arbitration, it attempts to establish a new loop circuit by transmitting an OPNy. If the open recipient is upstream of the port in the Transmitted Close state, the OPN will be received and the port enters the Opened state. The open originator can send frames to the open recipient, but frames from the open recipient are intercepted by the port in the Transmitted Close state because it is still conditioned for frame reception.

When this loop circuit is closed, the port left in the Transmitted Close state receives the CLS and enters the Monitoring state. Because it does not retransmit the CLS, one of the ports in this loop circuit may be left in the Transmitted Close state effectively propagating the error condition until loop initialization occurs. Normally, if a port finds that it cannot accomplish productive work, loop initialization should be used to re-establish the integrity of the loop.

Some implementations transmitted an extra CLS when the above error was suspected. This is generally not good behavior because an additional CLS will continue to close all circuits that are subsequently formed. When the loop is perceived to be unstable, loop initialization is always the best solution to re-establish loop integrity.

14.4 Link, Frame, and Sequence Errors

An Arbitrated Loop environment is subject to all of the normal errors that can occur in nonloop environments. Frames can be lost, misrouted, corrupted, contain invalid transmission characters, or CRC errors. In addition, errors can affect the flow control mechanisms using R_RDY ordered sets and Acknowledge frames. None of these occurrences are unique to the Arbitrated Loop and the actions taken are the same for loop and non-loop environments.

14.4.1 Link Level Errors

Errors at the link level can either be temporary, such as loss-of-signal or loss-of-synchronization, or permanent (e.g., loss-of-synchronization for longer than R_T_TOV).

When FC-1 encounters an invalid transmission character, the LPSM shall substitute the current fill word for the transmission word in error. The objective is to count the error at this time and not to propagate it to another port on the loop.

If a loop failure is detected, the LPSM begins loop initialization. It is recommended that the port log the loop failure in the Link Error Status Block (LESB). Figure 114 summarizes the link level errors and actions taken.

14.4.2 Frame Errors

If a frame is lost for some reason (e.g., the SOF delimiter is corrupted), the sequence fails to complete in the allotted time and the sequence times out. If the sequence initiator is not maintaining a sequence-level timer, the error is detected when the upper level protocol timer expires. A frame can also be lost if the frame is delivered to the wrong port in Class-3 because no P_RJT is sent.

1. Port_01 wins arbitration, sends an OPN to Port_B2, and enters the Open state.

2. Port_B2 receives the OPN and enters the Opened state.

3. Normal frame transmission takes place between Port_01 and Port_B2.

1. Port_B2 completes frame transmission, sends a CLS to Port_01, and enters the Transmitted Close state.

2. The CLS propagates around the loop and is received by Port_01 which enters the Received Close state.

1. Port_01 completes its frame transmission, transmits a CLS, and enters the Monitoring state.

2. Due to a link error, the CLS is corrupted and never received by Port_B2.

3. Port_01 is in the Monitoring state and the loop circuit is closed at Port_01. Port_B2 is still in the Transmitted Close state.

4. Since Port_01 (the arbitration winner) is in the Monitoring state it allows received ARBs to pass.

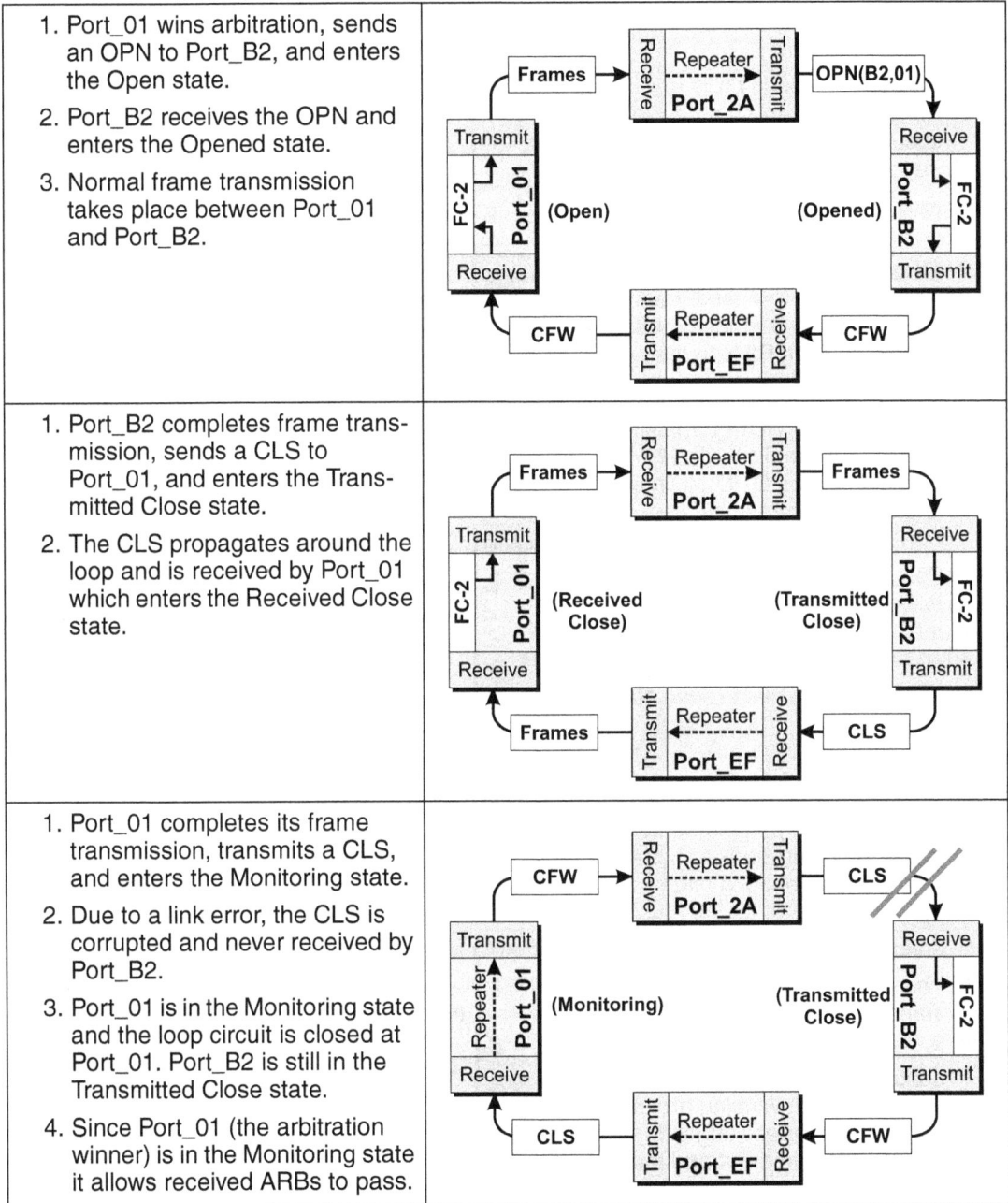

Figure 113. Port Left in Transmitted Close State (Part 1 of 2)

<table>
<tr>
<td>

1. Port_EF arbitrates and wins access to the loop.
2. Port_EF sends an OPN to Port_2A to establish a new loop circuit and enters the Open state.
3. Port_2A receives the OPN and enters the Opened state.
4. Three ports are now open on the loop: Port_EF is in the Open state, Port_2A is in the Opened state, and Port_B2 is in the Transmitted Close state

</td>
<td>

</td>
</tr>
<tr>
<td>

1. Frames and R_RDYs transmitted by Port_2A are discarded by Port_B2 (wrong D_ID), frames and R_RDYs transmitted by Port_EF arrive at Port_2A.
2. Port_EF completes frame transmission, sends a CLS, and enters the Transmitted Close state.
3. Port_2A receives the CLS, and enters the Received Close state.

</td>
<td>

</td>
</tr>
<tr>
<td>

1. When Port_2A completes frame transmission, it sends a CLS and enters the Monitoring state.
1. Port_B2 receives the CLS and enters the Monitoring state.
2. This time, Port_EF is left in the Transmitted Close state.
3. Because Port_EF is the current arbitration winner, it prevents any other port from winning arbitration eventually resulting in an arbitration wait time-out and the resultant loop initialization.

</td>
<td>

</td>
</tr>
</table>

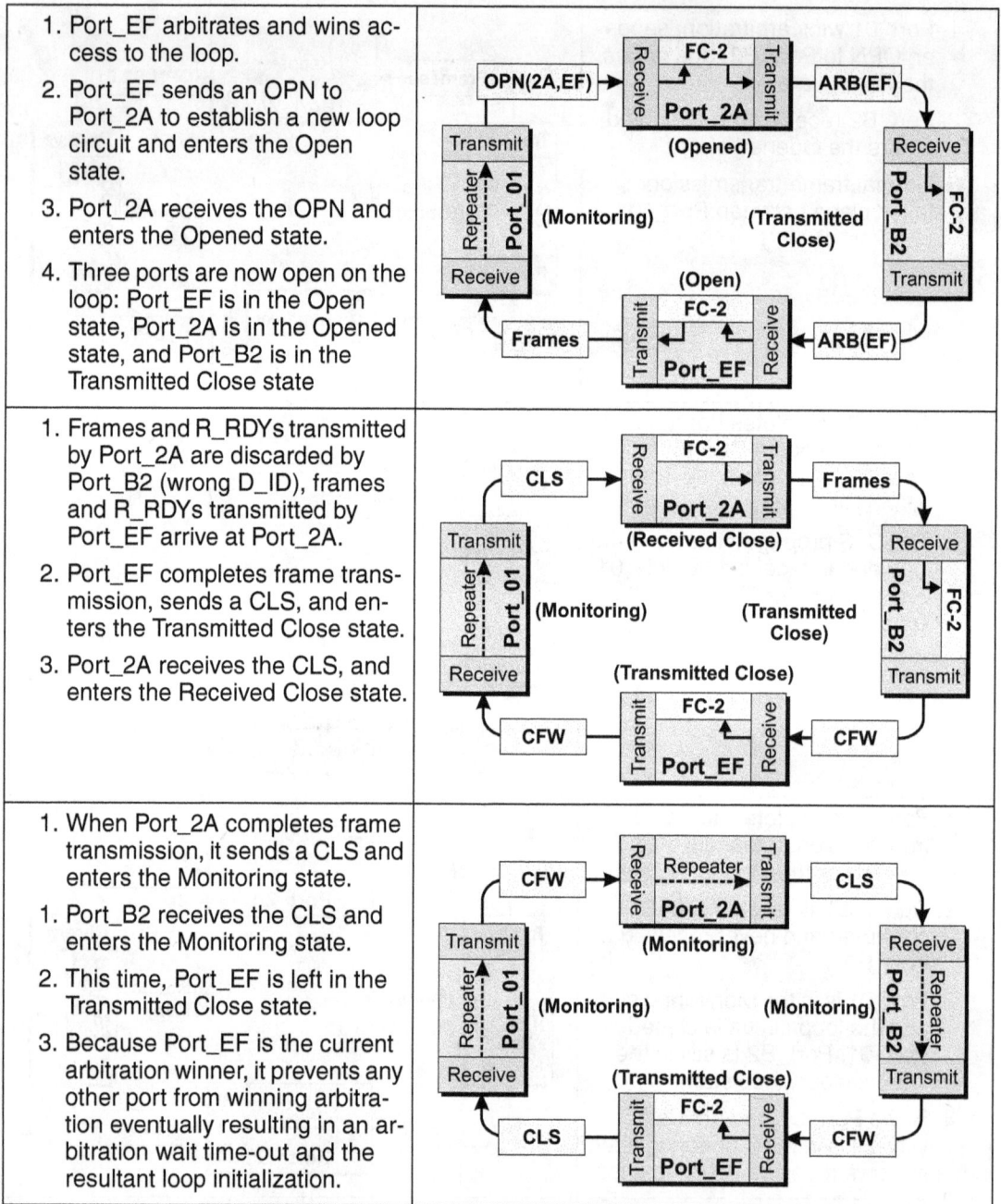

Figure 113. Port Left in Transmitted Close State (Part 2 of 2)

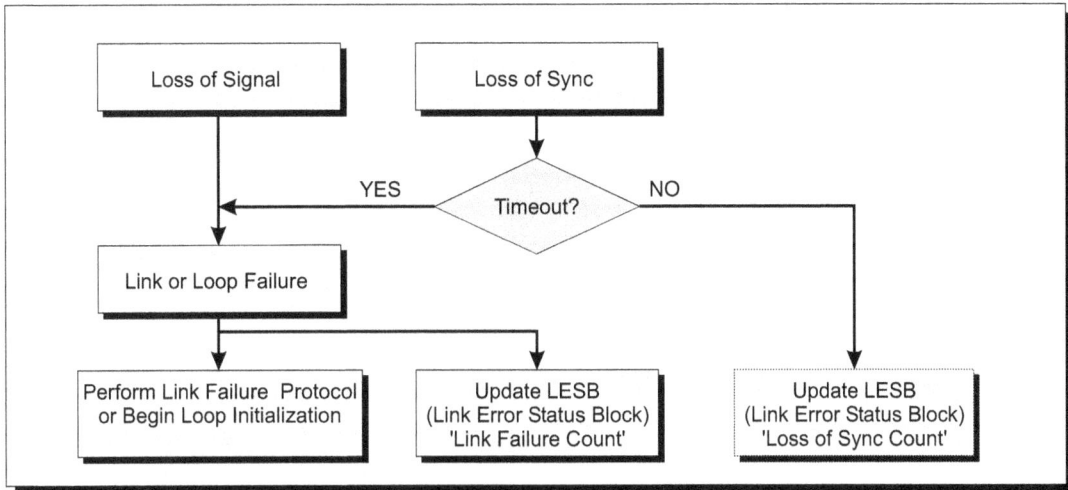

Figure 114. Link Level Errors

If a frame contains invalid transmission characters or a CRC error, the frame is discarded without notification to the originator of the frame. This is because the character in error can not be determined and any response could be sent to the wrong port. If the end of frame delimiter is corrupted, the frame is abnormally terminated by the next ordered set (current fill word, IDLE, etc.). The frame is again discarded and the sequence fails.

The results of invalid frames are shown in Figure 115 on page 271. Note that all invalid frames are discarded and, ultimately, the associated sequence may fail as well, depending on the error policy in use (the 'process' policy allows delivery of incomplete sequences).

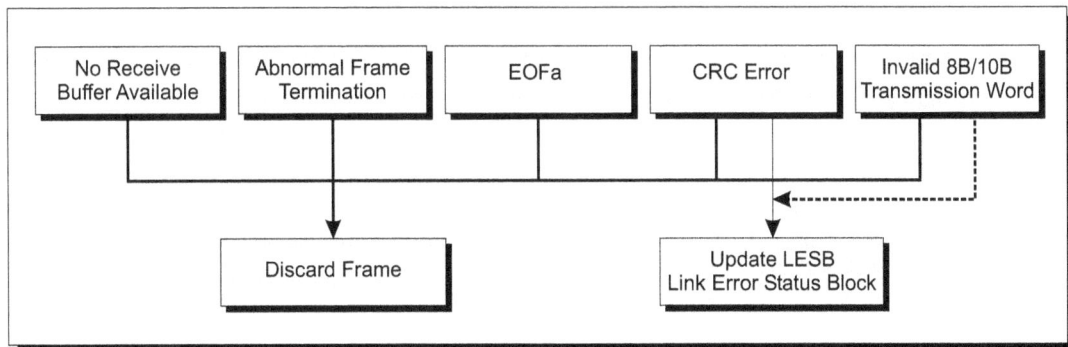

Figure 115. Frame Errors

If a valid frame is received, but a problem exists with the frame header content, a P_RJT is sent if appropriate for the class of service. Class-1, Class-2, and Class-4 utilize P_RJT to report invalid frames. For Class-3, the receiving port discards the frame without notification and depends on a higher level mechanism to detect the condition and take any appropriate action.

An illustration summarizing the different types of sequence errors is provided by Figure 116.

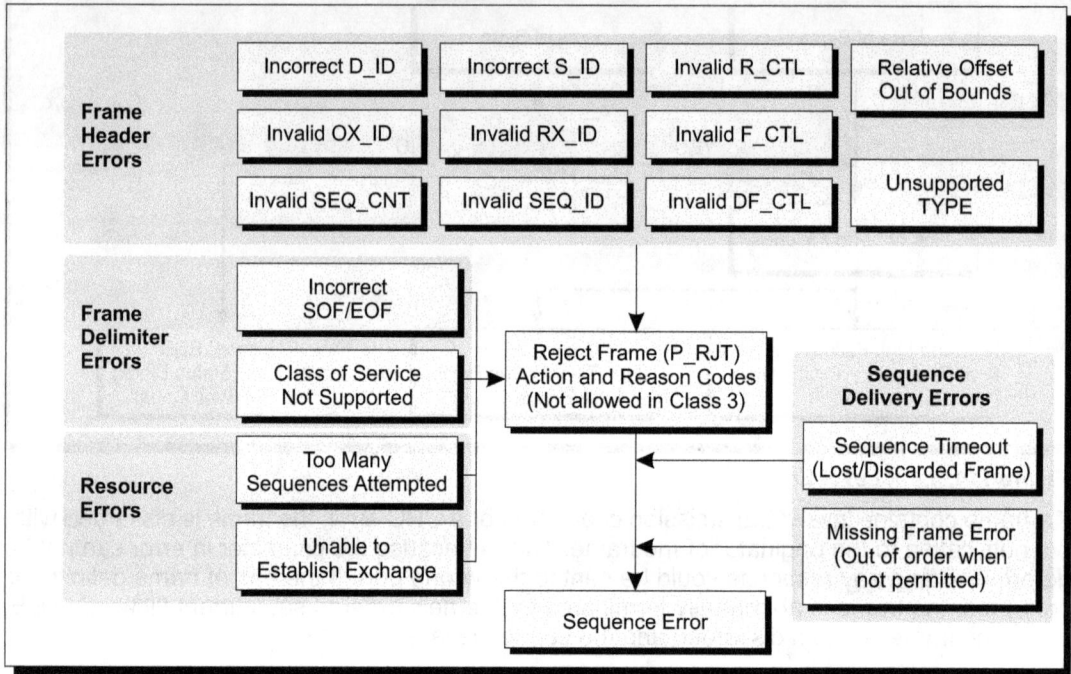

Figure 116. Sequence Errors

14.4.3 Acknowledge Errors

Because acknowledgments (ACKs) are frames, they are subject to all of the errors described for normal frames. acknowledgments may be lost, corrupted, or misrouted.

If an acknowledgment is lost, end-to-end credit may be incorrect. The history bit (bit 16 of the parameter field) indicates if all prior acknowledgments for that sequence have been sent. Therefore, a port can reclaim end-to-end credit even if one or more acknowledgments are lost.

Acknowledgments that are misrouted receive a port reject with a reason code of invalid Destination_ID. In this case, the sending port can determine that the ACK was not delivered and take the appropriate action.

14.4.4 Receiver Ready (R_RDY) Errors

If one or more R_RDYs are lost or corrupted, the available buffer-to-buffer credit associated with that R_RDY is lost. This may result in a performance degradation because it limits the number of frames that may be in flight at any point. If all of the available buffer-to-buffer credit is lost, the transmitter is unable to transmit frames and should close the loop. When the next loop circuit is established, the available buffer-to-buffer credit is set to the login buffer-to-buffer credit value, thereby recovering the lost credit.

If a spurious R_RDY is received, the buffer-to-buffer credit may increment incorrectly. This could result in a lost frame if the frame is transmitted when the receiver does not have a receive buffer available. In Class-3, the frame is discarded without notification; in Class-1, Class-2, or Class-4, a port busy is sent to notify the sending port of the error.

14.4.5 Sequence Delivery Failures

Any invalid frame header fields, frame loss, corruption, or discarding results in a sequence delivery failure. In an in-order delivery environment, the error may be detected by using the SEQ_CNT or relative offset in the parameter field of the frame header. An error is also indicated in an in-order environment if a frame with an SOFn delimiter is received without having previously received a frame with an SOFi delimiter for that sequence, or a new sequence is started without receiving an EOFt for the previous sequence. Sequence delivery errors may also be detected by a sequence time-out, or upper level time-out condition.

Loop operations are subject to the same error policies as used during point-to-point and fabric operations. When a sequence error occurs, the error policy is used to determine the recovery action. Figure 117 illustrates the error policy options available when a sequence error occurs.

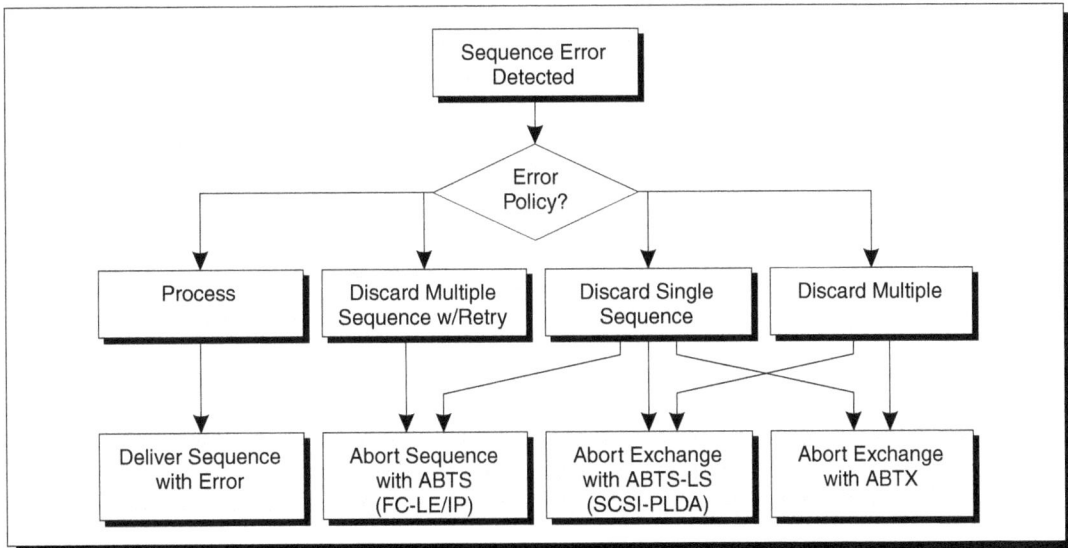

Figure 117. Fibre Channel Error Policies

The 'process' policy is used when the sequence is to be delivered even if it contains errors or is incomplete. This policy might be used for a video stream where frame errors are ignored.

Class-1 may use the 'discard multiple with immediate retry' policy during certain operations.

The 'discard single' error policy may be used when the sequences within an exchange are unrelated. An example of this type of operation occurs when the Transmission Control Protocol/Internet Protocol (TCP/IP) is being transported via Fibre Channel. In the Fibre Channel

---

Link Encapsulation (FC-LE) protocol, each sequence represents a separate IP packet and if one is not delivered, the TCP level takes care of retransmitting the appropriate packet.

The 'discard multiple' error policy is used by the SCSI-3 FCP standard. This error policy is normally used when sequences within an exchange are dependent upon one another. If a sequence fails, all subsequent sequences within that exchange are discarded. For example, if the FCP_DATA sequence of a SCSI read command fails, any subsequent status for that exchange is also invalid.

Disks supporting the SCSI Fibre Channel Protocol (FCP) normally abort the entire exchange when a sequence error is detected using the 'abort sequence' protocol with the 'last sequence' bit set (ABTS-LS). This protocol is illustrated in Figure 118 on page 274. The exchange may be retried by the upper level protocol after taking the appropriate recovery actions.

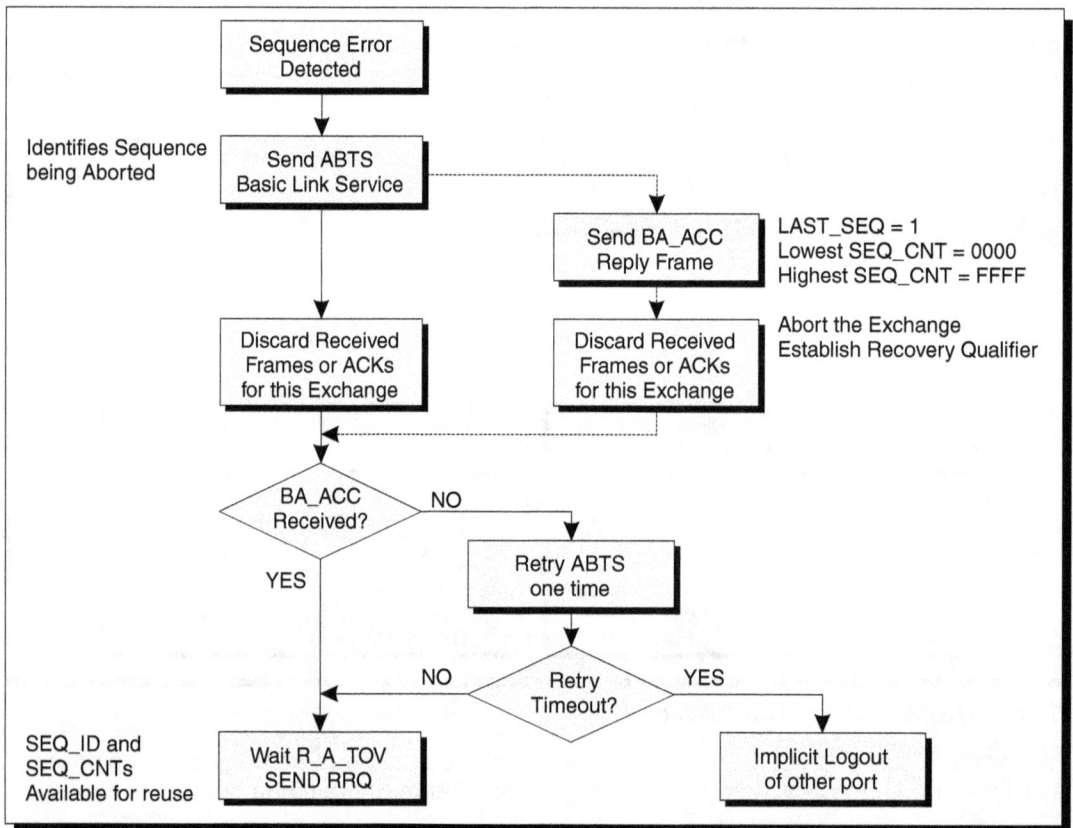

Figure 118. Abort Sequence - Last Sequence (ABTS) Protocol

Tapes supporting the Fibre Channel Protocol (FCP) for SCSI normally abort only the sequence on which the error is detected

---

15. Arbitrated Loop Hubs

A Fibre Channel Arbitrated Loop Hub is a device for interconnecting arbitrated loop ports. There are a number of various hub types available today which represent different cost targets and design points. But, before going into these, let's look at what a simple arbitrated loop hub is and how it works.

As has been seen elsewhere in this document, loops may be wired port to port in a cascading configuration. However, if any loop port fails or is not powered on, the loop is not operational.

Hubs are capable of automatically bypassing a loop port (or a loop segment containing more than one loop port) when a loss of signal is detected at the hub. This would occur if no loop port is connected, a connected loop port is powered off, or a loop segment is broken. A hub solves this problem by using port bypass circuits to detect and bypass a non-operational loop segment. The port bypass circuit either opens the loop to insert the active loop ports or closes the loop, ensuring the loop is operational. Hubs provide the ability to hot-plug loop ports in and out of the loop just like the port bypass circuits are used on a backplane for disk and tape device. A block diagram of a simple hub providing this bypass function is shown in Figure 119.

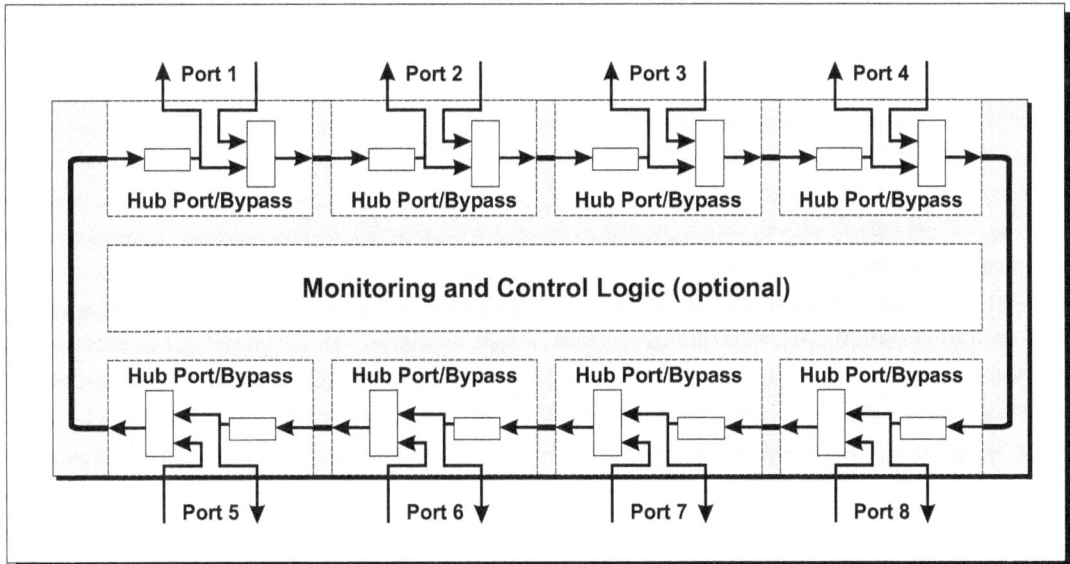

Figure 119. Fibre Channel Hub

The hub provides the bypass function for each of its ports and control logic to determine when an attached loop port (or loop segment) should be bypassed. The means by which a hub decides to bypass the attached loop segment is a function of the design of the hub. The hub may simply monitor transmitted output of the attached loop segment to determine if the loop segment is working correctly. If no transmitted signal is received, the segment is bypassed. Hubs may also monitor the received signal for a LIP(F8) which indicates that an attached loop segment has detected a failure. As long as this failure persists, the hub could bypass this segment and reactivate the segment when the LIP(F8) is changed to a LIP(F7).

More sophisticated approaches may monitor information sent to the segment and verify that the segment is generating appropriate responses. The hub may also interpret the LPE and LPB primitive sequences to control the bypass function.

The port on a hub is just an attachment point and one or more loop ports may be attached to one hub port. Hubs typically provide between six and 16 ports each and can normally be stacked or cascaded to support larger configurations of up to 127 ports. Normally, the hubs themselves are transparent to the loop ports and provide no additional addressing to an arbitrated loop environment. However, some hubs contain embedded NL_Ports that can be accessed for monitoring and management purposes.

A hub changes the electrical loop into a physical star wiring environment and makes it possible to physically cable a loop. Without a hub, the cables must be separated to go from the transmitter of one loop port to the receiver of the adjacent loop port (although many devices provide dual loop capability for redundancy, it is usually not desirable to contain both loops in the same cable plant). With a hub, the normal bi-directional Fibre Channel cables may be used (in this case, the loop is contained in each direction of the cable).

Many arbitrated loop hubs offer a mix of electrical and optical ports to facilitate mixing the two media types within the same loop. For example, one or more systems could use optical links to connect to the hub, while one or more disk enclosures are connected to the hub using electrical cables. This flexibility may be provided through a fixed set of media interfaces or provided by pluggable GBIC modules.

Figure 120 on page 277 illustrates an Arbitrated Loop with three servers and three storage devices connected to a hub. While this configuration lacks the appearance of an Arbitrated Loop, it is in fact still a loop. The hub provides a centralized wiring point changing the functional loop into a physical star configuration.

Hubs provide considerable flexibility in configuring Arbitrated Loops while at the same time providing loop robustness. It should be remembered, however, that hubs themselves are electronic devices and may fail. In high-availability applications, the need for redundant loops and dual ported devices is expanded to include redundant hubs.

15.1 Insertion Modes of Hubs

There are several different ways that hubs may decide when to insert loop segments into a loop. The following sections provides several examples.

Insert on Valid Transmission Word. The hub may simply decide to insert a loop segment when any valid transmission word is received.

If a port transmits IDLE, LIP, any other ordered set containing a K28.5 character, or any other valid 8B/10B encoded character during power-up, this type of hub may add the loop segment

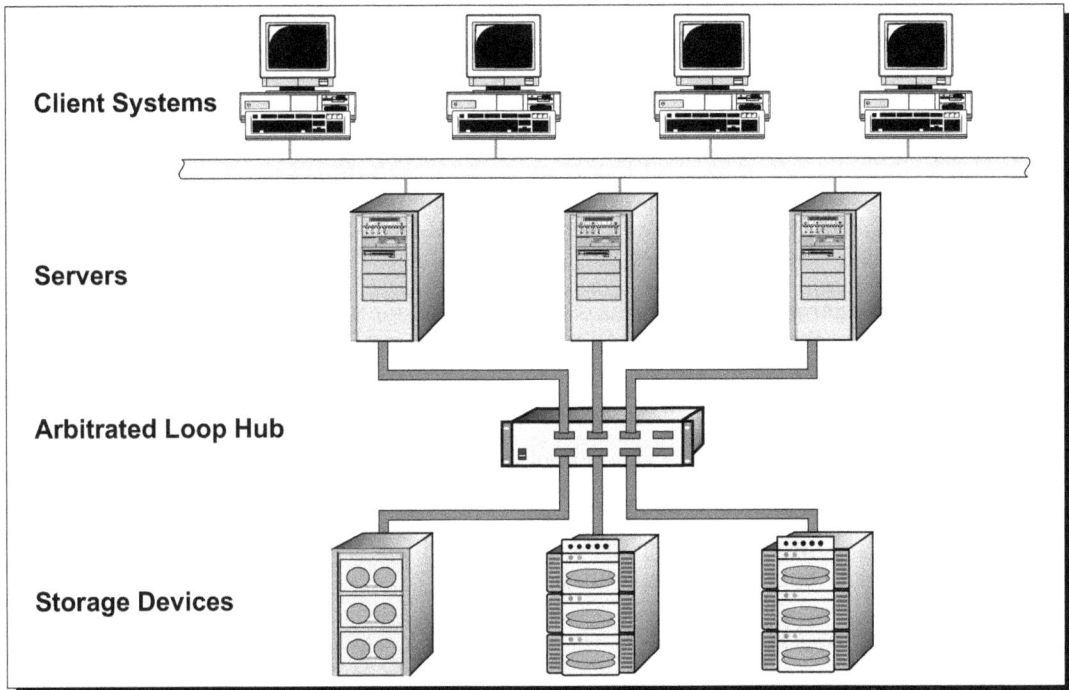

Figure 120. Arbitrated Loop with Hub

into the loop before the port(s) are ready to participate. This would make the loop non-functional while the port(s) are becoming ready.

Simply inserting on any valid transmission word may allow non-loop capable ports to join the loop. When a non-loop capable port attempts initialization, it transmits valid Fibre Channel transmission words.

Insert on Valid Ordered Set. A hub may insert a loop segment when ordered sets have been received for a minimum time period.

However, if a port transmits IDLE, LIP, or any other ordered set containing a K28.5 character during power-up, this type of hub may add the loop segment into the loop before the port(s) are ready to participate. This would make the entire loop non-functional while the port(s) are becoming ready.

This approach may also allow non-loop capable ports to join the loop. When a non-loop capable port attempts initialization, it transmits valid Fibre Channel ordered sets (OLS, NOS).

Insert on LIP. Hubs may be more selective by waiting for a valid, loop-specific ordered set such as the Loop Initialization Primitive (LIP) sequence before inserting an attached loop segment. This ensures that the hub does not insert a non-loop capable port into the loop. Howev-

---

er, if the hub inserts on any LIP, it is possible the hub may insert a broken segment if LIP(F8) is being received.

Insert after Diagnostic Verification. Hubs may use even more sophisticated methods to determine when to insert a loop segment.

A hub may be able to determine that the loop segment is operational by transmitting an ordered set that is not used by an loop port, but which would be forwarded by all loop ports (e.g., transmit a LIP(F0,F0)). Once this LIP is received by the hub, it could add the loop segment since all loop ports on the segment are now ready to participate on the loop.

Insert Under Management Control. Hubs may also wait for an external input (i.e., operator, SCSI Enclosure Services (SES), or SNMP request) to insert a loop segment into the Loop.

15.2 Removal Modes of Hubs

Hubs may automatically bypass a loop segment if it detects the following conditions:

1. If loss of signal or synchronization (>R_T_TOV), the loop segment is isolated.
2. If LIP(F8) is received, the loop segment is isolated since at least one loop port on this loop segment is reporting a loop failure.

15.3 Sophisticated Hubs

Considerable sophistication may be built into a hub, usually at additional cost. One of the purposes of a hub is to provide a number of functions, but for less cost than a Fibre Channel switch. A comparison between hubs and switches can be found in Figure 26.

ITEM	HUBS	SWITCH
Power supplies	Usually two for redundancy	Usually two for redundancy
Memory	Minimal (possible speed matching buffers if using re-clocker)	Considerable memory for each FL_Port to support a number of frames
Media adapters	GBICs, GLM, Electrical	GBICs, GLM, Electrical
Enclosure	Sheet metal	Sheet metal
Fabric Services	None required (could provide an F/NL_Port once private loop ports disappear)	Required to support large address space
Maximum number of N*_Ports	126	Approximately 14 million
Throughput	Maximum full duplex circuit (e.g., at 1Gbs, 200MB/s)	Number of ports times data rate
Error Isolation	Remove failing loop segment	Remove failing loop or N_Port
Media Converters	Optical and electrical supported	Optical and electrical supported

Table 26. HUB and Switch Comparison

Simple hubs may not re-time the signal; sophisticated hubs usually re-time, eliminating signal jitter and providing automatic clock speed matching on every port. As a result, these hubs can be cascaded, providing increased scalability and flexibility in network design. It was already indicated that sophisticated hubs may provide considerable loop management capabilities (e.g., configuration, error, and performance statistics); automatic LIP(F7) insertion, LIP(F8) bypass, automatic port bypass and character integrity checks.

15.3.1 Switching Hubs

Some hubs are capable of providing more performance for a loop environment. As shown in this book, only two loop ports are allowed to communicate with each other at any given time (excluding the replicate mode). With a "switching" hub, multiple loop segments may be created to allow more than two loop ports to simultaneously communicate. These hubs provide the following operational characteristics (note: for this to function properly, since there are no hub port frame buffers, a login BB_Credit of zero must be used):

1. During the initialization process, all loop segments are combined into one large loop of up to 126 NL_Ports and 1 FL_Port.

2. During the initialization process, the hub port identifies the AL_PAs that are contained in each loop segment (the difference in the loop initialization AL_PA bits of what the hub port transmits and what it receives back).

3. After the initialization process, the hub ports become repeaters on each loop segment. Any port that arbitrates on a loop segment only interferes with the other ports on the same loop segment. Once a port wins arbitration, it transmits the usual OPN(yx). If the open recipient is on the same loop segment, the OPN(yx) is delivered directly and a loop circuit is created; if the open recipient is on another loop segment, a connection is made between the two loop segments through the hub and the OPN(yx) is transferred to the other hub port where the open recipient resides. The hub port arbitrates on this loop segment using the x value of the OPN(yx) (i.e., the open originator) and when it wins, forwards the OPN(yx) to the destination port. Since a login BB_Credit of zero is required, the open originator waits for the R_RDY which provides credit to send frames.

Switching hubs such as this need to avoid possible deadlock conditions where a port one loop segment is attempting to open a port on a different loop segment where some other port has already won arbitration and want to open yet another port.

15.4 Hub Summary

Fibre Channel Arbitrated Loop hubs facilitate loop implementation by aggregating loop ports via a physical star configuration. Loop hubs typically provide 6 to 12 ports, and can be used to build larger loops via cascading hubs. hubs provide greater control and reliability and are usually found in a wiring closet (i.e., cable concentrator) to facilitate management of a Fibre Channel network. Hubs employ port bypass circuits at each port to keep dysfunctional L_Ports from disrupting loop traffic. Most hubs provide status and diagnostic LED's at each port.

15.5 Chapter Summary

Arbitrated Loop Hubs

- Provide significant enhancements to the loop
- Physical cabling flexibility
  - Allows use of standard cables
  - May provide media flexibility through use of GBICs
- Automatic bypassing of faulty loop segments
  - Hub makes decision to bypass loop segment
  - Criteria based on received signal, or
  - Hub may validate loop segment before insertion into loop
- May provide signal reconditioning
  - Signal amplitude regeneration
  - Signal timing restored

Hub Insertion Modes

- Insert on valid transmission word or valid ordered set
  - May admit non-loop ports
  - May admit ports prematurely
- Insert on loop-specific ordered set such as LIP
  - May admit broken loop segments - LIP(F8)
- Insert after validation
  - Validate loop segment using LIP(F0,F0) or similar ordered set
- Insert on management directive
  - Wait for external input to insert loop segment

Hub Deletion Modes

- Hub may bypass a loop segment on
  - Loss of signal or loss of synchronization
  - Receipt of LIP(F8)
  - Receipt of LPB for loop port/segment
  - If a link error threshold is exceeded
  - Under management directive
- Most hubs provide visual indication of bypassed segments
  - Light on hub panel
  - Via management interface

Switching Hubs

- Switching hubs may allow for configuration changes
  - Controlled by external inputs
  - Ethernet control port, for example
  - Allows loop to be configured into different segments
- Switching hubs may dynamically connect loop segments
  - Dynamically segments and joins loop segments
  - Driven by arbitrated loop protocols directly
  - May impose constraints on ports (such as use of zero login credit)
  - Treated as one large loop during initialization

16. High-Availability Loops

Arbitrated Loop shares a number of characteristics in common with other loop and ring topologies. One of the most apparent characteristics for high-availability applications is the potential for a failure in a single port to cause the entire loop to become inoperable. Each port in the loop is responsible for performing the correct loop protocols and retransmitting information intended for other ports. If one port fails, loop protocols cannot be completed and frame transmission is impossible.

Some applications may be able to tolerate this type of potential catastrophic failure. Personal workstations, or small loop configurations that experience a failure on the loop may simply be out of service until they are repaired. Many applications, such a storage subsystems and workgroup clustering, require that the loop continue to operate even if one or more of the ports on the loop is not operational. Before examining techniques that can be used to make loop configurations more robust, it is important to look at typical applications to understand the nature of the configuration and type of fault tolerance desired.

This chapter examines several approaches to enhancing loop robustness to satisfy the requirements of different applications such as storage subsystems and workgroup networking.

16.1 Single-Loop Configurations

A basic starting point for arbitrated loops in a storage environment is a single loop with one or more SCSI initiators and a number of attached peripheral devices. An block diagram of this configuration is shown in Figure 121 on page 282. The devices may be in the same enclosure as the initiator(s) or in one or more separate enclosures depending on the number and size of the devices in the configuration.

The connections between ports within a single enclosure will probably use copper interconnections in all but unique circumstances. This is due to the short distances involved and the significant economy offered by electrical interconnections. Small configurations may use individual cables to connect the ports, while printed circuit backplane wiring will likely be used in larger configurations. When it is necessary to connect enclosures together, either electrical or optical interfaces can be used depending on the distances. Distances up to 30 meters per fibre can use electrical cables to save costs, while longer distances require optical cables.

In a single-loop configuration, the failure of an initiator, any of the ports, or the loop itself may be catastrophic. While it may be acceptable for the subsystem to fail if the initiator fails in a single initiator environment, it is generally not acceptable for the entire subsystem to fail if a single port fails or is powered off, or if the device is removed for servicing. What is needed is a way to bypass the problem port and allow the rest of the loop to continue operating.

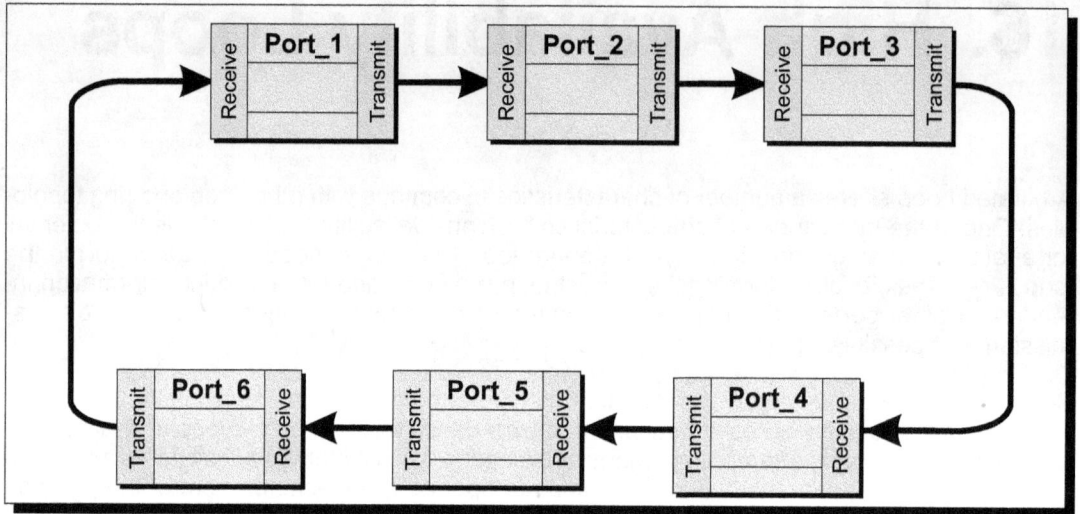

Figure 121. Single-Loop Configuration

16.2 Port Bypassing

The loop topology requires that all ports on the loop are functional so that the loop itself can function. If any port on the loop is not functional, the entire loop might experience a catastrophic failure. This is not unique to Fibre Channel's Arbitrated Loop, but rather a characteristic inherent in all loop and ring topologies.

Most high-availability implementations must provide a means to ensure that the failure of a single port on the loop does not cause the entire loop to fail. Some means must be provided to bypass a failed port and allow the remaining ports to continue to operate. The simplest method of accomplishing this is to provide a bypass function to allow a faulty port to be disconnected from the loop and the loop signals routed past the failing port.

An example of an electrical port bypass circuit (PBC, also sometimes referred to as a loop resiliency circuit, LRC) for use with copper interfaces is shown in Figure 122 on page 283. The incoming signal is fed to a receiver which delivers the signal to both the port's receive input and a multiplexer function. The control input to the port bypass circuit determines whether the received signal or the port's transmit output is selected for transmission to the next port on the loop. If the multiplexer retransmits the received input, the port is bypassed and has no effect on loop operations.

The port bypass circuit's control input is normally conditioned so that the bypass is activated when the port is removed or powered off. The port can also control the bypass based upon internal conditions, or receipt of the bypass primitive sequences (LPB/LPE). In some configurations, additional control logic may be provided to allow an external entity such as a maintenance facility to control the state of the port bypass circuit, either by using Arbitrated Loop specific primitive sequences, or via other control inputs.

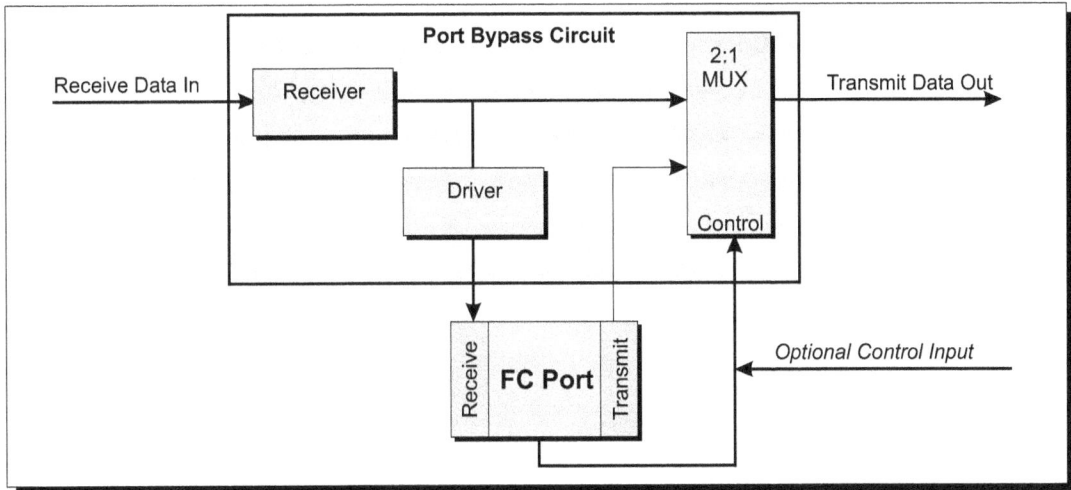

Figure 122. Port Bypass Circuit

Four primitive sequences are provided to control the port bypass circuits. They allow individual port bypass circuits to be activated or deactivated, as well as allowing all of the port bypass circuits to be activated or deactivated by a single primitive sequence. These controls facilitate diagnosis of a failed location by selectively bypassing and enabling individual ports on the loop until the failure is located.

Figure 123 on page 284 shows a single-loop configuration with port bypass circuits added to each port on the loop. Now, if one of the loop entities fails, the port bypass circuit is automatically activated allowing the rest of the loop to continue operating. The port bypass circuit can be used to alleviate problems caused by port failures, ports that are powered off, ports that have been removed for service, or configurations that are partially populated.

While this is a significant improvement in the availability of the subsystem, it does not completely solve the problem because a failure in loop cabling or one of the port bypass circuits can still cause the entire loop to be inoperative. To cover these cases, it is necessary to provide additional redundancy through the use of dual-loop configurations.

16.2.1 Bypassing, Jitter, and Repeaters

Each port bypass circuit contributes some amount of jitter to the transmitted signal. In a well-designed implementation, this added jitter is not significant and does not affect the error rate. When the signal is processed by the next device on the loop, the data is reclocked by the clock in that port and the jitter is effectively removed.

When consecutive port bypass circuits are enabled with no reclocking between them, the jitter contributed by each is cumulative with each one adding a additional jitter to the signal. If a large number of consecutive port bypass circuits are enabled, it is possible for the accumulated jitter to create problems. This could occur if an enclosure intended for a large number of devices is only partially populated. For example, a disk subsystem may provide space to mount

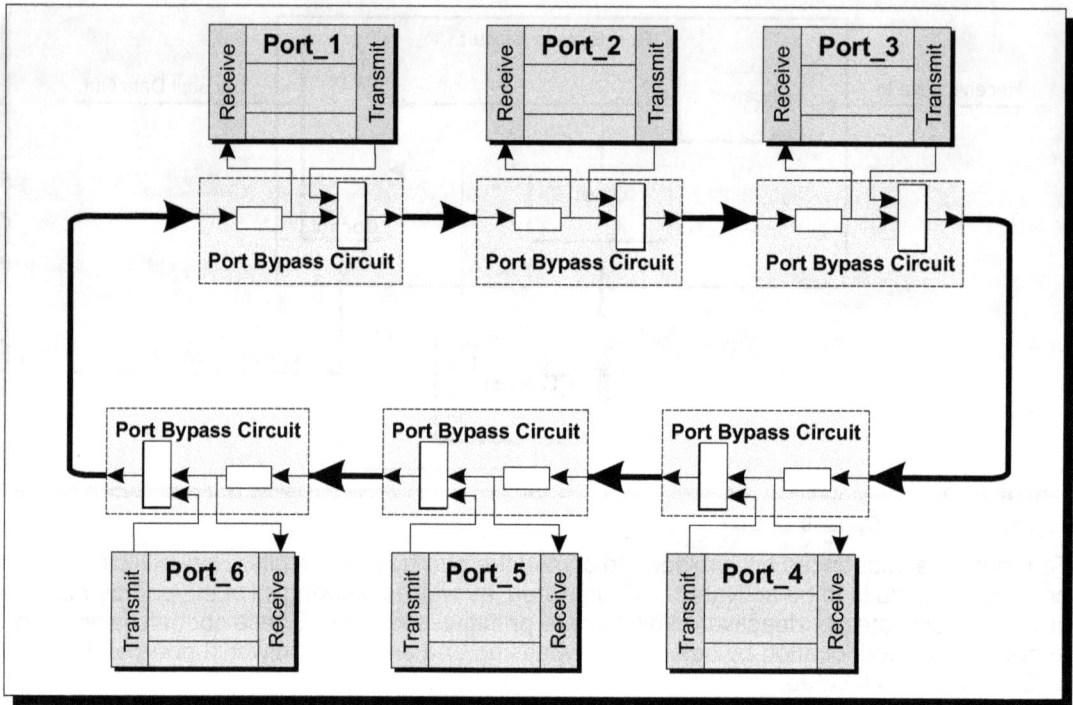

Figure 123. Single-Loop With Port Bypass Circuits

16 disk drives total. Each disk has an associated port bypass circuit resulting in a total of 16 port bypass circuits. An entry level configuration may only be populated with four disk drives, leaving the other 12 slots available for future expansion. When this is done, there may be a series of 12 consecutive port bypass circuits active, one for each of the vacant drive slots.

To correct this potential problem, the drive may be positioned to limit the number of consecutive bypass circuits. If this is not possible, a circuit called a repeater may used after a predetermined number of port bypass circuits. The repeater receives the incoming bit stream, recovers the clock with a phase locked loop, and uses the filtered phase locked loop to reclock the transmit data. This has the effect of attenuating the accumulated jitter and restoring the signal levels and quality. Because the signal is not being retimed (the same clock is being used), no elasticity buffer is required and fill word insertion and deletion does not occur.

16.2.2 Alternative Bypass Techniques

While discussions in this chapter have centered around using an active electrical port bypass circuit, other approaches are possible and may be appropriate in some cases. For example, a mechanical switch or specialized connector can complete the loop circuit when a device is removed. This doesn't address the case of a device failure, but does allow for device removal.

A coaxial relay may offer another potential mechanism for bypassing a device on the loop. The relay can be powered from the device so that when the device is removed or powered off, the relay closes and completes the loop circuit. Mechanical bypass techniques do not redrive the signal and may lead to unacceptable signal degradation under some conditions.

Optical links do not lend themselves to electrical bypassing, unless the optical signal is converted to electrical signals to facilitate the bypassing, and then reconverted to optical for retransmission. Optical bypass switches have been developed for other loop type topologies such as FDDI and may be developed for Fibre Channel.

16.3 Placement and Control of the Bypass Function

Once the decision has been made to incorporate a bypass function into a loop configuration, the next decision to be made is where to locate the function. Depending on the physical configuration, different solutions may be needed under different circumstances. One thing that is obvious is that the bypass function should not be part of the port, nor receive its power from the device, because this would defeat the purpose of the bypass.

As an example, a disk subsystem consisting of a number of devices that plug into a backplane may choose to locate the bypass function on the backplane itself, preferably as a pluggable unit (so the bypasses can be serviced without replacing the backplane).

The backplane approach will not work for a loop used as a high-performance network with distributed devices because there is no backplane present. In this case, a hub may be used to provide the bypass function.

16.3.1 Bypassing on the Backplane

When a backplane is used to connect a number of devices, it offers a convenient place to locate the bypass function. There may be a temptation to mount the port bypass circuits directly on the backplane to simplify the wiring, but this could be a mistake if the port bypass circuit itself fails (although some studies indicate that the backplane fails more often than the port bypass circuits). In this case, the entire backplane would have to be replaced, during which time the entire enclosure may be out of service.

If the port bypass circuits for each loop are mounted on a replaceable unit that plugs into the backplane, the port bypass circuits can be replaced without affecting operations on the other loop. High-availability applications may want to provide separate power supplies for the port bypass circuits associated with each loop so that a power failure only affects one loop (n+1 power designs obviate this requirement).

The Arbitrated Loop standard defines LPB and LPE primitive sequences to activate and deactivate the bypass function on a port-by-port basis. When the LPSM recognizes the appropriate primitive sequence, it activates or deactivates an external control signal usually connected to the port bypass circuit. The device should also activate the bypass control signal when an internal error occurs that may affect loop operations. The LPB and LPE also affect the behavior of the port. Because the port that receives LPB and activates the port bypass circuit does not know that the circuit is present or working, the port must act as a pure repeater (i.e., it does not originate any non-fill words onto the loop.

The port bypass circuit should enter the bypass mode if the device is removed or powered off. This may require the use of a pull-up or pull-down resistor to ensure that the control input is maintained at the proper level.

Some applications may provide additional control to the port bypass circuit. This is because some device failures may prevent the device from controlling the port bypass circuit. This could result in a nonfunctional loop even though the bypass is present. By providing additional control logic, the port bypass circuit can be activated independent of the device. The control input to the port bypass circuit is connected as a 'wired-or' circuit with both the device and the external control logic connected to the control input of the bypass. Either the device or the external control logic can activate the port bypass circuit, and both must deactivate their respective control signals before the bypass is deactivated.

Incorporating external logic to control the port bypass circuit can be used to prevent a port added to the loop from starting initialization at an inappropriate time. Because the external logic controls the bypass as well as the port, the port can only request that the bypass be deactivated. The external logic can override that request and prevent the port from entering the loop. Even if the port transmits the LIP sequence in a attempt to force loop initialization, the port bypass circuit prevents it from appearing on the loop.

16.3.2 Arbitrated Loop Hubs

Arbitrated loop hubs may be used to provide an automatic bypassing function when connecting loop ports together. Hubs were discussed earlier in *Arbitrated Loop Hubs* on page 275.

16.4 Dual-Loop Configurations

Single loop configurations are susceptible to failures of the loop ports, loop interconnections such a backplane wiring and cables, and the port bypass circuits themselves. To tolerate these types of failures, it is necessary to provide additional redundant elements. This is normally accomplished by use of a redundant loop. An example of a dual-loop configuration is shown in Figure 124 on page 287.

Dual-loop configurations provide a significant improvement in the overall availability by providing redundant paths to every device. If one of the loops fails, devices can still be accessed by using the other loop. This provides fault tolerance for failures in the loop ports, backplane wiring, cabling, or the port bypass circuits.

High-availability configurations require a great deal of attention to many details that are beyond the scope of the Arbitrated Loop and not discussed here. For example, the requirements for redundant power and cooling, and the ability to perform concurrent maintenance on one part of the configuration while operations continue on those portions of the configuration that are not being serviced. Details such as packaging and the packaging of replaceable units are important considerations if concurrent maintenance is a goal.

The dual-loop configuration illustrated in Figure 124 requires that each device provide two loop interfaces allowing it to be attached to both loops. There are a number of different approaches that can be taken when implementing dual-loop capabilities on a device. Another example of a dual-loop configuration is shown in Figure 125 on page 288.

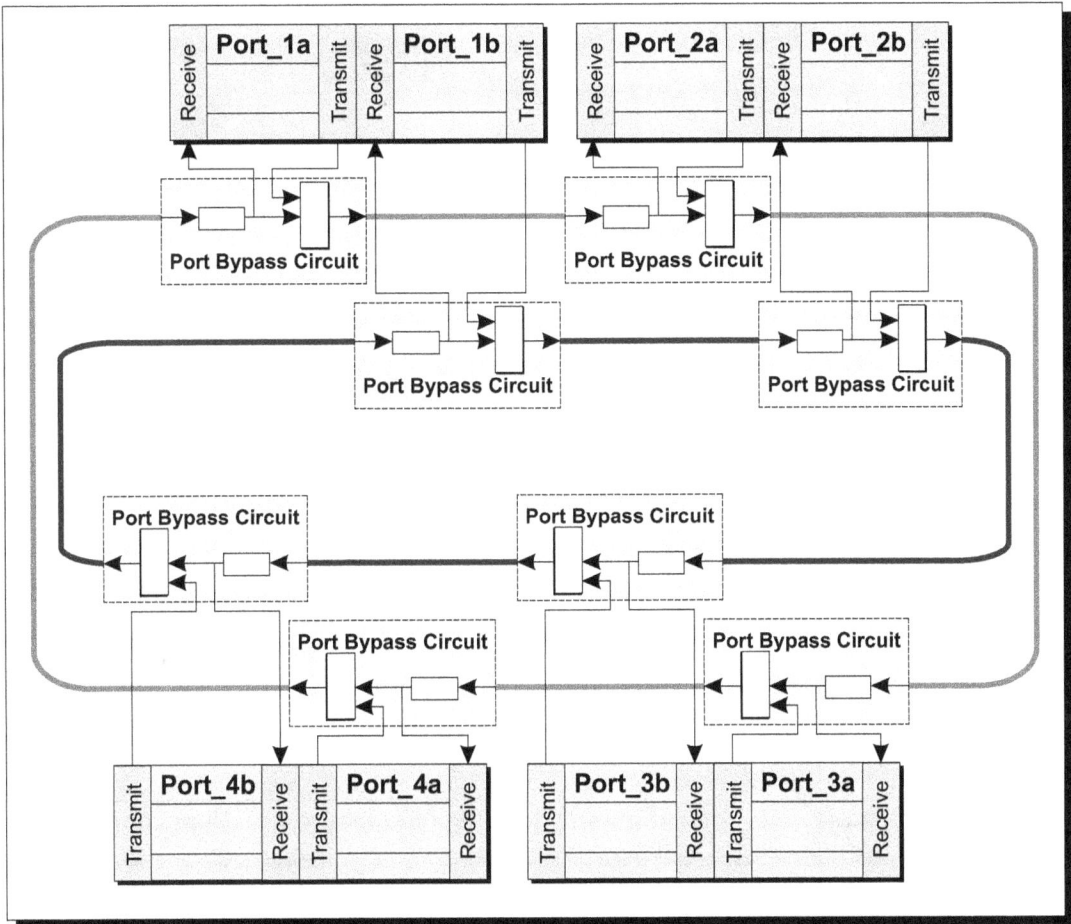

Figure 124. Dual Loops With Port Bypass Circuits

16.4.1 Dual-Loop Single-Port

Many first-generation Fibre Channel disk drives used a configuration with dual loop interfaces and a single FC-2. The advantage of this implementation is that for relatively low cost (i.e., about 10% premium for one FC-2 with dual-loop capabilities verses a single loop), the subsystem can realize twice the bandwidth as each loop is independent and two ports on each loop may simultaneously transmit and/or receive and a redundant path is provided. An example of a dual-loop single-port design is shown in Figure 126 on page 289.

In this approach, dual loop interfaces are provided, but there is only a single frame transmit and receive function (FC-2). Each loop interface contains only those functions needed to support loop protocol operations. The loop interface contains the physical drivers and receivers, serializer and deserializer functions, and all or part of the loop port state machine (LPSM).

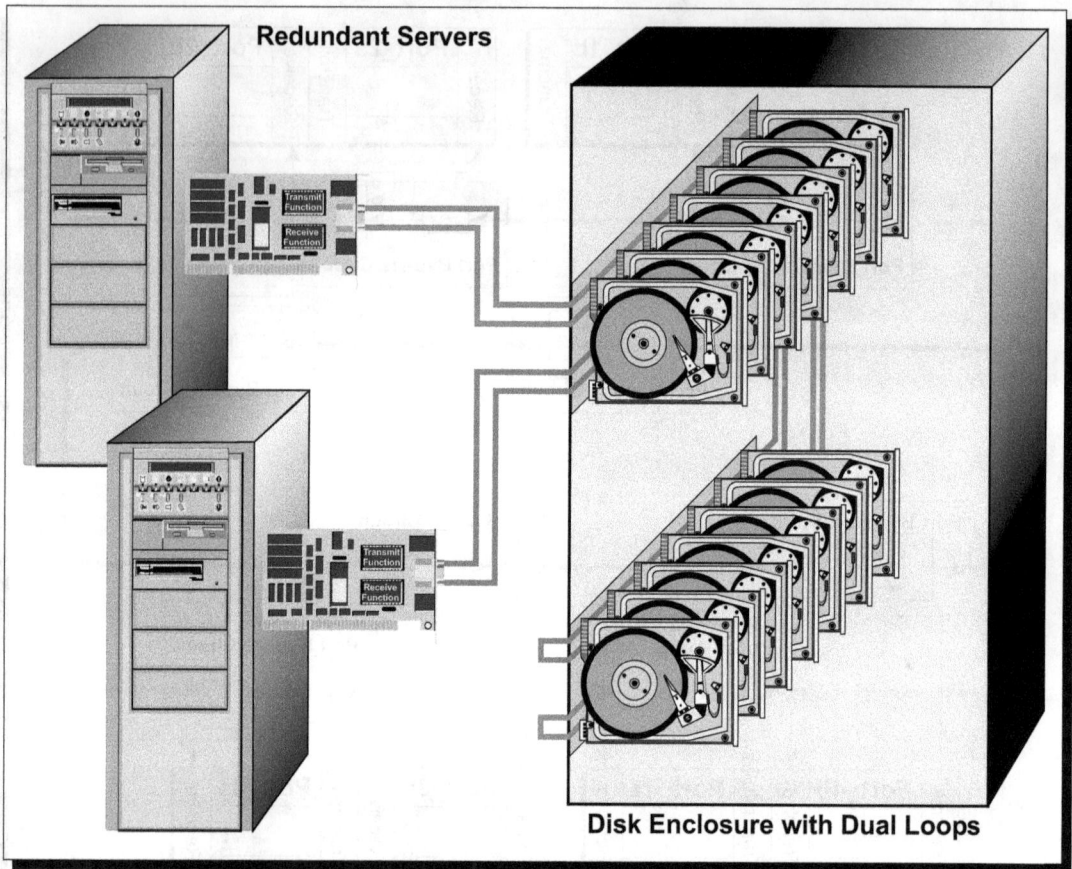

Figure 125. Dual Arbitrated Loops with Dual-Ported Disks

This allows each loop interface to support the required loop protocols and successfully perform loop operations.

Because there is a single FC-2 function, frame transmission and reception can only occur through one loop interface at any point. Whenever a loop circuit is open the frame transmission and reception logic is connected to one of the loop interfaces, and is not available to the other loop interface. Sharing the frame transmission and reception function in this manner leads to a number of interesting consequences, all having to do with the behavior of the loop interface that does not have access to the FC-2 function.

When the node wishes to arbitrate, it can arbitrate on either of the loop interfaces or on both simultaneously. If the node arbitrates on one loop interface, the operation is no different than what occurs with a single-ported device. If, however, the node arbitrates on both loop interfaces, it begins sending ARB(x) on each loop (the 'x' values may be different on each loop). Arbitrating on both loops allows the node to begin communications on the first loop that is available

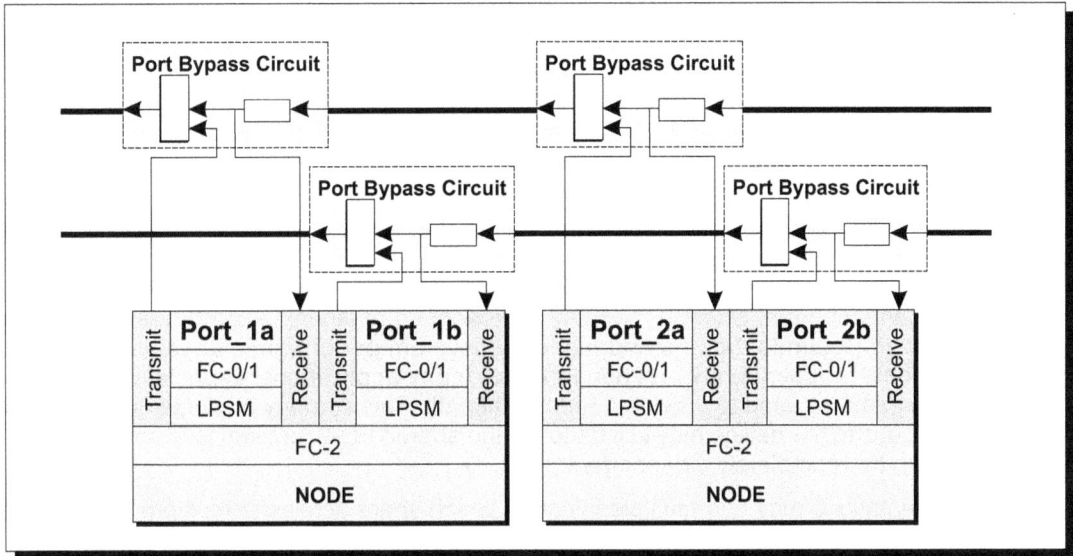

Figure 126. Dual-Loop, Single Port Design

(this allows for dynamic load balancing). One of the loops may be free and arbitration could be won immediately and the FC-2 is logically connected to that loop interface so frame transmission and reception can begin. But what happens on the other loop interface?

Once a port begins arbitrating, it is not permitted to withdraw its arbitration request unless it knows that it is not the last port arbitrating in the current access fairness window. If it is not sure, the only possible action for the LPSM is to continue arbitrating until it wins arbitration. When this occurs, the LPSM may send an OPNy to itself followed by a minimum of two fill words, a CLS, and enter the Transmitted Close state. When the CLS is received, the LPSM enters the Monitoring state making the loop available for the next port. Although this requires a round-trip delay on the loop, it is used to guarantee that the access fairness protocol is processed correctly.

If the loop interface receives an OPN while the FC-2 is logically connected to the other loop the LPMS must accept the OPN and go to the Opened state. If it allows the OPN to pass, the open originator will receive its own OPN back and conclude the destination port no longer exists on the loop.

When the LPSM enters the OPN state, it finds that the FC-2 is unavailable because it is in use by the other loop interface. Since no receive buffers are available, no R_RDYs can be sent. Instead, the port sends an immediate CLS which is interpreted by the open originator as a busy condition. Sending an immediate CLS is only allowed when the login BB_Credit granted by the open recipient is zero. Otherwise, R_RDYs must be sent to equal or exceed the login BB_Credit. If this approach is used with a non-zero login BB_Credit, frames may be lost if the port is opened while the FC-2 is in use by the other loop interface because frames may already be in transit by the time the OPN is received.

Another effect of the dual-loop, single-port approach appears during loop initialization. If loop initialization occurs on one of the loops, the FC-2 must be connected to that loop to process the initialization frames. This connection must be maintained for the duration of the loop initialization or else the initialization process could fail. During this time, the FC-2 is unavailable for use on the non-initializing loop and no activity can occur at this port on that loop. If all of the ports exhibit this behavior, then loop initialization on one loop completely stops activity on the other loop for the entire duration of the loop initialization process.

Using a shared FC-2 provides the advantages associated with dual interfaces and allows the device to attach to multiple loops for improved availability. Many devices are not capable of supporting multiple simultaneous operations and don't require the functionality provided by two fully independent ports. Sharing the FC-2 represents a reasonable compromise between cost and function (redundant paths and higher subsystem performance because two ports may communicate independently on each loop) for many applications, especially where the second loop is primarily used to provide a redundant path. This strategy provides dual-loop capability, but access to the device may still be lost if the shared FC-2 function fails so it is slightly less robust than two completely independent ports.

Some implementations may use multiple initiators which share access to multiple disk drives. One approach is to bypass those disk drives which are not actively used on that loop. This prevents the problem of receiving an unexpected OPN and minimizes the delay through the port.

16.4.2 True Dual-Porting

Another approach to dual-loop attachment is to provide two completely independent ports. Each port is fully functional and capable of operating independently of the other port. This type of dual porting could be implemented by using two Fibre Channel adapter cards in a host system, or designing two complete ports into I/O devices. An example of a node with two fully functional ports is shown in Figure 127 on page 291.

Because the ports are connected to separate loops and operating completely independently of one another, they may or may not have the same AL_PA values. If the AL_PA values are assigned by providing preferred addresses via jumpers or switches, then the two ports can have the same AL_PA values. If the AL_PA values are assigned dynamically by using soft addresses during loop initialization, they may or may not have the same AL_PA value, but this should not be an issue because nodes are found by using their node names, not the AL_PA values.

The benefit of having two fully functional ports is that, potentially twice as many operations may be performed compared to a single port design. There is also the advantage that a failure in one of the ports or in one of the loops is less likely to affect the operation of the other port. The disadvantage of this approach is that twice as much logic is required, adding to the cost of the product. Finally, with two independent ports, initialization of one loop should not have an effect on operations on the other loop.

16.4.3 Redundant Loops with Hubs

When an arbitrated loop configuration consists of redundant loops and hubs are used to connect the devices, redundant hubs are required. This provides redundancy in the event that one of the hubs should fail. An illustration of dual-loop configuration with two Hubs, multiple host

---

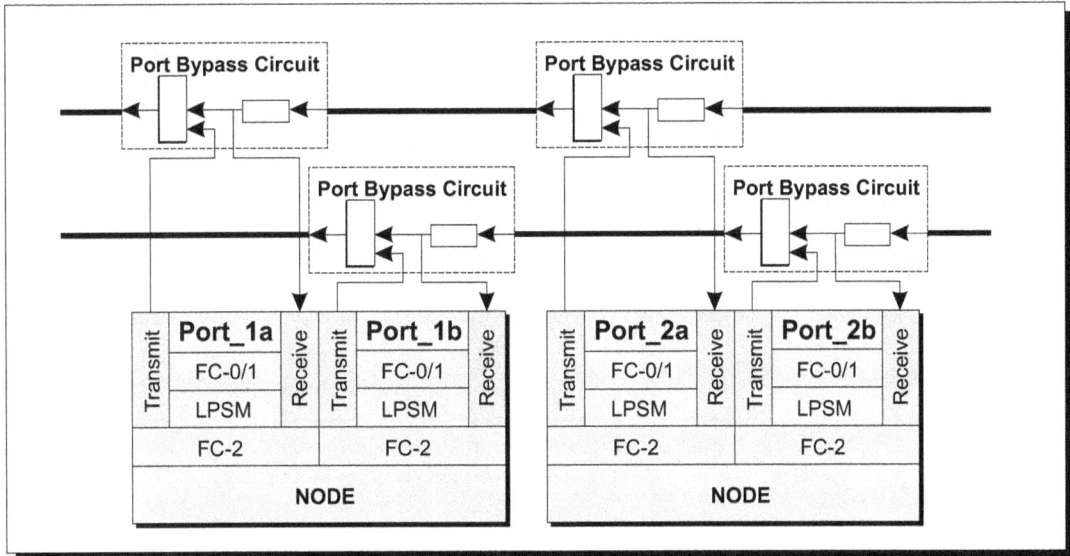

Figure 127. Dual Ported Node With Two Fully Functional Ports

bus adapters, and multiple storage devices where each disk drive is attached to both loops is shown in Figure 128.

16.5 Concurrent Maintenance and Hot Swapping

Many high-availability applications require that maintenance be performed concurrently with normal operations with little or no interference to ongoing operations. This requires that the product be designed with the idea of concurrent maintenance and hot swapping in mind. Field replaceable units must be accessible without impacting current operations and the removal and replacement of replaceable units must be accomplished, in most cases, without removing power from the product being serviced (hot swapping).

Hot swapping is particularly challenging in loop topologies because a basic characteristic of the topology is that information is flowing through intermediate nodes on its way to the ultimate destination. If the service person removes a device from an operational loop, some portion of the loop data may be removed along with the device. Similarly, when a device is added into an operational loop, the loop must be broken temporarily and expanded to allow the new device to be inserted into the loop. Both of these conditions may result in a temporary error condition requiring the invocation of error recovery processing. This may or may not be apparent to the user depending on the timing of the event and time required to perform the recovery process.

Devices can be added or removed from a loop environment without causing errors if loop activity can be temporarily suspended prior to adding or removing devices. In some environments, the operating system may provide a command that suspends activity on the subsystem. In this case, the system level function provides the desired result, ensuring that activity is suspended during maintenance.

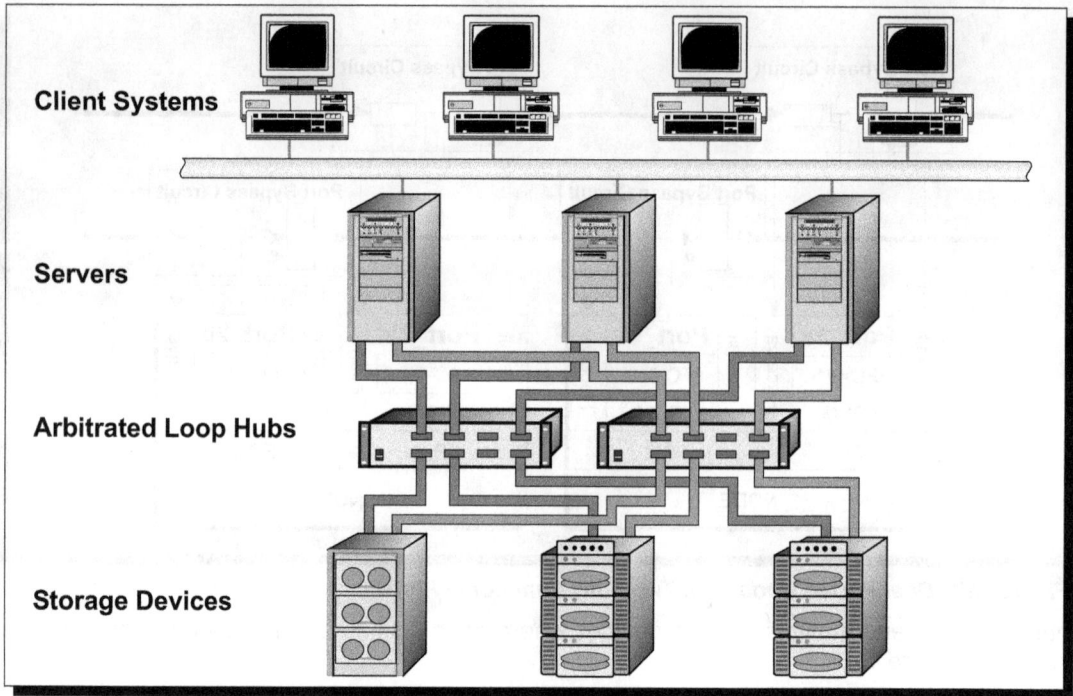

Figure 128. Dual Arbitrated Loops with Redundant Hubs

If no system level function is available, the subsystem is responsible for temporarily suspending loop activity. All that is required to suspend loop activity is for one of the ports on the loop to win arbitration and hold the loop until the addition or removal is complete. Even though the loop itself is interrupted, and link level errors occur, the I/O activity is not affected provided the disruption does not cause timeout errors.

One approach might be to provide a "service" switch on the control panel of the subsystem. When it is necessary to add or remove devices from the loop, the service switch is activated causing one of the ports on the loop (such as the initiator) to arbitrate and light an indicator after arbitration has been won. This provides a visual indication to the user that it is now safe to add or remove devices. Once maintenance is complete, the switch is be returned to the normal position and loop activity resumes.

This process could be automated for those products having a door or cover that must be opened to service the product. When the door is opened, an interlock switch is automatically set to the service position signalling a designated port to arbitrate for the loop. Again, a visual indication could be used to signal when it was safe to add or remove devices. In most cases, the loop activity could be suspended before the user could add or remove a device, even without a visual indication.

Any action that holds the loop for a significant time, such as those described above, may in itself create loop errors due to time-out conditions. If this is a possibility, all affected devices may have to receive notification that they should suspend timing until the service activity is complete. The only mechanism currently available that could be used to provide such a notification with today's designs is the MRK(tx) primitive signal. This requires defining a specific MRK(suspend timers,x) that would be interpreted by all ports as an indication to suspend their timers, and perhaps, loop failure detection until a MRK(resume timers,x) is received.

Synchronizing activation or deactivation of a port bypass circuit with loop activity may be automated under some situations. If a device detects an internal error and is preparing to activate the port bypass circuit, it can arbitrate, and after winning arbitration, transmit LIPs to notify other ports the loop configuration has changed, and activate the port bypass circuit. At this time, no other loop activity is in progress and activation of the port bypass circuit is nondisruptive.

When a new device is added to the loop, that device attempts to deactivate the port bypass circuit after completion of its internal self-test routines. If deactivation of the port bypass circuit is not synchronized to loop activity, errors may occur. To prevent errors, deactivation of the port bypass circuit should be synchronized with loop activity. Rather than automatically deactivating the port bypass circuit on completion of self-test one approach is to have the device wait for an appropriate LPE(fx) sequence. Periodically the initiator arbitrates and upon winning arbitration sends the LPE(fx) sequence to indicate that any port wishing to join the loop can reset the Bypass variable and deactivate their port bypass circuit. In this way, deactivation of the port bypass circuits is synchronized to other loop activity and no frame errors occur.

Another approach that has been incorporated in the Arbitrated Loop standard is to allow a port that does not have an AL_PA assigned to use the hard address (if it has one) to arbitrate and quiesce the loop. Using this 'trusted' address allows the port to arbitrate, and upon winning begin loop initialization to verify or obtain a proper AL_PA. This ensures that the LIP is only issued when no other loop activity is taking place.

One other approach has been discussed (but has not been accepted into the Arbitrated Loop standard) is to use a MRK(tx) where 't' indicates that a port without an AL_PA desires that a port with an AL_PA arbitrates and wins (to quiesce the loop), and then transmit a LIP for loop initialization. If the MRK(tx) is returned to the port (this could also be a MRK(tx) from another port which is attempting the same procedure) it may mean that no other port is going to assist this port. The port may then wish to wait for LP_TOV and issue its own LIP to initialize the loop. If the MRK(tx) is not returned, the port can assume that another port will assist in the initialization process.

16.6 Summary

Through the use of port bypass circuits, redundant loops, and redundant hubs, the arbitrated loop can provide a high degree of availability while still providing low-cost connectivity. This unique combination of high-performance, high-availability, and extended connectivity have made the arbitrated loop a natural interface for storage device and subsystems.

16.7 Chapter Summary

High-Availability Loops

- Standard only requires a single loop
  - No requirement for redundant loop
  - No requirement for port bypass circuit
  - Enhancements are viewed as value add for vendors
- Many applications require more robustness than provided by a single loop
  - Disk subsystems
  - Processor clustering
  - High-availability networks
- How can the needed robustness be achieved?

Loop Robustness

- Many approaches to high-availability
  - Port bypass circuit
  - Dual loops with dual-ported devices
- Different approaches to dual-porting
  - Completely independent ports with full functionality
  - Ports with shared FC-2 function (port and a half designs)
  - Ports with two-loop switch implementations
- Fibre Channel Hub
  - For physically separated ports (systems, or networks)

Port Bypass Circuit

- Electrical circuit to allow bypassing a port
  - Simple combinatorial logic
  - No data reclocking - beware of jitter buildup
  - One common package provides four circuits per module
- Activated when:
  - The port fails
  - Power is removed from device
  - Device is removed
  - Bypassing device for management purposes
- Not part of device, often part of the backplane

Dual-Loop Configurations

- Required for high-availability applications:
  - Dual loops in case a loop fails
  - Port bypass circuits on each loop
  - Dual ports on devices
- Different approaches are possible
  - Dual ports allow simultaneous operations on both loops
  - Dual loop designs allow limited operations on both loops, frame transmission or reception on one at a time
  - Switched fail-over designs allow static connection to either loop

Fibre Channel Hubs

- Hub is a separate device that provides loop robustness
  - Provides port bypass function automatically
  - May reclock data to attenuate jitter
  - May attach to network or maintenance facility for control and management (SNMP)
- Provides port bypass function when individual ports are separated (no backplane available)
  - Systems to peripherals
  - Fibre Channel networks
  - Within a subsystem to attach racks and provide jitter reduction
- Hubs are commonplace in networks

17. PLDA Technical Report

The *Private Loop Direct Attach (PLDA) Technical Report* is a profile document describing the behavior of SCSI devices operating on a private arbitrated loop, or communications with private ports operating on a public loop. The original intent of the technical report was to define the behavior of Fibre Channel attached disk drives and their controllers, but the scope has since been expanded to include other types of peripheral devices.

17.1 What Is a Profile?

Profiles are documents that define proper subsets of relevant standards. They are created to facilitate interoperability of products from different suppliers. Profiles provide a formalized means of identifying which optional behaviors or functions defined by the standards must be used and which optional behavior or functions cannot be used between compliant implementations. A standard as comprehensive and wide reaching as the Fibre Channel family of standards includes numerous optional features and behaviors. If one implementation required the use of a particular option while another did not support that option, the two implementations would not interoperate, even though both are compliant with the standard. Profiles, such as the PLDA document, provide a practical guideline to implementers to ensure that different designs implement a compatible subset of the standards.

A profile is not a standard and does not redefine behaviors or functions described in the associated standards. Rather, a profile defines a subset of the standard required for interoperability. A profile does not relieve an implementation from observing mandatory behaviors required by the associated standards. If a design fails to implement one of more aspects of the associated standard, it may be compliant with the profile, but not compliant with the standard.

Some implementations may choose to omit certain behaviors required by the associated standards. When this is done, the design may function within the scope of the profile environment, but fail to operate correctly outside of that environment. The PLDA document describes an environment wherein implementations may operate even though they have not implemented all of the behaviors required by the associated standards.

Because all of the capabilities and functions described by the PLDA document are already part of the associated standards, a separate standard was not required. Some new behaviors, using existing capabilities, are required by the PLDA document (for example, see *SCSI Target Discovery* on page 306).

17.2 PLDA Background

In 1994 a group of industry representatives from the disk drive and storage subsystem community initiated a series of working meetings to develop a set of guidelines for private loop directly attached Fibre Channel devices. Their goal was to define a simplified subset of features and operational characteristics drawn from the relevant Fibre Channel, Fibre Channel Arbitrat-

---

ed Loop, and Small Computer System Interface (SCSI-3) standards. There were two principal objectives behind this activity:

- The first was to foster interoperability between Fibre Channel direct attach products from different suppliers by providing a common set of functions and behaviors that all ports were required to support.
- The second goal was to simplify the design of ports operating in this environment by limiting the features and capabilities to the minimum necessary to implement viable products. The scope of their initial activities was intentionally limited to a specific environment—private loop disk devices using Arbitrated Loop as their native device interface

This activity progressed through a series of informal working meetings into late 1995 when the decision was made to formalize the work as an ANSI technical report called the *Private Loop Direct Attach Technical Report*, or PLDA for short. ANSI Technical Reports are used to provide clarification or supplemental information regarding the application of standards.

17.3 Relevant ANSI Standards

The *Private Loop Direct Attach* document defines a subset of features and behaviors which selects from multiple ANSI approved standards and standards under development. The following documents are the primary document set associated with the PLDA profile:

- *Fibre Channel Physical and Signalling (FC-PH)*
- *Fibre Channel Physical and Signalling (FC-PH-2)*
- *Fibre Channel Physical and Signalling (FC-PH-3)*
- *Fibre Channel Arbitrated Loop (FC-AL and FC-AL-2 by implication)*
- *SCSI-3 Fibre Channel Protocol (SCSI FCP)*

The following sections examine the key PLDA identified behaviors or functions associated with each of these documents.

17.3.1 Fibre Channel Feature Set

The PLDA Technical Report selects an appropriate set of Fibre Channel features based on the specific requirements associated with private loop ports. The principal goals in identifying this subset of features was to reduce cost by minimizing the functionality required without compromising data integrity or performance.

The *Private Loop Direct Attach* profile takes advantage of the in-order frame delivery characteristic of private loop environments. This is an inherent characteristic of private loop behavior which may significantly simplify designs specifically tailored for this application.

FC-PH Common Service Parameters. PLDA, as is the case with all loop operations, requires use of the Alternate BB_Credit management model and allows a port to grant Login BB_Credit values that are either zero or nonzero. Ports that grant a nonzero Login BB_Credit must ensure that they are always able to satisfy that Login BB_Credit whenever a new loop circuit is opened. For more information on the alternate BB_Credit management model, see *Buffer-to-Buffer Flow Control* on page 136.

The use of continuously increasing relative offset is required by the PLDA profile for FCP_DATA sequences (information category=1). This means that each FCP_DATA frame must have the relative offset present bit (bit 3 of the F_CTL field) set in the frame header and a valid relative offset value present in the parameter field. Using continuously increasing relative offset provides additional error detection capabilities in the event of frame loss.

The use of random relative offset is prohibited. Non-sequential SCSI transfers may be accomplished by the use of multiple data sequences, each of which uses continuously increasing relative offset within the sequence. The starting offset for each sequence can be established through use of the FCP_XFER_RDY information unit for write type commands, or the relative offset value in the first frame of each data sequence for read type commands.

The PLDA document requires a minimum Buffer-to-Buffer receive data field size of 256 bytes or greater (up to the 2112 byte limit defined in FC-PH). This is the parameter establishing the receive data field size for Class-3 frames. While a port could technically support 256-byte frames, most implementations will support larger data field sizes for improved performance.

Node_Name and Port_Name. Devices complying with the PLDA profile must report a unique Node_Name. Each port on that device must also report a unique Port_Name. A dual-ported disk drive has one Node_Name and two Port_Names for a total of three unique names.

Furthermore, the Node_Name and Port_Names must be based on a registered format. They must contain a registered identifier which is managed by a recognized registration authority (e.g., IEEE). This ensures that Node_Names and Port_Names assigned by different companies will be unique.

FC-PH Class-3 Service Parameters. One of the key decisions made in the private loop activity was the decision to use Class-3 service. It was felt that this would provide the simplest implementation consistent with the highest performance potential.

Because Class-3 service does not provide delivery confirmation or notification of nondelivery, all logic and firmware associated with the generation and management of Acknowledge, Busy, and Reject could be eliminated. Use of Class-3 also meant that there would be no end-to-end flow control and no requirement for EE_Credit management because all flow control in Class-3 uses the Buffer-to-Buffer flow control mechanism.

Eliminating the ACKs removed what could have been a significant amount of loop traffic and overhead. Because a port is not permitted to send an ACK until the received frame or frames have been validated, the ACK may not be available immediately. If the port generates the ACK after the loop circuit has been closed, an entirely new loop circuit could be required just to send the ACK. This could seriously degrade overall loop performance with the ACKs consuming almost as much loop time as the productive work.

Most general-purpose host adapter designs contain the necessary functionality to create and send ACKs concurrently with frame transmission and reception. Implementations designed to reduce the amount of logic required in the Fibre Channel port may only be capable of supporting half-duplex operation—they may be able to send or receive device data frames but not both. Early developers assumed that this would prevent them from sending ACKs, but even in half-duplex, ACKs may be transmitted without requiring a separate loop circuit.

If a loop circuit ends before all outstanding ACKs are sent (although possible, not very likely), it is possible that a new loop circuit with a different port could be established. When this occurs, the port has to buffer the original ACKs until a loop circuit can be established with the correct port. This could ultimately lead to the need for a port to buffer a significant number of ACKs before it is able to establish an appropriate loop circuit and send the ACKs.

One disadvantage of Class-3 service is that it doesn't provide explicit confirmation of frame or sequence delivery. The original assumption was that the SCSI upper level protocol provided sufficient confirmation due to the nature of the protocol. That is, all SCSI tasks begin with a command and end with status. This is a valid, although somewhat overly simplistic view of things as shall be seen later.

Basic Link Services. The PLDA profile prohibits the use of all basic link services except Abort Sequence (ABTS) which can only be issued by the SCSI initiator. The ABTS is used by the SCSI initiator to abort a failed operation due to a sequence delivery error or SCSI command level timeout.

Extended Link Services. The PLDA profile only requires a limited subset of the extended link services defined by the various versions of the Fibre Channel. They are:

- Discover Address (ADISC): returns the Node_Name, Port_Name, and hard address of a port.
- Discover N_Port Parameters (PDISC): returns the login parameters and login state of a port.
- Logout (LOGO): logout a port. The LOGO is also used in response to some frames to indicated that a PLOGI is needed.
- N_Port Login (PLOGI): login with a port.
- Process Login (PRLI): communicate the FCP service parameters and establish an FCP-level binding between ports.
- Process Logout (PRLO): remove the FCP-level binding between ports.
- Report Node Capabilities (RNC): obtain capabilities of a port, including which Fibre Channel documents and levels are supported.
- Third Party Process Logout (TPRLO): perform a process logout on behalf of another port. For example, one initiator could perform the process logout on behalf of another, failed initiator.

Several additional extended link services may optionally be used. They are:

- Read Exchange Status Block (RES): prohibited for disk type devices, allowed for streaming devices.
- Read Link Error Status Block (RLS): may optionally be issued by a SCSI initiator to retrieve link error information.
- Request Sequence Initiative (RSI): prohibited for disk type devices, allowed for streaming devices.
- Read Sequence Status Block (RSS): prohibited for disk type devices, allowed for streaming devices.

Other than Read Link Error Status Block (RLS), the optional extended link services are limited to non-disk type devices. They were included to allow non-disk type devices to perform more sophisticated problem determination and error recovery, if desired.

17.4 Exchange and Sequence Management

This section describes the exchange and sequence management behaviors required of ports that conform to the PLDA profile.

17.4.1 Exchange Management

The SCSI initiator is the originator of all SCSI FCP exchanges. The only exchanges that may be originated by a SCSI target are associated with the logout (LOGO) and Process Logout (PRLO) extended link services (and, in the case of non-disk devices, certain other optional extended link services).

Exchange Originator. The originator of each exchange is required to assign an originator exchange ID (OX_ID) for that exchange. The OX_ID value must be unique between that originator and responder pair of ports. Because originators may assign OX_ID values independently of other originators, there is no guarantee the OX_ID values from different originators are unique at a responder. This is no different than the SCSI parallel bus case where different initiators may assign the same queue tag value to operations that are sent to the same target. The responder must qualify the OX_ID value with the address identifier of the originator to uniquely identify the exchange.

Likewise, the originator of an exchange is not assured of responder exchange ID (RX_ID) uniqueness across multiple responders and must qualify the RX_ID with the address identifier of the responder to uniquely identify the exchange.

Because the environment defined by the PLDA profile ensures in-order delivery of frames and assumes that frames are processed in the order received, a set of simplifying assumptions can be made regarding when an exchange is open. The exchange originator can consider the exchange open from the time that the first frame of the first information unit (frame with the First_Sequence bit in the F_CTL field set to a one) is sent until one of the following occurs:

- The last frame of the last information unit (frame with the Last_Sequence bit in the F_CTL field set to 1) is received.
- The exchange is aborted using ABTS and a response to the ABTS is received.
- A LOGO is sent to, or received from, the exchange responder.

Exchange Responder. The exchange responder may assign an RX_ID or use the value of x'FFFF'. If the exchange responder assigns an RX_ID value, it must be unique between that responder and the exchange originator.

An exchange responder in a multiple originator environment is not assured of OX_ID uniqueness across multiple originators. Therefore, the responder must qualify the OX_ID with the address of the exchange originator (or assign a unique RX_ID to the exchange). As stated in the Fibre Channel Protocol for SCSI standard, exchange responders are not required to check for

OX_ID uniqueness with a given originator (a condition analogous to duplicate queue tags in the SCSI parallel bus topology).

An exchange responder considers the exchange open from receipt of the first frame of the first information unit (frame with the First_Sequence bit in the F_CTL field set to 1) until one of the following occurs:

- The last frame of the last information unit (frame with the Last_Sequence bit in the F_CTL field set to one) is sent.
- The exchange is aborted using ABTS.
- A LOGO is sent to, or received from, the exchange originator.

17.4.2 Sequence Management

The following section summarizes the sequence management requirements for ports operating in accordance with the *Private Loop Direct Attach* profile.

When Is a Sequence Open? The sequence initiator (the port sending the sequence) considers a sequence open from the time that the first frame of the sequence (the frame with the SOFi3 delimiter) is sent until one of the following occurs:

- The last frame of the sequence (the frame with the EOFt delimiter) is sent and $R\_A\_TOV_{SEQ\_QUAL}$ has elapsed (see *Resource Allocation Timeout (R_A_TOV)* on page 310 for a definition of this timeout value).
- The sequence is aborted using ABTS.
- A LOGO or PRLO is sent to, or received from, the sequence recipient.

The sequence recipient considers a sequence open from the receipt of the first frame of the sequence (the frame with the SOFi3 delimiter) until one of the following occurs:

- The last frame of the sequence (the frame with the EOFt delimiter) is received.
- The sequence is aborted using ABTS.
- A LOGO or PRLO is sent to, or received from, the sequence initiator.

Sequence_ID Usage. For sequences which transfer sequence initiative (other than the FCP_RSP which is described separately below) sequence ID reuse is defined by the following two rules:

- An NL_Port may reuse a SEQ_ID for the same exchange following confirmation of sequence delivery (see *FCP Sequence Delivery Confirmation* on page 305 for a list of FCP sequences for which delivery can be determined).
- An NL_Port may also reuse the SEQ_ID within a different exchange (to the same, or a different destination NL_Port) immediately following transmission of the last frame of the sequence without waiting for confirmation of sequence delivery. The next sequence sent by the sequence initiator is not considered a consecutive sequence because it is part of a different exchange.

For sequences which do not transfer sequence initiative, the rules governing reuse of the sequence ID are more complicated.

It is recommended that consecutive sequences for the same exchange follow the FC-PH rules for streamed sequences (examples of this occur when multiple FCP_DATA sequences are used during a single read operation and between the last FCP_DATA sequence and the FCP_RSP sequence of read-type commands). The rules for streamed sequences are summarized in the following list:

The first sequence of a group of consecutive sequences is not considered a streamed sequence. It may use any eligible SEQ_ID and the SEQ_CNT may be either x'0000' or continuously increasing (incremented by one from the last frame of the previous sequence of that exchange).

- The second, and subsequent, sequences of a group of consecutive sequences within the same exchange may optionally be treated as streamed sequences (optional because R_A_TOV$_{SEQ\_QUAL}$=zero and the prior sequence is no longer open). If they are treated as streamed sequences, the following rules apply ('x' is the number of open sequences per exchange from PLOGI):

  - x+1 different consecutive SEQ_IDs shall be used.

  - The x+1 different SEQ_IDs may be assigned by the sequence initiator in any order (they are not required to be monotonically increasing).

  - A SEQ_ID may be reused after 'x' (where 'x' is the number of open sequences per exchange from PLOGI) different intervening SEQ_IDs have been used, provided that R_A_TOV$_{SEQ\_QUAL}$ has expired for all frames in the prior use of that SEQ_ID. The value for R_A_TOV$_{SEQ\_QUAL}$ is defined in *Resource Allocation Timeout (R_A_TOV)* on page 310.

  - The sequence count (SEQ_CNT) across streamed sequences shall be continuously increasing. The SEQ_CNT of the first frame of the streamed sequence shall be incremented by one from the SEQ_CNT of the last frame of the previous sequence.

- If the second, and subsequent sequences of a group of consecutive sequences are not treated as streamed sequences, the following rules apply:

  - A minimum of two different consecutive SEQ_IDs shall be used by the sequence initiator.

  - The SEQ_CNT across consecutive sequences may optionally be continuously increasing. The SEQ_CNT of the first frame of a consecutive sequence may be incremented by one from the SEQ_CNT of the last frame of the previous sequence or restart at x'0000'.

- Because frame delivery is not confirmed, the sequence initiator shall not reuse a SEQ_CNT within a given sequence. For sequences with a beginning SEQ_CNT of x'0000', the SEQ_CNT is not allowed to wrap on reaching x'FFFF'. For sequences with a beginning SEQ_CNT of 'n' (where n is not x'0000') the SEQ_CNT may wrap on reaching x'FFFF' and continue from x'0000' up to a value of N-1.

- When there is additional data still to transfer and all of the data frames associated with a given sequence have been sent, or all permissible SEQ_CNT values used, the sequence initiator shall begin a new sequence to continue sending additional data.

- The sequence initiator shall not be required to send the maximum allowed number of data frames per sequence, even if there is additional data to send (for example, if the maximum sequence size is 1000 frames, the sequence initiator may end the current sequence after 600 frames and start a new sequence to send any remaining frames).

During a read-type command with at least one FCP_DATA sequence, the FCP_RSP sequence may optionally be considered a streamed sequence and observe the rules for streamed sequences listed above. In any case, the FCP_RSP shall not use the same SEQ_ID as the proceeding FCP_DATA sequence.

A SCSI target may reuse a SEQ_ID for a read FCP_DATA sequence immediately following transmission of the final FCP_RSP of an exchange.

Sequence Errors. There are many ways in which errors can be detected during receipt of a sequence. The following list identifies some of the conditions that indicate a sequence error has occurred:

- if a frame with an SOFi3 delimiter is received and the SEQ_CNT is not equal to x'0000' or incremented by one from the SEQ_CNT of the last frame of the previous sequence of that exchange

- if the SEQ_CNT of a received frame with an SOFn3 delimiter is not incremented by one from the previous frame received for that sequence (i.e., a frame was lost). This should also detect the case where a frame with an SOFn3 delimiter is received for a SEQ_ID not currently open because the SEQ_CNT of the previous frame for that sequence is undefined.

- if a frame with an SOFi3 delimiter is received and the previous sequence of that exchange is still open (see *When Is a Sequence Open?* on page 300 for a definition of when a sequence is open)

- if the relative offset in the parameter field of a received frame with an SOFn3 delimiter is not equal to the (relative offset + the payload size) of the previous frame received for that sequence

- The next frame of a sequence is not received within E_D_TOV

- If, during the same sequence initiative, a sequence is received that has the same SEQ_ID as the previous sequence of that exchange

When a sequence error is detected by the sequence recipient, it shall take the appropriate action as described in *Error Detection and Recovery* on page 311.

17.4.3 Arbitrated Loop Feature Set

The PLDA profile imposes relatively few restrictions on the use of Arbitrated Loop capabilities.

For example, a port is allowed to implement either a full-duplex or half-duplex design. Those ports that implement a full-duplex design can use the OPN(yx) full-duplex open, while those that implement a half-duplex design use the OPN(yy) half-duplex open. There is no problem with interoperability because the half-duplex port is always able to control the nature of the loop circuit.

The use of login BB_Credit of zero or nonzero is allowed. Again, there is no problem with interoperability because the alternate BB_Credit management mechanism ensures that the two options interoperate correctly. Use of unfairness and transfer are allowed. Again these behaviors do not have an affect on interoperability between ports.

One restriction that the PLDA profile does impose on use of Arbitrated Loop features is that a target device is prohibited from originating the port bypass primitive sequences. The SCSI initiator is the only port allowed to originate these sequences.

17.5 SCSI Operation

The PLDA profile prohibits use of most of the more advanced features present in the SCSI Fibre Channel Protocol (FCP) standard.

The only information units an initiator is allowed to use are the T1 (FCP_CMND) and T6 (FCP_DATA out). The target is restricted to using the I1 (FCP_XFER_RDY on write-type commands, I3 (FCP_DATA in), and I4 (FCP_RSP). An example of a write-type command is shown in Figure 129 on page 303.

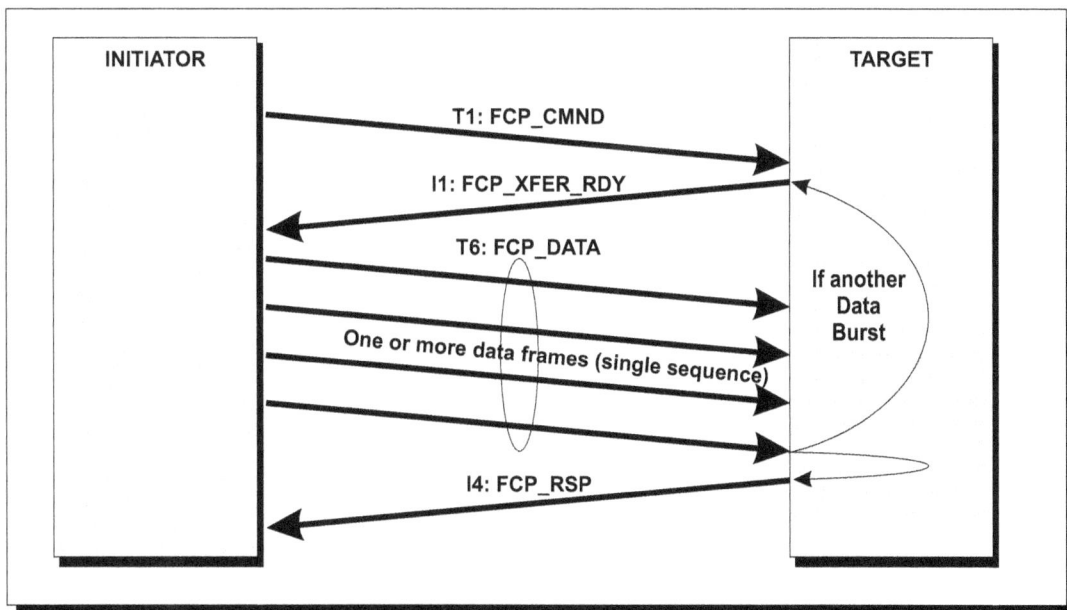

Figure 129. PLDA FCP Write I.U. Usage

If the target decides to break the write data transfer into multiple bursts, each burst is initiated by an I1 FCP_XFER_RDY information unit. This causes the initiator to send a single T6 (FCP_DATA out) information unit to transfer the requested data. The T6 may consist of one or

more frames depending on the amount of data requested by the target and the frame size being used. If the data transfer consists of multiple bursts, each is requested by an I1 information
unit from the target and results in a T6 FCP_DATA out sequence consisting of one or more
frames. When all of the data has been transferred, or an error detected by the target, an I4 is
sent to return the SCSI status byte and any autosense information.

Read-type commands compliant with the PLDA profile do not use the I2 (FCP_XFER_RDY) information unit because a preamble for the following data is not required (i.e., in Fibre Channel,
each frame is self-defining). Instead, the target begins an I3 (FCP_DATA in) sequence to
transfer a burst of read data. If the target is transferring the data in multiple bursts, it uses multiple I3 sequences, one per burst. After all of the data has been sent, the target sends an I4 information unit to end the command. An example of a read-type command is illustrated in
Figure 130 on page 304.

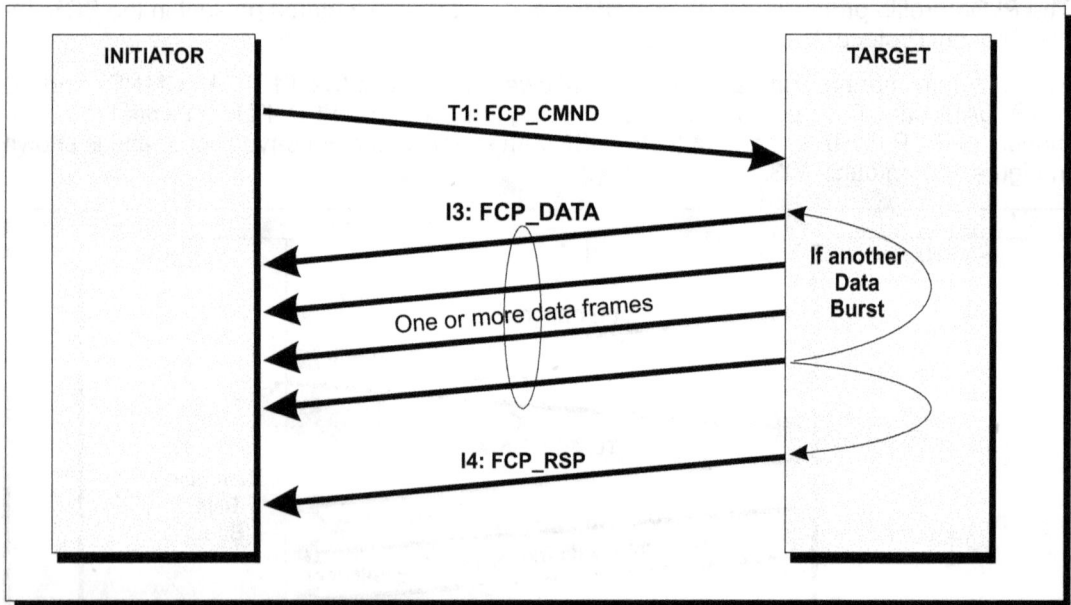

Figure 130. PLDA FCP Read I.U. Usage

Because there is no transfer of sequence initiative following an I3 information unit, the target
has no way of knowing if the I3 sequence was received successfully. In fact, the target does
not know if the I4 was received by the initiator either. This may have implications for some
command queueing situations. For example, if the target is executing a set of commands with
the ordered queue type, it is permitted to begin execution on the next command in the queue
once the previous command has completed. In this case, the target considers the command
complete once the FCP_RSP is sent, without knowing if it reached the initiator.

The combination of Class-3 service and FCP defined information units may lead to difficulties
in some cases where the order of command execution is important if multiple commands are

issued to the target without waiting for confirmation that prior commands have been received successfully by the target.

17.5.1 FCP Sequence Delivery Confirmation

The PLDA technical report describes operations in a Class-3 environment. Consequently, there are no Acknowledgments to provide direct confirmation of sequence delivery. In many cases, sequence delivery can be inferred following transmission of most sequences that transfer sequence initiative. For example,

- The SCSI initiator sends a control type FCP_CMND to the target. It knows the target received the command if the target sends the associated FCP_RSP for that exchange.

- The SCSI initiator sends a write type FCP_CMND to the target. It knows the target received the command if the target sends a write XFER_RDY or FCP_RSP for that exchange.

- The SCSI initiator sends a read type FCP_CMND to the target. It knows the target received the command if the target sends the read data or FCP_RSP for that exchange.

- The SCSI initiator sends a write FCP_DATA sequence to the target. It knows the target received the data if the target sends a write XFER_RDY or the FCP_RSP for that exchange.

- The target sends a write XFER_RDY to the initiator. It knows the initiator received the transfer ready if the initiator sends the requested data.

- Delivery of the following can not be determined directly (delivery failure is detected by a timeout condition or other mechanism):

  - The target sends a read FCP_DATA sequence to the initiator. The fact that delivery of a Read FCP_DATA sequence can't be determined by the target places the burden of error detection on the SCSI initiator that has to determine that all of the read data was in fact received.

  - The target sends the FCP_RSP to the initiator. Once the target sends the FCP_RSP, it has completed the command and is not required to maintain any resources associated with that command.

In all but the last two cases, sequence delivery can be assumed because the target or initiator performed the next step of the protocol. However, if some or all of the read data is lost, it is up to the SCSI initiator to detect that an error occurred. Frame level errors, or lost frames within a sequence can be detected by normal Fibre Channel checks. Loss of an entire sequence may not be detected except by the initiator counting the number of bytes received.

Loss of the FCP_RSP results in an upper level timeout because the command never completes at the initiator, even though it has completed at the target. The initiator can not determine if the target executed the command successfully without invoking an error recovery process.

17.6 PLDA Defined Functions

The *Private Loop Direct Attach* profile defined some new functions and timers that are required by ports conforming to this profile. These are intended to provide error detection and timeout mechanism specific to this loop application.

17.6.1 SCSI Target Discovery

Whenever the possibility of a configuration change is detected, a SCSI initiator may want to rediscover the new configuration to confirm that the configuration is still as expected. An initiator may validate the configuration using the SCSI target discovery procedure as shown in Figure 131 on page 307.

To determine whether or not an OPN was successful in the target discovery procedure, an NL_Port must be able to detect one of the following conditions:

- The open originator receives its own OPN back (the open recipient failed to recognize the OPN and remove it from the loop).

- R_RDY has not been received within E_D_TOV of sending an OPN.

- A CLS was received in response to the OPN. In this case, the target discovery procedure should be retried later.

If the SCSI target discovery procedure revealed that there was a hard-address conflict (i.e., some NL_Port was unable to acquire its hard address), then an application may choose to operate in spite of that conflict. If this is the case, then the discovery procedure can continue with the PRLI and subsequent SCSI INQUIRY command. If the application is not tolerant of hard address conflicts, the SCSI initiator may choose not to use that NL_Port.

The target discovery procedure is designed to avoid the abnormal termination of all open exchanges when a new port is inserted into the loop, or when a port powers on. While not all initiators may perform the exact steps illustrated in Figure 131, a SCSI initiator is required to issue ADISC or PDISC to all SCSI targets it is logged in with within RR_TOV of receiving LIP if it wants to remain logged in with those SCSI targets.

Ports are not required to respond to Class-3 frames having a D_ID that does not match their full 24-bit N_Port identifier. The SCSI target discovery process may cause timeouts if a SCSI initiator sends a frame to a Public NL_Port using a D_ID of x'0000'+AL_PA or to a Private NL_Port using a D_ID with the upper 16 bits nonzero. For expediency during the discovery process, SCSI initiators should be able to originate multiple PDISC or ADISC exchanges without waiting for the responses from other ports. This will help mask the timeouts associated with any AL_PA values not corresponding to operational ports.

Ports may be limited in the number of concurrent exchanges that can be created during the target discovery process. This is because exchanges that were open prior to the loop initialization remain open during the discovery process. New exchanges created to support the discovery process are in addition to those in existence prior to the loop initialization. In some cases, it may be necessary to reserve one or more exchanges to support the discovery process in the event of a loop initialization.

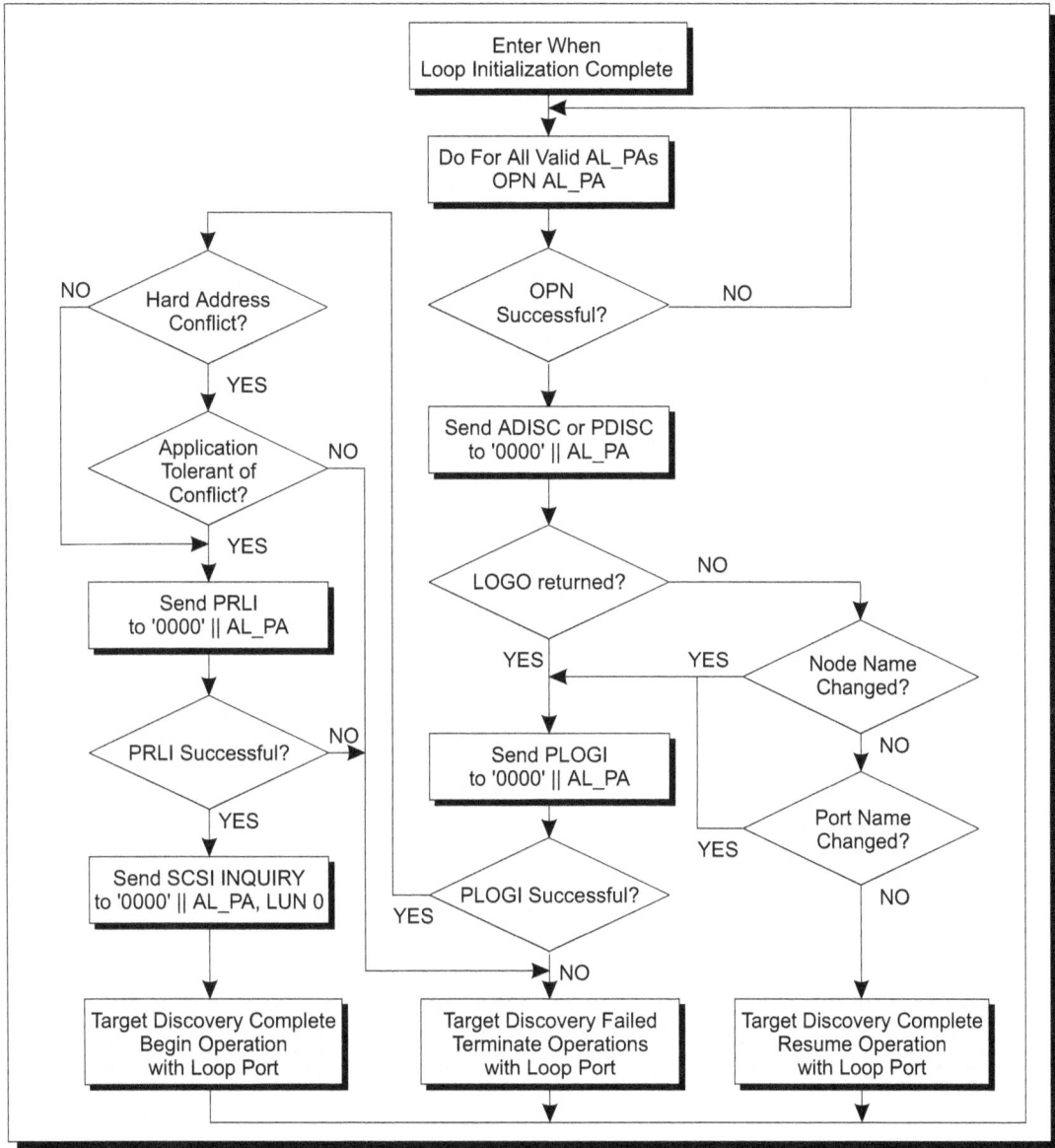

Figure 131. PLDA Target Discovery Procedure

17.6.2 Changing Login Parameters

If a node is preparing to change the login parameters of any NL_Port associated with that node, it must perform an explicit logout with all NL_Ports currently logged-in with that NL_Port

---

before allowing the new parameters to take effect. If there are open and active sequences with the NL_Ports to be logged out, the port discards any frames received in those sequences and sends a LOGO, if one has not already been sent.

17.6.3 Exchange Authentication Following LIP

Following transmission of the CLS signalling completion of loop initialization, SCSI initiators are required to authenticate each SCSI target they are logged in with. Following loop initialization, a SCSI initiator suspends execution of all open tasks with a SCSI target until authentication is complete. After transmission or forwarding of a LIP, only frames related to SCSI target authentication (i.e., ADISC, PDISC, or PLOGI) shall be transmitted to that SCSI target before any frames for other exchanges to that SCSI target are transmitted.

The ADISC or PDISC request must be received by the target within RR_TOV of the completion of loop initialization or the target may terminate all open exchanges for that initiator. If the [N_Port_ID:Port_Name:Node_Name] in the ACC match the previous values for that AL_PA the initiator may resume all tasks with that target. If the [N_Port_ID:Port_Name:Node_Name] do not match the previous values for that AL_PA, the initiator may transmit a LOGO to that port to terminate all open exchanges (the initiator may also transmit a PLOGI that also serves to terminate all open exchanges).

The SCSI initiator exchange portion of the authentication is complete when the ACC to an ADISC or PDISC has been received. If the SCSI initiator fails to receive an ACC within R_A_TOV, it implicitly logs out the SCSI target and terminates all tasks for that target.

Following loop initialization, any frames received (other than ACC to an ADISC, PDISC, or PLOGI, or a LOGO request) from a SCSI target that has not been authenticated are discarded. This means they shall not be considered part of any valid exchange, and the only action taken in response to these frames is to transmit R_RDYs to maintain the BB_Credit.

If a SCSI initiator receives a LOGO from an NL_Port during this procedure, it terminates all open exchanges with that NL_Port and sends an ACC.

SCSI Target Exchange Authentication. Following completion of loop initialization, SCSI targets are required to wait for exchange authentication by the SCSI initiators that they have completed PLOGI with. For each SCSI initiator that has open tasks, a SCSI target suspends tasks associated with that SCSI initiator until an ADISC or PDISC is received from that SCSI initiator.

Following transmission or forwarding of a LIP, only frames related to SCSI initiator authentication (i.e., ACC to an ADISC or PDISC) shall be transmitted to that SCSI initiator before frames for other exchanges to that SCSI initiator are transmitted. Any frames received (other than ADISC, PDISC, or PLOGI) from a SCSI initiator that has not been authenticated shall be discarded. Only R_RDYs to maintain BB_Credit shall be sent in response to those frames.

For each initiator that sends ADISC or PDISC, if the [N_Port_ID:Port_Name:Node_Name] triplet for that SCSI initiator matches the triplet of a logged-in SCSI initiator, the SCSI target sends an ACC to the extended link service. The SCSI target may then resume tasks associated with that SCSI initiator. If the [N_Port_ID:Port_Name:Node_Name] does not match the triplet of a logged-in SCSI initiator, the SCSI target transmits LOGO to that SCSI initiator and terminates all exchanges associated with that SCSI initiator.

If a SCSI target does not receive a PDISC or ADISC from each logged-in SCSI initiator within RR_TOV of completing loop initialization, it may implicitly logout that SCSI initiator and terminate all exchanges associated with that SCSI initiator.

SCSI target authentication is complete when the ACC to an ADISC or PDISC has been transmitted.

17.6.4 Private Loop Direct Attach Defined Timers

The *Fibre Channel Arbitrated Loop* standard was written to support a wide range of applications, each of which may have its own particular timing considerations. Consequently, the time allowed for actions such as forwarding a loop initialization sequence, although LP_TOV is used to monitor each step of the loop initialization. The *Private Loop Direct Attach* profile defines a number of timers not present in the *Fibre Channel Arbitrated Loop* standard and assigns timeout values to certain events. These timers, and their associated values, add a degree of consistency to the private loop environments consisting of disk or tape devices. Table 27 on page 309 summarizes the added timers.

Timer	Implemented by:		Description	Value
	Initiator	Target		
AW_TOV	Y	Y	Minimum time to wait for access to loop before LIP allowed	1 sec.
LIS_HOLD_TIME	Y	Y	Maximum time for each node to forward a loop initialization sequence	1 ms.
E_D_TOV	Y	N	Maximum time permitted for the next expected event within a sequence.	2 sec.
R_A_TOV$_{SEQ\_QUAL}$	Y	N	Minimum time allowed for reuse of sequence qualifiers or transmission or RRQ	0 sec. (note 1)
R_A_TOV$_{ELS}$	Y	N	Maximum time allowed for response to an ELS	2 sec.
RR_TOV	N	Y	Minimum time a target waits for ADISC/PDISC after LIP or sequence initiative transfer before optionally logging out a SCSI initiator	2 sec.
ULP_TOV	Y	N	Minimum time an initiator waits for SCSI status before the ULP initiates recovery	>E_D_TOV

1 The division of R_A_TOV usage as specified in this table differs from FC-PH. This is due to the unique characteristics associated with the PLDA environment.

Table 27. Private Loop Timer Summary

Arbitration Wait Timeout Value (AW_TOV). AW_TOV is equal to the minimum time a private NL_Port must wait to win arbitration before it may assume a malfunction or excessive unfairness and optionally transmit a LIP sequence. This timer is specified to be one second. Howev-

---

er, FC-AL-2 has specified this timer to be LP_TOV (i.e., two seconds). Although not the same, this should not be considered an interoperability issue.

Loop Initialization Sequence Hold Time (LIS_HOLD_TIME). LIS_HOLD_TIME is the maximum amount of time between when a node receives a loop initialization sequence until it forwards it to the next node. The value for LIS_HOLD_TIME is equal to one millisecond.

Sequence Timeout (E_D_TOV). E_D_TOV is the maximum time permitted for a sequence initiator between the transmission of consecutive data frames within a single sequence. This is also the minimum time that a sequence recipient shall wait to receive the next frame within a single sequence before recognizing a sequence timeout. The value is two seconds.

E_D_TOV must include the time required to gain access to the loop in addition to the actual frame transmission time. Therefore, it always includes at least one AW_TOV period.

Resource Allocation Timeout (R_A_TOV). R_A_TOV has two separate components that are labeled $R\_A\_TOV_{SEQ\_QUAL}$ and $R\_A\_TOV_{ELS}$.

$R\_A\_TOV_{SEQ\_QUAL}$ is used to define the minimum amount of time that a sequence initiator shall wait before reusing the sequence qualifiers (SEQ_ID and SEQ_CNT). This value is also the minimum amount of time that a SCSI initiator waits following receipt of the ACC to ABTS before transmitting a Reinstate Recovery Qualifier (RRQ) ELS. $R\_A\_TOV_{SEQ\_QUAL}$ is equal to zero seconds.

Using a value of zero for this time out value assumes that a sequence initiator does not transmit any frames for a sequence after an ABTS is sent for that sequence. If a design uses a queueing mechanism for the transmission of sequences, the queue for a given sequence must be empty before an ABTS for that sequence can be sent, or the act of sending the ABTS purges the queue.

A value of twice $R\_A\_TOV_{ELS}$ is used to determine the minimum time that the originator of an Extended Link Service or FC-4 Extended Link Service requests waits for the response to that request. $R\_A\_TOV_{ELS}$ is equal to two seconds, therefore the minimum wait shall be twice this time, or four seconds. This value includes two AW_TOV periods to allow for the time required to send the ELS request and receive the response.

Resource Recovery Timer (RR_TOV). RR_TOV is the minimum time a target waits for a specific SCSI initiator to perform exchange authentication (see *Exchange Authentication Following LIP* on page 308) following the completion of the loop initialization protocol (i.e., the receipt of CLS while in the Open-Init state). RR_TOV is also the minimum time a target waits for an initiator response following transfer of sequence initiative from the target to the SCSI initiator (e.g., following transmission of the FCP_XFER_RDY during a write command). A suggested default value is two seconds.

On expiration of RR_TOV without exchange authentication occurring, a target may perform a LOGO with that initiator, terminate all open exchanges for that initiator, and reclaim the resources associated with those exchanges. The suggested default value of two seconds provides a sufficient amount of time for a SCSI initiator to complete the post-LIP processing and initiate the exchange authentication process with each target on the loop.

If a target has transferred sequence initiative for all open exchanges with a specific initiator and no activity has occurred on any of those exchanges for RR_TOV, the target may send LOGO to that initiator, terminate all open exchanges for that initiator, and reclaim the resources associated with those exchanges.

Upper Level Protocol Timeout (ULP_TOV). This is an operation-specific timer maintained by the upper level protocol. It is used to time the completion of exchanges associated with ULP operations. Because the time required varies depending on the operation, the value assigned for this timer is determined by operation being timed. Some operations may require extended times to complete (for example, Format Unit with Immediate = zero).

17.6.5 Clearing Effects of Reset Actions

Table 28 on page 312 summarizes which FCP SCSI target objects are cleared as a result of the listed actions. A 'Y' in the corresponding column indicates the object is cleared to its default or power-on value within the device on completion of the specified action.

17.7 Error Detection and Recovery

This section describes the error actions to be taken by the SCSI initiator and target on detection of an error condition.

Error Detection by SCSI Initiator. The ABTS protocol (described in *Disk Error Recovery Using ABTS* on page 313) is invoked by a SCSI initiator when any of the following conditions occur:

- A sequence error is detected (see *Sequence Errors* on page 302 for a list of sequence error conditions)
- ULP_TOV has expired and an exchange has not completed (see *Exchange Management* on page 299 for conditions indicating exchange completion).

Error Detection by SCSI Target. When a target detects a sequence error, it discards that sequence, and all remaining sequences of that exchange without processing. It is possible that no explicit notification of this action is provided to the SCSI initiator. This eventually causes the exchange to timeout when ULP_TOV expires.

Targets may implement the RR_TOV timer as described in *Resource Recovery Timer (RR_TOV)* on page 310 to facilitate recovery of resources that are allocated to a nonrespondent SCSI initiator. If a target implements an RR_TOV timer for this purpose, it may send a LOGO to the SCSI initiator and terminate all open exchanges for that initiator on detection of the following:

- The SCSI initiator has failed to perform target authentication within RR_TOV
- The SCSI initiator has failed to transmit the next expected sequence of an exchange for all open exchanges with a specific initiator within RR_TOV (e.g., FCP write data in response to an FCP_XFER_RDY)

	FCP SCSI Initiator Action Clears Object								
FCP SCSI Target Object	Power Cycle	Reset LIP(y,x)[3]	LOGO, PLOGI	ABTS w/Last Seq.	PRLI, PRLO	TPRLO[5]	SCSI Target Reset	Clear Task Set[4]	Abort Task Set[4]
PLOGI parameters									
For all logged-in SCSI initiator ports	Y	Y	N	N	N	N	N	N	N
Only for SCSI initiator port initiating action	N	N	Y	N	N	N	N	N	N
Open sequences terminated									
For all SCSI initiator ports with open sequences	Y	Y	N	N	N	Y	Y[2]	N	N
Only for SCSI initiator port initiating action	N	N	Y	Y	Y	N	N	Y[2]	Y[2]
BB_Credit_CNT	Y	Y	Y	N	N	N	N	N	N
Hard address acquisition attempted	Y[1]	Y[1]	N	N	N	N	N	N	N
PRLI parameters cleared									
For all logged-in SCSI initiator ports	Y	Y	N	N	N	N	N	N	N
Only for ports of specified TYPE	N	N	N	N	Y	Y	N	N	N
Only for port initiating action	N	N	Y	N	Y	N	N	N	N
Open tasks (exchanges) aborted									
All tasks for all SCSI initiator ports with open tasks	Y	Y	N	N	N	Y	Y	Y	N
All tasks, only for port initiating action	N	N	Y	N	Y	N	N	N	Y
Only specified task for port initiating action	N	N	N	Y	N	N	N	N	N
Target mode page parms restored from saved pages									
For all SCSI initiators	Y	Y	N	N	N	Y	Y	N	N
Only for port initiating action	N	N	Y	N	Y	N	N	N	N
Pre-existing Unit Attention condition cleared									
For all SCSI initiators	Y	Y	N	N	N	Y	Y	N	N
Only for port initiating action	N	N	Y	N	Y	N	N	N	N
Pre-existing ACA condition cleared									
For all SCSI initiators	Y	Y	N	N	N	Y	Y	N	N
Only for port initiating action	N	N	Y	N	Y	N	N	N	N

Notes:

1 If the NL_Port has an AL_PA different that its hard address and the NL_Port experiences a power cycle or recognizes LIP(AL_PD,AL_PS), the NL_Port shall relinquish its current AL_PA and attempt to acquire its hard address.

2 Tasks are cleared internally within the SCSI target, but open sequences must be individually aborted by the SCSI initiator via the ABTS_LS protocol that also has the effect of aborting the associated exchange.

3 This is also known as LIP(AL_PD,AL_PS). If the destination recognizes a selective hard reset LIP where the AL_PD matches the AL_PA of the receiving NL_Port, the receiving NL_Port shall perform the behavior described in this column.

4 For multiple-LUN SCSI targets, Clear Task Set, and Abort Task set affect only the addressed LUN, not the entire SCSI target.

5 Actions listed shall be performed when the Global bit = '1'b. If the Global bit = '0'b, then the actions listed under PRLI/PRLO should be performed for the designated SCSI initiator.

Table 28. Clearing Effects of Reset Actions

Targets compliant with the PLDA profile are not permitted to invoke the ABTS protocol.

17.7.1 Disk Error Recovery Using ABTS

The ABTS-Last_Sequence protocol is required by PLDA. This protocol uses ABTS to abort entire exchanges. The exchange is the unit of error recovery for PLDA compliant ports, rather than the sequence. The error recovery protocol that defines retransmission of exchanges after ABTS is beyond the scope of the PLDA profile because it depends on the application and device type. For an illustration of the ABTS procedure, see Figure 118 on page 274.

SCSI Initiator ABTS Behavior. Only a SCSI initiator is permitted to transmit ABTS. The PLDA profile does not address the protocol by which multiple SCSI initiators communicate or synchronize shared peripherals. ABTS may be transmitted even if sequence initiative is not held. Following the transmission of ABTS, any Device_Data frames received for that exchange shall be discarded until the BA_ACC with Last_Sequence bit set to one is received from the target.

ABTS may not take effect immediately. For example, if ABTS is sent following transmission of a read command, the target may send back all or some of the requested read data before replying with the ACC to the ABTS (or the data may already be in flight at the time the ABTS was sent). The SCSI initiator must receive this data and send the appropriate R_RDYs to replenish the BB_Credit in order for the target to send the ACC.

There are circumstances where a configuration change event could occur quickly. These events could result in link errors and a ULP_TOV timeout, but without causing loop initialization. A SCSI initiator shall attempt the ABTS protocol following ULP_TOV timeout.

The ABTS protocol shall be invoked:

1. For all open exchanges for all LUNs on a designated target:

   * Following receipt of "Function Complete" to target reset

   * Following receipt of CHECK CONDITION status with Sense Key=Unit Attention and ASC/ASCQ of "Power on, reset, or bus device reset occurred" (29 XX) or Microcode changed (3F 01)

2. For all open exchanges for the specified LUN on a designated target:

   * Following receipt of "Function Complete" to Abort Task Set

   * Following receipt of "Function Complete" to Clear Task Set

   * On receipt of CHECK CONDITION status with Sense Key=Unit Attention and ASC/ASCQ of "Command cleared by another initiator" (2F 00)

3. For a specific exchange on a specified LUN on a designated target:

   * On ULP_TOV timer expiration (no STATUS returned for a command within an application specified amount of time)

   * On recognition of any of the sequence errors described in *Sequence Errors* on page 302

Following receipt of the ACC in response to an ABTS, the SCSI initiator shall transmit RRQ. The RRQ may be transmitted as soon as R_A_TOV$_{SEQ\_QUAL}$ has elapsed.

If a proper BA_ACC, BA_RJT, LOGO, or PRLO is not received from the target within E_D_TOV, second level error recovery as described in *Second-Level Error Recovery* on page 314 is performed.

SCSI Target ABTS Behavior. When ABTS is received by a target, it aborts the designated exchange and returns one of the following responses:

- The target discards the ABTS and returns LOGO if the port issuing the ABTS is not currently logged in (no PLOGI).
- The target returns BA_RJT with Last_Sequence=1 if the received ABTS contains an RX_ID, other than x'FFFF', which is unknown to the target. The reason code shall be 'Logical Error' with a reason code explanation of 'Invalid OX_ID/RX_ID combination'.
- Otherwise, the target returns BA_ACC with Last_Sequence=1

After transmission of any of these responses, the target may reclaim any resources associated with the designated exchange after R_A_TOV$_{SEQ\_QUAL}$ has elapsed or a Reinstate Recover Qualifier (RRQ) extended link service request has been received.

When RRQ is received at the target, it responds according to the same rules stated above for the ABTS reply. If the exchange resources were not reclaimed on responding to the ABTS, they shall be reclaimed at the time the response to the RRQ is sent.

Targets shall qualify ABTS based only on S_ID concatenated with the OX_ID, not RX_ID, because the RX_ID is not guaranteed to be known by a SCSI initiator, even if one was assigned by the responder.

Second-Level Error Recovery. If a response is not received to the ABTS within E_D_TOV, the SCSI initiator shall:

- Send the ABTS a second time.
- If a response is not received to the second ABTS within E_D_TOV, the SCSI initiator shall explicitly logout (FC-PH N_Port Logout, LOGO) the target and may issue the selective reset LIP(AL_PD,AL_PS) to reset the target. All outstanding exchanges with that target are terminated at the SCSI initiator.

17.8 PLDA and Standards Compliance

Because the PLDA profile defines operations in a specific environment, not all of capabilities required by the Fibre Channel and *Fibre Channel Arbitrated Loop* standards are used. This may lead to a temptation to omit certain capabilities from a design. While a design that does this may operate in the PLDA environment, it may lead to interoperability problems outside of that environment.

Failure to implement all of the mandatory functions required by the applicable standards results in noncompliance to those standards, even if all of the function required by the profile are implemented. While some cost may be saved by this approach, failure to comply with the standards may mean that a design cannot claim compliance with the applicable standards and may be excluded from certain market opportunities.

17.8.1 Mandatory FC-PH Functions Not Required by PLDA

The following behaviors that are mandatory in the FC-PH standard do not appear to be required for compliance with the PLDA profile.

Class-1 and Class-2 Responses. The base FC-PH standard requires a port that receives a Class-1 or Class-2 frame and does not support those classes of service generate a port reject (P_RJT) in the same class of service as the received frame.

Class-1 and Class-2 are prohibited by the PLDA profile. This does not necessarily mean that a PLDA compliant port will never receive a Class-1 or Class-2 frame. If a PLDA compliant port does receive a Class-1 or Class-2 frame and fails to generate the correct response, it does not comply with FC-PH behavior.

NOP and RMC Basic Link Service Commands. The PLDA profile prohibits the use of the NOP and Remove Connection (RMC) basic link service commands. PLDA also prohibits a SCSI target from issuing the Abort Sequence (ABTS). None of these basic link service commands are optional in the FC-PH standard.

Maintenance of Status Blocks. The Fibre Channel FC-PH standard identifies a number of status block and defines the conditions for their maintenance. These status blocks are:

- Link Error Status Block for maintaining information pertaining to link errors
- Sequence Status Block that maintains the status of open sequences
- Exchange Status Block that maintains the status of open exchanges

The PLDA profile prohibits usage of the Read Sequence Status Block (RSS) and Read Exchange Status Block (RES) extended link services when communicating with a disk-type device. The FC-PH standard does not appear to make these optional link services. If they are not supported by a port, it may or may not result in a problem depending on the issuing port.

These extended link services may provide enhanced error recovery capabilities in some applications. The PLDA profile allows a SCSI initiator to invoke these link services when communicating with a non-disk type device.

17.8.2 Mandatory FC-AL Functions not Required by PLDA

The following items described by the *Fibre Channel Arbitrated Loop* standard do not appear to be required for PLDA compliant operation. Failure to implement these functions may result in noncompliance with that standard.

Support of MRK(tx). The *Fibre Channel Arbitrated Loop* standard defines certain types of the MRK(tx) ordered set. There is no requirement however, for any or all ports to process the MRK(tx). The standard does require that a port retransmit the MRK(tx) in the appropriate states (if a design implements a different LPSM, it must still retransmit the MRK(tx) at the appropriate times). The LPSM will retransmit MRK(tx) in certain states, however, there is nothing to prevent an open port from receiving the MRK(tx), processing it, and retransmitting it by requesting that MRK(tx) be transmitted.

Support of Open Replicate - OPN(fr) or OPN(yr). The PLDA profile prohibits use of either the broadcast open replicate OPN(fr) or selective open replicate OPN(yr) ordered sets.

The standard does require that a port retransmit the OPN(r). If a port did not retransmit the OPN(r), it may cause other ports on the loop that do support it and are operating outside of the PLDA profile to fail.

Open Half-Duplex - OPN(yy). The open half-duplex ordered set allows a half-duplex port to inhibit device data frame transmission by the open recipient. If a port does not support the OPN(yy), it may lead to frame loss if the open recipient has (or obtains) BB_Credit during the loop circuit. This is only a consideration when a half-duplex port opens a full-duplex port. Of course if a port transmits device data frames when it is not allowed to, is a protocol violation.

Half-duplex ports that grant a login BB_Credit value of zero may choose prevent the open recipient from sending frames (including link control frames) by not sending any R_RDYs after the OPN. This has the same effect as sending an OPN(yy) because frame transmission by the open recipient is prohibited. Transmitting no R_RDYs is contrary to the FC-AL-2 standard which requires that at least one R_RDY precedes the first frame of a loop circuit.

Loop Port Bypass/Enable (LPB/LPE). The Loop Port Bypass and Loop Port Enable primitive sequences provide mechanisms for error bypassing and problem determination. If a design does not implement these, it is possible that a broken node cannot be isolated from the loop (the loop is then broken). The recognition of these ordered sets can be discovered during the testing of the bypass circuit and only by a port implementing these ordered sets can these bypass circuits be tested.

Loop Initialization Positional Mapping (LIRP/LILP). Support of the positional mapping steps of loop initialization wass optional in the original *Fibre Channel Arbitrated Loop* standard (note that FC-AL-2 requires that these steps be implemented). In some implementations (such as a disk array, for example) positional mapping may not be required because the configuration is predetermined.

In other applications, positional mapping may provide the only available information about the position of AL_PA values around the loop. If positional mapping is not supported in this type of environment, the positions of those ports that do not support positional mapping is not known. This may result in reduced maintenance capabilities. Nonsupport of the positional mapping steps must be indicated during LISA sequence.

Fabric Login. Private loop ports do not attempt a fabric login (FLOGI). Therefore, they are not required to provide the functionality to send a FLOGI, or receive the ACC response.

OLD-PORT State. The *Fibre Channel Arbitrated Loop* standard states that a port which fails to receive LIP within three times the AL_TIME value enters the Old-Port state and behaves as a normal N_Port. Ports intended for loop only operations may choose not to implement this state. If that is the case, the port is not capable of operating outside of a loop environment and may fail to function in some cases allowed by the *Fibre Channel Arbitrated Loop* standard.

Normal N_Port operations (even point-to-point) differ somewhat from loop operations and require additional logic to support the appropriate differences. For example, in a nonloop environment, the alternate BB_Credit management model is not used and a port cannot use a login BB_Credit value of zero.

Full-Duplex Operation. Ports are not required to support full-duplex operation in an Arbitrated Loop environment. By not doing so, however, additional arbitration cycles are required and considerable performance may be lost. The decision to implement full-duplex or half-duplex is implementation specific and usually rests on the capability of the device behind the port.

LISM Origination. In order for the LISM sequence of loop initialization to function correctly, it is only necessary for one port on the loop to originate the LISM sequence. It is conceivable that targets (disk drives) could choose not to originate the LISM sequence provided that the initiator (or FL_Port if this is a public loop) does so. All ports must be capable of forwarding received LISM frames or else loop initialization will fail.

Transfer State. Transfer provides a mechanism for the arbitration winner to establish a series of loop circuits in succession without relinquishing control of the loop. Because a port is not required to use this capability, implementation of the Transfer state is optional if transfer is never used by that port. Ports that receive an OPN from a port in the Transfer state do not behave differently than would be the case in a normal OPN.

NOS/OLS/LR/LRR Origination/Recognition. It does not appear that these ordered sets are required if a port only operates in Class-3 on a private loop. They would be required if the port ever operates in a point-to-point or fabric environment. These ordered sets were not optional in the *Fibre Channel Arbitrated Loop* standard and failure to support them may result in noncompliance with the standard, however, in FC-AL-2, these ordered sets are no longer required (except in the Old-Port state and initialization process).

Transmission of R_RDY While in the Received Close State. If a port has received a CLS and is in the Received Close state, it does not have to transmit any R_RDYs in response to received frames. Because the other port is in the Transmitted Close or Transfer state, BB_Credit is not applicable at the other port.

Recognition of LIP(AL_PD,AL_PS). The selective reset form of the LIP causes the specified port to implement a vendor specific reset. This was intended to provide a way for a SCSI initiator (for example) to reset a SCSI target device. Ports that do not support this function perform normal LIP processing, but without the associated reset.

Performing Loop Initialization. Some applications cannot tolerate the interruption caused by loop initialization. One approach that has been taken to alleviate this interruption is to simply not perform loop initialization at all. In this case, all ports have hard addresses and default to using those addresses for their AL_PA values.

17.9 Loop Tenancy Management

The PLDA document does not address how SCSI operations are mapped to loop tenancies (unless the transfer function is used, each loop circuit corresponds to a loop tenancy). Any of the loop tenancy options for control-type commands in Figure 74 on page 213, write-type commands shown in Figure 76 on page 216, and read-type commands shown in Figure 81 on page 224 may be used. In addition, frames for more than one exchange may be sent during a single loop tenancy, complicating the picture further.

This lack of a specific definition of a relationship between command processing and loop tenancies leaves the door open to possible ambiguities. Assume, for example, that a SCSI initiator wins arbitration and sends a command to a target device. After the command is sent, does the initiator close the loop circuit or leave it open?

- If the initiator is communicating with a half-duplex port that needs to end the current loop circuit to change direction, then closing the loop circuit is appropriate.
- If the initiator is communicating with a full-duplex port and sends a CLS, it may prevent the full-duplex port from sending available frames. This is due to the initiator's inability to send R_RDY to replenish the BB_Credit at the target once a CLS has been sent.
- If the initiator is communicating with a port that supports the Dynamic Half Duplex ordered set, then it should send the DHD and wait for a response from the target.

The default behavior for the open originator is to send the initial CLS after it has completed its frame transmission. If the open recipient has additional frames to send after it has received the CLS and exhausted the available BB_Credit, it must establish a new loop circuit to send those frames. Again, DHD could be used to alleviate this problem.

17.10 PLDA Summary

The Private Loop Direct Attach profile provides a set of implementation guidelines for use when communicating with other ports conforming to that profile. For the designer, this is the starting point for developing the design specification because the PLDA document describes exactly which functions are required and which functions may not be used between compliant ports. In addition to the behaviors and functions required by the PLDA document, the designer also has to ensure that those functions that are mandatory in the associated standard are implemented if the design is to operate outside of the private loop environment.

17.11 Chapter Summary

What is PLDA?

- The Private Loop Direct Attach technical report is a 'profile' document
  - It defines a subset of available options selected from multiple standards
  - Targeted to a specific environment (e.g., Arbitrated Loop)
  - Provides a starting point for implementers
- Does not define new standards related behavior
  - That would be done by incorporation into the relevant standard
  - Does not relieve the design of behavior required by the associated standards

Why Create Profiles?

- Product design is affected by multiple standards
- Each standard may provide multiple options
- Interoperability problems may arise if -
  - One vendor uses an optional feature not support by a different vendor
  - Incompatible values chosen for variables such as timers
- Profile defines an environment which selects from relevant standards
  - Defines required, allowable, prohibited options and defines values where appropriate
  - Does not preclude use of options in other environments

Relevant Standards

- Designers of SCSI products intended for Arbitrated Loop environments faced with multiple standards
  - Fibre Channel Physical and Signaling
  - Fibre Channel Physical and Signaling-2
  - Fibre Channel Physical and Signaling-3
  - Fibre Channel Arbitrated Loop (FC-AL)
  - SCSI Architecture Model (SAM)
  - SCSI Primary Commands (SPC)
  - SCSI Block Commands (SBC)
  - SCSI Stream Commands (SSC)
- Each with a multiplicity of options and features

Simplifying the Choices

- Fibre Channel and SCSI standards are incredibly rich
  - Support a wide range of environments
- PLDA simplifies the choices by selecting from:
  - Fibre Channel FC-PH, FC-PH2, and FC-PH3 options and features
  - Arbitrated Loop options and features
  - SCSI-3 Fibre Channel Protocol (FCP)
  - SCSI-3 Architectural Model
  - SCSI Block Commands, SCSI Stream Commands, SCSI Media Changer Commands

Fibre Channel Feature Set

- PLDA requires Class-3 service only
  - No FC-2 Acknowledgment to frames
  - Improves utilization of loop bandwidth
  - Simplifies design of ports
  - Upper Level Protocol (SCSI) provides confirmation of operation via SCSI status
- Requires use of Continuously Increasing Relative Offset
  - Parameter field of frame header contains offset of data in frame
  - Provides enhanced error detection
  - Allows out-of-order data transmission on read-type commands

Fibre Channel Feature Set

- Node_Names and Port_Names must use a registered name format
  - Contain a field controlled by a registration authority (IEEE)
  - Facilitates identification of device changes such as disk drive replacement
  - Goal is to insure data integrity during reconfigurations
- Following loop initialization, initiator performs target discovery procedure
  - Command execution is suspended until initiator verifies target's identity

Arbitrated Loop Feature Set

- PLDA applies only to the Arbitrated Loop
- Take advantage of Arbitrated Loop's advantages
  - Low-cost connectivity
  - In order delivery of frames
- PLDA applies only to private NL_Ports
  - NL_Ports that do not Login with the Fabric
- Loop may contain both public and private NL_Ports
  - PLDA only describes behavior used when communicating with private NL_Ports
  - Public NL_Port behavior is described by the Fabric Loop Attach (FLA) document

Arbitrated Loop Feature Set

- Both half-duplex and full-duplex operations are supported
  - Both may coexist on the same loop
  - OPN ordered set specifies mode of operation
  - Full interoperability between half-duplex and full-duplex designs
  - Half-duplex designs can reduce complexity and cost
  - Full-duplex implementations may improve performance
- Use of Fairness and Transfer state is optional
  - Allows optimization of loop utilization in different applications
  - No special loop protocols are involved, therefore, no interoperability impact

Arbitrated Loop Feature Set

- Use of both zero and non-zero flow control buffer-to-buffer (BB_Credit) credit is allowed
  - Zero BB_Credit simplifies designs and buffer management
  - Non-zero BB_Credit offers improved performance
- Arbitrated Loop protocols insure interoperability of the two methods

SCSI FCP Feature Set

- Use a simplified subset of FCP information units
  - FCP_CMND (LUN, queue type, CDB)
  - FCP_XFER_RDY on write (data pointer offset, number of bytes requested by the target)
  - FCP_DATA corresponds to a SCSI burst
  - FCP_RSP contains Status and Sense data
- Simplifies port designs while providing familiar SCSI mode of operation
  - Simplifies migration from bus-oriented SCSI to Fibre Channel
  - Each Information Unit corresponds to a Fibre Channel Sequence
  - All Sequences except data are single-frame

SCSI Command Sets

- Command sets and SCSI features are defined
- Minimum command set defined for
  - Disk (Block) type devices
  - Stream (Tape) type devices
  - Media changer devices
- Optional commands/command options defined for
  - Disk (Block) type devices
  - Stream (Tape) type devices
- Auto Contingent Allegiance (ACA) discovered via Inquiry command
- Allows different products to implement to the same minimum set of commands

Clearing Effects of Actions

- Defines which objects (Login parameters, Tasks, mode pages, Unit Attention, ACA) are cleared as a result of various actions, such as
  - Power cycle
  - Reset LIP
  - Port Login/Logout (PLOGI/LOGO), Process Login/Logout (PRLI/PRLO/TPRLO)
  - SCSI Target Reset, Clear Task Set, Abort Task Set
- Removes ambiguity regarding effects of actions
- Clarifies handling of multi-ported devices

A. LPSM State Tables

The following sections contain information regarding processing associated with each of the LPSM states. The Fibre Channel Arbitrated Loop (FC-AL) standard contains detailed state transition tables which were used to derive the tables in this section. Where possible, the tables follow the FC-AL organization to facilitate cross-referencing to the standard.

Interpreting the State Tables

The state tables are processed from top to bottom, left to right. Received primitive signals and sequences normally take precedence over the L_Port controls with certain exceptions. The FC-AL standard does not identify those cases where L_Port controls override received conditions, but does identify REQ(bypass L_Port) and REQ(initialize) as two examples.

The items listed in the 'Entry Actions' row are performed upon entry to the state prior to recognizing any of the conditions listed in subsequent rows.

The column labeled 'Condition' contains inputs to the LPSM. The numbers in the left-most column are used for cross-references within the explanatory text associated with each state (e.g., see monitoring state, line 14).

The inputs are subject to the statements contained in the 'Qualifier' column. Where multiple qualifier entries are present for a single input condition, the qualifiers are processed from top to bottom, until the first valid condition is met. No further processing is performed once the first qualifying statement has been processed.

When a condition and qualifier (if present) have been met, the row is processed left to right. That is, the 'New CFW' action is taken, followed by the 'Variables', then the 'Transmit', and finally the 'Next State' column.

The column labeled 'New CFW' indicates the value that the current fill word assumes as a result of the input condition and qualifier. A '—' in this column indicates that the current fill word value is not affected by the condition. If the fill word is updated and transmitted as a result of the inputs, the update occurs first, and then the updated fill word is transmitted.

The column labeled 'Variables' identifies actions that affect the state of the control variables associated with the LPSM.

The 'Transmit' column specifies the word or words that are to be transmitted as a result of the inputs.

- An entry of 'FC-PH' indicates that normal FC-PH framing protocol, primitive signals, or primitive sequences are to be sent.

- A '—' indicates a transmitted word is not produced by the input condition. Either the condition has no effect on transmitted words, or causes an immediate state transition.

A '—' in the 'Next State' column indicates that the current state of the LPSM is unaffected by the input.

A value of '1' in the table is equivalent to the associated bit or condition being set, active, or true. A value of '0' in the table is equivalent to the associated bit or condition being reset, inactive, or false.

Repeat is a symbol that is defined to simplify the LPSM description (especially in the monitoring state). Repeat is 1, if Participate is 0 or Bypass is 1 or both. Repeat is 0, if Participate is 1 and Bypass is 0. When Repeat is 1, the LPSM repeats most incoming transmission words (except for normal fill word processing—updating the CFW appropriately) without responding to them. When Repeat is 0, the LPSM actively participates on the Loop. The combined values of the Participate and Bypass variables record the four L_Port operational modes:

1. Participating (Participate = 1, Bypass = 0) — the L_Port has an AL_PA and is enabled on the Loop. The L_Port may use the loop and respond to all requests directed to it. This is the normal operational mode in which most loop access occurs. In this mode, Repeat is 0.

2. Non-Participating (Participate = 0, Bypass = 0) — the L_Port does not have an AL_PA, but is enabled on the loop. The L_Port repeats transmission words (except for normal fill word processing—updating the CFW appropriately) and only responds to a limited number of requests such as loop initialization. If the L_Port wishes to obtain an AL_PA and participate in the loop, the L_Port may initiate loop initialization; it attempts to obtain an AL_PA if loop initialization occurs. In this mode, Repeat is 1.

3. Participating Bypassed (Participate = 1, Bypass = 1) — the L_Port has an AL_PA, but is bypassed (i.e., not enabled) from the loop. The L_Port activates its optional port Bypass circuit if one is present. The L_Port also repeats transmission words (except for normal fill word processing—updating the CFW appropriately) in case no Port Bypass circuit is present. The L_Port responds to an LPE(yx) directed to its AL_PA. In this mode, Repeat is 1.

4. Non-Participating Bypassed (Participate = 0, BYPASS = 1) — the L_Port does not have an AL_PA and is bypassed (i.e., not enabled) from the Loop. The L_Port activates its optional Port Bypass Circuit if one is present. The L_Port also repeats transmission words (except for normal fill word processing—updating the CFW appropriately) in case no Port Bypass circuit is present. The L_Port does not respond to any primitive signal or primitive sequences directed to a specific AL_PA. In this mode, Repeat is 1.

1.1 Symbols

Logic symbols are represented in state tables and diagrams as follows:

— the logical 'or' is represented as '|';
— the logical 'and' is represented as '&';
— the logical negation is represented as '~' (tilda);
— the 'less-than' is represented as '<';
— the 'greater-than' is represented as '>';
— comparisons are represented as '=' (equal) and '<>' (not equal);
— setting a variable is done using the colon equal operator, ':='; and,
— the concatenation symbol is represented as '||'.

M O N I T O R I N G   S T A T E

ENTRY ACTIONS

Access = n/c	Duplex = 0	DHD_Rcv = n/c
ARB_Pend = 0	Replicate = 0	Bypass = n/c
ARB_Won = 0	CFW = n/c	Err_Init = 0
ARBf_Sent = 0		Xmit_2_Idles = n/c
Available BB_Credit = n/c	Available EE_Credit = n/c	

INPUTS		OUTPUTS			
Condition	Qualifier	New CFW	Actions	Transmit	Next State
Errors, Elasticity Word, Valid Data Words					
1. Loss of Synchronization	<R_T_TOV	—		CFW	—
2. Loop Failure	Repeat=0	—		—	Initializing
	Repeat=1	—		LIP(F8)	—
3. Invalid Transmission Character or Word		—		CFW	—
4. Running Disparity Error at Ordered Set		—		CFW	—
5. Elasticity Word Required		—		CFW	—
6. Valid Data Word	FL_Port	—		Same word	—
	NL_Port & Replicate=0	—		Same word	—
	NL_Port & Replicate=1	—	Receive word	Same word	—
Valid Ordered Sets					
7. Start of Frame (SOF)	FL_Port	—		Same word	—
	NL_Port & Replicate=0	—		Same word	—
	NL_Port & Replicate=1	—	Receive word	Same word	—
8. End of Frame (EOF)	FL_Port	—		Same word	—
	NL_Port & Replicate=0	—		Same word	—
	NL_Port & Replicate=1	—	Receive word	Same word	—
9. IDLE	Repeat=0 & ARBf_Sent=0	IDLE	Access=1	CFW	—
	Repeat=0 & ARBf_Sent=1	ARB(FF)		CFW	—
	Repeat=1	IDLE		CFW	—
10. R_RDY		—		Same word	—
11. ARB(yx)	y<>x	—		CFW	—
12. ARB(FF)	Repeat=0 & (CFW<>IDLE or Xmit_2_Idles=0)	ARB(FF)		CFW	—
	Repeat=0 & (CFW=IDLE & Xmit_2_Idles=1)	—		CFW	—
	Repeat=1	ARB(FF)		CFW	—

Table 29. Monitoring State (Part 1 of 4)

INPUTS		OUTPUTS			
Condition	**Qualifier**	**New CFW**	**Actions**	**Transmit**	**Next State**
13. ARB(F0)	Repeat=0 & CFW=(IDLE or ARB(FF))	—	Xmit_2_Idles=1	CFW	—
	Repeat=1 & CFW=(IDLE or ARB(FF))	ARB(F0)		CFW	—
	CFW<>(IDLE or ARB(FF))	ARB(F0)	ARBf_Sent=0 Xmit_2_Idles=1	CFW	—
14. ARB(x)	Repeat=0 & x<>AL_PA & (CFW<>IDLE or Xmit_2_Idles=0)	ARB(x)	ARBf_Sent=1	CFW	—
	Repeat=0 & x<>AL_PA & CFW=IDLE & Xmit_2_Idles=1	—	ARBf_Sent=0	CFW	—
	Repeat=0 & x=AL_PA	IDLE	ARBf_Sent=0	CFW	—
	Repeat=1	ARB(x)		CFW	—
15. OPN(fr) or OPN(yr)	Participate=0	—		Same word	—
	Participate=1 & FL_Port	—		Same word	—
	Repeat=0 & Participate=1 & NL_Port & f=x'FF'	—	Replicate=1	Same word	—
	Repeat=1 & Participate=1 & NL_Port & f=x'FF' &	—		Same word	—
	Repeat=0 & Participate=1 & y=AL_PA	—	Replicate=1	Same word	—
	Repeat=1 & Participate=1 & y=AL_PA	—		Same word	—
	Participate=1 & all other OPN(r)	—		Same word	—
16. OPN(yx) or OPN(yy)	Repeat=0 & y=AL_PA	—		—	Opened
	Repeat=0 & y<>AL_PA	—		Same word	—
	Repeat=1	—		Same word	—
17. CLS	Replicate=0	—		Same word	—
	Replicate=1	—	Replicate=0	Same word	—
18. DHD		—		Same word	—
19. MRK(tx)	Repeat=0 & x=AL_PA	—		CFW	—
	Repeat=0 & x<>AL_PA	—		Same word	—
	Repeat=1	—		Same word	—

Table 29. Monitoring State (Part 2 of 4)

INPUTS		OUTPUTS			
Condition	Qualifier	New CFW	Actions	Transmit	Next State
Valid Primitive Sequences					
20. LIP	Bypass=0	—		—	Open-Init
	Bypass=1	—	Participate=0 ARBf_Sent=0	Same word	—
21. LPB(yx) or LPB(fx)	x=AL_PA & Repeat=0	—		CFW	—
	x=AL_PA & Repeat=1	—		Same word	—
	y<>AL_PA	—		Same word	—
	y=AL_PA	—	Replicate=0 Bypass=1 ARBf_Sent=0	Same word	—
	y=x'FF'	—	Replicate=0 Bypass=1 ARBf_Sent=0	Same word	—
22. LPE(yx) or LPE(fx)	x=AL_PA & Repeat=0	—		CFW	—
	x=AL_PA & Repeat=1	—		Same word	—
	y<>AL_PA	—		Same word	—
	y=AL_PA	—	Bypass=0	Same word	—
	y=x'FF'	—	Bypass=0	Same word	—
23. Other Ordered Set		—		Same word	—
L_Port Controls					
24. REQ(monitor)		—		—	—
25. REQ(arb own AL_PA)	Access=0	—		—	—
	Access=1 & Repeat=0	—		—	Arbitrating
	Access=1and Repeat=1	—		—	—
26. REQ(arbitrate FF)	Repeat=0 & CFW=IDLE	—	ARBf_Sent=1 (when 6 IDLES sent)	—	—
	Repeat=0 & CFW<>IDLE	—		—	—
	Repeat=1	—		—	—
27. REQ(open yx)		—		—	—
28. REQ(open yy)		—		—	—
29. REQ(open fr)		—		—	—
30. REQ(open yr)		—		—	—
31. REQ(close)		—		—	—
32. REQ(send DHD)		—		—	—
33. REQ(transfer)		—		—	—
34. REQ(old-port)		—		—	Old_Port

Table 29. Monitoring State (Part 3 of 4)

INPUTS		OUTPUTS			
Condition	Qualifier	New CFW	Actions	Transmit	Next State
35. REQ(participating)		—		—	Initializing
36. REQ(nonparticipate)		—	Participate=0 ARBf_Sent=0	12 LIPs[1] LIP(F7,F7)	—
37. REQ(mark as tx)	Repeat=0	—		MRK(tx)[2]	—
	Repeat=1	—		—	—
38. REQ(bypass L_Port)		—	Replicate=0 Bypass=1 ARBf_Sent=0	—	—
39. REQ(bypass L_Port y)		—		—	—
40. REQ(bypass all)		—		—	—
41. REQ(enable L_Port)		—	Bypass=0	—	—
42. REQ(enable L_Port y)		—		—	—
43. REQ(enable all)		—		—	—
44. REQ(initialize)		—		—	Initializing

1. The L_Port may optionally transmit 12 LIPs to notify all other L_Ports that it is yielding its AL_PA.
2. MRK(tx) is transmitted at the next appropriate fill word; i.e., normal FC-PH spacing rules require two fill words before and after an ordered set.

Table 29. Monitoring State (Part 4 of 4)

A R B I T R A T I N G   S T A T E

ENTRY ACTIONS

Access = n/c	Duplex = 0	DHD_Rcv = n/c
ARB_Pend = n/c	Replicate = n/c	Bypass = n/c
ARB_Won = 0	CFW = n/c	Err_Init = n/c
ARBf_Sent = n/c		Xmit_2_Idles = n/c
Available BB_Credit = n/c	Available EE_Credit = n/c	

INPUTS		OUTPUTS			
Condition	**Qualifier**	**New CFW**	**Actions**	**Transmit**	**Next State**
Errors, Elasticity Word, Valid Data Words					
1. Loss of Synchroniza-tion	<R_T_TOV	—		CFW	—
2. Loop Failure		—		—	Initializing
3. Invalid Transmission Character or Word		—		CFW	—
4. Running Disparity Er-ror at Ordered Set		—		CFW	—
5. Elasticity Word Re-quired		—		CFW	—
6. Valid Data Word	FL_Port	—		Same word	—
	NL_Port & Replicate=0	—		Same word	—
	NL_Port & Replicate=1	—	Receive word	Same word	—
Valid Ordered Sets					
7. Start of Frame (SOF)	FL_Port	—		Same word	—
	NL_Port & Replicate=0	—		Same word	—
	NL_Port & Replicate=1	—	Receive word	Same word	—
8. End of Frame (EOF)	FL_Port	—		Same word	—
	NL_Port & Replicate=0	—		Same word	—
	NL_Port & Replicate=1	—	Receive word	Same word	—
9. IDLE	Xmit_2_Idles=0	own ARB(x)	ARB_Pend=1	CFW	—
	Xmit_2_Idles=1	IDLE		CFW	—
10. R_RDY		—		Same word	—
11. ARB(yx)	y<>x	—		CFW	—

Table 30. Arbitrating State (Part 1 of 3)

INPUTS		OUTPUTS			
Condition	Qualifier	New CFW	Actions	Transmit	Next State
12. ARB(x) or ARB(F0) or ARB(FF)	x<AL_PA & (CFW<>IDLE or Xmit_2_Idles=0)	ARB(x)		CFW	—
	x=x'F0' & (CFW<>IDLE or Xmit_2_Idles=0)	own ARB(x)	ARB_Pend=1 Xmit_2_Idles=1	CFW	—
	(x>AL_PA or x=x'FF') & (CFW<>IDLE or Xmit_2_Idles=0)	own ARB(x)	ARB_Pend=1	CFW	—
	x=AL_PA & (CFW<>IDLE or Xmit_2_Idles=0)	—		—	Arbitration won
	CFW=IDLE & Xmit_2_Idles=1	—		CFW	—
13. OPN(fr) or OPN(yr)	FL_Port	—		Same word	—
	NL_Port & f='FF'	—	Replicate=1	Same word	—
	NL_Port & y=AL_PA	—	Replicate=1	Same word	—
	All other OPN(r)	—		Same word	—
14. OPN(yx) or OPN(yy)	y<>AL_PA	—		Same word	—
	y=AL_PA	—		—	Opened
15. CLS	Replicate=0	—		Same word	—
	Replicate=1	—	Replicate=0	Same word	—
16. DHD		—		Same word	—
17. MRK(tx)	x=AL_PA	—		CFW	—
	x<>AL_PA	—		Same word	—
Valid Primitive Sequences					
18. LIP		—		—	Open-Init
19. LPB(yx)	x=AL_PA	—		CFW	—
	y<>AL_PA	—		Same word	—
	y=AL_PA	—	Bypass=1	—	Monitoring
	f=x'FF'	—	Bypass=1	—	Monitoring
20. LPE(yx) or LPE(fx)		—		Same word	—
21. Other Ordered Set		—		Same word	—
L_Port Controls					
22. REQ(monitor)		—		—	—
23. REQ(arb own AL_PA)		—		—	—
24. REQ(open yx)		—		—	—
25. REQ(open yy)		—		—	—
26. REQ(open fr)		—		—	—
27. REQ(open yr)		—		—	—
28. REQ(close)		—		—	—
29. REQ(send DHD)		—		—	—

Table 30. Arbitrating State (Part 2 of 3)

INPUTS		OUTPUTS			
Condition	Qualifier	New CFW	Actions	Transmit	Next State
30. REQ(transfer)		—		—	—
31. REQ(old-port)		—		—	—
32. REQ(participating)		—		—	—
33. REQ(nonparticipate)		—		—	—
34. REQ(mark as tx)		—		MRK(tx)[1]	—
35. REQ(bypass L_Port)		—		—	—
36. REQ(bypass L_Port y)		—		—	—
37. REQ(bypass all)		—		—	—
38. REQ(enable L_Port)		—		—	—
39. REQ(enable L_Port y)		—		—	—
40. REQ(enable all)		—		—	—
41. REQ(initialize)		—		—	Initializing

1. MRK(tx) is transmitted at the next appropriate fill word; i.e., normal FC-PH spacing rules require two fill words before and after an ordered set.

Table 30. Arbitrating State (Part 3 of 3)

ARBITRATION WON STATE

ENTRY ACTIONS

Access = n/c	Duplex = n/c	DHD_Rcv = n/c
ARB_Pend = n/c	Replicate = n/c	Bypass = n/c
ARB_Won = n/c	CFW = n/c	Err_Init = n/c
ARBf_Sent =n/c		Xmit_2_Idles = n/c
Available BB_Credit = n/c	Available EE_Credit = n/c	

INPUTS		OUTPUTS			
Condition	Qualifier	New CFW	Actions	Transmit	Next State
Errors, Elasticity Word, Valid Data Words					
1. Loss of Sync	<R_T_TOV	—		n/a	n/a
2. Loop Failure		—		n/a	n/a
3. Invalid Transmission Character or Word		—		n/a	n/a
4. Running Disparity at Ordered Set		—		n/a	n/a
5. Elasticity Word Required		—		n/a	n/a
6. Valid Data Word		—		n/a	n/a
Valid Ordered Sets					
7. Start of Frame (SOF)		—		n/a	n/a
8. End of Frame (EOF)		—		n/a	n/a
9. IDLE		—		n/a	n/a
10. R_RDY		—		n/a	n/a
11. ARB(yx)		—		n/a	n/a
12. ARB(F0)		—		n/a	n/a
13. ARB(x)		—		n/a	n/a
14. OPN(fr) or OPN(yr)		—		n/a	n/a
15. OPN(yx) or OPN(yy)		—		n/a	n/a
16. CLS		—		n/a	n/a
17. DHD		—		n/a	n/a
18. MRK(tx)		—		n/a	n/a
Valid Primitive Sequences					
19. LIP		—		n/a	n/a
20. LPB(yx) or LPB(fx)		—		n/a	n/a
21. LPE(yx) or LPE(fx)		—		n/a	n/a
22. Other Ordered Set		—		n/a	n/a

Table 31. Arbitration Won State (Part 1 of 2)

INPUTS		OUTPUTS			
Condition	Qualifier	New CFW	Actions	Transmit	Next State
L_Port Controls					
23. REQ(monitor)		—		n/a	n/a
24. REQ(arb own AL_PA)		—		n/a	n/a
25. REQ(open yx)		—		OPN(yx)	Open
26. REQ(open yy)		—		OPN(yy)	Open
27. REQ(open fr)		—	Replicate=1	OPN(fr)	Open
28. REQ(open yr)		—	Replicate=1	OPN(yr)	Open
29. REQ(close)		—	y=own AL_PA	OPN(yy)[1]	Open[1]
30. REQ(send DHD)		—		n/a	n/a
31. REQ(transfer)		—		n/a	n/a
32. REQ(old-port)		—		n/a	n/a
33. REQ(participating)		—		n/a	n/a
34. REQ(nonparticipate)		—		n/a	n/a
35. REQ(mark as tx)		—		n/a	n/a
36. REQ(bypass L_Port)		—		n/a	n/a
37. REQ(bypass L_Port y)		—		n/a	n/a
38. REQ(bypass all)		—		n/a	n/a
39. REQ(enable L_Port)		—		n/a	n/a
40. REQ(enable L_Port y)		—		n/a	n/a
41. REQ(enable all)		—		n/a	n/a
42. REQ(initialize)		—		n/a	n/a

1. OPN(yy) is used to ensure correct processing of the Access Fairness protocol when a port wins arbitration, but no longer requires access to the loop.

Table 31. Arbitration Won State (Part 2 of 2)

OPEN STATE

ENTRY ACTIONS

Access = 0 if using fairness	Duplex = 1	DHD_Rcv = n/c
Access = 1 if not using fairness	Replicate = n/c	Bypass = n/c
ARB_Pend = 0	CFW = ARB(F0)	Err_Init = n/c
ARB_Won = 1		Xmit_2_Idles = n/c
ARBf_Sent = n/c		

Available BB_Credit = Login BB_Credit[1]
Available EE_Credit = Available EE_Credit of destination N*_Port

Transmit at least 6 CFWs (including at least one R_RDY)

INPUTS		OUTPUTS			
Condition	Qualifier	New CFW	Actions	Transmit	Next State
Errors, Elasticity Word, Valid Data Words					
1. Loss of Synchronization	<R_T_TOV	—		FC-PH	—
2. Loop Failure		—		—	Initializing
3. Invalid Transmission Character or Word		—		FC-PH	—
4. Running Disparity Error at Ordered Set		—		FC-PH	—
5. Elasticity Word Required		—		n/a	—
6. Valid Data Word		—		FC-PH	—
Valid Ordered Sets					
7. Start of Frame (SOF)		—		FC-PH	—
8. End of Frame (EOF)		—		FC-PH	—
9. IDLE		IDLE	Access=1	FC-PH	—
10. R_RDY	number of R_RDYs discarded < login BB_Credit used?	—		FC-PH	—
	number of R_RDYs discarded = login BB_Credit used?	—	Increment available BB_Credit + 1	FC-PH	—
11. ARB(yx)		—		FC-PH	—
12. ARB(F0)		IDLE	Xmit_2_Idles=1	FC-PH	—
13. ARB(x)		—		FC-PH	—
14. OPN(fr) or OPN(yr)		—		FC-PH	—
15. OPN(yx) or OPN(yy)		—		FC-PH	—
16. CLS		—		FC-PH	Received Close
17. DHD		—		FC-PH	—
18. MRK(tx)		—		FC-PH	—

Table 32. Open State (Part 1 of 3)

INPUTS		OUTPUTS			
Condition	**Qualifier**	**New CFW**	**Actions**	**Transmit**	**Next State**
Valid Primitive Sequences					
19. LIP		—		—	Open-Init
20. LPB(yx) or LPB(fx)	x=AL_PA	—		FC-PH	—
	y<>AL_PA	—		FC-PH	—
	y=AL_PA	—	Bypass=1	—	Monitoring
	f=x'FF'	—	Bypass=1	—	Monitoring
21. LPE(yx) or LPE(fx)		—		FC-PH	—
22. Other Ordered Set		—		FC-PH	—
L_Port Controls					
23. REQ(monitor)		—		—	—
24. REQ(arb own AL_PA)		—		—	—
25. REQ(open yx)		—		—	—
26. REQ(open yy)		—		—	—
27. REQ(open fr)	Replicate=0	—		—	—
	Replicate=1			OPN(fr)[2]	—
28. REQ(open yr)	Replicate=0	—		—	—
	Replicate=1			OPN(yr)[2]	—
29. REQ(close)		—		CLS[2]	Transmitted Close when CLS is sent
30. REQ(send DHD)	Duplex=0	—		—	—
	Duplex=1	—	Duplex=0	DHD[2]	—
31. REQ(transfer)	Access=0	—		CLS[2]	Transmitted Close when CLS is sent
	Access=1	—		CLS[2]	Transfer when CLS is sent
32. REQ(old-port)		—		—	—
33. REQ(participating)		—		—	—
34. REQ(nonparticipate)		—		—	—
35. REQ(mark as tx)		—		MRK(tx)[2]	—
36. REQ(bypass L_Port)		—		—	—
37. REQ(bypass L_Port y)		—		LPB(yx)[3]	—
38. REQ(bypass all)		—		LPB(fx)[3]	—

Table 32. Open State (Part 2 of 3)

INPUTS		OUTPUTS			
Condition	Qualifier	New CFW	Actions	Transmit	Next State
39. REQ(enable L_Port)		—		—	—
40. REQ(enable L_Port y)		—		LPE(yx)[3]	—
41. REQ(enable all)		—		LPE(fx)[3]	—
42. REQ(initialize)		—		—	Initializing

1. The available BB_Credit is set to the value remembered from N_Port login with the open recipient. The remembered login BB_Credit value is <0..n..Login_BB_Credit received>.
2. This word can only be transmitted at the next appropriate fill word interval and must be preceded and followed by a minimum of two fill words.
3. This word is transmitted at the next fill word.

Table 32. Open State (Part 3 of 3)

OPENED STATE

ENTRY ACTIONS

Access = n/c

ARB_Pend = n/c

ARB_Won = 0

ARBf_Sent = n/c

Duplex = 0 if OPN(yy)

Duplex = 1 if OPN(yx)

Replicate = 0

CFW = n/c

DHD_Rcv = 0

Bypass = n/c

Err_Init = n/c

Xmit_2_Idles = n/c

Available BB_Credit = Login BB_Credit[1]

Available EE_Credit = Available EE_Credit of destination N*_Port

INPUTS		OUTPUTS			
Condition	Qualifier	New CFW	Actions	Transmit	Next State
Errors, Elasticity Word, Valid Data Words					
1. Loss of Synchronization	<R_T_TOV	—		FC-PH	—
2. Loop Failure		—		—	Initializing
3. Invalid Transmission Character		—		FC-PH	—
4. Running Disparity Error at Ordered Set		—		FC-PH	—
5. Elasticity Word Required		—		n/a	—
6. Valid Data Word		—		FC-PH	—
Valid Ordered Sets					
7. Start of Frame (SOF)		—		FC-PH	—
8. End of Frame (EOF)		—		FC-PH	—
9. IDLE	ARB_Pend=0	IDLE	Access=1	FC-PH	—
	ARB_Pend=1 & Xmit_2_Idles=0	own ARB(x)		FC-PH	—
	ARB_Pend=1 & Xmit_2_Idles=1	IDLE		FC-PH	—
10. R_RDY	Number of R_RDYs discarded < login BB_Credit used?	—		FC-PH	—
	Number of R_RDYs discarded = login BB_Credit used?	—	Increment avail. BB_Credit + 1	FC-PH	—
11. ARB(yx)	y<>x	—		FC-PH	—
12. ARB(F0)	ARB_Pend=0 & (CFW<>Idle or Xmit_2_Idles=0)	ARB(F0)	Xmit_2_Idles=1	FC-PH	—
	ARB_Pend=1 & (CFW<>Idle or Xmit_2_Idles=0)	own ARB(x)	Xmit_2_Idles=1	FC-PH	—
	CFW=Idle & Xmit_2_Idles=1	—		FC-PH	—

Table 33. Opened State (Part 1 of 3)

INPUTS		OUTPUTS			
Condition	Qualifier	New CFW	Actions	Transmit	Next State
13. ARB(x)	ARB_Pend=0 & x<>AL_PA & (CFW<>Idle or Xmit_2_Idles=0)	ARB(x)		FC-PH	—
	ARB_Pend=0 & x=AL_PA & (CFW<>Idle or Xmit_2_Idles=0)	IDLE		FC-PH	—
	ARB_Pend=1 & x>=AL_PA & (CFW<>Idle or Xmit_2_Idles=0)	own ARB(x)		FC-PH	—
	ARB_Pend=1 & x<AL_PA & (CFW<>Idle or Xmit_2_Idles=0)	ARB(x)		FC-PH	—
	CFW=Idle & Xmit_2_Idles=1	—		FC-PH	—
14. OPN(fr) or OPN(yr)		—		FC-PH	—
15. OPN(yx) or OPN(yy)		—		FC-PH	—
16. CLS		—		FC-PH	Received Close
17. DHD		—	DHD_Rcv=1	FC-PH	—
18. MRK(tx)		—		FC-PH	—
Valid Primitive Sequences					
19. LIP		—		—	Open-Init
20. LPB(yx) or LPB(fx)	y<>AL_PA	—		FC-PH	—
	y=AL_PA	—	Bypass=1	—	Monitoring
	f=x'FF'	—	Bypass=1	—	Monitoring
21. LPE(yx) or LPE(fx)		—		FC-PH	—
22. Other Ordered Set		—		FC-PH	—
L_Port Controls					
23. REQ(monitor)		—		—	—
24. REQ(arb own AL_PA)		—		—	—
25. REQ(open yx)		—		—	—
26. REQ(open yy)		—		—	—
27. REQ(open fr)		—		—	—
28. REQ(open yr)		—		—	—
29. REQ(close)		—		CLS[2]	Transmitted Close (when CLS sent)
30. REQ(send DHD)		—		—	—
31. REQ(transfer)		—		—	—

Table 33. Opened State (Part 2 of 3)

INPUTS		OUTPUTS			
Condition	Qualifier	New CFW	Actions	Transmit	Next State
32. REQ(old-port)		—		—	—
33. REQ(participating)		—		—	—
34. REQ(nonparticipate)		—		—	—
35. REQ(mark as tx)		—		MRK(tx)[2]	—
36. REQ(bypass L_Port)		—	Bypass=1	—	Monitoring
37. REQ(bypass L_Port y)		—		—	—
38. REQ(bypass all)		—		—	—
39. REQ(enable L_Port)		—		—	—
40. REQ(enable L_Port y)		—		—	—
41. REQ(enable all)		—		—	—
42. REQ(initialize)		—		—	Initializing

1. The available BB_Credit is set to the value remembered from N_Port login with the open recipient. The remembered Login BB_Credit value is <0..n..Login_BB_Credit received>.
2. This word can only be transmitted at the next appropriate fill word interval and must be preceded and followed by a minimum of two fill words.

Table 33. Opened State (Part 3 of 3)

ENTRY ACTIONS

Access = n/c	Duplex = 0	DHD_Rcv = n/c
ARB_Pend = n/c	Replicate = n/c	Bypass = n/c
ARB_Won = n/c	CFW = n/c	Err_Init = n/c
ARBf_Sent = n/c		Xmit_2_Idles = n/c

Available BB_Credit = 0
Available EE_Credit: continue to process for closed N*_Port until CLS received. Then save the available EE_Credit for that port.

INPUTS		OUTPUTS			
Condition	**Qualifier**	**New CFW**	**Actions**	**Transmit**	**Next State**
Errors, Elasticity Word, Valid Data Words					
1. Loss of Synchronization	<R_T_TOV	—		CFW	—
2. Loop Failure		—		—	Initializing
3. Invalid Transmission Word		—		CFW	—
4. Running Disparity Error at Ordered Set		—		CFW	—
5. Elasticity Word Required		—		n/a	—
6. Valid Data Word		—		CFW	—
Valid Ordered Sets					
7. Start of Frame (SOF)		—		CFW	—
8. End of Frame (EOF)		—		CFW	—
9. IDLE	ARB_Pend=0	IDLE	Access=1	CFW	—
	ARB_Pend=1 & Xmit_2_Idles=0	own ARB(x)		CFW	—
	ARB_Pend=1 & Xmit_2_Idles=1	IDLE		CFW	—
10. R_RDY		—		CFW	—
11. ARB(yx)	y<>x	—		CFW	—
12. ARB(F0)	ARB_Won=1 & (CFW<>IDLE or Xmit_2_Idles=0)	IDLE	Xmit_2_Idles=1	CFW	—
	ARB_Won=0 & ARB_Pend=0 & (CFW<>IDLE or Xmit_2_Idles=0)	ARB(F0)	Xmit_2_Idles=1	CFW	—
	ARB_Won=0 & ARB_Pend=1 & (CFW<>IDLE or Xmit_2_Idles=0)	own ARB(x)	Xmit_2_Idles=1	CFW	—
	CFW=IDLE & Xmit_2_Idles=1	—		CFW	—

Table 34. Transmitted Close State (Part 1 of 3)

INPUTS		OUTPUTS			
Condition	Qualifier	New CFW	Actions	Transmit	Next State
13. ARB(x)	ARB_Won=1	—		CFW	—
	ARB_Won=0 & ARB_Pend=0 & x<>AL_PA & (CFW<>IDLE or Xmit_2_Idles=0)	ARB(x)		CFW	
	ARB_Won=0 & ARB_Pend=0 & x=AL_PA & (CFW<>IDLE or Xmit_2_Idles=0)	IDLE		CFW	—
	ARB_Won=0 & ARB_Pend=1 & x>=AL_PA & (CFW<>IDLE or Xmit_2_Idles=0)	own ARB(x)		CFW	—
	ARB_Won=0 & ARB_Pend=1 & x<AL_PA & (CFW<>IDLE or Xmit_2_Idles=0)	ARB(x)		CFW	—
	ARB_Won=0 & CFW=IDLE & Xmit_2_Idles=1	—		CFW	
14. OPN(fr) or OPN(yr)		—		CFW	—
15. OPN(yx) or OPN(yy)		—		CFW	—
16. CLS	ARB_Won=1	—		CFW	Monitoring[1]
	ARB_Won=0 & ARB_Pend=0	—		CFW	Monitoring[1]
	ARB_Won=0 & ARB_Pend=1	—		CFW	Arbitrating
17. DHD		—		CFW	—
18. MRK(tx)	x=AL_PA	—		CFW	—
	x<>AL_PA	—		Same word	—
Valid Primitive Sequences					
19. LIP		—		—	Open-Init
20. LPB(yx) or LPB(fx)	x=AL_PA	—		CFW	—
	y<>AL_PA	—		CFW	—
	y=AL_PA	—	Bypass=1	—	Monitoring
	f=x'FF'	—	Bypass=1	—	Monitoring
21. LPE(yx) or LPE(fx)		—		CFW	—
22. Other Ordered Set		—		CFW	—
L_Port Controls					
23. REQ(monitor)		—		—	Monitoring
24. REQ(arb own AL_PA)		—		—	—
25. REQ(open yx)		—		—	—

Table 34. Transmitted Close State (Part 2 of 3)

INPUTS		OUTPUTS			
Condition	Qualifier	New CFW	Actions	Transmit	Next State
26. REQ(open yy)		—		—	—
27. REQ(open fr)		—		—	—
28. REQ(open yr)		—		—	—
29. REQ(close)		—		—	—
30. REQ(send DHD)		—		—	—
31. REQ(transfer)		—		—	—
32. REQ(old-port)		—		—	—
33. REQ(participating)		—		—	—
34. REQ(nonparticipate)		—		—	—
35. REQ(mark as tx)		—		MRK(tx)[2]	—
36. REQ(bypass L_Port)		—		—	—
37. REQ(bypass L_Port y)		—		—	—
38. REQ(bypass all)		—		—	—
39. REQ(enable L_Port)		—		—	—
40. REQ(enable L_Port y)		—		—	—
41. REQ(enable all)		—		—	—
42. REQ(initialize)		—		—	Initializing

1. The appropriate state is entered when at least login BB_Credit is available.
2. This word can only be transmitted at the next appropriate fill word interval.

Table 34. Transmitted Close State (Part 3 of 3)

ENTRY ACTIONS

Access = n/c	Duplex = n/c	DHD_Rcv = n/c
ARB_Pend = n/c	Replicate = n/c	Bypass = n/c
ARB_Won = n/c	CFW = n/c	Err_Init = n/c
ARBf_Sent = n/c		Xmit_2_Idles = n/c
Available BB_Credit = 0		

Available EE_Credit: continue to process until CLS sent. Then save available EE_Credit for that port.

INPUTS		OUTPUTS			
Condition	**Qualifier**	**New CFW**	**Actions**	**Transmit**	**Next State**
Errors, Elasticity Word, Valid Data Words					
1. Loss of Synchronization	<R_T_TOV	—		FC-PH	—
2. Loop Failure		—		—	Initializing
3. Invalid Transmission Word		—		FC-PH	—
4. Running Disparity Error at Ordered Set		—		FC-PH	—
5. Elasticity Word Required		—		n/a	—
6. Valid Data Word		—		FC-PH	—
Valid Ordered Sets					
7. Start of Frame (SOF)		—		FC-PH	—
8. End of Frame (EOF)		—		FC-PH	—
9. IDLE	ARB_Pend=0	IDLE	Access=1	FC-PH	—
	ARB_Pend=1 & Xmit_2_Idles=0	own ARB(x)		FC-PH	—
	ARB_Pend=1 & Xmit_2_Idles=1	IDLE		FC-PH	—
10. R_RDY		—		FC-PH	—
11. ARB(yx)	y<>x	—		FC-PH	—
12. ARB(F0)	ARB_Won=1 & (CFW<>IDLE or Xmit_2_Idles=0)	IDLE	Xmit_2_Idles=1	FC-PH	—
	ARB_Won=0 & ARB_Pend=0 & (CFW<>IDLE or Xmit_2_Idles=0)	ARB(F0)	Xmit_2_Idles=1	FC-PH	—
	ARB_Won=0 & ARB_Pend=1 & (CFW<>IDLE or Xmit_2_Idles=0)	own ARB(x)	Xmit_2_Idles=1	FC-PH	—
	CFW=IDLE & Xmit_2_Idles=1	—		FC-PH	—

Table 35. Received Close State (Part 1 of 3)

INPUTS		OUTPUTS			
Condition	Qualifier	New CFW	Actions	Transmit	Next State
13. ARB(x)	ARB_Won=1	—		FC-PH	—
	ARB_Won=0 & ARB_Pend=0 & x<>AL_PA & (CFW<>IDLE or Xmit_2_Idles=0)	ARB(x)		FC-PH	—
	ARB_Won=0 & ARB_Pend=0 & x=AL_PA & (CFW<>IDLE or Xmit_2_Idles=0)	IDLE		FC-PH	—
	ARB_Won=0 & ARB_Pend=1 & x>=AL_PA & (CFW<>IDLE or Xmit_2_Idles=0)	own ARB(x)		FC-PH	—
	ARB_Won=0 & ARB_Pend=1 & x<AL_PA & (CFW<>IDLE or Xmit_2_Idles=0)	ARB(x)		FC-PH	—
	ARB_Won=0 & CFW=IDLE & Xmit_2_Idles=1	—		FC-PH	—
14. OPN(fr) or OPN(yr)		—		FC-PH	—
15. OPN(yx) or OPN(yy)		—		FC-PH	—
16. CLS		—		FC-PH	—
17. DHD		—		FC-PH	—
18. MRK(tx)		—		FC-PH	—
Valid Primitive Sequences					
19. LIP		—		—	Open-Init
20. LPB(yx) or LPB(fx)	x=AL_PA	—		FC-PH	—
	y<>AL_PA	—		FC-PH	—
	y=AL_PA	—	Bypass=1	—	Monitoring
	f=x'FF'	—	Bypass=1	—	Monitoring
21. LPE(yx) or LPE(fx)		—		FC-PH	—
22. Other Ordered Set		—		FC-PH	—
L_Port Controls					
23. REQ(monitor)		—		—	—
24. REQ(arb own AL_PA)		—		—	—
25. REQ(open yx)		—		—	—
26. REQ(open yy)		—		—	—
27. REQ(open fr)		—		—	—
28. REQ(open yr)		—		—	—

Table 35. Received Close State (Part 2 of 3)

Chapter

INPUTS		OUTPUTS			
Condition	Qualifier	New CFW	Actions	Transmit	Next State
29. REQ(close)	ARB_Pend=0	—		CLS[1]	Monitoring when CLS sent
	ARB_Pend=1	—		CLS[1]	Arbitrating when CLS sent
30. REQ(send DHD)		—		—	—
31. REQ(transfer)		—		—	—
32. REQ(old-port)		—		—	—
33. REQ(participating)		—		—	—
34. REQ(nonparticipate)		—		—	—
35. REQ(mark as tx)		—		MRK(tx) at next appr. Fill Word[2]	—
36. REQ(bypass L_Port)		—	Bypass=1	—	Monitoring
37. REQ(bypass L_Port y)		—		—	—
38. REQ(bypass all)		—		—	—
39. REQ(enable L_Port)		—		—	—
40. REQ(enable L_Port y)		—		—	—
41. REQ(enable all)		—		—	—
42. REQ(initialize)		—		—	Initializing

1. When login BB_Credit buffers are available, then CLS can be transmitted at the next appropriate fill word interval and must be preceded and followed by a minimum of two fill words.
2. This word can only be transmitted at the next appropriate fill word interval and must be preceded and followed by a minimum of two fill words.

Table 35. Received Close State (Part 3 of 3)

TRANSFER STATE

ENTRY ACTIONS

Access = n/c   Duplex = 0   DHD_Rcv = n/c
ARB_Pend = n/c   Replicate = n/c   Bypass = n/c
ARB_Won = n/c   CFW = n/c   Err_Init = n/c
ARBf_Sent = n/c   Xmit_2_Idles = n/c
Available BB_Credit = 0
Available EE_Credit: continue to process for closed N*_Port until CLS received. Then save the available EE_Credit for that port.

INPUTS		OUTPUTS			
Condition	Qualifier	New CFW	Actions	Transmit	Next State
Errors, Elasticity Word, Valid Data Words					
1. Loss of Synchronization	<R_T_TOV	—		CFW	—
2. Loop Failure		—		—	Initializing
3. Invalid Transmission Word		—		CFW	—
4. Running Disparity Error at Ordered Set		—		CFW	—
5. Elasticity Word Required		—		n/a	—
6. Valid Data Word		—		CFW	—
Valid Ordered Sets					
7. Start of Frame (SOF)		—		CFW	—
8. End of Frame (EOF)		—		CFW	—
9. IDLE		IDLE	Access=1	CFW	—
10. R_RDY		—		CFW	—
11. ARB(yx)		—		CFW	—
12. ARB(F0)		IDLE	Xmit_2_Idles=1	CFW	—
13. ARB(x)		—		CFW	—
14. OPN(fr) or OPN(yr)		—		CFW	—
15. OPN(yx) or OPN(yy)		—		CFW	—
16. CLS		—		—	Open or Monitoring per L_Port Controls
17. MRK(tx)	x=AL_PA	—		CFW	—
	x<>AL_PA			Same word	

Table 36. Transfer State (Part 1 of 2)

INPUTS		OUTPUTS			
Condition	Qualifier	New CFW	Actions	Transmit	Next State
Valid Primitive Sequences					
18. LIP		—		—	Open-Init
19. LPB(yx) or LPB(fx)	x=AL_PA	—		CFW	—
	y<>AL_PA	—		CFW	—
	y=AL_PA	—	Bypass=1	—	Monitoring
	f=x'FF'	—	Bypass=1	—	Monitoring
20. LPE(yx) or LPE(fx)		—		CFW	—
21. Other Ordered Set		—		CFW	—
L_Port Controls					
22. REQ(monitor)	When CLS rcvd	—		CFW	Monitoring[1]
23. REQ(arb own AL_PA)		—		—	—
24. REQ(open yx)	When CLS rcvd	—		OPN(yx)	Open[1]
25. REQ(open yy)	When CLS rcvd	—		OPN(yy)	Open[1]
26. REQ(open fr)	When CLS rcvd	—	Replicate=1	OPN(fr)	Open[1]
27. REQ(open yr)	When CLS rcvd	—	Replicate=1	OPN(yr)	Open[1]
28. REQ(close)		—		—	—
29. REQ(transfer)				—	—
30. REQ(old-port)		—		—	—
31. REQ(participating)		—		—	—
32. REQ(nonparticipate)		—		—	—
33. REQ(mark as tx)		—		MRK(tx)[2]	—
34. REQ(bypass L_Port)		—	Bypass=1	—	Monitoring
35. REQ(bypass L_Port y)		—		—	—
36. REQ(bypass all)		—		—	—
37. REQ(enable L_Port)		—		—	—
38. REQ(enable L_Port y)		—		—	—
39. REQ(enable all)		—		—	—
40. REQ(initialize)		—		—	Initializing

1. These transitions can only be honored when CLS is received and when login BB_Credit buffers are available.
2. This word can only be transmitted at the next appropriate fill word interval and must be preceded and followed by a minimum of two fill words.

Table 36. Transfer State (Part 2 of 2)

INITIALIZING STATE

ENTRY ACTIONS

Access = 1	Duplex = 0	DHD_Rcv = 0
ARB_Pend = 0	Replicate = 0	Bypass = 0
ARB_Won = 0	CFW = IDLE	Err_Init = n/c
ARBf_Sent = 0		Xmit_2_Idles = 0
Available BB_Credit = 0	Available EE_Credit = n/c	Transmit LIPs

INPUTS		OUTPUTS			
Condition	Qualifier	New CFW	Actions	Transmit	Next State
Errors, Elasticity Word, Valid Data Words					
1. Loss of Synchronization	<R_T_TOV	—		LIP	—
2. Loop Failure		—		LIP	—
3. Invalid Transmission Word		—		LIP	—
4. Running Disparity Error at Ordered Set		—		LIP	—
5. Elasticity Word Required		—		n/a	—
6. Valid Data Word		—		LIP	—
Valid Ordered Sets					
7. Start of Frame (SOF)		—		LIP	—
8. End of Frame (EOF)		—		LIP	—
9. IDLE		—		LIP	—
10. R_RDY		—		LIP	—
11. ARB(yx)		—		LIP	—
12. ARB(F0)		—		LIP	—
13. ARB(x)		—		LIP	—
14. OPN(fr) or OPN(yr)		—		LIP	—
15. OPN(yx) or OPN(yy)		—		LIP	—
16. CLS		—		LIP	—
17. DHD		—		LIP	—
18. MRK(tx)		—		LIP	—
Valid Primitive Sequences					
19. NOS		—		LIP	—
20. OLS		—		LIP	—
21. LR		—		LIP	—
22. LRR		—		LIP	—
23. LIP		—		—	Open-Init

Table 37. Initializing State (Part 1 of 2)

INPUTS		OUTPUTS			
Condition	Qualifier	New CFW	Actions	Transmit	Next State
24. LPB(yx) of LPB(fx)	x=AL_PA	—		LIP	—
	y<>AL_PA	—		Same word	—
	y=AL_PA	—	Bypass=1	—	Monitoring
	f=x'FF'	—	Bypass=1	—	Monitoring
25. LPE(yx) or LPE(fx)	x=AL_PA	—		LIP	—
	x<>AL_PA	—		Same word	—
26. Other Ordered Set		—		LIP	—
L_Port Controls					
27. REQ(monitor)		—		—	—
28. REQ(arb own AL_PA)		—		—	—
29. REQ(open yx)		—		—	—
30. REQ(open yy)		—		—	—
31. REQ(open fr)		—		—	—
32. REQ(open yr)		—		—	—
33. REQ(close)		—		—	—
34. REQ(send DHD)		—		—	—
35. REQ(transfer)		—		—	—
36. REQ(old-port)		—		—	Old-Port
37. REQ(participating)		—		—	—
38. REQ(nonparticipate)		—		—	—
39. REQ(mark as tx)		—		—	—
40. REQ(bypass L_Port)		—	Bypass=1	—	Monitoring
41. REQ(bypass L_Port y)		—		LPB(yx)	—
42. REQ(bypass all)		—		LPB(fx)	—
43. REQ(enable L_Port)		—		—	—
44. REQ(enable L_Port y)		—		LPE(yx)	—
45. REQ(enable all)		—		LPE(fx)	—
46. REQ(initialize)		—		—	Initializing

Table 37. Initializing State (Part 2 of 2)

OPEN-INIT STATE

ENTRY ACTIONS

Access = 1

ARB_Pend = 0

ARB_Won = 0

ARBf_Sent = 0

Available BB_Credit = n/c

Alternate_BB_Credit = 1

Duplex = 0

Replicate = 0

CFW = IDLE

Available EE_Credit = n/c

DHD_Rcv = 0

Bypass = 0

Err_Init = 0 (first time)

Err_Init = n/c (on re-entry)

Xmit_2_Idles = 0

Transmit at least 12 LIPs; ignore received LIPs for AL_Time or until ARB(F0) or CLS is received.

OPERATIONAL CONDITIONS

If LIP(F8) and Err_Init=0, Err_Init=1, continue with LISM process

If LIP(F8) and Err_Init=1, transmit LIP(F8) for LP_TOV or until LIP(F7) recognized.

If LP_TOV timeout, go to Initializing state and transmit LIP(F7).

INPUTS		OUTPUTS			
Condition	Qualifier	New CFW	Actions	Transmit	Next State
Errors, Elasticity Word, Valid Data Words					
1. Loss of Synchronization	<R_T_TOV	—		FC-PH	—
2. Loop Failure		—		—	Initializing
3. Invalid Transmission Word		—		FC-PH	—
4. Running Disparity Error at Ordered Set		—		FC-PH	—
5. Elasticity Word Required		—		n/a	—
6. Valid Data Word		—		FC-PH	—
Valid Ordered Sets					
7. Start of Frame (SOF)		—		(see text)	—
8. End of Frame (EOF)		—		(see text)	—
9. IDLE		—		FC-PH	—
10. R_RDY		—		FC-PH	—
11. ARB(yx)		—		FC-PH	—
12. ARB(F0)	Loop Master	—		FC-PH	—
	Other L_Ports	—		ARB(F0)[1]	—
13. ARB(x)		—		FC-PH	—
14. OPN(fr) or OPN(yr)		—		FC-PH	—
15. OPN(yx) or OPN(yy)		—		FC-PH	—

Table 38. Open-Init State (Part 1 of 3)

INPUTS		OUTPUTS			
Condition	Qualifier	New CFW	Actions	Transmit	Next State
16. CLS	Before LISA	—		—	Initializing
	After LISA & Loop Master	—		CFW	Monitoring
	After LISA & other L_Ports	—		CLS[1,2]	Monitoring (when CLS sent)
17. DHD		—		FC-PH	—
18. MRK(tx)		—		FC-PH	—
Valid Primitive Sequences					
19. NOS		—		—	—
20. OLS		—		—	—
21. LR		—		—	—
22. LRR		—		—	—
23. LIP		—		—	Re-enter Open-Init
24. LPB(yx) or LPB(fx)	x=AL_PA	—		FC-PH	—
	y<>AL_PA	—		Same word	
	y=AL_PA	—	Bypass=1	—	Monitoring
	f=x'FF'	—	Bypass=1	—	Monitoring
25. LPE(yx) or LPE(fx)	x=AL_PA	—		FC-PH	—
	x<>AL_PA	—		Same word	—
26. Other Ordered Set		—		FC-PH	—
L_Port Controls					
27. REQ(monitor)		—		—	—
28. REQ(arb own AL_PA)		—		—	—
29. REQ(open yx)		—		—	—
30. REQ(open yy)		—		—	—
31. REQ(open fr)		—		—	—
32. REQ(open yr)		—		—	—
33. REQ(close)	Non-master	—		—	—
	Loop master	—		CLS[1]	—
34. REQ(send DHD)		—		—	—
35. REQ(transfer)		—		—	—
36. REQ(old-port)		—		—	—
37. REQ(participating)		—		—	—
38. REQ(nonparticipate)		—		—	Monitoring
39. REQ(mark as tx)		—		—	—
40. REQ(bypass L_Port)		—	Bypass=1	—	Monitoring

Table 38. Open-Init State (Part 2 of 3)

INPUTS		OUTPUTS			
Condition	Qualifier	New CFW	Actions	Transmit	Next State
41. REQ(bypass L_Port y)		—		LPB(yx)	—
42. REQ(bypass all)		—		LPB(fx)	—
43. REQ(enable L_Port)		—		—	—
44. REQ(enable L_Port y)		—		LPE(yx)	—
45. REQ(enable all)		—		LPE(fx)	—
46. REQ(initialize)		—		—	Initializing

1. This word should only be sent when receive buffers are available.
2. Can only be transmitted at the next appropriate fill word. Must be preceded and followed by a minimum of two fill words.

Table 38. Open-Init State (Part 3 of 3)

OLD-PORT STATE

ENTRY ACTIONS

Access = n/c	Duplex = n/c	DHD_Rcv = n/c
ARB_Pend = n/c	Replicate = n/c	Bypass = n/c
ARB_Won = n/c	CFW = n/c	Err_Init = n/c
ARBf_Sent = n/c		Xmit_2_Idles = n/c
Available BB_Credit = 1	Available EE_Credit = n/c	
Alternate_BB_Credit = 0		

INPUTS		OUTPUTS			
Condition	Qualifier	New CFW	Actions	Transmit	Next State
Errors, Elasticity Word, Valid Data Words					
1. Loss of Synchronization	<R_T_TOV	—		FC-PH	—
2. Loop Failure		—		—	Initializing
3. Invalid Transmission Char.		—		FC-PH	—
4. Running Disparity Error at Ordered Set		—		FC-PH	—
5. Elasticity Word Required		—		n/a	—
6. Valid Data Word		—		FC-PH	—
Valid Ordered Sets					
7. Start of Frame (SOF)		—		FC-PH	—
8. End of Frame (EOF)		—		FC-PH	—
9. IDLE		—		FC-PH	—
10. R_RDY		—		FC-PH	—
11. ARB(yx)		—		FC-PH	—
12. ARB(F0)		—		FC-PH	—
13. ARB(x)		—		FC-PH	—
14. OPN(fr) or OPN(yr)		—		FC-PH	—
15. OPN(yx) or OPN(yy)		—		FC-PH	—
16. CLS		—		FC-PH	—
17. DHD		—		FC-PH	—
18. MRK(tx)		—		FC-PH	—
Valid Primitive Sequences					
19. NOS		—		OLS	—
20. OLS		—		LR	—
21. LR		—		LRR	—
22. LRR		—		IDLE	—

Table 39. Old-Port State (Part 1 of 2)

INPUTS		OUTPUTS			
Condition	Qualifier	New CFW	Actions	Transmit	Next State
23. LIP		—		—	Open-Init
24. LPB(yx) or LPB(fx)		—		FC-PH	—
25. LPE(yx) or LPE(fx)		—		FC-PH	—
26. Other Ordered Set		—		FC-PH	—
L_Port Controls					
27. REQ(monitor)		—		—	
28. REQ(arb own AL_PA)		—		—	—
29. REQ(open yx)		—		—	—
30. REQ(open yy)		—		—	—
31. REQ(open fr)		—		—	—
32. REQ(open yr)		—		—	—
33. REQ(close)		—		—	—
34. REQ(send DHD)		—		—	—
35. REQ(transfer)		—		—	—
36. REQ(old-port)		—		—	—
37. REQ(participating)		—		—	—
38. REQ(nonparticipate)		—		—	—
39. REQ(mark as tx)		—		—	—
40. REQ(bypass L_Port)		—		—	—
41. REQ(bypass L_Port y)		—		—	—
42. REQ(bypass all)		—		—	—
43. REQ(enable L_Port)		—		—	—
44. REQ(enable L_Port y)		—		—	—
45. REQ(enable all)		—		—	—
46. REQ(initialize)		—		—	Initializing

Table 39. Old-Port State (Part 2 of 2)

B. SCSI FCP Command Traces

This section contains annotated traces of SCSI FCP commands taken from an operational fibre channel arbitrated loop environment. These traces illustrate how all of the protocols and constructs discussed flow together to perform a complete command.

Before examining the traces, a few words about trace analysis may be helpful. Because every fibre channel port has a separate transmit and receive fibre, analyzers contain two channels to monitor both the transmit and receive activity. In the traces shown in this chapter, the analyzer is attached at the SCSI initiator interface. Consequently, it shows the loop activity from the initiator's perspective.

Along the left side of the traces is an event number (or trace entry) used to reference events contained in the traces. The observant reader will notice that some event numbers are missing from the traces. The particular analyzer used to capture these traces does not display repeated events to conserve space on the display. Instead, it may simply hide repeated events, or in some cases, summarize the time that a particular ordered set was recognized.

B.1 Write Command

The write command used for this example consists of the FCP_CMND, FCP_XFER_RDY, a single FCP_DATA, and the FCP_RSP information units. The command, transfer ready, and response are all single-frame sequences while the data consists of multiple frames (only some of which are shown in the trace). In this example, the initiator is AL_PA value x'EF' (output shown in left column) and the target disk drive is at AL_PA value x'71' (output shown in right column).

B.1.1 Write Command Frame

A SCSI FCP write command frame (FCP_CMND, or T1 information unit) is shown in Figure 132 on page 354. This is a single frame Class-3 sequence so the frame uses the SOFi3 and EOFt frame delimiters. The 'last frame of sequence' bit is also set in the F_CTL field.

This is the first information unit of the command, and the 'first sequence of exchange' bit is set in the F_CTL field of the frame header. As T1 information unit transfers sequence initiative, the sequence initiative bit in the F_CTL field of the frame header is also set. Transferring the sequence initiative allows the target to send an FCP_XFER_RDY when it is ready to begin the data transfer.

In this example, the command is directed to Logical Unit Number (LUN) zero. The execution management flags in the FCP_CNTL field indicate that this command transfers write data and the FCP_DL field indicates that '3000'x bytes will be transferred. The SCSI CDB starts in byte twelve of the payload of the frame. In this case, the CDB is a 10-byte write command beginning with Logical Block Address (LBA) x'00243771' and continuing for x'0003' logical blocks.

```
              Initiator Transmit Output                    Initiator Receive Input

00003C:ARBx   Port EF◄─── Initiator Arbitrates & Wins   | Idle 920 ns
00003E:    .                                    └──────►| ARBx   Port EF
000040:OPN    Full Duplex, Ports 71,EF ◄─────────────── |    ·──── Initiator opens Port 71
000041:ARBx   Port F0◄─┐                                 |    ·
000043:R_RDY           │                                 |    ·
000044:ARBx   Port F0  │                                 |    ·
000046:R_RDY           │                                 |    ·
000047:ARBx   Port F0  │  Initiator gives BB_Credit of 4 |    ·
000049:R_RDY           │                                 |    ·
00004A:ARBx   Port F0  │                                 |    ·
00004C:R_RDY           │                                 |    ·
00004D:ARBx   Port F0◄─┘                                 |    ·
00004F:    .                                              | ARBx   Port F0
000051:    .          Target gives BB_Credit of 1 ─────► | R_RDY
000052:    .                                              | ARBx   Port F0
000054:Idle 160 ns                                        |    ·
000056:    ┌ SOFi3                                        |    ·
000057:    │     R_CTL:06    D_ID:000071                  |    ·
000058:    │                 S_ID:0000EF          ◄────── | ── Initiator sends FCP_CMND frame
000059:    │     Type:08(FCP)    F_CTL:290000            |    ·
00005A:    │     Seq:88, DF_CTL:00, CNT0000              |    ·
00005B:    │     OX_ID:003F RX_ID:FFFF                    |    ·
00005C:    │     Parameter:00000000                      |    ·
00005D:    │        Payload:32($20) Bytes               |    ·
00005E:    │      ┌─────────────────────────┐            |    ·
           │      │ 00 00 00 00 00 00 00 00 │◄────────── | ── Logical Unit Number (LUN)
00005F:  ┌─┤      │ 00 00 00 01│2A 08 00 24 │◄────────── | ── SCSI CDB
000060:FCP_CNTL│  │ 37 71 00 00 03 00│00 00 │            |    ·
000061:  │ │      │ 00 00 00 00│00 00 30 00 │◄────────── | ── FCP_DL (Length in bytes)
000064:    │          CRC:13388FD9         └─────────────┘
000065:    └─ EOFt
000069:CLS    ◄──────────────── Initiator sends CLS      |    ·
00006A:Idle 80 ns                                         | Idle 920 ns
00006D:    .                                              | R_RDY
00006E:Idle 360 ns                                        | Idle 240 ns
000072:Idle 40 ns     Target sends CLS ─────────────►    | CLS
```

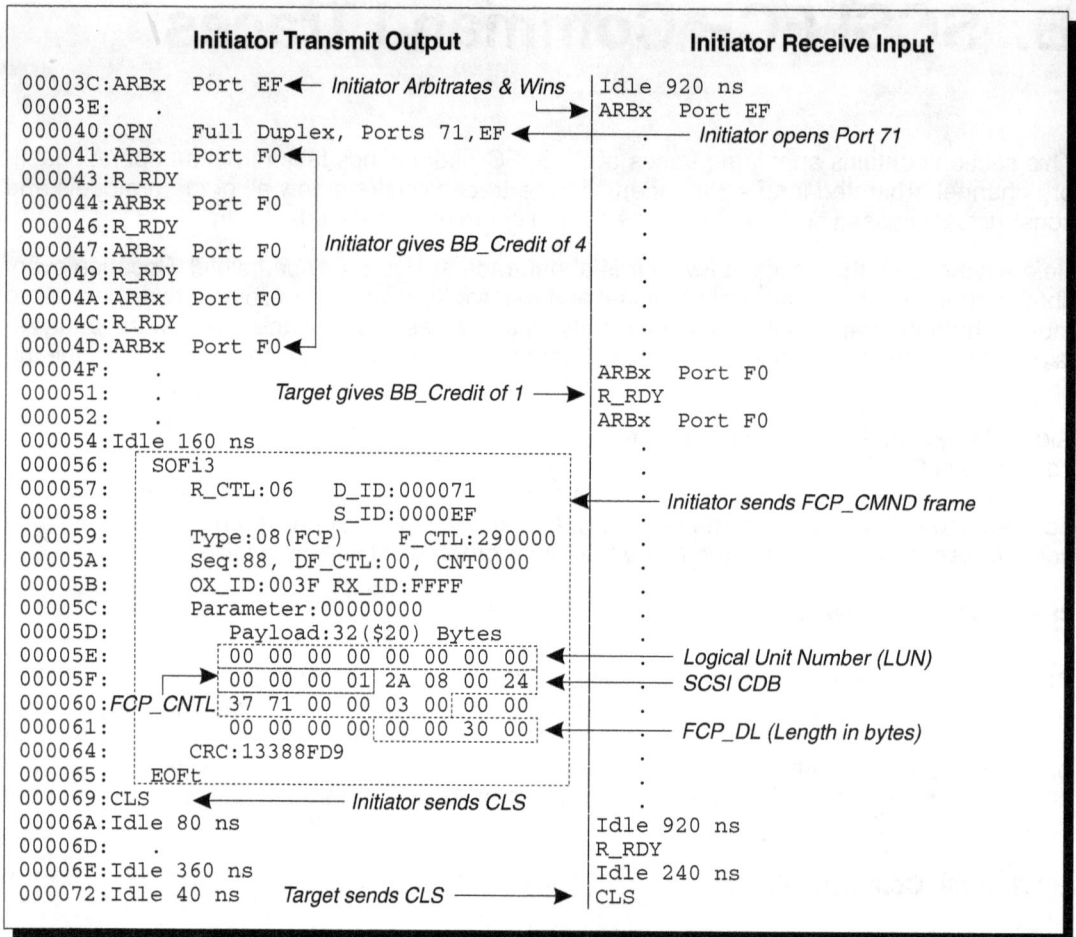

Figure 132. FCP Write Command Frame

B.1.2 Write Transfer Ready Frame

The write transfer ready frame (FCP_XFER_RDY, or I1 information unit) shown in Figure 133 on page 355 is sent when the target is ready to begin the data transfer. Because this is also a single-frame sequence, the SOFi3 and EOFt frame delimiters are used.

In this example, the target is requesting that the initiator send the data beginning at Relative Offset x'00000000'. The number of bytes request is x'00003000', which is all of the data specified by the FCP_CMND information unit. Consequently, there will be a single data sequence consisting of however many frames are required to transfer the requested data.

The FCP_XFER_RDY transfers sequence initiative by setting the sequence initiative bit in the F_CTL field so that the initiator can send the requested data.

```
              Initiator Transmit Output                    Initiator Receive Input

000075:   .            Target Arbitrates & Wins ──▶ ARBx   Port 71
000076:Idle 200 ns                                        .
000078:ARBx   Port 71 ◀──────────────────────┐           .
00007A:   .            Target opens Port EF ──▶ OPN    Half Duplex, Port EF
00007B:   .                                     ARBx   Port F0
00007E:ARBx   Port F0 ◀──┐                               .
000080:R_RDY             │                               .
000081:ARBx   Port F0    │                               .
000083:R_RDY             │                               .
000084:ARBx   Port F0    │   Initiator gives             .
000086:R_RDY             │   BB_Credit of 4              .
000087:ARBx   Port F0    │                               .
000089:R_RDY             │                               .
00008A:ARBx   Port F0 ◀──┘                               .
00008C:   .                                     Idle 320 ns
00008E:Idle 320 ns                              Idle 240 ns
000090:Idle 440 ns                              ┌ SOFi3
000091:   . ─ Target sends FCP_XFER_RDY frame ─▶│  R_CTL:05    D_ID:0000EF
000092:   .                                     │             S_ID:000071
000093:   .                                     │  Type:08(FCP)    F_CTL:890000
000094:   .                                     │  Seq:FF, DF_CTL:00, CNT0000
000095:   .                                     │  OX_ID:003F RX_ID:FFFF
000096:   .                                     │  Parameter:00000000
000097:   .                                     │    Payload:12($C) Bytes
000098:   .        Data Relative Offset ───────▶│  ┌00 00 00 00│00 00 30 00┐
000099:   .                                     │  │ 00 00 00 00          │
00009A:   .            Burst Length ────────────│  └CRC:5BF64B62──────────┘▲
00009B:   .                                     │  EOFt                    │
00009C:Idle 280 ns                              Idle 280 ns
00009E:Idle 40 ns         Target sends CLS ──▶ CLS
00009F:Idle 160 ns                              Idle 280 ns
0000A2:R_RDY                                    Idle 40 ns
0000A3:Idle 40 ns                               Idle 80 ns
0000A5:CLS ◀────────── Initiator sends CLS      Idle 40 ns
```

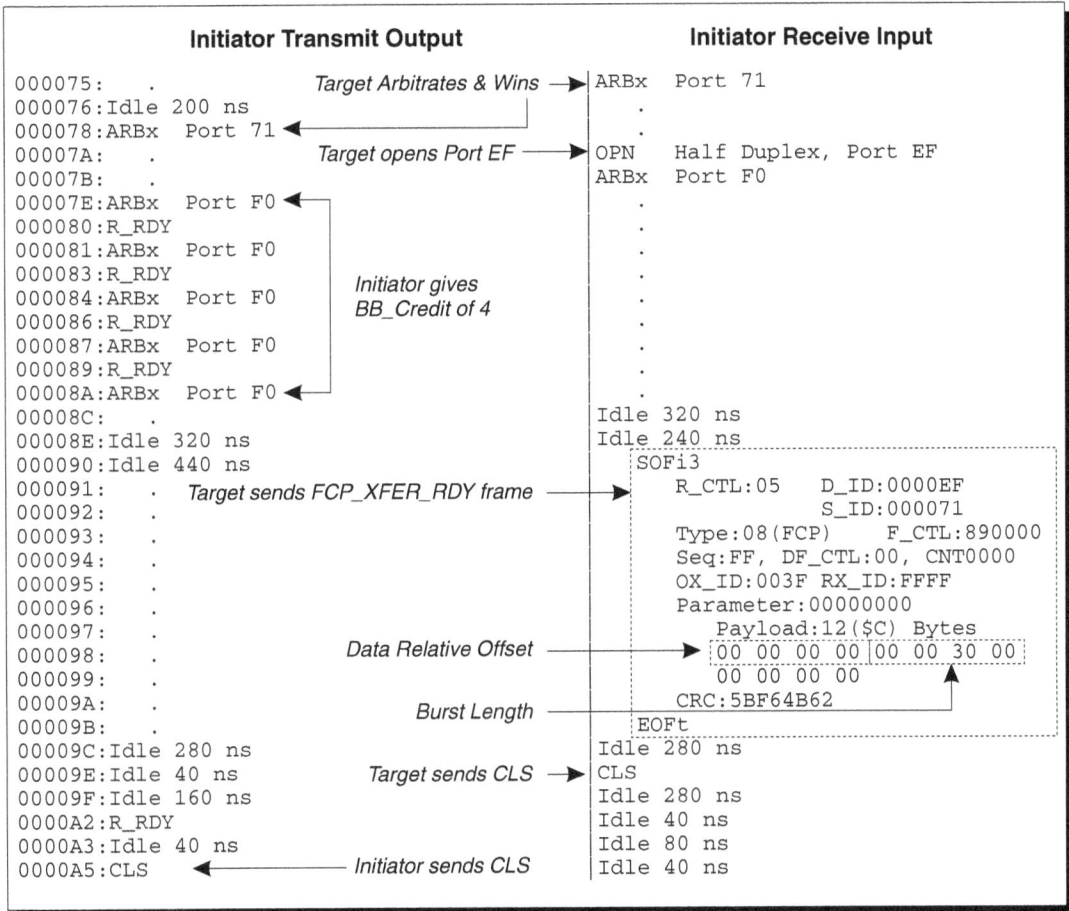

Figure 133. FCP Write Transfer Ready Frame

B.1.3 Write Data Frames

The write data sequence (FCP_DATA, or T6 information unit) is sent in response to the target's transfer ready.

In this example, the write data transfer requires 12 frames which have SEQ_CNTs of x'0000' through x'000B'. The first write data frame is shown in Figure 134 on page 356. Because this is a multi-frame sequence, the appropriate frame delimiters must be used for each frame depending on whether it initiates or terminates the sequence. All of the data frames associated with the data sequence are sent during a single loop tenancy. The initiator arbitrates prior to sending the first data frame and maintains the loop circuit until all of the data frames have been sent. This simply reflects the implementation of the initiator protocol chip as the data could have been transferred during multiple loop circuits.

```
              Initiator Transmit Output                    Initiator Receive Input

0000A8:ARBx    Port EF ◄─ Initiator Arbitrates & Wins   Idle 840 ns
0000AA:    .                              └──────►       ARBx    Port EF
0000AC:OPN     Full Duplex, Ports 71,EF ◄──────────      .  ──── Initiator opens Port 71
0000AD:ARBx    Port F0 ◄─┐                                .
0000AF:R_RDY                                              .
0000B0:ARBx    Port F0                                    .
0000B2:R_RDY                                              .
0000B3:ARBx    Port F0        Initiator gives BB_Credit of 4   .
0000B5:R_RDY                                              .
0000B6:ARBx    Port F0                                    .
0000B8:R_RDY                                              .
0000B9:ARBx    Port F0 ◄─┘                                .
0000BC:    .                                             ARBx    Port F0
0000BE:    .         Target gives BB_Credit of 1 ───►    R_RDY
0000BF:    .                                             ARBx    Port F0
0000C2:Idle 160 ns
0000C4:    ┌ SOFi3                                        .
0000C5:    │    R_CTL:01    D_ID:000071                   .
0000C6:    │               S_ID:0000EF        ◄────── Initiator sends first FCP_DATA frame
0000C7:    │    Type:08(FCP)      F_CTL:010000            .
0000C8:    │    Seq:87, DF_CTL:00, CNT0000                .
0000C9:    │    OX_ID:003F RX_ID:FFFF                     .
0000CA:    │    Parameter:00000000                        .
0000CB:    │       Payload:1056($420) Bytes              .
0000CC:    │       FF FF FF FF FF FF FF FF                .
0000CD:    │       FF FF FF FF FF FF FF FF                .
0000CE:    │       FF FF FF FF FF FF FF FF      Idle 10.1 us
0000CF:    │       FF FF FF FF FF FF FF FF  ◄────── Payload contains the write data
0000CF:    │       FF FF FF FF FF FF FF FF                .
0000CF:    │       FF FF FF FF FF FF FF FF                .
0000CF:    │       FF FF FF FF FF FF FF FF                .
0000CF:    │       FF FF FF FF FF FF FF FF                .
0000D0:    │    CRC:FFD05155                              .
0000D1:    └ EOFn                                         .
0000D2:Idle 1.1 us                                       Idle 1.0 us
```

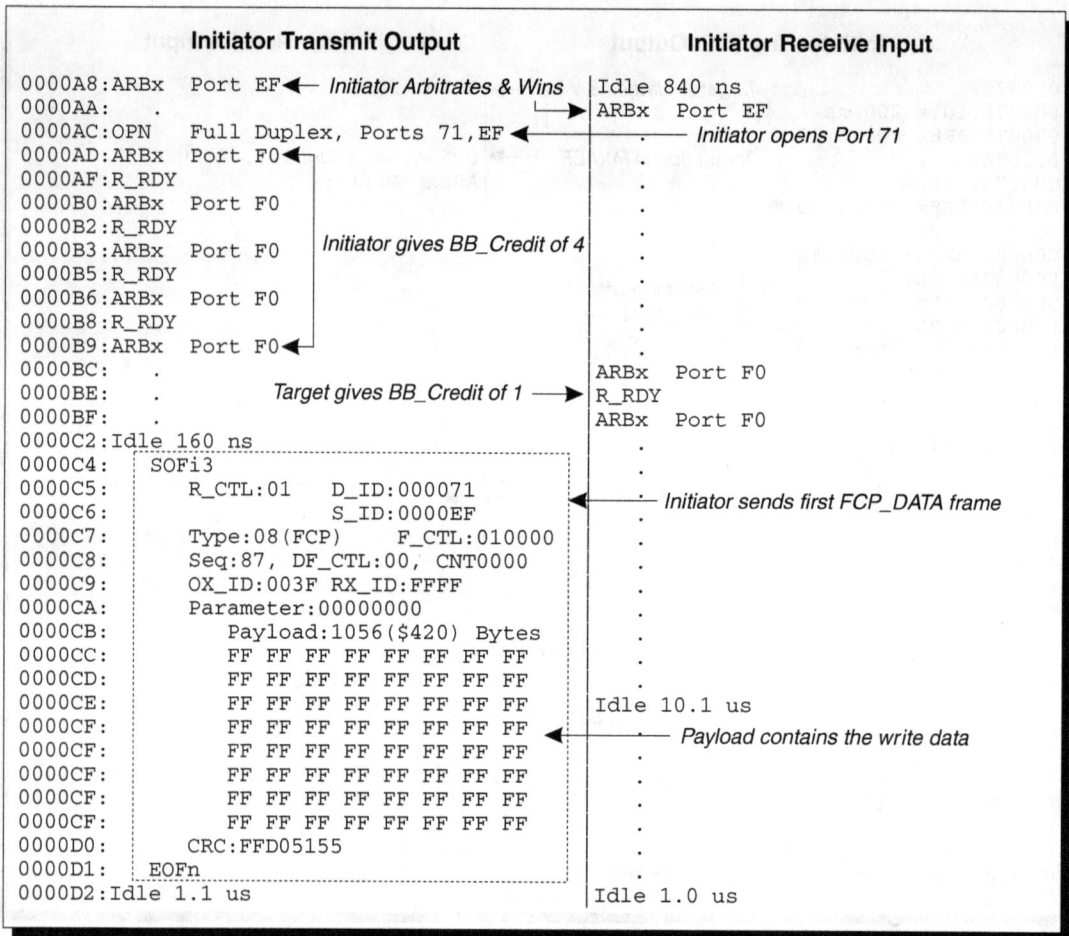

Figure 134. FCP Write First Data Frame

The second through 11th data frames continue the process of transferring the write data. As each frame is sent, the SEQ_CNT is incremented by one. Because these frames are in the middle of the FCP_DATA sequence, they use the SOFn3 start-of-frame delimiter and EOFn end-of-frame delimiter. The second and 11th write data frames are shown in Figure 135 on page 357; the intervening data frames are not shown.

As each frame is sent, the relative offset value in the parameter field of the frame header is updated. The use of continuously increasing relative offset is required by the Private Loop Direct Attach profile. It is interesting to note that the relative offset present bit in the F_CTL field of the frame header is not set, indicating that the parameter field does not contain a valid relative offset value. This is a bug in the operation of the initiator shown in this trace and is representative of the type of problem that may be encountered during the development phase of a project.

```
        Initiator Transmit Output              Initiator Receive Input

0000D4:Idle 40 ns    Target gives BB_Credit of 1 ──▶ R_RDY
0000D5:Idle 4.4 us                               Idle 4.6 us
0000D8:    SOFn3                                  Idle 10.8 us
0000D9:      R_CTL:01    D_ID:000071             .
0000DA:                  S_ID:0000EF        ◀──── · Initiator sends second FCP_DATA frame
0000DB:      Type:08(FCP)    F_CTL:010000        .
0000DC:      Seq:87, DF_CTL:00, CNT0001 ◀──────── · SEQ_CNT increment by one
0000DD:      OX_ID:003F RX_ID:FFFF               .
0000DE:      Parameter:00000420                  .
0000DF:         Payload:1056($420) Bytes         .
0000E0:         FF FF FF FF FF FF FF FF           .
0000E0:         FF FF FF FF FF FF FF FF           .
0000E0:         FF FF FF FF FF FF FF FF           .
0000E0:         FF FF FF FF FF FF FF FF      ◀──── · Payload contains the write data
0000E0:         FF FF FF FF FF FF FF FF           .
0000E0:         FF FF FF FF FF FF FF FF           .
0000E0:         FF FF FF FF FF FF FF FF           .
0000E0:            FF FF FF FF FF FF FF FF        .
0000E1:      CRC:08D21110                         .
0000E2:    EOFn                                   .
0000E3:Idle 1.2 us                               Idle 1.1 us
```

Frames 3 through 10 not shown

```
000176:Idle 40 ns    Target gives BB_Credit of 1 ──▶ R_RDY
000177:Idle 4.4 us                               Idle 4.5 us
00017A:    SOFn3                                  Idle 10.8 us
00017B:      R_CTL:01    D_ID:000071        ◀──── · Initiator sends 11th FCP_DATA frame
00017C:                  S_ID:0000EF              .
00017D:      Type:08(FCP)    F_CTL:010000        .
00017E:      Seq:87, DF_CTL:00, CNT000A ◀──────── · SEQ_CNT has incremented to frame 11
00017F:      OX_ID:003F RX_ID:FFFF               .
000180:      Parameter:00002940                  .
000181:         Payload:1056($420) Bytes         .
000182:         FF FF FF FF FF FF FF FF           .
000182:         FF FF FF FF FF FF FF FF           .
000182:         FF FF FF FF FF FF FF FF           .
000182:         FF FF FF FF FF FF FF FF      ◀──── · Payload contains the write data
000182:         FF FF FF FF FF FF FF FF           .
000182:         FF FF FF FF FF FF FF FF           .
000182:         FF FF FF FF FF FF FF FF           .
000182:            FF FF FF FF FF FF FF FF        .
000183:      CRC:C0E10918                         .
000184:    EOFn                                   .
```

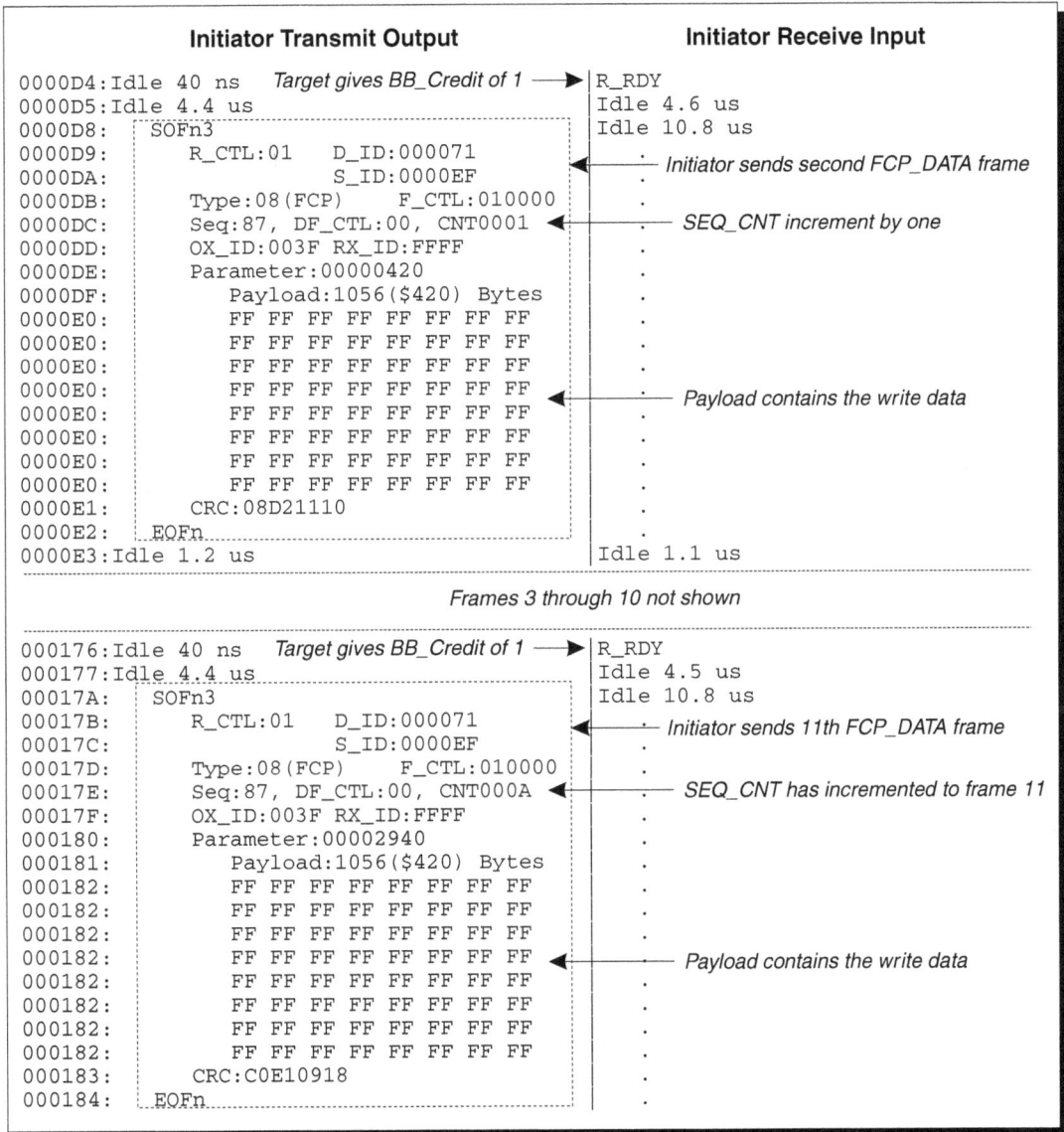

Figure 135. FCP Write Data Frames 2-11

The last write data frame of this command (SEQ_CNT=000B) is shown in Figure 136 on page 358. Because this frame ends the data sequence, the 'last frame of sequence' bit is set in the F_CTL field of the frame header and the frame uses the end-of-frame terminate (EOFt) delimiter.

Sequence initiative is transferred by this frame, even though the Sequence Initiative bit was set in earlier frames of the sequence (it is only meaningful on the last frame of the sequence). Transfer of the initiative allows the target to send the FCP_RSP containing the SCSI status which is the next sequence of this command.

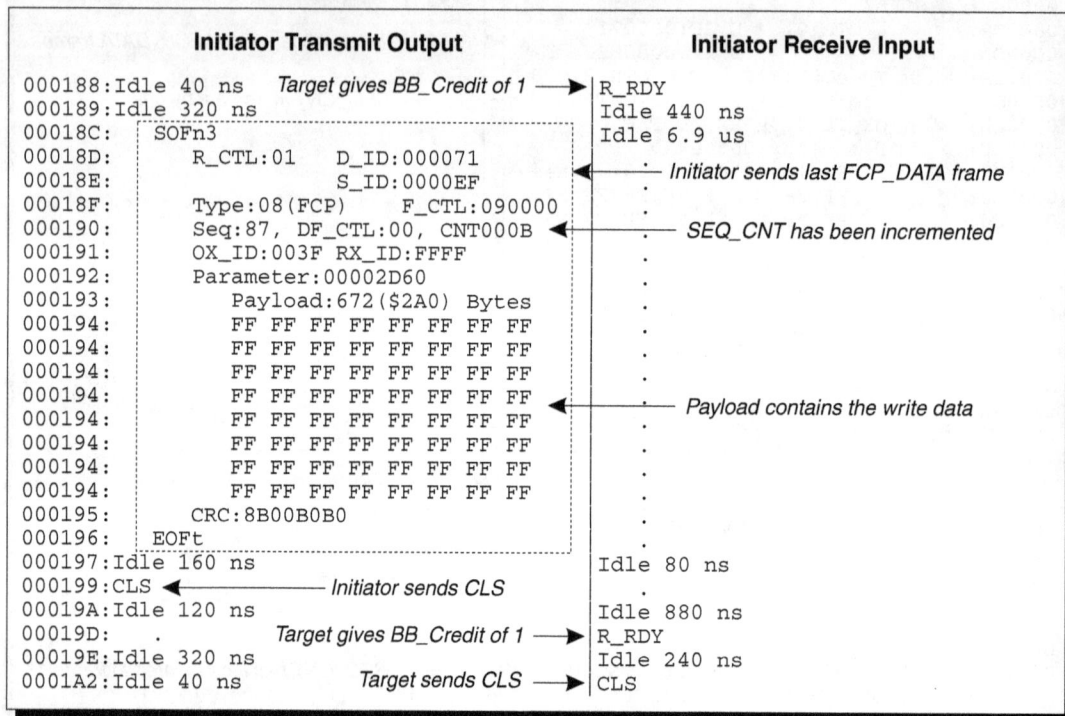

```
             Initiator Transmit Output                    Initiator Receive Input

000188:Idle 40 ns      Target gives BB_Credit of 1 ──▶ R_RDY
000189:Idle 320 ns                                      Idle 440 ns
00018C:    SOFn3                                         Idle 6.9 us
00018D:       R_CTL:01    D_ID:000071
00018E:                   S_ID:0000EF         ◀──── Initiator sends last FCP_DATA frame
00018F:       Type:08(FCP)    F_CTL:090000         .
000190:       Seq:87, DF_CTL:00, CNT000B ◀──── SEQ_CNT has been incremented
000191:       OX_ID:003F RX_ID:FFFF              .
000192:       Parameter:00002D60                 .
000193:          Payload:672($2A0) Bytes         .
000194:          FF FF FF FF FF FF FF FF          .
000194:          FF FF FF FF FF FF FF FF          .
000194:          FF FF FF FF FF FF FF FF          .
000194:          FF FF FF FF FF FF FF FF    ◀──── Payload contains the write data
000194:          FF FF FF FF FF FF FF FF          .
000194:          FF FF FF FF FF FF FF FF          .
000194:          FF FF FF FF FF FF FF FF          .
000194:          FF FF FF FF FF FF FF FF          .
000195:       CRC:8B00B0B0
000196:    EOFt                                        .
000197:Idle 160 ns                                     Idle 80 ns
000199:CLS ◀──────── Initiator sends CLS                .
00019A:Idle 120 ns                                     Idle 880 ns
00019D:    .          Target gives BB_Credit of 1 ──▶ R_RDY
00019E:Idle 320 ns                                     Idle 240 ns
0001A2:Idle 40 ns          Target sends CLS ──▶ CLS
```

Figure 136. FCP Write Last Data Frame

B.1.4 Write Response Frame

The write response frame (FCP_RSP, or I4 information unit) is sent when the target has completed the command and is returning the SCSI status (and autosense information if a check condition occurred). An example of a response frame is shown in Figure 137 on page 359. In this case, the command completed successfully as indicated by a SCSI status byte of x'00'.

This frame also contains a bug. The Fibre Channel Protocol for SCSI standard states that the response length and sense length fields are always present in the FCP_RSP, even if their associated validity bits indicate the fields do not contain valid information. In this example, the payload of the frame does not contain the length fields as required.

The FCP_RSP ends the SCSI write command. In this example, the entire operation used four loop tenancies to complete the operation. The target device is a half-duplex design which requires a new loop tenancy to accommodate each change of direction.

```
                    Initiator Transmit Output              Initiator Receive Input

0001A5:Idle 240 ns        Target Arbitrates & Wins  ───►  ARBx  Port 71
0001A8:ARBx  Port 71 ◄───                                   .
0001AA:    .              Target opens Port EF      ───►  OPN   Half Duplex, Port EF
0001AB:    .                                              ARBx  Port F0
0001AD:ARBx  Port F0 ◄───┐                                 .
0001AF:R_RDY             │                                 .
0001B0:ARBx  Port F0     │                                 .
0001B2:R_RDY             │                                 .
0001B3:ARBx  Port F0     │  Initiator gives               .
0001B5:R_RDY             │  BB_Credit of 4                .
0001B6:ARBx  Port F0     │                                 .
0001B8:R_RDY             │                                 .
0001B9:ARBx  Port F0 ◄───┘                                 .
0001BC:    .                                              Idle 320 ns
0001BE:Idle 760 ns                                       Idle 720 ns
0001C0:Idle 440 ns                                  ┌─────────────────────────────────
0001C1:    .              Target sends FCP_RSP frame│ SOFi3
0001C2:    .                                  ───►  │   R_CTL:07    D_ID:0000EF
0001C3:    .                                        │               S_ID:000071
0001C4:    .                                        │   Type:08(FCP)      F_CTL:980000
0001C5:    .                                        │   Seq:FF, DF_CTL:00, CNT0000
0001C6:    .                                        │   OX_ID:003F RX_ID:FFFF
0001C7:    .                                        │   Parameter:00000000
0001C8:    .                                        │      Payload:12($C) Bytes
0001C9:    .                                        │      00 00 00 00 00 00 00 00
0001C9:    .                                        │      00 00 00 00
0001CA:    .              SCSI Status Byte ─────────│   CRC:89EE59A7  ▲
0001CB:Idle 80 ns                                   │ EOFt
0001CD:    .              Target sends CLS  ───►    │ Idle 280 ns
0001CE:Idle 240 ns                                  └ CLS
0001D1:R_RDY                                          Idle 80 ns
0001D2:Idle 40 ns                                      .
0001D4:CLS ◄────────────── Initiator sends CLS       Idle 80 ns
                                                       .
```

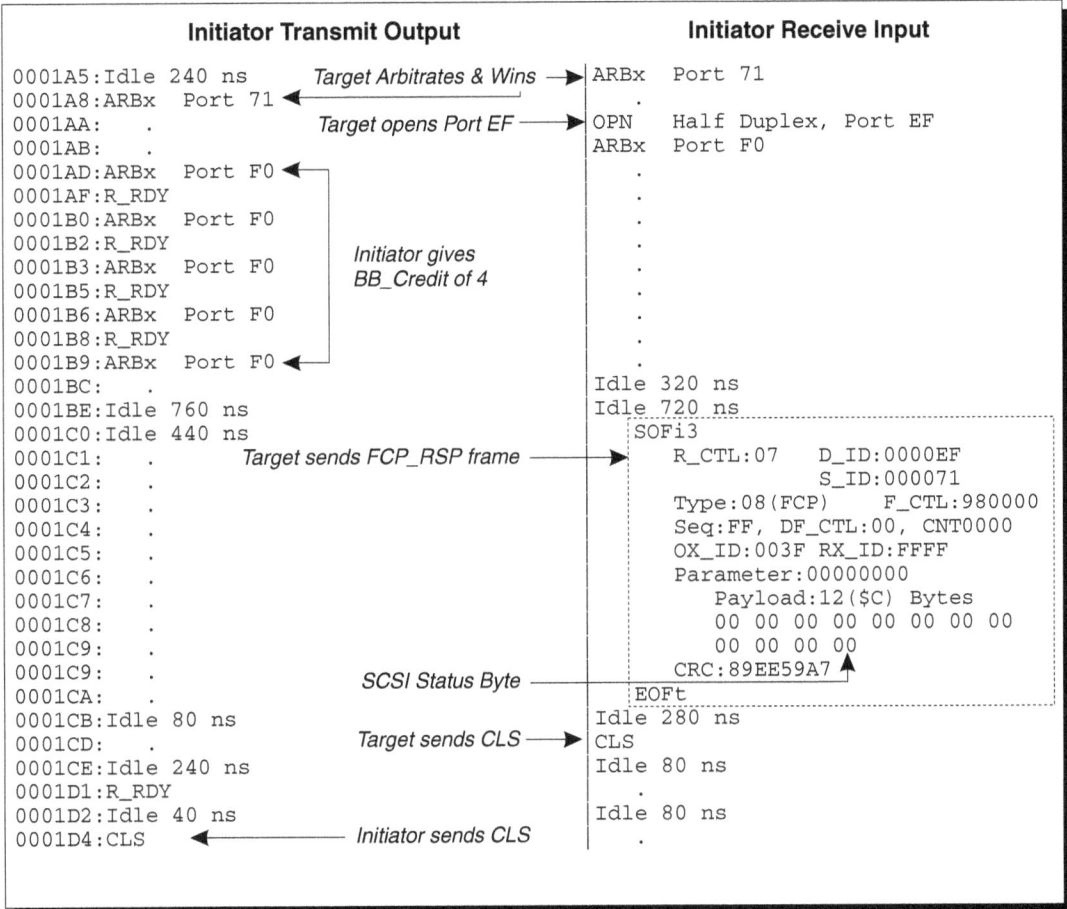

Figure 137. FCP Write Response Frame

B.2 Read Command

The read command used for this example consists of the FCP_CMND, a single FCP_DATA, and the FCP_RSP information units. This read command does not use the transfer ready information unit. The command and response are both single-frame sequences while the data sequence consists of multiple frames (some of which are omitted in the trace).

B.2.1 Read Command Frame

The read command frame (FCP_CMND, or T1 information unit) is shown in Figure 138 on page 360. This command is a 10-byte read which reads back the data written in the previous write command example.

```
            Initiator Transmit Output                    Initiator Receive Input

0001D7:ARBx   Port EF◄─── Initiator Arbitrates & Wins        .
0001D8:    .                                            Idle 880 ns
0001DA:    .                                        ┌──►ARBx   Port EF
0001DC:OPN    Full Duplex, Ports 71,EF◄──────┘        .  ─── Initiator opens Port 71
0001DD:ARBx   Port F0                                     .
0001DF:R_RDY ◄──┐                                         .
0001E0:ARBx   Port F0                                     .
0001E2:R_RDY    │                                         .
0001E3:ARBx   Port F0    Initiator gives BB_Credit of 4   .
0001E5:R_RDY    │                                         .
0001E6:ARBx   Port F0                                     .
0001E8:R_RDY ◄──┘                                         .
0001E9:ARBx   Port F0                                     .
0001EB:    .                                            ARBx   Port F0
0001ED:    .    Target gives BB_Credit of 1 ──────►    R_RDY
0001EE:    .                                            ARBx   Port F0
0001F1:Idle 160 ns
0001F3:    ┌ SOFi3                                        .
0001F4:    │     R_CTL:06    D_ID:000071       ◄─── ─ ── Initiator sends FCP_CMND frame
0001F5:    │                 S_ID:0000EF                  .
0001F6:    │   Type:08(FCP)     F_CTL:290000              .
0001F7:    │   Seq:8A, DF_CTL:00, CNT0000                 .
0001F8:    │   OX_ID:403F RX_ID:FFFF                      .
0001F9:    │   Parameter:00000000                         .
0001FA:    │     Payload:32($20) Bytes                    .
0001FB:    │    00 00 00 00 00 00 00 00 ◄──────── ── ─── Logical Unit Number (LUN)
0001FC:    │ ┌►00 00 00 02 28 08 00 24 ◄─────────── ─── SCSI CDB
0001FD:FCP_CNTL 37 71 00 00 03 00 00 00                  .
0001FE:    │    00 00 00 00 00 00 30 00 ◄──────── ── ─── FCP_DL (Length in bytes)
000201:    │   CRC:C2BF7159                              .
000202:    └ EOFt                                         .
000203:Idle 120 ns                                        .
000206:Idle 40 ns                                       Idle 40 ns
000207:CLS  ◄────────── Initiator sends CLS               .
000208:Idle 120 ns                                     Idle 880 ns
00020B:    .    Target gives BB_Credit of 1 ──────►    R_RDY
00020C:Idle 320 ns                                     Idle  240 ns
000210:Idle 40 ns    Target sends CLS ──────────►     CLS
```

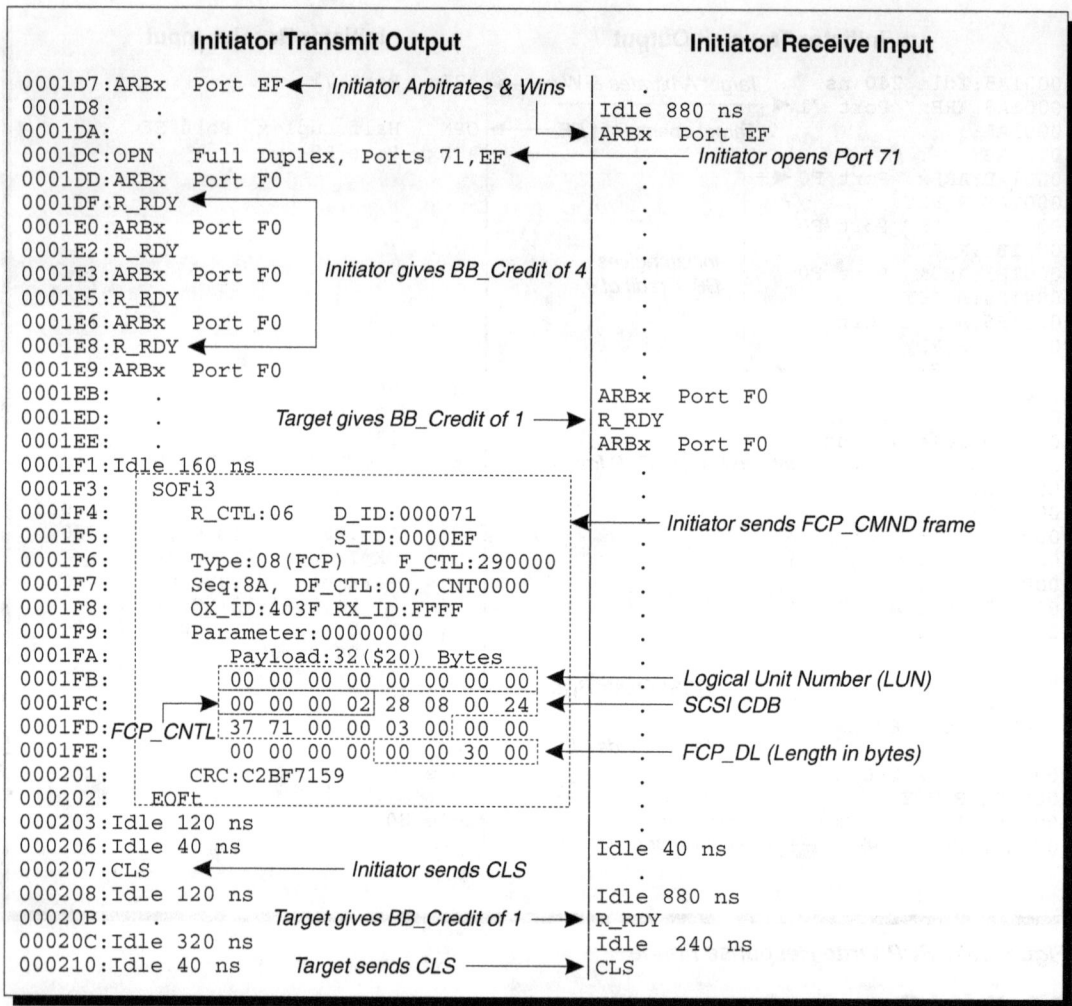

Figure 138. FCP Read Command Frame

B.2.2 Read FCP_DATA Frames

The read data frames (FCP_DATA, or I3 information unit) are sent as soon as the target is ready to begin the data transfer. No read transfer ready is used in this example which is following the behavior proscribed in the Private Loop Direct Attach profile (see *PLDA Technical Report* on page 295). If the target desired to perform an out-of-order data transfer, it could accomplish that by use of the relative offset value contained in the parameter field of the frame header. While the PLDA document requires use of continuously increasing relative offset within a sequence, multiple sequences could be used to transfer the data out-of-order, if desired.

In the read command example shown, the write data transfer is accomplished in a single sequence consisting of 12 data frames having SEQ_CNTs of x'0000' through x'000B'. The first read data frame of this sequence is shown in Figure 139.

```
              Initiator Transmit Output                    Initiator Receive Input

000213:Idle 200 ns      Target Arbitrates & Wins ──►│ARBx   Port 71
000216:ARBx   Port 71 ◄─────────────────────────     .
000218:    .            Target opens Port EF ──────►│OPN    Half Duplex, Port EF
000219:    .                                          ARBx   Port F0
00021C:ARBx   Port F0 ◄─┐                             .
00021E:R_RDY            │                             .
00021F:ARBx   Port F0   │                             .
000221:R_RDY            │ Initiator gives             .
000222:ARBx   Port F0   │ BB_Credit of 4              .
000224:R_RDY            │                             .
000225:ARBx   Port F0   │                             .
000227:R_RDY            │                             .
000228:ARBx   Port F0 ◄─┘                             .
00022A:    .                                          Idle 320 ns
00022C:Idle 320 ns                                    Idle 240 ns
00022E:Idle 10.8 us                                   SOFi3
00022F:    .            Target sends FCP_RSP frame ──►    R_CTL:01    D_ID:0000EF
000230:    .                                                         S_ID:000071
000231:    .                                             Type:08(FCP)     F_CTL:800008
000232:    .                                             Seq:00, DF_CTL:00, CNT0000
000233:    .                                             OX_ID:403F RX_ID:FFFF
000234:    .                                             Parameter:00000000
000235:    .                                                 Payload:1056($420) Bytes
000236:    .                                                 FF FF FF FF FF FF FF FF
000237:    .                                                 FF FF FF FF FF FF FF FF
000238:    .                                                 FF FF FF FF FF FF FF FF
000238:    . Frame payload contains the read data ──►        FF FF FF FF FF FF FF FF
000238:    .                                                 FF FF FF FF FF FF FF FF
000238:    .                                                 FF FF FF FF FF FF FF FF
000238:    .                                                 FF FF FF FF FF FF FF FF
000238:    .                                                 FF FF FF FF FF FF FF FF
000239:Idle 40 ns                                        CRC:A77B7E84
000239:    .                                             EOFn
00023A:    .                                          Idle 320 ns
```

Figure 139. FCP Read First Data Frame

The second through 11th data frames of the sequence continue the process of transferring the write data. As each frame is sent, the SEQ_CNT is incremented by one and the relative offset in the parameter field of the frame header is updated. These frames are shown in Figure 140 on page 362 (frames three through 10 are not shown).

It is important to note that the correct frame delimiters (and F_CTL bits) must be used for each frame of this multi-frame sequence. The first frame begins with the SOFi3 and ends with the EOFn. The middle frames use the SOFn3 and EOFn delimiters, with the last frame of the sequence using the SOFn3 and EOFt delimiters. Incorrect use of delimiters constitutes an error.

Initiator Transmit Output	Initiator Receive Input
00023A:Idle 40 ns	
00023B: .	SOFn3
00023C:Idle 10.9 us	R_CTL:01 D_ID:0000EF
00023D: .	S_ID:000071
00023E: . *Target sends second FCP_DATA frame* →	Type:08(FCP) F_CTL:800008
00023F: .	Seq:00, DF_CTL:00, CNT0001
000240: .	OX_ID:403F RX_ID:FFFF
000241: .	Parameter:00000420
000242: .	Payload:1056($420) Bytes
000243: .	FF FF FF FF FF FF FF FF
000244: .	FF FF FF FF FF FF FF FF
000245: .	FF FF FF FF FF FF FF FF
000246: . *Frame payload contains the read data* →	FF FF FF FF FF FF FF FF
000246: .	FF FF FF FF FF FF FF FF
000246: .	FF FF FF FF FF FF FF FF
000246: .	FF FF FF FF FF FF FF FF
000246: .	FF FF FF FF FF FF FF FF
000246: .	CRC:50793EC1
000247: .	EOFn
000248:Idle 280 ns	Idle 320 ns

Frames 3 through 10 not shown

0002BC:Idle 360 ns	Idle 280 ns
0002C0:Idle 200 ns	SOFn3
0002C1: .	R_CTL:01 D_ID:0000EF
0002C2: .	S_ID:000071
0002C3: . *Target sends 11th FCP_DATA frame* →	Type:08(FCP) F_CTL:800008
0002C4: .	Seq:00, DF_CTL:00, CNT000A
0002C5:R_RDY ← *Initiator gives BB_Credit of 1*	OX_ID:403F RX_ID:FFFF
0002C6:Idle 10.6 us	Parameter:00002940
0002C7: .	Payload:1056($420) Bytes
0002C8: .	FF FF FF FF FF FF FF FF
0002C9: .	FF FF FF FF FF FF FF FF
0002CA: .	FF FF FF FF FF FF FF FF
0002CA: . *Frame payload contains the read data* →	FF FF FF FF FF FF FF FF
0002CA: .	FF FF FF FF FF FF FF FF
0002CA: .	FF FF FF FF FF FF FF FF
0002CA: .	FF FF FF FF FF FF FF FF
0002CA: .	FF FF FF FF FF FF FF FF
0002CA: .	CRC:984A26C9
0002CB: .	EOFn
0002CC:Idle 360 ns	Idle 280 ns

Figure 140. FCP Read Data Frames 2-11

The last frame of the read data sequence is shown in Figure 141 on page 363. While this frame ends the sequence, it does not transfer sequence initiative. This allows the target to send the FCP_RSP containing the SCSI status byte.

As was also the case with the write command discussed earlier, all frames of the data sequence are transferred during a single loop tenancy. The target arbitrates for access to the loop prior to the first data frame, then maintains the loop circuit until all of the data has been

Initiator Transmit Output   **Initiator Receive Input**

```
0002CC:Idle 360 ns                        Idle 280 ns
0002D0:Idle 200 ns                          SOFn3
0002D1:    .    Target sends last FCP_DATA frame ──►  R_CTL:01    D_ID:0000EF
0002D2:    .                                               S_ID:000071
0002D3:    .                                  Type:08(FCP)    F_CTL:880008
0002D4:    .                                  Seq:00, DF_CTL:00, CNT000B
0002D5:R_RDY ◄──────── Initiator gives BB_Credit of 1    OX_ID:403F RX_ID:FFFF
0002D6:Idle 6.7 us                           Parameter:00002D60
0002D7:    .                                    Payload:672($2A0) Bytes
0002D8:    .                                    FF FF FF FF FF FF FF FF
0002D9:    .                                    FF FF FF FF FF FF FF FF
0002DA:    .                                    FF FF FF FF FF FF FF FF
0002DA:    . · Frame payload contains the read data ──►  FF FF FF FF FF FF FF FF
0002DA:    .                                    FF FF FF FF FF FF FF FF
0002DA:    .                                    FF FF FF FF FF FF FF FF
0002DB:    .                                    FF FF FF FF FF FF FF FF
0002DB:    .                                    FF FF FF FF FF FF FF FF
0002DB:    .                                  CRC:0856EBCB
0002DB:    .                                  EOFt
0002DC:Idle 320 ns                        Idle 320 ns
0002DE:Idle 40 ns      Target sends CLS ──► CLS
0002DF:Idle 160 ns                         Idle 200 ns
0002E1:R_RDY ◄──────── Initiator gives BB_Credit of 1    Idle 40 ns
0002E2:Idle 40 ns                          Idle 40 ns
0002E4:CLS ◄──────── Initiator sends CLS    Idle 40 ns
```

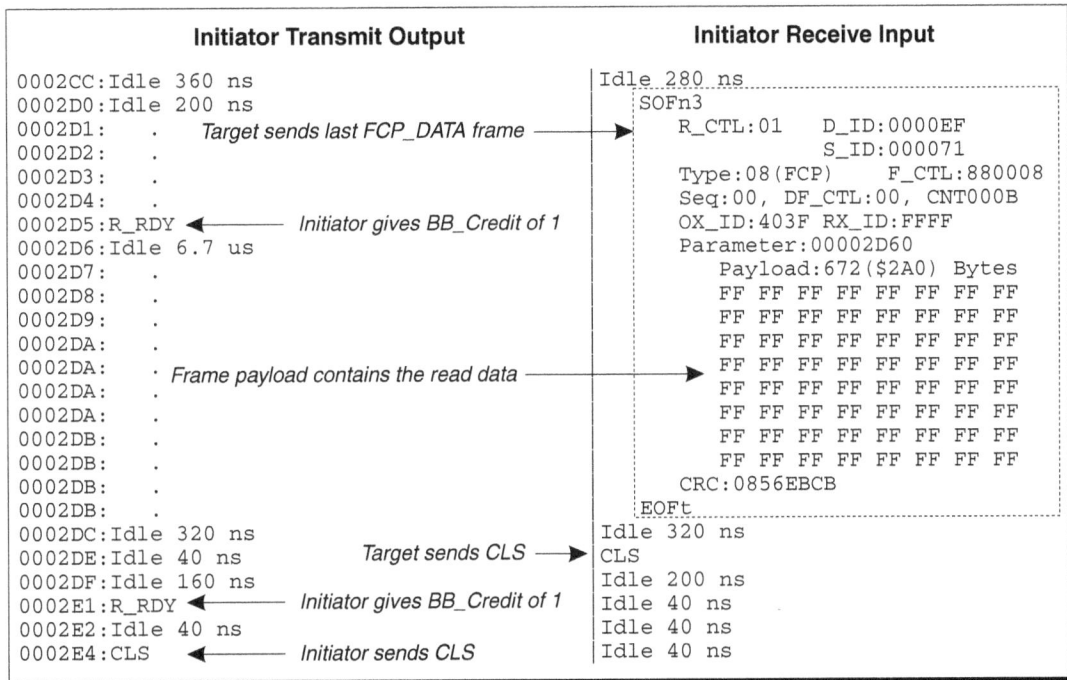

Figure 141. FCP Read Last Data Frame

sent. Interestingly, the loop circuit is closed after the data sequence and before the FCP_RSP is sent, even though there is no change of direction involved. This behavior is probably the result of tracing an early engineering drive which had not been optimized for performane at the time of the trace.

B.2.3 Read Response Frame

The read response frame (FCP_RSP, or I4 information unit) is sent when the target has completed the command and is returning the SCSI status. An example of a response frame is shown in Figure 142 on page 364. In this case, the SCSI status was good (x'00') indicating that the command was successul.

```
                Initiator Transmit Output                          Initiator Receive Input

0002E8:Idle 200 ns      Target Arbitrates & Wins →    ARBx   Port 71
0002EA:ARBx   Port 71 ◄                                 .
0002EC:       .         Target opens Port EF   →       OPN    Half Duplex, Port EF
0002ED:       .                                        ARBx   Port F0
0002EF:ARBx   Port F0 ◄                                 .
0002F1:R_RDY                                            .
0002F2:ARBx   Port F0                                   .
0002F4:R_RDY                                            .
0002F5:ARBx   Port F0         Initiator gives           .
0002F7:R_RDY                  BB_Credit of 4            .
0002F8:ARBx   Port F0                                   .
0002FA:R_RDY                                            .
0002FB:ARBx   Port F0 ◄                                 .
0002FD:       .                                        Idle 360 ns
000300:Idle 280 ns                                     Idle 200 ns
000302:Idle 400 ns                               ┌─────────────────────────────────────────┐
000303:       .         Target sends FCP_RSP frame →  │ SOFi3
000304:       .                                       │   R_CTL:07    D_ID:0000EF
000305:       .                                       │              S_ID:000071
000306:       .                                       │   Type:08(FCP)   F_CTL:980000
000307:       .                                       │   Seq:FF, DF_CTL:00, CNT0000
000308:       .                                       │   OX_ID:403F RX_ID:FFFF
000309:       .                                       │   Parameter:00000000
00030A:       .                                       │     Payload:12($C) Bytes
00030A:       .                                       │     00 00 00 00 00 00 00 00
00030A:       .                                       │     00 00 00 00
00030B:       .         SCSI Status Byte  ──────────  │   CRC:9F4EA192 ▲
00030C:Idle 360 ns                                    │ EOFt
000310:Idle 40 ns      Target sends CLS  →            └─────────────────────────────────────────┘
000311:       .                                       Idle 240 ns
000312:Idle 120 ns                                    CLS
000314:R_RDY                                          Idle 280 ns
000315:Idle 40 ns                                        .
000316:       .                                       Idle 40 ns
000317:CLS    ◄─────── Initiator sends CLS            Idle 40 ns
                                                      Idle 40 ns
```

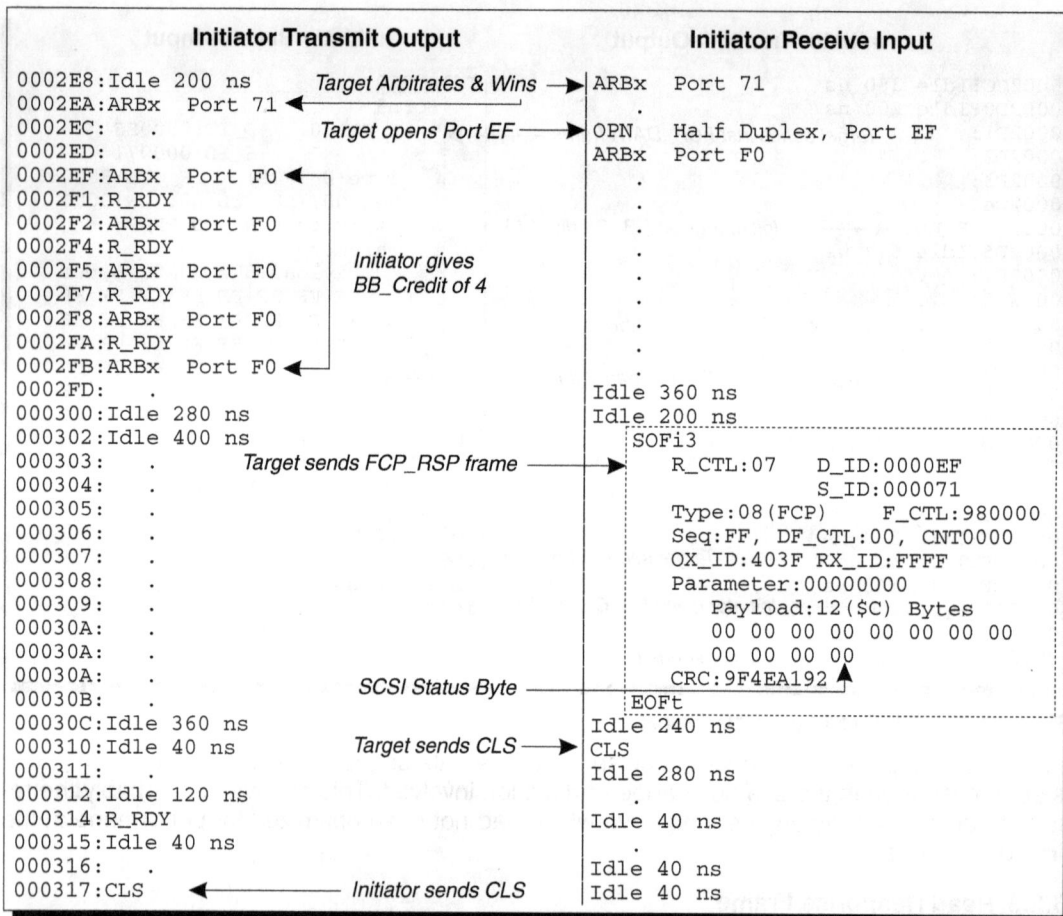

Figure 142. FCP Read Response Frame

C. FC-AL-2 Changes

This annex contains a list of major changes from the first version (FC-AL-1) to the second version (FC-AL-2) of the Fibre Channel Arbitrated Loop standards. Note that the second version is a complete replacement of the first version.

Dynamic Half Duplex (DHD). Dynamic Half Duplex (DHD) was added as a new ordered set to allow all traffic to be transmitted by the open recipient even though the L_Port which transmitted the OPN has finished its frame transmission. Normally, the L_Port would have sent CLS, but since there is no more flow control, the open recipient eventually runs out of credit and may not be able to finish transmitting all of its frames. The only option is then for open recipient to re-arbitrate for access to the loop to send the remaining frames. DHD shuts down the data frames only (i.e., R_RDY and ACKs, BSYs, RJTs will continue to be transmitted).

To use DHD, both L_Ports of the circuit must support it via a login bit. If it is supported, the open originator may transmit DHD in lieu of CLS to indicate to the L_Port in the open recipient that it will no longer transmit any data frames in this circuit. When the open recipient receives DHD, it can transmit all of its data frames and continue to receive flow control until it is finished. Once the open recipient completes its data frame transfer, it transmits CLS to start closing the Loop.

Old-Port State. The Old-Port state was made optional. Some implementations chose not to operate in a non-loop environment. To make these compliant with the standard, the Old-Port state was made optional. The intent of this state was to accommodate N_Ports and F_Ports which did not understand the loop protocol. Although still not required, the Old-Port state may be used to allow two L_Ports to go to this state when they realize that there are only two active L_Ports on the loop. The Old-Port state is required when two FL_Ports are the only L_Ports on a loop and they become E_Ports (expansion ports between two switches).

Bypassed Ports/Repeat Variable. Considerable cleanup was made to modify the behavior for bypassed L_Ports. The redefined variable Repeat was made consistent to indicate that an L_Port is either participating or not participating and bypassed or enabled.

Repeat is a symbol that was defined to simplify the LPSM description and is a combination of Participate and Bypass as shown in Table 40 on page 366.

Participate is a new history variable that was added since most implementations used it. In FC-AL-1, if the L_Port had an AL_PA, it was participating; in FC-AL-2, this information was changed to use Participate. This change was made to solve some interoperability issues: bypassed and participate was not easily understood in FC-AL-1 and although most implementation ignored non-active L_Ports, it was a potential problem.

Repeat	Participate	Bypass	Action
0	1	0	LPSM actively participates on the loop.
1	0	0 or 1	LPSM repeats most incoming transmission words (except for normal fill word processing -- updating the CFW appropriately) without responding to them. LPSM does not have an AL_PA.
1	1	1	LPSM repeats most incoming transmission words (except for normal fill word processing -- updating the CFW appropriately) without responding to them. LPSM keeps AL_PA until a LIP is recognized.

Table 40. Repeat Definition

Holding a Loop Circuit Open. FC-AL-1 had stated that once an L_Port wins arbitration, it may keep ownership of the Loop without re-arbitrating as long as there was no other port arbitrating (the L_Port in the OPEN state always 'sees' the next L_Port to win arbitration--if there is one). As part of this change, the paragraph which described this behavior was removed, although the spirit lives on (i.e., there is no reason for an L_Port to relinquish control of the Loop unless it 'sees' another L_Port arbitrating). Some implementations may choose to keep the loop until another port begins to arbitrate.

Arbitrated Loop Hubs. The definition and description of Hubs was added. These were supposed to be transparent to the loop, but the standard now indicates their presence.

Trusted AL_PA. The concept of a 'trusted' AL_PA was added to make hard addresses more functional. L_Ports may now attempt to arbitrate with their hard address (a 'trusted' address) to quiesce the loop prior to transmitting LIPs). This avoids any loss of frames which may otherwise be in transit on the loop.

ARB(FF). ARB(FF) was added as an alternative to IDLE. The IDLE was considered to be too 'noisy' for some implementers and they wanted a different fill word which did not have as many transitions. ARB(FF) was chosen to accomplish this. All existing L_Ports would still make the proper fill word substitution on ARB(FF). L_Ports which use ARB(FF) can only modify received IDLEs after 6 IDLEs have been transmitted.This rule assures that the fairness window is managed correctly.

Access Fairness Fixes. Even though there were several access fairness problems known in FC-AL-1, the standard was released. These were the first addressed in FC-AL-2 and include the following:

1. If an L_Port is arbitrating when it receives an OPN, it now continues to arbitrate (i.e., modifies the CFW) until it wins. It may only withdraw its arbitration request if it is sure that it is not the last arbitrating L_Port in the current fairness window. This fixes the case where L_Port n-1 wins arbitration and opens L_Port n which was also arbitrating. In FC-AL-1, n would stop arbitrating and if at the same time, n-1 was removed from the loop, no L_Port would reset the fairness window (until the 2 second timer expired). The change is to continue to modify the CFW according to normal rules as long as REQ(arb own AL_PA) is active in the Opened, Transmitted Close, and Received Close states.

2. ARB_PEND is used as a history variable in FC-AL-2 to remember that the L_Port was arbitrating. When the circuit is closed, the L_Port will return to the Arbitration state (instead of the Monitoring state).

3. The Arbitration Won state was minimized since now the L_Port (when it wins arbitration and no longer needs access to the loop (or it could have been arbitrating on multiple loops and only needs one)) must go through the Open state to return the loop (e.g., transmit OPN, CLS).

4. An addition was made to each state to assure that at least two IDLEs are forwarded to reset the fairness window (this avoids losing a single IDLE for clock skew). The LPSM uses a new history variable called 'Xmit_2_Idles' which is set when an ARB(F0) is detected. The variable is reset when two IDLEs have been forwarded.

5. If ARB(x) is received in the MONITORING state with x = AL_PA (an error since someone is using the same address) to avoid the fairness window from not being reset, the bullet 'x = AL_PA ...,' the CFW is changed to IDLE.

6. The L_Port in the OPEN state now does not reset the fairness window until it receives IDLE (it used to reset it when it transmitted IDLE). It was viewed to give the L_Port in the OPEN state a slight edge over other L_Ports; now the rule is the same -- when the L_Port receives the IDLE, it sets Access.

7. An L_Port may now start arbitrating late in the window (i.e., even when it has already passed an ARB(F0).

Ordered Set Recognition. Considerable effort was put into FC-AL-2 to provide rules for receiving loop constructs. FC-AL-1 only indicated what was to be transmitted, now rules were added to what must be checked by the recipient. For example, the initialization sequences (LISM, LIFA, LIPA, LIHA, LISA, LIRP, and LILP) all have new rules for what the receiver has to check. Also, the ARB and LIP ordered sets were defined for the recipient. For ARB, ARB(yx) was defined where x must equal y (if this is not true, the ordered set is usually replaced with the CFW. For LIP, the first two characters define a LIP with respect to LIP recognition; the last two characters indicate which LIP. LIP(ba) was added to indicate a future (as yet undefined) LIP. This change was to accommodate implementations which used undefined LIPs.

Initialization Definition. The entire Initialization and Open-Init states were redefined as discrete state diagrams to show the Initialization process. The purpose of this change was to minimize interoperability issues (some implementation had exceeded the requirements of FC-AL and consequently were not interoperable with those implementations which had adhered to the standard).

Timer Changes and Definitions. A new timer called LP_TOV (Loop Time-Out Value) of 2 seconds was added to monitor events like initialization, when to expect an R_RDY or CLS after transmitting OPN, when to restart the Initialization process, etc.

AL_Time was defined to be -0% to +20% (i.e., 15msec to 18msec). Also, the notion of start, minimum, maximum, and expire was added to the AL_Time.

LIRP and LILP Made Mandatory. LIRP and LILP are now required (optional for FC-AL-1). Early Tachyon (HP) chips performed the Initialization process in the 6 word clock skew management buffer and could not accept frames which did not fit into this buffer. LIRP and LILP have 132 byte payloads; FC-AL-1 grandfathered these implementations for one generation.

Fill Word Management. An annex was written to show an implementation of fill word management.

LPB(fx) Added. LPB(fx) was added to bypass all ports except the transmitter of LPB(fx). The purpose of the bypass primitive sequence is to be able to bypass all L_Ports (except the L_Port which transmitted LPB(fx). This may be the only way to bypass an L_Port which does not have an AL_PA (non-participating L_Ports still monitor the loop and will accept a broadcast (i.e., x'FF') AL_PA).

Loop Initialization. Modified initialization to use LISM instead of IDLE to flush the loop of all LIPs. Some implementers felt that the IDLE flush for AL_Time was too long; once that was realized, the IDLE flush was removed since the LISM accomplishes the same purpose.

Loop Initialization. The requirement to LIP was softened and a description was added of a controlled configuration (where few LIPs are used) in an annex. This was done to allow closed configurations to be controlled (i.e., the L_Ports do not decide to initialize when they decide that initialization should be performed).

Unexpected ARB(x) Received. The Opened and Received Close states were modified to transmit CLS at the next appropriate fill word if an ARB(x) (where x = AL_PA of the L_Port) is received. This implies an error situation which could happen if the open recipient was arbitration (and continues to arbitrate) and the open originator disappeared (such that the ARB(x) circulated the loop).

Change to OPEN State. Added change to Open state to allow OPN(fr) to be issued subsequent to OPN(yr) (previously, if OPN(fr) was to be used, it could not follow an OPN(yr)).

Loss of Sync Handling. Changed the state tables to use the CFW (instead of IDLE) when Loss of Sync is detected.

Monitoring State. Changed the Monitoring state when bypassed. If Loss of Signal or a Loop Failure is detected, FC-AL-2 now transitions to the Initialization process to send LIP(F8). In FC-AL-1, a bypassed L_Port did not report anything. Of course if an L_Port is physically bypassed, the LIP(F8) does not actually get transmitted on the loop. In FC-AL-1 a timeout would have had to occur to recognize that something was wrong; going to the Initialization process (if there is no physical bypass), will notify all L_Ports on the loop immediately when an error is detected. Other changes made in this area are to not remove ordered sets which have the L_Port's AL_PA when the L_Port is bypassed. In FC-AL-1, these ordered sets were removed. An L_Port keeps its AL_PA (even though it is bypassed) until a LIP is recognized (then it loses its AL_PA since it does not participate in the Initialization process). As long as it still has an AL_PA: in FC-AL-1, the logic was to remove any ordered sets that this L_Port had originated; in FC-AL-2 (except for the loop error described above), a bypassed L_Port will attempt to make no changes to any transmission word which it is 'repeating' (so that the behavior of a physically bypassed and logically bypassed L_Port is as close to the same as possible (clock skew management in an L_Port would make them not identical).

Selective Reset LIP. Modified the selective reset LIP (LIP(AL_PD,AL_PS)) to include public L_Ports. Also added LIP(FF,AL_PS) to include a reset of all L_Ports (except the one at AL_PS). This broadcast reset should be used cautiously and only when all other possible attempts to recover a loop have been exhausted.

NOS/OLS/LR/LRR Removed. NOS/OLS/LR/LRR was removed from all states after the Initialization process in FC-AL-2. They were only there because some committee members insisted that the loop supports all of the FC-PH protocol. These primitive sequences were not needed in FC-AL-1 (except when going to the Old-Port state), and since no one implemented them they were removed from those states where they are not used.

Power-On. New definition of power-on was added. In FC-AL-1 this was left to the implementation based on what FC-PH stated (which was not much). FC-AL-2 now specifies the process as well as the transmission words which need to be transmitted. In FC-AL-1, all L_Ports were required to go through the Initialization process; in FC-AL-2 this was made optional via SCSI mode page control. For certain controlled environments, trusted hard AL_PAs may be used instead of the Initialization process. Also initiator transmitted LIPs and error LIPs (i.e., LIP(F8)) are the only LIPs transmitted on the loop.

BB_Credit Clarification. The rules for managing BB_Credit were more clearly defined.

State Descriptions. The state descriptions in 8.4 were updated to reflect the state tables in 9. In FC-AL-1, the objective was to minimize text descriptions (only where needed to enhance the tables) and that the tables would be self-defining. The committee decided for FC-AL-2, all transitions from the tables should be described.

D. Notes on FC-AL-1

This appendix contains a list of errors, omissions, clarifications, and comments pertaining to the Arbitrated Loop standard.

D.1 Notes on Version 4.5

Version 4.5 of the FC-AL document is the version forwarded for adoption as an ANSI standard. Since it was forwarded, a number of clarifications have been observed and are presented here for the reader's attention.

- Page 42, Table 7, the entry for REQ(open fr) is incorrect. It should look like the entry for (REQ(open yr) except OPN(yr) should be OPN(fr). The text under item 16 on page 30 that starts "If Replicate is TRUE..." says that OPN(fr) is permitted while in the open state. Under the document precedence rules, the text is correct and the table is incorrect.

- Page 31, near the top, the line that starts "If Replicate is TRUE (1), all received Transmission Words (except CLS and any Primitive Sequence) shall be discarded." If discarded is interpreted as not processed, then access fairness does not function correctly. For clarity, this should read "... except IDLE, ARB(F0), CLS, and any Primitive Sequence)..."

- Page 47, Table 12, Elasticity Word n/a. If a LPB or LPE sequence is recognized, the L_Port begins transmitting the same sequence as received. This continues as long as the primitive sequence is recognized on the receive input. This is not a repeating state so the received words are not retransmitted, rather an identical sequence is transmitted.

- Page 28, statement starting: "If LPE(yx) (y = AL_PA of the L_Port) or LPE(fx) is recognized..." and Page 38, Table 4 entries for the above conditions. Neither statement states what should be transmitted if the LPE was not originated by this port and is not intended for this port. If the LPE is received while in the monitoring state and x <> AL_PA of this L_Port, the LPSM should transmit the same word as received. Neither the text on page 28 nor Table 4 covers this. This is corrected in FC-AL, rev. 5.0.

- There is an interesting behavior in the state tables for the initializing and open-init states. Any state that does not retransmit the same word in the "Any Other O.S." entry but attempts to retransmit sequences such as LPB or LPE will delete the first two occurrences of the ordered set before retransmitting it. Clause 9, Note 1 says that primitive sequence handling is based on the point of recognition (i.e. third consecutive occurrence) which means that the first two occurrences are "Any Other O.S.". For example, in table 12 (Initializing) assume that LPE(fx) is being received. When the first two LPE(fx) ordered sets are received they are 'Any Other O.S.' and a LIP is transmitted in their place. When the primitive sequence is recognized at the third O.S., the table says to output the same word. If taken literally, each L_Port will absorb the first two transmission words of the sequence as it propagates around the loop. This behavior shouldn't causes any problems since the primitive sequences are either regenerated (LIPs for example) or transmitted continuously until they propagate around the loop.

- Page 35, under item 21, 2nd bullet starting: "if LPB(yx) is recognized, where y = AL_PA of the L_Port, the LPSM shall set the Bypass Circuit (if present); set LP_Bypass to TRUE (1); and make the transition to the monitoring state. (See items 12 and 13.) Any other LPB(yx) shall be retransmitted;" As stated, there is no way to purge the LPB(yx) from the loop. The statement should add "if x=AL_PA, the LPB(yx) is discarded and LIP is transmitted." The state transition table is correct, however.

- Page 35, under item 21, same comment for the next item, third bullet starting: "if LPE(yx) or LPE(fx)..." As stated, there is no way to purge the LPE(yx) or LPE(fx) from the loop. The statement should also add "if x=AL_PA, the LPE(yx) or LPE(fx) is discarded and LIP is transmitted." The state transition table is correct, however.

- Page 31, Item 17, last paragraph: "only the L_Port which received EOFdt shall transmit CLS." If this is taken literally, only the L_Port receiving the EOFdt would transmit a CLS. The other port in the loop circuit would never send a CLS and the loop circuit would never end. This phrase should read "only the L_Port which received EOFdt shall transmit the first CLS and go to the transmitted close state. The other port shall wait until the CLS is received before transmitting a CLS of its own from the received close state."

- Page 38, Table 4 "LPB (LPEyx | LPEfx)" should be "LPE (LPEyx | LPEfx)". This is corrected in FC-AL rev. 5.0.

Also affecting Page 38, Table 4; neither statement for the above entries states what should be transmitted if the LPE was not originated by this port and is not intended for this port. If the LPE is received while in the monitoring state and x <> AL_PA of this L_Port, the LPSM should transmit the same word as received. Neither the table 4 nor the text on page 28 starting: "If LPE(yx) (y = AL_PA of the L_Port) or LPE(fx) is recognized..." covers this. This is corrected in FC-AL, rev. 5.0.

D.2 Notes on Version 5.2

Revision 5.2 of the Arbitrated Loop document incorporates a number of minor additions and corrections to the standard. It is commonly referred to as FC-AL2.

Glossary

AL_PA   *See Arbitrated Loop Physical Address.*

Alias Address   An address identifier recognized by a port in addition to its Native Address Identifier.

Alias AL_PA   An AL_PA value recognized by an Arbitrated Loop port in addition to its assigned AL_PA.

Arbitrated Loop   A Fibre Channel topology structured as a loop and requiring a port to successfully arbitrate prior to establishing a circuit to send and/or receive frames.

Arbitrated Loop Physical Address   A one-byte value used to identify a port in an Arbitrated Loop topology. The value of the AL_PA corresponds to bits 7:0 of the 24-bit Native Address Identifier.

Available BB_Credit   A value used by a transmitter to determine permission to transmit frames, and if so, how many. The transmitter may transmit a frame when available BB_Credit is greater than zero.

Available_receive_buffers   The current number of buffers in a receiving port which are available for receiving frames at link rate.

Arbitration Wait Timeout Value   The minimum time that an L_Port waits while arbitrating before originating a loop initialization.

AW_TOV   *See Arbitration Wait Timeout Value.*

Byte   A group of eight data bits.

Circuit   *See Loop Circuit.*

Close   An Arbitrated Loop protocol used to terminate a loop circuit.

Current Fill Word   The fill word that the LPSM uses when a fill word is to be transmitted.

DMA   Direct Memory Access. A hardware function providing direct access to memory for reading or writing data.

Error Detect Timeout Value   The minimum time that an L_Port waits for sequence completion before initiating recovery.

E_D_TOV   *See Error Detect Timeout Value.*

FC-AL   The Fibre Channel Arbitrated Loop standard.

FC-PH   The Fibre Channel Physical and Signalling standard ANSI X3.230.

FCP   The mapping of SCSI-3 operations to Fibre Channel.

FIFO   A First-In, FIrst-Out data buffer.

Fill Word   A transmission word that is either an IDLE or ARB ordered set.

Frame   A data structure used to transport information from one Fibre Channel port to another.

Full-Duplex   A mode of communications allowing simultaneous transmission and reception of frames.

Half-Duplex   A mode of communications allowing either transmission or reception of frames at any point in time, but not both (other than link control frames which are always permitted).

Hard Address   The AL_PA which an NL_Port attempts to acquire in the LIHA Loop Initialization Sequence.

Information Unit   A unit of information defined by an FC-4 mapping. Information Units are transferred as a Fibre Channel Sequence.

Link   A connection between two Fibre Channel ports consisting of a transmit fibre and a receive fibre.

LIS_HOLD_TIME   The maximum time allowed for each node to forward a loop initialization sequence.

LM_TOV   *See Loop Master Timeout Value.*

Login BB_Credit   On an Arbitrated Loop, a value equal to the number of receive buffers that a receiving NL_port guarantees to have available when a loop circuit is established. Login BB_Credit is communicated in the FLOGI, PLOGI, or PDISC link services.

Loop Circuit   A temporary point-to-point like path that allows bidirectional communications between loop-capable ports. The loop circuit begins when the arbitration winner port enters the OPEN state and ends when that port receives a CLS while in the transfer or transmitted close states, or sends a CLS while in the received close state.

Loop_ID   Loop_IDs are seven-bit values numbered contiguously from zero to 126 decimal and represent the 127 legal AL_PA values on a loop (not all of the 256 hex values are allowed as AL_PA values per FC-AL).

Loop Failure   Loss of synchronization for greater than R_T_TOV or loss of signal.

Loop Master Timeout Value   The minimum time that the loop master waits for a loop initialization sequence to return.

Loop Port State Machine   A logical entity which performs the Arbitrated Loop specific protocols.

Loop Tenancy   The period of time between when a port wins arbitration and when it returns to the monitoring state.

LPSM   *See Loop Port State Machine.*

L_Port   A node or fabric port capable of performing Arbitrated Loop functions and protocols. NL_Ports and FL_Ports are loop-capable ports.

Node   An entity with one or more N_Ports or NL_Ports.

Non-L_Port   A Node or Fabric port that is not capable of performing the Arbitrated Loop functions and protocols. N_Ports and F_Ports are not loop-capable ports.

Non-Participating Mode   A mode within an L_Port that inhibits that port from participating in loop activities. L_Ports in this mode continue to retransmit received transmission words but are not permitted to arbitrate or originate frames. An L_Port in the non-participating mode may or may not have an AL_PA.

Open   An Arbitrated Loop protocol used to establish a loop circuit.

Open Originator   The L_Port on an Arbitrated Loop that won arbitration, sent an OPN ordered set, and entered the OPEN state.

Open Recipient   The L_Port on an Arbitrated Loop that received an OPNy ordered set and entered the OPENED state.

Participating Mode   A mode within an L_Port that allows the port to participate in loop activities. A port must have a valid AL_PA to be in participating mode.

PLDA   *See Private Loop Direct Attach.*

Port_Name   A 64-bit unique identifier assigned to each Fibre Channel port. The Port_Name is communicated during the login and port discovery processes.

Preferred Address   The AL_PA which an NL_Port attempts to acquire first during loop initialization.

Previously Acquired Address   During loop initialization, the AL_PA which was in use prior to receipt of LIP. Immediately following power-on and between the time one loop initialization completes and the next one begins, an NL_Port may not have previously acquired address unless it remembers it while power is removed.

Private Loop Direct Attach   A technical report which defines a subset of the relevant standards suitable for the operation of peripheral devices such a disks and tapes on a private loop.

Private NL_Port   An NL_Port which does not attempt login with the fabric and only communicates with other NL_Ports on the same loop.

Public NL_Port   An NL_Port that attempts login in with the fabric and can observe the rules of either public or private loop behavior. A public NL_Port may communicate with both private and public NL_Ports.

Request Rate   The rate at which requests are arriving at a servicing entity.

Resource Allocation Timeout Value   Minimum time that an L_Port waits before reinstating the Recovery Qualifier.

R_A_TOV   *See Resource Allocation Timeout Value.*

Resource Recovery Timeout Value   Minimum time that the Private Loop Direct Attach technical report requires a Target to wait for an ADISC or PDISC Extended Link Service following a LIP before it is allowed to implicitly logging out a SCSI Initiator.

RR_TOV   *See Resource Recovery Timeout Value.*

Service Rate   The rate at which an entity is able to service requests (e.g., the rate a which an Arbitrated Loop is able to service arbitration requests).

Topology   An interconnection scheme that allows multiple Fibre Channel ports to communicate. For example, point-to-point, Arbitrated Loop, and switched fabric are all Fibre Channel topologies.

Transfer   An optional procedure that may be used by an L_Port in the OPEN state to establish a series of sequential circuits with other L_Ports without re-arbitrating for each circuit.

Transmission Character   A 10-bit character encoded according to the rules of the 8B/10B algorithm.

Transmission Word   A 40-bit group consisting of four 10-bit transmission characters.

ULP process   A function executing within an FC node which conforms to Upper Layer Protocol (ULP) defined requirements when interacting with other ULP processes.

Upper Level Timeout Value   The minimum time that a SCSI ULP process waits for SCSI Status before initiating ULP recovery.

ULP_TOV   *See Upper Level Timeout Value.*

Index

Out-of-Order delivery 40

P

Participating 63
PDISC 298, 306, 308, 309
Phase locked loop 27
PLL, see Phase locked loop
PLOGI 298, 301, 308, 312, 314, 320
Point-to-point circuit 31
Port address 42
Port Bypass circuit 282, 293
Port_Name 72, 75, 297, 375
Preferred Address 375
Private
    loop 40
    loop device 375
    NL_Port 375
    ports 42
Private Loop Direct Attach 295
    MRK(tx) support 315
    OPNr support 316
PRLI 298, 306, 312, 320
PRLI, see Process Login
PRLO 298, 299, 300, 312, 314, 320
Process Login 208
Public
    devices 41
    loop 40
    NL_Port 375

Q

Queue type 203

R

R_A_TOV 301, 309, 310, 314, 375
R_RDY 29, 30, 36, 51, 52, 53, 54, 57, 60, 92, 109,
       110, 135, 138, 139, 140, 142, 143, 144,
       145, 146, 147, 148, 149, 150, 152, 153,
       159, 160, 162, 163, 165, 167, 168, 169,
       170, 171, 175, 177, 181, 186, 188, 189,
       212, 213, 214, 215, 217, 219, 224, 230,
       233, 242, 243, 248, 252, 253, 260, 261,
       265, 268, 270, 272, 273, 279, 289, 308,
       313, 316, 317, 318, 365, 367

discarding 144
Read Commands 222
Reject 43
Relative offset
    present bit in F_CTL 297
    random 297
Repeat 64
Repeater 283
Replicate 63
Replicate Mode 106, 130
Request Rate 237, 375
RES 298, 315
Resets
    Abort Task Set 312
    ABTS 312
    Clear Task Set 312
    LIP(y,x) 312
    LOGO 312
    PLOGI 312
    Power Cycle 312
    PRLI, PRLO 312
    Target 312
    TPRLO 312
Resource Allocation Timeout Value 375
Response frame 205
RLS 298, 299
RNC 298
Rrelative offset
    continuously increasing 297
RRQ 309, 310, 314
RSI 298
RSS 298

S

SBCON 6
SCSI
    autosense 203, 205
    status byte 205
    Storage Controller Commands 203
SCSI CBD 203
Selective Reset LIP 54, 55, 56, 72
SEQ_CNT 209
SEQ_ID 209, 300
Sequence Initiative 313
Sequence Initiative, see F_CTL, Sequence Initia-

tive
Sequence Initiator 300
Service Rate 236, 375
SOFf, *see Start-of-Frame, Fabric*
SOFiL 74
Soft assigned AL_PA 82
Start of Frame Loop Initialization (SOFiL) 74
Start-of-Frame
    Fabric 50
States
    initializing 88
    old-port 90
Stealth mode 40

T

Target authentication 308
Task attributes 203
Task management functions 203
TCP/IP 6
Tenancy, see Loop Tenancy
Timers
    AL_Time 88, 90
    arbitrated loop 261
    Arbitration Wait (AW_TOV) 125, 309, 310, 373
    E_D_TOV 302, 306, 309, 310, 314
    Error Detect (E_D_TOV) 80, 82, 85, 373
    LIS_HOLD_TIME 309, 310, 374
    Loop Master (LM_TOV) 374
    R_A_TOV 301, 309, 310, 314
    R_T_TOV 92, 103
    Resource Recovery (RR_TOV) 306, 308, 309, 310, 375
    Upper Level Protocol (ULP_TOV) 309, 311, 313, 376
TPRLO 298, 320
Transfer 317
Transfer Function 249
Transfer Ready frame 204
Translative mode 40

U

Unfair Port 125

V

Velocity Factor 230

W

Write commands 215

X

Xmit_2_IDLEs 64

Index

383